THE USSR IN 1990: A RECORD OF EVENTS

Published in cooperation
with Radio Free Europe/Radio Liberty

The USSR in 1990: A Record of Events

Compiled by

Vera Tolz

Edited by MELANIE NEWTON

Foreword by Iain Elliot

Routledge
Taylor & Francis Group
LONDON AND NEW YORK

First published 1992 by Westview Press

Published 2019 by Routledge
52 Vanderbilt Avenue, New York, NY 10017
2 Park Square, Milton Park, Abingdon, Oxon OX14 4RN

Routledge is an imprint of the Taylor & Francis Group, an informa business

Library of Congress Cataloging-in-Publication Data
Tolz, Vera.
The USSR in 1990 : a record of events / compiled by Vera Tolz : edited by Melanie Newton.
p. cm.
Includes bibliographical references and index.
1. Soviet Union—Politics and government—
1985– —Chronology. 2. Soviet Union—History
—1953– —Chronology. I. Newton, Melanie.
DK286.U87 1992
947.085 4—dc20 91-40048
CIP

ISBN 13: 978-0-367-29703-9 (hbk)
ISBN 13: 978-0-367-31249-7 (pbk)

Contents

Foreword

Why, one might ask, a chronology of the year 1990 in the USSR when we already know about the putsch of August, 1991, and the collapse of the Communist empire? It is precisely because one extraordinary event follows the other with such baffling rapidity that all who are actively concerned with contemporary developments in that part of the world need a carefully compiled daily record at their fingertips. To understand the dynamics of change, one first needs the facts; to explain why, one must first ask what, when, and where? The answers are readily available here.

Historians and political scientists are often accused of selecting only the evidence that supports their thesis, while conveniently forgetting those awkward facts that cannot be made to fit. In her masterly chronology of the significant developments of 1990, Vera Tolz has avoided any such pitfalls. Her task was to achieve an objective compilation of events judged solely on the criteria of their long-term importance for the USSR and the world. In this she has succeeded admirably, adding her own expert analysis and drawing on that of her colleagues when necessary. The selection is balanced, comprehensive, and eminently sensible. Melanie Newton has completed the editing with her usual thoroughness and skill. The name index and subject index, together with the chronological presentation of the text, allow one to find a specific item of information rapidly. But a leisurely browse through the contents will also reap a rich reward, for 1990 was indeed an amazing year.

In 1990 Mikhail Gorbachev entered his sixth year in power, and it was already clear that the reform process initiated by him in March, 1985, had run far beyond his control. The fragmentation of the USSR was proceeding apace, with the Baltic republics, Armenia, and Georgia leading the other republics in breaking away from the central government, and with the RSFSR itself, under Boris El'tsin, intent on pursuing an independent course. Republican parliaments adopted laws that clashed with Gorbachev's all-Union legislation, and some republics actively encouraged draft evasion, preventing the Soviet Army from raising its intended quota of young recruits for compulsory military service beyond their borders.

Added to this, the generals were offended by the undignified withdrawal of Soviet troops from Eastern Europe and the lack of decent quarters to house them on their return. Ethnic hostilities within the ranks of the armed forces were exacerbated by the growing use of military units to police republics seeking independence. The officer corps, although less subject to ethnic tensions because of being drawn mainly from Russians or members of the other Slav nations, was itself evidently divided on how far to support liberal reforms and the loss of Party control. Defense Minister Dmitrii Yazov did not attempt to conceal his repressive views. The KGB, under another budding putschist, Vladimir Kryuchkov, produced a draft law on the role of the security organs that was hotly debated by reformist deputies, and republican leaderships began to separate their domestic security organizations from the all-Union KGB. The appointment of Boriss Pugo to head the MVD internal troops reinforced the reactionary elements around Gorbachev.

The Nagorno-Karabakh dispute between Armenia and Azerbaijan escalated. Baku suffered hundreds of casualties when Soviet troops violently occupied the city in January. More than twenty people were killed and several hundred injured in the riots that shook the Tajik capital of Dushanbe in February, and interethnic clashes caused bloodshed in Kirgizia, Moldavia, and other republics. Gorbachev's reluctant drafting of a new Union treaty came too late, and the draft was too limited in its scope to satisfy the aspirations of most republican leaders.

The Twenty-eighth Congress of the CPSU in July adopted statutes allowing more initiative to Communist leaders at the republican level and making the Party first secretary of each republic ex officio a member of the Politburo, which, however, was by then much degraded in its powers and no longer the center of policy formation. The membership of the CPSU continued to fall as it steadily lost control over the instruments of government, while several opposition movements emerged. The CPSU lost its monopoly on power with the abolition of Article 6 of the USSR Constitution, and the Supreme Soviet eventually adopted legislation to promote the development of a multiparty system.

The trends already evident in 1990 may have pointed the way for the hard-line Communists who plotted the August putsch of 1991. Gorbachev had failed to hold the USSR together and had failed to reassert the authority of the CPSU. Moreover, he had presided over a disastrous decline in the economy. The Shatalin plan, although not radical enough for some pro-market reformers, delegated more responsibility to the republics than Gorbachev and his immediate advisers were prepared to accept. Gorbachev's attempts to run the economy by decree proved ineffective, and industrial output continued to fall.

Only in his foreign policy initiatives did Gorbachev appear to make some progress in 1990; yet here too internal pressures played a major role. German reunification brought immediate deutsche mark dividends, while the USSR's withdrawal of troops from Eastern Europe and its new willingness to reach agreements on reducing arms made the United States and Western Europe more inclined to help Gorbachev overcome his domestic problems. There was also a clear economic incentive behind the dramatic improvement in relations with South Korea and Saudi Arabia. Nonetheless, the surprise resignation of Eduard Shevardnadze in December emphasized that the reactionary forces still ensconced in positions of power were actively opposing reforms in foreign policy also.

Regular readers of the RFE/RL Research Institute's weekly publication *Report on the USSR* and of the *RFE/RL Daily Report*, from which this book draws much of its material, will have followed in detail how the trends covered here have culminated in the even more momentous events of 1991. This is indeed history in the making, and in presenting it in the form of a carefully documented day-by-day record, the compilers have performed an invaluable service.

IAIN ELLIOT

Preface

The USSR in 1990: A Record of Events is the second volume in an annual chronology of developments in and relating to the Soviet Union. Like *The USSR in 1989: A Record of Events*, it is essentially a reference work whose purpose is to bring together in a single volume a wealth of detailed information, thereby making it more easily accessible to anyone interested in Soviet affairs. The volume is organized on a day-by-day basis and divided into chapters for each month. Headlines are used for each entry to facilitate locating information. Entries for a given day have been arranged roughly in descending order of importance. Where a story runs over several days or even weeks—as is often the case with state visits, parliamentary sessions, and ethnic disputes—its sequential parts have been grouped together in a single entry on the day it began.

For its information, *The USSR in 1990: A Record of Events* draws on the wide range of Soviet and non-Soviet media reports at the disposal of RFE/RL. As a consequence of the campaigns of the USSR's constituent republics for independence, many republican media organizations were able to increase the scope of their reporting in 1990, and quite a number of new ones were established. This, combined with the fact that the broadcasting services of RFE/RL took advantage of the new press freedom to engage a number of free-lance correspondents in the USSR and to conduct telephone interviews with Soviet politicians and public figures, meant that information about many events could be obtained directly from the republics rather than through the filter of the central media. These new circumstances are reflected in the contents of the present volume.

The quantity of information issuing from the USSR in 1990 was even greater than that in 1989. Once again, this inevitably meant that some degree of selection had to be exercised in compiling the volume. While naturally seeking to cover all the major events in or involving the Soviet Union that were in the public eye during 1990—itself a daunting task—the compiler also tried to focus on some of the less topical but nonetheless interesting developments that may have escaped notice elsewhere. The selection of items in the latter category, while taking into account their relative importance and the general scope of the volume, obviously reflects to some extent the compiler's own areas of interest.

Frequently, an event or topic that is dealt with in the volume has been described or analyzed more fully in an article that appears in the RFE/RL Research Institute's weekly publication *Report on the USSR*. For reasons of space, these articles have been referred to simply by their "RL" numbers. To illustrate, the entry headlined "Law on Freedom of Conscience Adopted" on page 589 carries a reference to RL 480/90. To assist the reader who may wish to locate RL 480/90, there is a Key at the back of the volume showing in which issue of *Report on the USSR* the article was published.

A comprehensive index is an essential part of any reference work of this kind if users of it are to find information quickly and easily. *The USSR in 1990: A Record of Events* contains two indexes—one of persons only and one of subjects and proper names other than those of persons. Because some persons are mentioned literally hundreds of times in the volume, the index entries of their names are further subdivided into subject categories.

MELANIE NEWTON AND VERA TOLZ

Acknowledgments

Though only the names of the two principals—the compiler, Vera Tolz, and the editor, Melanie Newton—appear on the cover of this volume, many other people were involved both directly and indirectly in its preparation. A particularly valuable contribution was made by the analysts on the staff of the RFE/RL Research Institute, whose specialized knowledge and writings helped to make authoritative coverage of such a vast range of topics possible. Their commentaries for the *RFE/RL Daily Report* were drawn on extensively. Of enormous help too were the summaries of news agency reports put together by RFE/RL's News and Current Affairs Division, the reports filed by RFE/RL's own correspondents, and the numerous telephone interviews with people in the Soviet Union conducted by members of RFE/RL's broadcasting services.

Without the continuing encouragement of E. Eugene Pell, president of RFE/RL, Inc., *The USSR in 1990: A Record of Events* could not have been produced. Both this volume and its predecessor, *The USSR in 1989: A Record of Events,* manifest his interest in making part of the immense flow of information now emanating from the Soviet Union and being evaluated by RFE/RL in connection with its broadcasts available to the Western public in a convenient, lasting, and usable form.

The preparation of the volume was under the general charge of Robert Farrell, assistant director of the Publications Department of the RFE/RL Institute, who conceived the idea for the series. Karen Whitehouse and Elizabeth Hayes typeset and copyfit the text on a Macintosh® using Microsoft Word® and PageMaker®. Emily Heyser took on the overwhelming task of proofreading the entire text. The kind help of Rebecca Ritke, acquisitions editor at Westview Press, is gratefully acknowledged. She, Libby Barstow, and Connie Oehring patiently and conscientiously shepherded the volume through the complicated process of production. Finally, a public expression of gratitude is owed to the indexer, Jane McGraw, whose labors contributed significantly to the volume's usefulness as a reference work.

MN
VT

Acknowledgments

The Month of January

Monday, January 1

Gorbachev Broadcasts New Year's Message to United States

In a New Year's message televised in the United States, Soviet leader Mikhail Gorbachev said this year could be the turning point in efforts to limit arms. He said US-Soviet cooperation should be based on "universal human values." In his companion television message for the USSR, US President George Bush said lasting peace resulted from respecting human rights and sharing democratic values (*Reuters*, *UPI*, *Pravda*, January 1).

Mass Unrest on Soviet-Iranian Border

TASS (January 2) reported that from December 31 through January 1 "extremists" rioted along a 137-kilometer stretch of the border between Iran and the Nakhichevan ASSR (part of Azerbaijan), causing extensive damage to watchtowers, communications lines, and technical installations, and threatening border guards. TASS claimed that the rioters were trying to aggravate the already tense situation in the Transcaucasus and that many of them were under the influence of alcohol or drugs. *The Washington Post* quoted a spokesman for the Azerbaijani Popular Front as saying that the demonstrations by ethnic Azerbaijanis on both sides of the border had been peaceful and that the demonstrators were merely calling for the easing of official restrictions on cross-border traffic. Some officials and journalists in Azerbaijan described the unrest as a land dispute. On January 3, the Soviet authorities were reported to have sent reinforcements to maintain order on the border between Azerbaijan and Iran. The chief of the KGB in the Transcaucasus Border District, Iokubas Petrovas, told *Izvestia* the situation was tense along nearly the whole length of the 790-kilometer border with Iran. Later reports said little was left of the border installations following the riots (*UPI*, *TASS*, in English, January 5).

On January 5, the Party first secretary in the Nakhichevan ASSR, Geidar Isaev, was reported to have retired from his post for health reasons. He was replaced by Afiyaddin Dzhalilov (*Reuters*, January 5). The same day, Iranian and Soviet Foreign Ministry officials met in Moscow to discuss the demonstrations along their common border. CPSU Central Committee Secretary Andrei Girenko went to Azerbaijan with a delegation to discuss ways of resolving the problems. A border official said on Soviet television that earlier reports that the border demonstrators had been drunk or on drugs were not true (*IRNA, UPI*, January 6).

On January 7, rallies were reported to have taken place in the Nakhichevan ASSR criticizing the Soviet and Azerbaijani authorities' responses to demands for the border to be opened. A spokesman for the Nakhichevan branch of the Azerbaijani Popular Front told RFE/RL by telephone that the front thought the authorities' proposals were too vague and did not meet the demands for free travel between Soviet and Iranian Azerbaijan (RL Azerbaijani service, January 7). The same day the Iranian news agency IRNA said a rally to press demands for an open border had also been held on Iran's side of the border.

On January 8, in Baku, Azerbaijani Party leaders and law-enforcement officials discussed "how it could happen" that Azerbaijanis had violated the USSR state border. The meeting was attended by Girenko. He said the situation in Azerbaijan was tense, despite progress in housing and on ecological and other issues (*TASS*, in English, January 8). The same day, *Sovetskaya Rossiya* carried an article saying that Azerbaijani demands for the development of cross-border contacts and trade with Iran were largely justified. The same day, *Izvestia* reported that on January 7 Azerbaijanis campaigning against border restrictions had torn down barriers on the frontier with Turkey.

On January 9, the Iranian delegation arrived in Baku from Moscow to discuss cross-border contacts. Reuters quoted IRNA as saying Iranian Deputy Foreign Minister Mahmoud Vaezi had told Soviet Foreign Minister Eduard Shevardnadze in Moscow that Iran was ready to facilitate visits by Soviet Muslims to Iran. Soviet television said Vaezi and Shevardnadze had declared their readiness to develop private cross-border travel as well as economic and cultural contacts.

On January 10, the Presidium of the USSR Supreme Soviet said those responsible for violating Soviet and Iranian border regulations in the Nakhichevan ASSR would be punished (*TASS*, January 10).

On January 11, the Azerbaijani Popular Front said thousands of people had attended rallies in Nakhichevan to protest about the actions of Soviet border troops. A popular front spokesman told Radio Liberty that about 500 border troops with dogs had made about fifty demonstrators in Nakhichevan leave the Iranian border area on January 10 (RL Azerbaijani service, January 11). See RL 19/90 and RL 20/90.

Bells Chime at St. Basil's in Moscow

Church bells at St. Basil's Cathedral in Moscow rang out across Red Square for the first time in decades. Western correspondents reported that thousands had gathered outside the cathedral to hear a concert performed by bell-ringer Ivan Danilov (*Reuters*, *AP*, *Pravda*, January 1).

Record Soviet Jewish Emigration Figures in 1989

An Israeli immigration agency reported that 71,509 Jews emigrated from the Soviet Union in 1989, the highest figure ever. The majority of those emigrating went to the United States. Today 125 Soviet Jews emigrating to Israel arrived in Tel Aviv on a direct chartered flight from Moscow. Western reports said it was the first time since the founding of the Jewish state that emigrants had flown directly from the Soviet Union to Israel.

New Dailies and Radio Station Start Up

The first issue of the new Russian-language newspaper *Rabochaya tribuna* appeared in Moscow. The new daily published by the CPSU Central Committee is a merger of *Sotsialisticheskaya industriya* and *Stroitel'naya gazeta*. A Ukrainian-language edition of the newspaper, *Robitnycha tribuna*, is to be published four times a week in the Ukrainian town of Zheltye vody. A new radio station, *Novaya volna*, will broadcast for five hours daily in the Siberian city of Novosibirsk. The radio is to broadcast in several languages, including Ukrainian, Kazakh, and Tatar. *Pravda* changed its masthead, removing three medals—two Orders of Lenin and one Order of the October Revolution—that have adorned its front page for decades.

USSR Defense Ministry Statement on Weapons Cuts

The USSR Ministry of Defense announced details of the destruction of weapons in accordance with the US-Soviet medium-range nuclear forces treaty. TASS said that, as of December 31, 1989, the USSR had destroyed about 80 percent of its medium- and shorter-range missiles and nearly 70 percent of its launchers for such missiles. The INF treaty calls for the United States and the USSR to eliminate over a three-year period all ground-launched nuclear missiles that have a range of 500–5,500 kilometers.

Tuesday, January 2

Renewed Violence in Nagorno-Karabakh

TASS said one person was killed today after a convoy carrying Azerbaijanis was ambushed in the Nagorno-Karabakh Autonomous Oblast. TASS said the convoy was stoned and fired upon in Stepanakert, which has a mostly Armenian population. MVD troops accompanying the Azerbaijanis returned fire in self-defense. TASS said four Stepanakert citizens were hurt and one died later. Several passengers in a convoy bus were also reported to have been injured.

On January 4, the USSR Supreme Soviet Presidium named Vladimir Foteev, who is a Presidium member, chairman of the "Union Monitoring and Observation Commission" for the Nagorno-Karabakh Autonomous Oblast. The USSR Supreme Soviet voted to set up the commission on November 28 after voting to dissolve a special committee that had administered Nagorno-Karabakh and to restore most control over the oblast to local Azerbaijani officials (*TASS*, in English, January 4).

On January 7, saboteurs blew up a highway bridge between Askeran and Agdam. There were also several other incidents in which people were taken hostage and machine guns fired on guards (*TASS*, January 8).

On January 8, Armenian Party officials in Stepanakert staged a walkout in order to avoid a meeting with a visiting delegation from Baku that included republican Party First Secretary Abdul-Rakhman Vezirov and CPSU Central Committee Secretary Andrei Girenko. Three people were injured in the city when troops tried to clear the road from the airport for the delegation (*TASS*, *Reuters*, January 9).

On January 10, Soviet television said grenades and ground-to-ground missiles were being smuggled from Armenia into Nagorno-Karabakh. "Vremya" did not say when the weapons had been found or where. The same day, the Presidium of the USSR Supreme Soviet ruled that the Supreme Soviets of both Armenia and Azerbaijan had violated the law in their actions concerning Nagorno-Karabakh. TASS quoted a Presidium decree as saying the Armenian Supreme Soviet had acted unconstitutionally in declaring Nagorno-Karabakh a part of Armenia on December 1 and in including Nagorno-Karabakh in the republic's 1991 budget. The Presidium also found illegal parts of a resolution passed by the Azerbaijani Supreme Soviet on December 4, which set up a body to take control of Nagorno-Karabakh in violation of a USSR Supreme Soviet decision that Armenians should be represented on the governing committee of the autonomous oblast. For the text of the decree, see *Pravda*, January 16.

On January 12, TASS reported that a Soviet military officer had died as a result of gunshot wounds suffered while his unit was trying to restore order in the Shaumyan Raion of Nagorno-Karabakh.

Wednesday, January 3

Romanian Front Member Says Moscow Reluctantly Backed Ceausescu Overthrow

A member of Romania's National Salvation Front Council, Silviu Brucan, said senior Soviet officials had reluctantly agreed to support Romania "in case of" President Nicolae Ceausescu's ouster several weeks before he was overthrown. He made the remark in an interview broadcast by British Television (Channel 4), but did not give details. He insisted, however, that the uprising in Romania had been completely spontaneous (*Reuters*, January 3). On January 4, the Soviet Union denied that it had offered such support. Soviet Foreign Ministry spokesman Gennadii Gerasimov told a Moscow news conference "our research at the Foreign Ministry has led us to the conclusion that there was no official promise of that sort" (*Reuters*, January 4).

Russian Orthodox Sit-In in Lvov

Members of the Russian Orthodox Church were reported to have held a three-day sit-in in Lvov to protest against "a wave of violence" perpetrated against them by Ukrainian Catholics. The Russian Orthodox Church has condemned what it calls violent action taken against its believers in Western Ukraine by laymen representing the Ukrainian Catholic Church. Catholics in some areas of Ukraine have been taking over Orthodox churches that used to be Catholic, following a recent decision by the Soviet authorities to let Ukrainian Catholics register their parishes. The Ukrainian Catholic Church was forcibly merged with the Russian Orthodox Church in 1946 (*Central Television*, "Vremya," January 3).

Predictions for 1990

Literaturnaya gazeta (No. 1) carried several interviews with leading Soviet public figures and Western Sovietologists and writers on their predictions for 1990. Many interviewees, while hailing changes in Eastern Europe, were pessimistic about the situation in the Soviet Union. Economic journalist Vasilii Selyunin said, for example, that, since the authorities had still not introduced radical economic reforms, the Soviet economy would deteriorate further this year. Selyunin expressed special fears about the possible paralyzation of Soviet railroads this winter. Romanian émigré playwright Eugene Ionesco said that, although he hoped that the Soviet Union would move further towards democracy this year, interethnic conflicts and the country's economic problems made him pessimistic.

Thursday, January 4

Contrasting Statements on Noriega Trial

Soviet Foreign Ministry spokesman Gennadii Gerasimov likened the expected trial of General Manuel Antonio Noriega in the United States to "lynch law" and said no guilty verdict could justify the US intervention in Panama. Gerasimov questioned whether an American court had the right to try the Panamanian dictator, and said the United States had already committed several violations of international law by invading Panama last month and removing Noriega for trial. Gerasimov said that, "from the outside," the US capture of Noriega looked like government vengeance against a former CIA agent who had got away (*AP*, January 4). The same day, Moscow television journalist Igor Kudrin said on "Vremya" that the general would face a "just" court in the United States. He also quoted President Bush's statement that Washington had achieved all its goals in Panama and that Noriega's rights would be guaranteed during his trial.

USSR Protests about Neo-Nazi Activities in GDR

The Soviet Union protested about recent Neo-Nazi attacks on Soviet war memorials in East Germany. Soviet Foreign Ministry spokesman Gennadii Gerasimov said there was clear evidence of close connections between neofascists in East Germany and the West German right-wing Republican Party (*DPA*, *AFP*, January 4).

KGB Seeks to Expand Contacts with CIA

KGB Chairman Vladimir Kryuchkov told *Moscow News* (No. 1) that there could be joint US-Soviet action in the future in world "hot spots" and that for this purpose the KGB and the CIA might exchange intelligence information. Kryuchkov said the KGB would expand its contacts with the Central Intelligence Agency and other foreign secret services this year, mainly with the aim of combating terrorism, drug and narcotics trafficking, and smuggling.

Israeli Minister Weizman Arrives in Moscow

Israeli Science Minister Ezer Weizman arrived in Moscow on a visit. He is scheduled to meet with Soviet First Deputy Foreign Minister Yulii Vorontsov and scientists in Moscow and Leningrad. Weizman, a former Israeli defense minister, told TASS that Israel was interested in cooperating with the Soviet Union in space exploration (*Reuters*, *TASS*, January 4).

Marxism-Leninism No Longer Required at Soviet Universities

Soviet university students will no longer be required to study and take examinations in Marxism-Leninism starting this spring. The end of the mandatory courses was announced in *Uchitel'skaya gazeta*. Instead, the journal said, students will be required to attend a course in social sciences and also to take an examination in order to graduate. This will include, but not be limited to, a study of the history of the CPSU.

Friday, January 5

Shevardnadze Says Events in Romania "Extraordinary"

In an article published in *Komsomol'skaya pravda* on the eve of his visit to Romania, Soviet Foreign Minister Eduard Shevardnadze described recent events in Romania as "extraordinary." Noting that the Romanians had risen up and overthrown a totalitarian regime, he said Romanians were now exercising their right to choose their own path of development. In an interview in Moscow conducted by the Romanian media, Shevardnadze said that the Romanian revolution had enormous significance for Europe and for the world and that it was supported by Gorbachev (*Reuters*, *Radio Bucharest*, January 5).

***Pravda* Says Communist Authority Undermined by East European Events**

A commentary in *Pravda* said Communist authority had been seriously undermined by events in Eastern Europe. It said this authority could be restored only if Communist Parties renewed themselves and renounced past deviations from the principles of human and democratic socialism. The *Pravda* commentary also said the events of late 1989 showed that "the perverted command-bureaucratic model" of socialism was crumbling throughout Eastern Europe.

Two Ukrainian Oblast Party First Secretaries Dismissed

Communist Party first secretaries in two Ukrainian oblasts were reported to have lost their posts. Radio Moscow (2000) said Vladislav Mysnichenko had been released from his post as first secretary of the Kharkov Oblast Party Committee and replaced by Anatolii Myalitsa. Radio Moscow also said Nikolai Nivalov had been dismissed as first secretary of the Chernovtsy Oblast Party Committee after being accused of serious shortcomings in his leadership of the committee bureau and violations of Party ethics. It said his actions had done serious harm to the oblast Party organization. TASS said talks were under way to find a replacement for Nivalov.

Many Joint Ventures Signed in USSR, but Failure Rate High

According to TASS, more than 1,000 foreign firms have created formal joint ventures with Soviet partners but many of the enterprises have failed to start up or have gone bankrupt. TASS said the USSR Finance Ministry had registered 1,284 joint ventures, with a total charter capital of more than three billion dollars. Half of the Western investment in joint ventures went into light industry and service establishments, another 20 percent was invested in industrial services such as market engineering and maintenance, and about 15 percent was committed to heavy industry and machine tools. The news agency added, however, that the ventures were frequently plagued by legal, financial, and organizational problems. Western commercial attachés say the Soviet business climate remains hazardous for all but the biggest and most patient foreign partners (*Reuters*, January 5).

Hungarian Parliament Urges Withdrawal of Soviet Troops

Two Hungarian parliamentary committees proposed that the government be authorized to take steps for the withdrawal of Soviet troops from Hungary, possibly by the end of this year. Radio Budapest (1200) said the proposal was submitted to parliament by the committees of foreign affairs and defense.

USSR Establishes Diplomatic Relations with Antigua and Barbuda

The Soviet Union established diplomatic relations with the Caribbean state of Antigua and Barbuda. Antigua and Barbuda is a former British dependency, but has been an independent state since 1981 (*TASS*, January 6).

Saturday, January 6

Shevardnadze in Romania

Soviet Foreign Minister Eduard Shevardnadze arrived in Bucharest for a scheduled one-day visit. After meeting with Romanian leaders, Shevardnadze told a news conference that the two countries would begin discussions on opening the border. He said Romania's new leaders had the Soviet Union's support and that ties between the two countries did not depend on the existence of a Communist government in Romania. He said the member states of the Warsaw Pact did not need to have the same political system. At the press conference, Shevardnadze also said he agreed that the Comecon trading organization was in need of a drastic overhaul. Shevardnadze's remark came amid sharp criticism of the trading bloc from leading figures in Romania,

Poland, Czechoslovakia, and Hungary. Ion Iliescu, leader of the Romanian National Salvation Front Council, accepted an invitation from Shevardnadze to visit the Soviet Union (*DPA*, *Radio Bucharest*, *TASS*, January 6; *Pravda*, January 7).

Gorbachev Meets Leaders of pro-Moscow Lithuanian Party

Gorbachev met in Moscow with leaders of the pro-Moscow Lithuanian Communist Party. This meeting followed one on January 4 at which Gorbachev spoke with leaders of the Independent Lithuanian Communist Party. TASS also reported from Vilnius that on January 6 a rally was held in Vilnius to support the pro-Moscow Lithuanian Party (see *Pravda*, January 7).

Sunday, January 7

Soviet TV Broadcasts Orthodox Christmas Service

Soviet television broadcast the Russian Orthodox Christmas service live from Moscow's main cathedral. It was the first such service to be broadcast live by the state-run television. On January 6, Radio Moscow broadcast a Christmas message from Pimen, Patriarch of Moscow and All-Russia.

KGB Chairman Calls for Unity at Time of Tension

KGB Chairman Vladimir Kryuchkov urged "progressive elements in Soviet society" to preserve their sense of unity. In remarks that were carried by Radio Moscow, Kryuchkov said unity was a key condition for stabilization. He said it was of particular importance at a time when worries were increasing over the state of the economy and ethnic relations. He said the Soviet Union was going through a painful stage of transition. Kryuchkov reiterated that the *perestroika* process was also under way in the KGB (*Radio Moscow*, World Service, January 7).

Some 30 Million Soviet Citizens Engaged in Illicit Business

Soviet economist Tat'yana Koryagina said some 30 million Soviet citizens were engaged in illegal business activities. Interviewed in *Komsomol'skaya pravda*, Koryagina said the overall volume of such activities in financial terms amounted to 100 billion rubles. She said official data indicated that there were about 300 millionaires in the Soviet Union. According to her own estimates, however, the number of people who have made millions by engaging in illicit business is between 15,000 and 30,000.

Moscow News Carries Articles Attacking Conservatives

In *Moscow News* (No. 1), Belorussian writer Ales Adamovich called on Gorbachev to replace all conservative Party officials with liberals, pointing out that there was a striking difference between the open-mindedness of Gorbachev's foreign-policy team (Eduard Shevardnadze and Aleksandr Yakovlev) and the limitations of the conservatives responsible for domestic affairs.

The issue opened with an article by Shevardnadze on the United Nations, followed by a long interview with Yakovlev about the plans of the Politburo Commission for the Additional Study of Materials Connected with Repressions in the 1930s–50s. Yakovlev, who chairs the commission, promised to rehabilitate the peasant victims of collectivization, as Adamovich asked him to do in a speech to the first USSR Congress of People's Deputies in summer, 1989. Like virtually every issue of *Moscow News*, this one contained an article attacking Egor Ligachev. On this occasion, Uzbek writer Timur Pulatov accused Ligachev of discrimination against Uzbeks during the rule of Ligachev's protégé Inamzhon Usmankhodzhaev, who was recently sentenced for bribery. Pulatov said that the recent corruption trials of Uzbek officials and the demonstration in Leningrad on November 22, 1989, in the course of which reactionary CPSU officials attacked Yakovlev and Gorbachev, had reminded him that the essence of the Party apparatus remained unchanged.

Criticism of Ligachev continued on January 11, with an article in *Izvestia* by agricultural expert Gelii Shmelev censuring Ligachev for his dogmatic ideological stance on agriculture, which Shmelev charged was exactly the same as the one used by Stalin to justify collectivization.

Monday, January 8

CPSU Delegation Goes to Lithuania

A CPSU delegation led by the Politburo member responsible for ideology, Vadim Medvedev, arrived in Lithuania in advance of Gorbachev. Radio Moscow said Medvedev met with workers at the Zalgiris machine-tool factory in Vilnius and gave a speech. Medvedev was quoted as saying that the Lithuanian Party's decision to declare its independence was a blow to *perestroika*. Another member of the delegation, First Deputy Prime Minister Yurii Maslyukov, met with workers at the Ignalina nuclear power station. *Izvestia* (January 11) carried a report on Medvedev's visit. On January 12, *Izvestia* quoted Maslyukov as saying that Lithuania had the right to secede from the USSR but that the move would require a referendum.

Soviet Union Backs Bulgarian Ethnic Policy

The USSR said it backed Bulgaria's decision to restore the rights of Bulgarian ethnic Turks and other Muslims. Soviet Foreign Ministry spokesman Gennadii Gerasimov said in Moscow that the Bulgarian decision was an effort to set right the aberrations committed by the country's former leaders (*TASS*, January 8).

Ryzhkov Proposes "Experiment" to Comecon Summit in Bulgaria

The heads of government of the Comecon countries gathered in Sofia for what Soviet Prime Minister Nikolai Ryzhkov said would be an unusual meeting. Speaking on Radio Moscow's World Service, Ryzhkov said abandoning Comecon would harm all of its members, but he said Comecon must adapt to changes taking place in its member countries (*Reuters*, January 8).

On January 9, the Comecon summit began (*Pravda*, January 10). Delivering the opening speech, Ryzhkov proposed as "an experiment" the use this year of hard-currency settlement and world market prices in some 10–15 percent of intra-Comecon trade. In fact such arrangements have already been in operation in Comecon for ten years or more, with 10–15 percent of hard-currency trade in the intra-Comecon total consisting mainly of extra-plan deliveries of "hard" goods like energy and grain, which can be sold on world markets at prices attractive to the exporters and which are in short supply within Comecon. What Ryzhkov may have had in mind is that this year there should in addition be hard-currency settlement and world-price invoicing for 10–15 percent of "normal" (planned) trade. That trade contains a mix of hard and soft goods, and the proposed change would exert pressure on suppliers to change the mix towards a larger share of hard goods. This would, of course, tend to benefit the Soviet Union.

The summit ended on January 10. Ryzhkov said it had helped to define the positions of member nations and laid the foundations for the trading group's future (*Radio Sofia*, 1730, *TASS*, January 10).

Dissident Journalist Set Free

Western news agencies and *Izvestia* (January 9) reported that the Sverdlovsk Oblast Court had reduced the sentence of dissident journalist Sergei Kuznetsov to time already served. Kuznetsov himself informed RFE/RL that he had been freed, and he expressed his thanks for foreign intervention in his case. Last November, Kuznetsov was sentenced to three years of imprisonment on trumped-up charges of having slandered local police and resisted arrest. As a member of the opposition Democratic

Union, Kuznetsov was active in organizing meetings and demonstrations against the local Party leadership. The appeals court did not quash the charges against Kuznetsov, despite the lack of evidence against him; the reduction of his sentence seems to have been the result of a compromise between oblast Party First Secretary Leonid Bobykin and a broad front of local Party reformers, whose appeal to First Deputy Chairman of the USSR Supreme Soviet Anatolii Luk'yanov on Kuznetsov's behalf was apparently successful. Kuznetsov is now in the hospital undergoing treatment for the effects of his long hunger strike. His lawyer, Sergei Kotov, who has been nominated for a seat in the RSFSR Congress of People's Deputies, said he would continue to fight for the full rehabilitation of his client.

Soviet Troop Withdrawals to Continue This Year

The Soviet Union said it would reduce its armed forces by more than 185,000 men this year. Colonel General Oleg Moskovsky, deputy chief of the General Staff of the Soviet Armed Forces, said this was part of the promise to unilaterally cut Soviet forces by 500,000 by 1991. TASS and the Hungarian news agency MTI quoted Moskovsky as saying some 6,000 troops would be withdrawn from Hungary this year.

MVD Troops Sent to South Ossetia

Reports from Moscow said MVD troops had been sent to the South Ossetian Autonomous Oblast in Georgia following an escalation of tensions there between Ossetians and Georgians. The latest trouble followed the killing of an infant by gunmen in a town not far from the region's capital, Tskhinvali, last week (*Reuters*, *AFP*, January 8).

Tuesday, January 9

Rogachev Visits Beijing

Soviet Deputy Foreign Minister Igor Rogachev arrived in Beijing for talks with Chinese officials about Cambodia. They are reportedly to discuss Australia's proposal for the Vietnam-backed government in Phnom Penh to be replaced by an interim UN administration until free elections can be held (*Reuters*, January 9). On January 12, UPI quoted Rogachev as dismissing concerns that a new Sino-Soviet rift is developing over the political and economic reforms in the USSR and Eastern Europe. Rogachev said that Eastern Europe was not discussed during his visit and that Sino-Soviet relations were going smoothly.

Former Uzbek Official on Trial

Another former Uzbek official went on trial before the USSR Supreme Court in Moscow. TASS said Erezhep Aitmuratov, who was chairman of the Council of Ministers of the Karakalpak ASSR before becoming a Central Committee secretary in 1981, is charged with taking bribes totaling 80,500 rubles from seventeen subordinates. TASS said Aitmuratov had denied the charges.

Wednesday, January 10

Restrictions Eased on Soviet-Romanian Border

The Soviet Union has started removing obstacles along parts of its border with Romania. TASS also said new border crossing points had been opened between Romania and Moldavia and that requirements for crossing the border had been eased for residents in the border area. The opening of the border was promised by Soviet Foreign Minister Eduard Shevardnadze when he was in Bucharest earlier this week.

Thursday, January 11

Gorbachev Visits Lithuania

On January 11, Gorbachev began a three-day visit to Lithuania to try to resolve the controversy caused by the Lithuanian Communist Party's decision to become independent of the CPSU. On the eve of Gorbachev's visit, thousands of people demonstrated in Vilnius, demanding the republic's independence (*TASS*, Western agencies, January 10). Gorbachev began his visit by laying a wreath at a statue of Lenin in central Vilnius and then visited a factory. At both places he talked to crowds of people, many of whom spoke out in favor of Lithuanian independence, but Gorbachev suggested that all the Union republics should try to improve the USSR's situation and solve the country's problems together. During his talks with people, Gorbachev defended the concept of a Soviet federation. He said the Soviet people had never lived in a true federation. Talking to people at a Vilnius factory, Gorbachev called for the preparation of a law setting conditions for republics to secede. He stressed, however, that he personally was strongly against secession. The Soviet leader said that, if Lithuania were to seek its own way in the world, it could not survive, because it could not afford to pay world market prices for the commodities it needs. Gorbachev's wife, Raisa, who accompanied her husband, also talked to people, saying that, in the current situation, the Soviet people, like families, should not separate because of differences. Simultaneously, tens of thousands of people demonstrated on Vilnius's central square, demanding the complete independence of the republic. The demonstration was sponsored by "Sajudis" (*Reuters*, *AP*, January 11). Later the same day, Gorbachev met with Vilnius intellectuals.

On January 12, Gorbachev continued his visit to Lithuania with a trip to the city of Siauliai, where he talked with workers at a television factory, met with farmers, and held talks with local Communists (*TASS*, January 12). Before Gorbachev left Vilnius for Siauliai, he met with Lithuanian Communist officials still loyal to the CPSU (*Radio Vilnius*, *TASS*, January 12).

On January 13, before leaving Lithuania, Gorbachev addressed a meeting of both the Independent Lithuanian Communist Party and the pro-Moscow group (*TASS*, January 13). At the meeting, Vasilii Emel'yanov, editor of *Sovetskaya Litva*, told Gorbachev that Lithuanian Communists had had no choice but to declare their independence, because the people in the republic had completely lost faith in the CPSU. In response, Gorbachev urged Lithuanians to slow down their drive for independence and accused them of rushing towards "a nationalist wilderness" (*Pravda*, January 15). In his speech, Gorbachev commented on the possibility of a multiparty system in the USSR. Gorbachev said he was not afraid of a multiparty system as long as it arose from a normal historical process and fulfilled the needs of society, but he warned that it was not a panacea.

On January 15, "Sajudis" said Gorbachev's visit to Lithuania had not answered the main question—namely, how and by what stages Lithuanian independence would be restored (*Radio Vilnius*, January 15). For reports on Gorbachev's visit, see *Pravda*, January 12, 13, 14, and 15. See also RL 37/90.

Unrest in Chernigov

Izvestia and *Rabochaya tribuna* reported that the residents of the Ukrainian city of Chernigov had gone on the warpath against their local leaders, following an incident on January 6 in which two private Zhiguli cars crashed with a Volga owned by the oblast executive committee. The trunk of the Volga was found to contain a stash of goods in short supply such as sausage and spirits, and both the driver and his passenger, an executive committee official named Zaiko, were apparently inebriated. According to the newspaper reports, "passions flared," and a mass meeting was held to condemn official privileges in the face of a shortage of goods for ordinary people. In response, the Chernigov Oblast Committee announced that Zaiko had been fired and stripped of his Party membership and that his driver faced criminal charges. This was not enough, however, to mollify the angry citizens, who demanded not only the wholesale resignation of the oblast leadership but also "the liquidation" of the Komsomol and raion-level Party and executive committees and the conversion of administrative buildings into schools and hospitals. On January 22, Vasilii Lysovenko replaced Leonid Palazchenko as first secretary of the Chernigov Oblast Party Committee (*Radio Moscow*, January 22).

Azerbaijani Popular Front Takes over Lenkoran District

The Azerbaijani Popular Front in the Caspian port city of Lenkoran said it had taken over control of Lenkoran Raion. Popular front spokesman Hussein Gulu told Radio Liberty that front members had dissolved all Communist Party, local government, police, and judicial organs in Lenkoran Raion and taken over these functions. The spokesman said the popular front's action was in response to a move by the Armenian Supreme Soviet to include a budget for the Nagorno-Karabakh Autonomous Oblast in its own budget for 1990. The front condemned the Azerbaijani Party and government leadership's policy towards Nagorno-Karabakh as too cautious. TASS said the Azerbaijani Council of Ministers had denounced the popular front's actions in Lenkoran.

Latvia Drops Provision on Party's Leading Role

The Latvian Supreme Soviet dropped from Latvia's constitution the provision that guarantees the Communist Party a leading role in Latvian society. TASS quoted Latvian Party First Secretary Janis Vagris as saying the new wording of the constitution sets the stage for democratic elections to the Latvian Supreme Soviet. Latvia is the second Baltic republic to end the guarantee of the leading role of the Communist Party. Lithuania did the same early last month.

Soviet Official Says Some Reactors Still Unsafe

Deputy Chairman of the USSR State Committee for Safety in Industry and in the Atomic Power Industry Nikolai Shteinberg told *Izvestia* that some Soviet nuclear reactors still do not comply with safety standards, despite improvements made after the Chernobyl' accident. He said this applied to reactors of the Chernobyl' type and also to another, older type of reactor—the first generation of

VVER-440s. He said the latter operated reliably but lacked a containment vessel to prevent leakages and had "relatively weak" safety systems.

Armenian Supreme Soviet Votes to Veto Laws of USSR Supreme Soviet

The Armenian Supreme Soviet gave itself the authority to veto laws passed by the USSR Supreme Soviet, TASS reported. The Armenian legislature amended the republic's constitution to allow it to refuse to apply Soviet laws that it feels are against the republic's interests. Similar veto laws have been passed in several other Union republics, including the Baltic republics. The laws were declared illegal by the Presidium of the USSR Supreme Soviet in November, 1989.

Friday, January 12

Latvian Supreme Soviet Backs Lithuanian Independence

The Latvian Supreme Soviet adopted a resolution supporting Lithuania's drive for independence. Radio Riga said the Latvian resolution also recognized the right of the Lithuanian Communist Party to be independent of the CPSU. The radio quoted the resolution as saying that events in Lithuania were a practical implementation of *perestroika* and proved that the Lithuanian people, public organizations, and government were united in favor of independence. There were public demonstrations in Latvia on January 11 to show solidarity with Lithuania.

Strikes and Protests in Georgia

TASS, Radio Moscow, and Western agencies reported strikes and proindependence demonstrations in Georgia. Spokesmen for proindependence groups said the demonstrators wanted Moscow to send a Politburo member to Georgia to discuss their demands for independence. A leader of one proindependence group in Tbilisi, Irina Sarishvili, told AP that many businesses and most forms of public transport were on strike in the capital. On January 13, *Krasnaya zvezda* reported that hunger strikes were being held to back demands for independence.

Bush Praises Gorbachev

US President George Bush praised Gorbachev for easing East-West tensions, but he said it was still too early for sharp US military cuts in Europe. In a speech today, Bush said that he was excited about changes taking place in Eastern Europe but that Gorbachev was struggling against difficult odds (*Reuters*, January 12).

USSR Denies Intention to Upgrade Relations with Israel

The Soviet Union denied reports of its intention to upgrade its relations with Israel. Foreign Ministry spokesman Vadim Perfil'ev said that, during talks between Foreign Minister Eduard Shevardnadze and Israeli Science Minister Ezer Weizman last week, Shevardnadze had said only that the Soviet Union was ready to hold talks about changing the status of representation (*TASS*, January 12). Weizman told reporters in Tel Aviv that the Soviet Union had played a trick on him. He said Shevardnadze had told him he wanted to upgrade consular groups while in fact the Soviet Union had exploited his visit to Moscow to make its announcement about upgrading relations with the PLO. Shortly after Weizman's talks with Shevardnadze, the Soviet Union announced that it would allow the PLO to upgrade its Moscow representation to embassy level (*Reuters*, *AP*, January 12).

Saturday, January 13

Unrest in Baku; Soviet Troops Sent In

This week interethnic tensions in the Transcaucasus escalated still further. The Azerbaijani Popular Front said two helicopters from Armenia had fired machine guns on the Azerbaijani village of Shaumyan on January 12, causing casualties, including some deaths. *Komsomol'skaya pravda* reported on Armenian-Azerbaijani clashes in the Shaumyan and Khanlar areas near the Nagorno-Karabakh border on January 14. According to Soviet television of January 14, dozens of people from both sides were injured or killed in these areas. On January 16, Western agencies reported that open warfare had broken out between Armenians and Azerbaijanis in the two areas. Soviet television said both sides had been sending in volunteer fighters.

On January 13, TASS said that unrest had broken out in the Azerbaijani capital, Baku, and that Armenian homes had been attacked. The agency reported casualties. Meanwhile, thousands of people demonstrated in Baku, demanding full Azerbaijani control over Nagorno-Karabakh. In Nagorno-Karabakh itself the situation was reported to be tense (*TASS*, January 13).

On January 14, Radio Baku quoted a Communist Party official in the Azerbaijani city of Lenkoran as saying it was up to the central government in Moscow to resolve the situation in that city. City offices and the radio station in Lenkoran were taken over by the Azerbaijani Popular Front last week. Front spokesmen said they would retain control until their demands concerning

Nagorno-Karabakh were met. TASS said pogroms had been carried out in Baku on January 13. TASS reported that Chairman of the USSR Supreme Soviet Council of the Union Evgenii Primakov, Soviet Deputy Prime Minister Vitalii Doguzhiev, and CPSU Central Committee Secretary Andrei Girenko were in Baku. In Armenia, at least 300,000 people gathered in Erevan to demand greater protection for Armenians living in Azerbaijan. TASS reported that more than thirty people, mostly Armenians, had been killed in the pogroms in Baku. The same day, Soviet television said road and rail traffic from Azerbaijan to Nagorno-Karabakh had again been disrupted.

On January 15, the Presidium of the USSR Supreme Soviet declared a state of emergency in Nagorno-Karabakh "and some other regions." Radio Moscow's correspondent in Baku condemned the pogroms against Armenians there, saying it was as if a modern city had reverted to the Middle Ages (*Radio Moscow-1*, 0759, January 15). The same day, Soviet television said many Armenians from Baku had been evacuated to Krasnovodsk in Turkmenistan. The same day, Radio Liberty's Azerbaijani service quoted a spokesman for the Azerbaijani Popular Front as condemning the anti-Armenian pogroms. The World Council of Churches pledged solidarity with the Soviet Union's Armenian community and appealed to Gorbachev to protect it from attacks (*Reuters*, January 15). *Izvestia* quoted the USSR Ministry of Internal Affairs as saying that the situation in many parts of Azerbaijan was still "uncontrollable." The same day, Prime Minister Nikolai Ryzhkov said the conflict in the Transcaucasus would not be allowed to develop into a civil war. In an interview with *Komsomol'skaya pravda* on January 18, however, USSR Minister of Internal Affairs Vadim Bakatin described the fighting in the Transcaucasus as civil war. On January 16, the Soviet Union informed Iran and Turkey of the imposition of a state of emergency in parts of Azerbaijan (*TASS*, January 16).

On January 17, a spokesman for the Ministry of Internal Affairs said four more charred bodies had been found during the night in Baku, bringing the official death toll to sixty. Reports indicated that interethnic fighting was now going on throughout Nagorno-Karabakh. Fighting was also reported near Azerbaijan's second-largest city, Kirovabad. Meanwhile, Soviet troops in Azerbaijan and Armenia were given permission to open fire to defend themselves and protect weapons stockpiles, following attacks in which troops were killed or wounded (*Central Television*, January 17). *Izvestia* reported that about 17,000 members of the security forces were engaged in maintaining order in Baku. Radio Moscow reported that security forces sent to enforce the state of emergency had now taken up positions in areas of high tension; troops reportedly reached their destinations in Azerbaijan, despite roadblocks set up in some places by militants. A spokesman for the USSR Ministry of Internal Affairs said that the presence of the troops had considerably reduced the level of confrontation between the two sides (*TASS*, January 17). On January 17, Gorbachev met senior Armenian Party officials to discuss the situation in the Transcaucasus (*Radio Erevan*, January 17).

On January 18, Defense Minister Dmitrii Yazov told Radio Moscow that army reservists were being mobilized to help restore order in the Transcaucasus. He said that the call-up affected those with recent military service and no family ties. He said that a full mobilization of formations from certain oblasts was under way and that army units in the areas affected by the state of emergency were to be brought up to wartime strength. *Komsomol'skaya pravda* said that people in Erevan were convinced that border installations between the Nakhichevan ASSR and Iran had been destroyed recently with long-term goals in mind and that Azerbaijani militants in the area were receiving large supplies of weapons from across the border. The same day, a big demonstration took place in Baku. The main demand was the withdrawal of security forces from the city (RL Azerbaijani service, January 18). Speaking at a meeting with workers and peasants, Gorbachev defended the decision to declare a state of emergency in parts of the Transcaucasus (*TASS*, January 18).

Late at night on January 19, Soviet troops with tanks opened fire on resisting Azerbaijani activists and forced their way into the center of Baku, after representatives of the Azerbaijani Popular Front had refused to dismantle roadblocks and barricades. A TASS commentary earlier in the day said Azerbaijani nationalists had called for "the forcible overthrow of Soviet power, the secession of Azerbaijan, and the reunification of northern and southern Azerbaijan into a single Islamic state." According to the Baku military commander, eighty-three people, including fourteen soldiers and their dependents, were killed in the ensuing fighting. Azerbaijani Popular Front sources claimed that the death toll was far higher. Gorbachev said the emergency call-up of reservists had prompted protest demonstrations in several cities. He blamed the unrest on opponents of *perestroika* and on "Islamic extremists."

Five US senators urged Gorbachev to allow Nagorno-Karabakh residents "to freely choose their political and cultural associations within the Soviet Union." In a letter, the senators urged the USSR to guarantee safe passage for Armenians who wish to leave Azerbaijan (*Reuters*, January 19).

Sporadic fighting continued in Baku over the weekend. On January 20, the Nakhichevan ASSR declared that it had seceded from Azerbaijan and from the USSR and called upon the UN, Iran, and Turkey to safeguard its territorial integrity and "prevent a massacre." Also on January 20, Azerbaijani Party First Secretary Abdul-Rakhman Vezirov, whose resignation had earlier been called for by demonstrators in Baku, was removed from his post, and his duties were entrusted to Party Second Secretary Viktor Polyanichko and republican Prime Minister Ayaz Mutalibov, who met with Gorbachev in Moscow the same day to discuss conditions for a withdrawal of Soviet troops from Baku. In a television address that evening, Gorbachev argued that the military intervention in Baku was justified, insofar as all earlier attempts to resolve the situation peacefully had failed and "extremist forces" were attempting to seize power. He criticized the local leadership in Armenia and Azerbaijan for giving in to pressure from nationalist groups (RL Azerbaijani and Armenian services, *TASS*, in English, *AP*, *Reuters*, *Radio Baku*, January 20).

On January 21, the Iranian Foreign Ministry criticized the crackdown in Azerbaijan and denied Soviet reports that Iran had supplied arms to Soviet Azerbaijanis. The Azerbaijani Popular Front held a mass rally in Baku to mourn those killed the previous day and called for a general strike to last until the withdrawal of all Soviet troops from the city. In Armenia, thousands attended the funeral of Movses Gorgisyan, who was killed in fighting along the Armenian border with Nakhichevan (*Reuters*, *AP*, *TASS*, January 21).

An an extraordinary session on January 22, the Azerbaijani Supreme Soviet called for the withdrawal as soon as possible of the troops sent to Azerbaijan under the state of emergency declared on January 19. The Azerbaijani Popular Front was more vehement, calling for the withdrawal of the troops within forty-eight hours. The funerals of some sixty people killed when troops forcibly entered the center of Baku on January 19 were attended by up to one million mourners. TASS reported that high-ranking Party officials from both Armenia and Azerbaijan had met in Armenia and agreed to end hostilities along the frontier between the two republics and withdraw armed bands from the area. Soviet Foreign Ministry spokesman Gennadii Gerasimov confirmed a Radio Teheran report that the USSR had begun closing the frontier between Azerbaijan and Iran (*TASS*, Western agencies, RL Azerbaijani service, January 22). *Izvestia* reported that more than 150 people had been detained in Baku over the weekend for ethnically motivated crimes.

On January 23, the military commandant of Baku issued an order banning strikes and public meetings and abolishing the National Defense Committee of the Azerbaijani Popular Front. Soviet Defense Minister Dmitrii Yazov was reported to be in Baku.

On January 24, Soviet troops and warships ended a blockade of the port of Baku with an artillery barrage. Azerbaijani seamen on tankers and other ships had blockaded naval ships in the harbor for several days because they believed the navy was trying to remove the bodies of people killed in last weekend's clashes. The Soviet authorities denied this. Meanwhile, a general strike continued in Baku to back demands for the withdrawal of Soviet troops. Forty-three members of the National Defense Committee were reported to have been arrested; files were seized and telephone lines severed in a raid on the headquarters of the popular front. Vezirov was expelled from the CPSU, and a plenum of the Azerbaijani Party Central Committee elected Mutalibov as his successor. In Moscow, Soviet and Iranian officials discussed their sensitive border situation while people in Iran held mourning services for Muslim victims of the Transcaucasian violence. The Armenian Pan-National Movement joined in criticizing the Soviet army intervention in Baku. Western correspondents quoted a statement from the front as saying the army action had violated Azerbaijani sovereignty (Western agencies, *TASS*, *Central Television*, January 24).

On January 25, two ceasefires were announced between battling Azerbaijani and Armenian forces. One covered the entire border between Armenia and the Nakhichevan ASSR. The second covered Armenian and Azerbaijani districts around the Azerbaijani city of Kazakh along the main Azerbaijani-Armenian border. Although scattered clashes were still being reported, TASS said life was gradually returning to normal in Baku and other areas. It added, however, that, owing to "extremist actions," most enterprises in Baku remained idle (*TASS*, in English, *Central Television*, January 25).

On January 26, *Izvestia* quoted USSR Defense Minister Dmitrii Yazov as accusing officials of the Azerbaijani Ministry of Internal Affairs of helping the Azerbaijani

Popular Front resist the entry of Soviet troops into Baku. Yazov said Soviet troops had been sent in to thwart plans by the popular front to seize total power in Azerbaijan. He said there were still some 40,000 heavily armed militants on the loose in Azerbaijan. Baku's military commandant said the death toll from the unrest had risen to 125, including twenty-seven members of the security forces. In Moscow, a leader of the Azerbaijani Popular Front, E'tibar Mamedov, was detained after arriving from Baku (Western agencies, *TASS*, January 26). People's deputy Sergei Stankevich said on "Vzglyad" that the Interregional Group of Deputies had expressed concern that the USSR Supreme Soviet (now in recess) had not been consulted before troops were sent to Baku. He said the Interregional Group had called on the authorities to open a dialogue with all those involved in the conflict and to call an emergency session of the Supreme Soviet or of the Council of Nationalities.

Komsomol'skaya pravda reported on January 27 that forty "extremist" leaders had been arrested in Azerbaijan since the state of emergency was declared. The same day, Yusuf Samedoglu, one of the leaders of the Azerbaijani Popular Front, proposed negotiations with Moscow on the withdrawal of troops from Baku in return for guaranteeing to maintain law and order in the city. Representatives of the Azerbaijani Popular Front and the Armenian Pan-National Movement also agreed to hold talks in Riga on January 31.

On January 29, TASS reported that the situation in Azerbaijan was gradually stabilizing under the control of troops and law-enforcement agencies, although leaflets were being circulated in Baku calling for the continuation of strikes.

On January 31, delegations from the Armenian Pan-National Movement and the Azerbaijani Popular Front arrived in Riga to start negotiations mediated by the independent Baltic Council. See RL 55/90.

Kazakh Muslims Set Up Religious Board

A Muslim religious board was set up in Kazakhstan. TASS said the founding meeting was attended by more than 250 delegates, who unanimously elected Mufti Ratbek Nysanbai-Uly as head of Kazakh Muslims. TASS quoted the Mufti as saying "we will be able to devote more attention to solving the problems of Kazakh Muslims." The report said the meeting noted that Kazakhstan now has sixty-three mosques. It said fifteen new mosques were opened in the republic last year, while others were "returned to believers."

More Demonstrations in Ukraine

There were more reports of demonstrations in Ukraine, this time in the city of Chernovtsy. A member of the Ukrainian Helsinki Union, Anatolii Dotsenko, said the protest was against the privileges enjoyed by Party officials. He told RFE/RL by telephone that up to 3,000 people had joined a demonstration on January 11 outside the Chernovtsy Oblast Party headquarters. Last week there were demonstrations against official privileges in Chernigov.

Latvian Green Party Holds Founding Congress

Some 200 members of the Latvian Green Party held their founding congress in the Latvian resort of Jurmala. TASS quoted a draft of the party statutes as saying the new party was an independent political alliance that would use all available means to protect the environment.

Party Leadership in Volgograd Oblast Forced to Resign

Ogonek (No. 1) carried a lengthy article strongly criticizing the policies of the first secretary of the Volgograd Oblast Party Committee, Vladimir Kalashnikov. Kalashnikov was portrayed as continuing to follow Brezhnev's line of suppressing people's initiative. He was also accused of corruption. The journal said that, as a result of Kalashnikov's policies, many people in the oblast had left the Party and young people had been discouraged from joining. On January 24, Kalashnikov was reported to have lost his post. He was replaced temporarily by Vyacheslav Ronshin (*Central Television*, 2230, January 24).

On January 29, "Vremya" showed footage of a demonstration held in Volgograd on January 28. Speakers called for the resignation of the entire oblast Party committee buro, the convening of an extraordinary oblast Party conference to elect new leaders, and the granting of independence to local prosecutors, police, and the KGB. *Izvestia* (January 25) reported that a number of Volgograd Oblast Party Committee officials, including the recently elected temporary first secretary, had obtained their apartments illegally. The demonstration coincided with a commentary in *Pravda* (January 28) saying that Kalashnikov and his associate, Vladimir Balandin, had blamed the media and certain "dark forces" for their unpopularity with citizens.

On January 30, the Volgograd Oblast Party Committee dismissed its leadership and called a special Party conference to choose new officials. "Vremya" said the Party plenum had elected an interim buro to organize the conference and meted out "strict Party punishment" to several leaders for abuse of office in allocation of housing. Among these was Ronshin. See RL 82/90.

Sunday, January 14

Pravda Says US Spy Caught and Sentenced to Death

Pravda said a Soviet diplomat code-named "Donald," who spied for the FBI and the CIA, had been caught red-handed and had been sentenced to death after confessing. The newspaper said he was one of the most important of some thirty Western spies caught by the Soviet Union in recent years.

Pravda Reports Emigration Figures for 1989

Pravda reported that 228,600 people emigrated from the USSR in 1989. That is more than twice as many as in the previous year. Most went to Israel, West Germany, the United States, and Greece. It gave figures for emigration to these four countries in 1989 as 102,000, 95,700, 13,900, and 10,000 respectively.

No Sabotage on Railroads

An investigation has revealed that sabotage is not responsible for the massive bottlenecks currently afflicting the Soviet railroad system, according to a report in *Sovetskaya Rossiya*. Rumors swept the Moscow press in October, 1989, that enemies of *perestroika* were bribing rail workers to get them to stop work, thereby exacerbating the current shortages—in particular, of soap. The investigation was carried out by the KGB, the USSR Prosecutor's Office, and the new MVD Department to Combat the Criminal Disruption of Freight. It concluded that the current problems were caused by "incorrigible mismanagement more than anything else."

Most Moldavians Do Not Want to Join Romania

Moldavian Party First Secretary Petru Lucinschi was quoted on Radio Moscow's World Service as saying that most residents of Moldavia did not want to be reunited with Romania, but he added that they did want closer contacts with Romania.

Anan'ev Says He Will Continue Resisting RSFSR Writers' Union Decision

Moscow News (No. 2) carried an interview with the chief editor of the journal *Oktyabr'*, Anatolii Anan'ev. In 1989, the Secretariat of the RSFSR Writers' Union tried to dismiss Anan'ev from his post after accusing him of Russophobia. Anan'ev refused to go, however, saying that as a people's deputy he could not be dismissed from his post without the approval of the USSR Supreme Soviet. Anan'ev told *Moscow News* that he would continue his fight to remain at *Oktyabr'*. Meanwhile, Russian nationalist poet

Stanislav Kunyaev leveled another attack on Andrei Sinyavsky's *Progulki s Pushkinym*. The publication of this work in *Oktyabr'* was one of the pretexts used by the union's Secretariat to seek Anan'ev's dismissal (*Literaturnaya Rossiya*, No. 2).

***Moscow News* Carries Interview with Markus Wolf**

Moscow News (No. 2) carried an interview with Markus Wolf, former chief of the intelligence service at the East German Ministry of State Security. In the interview, Wolf discussed his recently published book *Die Troika* and his decision to leave the GDR security forces.

Moscow News* Poll on *Perestroika

Moscow News (No. 2) carried an opinion poll on people's attitudes towards Gorbachev's policies. Of the 922 residents of Moscow polled, 71 percent said they thought that current policies were generally correct but that the reforms should be speeded up. Eighty-two percent said that the economic situation had worsened in the past three or four years. Thirty-three percent complained about a deterioration in their own standard of living, while 24 percent said their standard of living had improved. Asked whether the Soviet Union should resist if an East European country wanted to leave the Warsaw Pact, 64 percent said that it should not. Fifty-seven percent reacted positively to the idea of introducing privately owned enterprises. Only 4 percent, however, thought that in ten years' time a Capitalist system would exist in the USSR.

Monday, January 15

Abalkin on Soviet Economy

Deputy Prime Minister Leonid Abalkin said his country's economy must improve this year, or the Soviet people would lose confidence in their leaders. Abalkin spoke to reporters in Amsterdam at the start of a two-day visit to the Netherlands. He said improving the situation for Soviet consumers by the end of this year was his top priority (*Reuters*, *AP*, January 15). On January 16, in a speech in The Hague, Abalkin said the USSR should abolish the state-ownership system and set up stock and commodity markets.

Government Commission Arrives in Novokuznetsk

A USSR government commission went to Western Siberia for talks about the situation of miners. Many miners have said the government has been slow to meet their demands for better conditions. The commission, led by Deputy Prime Minister Lev Ryabev, began work in the city of Novokuznetsk in the Kemerovo Raion. TASS said they would study the implementation of government pledges made to miners last July after a wave of strikes. It will also examine the implementation of a government decree issued last August on the improvement of miners' living and social conditions. Ryabev is in charge of the USSR Council of Ministers' Bureau for the Fuel and Energy Complex.

Brazauskas Elected Chairman of Lithuanian Supreme Soviet

The first secretary of the Independent Lithuanian Communist Party, Algirdas Brazauskas, was elected chairman of the Presidium of the Lithuanian Supreme Soviet. Two candidates were nominated to oppose Brazauskas, but only four deputies out of 251 voted against him. Vytautas Astrauskas, who had been chairman of the Presidium of the Supreme Soviet since December, 1987, resigned today (*Radio Vilnius*, January 15).

Only Permanent Residents Allowed to Vote in Lithuania

The Lithuanian Supreme Soviet ruled that only permanent residents of Lithuania would be allowed to vote in local and republican elections. The decision, if upheld, means that most Soviet soldiers stationed in Lithuania will not be allowed to vote in the Lithuanian Supreme Soviet elections next month. Thousands of Lithuanians had signed a petition calling for a referendum on the issue. Deputies said that the signatories sought to bar Soviet soldiers from voting, and that therefore today's action by the Lithuanian Supreme Soviet made a referendum unnecessary (*Radio Vilnius*, *AP*, January 15).

The Lithuanian Supreme Soviet also decided by an overwhelming majority to declare two measures of the central authorities invalid on the territory of the Lithuanian SSR. The first was the USSR Law on Constitutional Compliance; the second was the decree of the Council of Ministers transferring the USSR Savings Bank to the control of the USSR State Bank. This decree had angered the Balts because it was adopted after the USSR law on Baltic economic autonomy, which states that all banking operations, except those of the USSR State Bank, are to be the prerogative of the republics (*Radio Vilnius*, January 15).

Protest against Gorlovka Chemical Plant

Radio Moscow said a rally had been held in Gorlovka in the Donets Basin on January 14 to demand the closure of a local defense industry chemical plant. The radio said the chemical plant was near a coal mine where three miners had died and some 300 had been poisoned after gas leaking from a pipeline serving the chemical plant reached the mine shaft. The radio did not say when the miners were killed but said that the pipeline had been leaking since 1983. It said that the mine had been closed as a result of the pipeline leakage and that some 1,000 miners had lost their jobs (*Radio Moscow-2*, 0839, January 15).

Ogonek on Murder of Last Russian Tsar

Another installment of Edvard Radzinsky's study on the execution in 1918 of the family of the last tsar appeared in *Ogonek* (No. 2). Radzinsky mentions the existence of an unknown tape of a report on the execution that was made in 1964 by two former members of the Urals Cheka, G. P. Nikulin and I. Rodzinsky, who participated in the executions. The tape, which has been kept in the closed section of the Central Party Archives, contains Rodzinsky's statement that documents offered by the Urals Soviet as proof that White Army officers and Russian monarchists abroad tried to arrange the escape of Nicholas II and his family to the West were simply fabricated by the Urals Soviet and the local Cheka. Radzinsky also reports for the first time in the Soviet press that there are indications that the decision to execute the tsar's family was made by Lenin and Yakov Sverdlov, and he quotes Leon Trotsky in support of this view. This is the first time that a statement by Trotsky has been used as evidence by a Soviet writer. The same issue of *Ogonek* contains an interview with the head of the Romanov family, Grand Duke Vladimir Kirillovich, who lives in France.

Iran Says Soviet Azerbaijanis Cross into Iran

The Iranian media said more than thirty Soviet Azerbaijanis had crossed the Araks River into Iran during a demonstration on January 14 held to demand closer ties between Soviet and Iranian Azerbaijanis (*AP*, January 15). On January 19, the Iranian news agency IRNA said thousands of Soviet Azerbaijanis had crossed the border into Iran to take part in Muslim prayer services. The news agency said many of the travelers were children and elderly people (*Reuters*, *DPA*, January 19).

Tuesday, January 16

Nenashev Gives Press Conference

On January 16, Soviet television broadcast a press conference given by Gosteleradio chief Mikhail Nenashev, who said that television should make a greater contribution to stabilizing the situation in the USSR. The most interesting part of the press conference was the question and answer session, in which Nenashev made clear that he disagreed with the most radical proposals for liberalizing the Soviet media and probably did not support the draft law on the media that has been published for nationwide discussion. He opposed the creation of private television and radio channels, arguing that the broadcast media were "strategic weapons" as well as information sources and implying that they could be used to destabilize the country still further.

Former Uzbek Party Official Cleared of Charges

A former Uzbek Communist Party secretary, Rano Abdullaeva, has been cleared of charges that she accepted a bribe of 5,000 rubles. TASS said Abdullaeva had been released on January 15 after being cleared by the USSR Supreme Court. TASS quoted her as telling journalists that she was not satisfied, because those who fabricated the charges against her had not been brought to justice. Abdullaeva's case was handled by the Tel'man Gdlyan investigation group, which claimed she was involved in sixteen instances of bribe-taking. See RL 202/90.

El'tsin in Japan

People's deputy Boris El'tsin is on a lecture tour in Japan. Speaking in Tokyo, El'tsin said that this was not the right time for the USSR to return the disputed Kurile Islands to Japan but that the Soviet-Japanese territorial dispute should be settled by future generations of leaders in both countries "in a changed world political climate." According to *Tokyo Kyodo* of January 16, El'tsin said that the islands should be gradually opened to Japanese investment over the next three to four years and that they should be demilitarized within another five to seven years. A Soviet-Japanese peace treaty could be signed when the islands were returned sometime around 2010.

Rostropovich and Vishnevskaya Have Citizenship Restored

The Presidium of the USSR Supreme Soviet restored Soviet citizenship to exiled cellist Mstislav Rostropovich and his wife, opera singer Galina Vishnevskaya. A Presidium decree also rescinded an earlier decree that stripped both of them of Soviet state awards (*TASS*, January 16). On January 17, TASS carried a statement by Rostropovich and Vishnevskaya saying that the restoration of their Soviet citizenship would help them to maintain close cultural contacts with their homeland but that they had no plans to return permanently to the USSR. The statement said that the two had been forced to leave the Soviet Union because of their friendship with Aleksandr Solzhenitsyn, and it expressed hope that Solzhenitsyn would soon be fully rehabilitated in his homeland.

Pravda Says Communism Not a Lost Cause in Romania

Pravda said it was understandable that many Romanians had rejected communism, but it said the Romanian Communist Party was nonetheless not a lost cause. The commentary said a decision to outlaw the Communist Party in Romania did not reflect the opinion of all Romanians. It said Romania's National Salvation Front Council had taken the decision in a moment of weakness when pressed by protesters in Bucharest last week who were "excited by emotions."

Wednesday, January 17

Vatican Delegation in Moscow

TASS reported that a Vatican delegation headed by Cardinal Willebrands had completed five days of talks with representatives of the Russian Orthodox Church. The main topic of discussion was the situation of Orthodox believers and Eastern Rite Catholics in Western Ukraine. At a press conference after the talks ended, the Vatican delegation reported that it had also met with representatives of the Eastern Rite Catholic Church. Both the Vatican delegation and the Russian Orthodox participants in the discussion said they hoped to maintain contacts with each other in order to broaden the consensus they were able to reach (*RFE/RL Special*, January 18).

"Democratic Union" Calls for Election Boycott

On January 17, the informal group Democratic Union called on its supporters to stage demonstrations against the forthcoming elections to local and republican soviets. The Democratic Union is a radical leftist organization whose members reject any cooperation with the Communist Party, even with reformist forces in it, and are against any sort of constructive contribution to the social and political life of the USSR while the CPSU remains in power. According to the Tanjug news agency, the Democratic Union said that, after the elections to the soviets, the CPSU would start putting all the blame for the country's problems on democratically elected representatives.

Thursday, January 18

Gorbachev Meets Workers and Peasants

Mikhail Gorbachev attended a meeting of more than 1,000 workers, farmers, engineers, and technicians held by the Party Central Committee. In his address, Gorbachev said the USSR needed *perestroika* "as we need air." In response, several workers criticized Gorbachev's reforms. TASS quoted a worker from Moscow as saying the CPSU and government leadership should be honest and admit that there would be no real improvements in the near future. Others complained that the working class had not benefited from reforms. See *Pravda*, January 19 and 20.

Tyumen Oblast Party Leadership Resigns en Bloc

Gennadii Bogomyakov, first secretary of the Tyumen Oblast Party Committee, retired today, and the entire Party buro stepped down. TASS said the move was not unexpected, because Western Siberia had been plagued by production shortfalls of crude oil, foodstuffs, and other commodities. TASS said local residents were blaming the problems on the local Party leadership. On January 19, an interim Party leadership was elected in Tyumen. TASS said the new first secretary was Viktor Kitaev, formerly a secretary of the Tyumen Oblast Party Committee.

Niyazov Elected Chairman of Turkmen Supreme Soviet

Turkmen Party First Secretary Saparmurad Niyazov has been elected chairman of the Turkmen Supreme Soviet. Radio Moscow said the new Supreme Soviet met for the first time in the capital, Ashkhabad (*Radio Moscow*, 1800, January 18).

USSR Confirms Reports of Military Cuts at Cam Ranh Bay

The Soviet Union said it had begun to reduce its military presence at Cam Ranh Bay in Vietnam. Foreign Ministry spokesman Vadim Perfil'ev said in Moscow that MiG-23 and Tupolev-16 planes had been removed from the base at the end of last year. He said the USSR hoped the cutbacks would help defuse military and political tensions and strengthen trust in Southeast Asia (*TASS*, January 18).

Friday, January 19

El'tsin Says *Perestroika* Has Failed, Warns of Revolt

In an interview with the Dutch weekly *Elsevier*, reformist people's deputy Boris El'tsin said *perestroika* had failed and he warned of violent revolution unless radical changes were implemented. El'tsin said Gorbachev had not gone far enough in restructuring the economy, cutting defense spending, and making the Soviet space program profitable. He said the government must agree to fundamental changes in its relations with the republics to avoid a revolution. El'tsin said it was vital to end the constitutional guarantee of the leading role of the Communist Party, and he said he would make this his top priority at the next Party congress (*Reuters*, January 19).

Supplies Low in Armenia because of Blockade

A Moscow television report said supplies of food and fuel were running out in Armenia and factories were on the brink of closure because of a lack of materials to work with. The report said this was the result of a blockade imposed by Azerbaijan for the past ten days on rail shipments into Armenia. The report quoted an official of the Armenian electrical power industry as saying that fuel was running out at power stations in Armenia and that he did not think there would be enough electricity for more than one or two days. The report also said 5,000 refugees had arrived from Azerbaijan and more were expected (*Central Television*, 1900, January 19).

Gorbachev Renews Offer to End Nuclear Testing

Gorbachev renewed an offer to end all nuclear tests in the Soviet Union if the United States did the same. Gorbachev told an international forum on the environment meeting in Moscow that reducing military activity "is vital not only for reducing the threat of war but also to preserve the environment." The United States has rejected previous offers to end testing, saying tests are necessary to maintain and upgrade missile systems. Gorbachev also suggested creating an international "green cross" relief agency to respond to ecological disasters (*Reuters*, *TASS*, in English, January 19; *Pravda*, January 20).

Soviet Miners in US Say Their Strikes Were Not Very Successful

Coal miners from the Soviet Union visiting the United States said they did not believe their strikes last year had been very successful. Miner Gennadii Sharov said, "We're not fighting against an owner but against a government system. To win we have to change laws. It isn't just a strike for coal miners but for the nation." The miners are touring coal fields in the Appalachian region of West Virginia after meeting leaders of the United Mine Workers of America and of the American union organization AFL-CIO in New York and Washington (*AP*, January 19).

On January 26, at a Washington news conference marking the end of the miners' month-long visit to the United States, the AFL-CIO announced that it was offering material assistance to the strike committees of Soviet miners. The AFL-CIO said it would give the Soviet miners computers, communications equipment, medical supplies, and other needed materials. One of the miners, Sergei Naidenov, said free trade unions were needed in the USSR because official unions were "not living up to expectations" (*AP*, *RFE/RL Special*, January 26).

USSR Buys More US Soybean Meal and Wheat

The US Department of Agriculture said the Soviet Union had bought 100,000 tons of US soybean meal. Reporters said the sale had been conducted by private companies and was worth about 19 million dollars. This brings the total deliveries of US soybean meal to the Soviet Union to 895,000 tons for the current market year. The sale came one day after the Soviet Union had bought 525,000 tons of US wheat to bring its total for the current market year to more than 2.2 millions tons (*Reuters*, January 19).

USSR Opens Bank in China for First Time since Relations Soured

The Soviet Union has opened a bank in Beijing for the first time since relations between the two nations soured in the early 1960s, a bank official said. The official said Vneshtorgbank began business on January 12 but still had no permanent offices in China (*Reuters*, January 19).

Muslims to Send One Million Korans to Moscow

The Saudi Arabian–based Muslim World League is sending one million Korans to the Soviet Union, the weekly newspaper *Al-Muslimoon* said. It also said that, in another project, backed by Saudi Arabia's King Fahd, 600,000 Korans were being printed in Turkmen (*Reuters*, January 19).

Saturday, January 20

New Informal Political Group in Tajikistan

An informal political group calling itself "Rastokhez" (Renaissance) has been established in Dushanbe, with members in a number of cities throughout Tajikistan. The head of the organization, Bagir Abduljabar, told RFE/RL on January 19 that "Rastokhez" had not yet been registered but that it was being allowed to function and its draft program had been published. The group, which is open to anyone regardless of nationality, seeks to become involved in all aspects of the political, public, and cultural life of Tajikistan and to help solve the republic's ecological problems. Abduljabar indicated that "Rastokhez" would also advance the cause of economic autonomy for Tajikistan. Although he pointed out that his group was not a copy of the Baltic popular fronts, he said there were some similarities.

Traditional New Year Becomes Holiday in Uzbekistan

The traditional Persian New Year, Navroz, was declared a public holiday in Uzbekistan. An Uzbek journalist told RFE/RL that the decision to make Navroz a holiday (this year it will be celebrated on March 21) was announced by Uzbek First Secretary Islam Karimov at a meeting today with Tashkent city Party officials.

Sunday, January 21

Democratic Platform Created within CPSU

More than 450 progressive Communists from across the USSR met in Moscow over the weekend to set up a pressure group for democratic change within the CPSU. Delegates came from seventy-eight cities and represented about 100 of the USSR's new informal political clubs. The group's charter declaration calls for the transformation of the CPSU into "a genuinely democratic parliamentary party operating under a multiparty system." It also calls for a market economy, the extension of private ownership, and "democratic Socialist" values. The group's most immediate demand is for delegates to the next Party Congress to be chosen more democratically. In the past, delegates were nominated from above, but there is now strong pressure for them to be elected from below—perhaps on the basis of alternative political platforms. Some participants in the meeting said they might split off from the CPSU altogether and form a Social Democratic Party if the leadership of the CPSU delayed introducing reforms in the Party (*Radio Moscow*, January 20, 2200; *Central Television*, "Sem' dnei," January 22, 2100). See RL 53/90.

Human Chain Formed in Ukraine to Mark Unification Anniversary

Tens of thousands of Ukrainians marked the anniversary of Ukrainian unification by linking hands to form a chain from Lvov to Kiev. The event was organized by the Ukrainian Popular Movement for *Perestroika*, "Rukh," and was held to mark the seventy first anniversary on January 22 of the unification of formerly Russian-ruled

Ukraine with Western Ukraine, which until 1918 was part of the Austro-Hungarian empire. January 22 is also the seventy-second anniversary of the proclamation in Kiev of the independent Ukrainian People's Republic. A rally was held in Kiev to mark the anniversaries. TASS said participants in the rally spoke of unification not only of Ukrainians but also of Russians, Jews, and other nationalities that have Ukraine as their fatherland. Some of the Kiev demonstrators called for an independent Ukraine and for a government made up of "Rukh" supporters (*TASS*, Western agencies, RL Ukrainian service, January 21). See RL 57/90.

Changes in the Political Leadership of the Warsaw Pact

The chairmanship of the Political Consultative Committee of the Warsaw Pact will no longer be held by the Communist Party general secretary of a member country. In an interview with *Pravda*, Chief of the General Staff of the Soviet Armed Forces Mikhail Moiseev said that, owing to the creation of multiparty systems in some East European countries, in future the prime minister or the president of a Warsaw Pact member state would supervise the work of the Political Consultative Committee.

New Unofficial Group in Turkmenistan

Information reached the West that a new unofficial organization had been founded in Turkmenistan, according to *Turkmenskaya iskra* (January 21). The newspaper attacked an unofficial organization called "Agzybirlik" (Unity) for promoting divisiveness in Turkmenistan. *Turkmenskaya iskra* took the line that conservative Communist Party leaders elsewhere have adopted recently—namely, that many of the new group's rank and file are reasonable but that the leadership is dangerously radical.

Some 60,000 Killed in Soviet Road Accidents Last Year

Pravda said about 60,000 people had been killed and 319,000 injured in road accidents in the USSR in 1989. Commenting on the figures, *Pravda* said the police could not improve safety on the roads without the help of the general public.

Monday, January 22

Russian Bible Society Reestablished

According to a Keston College press release, a Russian Bible Society has been reestablished in Moscow on the initiative of the Baptist publishing group "Protestant." The president of the new society is Sergei Averintsev, a corresponding member of the USSR Academy of Sciences and a USSR people's deputy. The society has already been registered as an independent organization. The Latvian Bible Society was reestablished in mid-January, and similar societies are expected to appear in other parts of the Soviet Union.

Sakharov Honored Forty Days after His Death

Many Moscow residents honored the late Soviet human-rights activist Andrei Sakharov by laying flowers at his grave, gathering outside his Moscow home, and holding public meetings. TASS said the tributes were in keeping with a Russian tradition of honoring a deceased person forty days after his death. Sakharov died on December 14.

Tuesday, January 23

***Izvestia* Questions Whether *Perestroika* Will Last**

An article in *Izvestia* written by parliamentary commentator Vyacheslav Shchepotkin questioned the future of Gorbachev's reform program. Shchepotkin wrote that Soviet society today was "right at the point where it must answer the question: Will there be *perestroika* or not?" The article focused on the conflict in the Transcaucasus. Shchepotkin said the only way to bring a halt to the conflict was "the resolute and energetic imposition of law and order . . . a real dictatorship of the law." He added: "Millions of people have staked all their hopes and energy on the *perestroika* card. This is why we are telling the head of state: Act! Real democracy must be capable of defending itself."

Red Cross Team Finds Psychological Distress in Chernobyl' Area

An International Red Cross team said psychological distress remained a major health problem in the areas affected by the Chernobyl' nuclear accident. In a statement released in Geneva, the team said the Soviet authorities had provided very little information at the time of the accident, giving rise to mistrust, which in turn led to psychosomatic ailments. The statement said a team just back from a nine-day visit to parts of the RSFSR, Belorussia, and Ukraine had found many widely held misconceptions about radioactivity, and it suggested that trained volunteers could help allay fears by giving advice. It also said fears about food contamination could be eased by giving people Geiger counters to check their food (*AFP*, *DPA*, *Reuters*, *UPI*, January 23).

Latvian Party Plenum Shows Sharp Differences of Opinion

Latvia's Communist Party Central Committee held a plenum that, according to the Soviet media, revealed sharp differences of opinion among the republic's Communists. Radio Moscow said Party unity was now a matter of concern for friends and foes alike. It did not go into detail, but it said the plenum discussed the results of the Party campaign for Latvian sovereignty. Some leading Communists have called on the Party to consider formally splitting from Moscow, as some Lithuanian Communists have done (*Radio Moscow*, 1700, *Central Television*, "Vremya," 1900, January 23).

Drug Traffickers Sentenced in Tashkent

Pravda said the KGB in Uzbekistan had broken up a smuggling operation involving senior Soviet consular officials in Afghanistan. The *Pravda* report said the Uzbekistan Supreme Court had sentenced drug traffickers and smugglers of antiques and other goods to imprisonment and confiscation of property. It said the smuggling involved the Soviet consul general in Kabul, the consul in Mazar-i-Sharif, and residents of the Uzbek border town of Termez.

Soviet Reaction to NSC Proposals

TASS reacted negatively to the decision by the US National Security Council to review the list of technology the export of which to Eastern Europe is at present restricted. TASS said: "This announcement testifies to the fact that the United States is still not ready to fully renounce discriminatory practices in international trade." It added that the United States had been "forced" to review the COCOM list by West European countries that want to expand business with the East. While conceding that the decision represented an attempt by the Bush administration to rethink international political and military realities, it argued that any step the United States took to ease trading restrictions ultimately reflects its own interests and is not designed to help relieve the consumer goods shortages in the East.

Marju Lauristin Quits Communist Party

One of the leaders and founders of the Estonian Popular Front, Supreme Soviet deputy Marju Lauristin, has resigned from the Communist Party. Lauristin is a founding member of the new Estonian Social Democratic Independence Party and a long-time advocate of Estonian sovereignty. Lauristin has been active in dissident and opposition activities in Estonia since the 1960s, when she was a member of the New Left movement (RFE Estonian service, January 23).

Israel and USSR Sign Trade and Economic Ties Protocol

Israel and the Soviet Union have signed a protocol on developing trade and economic ties between the two countries. TASS said the protocol was signed in Moscow by Vladislav Malkevich, chairman of the USSR Chamber of Commerce and Industry, and Dan Gillerman, president of the Israeli Federation of Chambers of Commerce.

Meskhetians Demonstrate in Moscow

A group of Meskhetians demanding the right to return to their homeland demonstrated outside the Moscow television center. One of the placards they were carrying asked Gorbachev: "Where should we live today?" Another sign demanded that the Communist Party "move from words to deeds." A commission of the USSR Supreme Soviet recommended in December, 1989, that the Meskhetians be allowed gradually to return to their homeland in Georgia. The decision is now up to the Presidium of the Supreme Soviet. The Meskhetians were deported from Georgia in 1944. Some 60,000 Meskhetians fled Uzbekistan last year following interracial violence in which almost 100 people, most of them Meskhetians, were killed (*Central Television*, January 24, 1400).

Wednesday, January 24

Bush Declares Support for Gorbachev

US President George Bush expressed support for Gorbachev. Bush told a White House press conference that Gorbachev faced ethnic and internal problems of enormous proportions. Bush said he hoped Gorbachev not only survived but stayed strong. He said it was in the interests of the United States for *perestroika* to succeed (*Reuters*, January 24).

Ecological Association Set Up in Leningrad

An ecological association has been set up in Leningrad by large industrial enterprises and research organizations. TASS said that the enterprises and organizations had created a one-million-ruble fund and that more money would be allocated by state and public organizations. TASS quoted the director of the new association, Yurii Erdyakov, as saying the work of the association would be coordinated by a council composed of scientists and specialists from enterprises, who would attach great importance to monitoring the ecological situation in the Soviet Union.

Thursday, January 25

Lauristin Says Baltic Independence Movement Is Helping *Perestroika*

A leader of the Estonian Popular Front, Marju Lauristin, said the Baltic independence movement was helping, not hindering, Gorbachev's reform efforts. She was quoted by AP as saying in Stockholm that not to grant independence would amount to stopping halfway in rebuilding Soviet society. Lauristin said the Baltic republics now enjoyed greater economic autonomy from Moscow, but she added that this should be followed by greater political freedom.

Ukrainian Official Fired for Abuse of Position

A top official in Zhitomir Oblast in Ukraine has been fired for abusing his position and for other violations. TASS said Vasilii Yamchinsky had been released from his posts as chairman of the Zhitomir Soviet Executive Committee and as a member of the oblast Party committee buro. TASS said Yamchinsky had violated housing regulations by allowing his daughter and her family to jump the queue for an apartment.

Further Derailment on Armenian-Georgian Railway

Radio Erevan reported the second incident this week on a rail connection between Armenia and Georgia being used to keep Armenia supplied with goods. A brief report said several people had been hurt in a train derailment. The Soviet central media said on January 24 that a train had been derailed earlier in the week halfway between Tbilisi and the Armenian border in an Azerbaijani-populated area of Georgia. They said a section of the track had been removed. Trains have been arriving along the Georgian line carrying supplies and fuel that cannot get through via Azerbaijan.

Meeting in Ukraine on Transcaucasian Conflict

Some 10,000 people attended a meeting in Lvov on the situation in the Transcaucasus organized by an independent group called the Lvov Strike Committee, or Committee in Defense of Citizens' Rights. The unsanctioned meeting expressed its solidarity with "the democratic forces of the peoples of the Transcaucasus" and condemned the imposition of a state of emergency in the region, the military intervention, and the use of Ukrainians and soldiers of other nationalities to "solve an interethnic conflict" by force. (The name of one Ukrainian soldier killed in the region has already become known to activists in Lvov.) The Lvov Strike Committee proposed to appeal to Ukrainian soldiers to refuse to "carry out criminal imperial gendarme functions" in Azerbaijan and urged Ukrainians to protest against the use of "our countrymen" in "the suppression of national movements" (RL Ukrainian service, January 26).

Soviet Trade Delegation Arrives in Israel

A six-member Soviet delegation arrived in Israel for trade talks with Israeli Finance Minister Shimon Peres. The delegation will also draft agreements to be signed by Peres on a visit to the Soviet Union. No date has been set for that trip. The head of the Soviet delegation, Yurii Olkhovikov, said talks would cover trade, aviation, agriculture, tourism, and education (*Reuters*, *AP*, January 25).

Aeroflot Orders European Airbus

Today's *Journal of Commerce* reported that Aeroflot had signed a lease-purchase agreement with the European Airbus consortium for five A310-300 wide-body jets. The deal is estimated at about 300 million dollars, and the first jet is expected to be delivered in November, 1991. The planes will probably be used on Aeroflot's international routes, which the airline has been expanding rapidly in recent years.

Proposals Published for Cleaning Up the Environment

Writing in this week's issue of *Ekonomika i zhizn'* (No. 4), a group of authors explored possible market mechanisms to help clean up the environment. The authors suggested that the government establish a system of taxes and subsidies that would raise the costs of using "dirtier" raw materials while encouraging the recycling of wastes. Similarly, taxes could discourage the use of harmful products such as highly toxic pesticides. Another interesting proposal was for local governments to establish limits on pollution output and resource consumption based on local conditions. By establishing a maximum load that can be placed on the environment, this approach would help prevent the creation of any more ecological "disaster zones" like the Kuzbass.

Friday, January 26

"Vzglyad" Shows Attack on Liberal Writers

The television program "Vzglyad" showed a film of the attack in the Moscow Writers' Club on January 18 on members of the liberal "April" writers' committee by members of the club of the journal *Nash sovremennik*, among them a correspondent of the Moscow suburban newspaper *Luberetskaya pravda*. One of the interlopers read a statement to the effect that Politburo member Aleksandr Yakovlev had been "a hireling" of world Zionism since he was ambassador to Canada in the 1970s. While the investigator in charge of the case said there was no evidence that "Pamyat'" was involved, writer Anatolii Kurchatkin, who was one of those beaten up, said the attack represented a continuation of a right-wing offensive that included the "Pamyat'" demonstration on Red Square on November 12, the sixth plenum of the RSFSR Writers' Union on November 12 and 13, and the demonstration of Party officials on Leningrad's Palace Square on November 22, 1989. See also *Komsomol'skaya pravda*, January 21, and *Literaturnaya gazeta*, No. 4, 1990.

Belorussian Becomes Official Language of Belorussia

The Belorussian Supreme Soviet adopted a law making Belorussian the official language of the republic, with Russian as the language for interethnic communication. The law stipulated that every citizen in the republic has the right to speak Russian and to receive a Russian-language education (*TASS*, January 26).

Saturday, January 27

Complaints about Anti-Semitism in USSR

Speaking on the Saturday night television show "Do i posle polunochi" (Before and after Midnight), two progressive members of the Congress of People's Deputies called on viewers to prevent the Jewish pogroms that members of "Pamyat'" had announced would take place in Moscow and Leningrad on May 5. (A few hours earlier, "Pamyat'" had staged a demonstration near the Moscow television center, protesting coverage of its activities by the program "Vzglyad" the previous evening [*Pravda*, January 28].) While acknowledging that "Pamyat'" previously had distributed leaflets announcing pogroms that had subsequently failed to materialize, USSR people's deputies Yurii Shchekochikhin and Arkadii Murashov warned that the situation was becoming increasingly dangerous. Shchekochikhin said he had sent a parliamentary request to USSR Minister of Internal Affairs Vadim Bakatin protesting the police's refusal to undertake any action against members of "Pamyat'" who organized a riot in the Moscow Writers' Club on January 18.

Earlier today, Leningrad KGB chief Anatolii Kurkov stated on the local television channel that there was "no danger whatsoever" of pogroms. Kurkov added that the KGB knew everyone who professed anti-Semitic views and that, if the anti-Semites tried to make trouble, his organization was ready to take "the most decisive measures."

On January 30, TASS, Radio Moscow, and Soviet television reported that a Communist Party commission in Odessa Oblast had asked for "Pamyat'" to be banned because of its anti-Semitic activities. The report said the group's activities in Ukraine were poisoning inter-ethnic relations. The Soviet media said "Pamyat'" and other extremist organizations had been distributing provocative leaflets in Odessa Oblast in the past few days. The report said local Party officials had dismissed rumors of impending pogroms in Ukraine.

On February 1, *Literaturnaya Rossiya* published an appeal by three Russian nationalist groups rejecting the rumors of Jewish "pogroms" and suggesting that the rumors had been spread by Zionist groups.

Lithuanian Christian Democratic Party Holds Congress

On January 27 and 28, the Lithuanian Christian Democratic Party held a founding congress in Kaunus. The congress was attended by 156 delegates, representing the 1,500 registered party members, and about 100 guests. Representatives of other European Christian Democratic parties also attended. The congress approved party statutes updating the prewar statutes of the Lithuanian Christian Democratic Party to meet current requirements (RFE Lithuanian service, January 28).

Intellectuals Most Popular Election Candidates

The results of a preelection opinion poll conducted recently by the Institute of Sociology of the USSR Academy of Sciences indicated that representatives of the intelligentsia—lawyers, scientists, and physicians—are the most popular candidates for the upcoming parliamentary elections in the RSFSR. Only 6 to 14 percent of voters support the candidacies of workers and peasants. The results of the poll were published in *Sovetskaya Rossiya*, which last year became a mouthpiece of the United Front of Workers of Russia. The front has complained about the fact that a large number of intellectuals were elected to the first USSR Congress of People's Deputies and it has campaigned for an increase in worker representation in the elections to the republican and local soviets.

Sunday, January 28

Calls for Withdrawal of Soviet Troops from Eastern Europe

Some 20,000 people demonstrated outside a Soviet army base in Czechoslovakia demanding that Soviet troops there leave. AP and Reuters quoted the Czechoslovak media as saying protesters had given the commander of the base in Olomouc a petition urging withdrawal as quickly as possible. On January 29, the Soviet Union's chief negotiator on conventional force reductions, Oleg Grinevsky, said the Soviet Union was willing to withdraw all its troops from Eastern Europe within five years if NATO withdrew its troops from Western Europe (*The Washington Post*, January 29). On January 30, *Krasnaya zvezda* cautioned against too hasty a withdrawal of Soviet troops from Eastern Europe, saying that a unilateral withdrawal of Soviet troops might upset military stability in Europe.

Goskomstat Report on 1989 Plan Fulfillment

Pravda carried the USSR State Committee for Statistics report on the Soviet economy in 1989. The salient growth data for that year were given as: GNP—3 percent; national income (produced)—2.4 percent; and industrial output—1.7 percent. The budget deficit was reported to have been reduced from 120 billion rubles to 92 billion rubles. These figures are in current prices. What Goskomstat was still unable to bring itself to admit was that, in real terms, output fell last year. See RL 71/90 and RL 62/90.

New Mufti Elected in Northern Caucasus

A two-day congress in Makhachkala of the Muslims of the Northern Caucasus ended with the election of a new mufti (*Radio Moscow*, January 28, 1900). The post had been vacant for more than six months, after the previous incumbent, Mahmud Gekkiyiev, was removed, following demonstrations by the faithful. Among the charges raised against Gekkiyiev was that no congress of the North Caucasian Muslim Religious Board had been held since the one that elected him in 1978. The main objection to him, though, was undoubtedly that in the past he sided too often with the authorities and in more recent years failed to take account of Moscow's less repressive attitude towards religion. There may also have been some resentment towards him on the grounds that he was not a Dagestani, having been born in Kabardino-Balkaria. The new mufti, B. Isaev, was chosen from among three candidates. Until now he has been imam of the mosque in Makhachkala.

Monday, January 29

Moscow Discusses Jewish Emigration with Arabs

The Soviet ambassador to Jordan, Aleksandr Zinchuk, said Moscow was discussing the issue of Soviet Jewish emigration to Israel with the Palestine Liberation Organization and with Arab governments. But, in remarks published in the *Jordan Times*, Zinchuk said there was very little the Soviet Union could do to control the flow of Soviet Jews to Israel. He noted that the United States had imposed quotas on Jewish immigration at a time when the Soviet Union was opening its doors for emigration. Zinchuk said now that immigration to the United States was curtailed, Soviet Jews were being compelled to turn to Israel. The PLO and a number of Arab states have expressed concern about Soviet Jews settling in the Israeli-occupied West Bank and Gaza Strip (*Reuters*, January 29). On January 31, Soviet Deputy Foreign Minister Gennadii Tarasov discussed Jewish emigration from the Soviet Union with PLO leader Yasser Arafat during a meeting in Tunis (*Reuters*, *AP*, January 31).

Brazauskas on Lithuania's Future

Lithuanian Party leader Algirdas Brazauskas has rejected accusations by the Moscow central authorities that the Lithuanian Communists are separatists and nationalists. Brazauskas said in an interview with the West German news magazine *Der Spiegel* that the Lithuanian Party only wanted to achieve *perestroika* within the Party. He said this was the only way for the Party to regain people's respect. He said Lithuania's future relations with the Soviet Union would remain close. Brazauskas said the fact that Lithuania received 80 percent of its raw materials from the Soviet Union could not be ignored.

Kuzbass Talks End, Conflict Commission Set Up

The latest round of talks between miners in the Kuzbass region and government officials about miners' demands ended with the creation of a commission to settle conflicts. TASS said this commission would deal with the settlement of miners' demands. The demands included calls for regional self-financing and full economic and legal independence for mines. After the mass strikes by miners last summer, the Soviet authorities pledged last summer to meet the miners' demands, which also include better pay, benefits, and working conditions. But the miners said this has not been done yet. TASS said the two sides failed to sign a joint document on the implementation of the government's pledges.

Modrow and Gysi in Moscow

East German Prime Minister Hans Modrow arrived in Moscow for talks with Gorbachev and Prime Minister Nikolai Ryzhkov. On January 31, Soviet television broadcast an interview with Modrow in which he complained about West German interference in East German internal affairs. Modrow also said there were alarming signals of neofascist activity in East Germany. On February 2, East German Communist Party Chairman Gregor Gysi arrived in Moscow. He held talks with Gorbachev and gave an interview to *Sovetskaya Rossiya*.

More than 100 Accused of Bribery in Kharkov

More than 100 leading officials in the Ukrainian town of Kharkov are to stand trial for misappropriation and bribery. The Soviet media said the accused officials had made over 6 million rubles by using or supplying state property to make expensive, made-to-measure clothes. Radio Moscow and TASS said that among those facing trial for bribery were employees of the administration of public services and supplies, the chief accountant of the Kharkov department of the Finance Ministry, the managers of clothing factories, and sixteen employees of the Ministry of Internal Affairs.

Russian-Language Region in Moldavia Votes for Independence

Reports from Moldavia said citizens of the Tiraspol Raion had voted to declare their administrative independence. TASS said a referendum on the issue had been organized by the United Council of Labor Collectives of Tiraspol, an organization dominated by Russian-speakers, who make up nearly 90 percent of Tiraspol's residents. TASS said 96 percent of those voting supported regional self-government and the incorporation of Tiraspol Raion into a Dnestr Autonomous Republic, if such a republic were formed.

Tuesday, January 30

Gorbachev Accepts Principle of Unity

Signifying a major departure in Soviet foreign policy, Gorbachev publicly accepted the likelihood of German reunification. Speaking to reporters before beginning talks in Moscow with East German Prime Minister Hans Modrow, Gorbachev acknowledged that it was "not unexpected" that the issue of German unity was back on the agenda and that "in principle, no one puts it in doubt." He did caution, however, that any move towards reunification must remain stable and gradual. He said, "It is necessary to act responsibly and not decide this issue on the streets" (*ADN*, in English, January 30).

Shevardnadze on Eastern Europe and *Perestroika*

Soviet Foreign Minister Eduard Shevardnadze said the USSR was concerned about the fate of Communist Parties in Eastern Europe. He said the failures and setbacks of those parties "by no means gladden us." But Shevardnadze said the Soviet Union respected the will of the peoples who were bringing to the fore "other political forces" in Eastern Europe. Shevardnadze also said he disagreed emphatically with the view that the Soviet Union's reforms had reached a deadlock. He said that *perestroika* remained the main direction in the development of the Soviet state and society and that there was no alternative to it (*APN*, in English, January 30).

Wednesday, January 31

***Izvestia* Interviews Gidaspov**

Izvestia carried an interview with Leningrad Party chief Boris Gidaspov, who gave lack of time due to his existing responsibilities as the reason for his decision not to stand for election to the Leningrad City Soviet. Gidaspov said his activities as chairman of the USSR Congress of People's Deputies Mandate Commission and as first secretary of the Leningrad Oblast and City Party Committees did not leave him enough time to contribute to the work of the Leningrad Soviet, but he argued that as a USSR people's deputy and Leningrad Party chief he had ample opportunity to participate in carrying out the decisions of the soviet. It seems unlikely, however, that Gidaspov will succeed in convincing Leningrad residents, among whom he is highly unpopular, that his decision to withdraw his candidacy was not motivated by a fear of not being elected. The *Izvestia* correspondent who interviewed Gidaspov also alluded to the possibility that he feared defeat. See also *Komsomol'skaya pravda*, January 30.

Congress of People's Deputies under Fire

Pravda published readers' letters saying that democracy was degenerating into "anarchy" and that the central authorities were showing "demoralizing indecision." The USSR Congress of People's Deputies, readers said, had disappointed the public because it was "more like a rally than an institution of supreme power," and they suggested that the chairman of the Supreme Soviet

(Gorbachev) "lacked authority" to deal with the country's problems. "It is time," readers wrote, "to use power."

Round-Table Talks of Leading Social Groups Proposed

The editor of *Komsomol'skaya pravda*, Aleksandr Drozdov, proposed that, in view of the failure of the Congress of People's Deputies to function effectively, the USSR Party should copy the East Europeans and institute round-table discussions with representatives of leading social groups. Round-table discussions have been used in Poland, East Germany, Czechoslovakia, and Hungary as a means for the government to negotiate with the opposition.

Department for Refugees Set Up

A department has been set up in the USSR State Committee for Labor and Social Problems to deal with the mass movement of people resulting from natural disasters, major accidents, and ethnic strife (*Izvestia*, January 31). The chief functions of the new department will be to keep a record of these people, to give them material assistance, and to find them work. According to the deputy chairman of the state committee, Viktor Buinovsky, there are currently over 500,000 refugees who have left their homes following ethnic strife. They include Meskhetian Turks, Armenians, and Azerbaijanis. Buinovsky also said that a draft law had been drawn up regulating questions connected with forced migration on the territory of the Soviet Union.

Controversy over Ukrainian Catholic Church Continues

Signs are emerging of a conflict between the Moscow Patriarchate and the Soviet state over the issue of the Ukrainian Catholic Church. On January 30, Soviet television announced that an agreement had been reached between the Vatican and the Russian Orthodox Church whereby the Cathedral of the Resurrection in Ivano-Frankovsk would be handed back to the Ukrainian Catholics. On January 31, however, Metropolitan Filaret, the Russian Orthodox exarch for Ukraine, delivered a statement on the "Vremya" newscast on behalf of the Synod of the Russian Orthodox Church, denying that any such agreement had been reached and strongly condemning the decision to hand back the cathedral to the Ukrainian Catholics. On February 1, the Synod of the Russian Orthodox Church asked Gorbachev to intercede in its dispute with the Ukrainian Catholic Church (*TASS*, February 1). See RL 7/90.

USSR Reassures US over Soviet Helicopters in Nicaragua

US Secretary of State James Baker said that the Soviet Union had assured the United States that a new shipment of Soviet helicopters to Nicaragua would not be used for military purposes. Earlier, a US official said four MI-17 helicopters that Nicaragua had recently received from the Soviet Union could be used for combat as well as for civilian purposes. In Moscow, Soviet Foreign Ministry spokesman Gennadii Gerasimov said the helicopters were civilian and did not represent a resumption of deliveries of military equipment (*Reuters*, January 31).

McDonalds Opens in Moscow

The American fast-food chain McDonalds opened its first Moscow restaurant. Thousands of people were served American-style hamburgers. Fifty children were admitted as the first customers on the orders of restaurant manager George Kohon. The restaurant has 700 seats inside and 200 outside (*AP*, *UPI*, January 31).

***Pravda* Publishes Round Table on Political Power in USSR**

Pravda carried a round-table discussion devoted to the powers of the central authorities under *perestroika*. During the discussion, scholar Vladimir Zots said that central power was in fact weak in the Soviet Union and that the current head of state "lacks the powers that the presidents of other developed countries have." Zots also said that, at present, the chairman of the USSR Supreme Soviet (Gorbachev) has virtually no legislative protection. He said there were no guarantees that the Congress of People's Deputies, influenced by left- or right-wing forces, would not demand the chairman's replacement. He noted that it was also theoretically possible for a Central Committee plenum to recall the Party general secretary.

Latvian Komsomol Paves Way for Autonomy

The Latvian Komsomol has taken the first step in severing itself from the all-Union Komsomol organization. This was reported by Radio Riga, which said that about 800 delegates at a congress of the Latvian Komsomol had voted to keep the old name of the organization in order to preserve its rights to Komsomol property "until a completely different youth organization evolves." The Latvian Komsomol adopted its own statutes to replace those of the all-Union organization. Last year, the Lithuanian Komsomol broke away from the central Komsomol organization, while the Estonian Komsomol decided to replace itself with another youth organization.

Castro Explains Ban on Soviet Publications

On January 31, *Literaturnaya gazeta* carried an article from a Spanish newspaper in which Cuban President Fidel Castro explained why he had banned the distribution of certain Soviet periodicals. According to the Cuban leader, he did this "without vacillation" because many Soviet publications now cast aspersions on Lenin, the revolution, and socialism itself. See RL 14/90 and RL 15/90.

The Month of February

Thursday, February 1

Bush Puts Forward New Proposals on Troop Cuts

On February 1, US President George Bush put forward new proposals for the Soviet Union and the United States to cut their troop strength in central Europe to 195,000 each (Western agencies, February 1). Soviet Foreign Ministry spokesman Gennadii Gerasimov said Bush's proposal was a step in the right direction (*Reuters*, February 1).

Anti-Zionist Committee Condemns "Pamyat'" Attack on Writers

Radio Moscow-1 (1700) broadcast a statement by the Soviet Anti-Zionist Committee condemning a recent incident in which members of "Pamyat'" used violence to break up a meeting in Moscow of the independent writers' group "April." During their attack on the writers, members of "Pamyat'" shouted anti-Semitic slogans. The Anti-Zionist Committee condemned the incident as a crude provocation designed to fan the flames of ethnic conflict. Set up in 1983, the Anti-Zionist Committee was intended both to defuse Western accusations that the Soviet Union's attacks on Israel were anti-Semitic and to provide Moscow with another channel to continue attacks on Tel-Aviv.

***Moscow News* Again Attacks Ligachev**

Moscow News (No. 5) carried an editorial by its outspoken deputy chief editor, Vitalii Tret'yakov, who attacked Politburo member Egor Ligachev for glorifying Stalin, disregarding the people's will, lying, and clinging to Socialist ideals. Ligachev has often been attacked in the press, particularly by *Moscow News*, but Tret'yakov went further than most, accompanying his editorial with a picture showing Ligachev giving a Nazi-like salute.

Ukrainian Unions Protest against Price Rises

The Ukrainian Council of Trade Unions protested against increases in cargo rates and in wholesale prices for electricity and diesel fuel. At a briefing in Kiev, trade unionists said complaints had been sent to Prime Minister Nikolai Ryzhkov. TASS said many of them demanded that the increases be repealed or suspended. The unions predicted that the price rises would result in reduced wages and benefits and in the suspension of some housing construction. They also said that increasing levels of popular discontent might lead to "mass labor conflicts."

Friday, February 2

Unrest Continues in Azerbaijan

On February 2, Azerbaijani Popular Front leaders held talks in Baku with the Soviet military commander and demanded the withdrawal of Soviet troops (*TASS*, February 2). The first round of face-to-face talks between the Azerbaijani Popular Front and the Armenian Pan-National Movement took place in Riga on February 2–3 under the auspices of the Baltic Council. They culminated in an agreement on a ceasefire along the border between the two republics and an exchange of hostages. The agreement was, however, declared void later in the day, when the Armenian side received information that the Armenian population of two villages in the Khanlar Raion of Azerbaijan had been forced to leave their homes (*Reuters*, *TASS*, February 3).

The Soviet media reported on February 4 that there were still isolated outbreaks of shooting in Armenia and that in Azerbaijan strikes were continuing and meetings were being held to demand the withdrawal of Soviet troops and the lifting of the state of emergency. *Izvestia* reported that, since the state of emergency was imposed, 148 people had been killed and 503 injured in the two republics.

On February 5, TASS reported picketing, continuing strikes, and demands for the lifting of the curfew in Baku, where public transport and light industry are still not operating at full strength. AFP reported that two Armenians had been sentenced in Baku to nine and ten years' imprisonment for possession of explosives. Consignments of fuel, food supplies, and building materials are again being transported by rail from Azerbaijan to Armenia. Western agencies reported that the Mingechaur hydroelectric power station in northwest Azerbaijan, which supplies all three Transcaucasian republics, had been damaged by an explosion on February 4. Soviet television on February 5 broadcast an appeal for assistance in finding housing and employment for refugees who have fled the recent violence in the Caucasus.

On February 6, Radio Erevan aired a report saying that an armored unit of the Soviet army had been sent to Armenia to help keep order. The radio also reported that the armored unit would be assigned to help lift the railroad blockade imposed by the Azerbaijanis against Armenia.

On February 8, TASS said that losses from the stoppages had reached 390.5 million rubles as of February 7. It also said that a road blockade was continuing in Nagorno-Karabakh and that road transport there was moving only with military escorts.

On February 12, TASS said that an agreement had been reached in talks involving Armenian and Azerbaijani leaders, the USSR Ministry of Railways, and the military command in the Transcaucasus on the resumption of rail traffic between Baku and Erevan. On February 13, Radio Moscow-1 (1900) said that, despite the agreement, rail traffic had not yet resumed.

On February 14, members of the Azerbaijani Popular Front and Russian refugees from Azerbaijan demonstrated, separately, in Moscow. Radio Moscow quoted *Izvestia* as saying the Azerbaijanis demanded that the state of emergency be lifted in Baku and troops removed from the city. The radio said the Russian refugees from Baku demanded that the Soviet government guarantee them normal living conditions. The same day, TASS reported that a crowd had blockaded the building in Erevan where the Armenian Supreme Soviet was ending its session. The demonstrators demanded the resignation of the chairman of the Armenian Supreme Soviet, Grant Voskanyan. The agency also said that, despite the state of emergency imposed in Nagorno-Karabakh, people there were still taking hostages and throwing stones. Reuters and AP quoted Teheran radio as saying the USSR and Iran had signed an agreement to ease travel between Azerbaijan and Iran.

On February 16, TASS said that the situation in the Nakhichevan ASSR within Azerbaijan remained calm but that there was a shortage there of some goods, including fuel and food. TASS also reported the discovery of twelve bodies bearing marks of violence in a common grave in central Azerbaijan. The agency said the bodies were identified as Armenians who had been taken from an old people's home in Kirovabad and who had been missing since February 9.

Izvestia on Situation in Moldavia

Izvestia said "a sharp deterioration" of the sociopolitical situation in Moldavia had led the Presidium of the Moldavian Supreme Soviet to ban some political activities. It said that, on January 31, the Presidium had ordered a six-month ban on activities that could lead to ethnic divisions. It said the Presidium had warned that the authorities would deal resolutely with unsanctioned protest demonstrations. The Presidium also said it would soon invite the leaders of all public movements in Moldavia to attend round-table talks.

Izvestia on Anti-Communist Position of Estonian Popular Front

Izvestia said the Estonian Popular Front had set out its opposition to the Communist Party more openly and clearly than ever before. An article in *Izvestia* said this stance was made clear during a lengthy radio broadcast of an election conference organized by the popular front. The newspaper said the usual criticism of the Party apparatus and conservative elements in the Party had turned into rejection and exclusion of all who regard themselves as Communists.

USSR and Hungary Reach Agreement on Troop Withdrawals

On February 2, the Soviet Union and Hungary agreed to the withdrawal of Soviet troops from Hungary in the shortest possible time. Reuters quoted a joint statement as saying both sides had agreed there was no military justification for the continued presence of Soviet troops in Hungary. The same day, there was a demonstration in the Polish city of Krakow to demand the withdrawal of Soviet troops from Poland.

Another Attempt to Defend Lenin

Speeches in defense of Lenin were delivered at a meeting of the CPSU Central Committee Ideological Commission held to mark the 120th anniversary of Lenin's birth (*Pravda*, February 1). Gosteleradio chief Mikhail Nenashev said: "Today we find ourselves in ideological confrontation with enemies of the Party and socialism, and in fact we have reached the very limit." It was clear from the majority of speeches at the meeting that the collapse of Communist Parties in Eastern Europe has led many of those who were previously at the forefront of *perestroika*, such as, for instance, Director of the Institute of Marxism-Leninism Georgii Smirnov, to feel that the rejection of traditional Soviet dogmas has gone too far. In his speech, Smirnov strongly attacked the Democratic Platform, an informal group of Communists, for consolidating on an anti-Leninist basis.

Gorbachev Meets with Coal Miners

Gorbachev met in Moscow with what TASS called "a large group" of miners from the Soviet Union's major coal-producing regions. TASS said they had a frank exchange that covered "drastic problems facing *perestroika*, society, and the CPSU." The agency said the miners offered critical suggestions and proposals and asked numerous questions. A report on the meeting appeared in *Pravda* on February 5.

Shevardnadze Proposes International Referendum on Reunification

Shevardnadze called for an international referendum of Europeans, Americans, and Canadians to decide the question of German reunification. TASS quoted Shevardnadze as saying the peoples of these countries had suffered so much during World War II that they should now have the right to a guarantee that German reunification would not pose a threat (*AP*, *Reuters*, February 2).

Former Leningrad Oblast Party Chief Expelled

Former Leningrad Oblast Party First Secretary Yurii Solov'ev was expelled from the CPSU for "lack of modesty" and unethical behavior. TASS said that the decision was taken after the Leningrad Oblast Party Committee Buro had heard the report of an investigation by the Party Control Commission on February 1. The report accused Solov'ev of irregularities in his purchase of a foreign-made car.

MVD Troops Withdrawn from Chernobyl' for Health Reasons

USSR Chief Military Prosecutor Aleksandr Katusev said he had ordered the immediate withdrawal of a Soviet MVD regiment from the Chernobyl' area because of health hazards. Katusev told Radio Moscow that more than 2,000 men of the Seventieth Regiment of MVD troops had been guarding the Chernobyl' nuclear power plant since 1987. He said he had ordered its withdrawal because "above all we must have healthy people." The Radio Moscow interviewer said the Prosecutor's Office had learned that three people had died of leukemia while working in the Chernobyl' zone since 1987, that more than 3,000 had suffered various blood disorders, and that 50 percent of those working there had suffered stomach disorders.

Estonia's Future Discussed

More than 4,500 Estonian officials met in Tallinn to discuss the Baltic republic's future. The meeting brought together local officials elected in December and members of the Estonian Supreme Soviet and the USSR Congress of People's Deputies. The gathering had no authority as a decision-making body but served as a forum for discussion (RFE Estonian service, February 2). The meeting called for the restoration of Estonia's independence on the basis of the Tartu peace treaty of 1920. The same day, it was announced that the Presidium of the Estonian Supreme Soviet had created a commission to start talks with the central Soviet authorities on the restoration of Estonian independence. The move was reported by Estonian radio.

Saturday, February 3

Georgian CP Proposes Abolition of Party's Leading Role

The Interfax news agency reported that the Georgian Communist Party Central Committee had decided at a plenum on February 2 to propose the abolition of Article 6 of the Soviet constitution at the CPSU Central Committee plenum this week.It is Article 6 of the constitution that guarantees the Party's leading role. Tanjug reported that the Georgian Communist Party had also advocated an alliance of independent Communist Parties in the various Union republics.

Kishinev and Vilnius Reject Autonomy Demands

The Presidium of the Moldavian Supreme Soviet rejected the decision by Tiraspol Raion, the population of which is mainly Russian, to declare itself an independent territory, TASS reported. The Presidium said the Tiraspol referendum and resulting declaration were a violation of the provisions of the constitution and therefore invalid. A day earlier, Vilnius rejected the latest Polish demands for autonomy in Lithuania for the same reason.

Demonstration in Uzbekistan

Some 10,000 people demonstrated in Kokand to demand an end to persecution of members of "Birlik," the Uzbek Popular Front. Leaders of "Birlik" told Radio Liberty's Uzbek Service that the meeting had also called for the immediate closure of a chemical plant there, the dropping of charges against Uzbek singer and poet Dadakhan Hasan, and a public investigation of those behind the Fergana riots last summer. Party and government officials from Fergana also attended the protest.

Committee for Defense of Soviet Power Established in Tallinn

A group of Russian-speaking people's deputies from Estonia criticized a declaration made on February 2 concerning Estonian independence. The group said the declaration was contrary to the vital interests of a major part of Estonia's population and could not be implemented without their participation. TASS said the Russian-speaking group, meeting in Tallinn, also established a "Committee for the Defense of Soviet Power and Civil Liberties" and chose a seven-member buro led by deputy Vladimir Yarovoi. The committee said its main goal was to defend the political and economic rights of Soviet citizens within a renewed Soviet federation or a newly created state-territorial formation.

Soviet Envoy Says No Direct USSR-Israel Flights

Soviet envoy Gennadii Tarasov said Moscow did not intend to allow direct flights to Israel for Jews emigrating from the Soviet Union. He said any rumors about such flights "do not correspond with reality." In January, however, Soviet and Israeli airlines made flights carrying Soviet Jewish emigrants directly from the Soviet Union to Israel. Tarasov's remarks came after talks this week with officials of the Palestine Liberation Organization in Tunis (*Reuters*, *AP*, February 3). On February 6, King Hussein of Jordan called for an urgent Arab summit to forge a united stand against the emigration of Soviet Jews to Israel. In an interview published in the Kuwaiti newspaper *Al-Watan*, Hussein said the influx represented a real danger to the Arab world and its future (Western agencies, February 6).

Desire to Emigrate Strong among Muscovites

Sixteen percent of Muscovites polled in December, 1989, expressed the desire to emigrate to the West, *Vechernyaya Moskva* reported. Citing the results of an opinion poll conducted among 9,000 residents of Moscow, the newspaper said young and professionally active people were most keen to emigrate. The desire to emigrate was expressed by 27 percent of people between the ages of eighteen and thirty and by 24 percent of those between thirty-one and fifty.

Sunday, February 4

Pro-Democracy Demonstration in Moscow

On the eve of the CPSU Central Committee plenum, 200,000 people marched through the center of Moscow and rallied outside the walls of the Kremlin. Believed to be the largest unofficial demonstration in the Soviet Union since the Bolsheviks came to power, the rally was called to protest against the Russian nationalist group "Pamyat'" and to demand democratic reforms in the Soviet Union. The demonstration was publicized in advance on February 2 by the late-night television show

"Vzglyad." Extensive coverage of the demonstration was given by Soviet television news on February 4. Banners carried by marchers called on Gorbachev to act more decisively and to remove Article 6, which guarantees the Party's monopoly on power, from the Soviet constitution. The rally was addressed by several well-known reformists; in a speech reported by the Western media but not shown on Soviet television, Boris El'tsin said that the Party must relinquish its monopoly on power and that this week's plenum was its last chance to democratize itself. Soviet television focused on Evgenii Evtushenko, who read a poem saying, "We are for freedom, but not for freedom for racists." Commentary by the moderator was critical of this poem, which was clearly directed at "Pamyat'" and other groups practicing anti-Semitism. Other speakers not shown on Soviet television were historian Yurii Afanas'ev and economist Gavriil Popov. In his speech, Afanas'ev called for the start of a peaceful, democratic "February Revolution" (Radio Liberty Russian service, February 5). On the demonstration, see also *Izvestia*, February 6. On February 7, the Moscow Voters' Association sponsored a demonstration near the TASS building in Moscow in protest about inadequate Soviet media coverage of the mass rally on February 4 (*TASS*, February 7).

Punishment Urged for Former Karelian Party Chief

The CPSU Central Committee has been urged to revoke the Central Committee membership of former Karelian Oblast Party Committee First Secretary Vladimir Stepanov. Radio Moscow said the buro of the Karelian Oblast Party Committee in the RSFSR had based its request on allegations that Stepanov had abused his official position. The buro also asked the Central Committee to consider Party punishment for Stepanov. The oblast Party buro alleged that Stepanov frequently took advantage of his post to buy new cars for himself and his son. The Party Control Commission is currently working to investigate abuses by Party officials involving cars.

United States and USSR Still Seen as Rivals

"The idea of rivalry cannot be avoided in relations between such large countries as the Soviet Union and the United States," *Pravda*'s New York correspondent wrote in the newspaper. Having reviewed the long history of Russian-American relations, the correspondent said, "It is important that this rivalry be kindly and humane and correspond to the spirit and level of our civilization."

Monday, February 5

CPSU Central Committee Plenum

A plenum of the CPSU Central Committee opened in Moscow. In his speech to the plenum on February 5, Gorbachev said the Communist Party should give up its constitutionally guaranteed monopoly on power and instead fight for and win its leading role in Soviet society. Gorbachev said that Soviet society was becoming increasingly pluralistic and that the Communist Party must be ready "to cooperate and maintain dialogue with all the organizations that base themselves on the USSR Constitution and the social system inherent in it." He said a multiparty system could eventually emerge in the USSR, but he reiterated his conviction that, at the present stage, the Communist Party was the organization best fitted to play an "integrating and consolidating" role in the USSR's multiethnic society. Gorbachev said a revised edition of the Party Rules should be drawn up within the next three to four weeks and the draft presented for discussion at another plenum of the Central Committee. He said the new Party Rules should be published for public discussion. Gorbachev said that there should be discussion on "creating the institution of a presidency" and that this post should be endowed with "all the requisite plenipotentiary powers necessary to implement the policy of restructuring." Gorbachev also proposed the creation of a streamlined Central Committee of only 200 full members that would act as a permanently functioning body. In his remarks on the nationalities question, Gorbachev said the draft Party platform for the Twenty-eighth Party Congress pointed to the need for "a further development of the treaty principle of the Soviet federation." Otherwise he confined his remarks on the nationality question largely to a defense of the declaration of the state of emergency in Azerbaijan (he attributed the problems in the Transcaucasus largely to "representatives of the shadow economy") and to a call for a speedy adoption of legislation delimiting the powers of the center and the republics (*TASS*, February 5; see *Pravda*, February 6–9).

The immediate reaction of the plenum participants to Gorbachev's proposals was mixed. Criticism came from Anatolii Kornienko, Party first secretary in the city of Kiev, and from Valentin Mesyats, Moscow Oblast Party first secretary. Both said the Party should not be on the defensive against other movements and that it should stand by its Marxist-Leninist ideals. Moscow City Party leader Yurii Prokof'ev said, however, that the USSR already had a multiparty system and that therefore there should be no delay in undertaking "an unequivocal review" of the Party's constitutionally guaranteed leading role. A representative of the Soviet coal miners, K. Fesenko, added that, in any case, the Party's constitutional role did not mean much for rank-and-file members like him. He said that all power was in the hands of the Party apparatus and that it was because of the opposition of the apparatus that *perestroika* was not moving forward. He called for all Party leaders, including the general secretary, to be directly elected by the Party grass roots. Radical deputy Boris El'tsin told the plenum that, while Gorbachev's speech contained some progressive ideas, it was a compromise that tried (and failed) to reconcile different positions. El'tsin presented an alternative draft platform. This included plans for a multiparty system, breaking the power of the Party apparatus and abolishing all official privileges. Soviet television reported that other speakers also called for the transfer of the USSR to a multiparty system.

The session on February 6 was addressed by Egor Ligachev, who claimed that Gorbachev, together with Nikolai Ryzhkov, Eduard Shevardnadze, and Aleksandr Yakovlev, was present at a Politburo meeting on April 7, 1989, that approved the dispatch to Tbilisi of army and MVD troops. This affirmation contradicts the findings of the Georgian SSR Supreme Soviet commission that investigated the events preceding the troops' intervention, which established that the meeting that took the decision to deploy troops was chaired by Ligachev and attended by Nikolai Slyun'kov, Vadim Medvedev, Anatolii Luk'yanov, Dmitrii Yazov, Georgii Razumovsky, and Vladimir Kryuchkov. The appropriate orders were then issued by Yazov, and the first contingent of troops arrived in Tbilisi on the evening of April 7. According to the account of the plenum proceedings published in *Pravda* on February 8, Shevardnadze challenged Ligachev's statement. Shevardnadze was quoted as saying, "In the interests of justice I want to say that there was no Politburo meeting on the use of troops."

The same day, the plenum heard more criticism of the draft platform presented by Gorbachev. Leningrad Party leader Boris Gidaspov said that the country's political and economic destabilization was increasing daily but that the platform contained no optimistic prospects (*TASS*, February 6).

Speaking at the plenum on February 6, Azerbaijani Party First Secretary Ayaz Mutalibov said there was still a civil war going on in the Transcaucasus. Armenian Party

First Secretary Suren Arutyunyan said the Soviet central authorities should again take over the administration of Nagorno-Karabakh (*TASS*, February 6).

The plenum adjourned on February 7. Speaking at the closing session, Gorbachev said that mistakes had been made under his leadership and that his policies might have incalculable consequences. But, he said, the Party and the government must continue to act resolutely (*TASS*, February 8). The plenum voted to relinquish the Party's constitutionally guaranteed monopoly on power and to recommend the creation of a presidential form of government. The much criticized platform presented to the plenum by Gorbachev was finally accepted almost unanimously and "without significant amendments." There was only one vote against (El'tsin's) and one abstention.

Politburo member Yakovlev spoke at a press conference on February 7 (*Radio Moscow*, February 8). Yakovlev confirmed that the plenum supported Gorbachev's proposal to "concentrate power in the hands of the president and his cabinet." Asked about the Politburo's future role, Yakovlev said it would confine itself to Party affairs. Regarding the establishment of opposition parties, an official at the press conference said it was to be hoped that all parties in the USSR would "adhere to Socialist positions." Yakovlev said the legality of a given party must be decided in accordance with the law and the constitution; "It is not," he said, "the Party's job to ensure it has an opposition."

The plenum also condemned the Lithuanian Communist Party for declaring its independence. (In his speech to the plenum on February 6, Shevardnadze, however, opposed strict sanctions against the Independent Lithuanian Communist Party.) In a resolution approved on February 7, the plenum said the Lithuanian Communists had undermined the unity of the CPSU and caused great damage to *perestroika*. The resolution also praised those Communists who had "maintained their loyalty" and formed a second Party organization in Lithuania, and it instructed the Politburo to support the Moscow-allied Party organization with financial and other aid. But in a bow to reality, the Central Committee called on members of the Independent Lithuanian Party to suspend their split until the Party Congress and requested that Lithuanian Party organizations jointly choose delegates to that meeting (*TASS*, February 7).

On February 9, Central Committee Secretary and chief editor of *Pravda* Ivan Frolov gave some details of the draft platform of the CPSU presented by Gorbachev at the plenum. Frolov revealed that the new Presidium, which, according to the platform, is to replace the Politburo, would contain about thirty members. They would include senior Party officials, representatives from the Union republics, and representatives from rank-and-file Party organizations (*TASS*, February 9). The full text of the draft platform was published in *Pravda* on February 13.

Soviet Army Company Goes AWOL to Protest Conditions

Nearly an entire company of Soviet soldiers from the Transcaucasian Military District went absent without leave on January 21 to protest the conditions under which they serve, Soviet television reported today. The report said about seventy men left their posts and made their way to Moscow State University. One of their complaints was that their company sergeant major was selling soldiers to local farmers as workers in exchange for brandy.

Tuesday, February 6

Sverdlovsk Party Chief Resigns

TASS and *Izvestia* reported the resignation of the Party first secretary of Sverdlovsk Oblast, Leonid Bobykin. Bobykin is a conservative who has been attacked in the press. He also failed to be elected to the USSR Congress of People's Deputies.

KGB Deputy Chief Briefs US Human-Rights Delegation

A US delegation of human-rights specialists was briefed on the democratization process in the Soviet Union by Vladimir Pirozhkov—chief of the KGB's Judicial Bureau. Pirozhkov, deputy to four KGB chairmen since 1971, briefed Richard Schifter, the assistant US secretary of state for human rights, on current Soviet reform efforts and described the restructuring process in the KGB (*Radio Moscow*, February 6).

Political Party Created in Vorkuta

A representative of the Vorkuta miners told Radio Liberty's Russian service that a new political party had been set up in Vorkuta. Called the Party of Labor Councils, the organization apparently regards itself as an alternative to the CPSU. Its creation highlights the increasing politicization of the miners' movement. Only last year, miners in Vorkuta and the Kuzbass insisted that their unofficial organizations were either trade unions or popular fronts but not political parties.

Academician Advocates Abolition of Republican Academies

Academician Nikolai Enikolopov called for the abolition of academies of sciences in the Union republics in an interview with the new supplement to *Izvestia*, *Soyuz* (No. 3). Enikolopov also spoke against plans to establish a Russian Academy of Sciences. Pointing out that the academies in the Union republics, even the small ones, attempt to duplicate the structure of the all-Union academy, Enikolopov complained that there were simply not enough outstanding scientists to fill all the vacancies in all the academies. The result was, he said, that mediocrities were being elected. Enikolopov suggested that the money currently being "wasted" on the republican academies be used to provide the all-Union academy with extra financial support. Enikolopov clearly sees the political implications of his proposal but he argued that scientific interests rather than political ones should be taken into account in deciding the question of the academies.

Shortage of Medicines Threatens Health

The Soviet Union is experiencing an acute shortage of medicines because many factories that produce them have been closed in recent months. According to a report by Radio Moscow (2100), the problem has been studied by the USSR Council of Ministers State Commission for Emergencies. According to the commission's findings, the decisions to close the plants were generally made by local authorities on the grounds that the enterprises were violating environmental norms. In many cases the factories that were shut down were the only ones in the USSR manufacturing a particular preparation. The "Nairit" enterprise in Erevan, for example, a manufacturer of heart medicines, painkillers, and vitamins, has long been criticized by environmentalists, who said it was a major cause of that city's air-pollution problems. It was finally closed by the Armenian Supreme Soviet at the end of 1989, thereby depriving the country of its products. The commission ordered that production be resumed at the closed plants and that an investigation be undertaken of why the plants had been closed rather than equipped with emission-reduction devices.

Metropolitan of Odessa Dies

TASS reported that Sergii, Metropolitan of Odessa and Kherson, had died on February 4 at the age of sixty-five. The metropolitan, whose secular name was Sergei Vasil'evich Petrov, was ordained as a monk-priest in 1951 and in 1958 was made an inspector at the Odessa Theological Seminary, he later served as rector of the seminary. He was elevated to bishop in 1960 and was made an archbishop three years later. In 1971, Archbishop Sergii became metropolitan of Odessa and Kherson and administrator of the Moscow Patriarchate. He was first deputy chairman of the commission of the Holy Synod entrusted with preparing the celebrations of the millennium of Christianity in Rus'.

Situation on Soviet-Iranian Border

In an interview with *Gudok*, Major General Gennadii Martynov, deputy head of the Political Administration of the KGB Border Troops, said the situation along the Soviet-Iranian border was gradually returning to normal. Large parts of the border fortifications were destroyed in January by Azerbaijanis demanding that the border be opened for them to visit friends and relatives in Iran. On February 9, *Krasnaya zvezda* and *Izvestia* said a person had been killed attempting to cross the border into the Soviet Union from Iran. The reports said he was part of a group of between four and fourteen people attempting to cross the border illegally. The reports said the infiltrators used firearms.

Demonstrations in Dnepropetrovsk Area

Radio Kiev-2 reported that 5,000 people had gathered in Gagarin Square in Dneprodzerzhinsk to protest against the airing of a biased program on Central Television allegedly aimed at securing the recall of Sergei Konev, a radical USSR People's Deputy and prominent "Rukh" organizer. The program, shown on January 29, libeled Konev and his backers. The protesters in Dneprodzerzhinsk passed a resolution demanding the resignation of their city's Party leadership, the chairman of the executive committee, and the city prosecutor. The action in this city in the industrial Dnepropetrovsk area is the latest in a series of demonstrations against local leaders that has swept Ukraine in the last month, forcing the resignation of numerous officials.

Wednesday, February 7

Theological Faculty Opened at Riga University

TASS reported that a theological faculty had been opened at Riga University. The faculty, whose students should be religious believers, has been created on the basis of the theological seminar of Latvia's Protestant Church. The teaching staff of the new faculty will also include Catholic and Russian Orthodox theologists.

Soviet Cooperative Accused of Exporting Vital Metals

TASS said the same Soviet firm that has been accused of trying to sell modern Soviet battle tanks to the West has now been caught trying to export strategic metals. The ANT cooperative was accused of trying to ship twelve T-72 tanks to a Western country after a shipment was intercepted on its way to a Black Sea port. Now, TASS said, the authorities in Murmansk have halted an ANT shipment of more than twenty tons of nickel and seventy tons of copper. On February 8, TASS said ANT had also been accused of trying to ship fifty tons of magnesium to Japan.

Lithuania Declares 1940 Decision to Join USSR Illegal

The Lithuanian Supreme Soviet declared null and void the republic's incorporation into the Soviet Union in 1940. TASS said the Lithuanian parliament had endorsed findings presented in August, 1989, by a special commission examining the Soviet-German Pact of 1939 that led to the incorporation of the Baltic states and Bessarabia into the USSR. According to RFE's Lithuanian service, the Lithuanian Supreme Soviet also called on the Soviet Union to begin bilateral negotiations to restore Lithuania's independence.

Ukrainian Party Resolution on 1932–33 Famine

The Ukrainian Communist Party issued a resolution on the famine in the republic in 1932–33. TASS quoted the resolution as saying that, after studying documents, Ukrainian historians had determined that the famine had been caused by the forced collectivization of peasants, the policy of eliminating the kulaks, lack of expertise, and poor technology. TASS quoted the resolution further as saying that the Ukrainian leadership at the time had been incapable of opposing Stalin's order to increase grain deliveries to the state and had therefore carried out his policies. The resolution was published in the Ukrainian press.

MVD Troops Given Right to Use Weapons

A draft decree on the rights and duties of Soviet MVD troops has been submitted to a committee of the USSR Supreme Soviet. Radio Moscow's Interfax news service said the draft gives troops the right, when necessary, to use rubber truncheons, tear gas, water cannon, and armored vehicles. The radio said that in emergencies—for example, to save citizens' lives—the troops would be allowed to use "weapons." The radio quoted the draft further as saying that MVD troops would do patrol duty at mass political rallies, at sporting events, and on other public occasions.

Controversy over Journal *Leningrad*

Literaturnaya gazeta (No. 6) and other Soviet periodicals reported details of the controversy over the journal *Leningrad*, which was a victim of the famous "Zhdanov Decree" of 1946 on the two Leningrad literary journals *Leningrad* and *Zvezda*. In the course of *perestroika*, the "Zhdanov Decree" has been renounced and the CPSU Central Committee has promised to give the journal *Leningrad* to the Leningrad writers' organization. Recently, however, the Leningrad Party leadership, citing a split within the Leningrad writers' organization as a reason, transferred *Leningrad* to the supervision of the Leningrad City and Oblast Soviets. *Literaturnaya gazeta* reported that the Party organization of the Leningrad Writers' Union had condemned the Leningrad Party leadership's decision and decided to stop paying Party dues until the controversy over the journal is settled in favor of the Leningrad writers' organization.

Thursday, February 8

Baker in Moscow

US Secretary of State James Baker began a second round of talks with Soviet Foreign Minister Eduard Shevardnadze in Moscow. Arms reduction, regional conflicts, and practical issues connected with the Soviet-US summit scheduled for June were on the agenda (*Reuters*, *AP*, February 8).

During the talks, Baker told Shevardnadze that the United States was no longer insisting on the removal of Afghan President Najibullah before any negotiated political settlement of the Afghan conflict. US reports said on February 9 that the United States was prepared to accept Najibullah's remaining as Afghan leader.

On February 9, Gorbachev met with Baker. During the talks, Gorbachev put forward a counterproposal on the reduction of conventional forces in Europe. President George Bush has proposed that the United States and the Soviet Union reduce their troop levels in Central Europe to 195,000 each. Gorbachev told Baker that the Soviet Union would accept that figure only if it applied to the whole of Europe (*TASS*, February 9).

On the last day of his visit to Moscow, Baker challenged a Supreme Soviet Committee in Moscow over the USSR's continued support for Cuba and Nicaragua. Baker made an unprecedented appearance before the Supreme Soviet's International Affairs Committee.

Several committee members questioned Baker about the US invasion of Panama and other issues (*AP*, *Reuters*, February 10). On February 12, Baker was quoted as criticizing Gorbachev's proposal on reducing conventional forces in Europe. Baker said the Soviet call to bar the stationing of US troops in Western Europe ignored the unequal positions of the two countries. He said that Soviet forces would still be stationed in Europe even if they withdrew from Eastern Europe but that US forces would be on the other side of the Atlantic and, therefore, could not be deployed as quickly. Baker was speaking at a joint conference of members of NATO and the Warsaw Pact in Ottawa (Western agencies, February 12).

Another Major Submarine Accident

Komsomol'skaya pravda said a Soviet nuclear-powered submarine had suffered a major accident that had caused damage to surrounding water and territory, but it was not clear whether this meant radioactive damage. The newspaper said the submarine was testing its ballistic missiles. The newspaper did not provide details of the accident or say where it occurred.

Gdlyan and Ivanov Face Loss of Immunity and Trial

Two Soviet criminal investigators who have been instrumental in bringing a number of senior officials to court may have to stand trial themselves. Soviet television said the USSR Prosecutor's Office would ask the Supreme Soviet to remove the immunity of people's deputies Tel'man Gdlyan and Nikolai Ivanov so that legal proceedings against them might be started. Gdlyan and Ivanov headed a team that investigated large-scale corruption among Soviet officials. The television report said the Collegium of the USSR Prosecutor's Office heard a report on the two investigators' methods at a session in Moscow. The report accused the investigators of making dozens of illegal arrests of members of suspects' families.

Donetsk Rally Demands Local Party Leaders Step Down

Demonstrators gathered at the oblast Party headquarters in the Ukrainian mining city of Donetsk to demand the resignation of local Party leaders. Soviet television showed the demonstration. The television report said speakers expressed especially sharp criticism over food shortages in the oblast. (Similar demonstrations to demand the resignation of local Party leaders have taken place in other parts of the Soviet Union.)

Call for Replacement of Komsomol by Independent Clubs

A significant group of activists of the all-Union Komsomol want the organization to be replaced by independent groups, TASS reported. The agency said that, at a recent meeting in Novosibirsk, an Interregional Group of Komsomol members had been set up by activists from the RSFSR, Ukraine, Kazakhstan, and other republics. The group advocates the disbandment of the all-Union Komsomol and its replacement by independent youth clubs, formed on Socialist and social-democratic platforms. Thus, the activists of the all-Union Komsomol seem to be following the initiative of the Baltic republics, which have started to disband their Komsomol organizations.

Political Organs to Be Dissolved in Navy

According to TASS, political organs in the Soviet Navy are to be disbanded. TASS said that "the institution of commissars" had been abolished in the Baltic Fleet. More than 200 Party officials have worked as captain's first assistants—the equivalent to the post of *zampolit* or deputy commander for political questions in the army—in the Baltic Fleet. TASS said that commissars were very unpopular among sailors and that the abolition of these posts was in line with the overall reorganization of the Party apparatus.

Orthodox Church Calls for Return of Solovki

TASS reported that the leadership of the Russian Orthodox Church had appealed to the Supreme Soviet to return the ancient Solovki Monastery to the Church. At one time used as a prison camp, this site has been the target of a massive restoration effort over the last three decades; to date, however, none of the historic architectural monuments has been completely restored.

Estonians Issue Another Appeal for Independence

A group of 100 prominent Estonians has issued a new appeal for restoration of the republic's independence. The appeal was published in the Estonian Party daily *Rahva Haal.* Signatories included Estonian Prime Minister Indrek Toome and ideology secretary Mikk Titma. The appeal calls for a free Estonia within a common European home and a multiparty democracy.

Friday, February 9

Gidaspov Proposes Russian Party Congress

Conservative Leningrad Party First Secretary Boris Gidaspov has set up an official committee for the formation of a Russian Communist Party. According to TASS, the committee consists primarily of Party officials from Leningrad industrial plants. Gorbachev has opposed the formation of an RSFSR Party organization.

Moscow Agrees to Withdraw Troops from Czechoslovakia

After talks between the Czech and Soviet deputy foreign ministers in Moscow, the Czechoslovak media announced that the Soviet Union had agreed to begin withdrawing troops from Czechoslovakia this month (*Radio Prague*, February 9).

KGB Dismisses Rumors of Coming Attacks on Jews

The KGB issued a rare appeal for calm, saying rumors in Moscow of impending pogroms against Jews and other minorities were groundless. The KGB statement also said, "It is important for the mass media to cover such sensitive issues in a more balanced way and not to circulate unverified information." Leaflets predicting pogroms in May have been distributed in Leningrad, Moscow, and Ukraine.

Lithuania Adopts Press Law

The Lithuanian Supreme Soviet adopted a press law abolishing censorship and granting publishing rights to individuals and organizations. TASS said the law would take effect on March 1.

UN Resolution on Settlement of Soviet Jews in Occupied Territories

A draft resolution presented to the United Nations Human-Rights Commission in Geneva urged Israel not to settle Soviet Jewish immigrants in the occupied territories. The resolution said such a move was illegal. The resolution was sponsored by a number of Western countries, including West Germany, Britain, and France. A vote on it is to be taken later this month (Western agencies, February 9). The same day, AP reported that the Soviet ambassador to Syria, Aleksandr Zotov, had urged Arab nations to take "active steps" to prevent Soviet Jews settling in Israeli-occupied areas. Zotov did not elaborate.

Saturday, February 10

West German Leaders in Moscow to Discuss Reunification

West German leaders said in Moscow that they expected to have a plan for the reunification of Germany by the end of the year for presentation to an all-European summit. West German Chancellor Helmut Kohl and Foreign Minister Hans-Dietrich Genscher spoke with reporters after meeting with their Soviet opposite numbers, Mikhail Gorbachev and Eduard Shevardnadze. Kohl said Gorbachev had told him the USSR would respect the decision of the two Germanies on the timing and methods of reunification (*Reuters*, *TASS*, February 10). On February 11, Soviet Foreign Ministry spokesman Gennadii Gerasimov said that, when they are deciding on reunification, the two German states should consider various things, including security concerns and psychological concerns—e.g., that Europeans still have memories of World War II.

On February 12, Soviet Foreign Ministry spokesman Vitalii Churkin said that, in his talks with Kohl, Gorbachev had rejected a West German proposal for a united Germany committed to the NATO alliance, but a West German spokesman said neither Gorbachev nor Shevardnadze had made any request for a neutral Germany in talks with Kohl and Genscher (*Reuters*, *AP*, February 12). Politburo member Aleksandr Yakovlev said Soviet troops would remain in a unified Germany as long as NATO forces were stationed there (*Radio Moscow*, World Service, 1500, February 12).

On February 15, Shevardnadze urged a slow pace for German unification to match the gradual development of democracy in East Europe. He was speaking to the Canadian Senate's Foreign Relations Committee in Ottawa. Shevardnadze added that the German question had re-emerged at a challenging time when many European countries, including the USSR, were in transition. Shevardnadze said Germany's neighbors were entitled to guarantees that a unified state would not try to redraw borders or revive Nazism (Western agencies, February 15).

First Synod of the Ukrainian Orthodox Church

TASS reported that the first synod of the Ukrainian Orthodox Church had taken place in Kiev. Described by a Russian Orthodox churchman as a "truly historic" meeting, the session was authorized by a decision of the Russian Orthodox Church itself. Few details are yet available, but the new Church will be in communion with the Russian Orthodox Church.

Shevardnadze Calls for Efforts to Break Down "Korean Wall"

Soviet Foreign Minister Eduard Shevardnadze said at a press conference in Moscow that, with the Berlin Wall open, international efforts should concentrate on breaking down "the Korean wall" (*Reuters*, February 10; *Pravda*, February 11). A joint US-Soviet statement on February 10, following the talks between Shevardnadze and US Secretary of State James Baker, expressed the desire "to reduce tensions on the Korean Peninsula and to support a North-South dialogue."

Pravda on the Problem of Soviet Refugees

Pravda said more than 30,000 Soviet refugees had been registered in Moscow. The group is part of the more than half a million refugees in the USSR, the majority of whom come from the center of ethnic conflict in the Transcaucasus. The newspaper said refugees registered in the Soviet capital would be moved to locations outside the city. It promised that all refugees able to work would be offered jobs within the next two months.

More Ukrainian Regional Party Leaders Resign

There were more resignations by regional Party leaders in Ukraine on February 10. TASS said Anatolii Vinnik had resigned as first secretary of Donetsk Oblast. On February 9, Radio Moscow reported the resignations of Ivano-Frankovsk Oblast Party First Secretary Ivan Postoronko and Khmelnitsky Oblast Party First Secretary Vladimir Dikusarov.

On February 14, Voroshilovgrad City Party First Secretary Yakovlev was released from his post. Radio Moscow-1 (1700) reported that the decision, at Yakovlev's request, had been made at a plenum of the city's Party committee. The same day, Soviet television said that a Party plenum in Donetsk had voted against the resignation of the oblast Party buro. Outside the Party building, demonstrators repeated calls for the ouster of the entire Party leadership.

On February 15, Radio Kiev said the Party first secretary in Voroshilovgrad Oblast, Ivan Lyakhov, had been relieved of his duties. The radio said the decision to release Lyakhov had been taken on February 14 at a plenum of the oblast Party committee. Lyakhov, a Russian, had held the position since February, 1987.

Bashkir Oblast Party Leaders Resign

Radio Moscow reported that the entire Party leadership of the Bashkir ASSR had resigned at a special plenum of the oblast Party committee. The mass resignations came after a vote of no confidence in the leadership's conduct of *perestroika*. First Secretary Ravmer Khabibullin was accused of intolerance to criticism. The plenum elected provisional leaders to prepare for an oblast Party conference in April.

On February 14, Radio Moscow-1 (2200) reported that at its first meeting the new provisional Party leadership in the Bashkir ASSR had voted to set aside 70,000 rubles of

Party funds to aid poor families. The leadership also took measures to fight crime and ensure citizens' legal defense and discussed how to supply the public with more food and consumer goods.

Sunday, February 11

Disturbances in Tajikistan

Radio Moscow reported on February 12 that a state of emergency had been declared in the capital of Tajikistan and an overnight curfew imposed by the Presidium of the republican Supreme Soviet. The declaration came in the wake of disturbances that began on February 11, when several thousand people demonstrated at the republican Party headquarters demanding that Armenian refugees leave Tajikistan. On February 12, Radio Moscow-1 (2200) reported that some seventy people had been injured and several killed in violence that included clashes with the police. The desperate housing situation in Dushanbe and other serious social problems, all well documented in the republican press, have been cited as the cause of the disturbances. Novosti (February 14) said living standards and unemployment in Dushanbe were among the worst in the Soviet Union and had been ignored by the authorities for years.

On February 13, the situation became worse in Dushanbe. Western agencies quoted Soviet sources as saying crowds had gathered in city streets and some groups were causing trouble. Radio Moscow's Interfax agency said demonstrators' demands included replacement of the republican Party leadership, removal of all Armenians from the city, the return to the republic of all income from its cotton industry, and the closing of the Tajik aluminum plant, which has been a source of contention with neighboring Uzbekistan because of the pollution caused by the plant. The demonstrators also demanded that the cities of Samarkand and Bukhara, both ancient centers of Tajik culture, be given to Tajikistan. Reports also said gangs of youths were arriving in Dushanbe from throughout the republic, and Soviet television admitted that the situation was out of control despite a curfew and the presence of troops. Interfax said that police and troops of the Ministry of Internal Affairs had been unable to prevent rioters from looting almost all the shops in the center of the city. A journalist in Dushanbe told Reuters that troops were firing over the heads of rioting youths because they had no orders to shoot to kill.

On February 14, speaking to the USSR Supreme Soviet, Gorbachev called for firm action against those who inflamed national passions and provoked clashes in the Union republics (*TASS*, February 14). Soviet television also reported that Tajikistan's three top leaders—Party First Secretary Kakhar Makhkamov, Prime Minister Izatullo Khaeev, and Chairman of the Presidium of the Supreme Soviet Gaibnazar Pallaev—had offered their resignations. This, according to Western news agencies in contact with sources in Dushanbe, was part of an agreement between the Tajik Central Committee and a citizens' committee elected by demonstrators. An earlier offer by Makhkamov to resign had been rejected by the Central Committee in an emergency session. A Tajik television official told *The Washington Post* that the agreement also called for the withdrawal of tanks and troops to begin on February 14. TASS reported, however, that paratroops had arrived in Dushanbe on that day after violence worsened. Interfax news service claimed that an army division had refused to move into the city, because its officers did not want to be blamed for any of the violence. Soviet media reported that on February 14 some 5,000 "extremists" were attacking troops and looting was continuing. *Trud* pointed out that many rioters were young men from Gissar Raion who have been living in temporary housing or tents since their homes were destroyed in an earthquake in January, 1989. Interfax quoted speakers at the Central Committee emergency session who claimed the attacks had been carefully planned by Muslim sects and members of informal groups. Central Television reported that the organizers of earlier disturbances had been freed from jail at the demand of the demonstrators. Another Tajik television official told AP that the situation in Dushanbe had eased after the formation of the citizens' committee whose members were drawn from the informal organization "Rastokhez" and other protest groups. A Novosti account said that a representative of "Rastokhez" had appeared on republican television with an appeal for calm. Novosti praised "Rastokhez" for distancing itself from the violence and appealing for reason and pointed out that republican officials had tried to ignore the organization.

On February 15, Radio Dushanbe and the central mass media reported that the situation in Dushanbe was returning to normal, although it was still tense. The local radio broadcast an appeal from the republican Communist Party Central Committee for the public to remain calm and not to assemble on the streets. Another demonstration was held in Dushanbe, however, at which the demonstrators reiterated demands for the resignation of the entire buro of the republican Party Central Committee. Interfax said an agreement between leaders of the demonstration and officials of the Tajik Communist Party on withdrawing troops from the center of Dushanbe and on reducing the number of security forces had been reached. The service reported the proclamation by the Presidium of the republic's Supreme Soviet of three days of mourning for those killed. On the situation in Dushanbe, see also *Izvestia* and *Sel'skaya zhizn'*, February 15.

On February 16, the situation in Dushanbe improved further, although tensions remained. According to TASS and radio reports from Dushanbe, the Party first secretary, prime minister, and chairman of the Supreme Soviet of Tajikistan again offered to resign. Soviet television reported, however, that the Tajik Communist Party Central Committee had rejected the resignations. TASS also said the authorities in Dushanbe were working to dispel rumors they said had fueled the rioting in the city. TASS said a special edition of the city's evening newspaper had been issued to keep people informed. Radio Moscow gave new figures for casualties in Dushanbe as twenty killed and 568 injured. *Krasnaya zvezda* disclosed that many of the victims had been shot and it quoted candidate Politburo member Boriss Pugo as saying it was not known who had done the shooting. The Soviet media also reported that the disturbances had caused many Russian-speaking people to leave Tajikistan.

On February 18, Radio Moscow said that in Dushanbe university and secondary-school students were staying away from classes. The same day, thousands of people rallied in the Tajik capital, demanding improvements in the environmental situation in the republic, greater economic autonomy, and better living conditions (*Reuters*, February 18). The rally was allowed by the authorities, despite a ban on gatherings. Speaking in Kabul the same day, the Soviet ambassador to Afghanistan said the Soviet Union was greatly concerned about intensified efforts from Afghan territory to destabilize Tajikistan. Ambassador Boris Pastukhov alleged that "special services" of the United States and Pakistan had helped create a group known as "the Union of Northern People." He said this group was trying to destabilize southern Soviet republics and was smuggling arms, subversive literature, money, and illegal drugs into the Soviet Union (*UPI*, February 19). Commenting on reports that arms were being smuggled into Tajikistan from Afghan territory, Afghan President Najibullah said his government had taken all necessary steps to stop such traffic. On February 20, the president of the Afghan resistance government in exile in Pakistan, Sibghatullah Mojaddedi, said in an interview with Reuters that the Afghan resistance was not fomenting unrest inside the Soviet Union.

On February 19, TASS said the situation in Dushanbe was gradually returning to normal. The report said that teaching had resumed at the university and most schools and that food-production and industrial enterprises were working. The same day, the local MVD gave journalists details of legal proceedings against people detained as a result of rioting in Dushanbe. TASS reported that criminal cases had been initiated against twenty rioters. Some court proceedings were scheduled to be televised.

On February 21, a group of senior Tajik Communists was reported to be under investigation for allegedly planning to oust the republic's prime minister, Khaeev. TASS quoted Tajik Party First Secretary Makhkamov as saying the group wanted to replace Khaeev with his deputy, Buri Karimov. Karimov heads the citizens' committee formed following the rioting in Dushanbe. See RL 93/90.

Resignation of Oblast Party Buro Demanded in Ul'yanovsk

TASS reported that thousands of people had demanded the resignation of the oblast Party buro at a meeting in Ul'yanovsk in central Russia. Speakers at the meeting said that the first and second secretaries in the oblast Party buro had "compromised" themselves, discredited the Party, and rendered poor service to *perestroika*.

Rallies in Ukraine and Moldavia

Tens of thousands of Ukrainians rallied in Kiev to denounce efforts to split the Ukrainian nation with appeals to ethnic prejudices, including anti-Semitism. The rally was organized by the Ukrainian popular movement for *perestroika*, "Rukh." Activists in "Rukh" told RFE/RL by telephone that the rally also called for support of "Rukh" and of other democratic candidates in Ukrainian local and republican elections on March 4. They also reported that the authorities in Kiev had officially registered "Rukh" as a legal organization. The same day, Radio Kiev broadcast an appeal by the local authorities for the public to remain calm; the appeal followed rumors of pogroms planned against Jews, Russians, and other non-Ukrainian nationalities. Another appeal to stop rumors of planned pogroms was issued on February 15, this time by the Ukrainian Prosecutor's Office (*TASS*, February 15).

In neighboring Moldavia, more than 100,000 people demonstrated to demand greater autonomy in the republic. The demonstrators applauded both popular front activists and sympathetic republican Party leaders (*Reuters*, February 11). On February 12, Deputy Chairman of the Moldavian Popular Front Azun Antu was allowed to speak on Moscow television. He called for the unification of all democratically oriented political movements in Moldavia. Antu was interviewed during the demonstration of February 11 in Kishinev.

Ryzhkov Visits Asia

Soviet Prime Minister Nikolai Ryzhkov arrived in Thailand on the first leg of a trip to Asia (*Reuters*, *AP*, February 11). Ryzhkov's visit completes a series of top-level Soviet diplomatic missions to countries around the USSR's southern borders during the last six months.

On February 12, Ryzhkov held formal talks in Bangkok on efforts to end the Cambodian conflict and improve Soviet-Thai trade relations. During his meeting with Thai Prime Minister Chatchai Chunhawan, Ryzhkov also discussed recent developments in Eastern Europe (*AFP*, February 12).

On February 13, Ryzhkov arrived in Australia, where he signed agreements on matters including port access for Soviet trawlers, consular guarantees, and commodities deals. Speaking in Canberra on February 14, Ryzhkov said it could take up to fifteen years for the Soviet Union to integrate fully with the economies of the rest of the world. He said the Soviet Union was making a "painful" transition from one social order to another (*Reuters*, February 14). Ryzhkov is the most senior Soviet official to visit Australia. On February 15, Ryzhkov and Australian Prime Minister Bob Hawke signed a fishing agreement and other bilateral pacts (*Reuters*, *AP*, *UPI*, February 15).

Talking to reporters in Canberra on February 15, Ryzhkov said that only the CPSU could solve the USSR's current problems, suggesting that other political movements were not yet sufficiently developed for the task (*Central Television*, February 15).

On February 16, Ryzhkov arrived in Singapore (*UPI*, *Reuters*, *AP*, February 16). Speaking to reporters, Ryzhkov said the focus of Soviet foreign policy was now shifting from Europe to Asia. He said the countries of the Asia-Pacific region would rise to prominence in the next century. He said Moscow needed to prepare for this and wanted to improve its economic ties with the region. Asserting that regional cooperation could not be complete without the Soviet Union, Ryzhkov urged that his country be admitted to a proposed eleven-nation Asia-Pacific forum (*Reuters*, *UPI*, February 17). Ryzhkov was also quoted as saying that the Soviet Union intended to keep possession of the disputed Kurile Islands. While acknowledging that the Kurile issue still stood in the way of better Soviet ties with Japan, he said the USSR believed that this should not continue to be an obstacle. See also an interview with Ryzhkov in *Pravda*, February 18.

On February 19, Soviet Foreign Ministry spokesman Gennadii Gerasimov also commented on the Kurile issue. Addressing a seminar in the Philippine capital, Manila, Gerasimov said the return of the disputed Kurile Islands to Japan was the subject of debate within the Soviet leadership. Gerasimov said that one wing of the leadership believed returning the islands could create "a dangerous precedent" for other postwar borders, while other officials and legislators were in favor of the move. Gerasimov reiterated that Moscow did not agree that returning the islands was "a prerequisite" for good relations with Japan, as Tokyo has argued (*AP*, February 19).

Crime Rising in Armed Forces and MVD

General Aleksandr Katusev, the chief military prosecutor, told Radio Moscow-1 (2230) that crime had risen 14.5 percent in units of the army, navy, and Ministry of Internal Affairs over the past year. He said that the authorities had increased their efforts to combat crime.

First Commercial Soviet Space Mission

On February 11, the USSR launched its first space mission intended to generate a profit. TASS reported that the *Soyuz TM-9* "space factory" was expected to make a profit of 25 million rubles on the manufacture of biotechnical materials in zero-gravity conditions. Other money-making activities proposed for the flight include bioengineering experiments and photographing the earth's surface.

Rostropovich Returns to Moscow

The celebrated cellist and conductor Mstislav Rostropovich returned to his native Moscow, where he received a jubilant welcome. He was accompanied by his wife, the opera singer Galina Vishnevskaya (*AP*, *Central Television*, February 11). Speaking on February 12, Rostropovich said the Soviet authorities should drop treason charges against Aleksandr Solzhenitsyn and apologize to him. The same day, Rostropovich played his first concert in Moscow since his exile (*AP*, February 12 and 13).

Democratic Platform Meets

A group of Communists advocating radical democratic reforms in the Soviet Union, who in January set up the Democratic Platform, met in Moscow to discuss the latest

CPSU Central Committee plenum. The group issued a statement, carried by AP, saying the reforms adopted at the plenum were inadequate, inconsistent, and contradictory. The statement asked Gorbachev and other Politburo members to meet with representatives of the Democratic Platform to discuss the future of the USSR.

Opinion Poll on Party Prestige

Gorbachev enjoys a 43 percent popularity rating in the USSR, but only 22 percent of Soviet citizens say they completely trust the Communist Party, according to a poll published in *Ogonek* (No. 6). The magazine added that the Party's prestige would be even lower if Gorbachev were not at its head.

Mufti on Artificial Obstacles to Pilgrimage to Mecca

The chairman of the Religious Board of Muslims of Central Asia and Kazakhstan, Mufti Mukhammad-Sadiq Mukhammad-Yusuf, has complained that the various excuses advanced by the authorities for not allowing more Soviet Muslims to make the pilgrimage to Mecca are "naïve" and that the authorities sound "as though they are dealing with small children." Up to now, only about twenty handpicked Muslims have been allowed to go to Mecca each year. Writing in *Ogonek* (No. 6), the mufti said the excuses cited ranged from the lack of diplomatic relations with Saudi Arabia to a lack of foreign currency.

Burlatsky Backs Presidency

Writing in *Izvestia*, political commentator Fedor Burlatsky backed Gorbachev's call for a presidential system. He argued that it was naïve to believe a presidential system was less democratic than a parliamentary one but he added that the power of a future Soviet president should be carefully restricted by the Constitution, much as presidential power is in the United States. He suggested that the Soviet parliament should have the right to dismiss the president by a vote of no confidence or impeachment.

Monday, February 12

Shevardnadze Calls for Naval, Space Arms Verification

Soviet Foreign Minister Eduard Shevardnadze told a session of a joint NATO–Warsaw Pact conference in Ottawa that Moscow wanted verification of naval and space-based arms to be included in confidence-building measures. He said that the mobility of naval weapons presented a great danger of surprise attack and should not be left out of the program. The conference, which is to consider an "open skies" treaty, continues this week (*DPA*, February 12; *Pravda*, February 14).

Moscow Calls for Security Council Meeting on Israel

The Soviet Union called for an immediate meeting of the UN Security Council to discuss Israel's settlement of Soviet Jewish emigrants in Israeli-occupied Arab territory, according to Reuters, AFP, and TASS reports. Both the Soviet Union and Arab countries have condemned this policy, and Soviet Foreign Ministry spokesman Gennadii Gerasimov indicated last week that he hoped Moscow and Washington could issue a joint declaration condemning it. US Secretary of State James Baker rejected the idea, thus prompting the current Soviet call for a UN session.

Lithuania Legalizes Private Property

The Lithuanian Supreme Soviet adopted a law that allows individuals to own property and to hire labor. TASS said that, under the new measure, all forms of ownership that were not expressly forbidden by law would be permitted. According to the law, property can be owned by individuals, families, farms, cooperatives, joint-stock companies, joint ventures, state and public bodies, or other entities (*TASS*, February 12). The new Lithuanian legislation is the first of its kind in the Soviet Union.

Interregional Group of Deputies Discusses Presidential System

At a meeting of the radical Interregional Group of Deputies, Gavriil Popov suggested that, owing to "the difficult situation in the country," the first Soviet president should be elected not by popular vote but by the Congress of People's Deputies (*TASS*, February 13). Other Interregional Group members told the meeting that the president should be elected in a direct, nationwide election. Sergei Stankevich repeated Fedor Burlatsky's call (*Izvestia*, February 11) for the drafting of impeachment procedures.

Tuesday, February 13

Georgia Mediates in Azerbaijani-Armenian Talks

The Soviet media said there had been a meeting in the Georgian capital, Tbilisi, between Armenians and Azerbaijanis about how to end the ethnic crisis in their republics. Radio Moscow's Interfax agency said that members of the popular fronts of both republics had taken part in the talks. The radio said the talks were being mediated by the National Democratic Party of Georgia.

Demonstration in Saratov Reported

Radio Moscow reported that major demonstrations had been held over the weekend in Saratov on the Volga River. The demonstrators were reported to be angry about the way the election campaign was being run in the city and about the fact that more than half of the candidates were Communists running unopposed. The radio said the demonstrators wanted the unopposed candidates to show civic courage and withdraw from the elections. It was reported that the demonstrators had also expressed lack of trust in the oblast and city election commissions and criticized local Party leaders (*Radio Moscow-1*, February 13, 0811).

KGB Says Three-Quarters of a Million People Shot between 1930 and 1953

Dealing with the rehabilitation of Stalin's victims, the KGB Collegium announced for the first time figures for those who suffered repression in the period between the 1930s and the 1950s. TASS quoted the KGB Collegium as saying the figures released had been determined on the basis of analysis of documents in the KGB's archives. According to the KGB Collegium, 3,778,234 people were sentenced for alleged counterrevolutionary activities or crimes against the state from 1930 to 1953. The KGB announcement said 786,098 of them, including many state and Party leaders, scientists, military leaders, and cultural figures, had been shot. While announcing these figures, the KGB Collegium stated that the present KGB staff had nothing to do with crimes committed by the secret police under Stalin.

Rise in Crime in USSR in 1989

The USSR Ministry of Internal Affairs said there were nearly 600,000 more crimes in 1989 than in 1988. A ministry report said the MVD and the USSR Prosecutor's Office had recorded 2,461,692 crimes last year and it noted that the increase had been observed in all parts of the country. The ministry said one in seven crimes committed was classified as serious (*TASS*, February 13).

Troop Cuts in Leningrad Military District Announced

According to TASS, the deputy commander of the Leningrad Military District, Major General Ivan Ryabchenko, stated in an interview with the newspaper *Trud* that military manpower in his district had in recent years been reduced by 5,000 and that the number of tanks had decreased by 700. He stated that all intermediate-range missiles had been eliminated from the district's arsenal. During a speech in Finland, meanwhile, Chief of the General Staff of the Soviet Armed Forces General Mikhail Moiseev made similar statements, informing his hosts that troops along the Soviet-Finnish border (which is encompassed by the Leningrad Military District) would be sharply reduced (*TASS*, February 13).

Wednesday, February 14

Idea of Far Eastern Republic Promoted

A group of people's deputies have put forward a plan to create a Far Eastern republic in the Soviet Union, Novosti press agency reported. Speaking at a meeting of deputies at the USSR Congress from the Far East and Siberia early this month, they said a new republic would be a way to improve the economy of the Far East and promote closer contacts with Japan, China, and the United States. The APN commentary made clear that the central authorities have expressed no support for the idea. The plan to create a Far Eastern republic has been included in the electoral platforms of informal groups campaigning for election in the area. Especially active in campaigning for the republic is the Khabarovsk Popular Front, whose popularity in the region, according to *Partiinaya zhizn'* (No. 2, 1990), has forced local Party officials to offer to set up a joint bloc of candidates for the elections for the front and other local informal groups.

More Recognition for Unofficial Movements

The question of alternative centers of political power received more attention in the official Soviet press. An article in *Moscow News* (No. 7) reported the number of social and political informal groups operating in the USSR had reached 2,000–3,000. The majority of these groups are expected to become full-fledged political parties as soon as a multiparty system is legalized in the USSR. Another contribution came in a commentary on February 14 by Mikhail Poltoranin, a USSR people's deputy and deputy chairman of the USSR Supreme Soviet Commission for the Affairs of Ethnic Turks, who said that, in the Transcaucasus and other parts of the USSR, popular fronts had become much more powerful forces than Party and government bodies. Calling on the authorities to admit this, Poltoranin proposed an all-Union conference of popular fronts sponsored by Moscow (APN, February 14).

Protests in Support of Gdlyan and Ivanov

A warning strike and a mass rally were held in the town of Zelenograd near Moscow to protest against moves to strip the investigators Tel'man Gdlyan and Nikolai Ivanov of their parliamentary immunity. Loss of immunity would enable the two to be prosecuted on charges that they used illegal methods in their investigations of corruption among officials in Uzbekistan, in the course of which they accused a number of Central Committee officials, among them conservative Politburo member Egor Ligachev, of involvement in the case. Leaders of the local strike committee told Radio Liberty that all the enterprises in the town had observed the strike, which involved some 60,000 workers. TASS said 20,000 attended the rally, which had official authorization.

Opposition to Military Draft in Estonia

According to TASS, a Tallinn newspaper reported that the Tallinn City Soviet has repudiated its responsibility for the enforcement of the military draft in the city. The TASS report claimed that the action violated both the Soviet and the Estonian constitutions. It charged that the soviet's decision followed similar actions by the Estonian Prosecutor's Office, which, according to the report, failed to prosecute draft evaders during and after the draft this fall. The report was particularly critical of Estonian informal groups that have taken stands against military service in the Soviet Armed Forces and claimed that one group had gone so far as to offer legal advice on draft evasion. The report chastised official organs for abetting such behavior and charged that their actions promoted lawlessness among the population.

Work on Arkhangelsk Nuclear Power Plant Halted

Radio Moscow reported that the Arkhangelsk city and oblast soviets had decided to halt work on the local atomic power plant. Construction of about one dozen nuclear power plants in the USSR has been halted over the past eighteen months, largely as a result of public protest. According to the report, the plant, which is located fifteen kilometers from the city center, was in the early stages of construction. Instead of atomic power, officials plan to rely on local gas and oil deposits for future energy needs.

Meanwhile, on February 10, *Izvestia* reported that 118 unplanned shutdowns of nuclear reactors took place in the USSR in 1989. The causes for the shutdowns were split about evenly between operator error and equipment breakdown.

Uzbekistan Takes Steps against Rumors

Komsomol'skaya pravda reported that the Presidium of the Uzbek Supreme Soviet had ordered that fines and imprisonment be imposed for the spreading of inflammatory rumors or for inciting "pogroms and the forcible eviction of citizens." The report said that the action had been taken because rumors were causing panic in the republic. People can also be penalized for disseminating material that threatens public order or that seeks to create panic among the population.

Thursday, February 15

Shevardnadze Proposes Plan for Afghan Settlement

In the wake of US Secretary of State James Baker's visit to Moscow, Soviet Foreign Minister Eduard Shevardnadze proposed a ten-point peace plan for Afghanistan. The plan, which was published in *Izvestia*, coincided with the first anniversary of the Soviet Union's military withdrawal from Afghanistan. Shevardnadze said that domestic restructuring in the Soviet Union had provided the impetus for a reevaluation of its Afghan policy. The Shevardnadze plan called for a broad dialogue between all Afghan forces at home and abroad to be buttressed by "a suspension of hostilities" and the establishment of an all-Afghan peace conference. It envisioned "a transitional period" during which the current military status quo would be maintained and which would conclude with the creation of a broad-based government. Consideration of the establishment of a unified administration or territorial armed forces would be set aside until after the election of the government. He called for all forces in Afghanistan to pledge compliance with the results of elections and suggested oversight of such elections by international observers. In the international arena, Shevardnadze proposed a conference involving the Soviet Union, the United States, Iran, and Pakistan, as well as representatives of the Kabul government and the resistance (the latter to be chosen by "a working group" of experts). The United Nations would also be represented. Finally, Shevardnadze called for the termination of all arms deliveries to Afghanistan, the eventual removal of weapons stockpiles from the country, and the ultimate establishment of Afghanistan as a neutral, demilitarized state. He ended by expressing Soviet willingness to confer with all groups in Afghanistan and calling for the release of Soviet prisoners of war still held in the region.

Law on Property Debated by Supreme Soviet

Deputy Prime Minister Leonid Abalkin submitted a draft law on property ownership and assured the USSR Supreme Soviet that it contained a provision preventing exploitation. Abalkin told the Supreme Soviet his draft did not mention "private property" or private ownership of "means of production," because public reaction to those phrases had been negative. He said the draft did allow private ownership of some means of production—for example, a farmer would be allowed to own a tractor (*TASS*, February 15). In the debates over the draft, USSR Justice Minister Veniamin Yakovlev defended the bill, saying it was necessary for the creation of a market economy. But some deputies asked whether such a fundamental change in Soviet law might not also bring problems. On February 16, the USSR Supreme Soviet approved the draft law in principle but referred it to a committee for further work (*TASS*, February 16). The law was adopted by the Supreme Soviet on March 6 and the text of the law was published in *Pravda* on March 10.

Latvian Parliament on Soviet Incorporation

The Latvian Supreme Soviet declared that Latvia's incorporation into the Soviet Union in 1940 had been invalid because it had not been endorsed by all the people. It said the incorporation had also led to Latvia's loss of independence (*TASS*, February 15). Lithuania and Estonia have also declared invalid their incorporation into the Soviet Union.

Armenian Supreme Soviet Backs Sending Troops to Baku

The Armenian Supreme Soviet said it had been "vital" for the Soviet leadership to send troops to Baku, even though the intervention in the Azerbaijani capital was "belated." Radio Moscow said this assessment was included in a document devoted to the clashes between Armenians and Azerbaijanis in Baku and in other parts of Azerbaijan. The document called them "genocide" against Armenians. According to the radio, the Armenian parliament sent telegrams to the USSR Supreme Soviet and Congress of People's Deputies asking for firm steps to stop the forced resettlement of Armenians from the town of Khanlar. Khanlar is in Azerbaijan, south of Kirovabad.

Friday, February 16

Falin Says More than 26 Million Died in World War II

Chief of the Central Committee International Department Valentin Falin said that 26,340,000 Soviet citizens had died in World War II, Reuters reported. Falin gave the figure during a debate in Brussels about the future of Europe and German unification. The figure is six million higher than the figure that the Soviet authorities have traditionally cited but that has recently been disputed by Soviet historians and demographers. Writing in Soviet scholarly journals about direct losses of the Soviet population in the war, they have given figures near to Falin's.

Parliamentary Group Formed to Preserve Union

A large bloc of Soviet parliamentarians said they had united to fight nationalist threats to split up the Soviet Union. Georgii Komarov, a Russian deputy from Kirgizia, announced in the morning session of the USSR Supreme Soviet that 103 deputies had joined the "Soyuz" group, whose aim is to resist "the breakup of the Soviet Union." Komarov made clear that his group especially wanted to defend Russians who lived in the Union republics. Reuters quoted liberal deputies, especially those from the Baltic republics, as denouncing "Soyuz." They were quoted as saying "Soyuz" was a reactionary force made up largely of conservative Russian nationalist groups opposed to greater autonomy for the other republics.

Orthodox Church Returned in Gomel, Belorussia

The Russian Orthodox Church of SS. Peter and Paul in Gomel, Belorussia, was reconsecrated by Filaret, Metropolitan of Minsk and Grodno. TASS said the church, taken over by the state in 1917, had been returned to parishioners a few days earlier. TASS quoted church officials in the republic as saying that in 1989 seventy-eight Orthodox communities had been registered in the republic and about twenty buildings returned to believers.

Stalin's Victims Rehabilitated in Kazakhstan

TASS said more than 30,000 people in Kazakhstan wrongly convicted during the repressions under Stalin had been rehabilitated. TASS quoted sources at the Kazakh security committee and the public prosecutor's office. It said documents showed that between 1930 and 1953, 35,000 people were convicted of counterrevolutionary activity and crimes against the state, of whom more than 5,000 were shot.

Latvian Parliament Debates State Symbols, Military Issues

The Latvian Supreme Soviet decided to restore the symbols that Latvia used before the state was incorporated into the USSR, including the national anthem, national colors, and coat of arms. TASS said the parliamentary deputies also approved the first reading of a draft law on alternative service for conscientious objectors.

Lithuanians Celebrate Declaration of Independence

Thousands of Lithuanians celebrated their country's declaration of independence in 1918. The celebrations also pressed claims to regain sovereignty, which was lost when Lithuania was incorporated into the Soviet Union in 1940. A spokesman for "Sajudis" said tens of thousands of people attended a rally in the city of Kaunas and thousands more assembled in the capital, Vilnius (*AP*, *Reuters*, February 16).

Saturday, February 17

Armenian Supreme Soviet Declares 1921 Decision on Nagorno-Karabakh Illegal

The Armenian Supreme Soviet has formally declared illegal the Soviet government's resolution of 1921 that made Nagorno-Karabakh part of Azerbaijan. The Armenian Supreme Soviet said the resolution violated the right of self-determination of Armenians in Nagorno-Karabakh (*Radio Erevan*, *TASS*, in English, February 17).

Shcherbitsky Dies

Soviet television announced that Vladimir Shcherbitsky, former first secretary of the Ukrainian Communist Party, had died on February 16 after a serious illness, just one day before his seventy-second birthday. Shcherbitsky's tenure as Ukrainian Party first secretary from 1972 to September, 1989, featured an often brutal suppression of dissent, the strangling of Ukrainian national assertiveness, rapacious industrial development, and the mishandling of the Chernobyl' nuclear accident in April, 1986.

Kiev Demands Closure of Chernobyl'

The Ukrainian Supreme Soviet called for the closure of the Chernobyl' power plant and complained to Moscow about its failure to include the Chernobyl' issue on the agenda of the current session of the USSR Supreme Soviet (*TASS*, February 17). This decision came at the end of a three-day session of the republican legislature devoted to environmental issues. TASS added that the Kiev legislators had sharply criticized both republican and central leaders for their "slow resolution of the aftereffects [of the accident]."

Lauristin Calls for Neutral, Demilitarized Estonia

A leader of the Estonian Popular Front, Marju Lauristin, was quoted as saying the front's long-term ideal was for Estonia to be an independent, neutral, demilitarized republic. In a report from Moscow, AFP quoted her as saying the front was not pushing for secession from the USSR, since it did not consider Estonia ever to have been an integral part of the USSR. She said Estonia wanted to return its ties with Moscow to the footing of the guarantees of the Tartu Treaty of 1920. In that treaty, Moscow renounced all claims to Estonian land.

Armenian Supreme Soviet Urges Condemnation of Blockade

The Armenian Supreme Soviet urged the USSR Supreme Soviet to condemn Azerbaijan's blockade of Armenia and Nagorno-Karabakh. The Armenian Supreme Soviet also urged the USSR prosecutor-general to bring to account those responsible for the blockade and called for the USSR Supreme Soviet to collect compensation from Azerbaijan for economic losses in Armenia (*Radio Erevan*, February 17).

On February 19, the USSR Supreme Soviet held a closed-door session to discuss ethnic strife in Azerbaijan and Armenia. Radio Moscow said the deliberations were being kept private at the wish of the deputies (*Radio Moscow-2*, February 19, 1800). On February 20, Western correspondents in Moscow reported that Azerbaijani delegates had walked out of the USSR Supreme Soviet session. The session was then adjourned (*The Los Angeles Times*, February 20).

Georgia Hosts Another Azerbaijani-Armenian Meeting

There was another round of Georgian-sponsored talks between Armenians and Azerbaijanis. This round focused on how to resolve the rail blockade between the two republics. The talks also involved representatives of the Caucasian railway security forces, the USSR Prosecutor's Office, and the USSR Ministry of Internal Affairs (*TASS*, February 17). On February 22, Radio Moscow reported that the blockade had prevented more than 6 million tons of supplies from reaching Armenia.

5,000 Lithuanians Return Military Enlistment Cards

Some 5,000 young Lithuanians were reported to have handed in their military enlistment cards during a protest in Vilnius on February 16 against service in the Soviet Armed Forces, Radio Vilnius said. The protest came amid celebrations marking the anniversary of the Lithuanian declaration of independence in 1918. The radio also said the protesters had signed an appeal to Soviet Defense Minister Dmitrii Yazov saying the Geneva Convention of 1949 gave individuals the right to refuse service in the forces of an occupying power.

Rally Jeers Novgorod Oblast Party Leader

Some 6,000 people joined a rally in the Russian city of Novgorod and jeered the oblast Party first secretary, Ivan Nikulin, when he tried to address the crowd. TASS reported the rally, saying it had expressed "a vote of no confidence" in the oblast Party buro. TASS said the rally had been called because of dissatisfaction over the fact that many oblast Party and government leaders were running unchallenged in the forthcoming elections.

Thousands Rally in Alma-Ata

Thousands of people were reported to have gathered in Alma-Ata for an officially sanctioned rally organized by independent groups. Radio Moscow said participants in the meeting made a wide range of proposals, including calls for Kazakhstan to be given economic independence. The radio said there were also calls for an end to "the plunder" of Kazakhstan's natural resources and for action to save the Aral Sea. Radio Moscow also said there were demands for the closure of Soviet nuclear testing facilities in Kazakhstan.

Soviet Homosexuals Form Pressure Group

A group of Soviet homosexuals formed an organization to launch a newspaper and to push for greater legal and social tolerance for the country's homosexuals. The group, called the Moscow Lesbian and Gay Union, announced its creation at a news conference in Moscow. Organizers said the group comprised about twenty members. One member, Evgeniya Debryanskaya, who is also an active member of the Democratic Union, said there was a need not only to change Soviet laws on homosexuality but also to change public attitudes so that homosexuals could live without hiding their sexual orientation. Homosexuality is still punishable as a criminal offense in the Soviet Union (*Reuters*, February 17).

Sunday, February 18

Demonstrations in Moscow and Leningrad

Two major unofficial meetings took place in Moscow on February 18, according to Radio Liberty's Russian service. At one meeting, representatives of informal groups of democratic orientation called for the unity of all democratic forces in the country. Radio Liberty also obtained information about the creation of a new informal group called Afghan Veterans for Democracy, which shares the platform of the Interregional Group of Deputies. This is an interesting development, given the past tendency of

Afghan veterans to join forces with conservative rather than reformist groups. A separate demonstration in the Soviet capital was held by Russian nationalist groups (*AP*, February 18). The crowd was addressed by anti-Zionist propagandist and advocate of the theory of a Judeo-Masonic conspiracy Aleksandr Romanenko. In his speech, Romanenko called the Interregional Group and other democratic informal groups Zionist organizations and proposed a campaign against them.

On February 17, thousands of people gathered in Leningrad for a demonstration sponsored by the unofficial election bloc "Democratic Elections-90." The demonstrators stressed that, if created, the Russian Communist Party should share the position of the Democratic Platform (*TASS*, February 17). (The Democratic Platform was created in January by a group of Moscow Communists, who called for the transformation of the CPSU into a West European–style social democratic party.)

Moscow News on East European Communist Parties

In an article in *Moscow News* (No. 7), historian Liliya Shevtsova discussed the fact that, at the first free elections in Eastern Europe, Communist Parties were expected to win very few votes. She said the only way for these parties to survive was to transform themselves into new social democratic parties. She also raised the question of the decline in prestige of the CPSU and said that the slow pace of restructuring within the Party was dangerous for the future of the USSR. Shevtsova said that the CPSU was still the best organized political force in the USSR and that its withdrawal from the political arena could lead the country into chaos. On February 21, Novosti published an article by its observer Eduard Ryabtsev, who said the CPSU may split into several parties if no consensus is reached before the next Party congress, which is scheduled for late June.

Debate over Soviet Aid to Cuba Continues

Moscow News (No. 7) carried the latest installment in the debate begun in 1989 on whether Moscow should continue its massive aid program to Cuba. Sergo Mikoyan, chief editor of *Latinskaya Amerika*, argued for continuing the aid, which he said actually saved Moscow money. (The USSR would be hard pressed to come up with the hard currency needed to buy the sugar it currently receives from Cuba on the world market.) Aleksei Izyumov, an economist, argued against, saying that Cuba gave the USSR nothing and should therefore be cut loose. The editors of *Moscow News* called for further articles on the subject to be submitted.

Union of Soviet Journalists Criticized

The Moscow city organization of the USSR Journalists' Union, representing 14,000 media people, has called for the dismissal of the union's top officials, according to *Moscow News* (No. 7). Nikolai Burym, one of those making this demand, told the weekly that the Journalists' Union had not changed its approach since "the period of stagnation." He pointed out that the union had failed to defend journalists and editors when they were attacked by Party officials. Burym blamed the chairman of the union's administration, Viktor Afanas'ev, who last year was ousted from his post as chief editor of *Pravda*, for this state of affairs. Burym disclosed that Afanas'ev had given the union's annual award to his first deputy, Ivan Zubkov, for "a direct contribution to the drafting of the press law," even though the Supreme Soviet rejected the draft written by Afanas'ev and Zubkov.

Existence of Blacklist of Radicals Denied

Vladimir Troepol'sky, a Gosteleradio official, has denied that his organization maintains "a black list" of certain "left-radical" USSR people's deputies (*Moscow News*, No. 7). He justified the sudden cancellation of a broadcast in which USSR people's deputies Nikolai Travkin, Vladimir Tikhonov, Evgenii Evtushenko, Svyatoslav Fedorov, and Yurii Karyakin participated on the grounds that they appeared very frequently in the Soviet media. He said Gosteleradio did not want Central Television to become a platform for the dissemination of only their views.

Gorky Rally Calls for Resignation of Local Leaders

About 6,000 people attended a rally in the city of Gorky and heard demands for the resignation of local Party and government leaders. The rally was organized by the "Candidates for Democracy" association. Radio Moscow-2 said that some speakers attacked the oblast and city Party and government leaders and that the organizers read a resolution calling on election candidates who had no rivals to drop out of the race.

Anti-Semitism Creates Foreign Policy Problem for Moscow

Commenting on an interview with First Deputy Foreign Minister Yulii Vorontsov, the editors of *Moscow News* (No. 7) noted that rising anti-Semitism was creating foreign policy problems for Moscow. These concerns were echoed by Moscow's Chief Rabbi Adol'f Shaevich. In an interview with the Rome daily *Il Messagero*, Shaevich said that anti-Semitism was spreading in the USSR. He deplored the fact that the Soviet authorities had done nothing to control the activities of anti-Semitic groups.

In the same issue of *Moscow News*, Major General Aleksandr Karbainov, deputy chief of the KGB Directorate for the Defense of the Soviet Constitution, said "Pamyat'" did not represent a threat to Soviet society. The KGB general said "Pamyat'" had no more than 200 members in Moscow and only about 1,000 in the whole country. He rejected the suggestion that this organization could ever gain mass support, noting that "Pamyat'" lacked basic organizational structures. Karbainov also said that, since the KGB's Fifth Directorate was abolished in 1989, his organization no longer concerned itself with informal groups.

Elections in Uzbekistan

Elections to local soviets and the republican Supreme Soviet took place in Uzbekistan. TASS reported that in the days leading up to the voting some people in Tashkent and other cities had found it advantageous to "stir up the already complex situation in Uzbekistan." It said some groups had been calling for an election boycott. Radio Moscow said that in one-third of the republic's electoral districts candidates were standing unopposed. TASS said voters in Uzbekistan had expressed disapproval over a lack of choice of candidates in elections. The agency said "many voters" had disclosed that they had struck out all the candidates on the ballots in protest at the lack of choice.

Monday, February 19

***Pravda* Editor Says Return to Capitalism Possible**

Writing in *Pravda*, the deputy chief of the newspaper's ideology department, Yurii Shabanov, said it was inevitable that some of the new parties likely to emerge in the USSR will call for the restoration of capitalism. Shabanov said: "Whichever of these programs is supported by the people, that will be the road society will take." This is the first time *Pravda* is known to have admitted the possibility that capitalism might be restored in the USSR.

Russian Komsomol Members to Form Republican Organization

Representatives of the Komsomol decided to form an RSFSR organization of the youth league. Until now, the RSFSR was the only Soviet republic without its own Komsomol organization. TASS said the formation of such an organization for the Russian Federation was "a pressing issue," as national self-consciousness has grown sharply in the federation. Debates are currently under way about the future of the all-Union Komsomol and of the organizations in the Union republics. Some representatives of the Komsomol have suggested the disbandment of the organization and its replacement with other, more democratic youth groups.

All-Union Chernobyl' Society Registered

Radio Moscow said a group had been formed to protect the rights of people harmed while dealing with the aftermath of the Chernobyl' nuclear accident. The radio said the all-Union voluntary society "Soyuz Chernobyl'" had been registered by the Ukrainian Council of Ministers.

Tuesday, February 20

Proposals for Presidential System Discussed

A draft proposal for the constitutional establishment of a presidential system in the Soviet Union was circulated in the Supreme Soviet. It includes a six-year presidential term and provides the president with the right to veto legislation adopted by the USSR Supreme Soviet, to declare a state of emergency in any part of the country, and to rule the country by decree when the working parliament is not in session. Some reformist deputies were alarmed by the draft's provisions. *The Washington Post* cited Sergei Stankevich as saying that the Soviet president would enjoy most of the powers of his French and US counterparts without many of the constitutional limitations. He added that the new legislation "will not be acceptable to anyone who believes in a constitutional system of checks and balances," because the president would be above both the executive power and the legislative power. But Gorbachev's supporters are vigorously backing the draft. Politburo member Aleksandr Yakovlev said that, as chairman of the Supreme Soviet, Gorbachev lacked the powers needed to protect the constitutional order from destructive forces, which, Yakovlev said, have surfaced during democratization. "Vremya" televised Yakovlev's remarks on February 20.

More Trouble in Ukraine for Party Authorities

Popular challenges to regional Party leaders in Ukraine are increasing. Radio Kiev-3 reported that approximately 20,000 people had assembled to demand the resignation of the Kirovograd Oblast Party Committee. In Zhitomir, the "Citizens' Front to Assist *Perestroika*" held a well-attended demonstration during which participants called for the immediate transfer of power in the oblast to "a provisional coordinating council." Radio Kiev noted that the Zhitomir authorities had organized "a countermeeting," which emphasized the consolidation of progressive forces for the sake of *perestroika*. Meanwhile, members of Party organizations and committees in Kiev passed a resolution demanding the resignation of Anatolii Kornienko, who only last summer replaced the discredited Konstantyn Masyk as Party secretary there. Finally, RFE/RL received reports about the formation in Kharkov of an umbrella organization of independent trade unions and workers' strike committees. The organization is said to include the strike committees set up by miners in Donetsk and Voroshilovgrad.

New Organization to Combat Drug Trafficking

The head of the USSR Ministry of Internal Affairs antidrug administration told *Sovetskaya Rossiya* that Moscow was setting up an interagency body to coordinate the fight against drug trafficking. Aleksandr Kotlyarov said this step was needed, otherwise the Soviet Union might soon become one of the world's main drug exporters. According to Genrikh Khmel', an official of the Main Administration for State Customs Control of the USSR Council of Ministers, foreign drug dealers are already trying to establish themselves inside the Soviet Union, and Moscow is grateful for the cooperation it is receiving from other governments in combating this development. On February 22, Soviet Deputy Foreign Minister Viktor Komplektov said drugs were entering the USSR from Afghanistan and Pakistan (*UPI*, *Reuters*, February 22).

Higher Salaries for Army Officers

The Soviet government has decided to raise the salaries of army officers and to pay compensation for housing and other services, according to Army General Dmitrii Sukhorukov. (A Soviet official told the *Washington Times* on February 19 that such raises would cost 1.2 billion rubles.) In an interview with TASS on February 20, Sukhorukov also hinted that more officers have been nominated for government awards. These steps appear to reflect growing official concern about discontent in the officer corps.

Marxism Cannot Answer All Questions

Pravda praised a new Soviet philosophy textbook for overcoming "the prejudice" that Marxism has an answer to all questions. The paper said that this idea, long an unquestioned part of Soviet ideology, had done enormous harm to philosophy in the USSR. The new two-volume textbook is intended for university-level instruction; its "humanistic" approach will further erode Marxist influence in Soviet academic and professional thinking.

Fifteen Injured in Nagorno-Karabakh

Soviet media reported that fifteen people had been injured on February 18 in an explosion on a bus in Nagorno-Karabakh. There were conflicting reports about whether the blast had been caused by a bomb or a mine. Radio Moscow said the authorities had extended a nighttime curfew by two hours as a result of the blast.

Baku Military Commandant Replaced

The Soviet news media said the military commandant in Baku, Lieutenant General Vladimir Dubinyak, had been replaced. Lieutenant General Boris Smyslov, first deputy head of USSR MVD forces, has taken over as the new commandant. Dubinyak had been in charge of the troops that last month broke through blockades to enter Baku and impose a state of emergency.

Wednesday, February 21

Gorbachev Rules Out Change in German Borders

In a *Pravda* interview, Gorbachev said that German unification must not lead to any border changes. He repeated the oft-expressed Soviet worry that unification could upset the balance between NATO and the Warsaw Pact. But he said if these concerns were dealt with, Moscow would not stand in the way of unification, something he said it had been in favor of since the 1950s. While clearly intended to put pressure on Chancellor Helmut Kohl to make a more definitive statement on German borders, Gorbachev's remarks also allowed him to allay mounting concerns about the impact of German unity on the Soviet Union and Eastern Europe.

Proceedings against "Pamyat'"

The Public Prosecutor's Office of the city of Moscow initiated a criminal case against the extreme Russian nationalist group "Pamyat'" on charges of "arousing national or racial hostility or discord." *Literaturnaya gazeta* (No. 8) reported that the Prosecutor's Office had initiated the case after the newspaper of the Moscow Power Engineering Institute, *Energetik*, published the text of the "Pamyat'" program, which calls for barring Jews and "those related to them" from receiving scientific degrees, awards, positions of authority, etc. *Vechernyaya Moskva*

(February 20) reported that the Prosecutor's Office was also investigating an incident involving "Pamyat'" that took place on January 18 at the Central House of Writers. On that occasion, a group of people connected with "Pamyat'" broke up a meeting of writers and shouted anti-Semitic slogans. The article in *Vechernyaya Moskva*, signed by the public prosecutor of Moscow, was cautious about bringing charges against "Pamyat'" in connection with the incident. The prosecutor emphasized that the investigation should be given time to determine what had really happened. He also defended the Ministry of Internal Affairs against accusations leveled against it by the writers, who said that the police had shown sympathy towards "Pamyat'."

Mounting Transport Problems

The Soviet Union is currently spending hard currency to charter ships to bring in food donated by the West German government, Moscow television reported. Moscow was forced to take this step because the Soviet merchant marine does not have the ships to do the job and the railway ministry says it can transport only about one-third of the food. Moscow television also said commissions of the USSR Supreme Soviet had received a report saying Soviet passenger rail service was facing "an emergency situation." Candidate Politburo member Evgenii Primakov told the parliamentarians that the problems of the railways involved the quality of the rail bed, transport control, and the repair and manufacture of wagons. USSR Minister of Railways Nikolai Konarev said the USSR had not increased production of passenger wagons despite falling deliveries from Eastern Europe. As a result, the USSR has a current shortfall of some 14,000 passenger rail cars.

More Oblast Party Leaders Replaced

Aleksei Balagurov, first secretary of the Murmansk Oblast Party Committee since October, 1988, resigned at his own request (*Central Television*, "Vremya," February 21). Balagurov failed to win election to the USSR Congress of People's Deputies last March. The former second secretary, Sergei Serokurov, was elected to serve as the interim first secretary. Five oblast Party committee first secretaries in the Checheno-Ingush ASSR have been forced to resign following public demonstrations; protests are continuing against a sixth (*UPI*, February 21).

Evgenii Eliseev, first secretary of the Kabardino-Balkar ASSR since October, 1985, and a USSR people's deputy, has been transferred to a post in the CPSU Party Control

Committee (*Central Television*,"Vremya," February 21). The chairman of the republican Supreme Soviet and the second secretary of the republican Party committee were nominated for Eliseev's post; the second secretary, Valerii Kokov, won.

New AIDS Figures Given

According to a report on "Vremya," half of all carriers of the AIDS virus in the USSR are children. The report asserted, moreover, that many of these children had been infected in the course of medical treatment, primarily through the use of unsterilized needles. (In most countries, with the exception of Romania, the predominant mode of transmission of pediatric AIDS is from infected mother to child.) As of the end of January, the AIDS toll in the USSR was: 446 HIV carriers, twenty-eight cases of AIDS, and nineteen AIDS-related deaths. The virus has been identified in eleven of the fifteen Soviet republics. So far, over 50 million Soviet citizens have been tested for the virus. According to Mikhail Narkevich, the official coordinating the USSR's program to combat AIDS, a bill has been submitted to the USSR Supreme Soviet to guarantee the rights of AIDS victims (*TASS*, February 21).

USSR MVD Group on Crimes in and around Nagorno-Karabakh

An investigative group of the USSR Ministry of Internal Affairs said local police organs were obstructing criminal investigations in and around Nagorno-Karabakh. TASS quoted the group's leader as saying employees of one internal affairs department were not pursuing or arresting people who had committed crimes, and nothing was being done to confiscate weapons. TASS did not specify which area was involved, but it did say employees of the district internal affairs department were not contributing, for example, to the investigation of a time-bomb explosion on the Shusha-Baku road last September.

Thursday, February 22

Gdlyan and Ivanov Reported Expelled from CPSU

The BBC World Service (0715 CET) reported that Tel'man Gdlyan and Nikolai Ivanov had been expelled from the CPSU. The USSR Prosecutor-General was reported to have asked the USSR Supreme Soviet to remove their parliamentary immunity so that legal proceedings could be started against them. Gdlyan was quoted by the BBC as saying that he was still a loyal Communist but that he had no desire to belong to a Party run by Gorbachev, whom he described as the chief protector of "the mafia" that now controls the Central Committee. The same day, Reuters quoted a spokeswoman for the Moscow Party Committee as confirming the expulsion. She said the two investigators had been expelled as the result of a decision by the primary Party organization at the USSR Prosecutor's Office. They were accused of "nonobservance of Party rules." See RL 111/90.

More Trouble Involving Meskhetians in Uzbekistan

Radio Moscow's World Service said police guarding Meskhetians in Uzbekistan were attacked by a crowd of Uzbeks, and four policemen were injured. Radio Moscow quoted the Interfax news agency as saying the incident took place two days ago in the Karabai settlement in Tashkent Oblast. It said police were trying to evacuate the Meskhetians after a crowd of about 1,000 young Uzbeks had assembled in the village square to demand their eviction. A separate Radio Moscow report said on February 22 that the Uzbek Supreme Soviet Presidium had put into effect a decree barring outdoor rallies and limiting all other public demonstrations "until the sociopolitical situation in Uzbekistan has stabilized."

On February 22, TASS reported that a USSR Supreme Soviet commission investigating issues involving the minority Meskhetian population had completed its work and would present its findings to the Supreme Soviet Presidium. It said this had been announced by Rafik Nishanov, chairman of the USSR Supreme Soviet Council of Nationalities, during a meeting in Moscow with representatives of the Meskhetian population. TASS said the Meskhetians had asked Nishanov to speed up the consideration of their request to return to their homeland in the Transcaucasus.

Leningrad City and Oblast Party Committees to Be Merged

A joint plenum of the Leningrad City and Oblast Party Committees decided to merge the two bodies. The plenum also decided that a joint city-oblast first secretary would be elected at a Party conference in April. Boris Gidaspov now serves as first secretary of both committees. The decision to merge the city and oblast committees came after a referendum among Leningrad's Communists (*Radio Moscow-1*, February 22, 1900).

Chairman of Supreme Soviet Elected in Kazakhstan

Kazakhstan's Communist Party first secretary, Nursultan Nazarbaev, was elected chairman of the Presidium of the republic's Supreme Soviet, TASS reported. Nazarbaev replaces Makhtari Sagdiev, who has retired on pension.

Nazarbaev is the fourth Soviet republican leader to combine the posts of chairman of the Supreme Soviet and Party first secretary. The others are in Lithuania, Georgia, and Turkmenistan.

New Soviet Proposal on Troop Reductions

The USSR put forward a new suggestion at the Vienna talks on troop reductions in central Europe. The head of the East German delegation, Klaus-Dieter Ernst, said the USSR had suggested limiting the total manpower of NATO and the Warsaw Pact to between 700,000 and 750,000 each. The suggestion was not put forward as a formal proposal. Ernst said this was because one Warsaw Pact member had expressed doubts that it could be negotiated in time for an arms treaty, which it is hoped will be concluded before the end of the year (*Reuters*, February 22).

Kirgiz Party Seeks to Stop Rumors

Mikhail Vasilenko, head of the Kirgiz Party Central Committee Agitation and Propaganda Department, said the authorities had banned the spreading of rumors before the elections. Vasilenko spoke to Reuters in the Kirgiz capital of Frunze. He said the measure was aimed at preventing ethnic unrest, which has recently broken out in several other republics. Vasilenko said those who spread false information with the aim of causing panic and destabilizing the situation would be punished. He said the Kirgiz Party leadership planned a meeting on February 24 to discuss the preelection situation. (Elections in Kirgizia are scheduled for February 25.)

Kapitsa against Restoring Ties with Israel at Present

Mikhail Kapitsa, deputy chairman of the Supreme Soviet International Affairs Committee, said he was against restoring USSR-Israeli diplomatic ties at present. He said such ties should be ruled out "as long as Israel continues to be an aggressor" and refuses to agree to an international Middle East peace conference including the PLO. Kapitsa spoke at a news conference in Brussels after meetings between a Supreme Soviet delegation and members of a parliamentary association for European-Arab cooperation. Kapitsa also reiterated that Jews leaving the Soviet Union should not be settled in the Israeli-occupied territories (*UPI*, *Reuters*, February 22).

Preparations for Nuclear Power Station near Finland Suspended

The Soviet Union suspended preparations for the construction of a nuclear power plant near the border with Finland. The plant was to have been built in the

Karelian Autonomous Republic, but TASS said survey work and technical and economic preparations for construction of the plant had been suspended by the Presidium of the Karelian Supreme Soviet. TASS said this work would remain suspended until a Soviet law on the utilization of nuclear energy and nuclear safety had been adopted. It added that scientists were preparing an alternative program to supply Karelia with energy.

Uzbek Academy Translating Koran into Uzbek

The Uzbek Academy of Sciences is compiling an Uzbek-language version of the Koran for publication in Tashkent in 1991. This will be the first Koran ever published in the Uzbek language, although copies of the Koran in Arabic are available in Uzbekistan.

Presidential Proposal Dates Back to 1964

Soviet television screened a discussion of the executive presidency Gorbachev has proposed. Taking part were two people's deputies, Fedor Burlatsky and lawyer Konstantin Lubenchenko. Burlatsky revealed that in 1964, when he was a Central Committee staff member, he had served on a group that proposed the creation of an executive presidency. The idea, he said, had met with derision from Party leader Nikita Khrushchev. Later that year, Khrushchev was ousted in a Kremlin coup, and Burlatsky lost his Central Committee post. Burlatsky recalled that he had raised the possibility again in June, 1988, in an article that appeared on the eve of the Nineteenth Party Conference, but his proposal was again ignored. Lubenchenko said a move to a presidential system was essential to break the power of the Communist Party leadership.

Senior Military Officials on Defense Cuts

In interviews marking Armed Forces Day, Chief of the General Staff Mikhail Moiseev and Minister of Defense Dmitrii Yazov reiterated their support for current Soviet efforts to cut military spending and restructure the nation's armed forces. But in an interview with *Izvestia*, Moiseev warned that the West's continued efforts to gain military technological superiority over the USSR compelled the Soviet Union to maintain parity across a broad spectrum of weapons systems.

Yazov told *Pravda* on February 23 that the provision of housing for military personnel was the most critical problem facing the Ministry of Defense. He claimed that more than 173,000 families of officers currently lacked apartments, while thousands had become little better than refugees as a result of nationalist-based disorders and harassment. See RL 146/90.

On February 23, TASS issued the traditional Armed Forces Day "prikaz" by Yazov. It suggested a hardening in the military leadership's attitude towards Gorbachev's defense policies. In his order of one year ago, Yazov lauded the results of "new thinking" in international affairs, claiming that Soviet peace initiatives had "pushed back the threat to world peace." In this year's order, however, Yazov warned that positive changes in the world had still not attained an irreversible character, that sources of aggression had not disappeared, and that, while the threat to peace had diminished, it had not been annihilated. Yazov also made a strong statement on the Soviet domestic situation, claiming that the armed forces "condemn separatist, nationalist, and extremist displays and resolutely oppose efforts to cheapen Communist ideals and falsify Soviet military history." See RL 121/90.

Izvestia Opens New Rubric on Public Rallies

Izvestia opened a new rubric devoted to public rallies. Justifying the introduction of the new rubric, called *Demonstrations: Democracy or Extremism?*, the newspaper said that "at times it looks as if the entire country has gathered for one meeting, one demonstration." The first contribution to the column was a critical evaluation of a demonstration held on February 18 near the Ostankino television center in Moscow by conservative Russian nationalist groups, who attacked Gorbachev's policies as pro-Western and anti-Russian.

Friday, February 23

Estonian Supreme Soviet Abolishes Party's Leading Role

The Estonian Supreme Soviet abolished the leading role of the Communist Party and named a committee to hold talks with the central authorities about secession. The committee will also ask for Estonia to be given the right to take part in European security talks as an independent state (*TASS*, February 23).

Soviet Leaders Advocate More Discipline

Speaking on Soviet television, Prime Minister Nikolai Ryzhkov said the USSR needed order and discipline for reforms to make progress. Ryzhkov said people were worried about how strikes and ethnic strife had affected the economy. He said the government would take strict measures to ensure a normal life. The same day, *Izvestia* quoted Politburo member Aleksandr Yakovlev as saying that what the USSR needed most was discipline and responsibility. Yakovlev said the power of the street was not democracy but tyranny. The same day, TASS quoted Politburo member Vadim Medvedev as saying stronger central power was needed in the USSR. Medvedev said he favored the introduction of a presidential system in order to achieve this.

Pro-Moscow Lithuanian Party on 1940 Incorporation

The Lithuanian Communist Party that is still loyal to Moscow criticized a Lithuanian Supreme Soviet decision that declares null and void the republic's incorporation into the USSR in 1940. The Party said the Supreme Soviet declaration distorted the historical truth of what happened in Lithuania in 1940 (*Radio Moscow*, World Service, February 23).

Gerasimov Criticizes US over Pacific Troop Reductions

Foreign Ministry spokesman Gennadii Gerasimov said troop cuts being considered by the United States in the Pacific region were too small. Gerasimov told a news conference in Tokyo that the Soviet Union planned to make bigger cuts in the region. He said the Soviet Union would reduce troop strength by 200,000 in Asia and remove fifty warships from its Pacific Fleet. Gerasimov was reacting to comments made in Tokyo earlier today by US Defense Secretary Richard Cheney. Cheney said the United States was considering a 10-percent troop reduction in Asia over the next three years. He said it would be a mistake to sharply reduce the US presence there, in view of the fact that the USSR had not acted to reduce tensions in Asia in the same way that it had in Europe (*Reuters*, *AFP*, February 23).

Kazakh Party Leader on 1986 Events in Alma-Ata

Kazakhstan Party First Secretary Nursultan Nazarbaev said the Party bore part of the responsibility for the riots in Alma-Ata in December, 1986. In an interview with *Pravda*, Nazarbaev said the trouble started when the Kazakh Party Central Committee chose as its new leader the only candidate offered by the apparatus, "in the worst traditions" of the Brezhnev era. (The Central Committee chose a Russian, Gennadii Kolbin, to replace a Kazakh, Dinmukhamed Kunaev, as Party first secretary.) Nazarbaev said this had brought a group of young people to the central square of Alma-Ata to ask questions, including why a Kazakh had not been chosen for the job. Nazarbaev said that, although there had been no excuse for the riots that followed, the Party's approach to personnel problems "was one of the many reasons behind them."

Draft of Soviet Income Tax Plan Published

TASS reported that the USSR Council of Ministers had publicized its new draft law on income taxes. The draft law would tax enterprises—both government and "private"—at a maximum rate of 55 percent of profits. The draft would also lower the tax on the incomes of low-paid workers and gradually increase the tax on people who have no children (excluding those who are childless for medical reasons). The government also plans to establish a tax office to enforce the new law. The penalty for those who try to cheat on their taxes will be as much as double the amount underpaid, plus a possible jail term.

Plans to Build Pesticide Plant in Western Ukraine Canceled

Plans to build a large pesticide factory in Western Ukraine have been canceled owing to protests from local residents. TASS said local residents had been protesting ever since they learned of plans to build the factory in Shumskoe, which is located in the most densely populated part of Ukraine. It said residents considered the factory an ecological hazard.

Russian Nationalists Denounce Reforms

The latest in a series of meetings held in Moscow by extreme Russian nationalists to denounce Gorbachev's reforms took place today. Speakers at the meeting accused the Politburo of being involved in a Zionist conspiracy and condemned attempts to bring Western capital into the Soviet Union. Nina Andreeva was among the speakers and was applauded when she demanded the resignation of Gorbachev, Shevardnadze, and Yakovlev (*The Washington Post*, February 24). A similar meeting took place in Moscow on January 31. At that gathering, described as a meeting of readers of the journal *Nash sovremennik*, speakers attacked nationalist movements in the Union republics. Some of them suggested that the Baltic republics were simply blackmailing Russia with threats of secession in order to get more financial support from the Russian people (*Atmoda*, February 12). Similar speeches were also delivered at a press conference of the board of the RSFSR Writers' Union on February 12 (*Literaturnaya Rossiya*, February 16).

Commentary Says Gorbachev Should Quit Party Post

A commentary published by Novosti press agency urged Gorbachev to give up his post as Party general secretary and to concentrate on the executive presidency as a full-time job. Novosti observer Aleksandr Ignatov said that the Communist Party was still blocking essential reforms and that only by dissociating himself from the Party would Gorbachev be able to stave off growing public discontent.

KGB Blocks Weapons Theft

TASS said the KGB's military counterintelligence service had prevented an attack on a military arms depot in Altai Krai. The attackers were apparently planning to steal weapons and ammunition and to sell them for 200,000 rubles to "one of the country's southern republics."

"Soyuz" Founder Says USSR Could Copy US Nationality Policy

A founder of the "Soyuz" faction in the USSR Congress of People's Deputies said that Moscow could learn from the way nationalities are integrated in the United States. Georgii Komarov, a deputy from Kirgizia, said nationalities in that republic, including Russians, had their own churches, schools, shops, and restaurants, which allowed their national cultures to thrive. Komarov said "Soyuz" had been formed earlier this month because many deputies were afraid that central and local government were losing control over events. He said "Soyuz" would support the most radical forces in their efforts to speed up the democratization of the USSR but also the most conservative forces in their efforts to maintain the country's territorial integrity. Deputies from the Baltic republics denounced "Soyuz" as a conservative faction whose goals were opposed to the interests of the non-Russian nationalities of the USSR.

Deteriorating Ethnic Relations in Army

In an interview published in *Argumenty i fakty* (No. 8), the head of the political department of an unidentified military formation claimed that ethnic relations were now the most serious problem facing the Soviet Armed Forces. According to Lieutenant Colonel V. Durnev, 80 percent of all criminal activities connected with *dedovshchina* (the abuse of junior soldiers by their seniors) in his unit last year were ethnically motivated. This percentage was, he claimed, far higher than in previous years. Durnev said that conscripts from the

Transcaucasus and Central Asia were especially likely to form groups along ethnic lines, a practice that led to conflict with other soldiers.

Sakharov More Popular Than Either Lenin or Gorbachev

A poll published in *Argumenty i fakty* (No. 8) showed the late Andrei Sakharov to be more popular than either Lenin or Gorbachev. The poll named Gorbachev as the most popular living Soviet figure. The poll, conducted in December and January by the Moscow Center for Sociological Research, placed Egor Ligachev at the bottom of the popularity scale. In 1989, the chief editor of *Argumenty i fakty*, Vladislav Starkov, became involved in a row with Gorbachev over the publication of an opinion poll indicating that Sakharov and other radical deputies were more popular than Party leaders. Gorbachev demanded Starkov's resignation but did not succeed in securing it.

Popov on Monetary Reform

Radical reformer Gavriil Popov proposed "a *perestroika* variant" of monetary reform, which, he argued, would both soak up the excess money currently in circulation in the Soviet economy and also be seen as socially just by the Soviet public (*Argumenty i fakty*, No. 8). Popov argued for the introduction of a new currency to be exchanged for the old at a rate of 1 to 1 with respect to a sum up to the equivalent of an individual's legal earnings for the preceding ten years. Earnings from legal private activities (auto repairs and the farming of private plots, for example) would also be exchanged at a rate of 1 to 1. Other money balances—which Popov assumed to be speculative income earned by "smart operators" (*del'tsy*)—would simply be destroyed by the government.

"Sajudis" Candidates Win in Elections

At the elections to the Lithuanian Supreme Soviet, candidates backed by "Sajudis" won the majority of seats. The results of the voting, which were announced on February 25, revealed that "Sajudis" candidates had won seventy-one seats. A "Sajudis" spokesman told RFE/RL that the preliminary results showed that ninety of the 141 seats had been decided. The spokesman said that there would be runoff elections for forty-five seats and that in six districts there would be a new vote because an insufficient number of voters had participated in those districts. Speaking to reporters on February 25 in connection with the elections, the chairman of "Sajudis," Vytautas Landsbergis, said he believed it was possible Lithuania would become independent of the USSR by the end of this year. On February 26, *Pravda* said "Sajudis" and the breakaway Lithuanian Communist Party would probably form a coalition government in the near future. See RL 119/90.

New Movement for Democratic Russia Created

A declaration published in *Ogonek* (No. 8) announced the creation of a new movement called "Civil Action" (*Grazhdanskoe deistvie*), which sets as its main goal the creation of a democratic and free Russia. Signed by leading Soviet reformers and people's deputies Yurii Afanas'ev, Gavriil Popov, and Anatolii Sobchak, as well as by former dissidents Larisa Bogoraz and Sergei Kovalev, the declaration called for the speeding up of democratic reforms in the USSR. It also said that the only way Russia could become democratic was for it "to meet the demands of other nationalities of the USSR for national revival." Referring to extreme Russian nationalists, the declaration also complained that a group of people that had instigated national discord and wanted to separate Russia from Western civilization had usurped the right to present itself as the only defender of the interests of the Russian people.

Mogilev Declared Radiation Disaster Zone

Izvestia reported that officials in Mogilev Oblast in Belorussia had declared the area "a radiation disaster zone." The paper said the population of Mogilev was determined to leave but had nowhere to go. No fewer than 7,000 families must be resettled this year, according to the report. The Belorussian government has submitted a Chernobyl' aid program to the USSR Supreme Soviet for its approval, but the status of the proposed package is unclear. Last week, according to TASS, the Belorussian press published an appeal by the republican government to international organizations asking for help in eliminating the consequences of the nuclear disaster. More than 2 million people live in areas known to be contaminated, and new hot spots are constantly being identified. See RL 152/90.

Shooting Interrupts Baku-Erevan Railway Transport

Radio Moscow said shooting at the Dzhulfa station in the Nakhichevan Autonomous Republic on February 23 had interrupted railway transport on the Baku-Erevan route for twelve hours. The radio said that "extremist operations" were causing great damage in the Transcaucasus and in the entire Soviet Union (*Radio Moscow-1*, February 24, 0900).

USSR Foreign Ministry Collegium Rejects United Germany in NATO

The USSR Foreign Ministry Collegium said a united Germany in NATO would bring about an unacceptable alteration in the military strategic balance between the Western alliance and the Warsaw Pact. The collegium is an advisory body of senior Soviet officials dealing with foreign policy matters. A statement issued after a meeting of the collegium rejected the argument that a united Germany in NATO would be in the interests of the Soviet Union because it would be under some kind of external control (*AP*, February 24).

Reuters reported on February 27 that a Central Committee adviser on German affairs had called for NATO's tactical nuclear weapons to be removed from a united Germany. Nikolai Portugalov claimed that Moscow was unwilling to accept a situation in which East Germany was demilitarized while West Germany retained the many nuclear weapons now deployed there by NATO. Daniel Proektor, a specialist on Germany, suggested to *Sovetskaya Rossiya* the same day that Soviet troops should be allowed to stay in East Germany following unification in order to ensure the security of the Warsaw Pact. The statements by both men reflect growing Soviet concern that the unification of Germany will further undermine the strategic position of the Soviet Union in Europe.

Estonians Celebrate Independence Anniversary

Estonians celebrated the anniversary of Estonia's declaration of independence from Russia in 1918 with church services, rallies, and concerts throughout the republic (*UPI*, February 24). Marju Lauristin, a leader of the Estonian Popular Front and a deputy of the USSR Supreme Soviet, said it would be best if negotiations on the future of the Baltic republics were part of the European Helsinki process. She spoke in an interview with DPA.

Conference of Reformist Communists in Leningrad

A conference of reformist Communists opened in Leningrad, TASS reported. The participants discussed the program of the Democratic Platform—a group of radical rank-and-file members of the CPSU who announced the creation of their own organization earlier this year. The participants called for a dialogue between the Democratic Platform and the CPSU. The journal *Politika* (No. 1) carried an article by one of the founder members of the Democratic Platform, Vladimir Lysenko, who proposed various ways to bring about the democratization of the CPSU.

Sunday, February 25

Prodemocracy Demonstrations in a Dozen Soviet Cities

Prodemocracy rallies were held in about a dozen Soviet cities. Western reporters estimated that between 100,000 and 300,000 people took part in a rally in Moscow. Rallies were also reported in Tbilisi, Tashkent, Khabarovsk, Vladivostok, and Minsk. Turnout was lower than the organizers—who included the Interregional Group of Deputies, reformist voters' clubs, and the CPSU's reform-oriented Democratic Platform—had hoped. The relatively low turnout seems to have been the result of a week-long barrage of official warnings that the demonstrations might result in violence. The warnings led to the cancellation of demonstrations in Leningrad and Rostov-on-Don. Reports said the Moscow demonstrators called for the speedier implementation of political reforms and an immediate end to the Communist Party's monopoly on power. Opposition was voiced to the creation of a stronger presidency, while demonstrators expressed support for Tel'man Gdlyan and Nikolai Ivanov, the two prosecutors who were expelled from the Party last week, following charges that they had used illegal methods in their investigations of official corruption (*TASS*, *Central Television*, Western agencies, February 25).

Popular Front Takes Over Belorussian TV Studio

A prodemocracy demonstration in Minsk drew 100,000 people, the largest rally of its kind ever seen in Belorussia. Reports reaching RFE/RL said that, after Belorussian television reneged on a promise to broadcast the event live, three members of the Belorussian Popular Front—including chairman Zyanon Paznyak—had entered the television studios and read speeches on the air in which they accused the Soviet government of lying about Chernobyl', called for the resignation of the Belorussian Communist Party leadership, and urged voters not to cast their ballots for Communist candidates in the elections on March 4.

Elections in Tajikistan

Elections were held for a new Supreme Soviet in Tajikistan. TASS reported that some representatives of informal organizations had complained that the elections were not democratic, but the news service said that the chairman of the republican electoral commission, Ivan Dedov, had denied the charge. Dedov pointed out that only four electoral districts had unopposed candidates—in the rest there were between two and seventeen contenders for each seat. On February 26, Radio Moscow reported the election results, according to which all the Tajik Communist Party candidates won seats in the Tajik parliament. The radio reported that new elections would be required in some districts. Radio Moscow also said that at a press conference in Dushanbe it was announced that thirty-five people had been arrested in connection with acts of violence.

Elections in Kirgizia

On February 25, Kirgizia held both republican and local elections. On February 26, TASS reported that in Frunze only one-third of the candidates competing for the 100 seats in the city soviet had been elected. The agency said a similar situation existed in several other regions of Kirgizia. On February 23, republican Party chief Absamat Masaliev told a meeting of representatives from Frunze's factories and scientific and educational institutions that economic problems could not be solved by mass rallies alone. According to a Radio Moscow report, participants in the meeting appealed to the population to reject the efforts of extremists to destabilize the situation (*Radio Moscow-1*, February 24, 1900).

Elections in Moldavia

Elections also took place in Moldavia. The main challenger to the Party was the Moldavian Popular Front. Partial results of the elections were announced on February 28. AP and AFP reported that runoff or repeat elections would be held in two weeks in 241 of the 380 districts sending representatives to the Moldavian Supreme Soviet. Moldavian Popular Front officials were quoted as saying that their members had won at least 65 of the 139 seats and were asking for recounts in some other districts. There were 1,892 candidates, some 80 percent of whom were CPSU members, competing for the 380 seats. Voter turnout averaged 83.5 percent. Petru Lucinschi, the first secretary of the Moldavian Communist Party, whose opponent's registration was declared illegal, ran unopposed and received 91.2 percent of the vote. Mircea Snegur, chairman of the Presidium of the Moldavian Supreme Soviet, also ran unopposed and received 88.2 percent of the vote.

Sweden Accuses USSR of Violating Swedish Waters

The Swedish navy said it had fired a depth charge at what it believed was a foreign submarine near the Musko naval base, according to Western news agencies. While the submarine apparently escaped undamaged, Stockholm accused the USSR of violating Swedish waters. A Soviet submarine ran aground near Sweden's Karlskrona naval station in 1981, but until recently Stockholm has avoided taking any effective action against the intruders. The latest move may have been prompted by a recently released report by the RAND Corporation documenting both the frequency of Soviet penetration of Swedish waters and Stockholm's failure to take strong action.

El'tsin against Multiparty System at Present

Radical deputy Boris El'tsin called the USSR a country defeated by socialism. El'tsin also said he was against the idea of a multiparty system in the USSR at the present stage. In an article in *The Sunday Times*, he said the mere existence of several parties would not solve any problems. He said the Soviet Union needed to "grow and mature towards a genuine, civilized, multiparty system."

5,000 Soviet Azeris Said to Demonstrate on Iranian Border

Iran said 5,000 Soviet Moslems demonstrated today on their side of the Araks border river in the biggest such rally since Soviet troops quashed unrest in Azerbaijan last month. Iranian television said the demonstration was held in Nakhichevan, near the Iranian border town of Poldasht (*Reuters*, February 26). On February 27, TASS reported that Soviet border police had arrested four Azerbaijanis returning from an illegal trip to Iran and had seized a pistol, ammunition, and a large sum of rubles and Iranian money. Four machine guns were also reported to have been found at the scene of the arrest.

Monday, February 26

Havel Visits Moscow; Agreement on Withdrawal Signed

Czechoslovak President Vaclav Havel began a visit to Moscow with talks in the Kremlin with Gorbachev. The talks focused on bilateral ties and the new situation in Eastern Europe. Gorbachev and Havel signed an agreement on the withdrawal of Soviet troops from Czechoslovakia. An agreement on bilateral relations was also signed (*Radio Prague*, *TASS*, February 26).

Construction of Radar Station in Western Ukraine Halted

Radio Moscow's World Service reported that, as a result of local protests, the authorities had halted the construction of a powerful new radar station in Western Ukraine near the Hungarian and Czechoslovak borders. The radio said the radar station was to be built in the Transcarpathian Oblast, near the city of Mukachevo. It said the oblast soviet had decided to invite a competent government commission to investigate. On February 27, Radio Kiev reported that USSR Defense Minister Dmitrii Yazov had agreed to halt construction of the radar station.

Moldavian Officials' Privileges Eliminated

TASS said that privileges for high-ranking Moldavian officials were being eliminated. The agency said this was being done by a commission set up in January by the Moldavian Supreme Soviet. TASS said that the raion and city executive committees were following the commission's orders to close down various kinds of special restaurants and special departments in consumer goods and food shops. TASS said that polyclinics and sanatoriums previously reserved for senior officials had been opened to the public. The commission will also review officials' access to state housing.

Tuesday, February 27

Executive Presidency Approved

The Supreme Soviet approved the proposal that the USSR should have an executive president. Gorbachev immediately announced that he would stand for the post (*TASS*, February 27). Some deputies from the Baltic republics refused to take part in the vote, saying their authority was restricted to preparing negotiations to restore independence to their republics (*TASS*, February 27).

***Pravda* Publishes Rules for Election of Congress Delegates**

Pravda published draft rules for the election of delegates to the Party congress. Party organizations were instructed that, in a departure from past practice, congress delegates would be elected from the grassroots instead of being nominated from above. Primary Party organizations would be allowed to nominate delegates but, because the CPSU has as many as 442,000 primary organizations, smaller bodies would, on the instructions of their superior Party bodies, join together for the purpose of electing delegates.

Moscow Offers to Help New Nicaraguan Government

In a remarkable turnaround, a Soviet Foreign Ministry spokesman welcomed the results of the elections in Nicaragua, which Manuel Ortega lost, as a step towards democracy, peace, and stability in the region. TASS commentaries on the election echoed this line, and Moscow offered economic aid to the new post-Sandinista government.

Soviet Magazine Publishes Russian Copies of Secret Protocols

After denying they existed, Soviet officials published photographs of a Russian-language copy of the secret protocols to the Molotov-Ribbentrop Pact and the Border and Friendship Treaty, which provided for the incorporation of the Baltic states into the USSR. In 1989, the protocols were denounced by a commission of the USSR Congress of People's Deputies, after being condemned in the Baltic republics. In the summer of 1989, Soviet journals carried photographs of the German-language version of the documents. The photographs of the Russian version appear in the first issue for 1990 of *Vestnik*, a joint-venture publication produced by the USSR and Austria.

Moscow May Sell Nuclear Power Plant to Pakistan

The Soviet ambassador to Islamabad told the Pakistani press that Moscow was considering selling that country a nuclear power plant, AFP reported. Viktor Yakunin was reported to have said that the USSR wanted to help Pakistan overcome its energy crisis. If its spent fuel were diverted for military research purposes, such a plant could complicate Pakistan's relations with the United States.

"Open Skies" Conference Ends without Agreement

Talks in Ottawa between NATO and the Warsaw Pact on aerial surveillance ended without an agreement. Moscow was unwilling to accept a NATO plan, supported by the majority of participants, calling for each alliance to use its own aircraft and technology and to circulate information only within the alliance. The Soviet Union wants surveillance by both alliances to be carried out with standardized technology and a common fleet of planes; it also wants the two sides to share any information gathered. The NATO proposal also calls for 150 flights a year for each alliance, while the Soviet Union wants only thirty-four. A NATO source reported that the Soviet position was opposed by the other twenty-two countries at the conference, but the chief Soviet negotiator, Viktor Karpov, claimed that France and three other smaller European countries supported the Soviet Union. Positions on both sides appear to have hardened, and there is now less optimism that an agreement can be reached when the conference reconvenes in Budapest this spring (*RFE/RL Special*, January 27).

Developments in Tajikistan

The Presidium of the Supreme Soviet of Tajikistan ruled further activity by the informal "Citizen's Committee" illegal, according to Radio Moscow-1 (1900). Set up by representatives of informal groups and the intelligentsia during demonstrations in Dushanbe on February 12–14, the committee undertook to negotiate with the republican authorities over the demonstrators' demands, particularly their call for the resignation of the republican leadership. The head of the republican Gosplan, Buri Karimov, who was elected chairman of the committee, and other republican officials were under investigation by Party authorities for their role during the Dushanbe disturbances. The report said the upcoming republican Central Committee plenum would discuss whether it was appropriate for Communist Party members who occupied high-ranking government posts to participate in the activities of informal organizations.

New Informal Group in Uzbekistan

A new movement called "Erk" (Will) has been set up within the Uzbek Popular Front, "Birlik," TASS reported. Members of "Erk" held a founding congress in Tashkent and elected the poets Erkin Vahidov and Muhammad Salih, both of whom recently won seats in the republican Supreme Soviet, to lead the new group. TASS said the new group's program called for Uzbekistan's economic and political autonomy within the framework of the USSR. For some time, "Birlik" has been split into moderate and radical wings; the program and leadership of the new group suggests that it embodies the moderate wing of "Birlik." The establishment of "Erk" as a distinct entity suggests that earlier divisions in "Birlik" have been formalized.

Government Accused of Cover-Up over Chernobyl'

Deputy chairman of the State Committee for Hydrometeorology Yurii Tsaturov had accused both the USSR and RSFSR governments of a massive cover-up after the Chernobyl' accident, *Rabochaya tribuna* said. Tsaturov said his committee had produced a map of the contamination in the Bryansk, Kaluga, and Orel areas three years ago, but government officials had classified it "Top Secret." In his interview, Tsaturov also discussed the rising number of accident-related diseases in that region and the shortages of medical staff, drugs, and equipment there.

In other Chernobyl'-related matters, the Belorussian ambassador to the UN repeated earlier appeals for international aid for his republic to help it recover from the accident: he said Belorussia needed 17 billion rubles to overcome the consequences of Chernobyl'. Also on

February 27, two films about Chernobyl' directed by Rollan Sergienko were premiered in Moscow (*AP*, *TASS*, February 27).

Soviet Bankers Convene

Soviet banking and financial officials held a three-day conference in Moscow to discuss restructuring the USSR's banking system. Radio Moscow said the bankers were trying to find a way to help boost living standards in the short run without exacerbating the problem of monetary overhang (excess cash in circulation).

Moscow Seeks High-Tech Joint Ventures

Speaking in Chicago, Central Committee member Konstantin Frolov said the Soviet Union was eager to cooperate with the West on scientific projects. Moreover, Moscow wants the West to help market Soviet innovations. Frolov suggested that US scientists were more pragmatic and eager to see their innovations applied in industry, while Soviet scientists were more interested in theoretical advances. If the latter had greater incentive to focus on more practical matters, he said, they could make significant global contributions. Frolov said he thought several Soviet technological advances—including laser technology and some new materials that might be useful in encasing radioactive materials—could be successfully marketed in the West.

Moscow Admits *Storozhevoi* Mutiny

Fourteen years after it happened, *Izvestia* reported the mutiny on the Soviet submarine-chaser *Storozhevoi* in the Baltic Sea, which took place in November, 1975. Reports of the incident at the time from local fishermen, relations and friends of the crew-members, and *samizdat* sources soon reached the West and were relayed into the Soviet Union by Western radios. Initially, Moscow refused to comment on the allegations, but a deputy commander of the Soviet Baltic Fleet subsequently termed the report "unthinkable" and a Western "hoax" (*Berlingske Tidende*, August 11, 1976). The *Izvestia* account mentioned Tom Clancy's novel *The Hunt for Red October*, which was loosely based on the *Storozhevoi* incident. On March 1, *Komsomol'skaya pravda* also reported the *Storozhevoi* mutiny.

Widespread Bribery by Cooperatives Reported

TASS quoted the USSR Ministry of Internal Affairs as saying there had been widespread bribery of officials by people seeking favorable treatment for private cooperative businesses. According to TASS, an MVD spokesman said officials of government agencies, state enterprises, banks, and inspection services were among those bribed. The spokesman said more than 250 such bribery cases were discovered last year and that was "just the tip of the iceberg."

Referendum Opposes Nuclear Power Plant

A referendum has called for a halt to construction of a nuclear power plant in the southern Urals. Radio Moscow said that 99 percent of those who took part in the referendum favored stopping work on the plant, which is in the Bashkir Autonomous Republic.

Gorbachev Meets with Baltic Representatives

Gorbachev met with representatives from the Baltic republics to discuss their push for independence. Two members of the Congress of People's Deputies from each of the three Baltic republics attended. One of them, Ulo Nugis, the chairman of the Estonian Union of Work Collectives, told the Estonian daily *Paevaleht* on February 28 that the meeting amounted to the first negotiations on independence for the Baltic republics. On March 1, leading Lithuanian, Latvian, and Estonian officials met to coordinate their efforts to achieve independence from Moscow (*Reuters*, March 1).

Wednesday, February 28

New Land Law Approved

The USSR Supreme Soviet passed new legislation concerning land ownership (*Radio Moscow-2*, February 28, 1230). The law takes effect March 15 and sets the framework for republics to broaden their own laws concerning land ownership. While extending the right to "own" land in perpetuity (including the right to pass land deeds to heirs), the law does not permit the selling, giving away, or exchange of land. The land will be leased free of charge but subject to a tax. The state can revoke the lease if the holder is deemed not to be using it rationally or if he causes excessive pollution.

Gorbachev Accused of Taking Bribes

Radio Vilnius broadcast excerpts from a speech made some time ago by former special investigator Tel'man Gdlyan accusing Gorbachev of having taken bribes from trade organizations when he was first secretary of the Stavropol Krai Party organization in the 1970s. Gdlyan demanded that criminal proceedings be started against Gorbachev, his wife, and Defense Minister Dmitrii Yazov for using state resources to build dachas in Yalta. Radio Vilnius also broadcast the translation of an interview with Gdlyan's colleague, Nikolai Ivanov, who stated that "the chief patron of the 'mafia' in the Soviet Union is none other than Gorbachev."

Controversy in Chuvash ASSR

The Party leadership of the Chuvash ASSR, including its first secretary, Aleksandr Petrov, survived a vote of no confidence at an extraordinary plenum of the republican Party organization, Radio Moscow reported. The vote had been demanded by members of a local voters' organization, "Alternativa," at a demonstration held on February 25. Petrov runs one of the most corrupt Party organizations in the USSR. The murder last year of a local investigative journalist—which was apparently arranged by one of Petrov's loyal subordinates—is one of the more egregious examples of misconduct by local officials in Chuvashia.

Grigoryants Not Allowed to Attend East-West Meeting

Sergei Grigoryants, editor of the *samizdat* journal *Glasnost'*, said Soviet officials had refused to let him attend an East-West meeting in Paris that is to discuss the problems of creating a free press in countries that have recently moved over to democracy. Grigoryants told AP in Moscow that, while his visa application had been rejected, editors of official Soviet publications had had no trouble going to the meeting, which is being organized by UNESCO. A UNESCO spokesman told RFE/RL it had asked the Soviet delegation to intervene so Grigoryants could honor the agency's invitation to attend.

Laptev Made Acting Head of Journalists' Union

Chief editor of *Izvestia* Ivan Laptev has replaced Viktor Afanas'ev as head of the USSR Union of Journalists; Laptev will serve until the next congress of the union. Afanas'ev resigned as chairman of the Board of the Journalists' Union after a series of complaints about his performance. (TASS reported his resignation on February 27.) A few weeks ago, 14,000 Moscow media employees demanded that Afanas'ev, who was removed last year from his post as chief editor of *Pravda*, be ousted from the union post as well (*Moscow News*, No. 7). Laptev is a strong supporter of Gorbachev's reforms, and under his direction *Izvestia* has on the whole followed a liberal line. In 1989, Laptev was involved in a sharp dispute with Afanas'ev over a conservative draft law on the press that had been devised by Afanas'ev and his associates.

Resettlement of Refugees

In *Sovetskaya Rossiya*, Prime Minister Nikolai Ryzhkov said that interethnic conflicts in the Soviet Union had created 500,000 refugees. As a result, the government has started to establish a program to assist refugees by providing them with housing, jobs, and facilities for children. Ryzhkov said the cost of the program would be enormous and must be shared by the republics that the refugees were forced to leave. "You drove out the people. You must accept responsibility, including material responsibility," he said.

Firearms Found in Raid on Nagorno-Karabakh Village

A raid by MVD and army troops uncovered a cache of firearms, radios, uniforms, and food in a village in Nagorno-Karabakh. TASS said the village of Kirovo in the Shusha district had until recently been a base for militants. The agency quoted an MVD investigator, Valerii Kadyrov, as saying troops had found firearms, grenades, antipersonnel mines, and other explosive devices under hay in the cellars of abandoned homes. It said criminal proceedings had been started in connection with the discovery.

The Month of March

Thursday, March 1

Warning Strikes in Donetsk

Miners in the Ukrainian city of Donetsk staged warning strikes to press for the resignation of local Party leaders. The cochairman of the Donetsk strike committee, Nikolai Volynko, was quoted by UPI as saying all the city's pits had joined the strikes, which lasted six hours. Volynko said a full-scale regional strike was planned for March 2 unless the resignation demand was met. In Kazakhstan, a Soviet government commission started checking how local officials had honored pledges made to striking coal miners in the Karaganda Oblast in 1989 (*TASS*, March 1). On March 2, however, Radio Moscow reported that only three pits out of the 121 in Donetsk participated in the strike. The radio said most miners were "reluctant to aggravate the economic situation further."

Dock Strike in Klaipeda

Radio Moscow World Service said dock workers had staged a two-hour warning strike in the Lithuanian port of Klaipeda. The radio said that the Klaipeda dockers had the support of dockers in other Baltic ports and that they were protesting against a Soviet government decision to hold port workers responsible for the security of imported cargoes between the port and railheads. The radio said loads worth more than 500,000 rubles had been lost en route last year. The dock workers felt they should not be held responsible for these losses.

Latvian Parliament Urges Changes in Law on Constitutional Oversight

TASS said the Latvian Supreme Soviet had decided to ask the USSR Congress of People's Deputies to amend the law on constitutional oversight. That law grants a committee meeting in Moscow the power to overturn republican laws and constitutional provisions if they clash with those of the USSR. The law was adopted last year against the wishes of the Baltic republics. TASS said the Latvian Supreme Soviet had also adopted a law allowing an alternative to military service for conscientious objectors. The law, which is the first of its kind to be adopted in the USSR, allows for thirty-six months of alternative service for most conscripts and eighteen months for university graduates.

Special Forces Prepared for Departure of Troops from Tajikistan

Tajik Minister of Internal Affairs Mamadayez Novzhuvanov told Moscow television that a new 500-man unit of troops from the Tajik MVD had been established in Dushanbe to take over the maintenance of public order when Moscow ended the state of emergency in the republic. He said Tajikistan also intended to ask the USSR MVD to create a special troop unit in Dushanbe. Novzhuvanov said these arrangements should reassure citizens about the Tajik government's ability to "ensure complete maintenance of public order."

Soviet Officials in Teheran for Economic Talks

Soviet Railways Minister Nikolai Konarev arrived in Teheran for talks that he said would include discussion of the possible sale of passenger planes to Iran. The Iranian news agency IRNA quoted Iranian Finance Minister Mohsen Nurbakhsh as saying the talks would cover cooperation in dam construction, steel production, and nuclear power research (*Reuters*, March 1). Konarev left Teheran on March 7 after an agreement had been reached for the Soviet Union to build two nuclear power plants in Iran (*Reuters, AP*, March 7).

Official of KGB Says It Is Undergoing Radical Transformations

The deputy chairman of the KGB said his organization was continuing to undergo radical transformations. Leonid Shebarshin, who heads the KGB's foreign intelligence service, said these included changes in personnel. He said the Fifth Directorate, which deals with dissidents, had been abolished and excessive "veils of secrecy" were being removed. (The abolition of the Fifth Directorate was announced in 1989.) Shebarshin said his service was now concerned with gathering information about world economies to help the USSR overcome its economic crisis. TASS said Shebarshin had made the comments at a recent meeting of a labor collective in Moscow.

***Pravda* Comments on Sino-Soviet Relations**

Pravda said the normalization of Sino-Soviet relations represented a move towards common sense that took into account modern realities. The newspaper said that, after the 1989 Sino-Soviet summit, the two states had turned their backs on the negative bilateral relations of the past. *Pravda* said it was evident that under present conditions it was impossible to return to the Sino-Soviet military-political union of the 1950s. The newspaper also rejected as "totally inadmissible" the model of Sino-Soviet relations that existed in the 1960s and 1970s.

US-Soviet Trade Talks

US and Soviet officials began two days of talks in London on an agreement aimed at reducing obstacles to bilateral trade. The talks are the second in a series that began in Washington in February. The talks include discussion of conditions under which the United States would grant the Soviet Union most-favored-nation trading status (*Reuters*, March 1).

Friday, March 2

USSR Reschedules Socialist Countries' Debts

The Soviet Union was reported to have rescheduled many debts of Socialist countries, including Poland and Cuba, and written off many others. Statistics published in *Izvestia* showed that the USSR was still owed a total of 85,000 million rubles, of which about half consisted of debts incurred by Socialist countries. The newspaper said "we should not seriously count on these debts being repaid soon," and it added that the USSR was likely to write off even more debts.

***Pravda* on Jewish Emigration**

Pravda accused Israel and the United States of fanning the controversy over Soviet Jewish emigration to Israel. The newspaper said it was pertinent to recall US concern over the rights of Soviet Jews, since now that emigration had begun the United States had closed its doors, forcing the émigrés to go to Israel. Israeli Prime Minister Yitzhak Shamir has refused to accept US conditions for providing money to help resettle the immigrants; the United States has offered loan guarantees to build needed housing but only on condition that Israel promises not to move settlers to the West Bank or the Gaza Strip.

Latvia Sets Up Own Bank

The Latvian Supreme Soviet adopted a banking law that set up a republican central bank with broad powers. TASS said the bank would have the exclusive right to issue currency and would represent Latvia's interests in relations with foreign banks. It said the bank would also be authorized to accept international credits and solicit loans. The Latvian deputies also set up a commission to work out measures for the restoration of Latvian economic independence. TASS said the commission's working groups were to discuss Latvia's plans with Soviet state organs. The deputies also banned Latvian judges from membership in parties and other sociopolitical organizations.

On March 1, DPA quoted the director general of Estonia's central bank, Rein Otsason, as saying the Soviet central authorities had imposed controls on banking activities in the Baltic republics. Otsason said this move was contrary to the program for Soviet republics to gain increased economic autonomy. Otsason said the regulations had come into effect on March 1 and stipulated that payment transactions made by banks in the Baltic republics must be routed through the Soviet central bank in Moscow.

One Million Commemorate Baku Dead

About a million people marched to Baku's Nagorny park to commemorate those killed in January when troops entered the city to quell ethnic unrest. Radio Moscow said the crowd was made up of people of various nationalities and religions. It included members of the Azerbaijani minorities in Georgia, Dagestan, and other Soviet republics. Soviet television showed film of the demonstration and reported plans to build a monument in Baku to those who died. Radio Moscow-1 (2200) said prayer services were held in all mosques, churches, and synagogues of Baku.

Katyn Families Demonstrate at Soviet Embassy in Warsaw

Some forty relatives of Polish officers killed in the massacre in the Katyn Forest during World War II demonstrated outside the Soviet embassy in Warsaw. A delegation of the "Katyn families" organization and other relatives of the Polish victims gave Soviet Ambassador Vladimir Brovikov a letter addressed to Prime Minister Nikolai Ryzhkov. Radio Warsaw quoted the letter as saying the families demanded that the Soviet government take "an official stand" on the Katyn slayings.

6,500 Fail to Register for USSR Military Draft

The USSR's chief military prosecutor, Aleksandr Katusev, said some 6,500 persons throughout the USSR had failed to report for the latest draft call-up. *Komsomol'skaya pravda* quoted Katusev as saying there was a rising trend towards draft dodging in the USSR. On February 10, the same figure was given by Chief of the General Staff of the Soviet Armed Forces Mikhail Moiseev in *Krasnaya zvezda.*

Saturday, March 3

***Pravda* Publishes Program of Democratic Platform**

Pravda published the program of the Democratic Platform in the form of a round-table discussion with its authors. The Democratic Platform is an amalgamation of progressive Communists representing over 150 different Party clubs and organizations from thirteen Union republics. The program calls, among other things, for the investment of real authority in the soviets and the transformation of the CPSU into a parliamentary party operating within a multiparty system.

Strikes among Archival Workers

In an article devoted to the deteriorating state of Soviet archives, *Ogonek* (No. 9) revealed that in January employees of dozens of republican, oblast, and krai archives had gone on strike. The striking archivists demanded an increase in salaries, an improvement in the conditions of preservation of archival materials, and the dismissal of the conservative leadership of the Main Archival Administration. Striking employees at Moscow's Central Archives of Ancient Manuscripts named the head of the archival administration, Fedor Vaganov, as the main obstacle to the reorganization of archival work. Criticism of Vaganov has been going on for almost two years now, and it is surprising that such an infamous figure, who made his career by writing books denouncing Nikolai Bukharin, is still in charge of Soviet archives.

Clashes in Uzbekistan

Reports from Uzbekistan said people had been killed and wounded in a clash between demonstrators and soldiers in the Parkent Raion of Tashkent Oblast in Uzbekistan. On March 3, Abdurashid Sharif, a spokesman for the Uzbek Popular Front "Birlik," was quoted by AP as saying that soldiers had fired on "peaceful demonstrators" in the city of Parkent. He said the demonstrators had been protesting about alleged fraud in last month's elections and demanding the resignation of elected officials. Sharif said protesters then stormed and burned the local police headquarters and broke windows at the Communist Party organization building. He said the soldiers then opened fire again, killing more civilians. In a conflicting report, *Komsomol'skaya pravda* said the trouble had started with an unsanctioned rally demanding the removal of Meskhetian refugees from the raion. It said Uzbek Prime Minister Mirakhmat Mirkasymov, had gone on television on March 3 to say that a mob "provoked to unlawful actions by irresponsible instigators had started to storm the headquarters of the raion police and other public buildings" and that as a result people had been wounded and killed. On March 5, AP and Reuters quoted the MVD as saying four people had been killed and ninety-two injured during the clashes. On March 8, *Izvestia* said an investigation commission had been set up to assess the violence that took lives in Parkent.

Armenian and Azerbaijani Delegations Debate Settlement

A meeting was held in Tbilisi between representatives of the Azerbaijani Popular Front and two Armenian informal organizations—the Karabakh Committee and the radical Union for Self-Determination, whose ultimate goal is the creation of an independent Armenian state. The meeting was organized by the Georgian National Democratic Party, which seeks Georgian independence. The Georgians proposed that a moratorium be placed on all territorial claims among the three Transcaucasian republics until they have gained independence (which presumably would include the demand by Azerbaijanis in Georgia for their own autonomous formation, as well as Armenian claims on Nagorno-Karabakh). This proposal was accepted by the Azerbaijanis, but the Armenian groups asked for a week to study it (*AP*, March 3).

The issue of Nagorno-Karabakh was also discussed today by the Presidium of the USSR Supreme Soviet. TASS quoted members of the Azerbaijani Organizing Council currently administering Nagorno-Karabakh (the council is composed exclusively of Azerbaijani and Russian officials) as stating that the sociopolitical situation in the oblast remained explosive and that the council itself was being boycotted. TASS said that transport was functioning again and power and water supplies were being restored but that strikes continued in Stepanakert.

On March 5, the USSR Supreme Soviet voted to urge Armenia and Azerbaijan to hold talks on ending the two-year conflict over Nagorno-Karabakh and to restore "trust and agreement." A spokesman for the Azerbaijani deputies characterized the resolution, which underscores "the sovereignty and territorial integrity" of both republics, as "not ideal," but, he said, "we have to stop talking and start moving forward." The resolution was bitterly opposed by the Armenians (*Reuters*, *TASS*, in English, March 5).

Sunday, March 4

Elections in RSFSR

After casting his ballot in the RSFSR elections, Mikhail Gorbachev told reporters that the number of Party members elected was less important than the number of people "who support *perestroika* and who are prepared to move this process forward" (*The Los Angeles Times* and

The Washington Post, March 5). According to Central Television of March 5, less than 15 percent of the races for seats in the RSFSR Congress of People's Deputies were decided in the March 4 elections. Politburo member and Chairman of the Presidium of the RSFSR Supreme Soviet Vitalii Vorotnikov defeated his sole competitor easily, winning 71.3 percent of the vote. Prominent reformers who won included Boris El'tsin; editor of *Argumenty i fakty* Vladislav Starkov; former political prisoner Sergei Kovalev; and Aleksandr Polit'kovsky, one of the hosts of the controversial television show "Vzglyad." In Leningrad, only two of approximately 150 candidates enjoying conservative backing advanced to the second round (*AP*, *Reuters*, *The Baltimore Sun*, *TASS*, March 5 and 6).

The runoff elections in the RSFSR on March 18 were also marked by major victories for reformers. "Democratic-Elections 90" in Leningrad said that its candidates had won 80 percent of Leningrad's seats in the RSFSR Congress of People's Deputies and controlled 65 percent of the seats in the Leningrad City Soviet. In Moscow, reformist candidates were said to have won ten of the fourteen seats to the RSFSR Congress decided in the runoffs (Western agencies, *Radio Moscow-1*, March 19). Officials who won election to city soviets included the chairman of the Leningrad City Soviet Executive Committee, Vladimir Khodyrev; the chairman of the Moscow City Soviet Executive Committee, Valerii Saikin; and the first secretary of the Moscow City Party Committee, Yurii Prokof'ev. USSR Minister of the Coal Industry Mikhail Shchadov was defeated by a miner in Vorkuta. Candidates running on Russian nationalist platforms, including Leningrad art critic Mark Lyubomudrov and Moscow poet Stanislav Kunyaev, lost in the runoff elections (Western agencies, March 20 and 21). See RL 92/90, RL 162/90, and RL 172/90.

On March 28, the RSFSR Supreme Soviet declared elections in some districts in the republic invalid because of irregularities, TASS reported. The news agency said about 10 million ballots had had to be declared invalid. It blamed local election commissions for this. It also said the shortcomings were due to poorly prepared provisions in the government's election laws. See RL 163/90.

Elections in Ukraine and Belorussia

The former political prisoners and long-time Ukrainian dissidents Vyacheslav Chornovil and Mykhailo and Bohdan Horyn won their bids for seats in the Ukrainian Supreme Soviet. All three ran in the West Ukrainian city of Lvov. Poet Ivan Drach, the chairman of "Rukh," was also elected in Lvov (Western agencies, *TASS*, March 4, 5, and 6).

Despite complaints about election malpractice by the authorities, first reports indicated that democratic candidates in Ukraine had scored further impressive victories in the runoff elections on March 18. In Kiev, candidates from the "Democratic Bloc" (an alliance formed by "Rukh," the Ukrainian Helsinki Union, and other independent groups) were reported to have won fifteen of the twenty-one contested seats. Among those elected were former political prisoner and Ukrainian Helsinki Union activist Oles' Shevchenko, "Rukh" activists Serhii Holovatyi and Larysa Skoryk, the controversial theater director Les' Tanyuk, and the poet and "Rukh" and Ukrainian Language Society activist Pavlo Movchan. In total, democratic candidates and their allies won seventeen of Kiev's twenty-two seats in the Ukrainian Supreme Soviet. In Lvov, all four contested seats were reported to have been won by "Democratic Bloc" candidates. See RL 115/90.

On March 5, Central Television reported that in Belorussia, Efrem Sokolov, first secretary of the Belorussian Communist Party, and Zyanon Paznyak, leader of the Belorussian Popular Front, had both won. A popular front spokesman said progressive candidates were winning in urban areas but Party officials in rural areas.

Runoff elections were held on March 17 in Minsk and on March 18 in the rest of Belorussia. RFE/RL was told that "Democratic Bloc" candidates had won fourteen of the forty-two Minsk constituencies that were not decided in the first round. That brings to twenty the total number of popular front–backed deputies who will be representing the Belorussian capital in the republican Supreme Soviet. Twelve more deputy mandates from Minsk, however, will have to be decided in repeat elections. Several popular front leaders lost their bids for election, including the deputy chairmen of "Adradzhen'e" Yurii Khadyka and Mikhas' Tkachou, and secretaries Vintsuk Vyachorka and Alyaksei Marachkin. They were the victims of a vicious smear campaign. Khadyka has decided to sue *Vechernii Minsk* correspondent Tat'yana Bumazhkova for slander. By scheduling the elections in Minsk on Saturday, a working day, rather than Sunday, the authorities achieved their goal of keeping the electorate away from the ballot boxes; voter turnout in some districts was reported to have barely exceeded 50 percent.

USSR Reveals Military Aid to Egypt in 1970s

Sovetskaya Rossiya reported that Soviet antiaircraft units and MiG-21s flown by Soviet pilots were deployed in Egypt from March, 1970, through March, 1971, and that during that time they managed to shoot down twenty-one

Israeli planes. The reports said Soviet personnel, twelve of whom were killed in action, wore Egyptian military uniforms. This story comes in the wake of other reports dealing with past Soviet military activities in the Third World and seems to be part of a broader effort to gain recognition and benefits for the military personnel (and their families) who took part in these actions. Until now, their activities have largely been kept secret in the USSR.

Chernobyl' Plant to Be Closed

The Ukrainian Supreme Soviet announced that the Chernobyl' nuclear power plant, the site of the world's worst nuclear accident, would be phased out of operation over the next five years and shut down. Until now, both Kiev and Moscow have resisted such a move because of the danger of domestic energy shortages and, as *The Washington Post* noted on March 4, the possibility that contracts with East European countries would not be fulfilled. The decision to close the plant is clearly an important victory for Ukraine's powerful ecological lobby.

Interview with Ratushinskaya Published

Komsomol'skaya pravda carried an interview with the poet and former Soviet political prisoner Irina Ratushinskaya. An active Christian, Ratushinskaya was sentenced to seven years in prison and five years of internal exile in 1983. She was released in 1986 and now lives in England. Until now, Ratushinskaya had been the subject of strong attacks in the Soviet press.

Another Wartime Grave in Poland

The existence of another mass grave dating from the time of the Soviet entry into Poland in 1944 has been disclosed. PAP said the grave, containing up to 1,000 bodies, was in the southeastern Tarnobrzeg region. It quoted local people as saying they recalled the Soviet NKVD bringing prisoners there in 1944 and killing them.

Top Tajik Officials Expelled from CPSU

Radio Moscow-2 (2230) said Tajik Deputy Prime Minister Buri Karimov and Culture Minister Nur Tabarov had been expelled from the CPSU. The radio said they were expelled on March 3 at a plenum of the republic's Party Central Committee. Karimov heads the outlawed "Provisional Citizen's Committee," which was formed after last month's riots in Dushanbe. TASS said earlier that a group of senior Tajik Communists was under investigation for allegedly trying to oust Prime Minister Izatullo Khaeev in favor of Karimov.

Karpov Accuses US of Wanting to Hide "Open Skies" Data

Viktor Karpov, the deputy foreign minister who headed the Soviet delegation to the "Open Skies" Conference in Ottawa, accused the United States of planning to use its technological edge to hide information obtained from military flights over Warsaw Pact countries under an "open skies" treaty. The first phase of "open skies" talks, aimed at reaching a treaty allowing surveillance flights by NATO and Warsaw Pact countries over each other's territories, ended in Ottawa last week with various issues unresolved. The talks resume in Budapest in late April. Karpov told *Pravda* that the United States "wants to use its technological advantages to obtain information it does not want to share with anybody." "There should be genuine openness and genuine equality," he said. Karpov said the Soviet Union was prepared to accept any state-of-the-art surveillance technology. But "this should be a mutually accepted technology, a technology that will enable the sides to compare information they get," he said. Karpov said the Soviet Union had proposed setting up a joint pool of planes that both sides could use to share information or creating two pools of planes—one for the Warsaw Pact, the other for NATO—but this has been rejected.

Soviet Fear of Nuclear Terrorism

Vice President of the USSR Academy of Sciences Evgenii Velikhov said the decision to send troops to Azerbaijan last January had been prompted by the fear that extremists might break into KGB-guarded nuclear weapons stockpiles located near Baku. Western intelligence sources have claimed that an estimated 100 nuclear weapons are stored near Baku. In an interview appearing in *Moscow News* (No. 10), Velikhov said that there had never been a danger that extremists could launch an attack with nuclear weapons, but he did not exclude the possibility that Azerbaijani extremists could, theoretically, seize the nuclear stockpiles and sell them to terrorists in the Third World. See RL 148/90.

Bukovsky's Novel Serialized in Soviet Journal

The Soviet journal *Teatr* (No. 2) started the serialization of the autobiographical novel *The Wind Returns* by exiled Soviet dissident Vladimir Bukovsky. *Moscow News* (Nos. 8–9) carried an abridged text of Bukovsky's foreword to this novel. Until now Bukovsky has been strongly attacked in the Soviet press. He was among those émigrés who until recently refused to believe that Gorbachev's policies were aimed at democratizing the Soviet Union.

KGB Attacks Reform and Gorbachev

The KGB issued a dramatic appeal to the Soviet parliament and to Gorbachev personally to halt the defamation of the army and the security organs in the Soviet press. The appeal, signed by "participants in a meeting of representatives of sections of the KGB central apparatus" was distributed by Novosti today. The appeal criticizes the Kremlin leadership for its weakness in combating negative tendencies in Soviet society, stating that the hesitation of the leadership to take appropriate action is incomprehensible, since the KGB has kept it informed of the growing tensions in the country. The KGB urged the Kremlin leadership to halt the decay of the Soviet federation and to prosecute those who try to discredit "the holy name of Lenin" and the October Revolution. The concern of the KGB apparatus derives from the fact that the security organs have come under increasing fire in recent months. A critical article about KGB activities in Rostov Oblast that appeared in *Ogonek* (No. 8) has provoked an almost hysterical reaction from local KGB officials. The KGB chairmen of Latvia and Lithuania, who have vigorously opposed the drive for independence in these republics, were both retired on the same day (*Radio Riga* and *Radio Vilnius*, March 7). See RL 169/90.

Lizichev Interviewed by *Literaturnaya Rossiya*

In a wide-ranging interview appearing in *Literaturnaya Rossiya* (No. 8), Head of the Main Political Administration of the Soviet Army and Navy (MPA) Aleksei Lizichev commented on the future of the army's political organs, whose status has been under fire of late, and discussed his relationship with uniformed radicals in the Soviet parliament. General Lizichev admitted that the future of the army political organs was uncertain, and he drew the questionable conclusion that, within the confines of a multiparty system, centralized political and educational work is especially important for the armed forces. He also praised the role of political officers during the recent disorders in the Transcaucasus and accused critics of the MPA of harboring confused notions concerning its functions. Lizichev stated that political officers now constitute 8 percent of the total officer corps and revealed that one-third have graduated not from military-political academies, but from combined-arms, tank, or other military schools.

The interview also demonstrated the continuing ambivalence of the military establishment towards the activities of its uniformed critics in the Soviet parliament. Lizichev disclosed that during last year's election campaign there were efforts within the military leadership to expel Colonel Viktor Podziruk—a radical critic of the armed forces who ran against a senior military commander—from the armed forces. Lizichev claimed to have intervened decisively on Podziruk's behalf, arguing that Podziruk's political activities were not proper grounds for dismissal.

First Western Computer Store Opens in Moscow

The first Soviet store selling Western computers opened in Moscow, sporting a US flag over the door and a huge red banner reading: "Business to business, person to person." But, despite the inviting sign, only those Soviet citizens with hard currency can buy the computers, which included IBM and other leading brands, and most trade is expected to come from Soviet research institutes and businesses rather than individuals (*Reuters*, March 5).

Religious Prisoners Still Being Held in USSR

Keston College issued a statement saying there were sixty-seven persons still being held in Soviet labor camps and "open prisons" because of their religious beliefs. Thirty-two of these are known to be in detention and thirty-five are unconfirmed.

Tuesday, March 6

Gorbachev Announces Opposition to NATO Membership for Germany

On March 5, the secretary general of NATO, Manfred Wörner, predicted that the Soviet Union would not oppose NATO membership for a united Germany, arguing that Gorbachev would overrule the hard-line position taken until now by Foreign Minister Eduard Shevardnadze (*Chicago Tribune*, March 5). On March 6, in Moscow, however, Gorbachev stated unequivocally that the Soviet Union would not accept the participation in any form of a unified Germany in NATO, claiming that such a development would upset the strategic balance in Europe (*TASS*, March 6; *Pravda*, March 7). Gorbachev's statements came during an interview following consultations with Hans Modrow, the East German Prime Minister. Gorbachev also expressed his support for German unification, but cautioned that for a number of historical reasons it should take place only in a carefully controlled, step-by-step process.

Controversy over Rationing Shows Split among Reformists

During the election campaign, several democratic candidates have advocated the idea of universal rationing in the Soviet Union. Such a system would be egalitarian, they argue, by providing everyone with an affordable, basic living standard, while thwarting speculation and reducing queuing. But, according to an article in *Ekonomika i zhizn'* (No. 6), such a system is not feasible, simply because there are not enough goods to ration.

Izvestia (March 1) also devoted a whole page to the question of rationing, pointing out that such liberal deputies as Il'ya Zaslavsky and Gavriil Popov of the Interregional Group advocate the idea. Economist Larisa Piyasheva, however, rejects the idea of rationing and has attacked Zaslavsky's views on it. *Izvestia* revealed that Piyasheva had been expelled from "Democratic Russia," an unofficial bloc of candidates standing for election, for her views.

Economist Nikolai Shmelev was quoted in *Izvestia* as siding with Piyasheva. Shmelev argued that rationing would lead to corruption and to abuses by officials distributing ration coupons. He added that rationing would cause Soviet citizens to live again like Gulag prisoners, working for their "small share of bread and a place on a plank-bed."

Defense Ministry Denies Troop Transfer to Baltic

The Soviet Defense Ministry denied that troops being pulled out of Czechoslovakia would be stationed in the Baltic republics. TASS said the statement had been made to counteract foreign news reports, which it said were groundless. The Latvian Supreme Soviet last week put on the record an open letter from one of its commissions, protesting about the possible transfer of Soviet troops from Central Europe to Latvia.

Party Calls for Updating Leninism

A new document issued by the CPSU said Lenin's basic ideas were still valid but should be brought into line with contemporary developments. The document, issued by the Party's Ideological Commission for the 120th anniversary of Lenin's birth, said Lenin's views should not be sacrosanct. The document said Lenin himself would have found this absurd. It also said Lenin's teaching had been distorted under Stalin. It said Leninism freed of distortions would become a major source of inspiration in the Party's drive for renewal and would protect the Party from conservatism and dogmatism (*TASS*, March 6; *Pravda*, March 7).

Gorbachev Sets Out Financial Claims to Lithuania

Gorbachev was reported to have outlined the huge financial compensation the Soviet authorities would demand in the event of a Lithuanian decision to declare independence. On March 6, Radio Vilnius and Lithuanian television said Gorbachev had presented figures on March 5 to Chairman of the Presidium of the Lithuanian Supreme Soviet and Lithuanian Communist Party leader Algirdas Brazauskas. The radio said Gorbachev put Lithuania's debt to the Soviet Union at 21 billion rubles, most of it for Soviet capital investment in Lithuania. Brazauskas was quoted as saying that this amount was one-third of Lithuania's national product and that it was very hard to see how the Baltic republic could settle this initially in hard currency. The claim is apparently aimed at convincing the newly elected Lithuanian Supreme Soviet not to advocate separation from the USSR when it meets this weekend in its first session. In another apparent attempt to convince Lithuania not to secede, Gorbachev told Brazauskas that the territorial borders of Lithuania were not clear. Brazauskas, however, told Lithuanian television that there was no need to be afraid of the economic consequences of secession. He was quoted as saying Lithuania would be far better off by itself and that the advantages would offset its debts to Moscow.

On March 8, Lithuanian economist Bronislavas Zaikauskas told Radio Vilnius that the issue of compensation should not be raised in negotiations with the Soviet Union on Lithuania's independence. He said that if any compensation was to be made, it was the USSR that should compensate Lithuania for the damage caused to the republic under Soviet power, particularly by the repression of Lithuanian citizens.

Proposal on Semipalatinsk Nuclear Testing Site

A joint session of the USSR Supreme Soviet's Committee for Defense and State Security and its Ecology Committee held hearings on proposals to close the Semipalatinsk nuclear weapons test site in Kazakhstan. Radio Moscow and TASS reported that three main proposals had been put forward. The first was offered by military representatives and some nuclear scientists, who called for "a transitional period" of three years, during which nuclear testing would continue at the site. According to Colonel General Vladimir Gerasimov, this would involve twenty-seven more explosions. Following this period, nuclear testing would be moved to a test site on Novaya Zemlya, an island in the Barents Sea. Gerasimov belittled calls for a nuclear testing moratorium, arguing that, in view of continued US nuclear testing and nuclear force modernization, a Soviet moratorium would amount to "unilateral disarmament." He said the Soviet Union was willing to halt testing if the United States did the same. A second proposal called for a one-year testing moratorium in order to allow the government time to consider the problem. A third proposal, reportedly advanced primarily by residents of Kazakhstan, called for a quick end to nuclear testing at Semipalatinsk.

Wednesday, March 7

Supreme Soviet Committee on Crime Made Permanent

The provisional Committee for the Struggle against Crime created in the summer of 1989 and chaired by Anatolii Luk'yanov has been transformed into a permanent USSR Supreme Soviet committee. Its chairman is Yurii Golik, dean of the Law Faculty of Kemerovo University and a member of the Supreme Soviet (*Radio Moscow-2*, March 7). Golik is also deputy chairman of the committee investigating the Gdlyan-Ivanov affair, a member of the Committee on Legislation, Legality, and Law and Order, and a member of the USSR Congress of People's Deputies Constitutional Oversight Commission. In connection with the new status of the committee on crime, the Committee on Legislation, Legality, and Law and Order has been renamed the Committee for Legislation.

Platform of "Soyuz" Group of Deputies

The recently formed "Soyuz" group of deputies, which is dedicated to preserving the integrity of the Soviet Union, has distributed the text of its platform to all members of the USSR Congress of People's Deputies (*APN*, March 7). The platform complained that some of the political forces trying to find a way out of the crisis in the Soviet Union were failing to take account of the following realities: the multinational composition of the population of the Union republics, the great differences in the level of economic development between various regions of the country, the underdeveloped state of democratic institutions, the low level of political and legal culture in the population, and the weakness of the law-enforcement system. The remedies the platform suggested were broadly in line with Gorbachev's policies—namely, a modernization of the federation; equality of rights for citizens on the whole territory of the country regardless of nationality; recognition of the right to self-determination including secession, but without absolutizing this principle ("which can lead to the idea of creating 'ethnically pure' states and in the final analysis to racism"); and economic autonomy, first and foremost for enterprises (rather than republics). While recognizing the need to revamp the federation, "Soyuz" warned, however, against hasty decisions and called for a temporary moratorium on reviewing its structure. "Soyuz" denied that it was a conservative group. A poll conducted in Moscow, Leningrad, Gorky, Irkutsk, Alma-Ata, and Tallinn between February 22 and 25 by the USSR Academy of Sciences Institute of Sociology for *The Guardian* and BBC "Newsnight" showed a surprising average of 52.5 percent—ranging from 71.1 percent in Tallinn to 37.5 percent in Alma-Ata—fully approving of the right of republics to secede. A further 13.7 percent partially approved, and only 7.3 percent fully disapproved (*The Guardian*, March 7).

General Moiseev Attacks Draft Resistance in Republics

In an interview with TASS, Chief of the General Staff of the Soviet Armed Forces General Mikhail Moiseev again denounced antimilitary sentiment in the non-Russian republics. With the approach of the annual spring call-up, opposition to the draft is intensifying in the Baltic republics and throughout the Caucasus and Central Asia, and Moiseev accused popular front movements in these areas of undermining Soviet defense efforts. He also repeated his earlier criticism of local law-enforcement agencies for their failure to prosecute draft evaders and called on the USSR Supreme Soviet to enforce the constitutional obligation to perform military service.

USSR Signs Trade Agreement with Panama

TASS reported that the USSR and Panama had signed an agreement on trade and commerce. The agreement focused on the exchange of commercial information and the participation of the two countries in working out joint trade projects and organizing trade fairs. Soviet exports to Panama in recent years have totaled only about 0.01 percent of total Soviet exports.

Supreme Soviet Committee on Conversion Publishes Report

The USSR Supreme Soviet Committee for Defense and State Security examined, among other issues, the current status of the program for converting defense industries into civilian ones. Deputy Chairman of Gosplan Valentin Smyslov gave a report on the outlook for the conversion program for 1990–95; he said there was hope that by 1995 the share of the defense budget in Soviet national income could be halved. He also noted that conversion concerns not only defense industries but also civilian ones that produce equipment for the armed forces. One of the most interesting points Smyslov made was that the retooling of existing defense production capacity and the creation of new civilian production capacity within the defense complex will have cost some 40 billion rubles by 1995 (*Radio Moscow-1*, March 7, 1930). See RL 75/90.

Soviet Coverage of Afghan Coup Attempt

Amid a welter of conflicting and unsubstantiated reports coming from various sources on the military coup attempt launched in Afghanistan on March 6, TASS reports on March 7 claimed that Gulbaddin Hekmatyar, head of the fundamentalist resistance group Hezb-i-Islami, was the organizer of an extensive underground network set up in Kabul to support the coup attempt. Soviet reports presented the revolt as a last-ditch effort to prevent a peaceful reconciliation among Afghanistan's warring parties, a process that, according to TASS, was gaining momentum under Najibullah's leadership. One TASS report also implied US complicity in the coup attempt, by claiming that Hekmatyar's "irreconcilables" and "those who have been supporting him from the wings for these many years" were behind the plot. The United States and Pakistan have long supplied resistance forces, and Hekmatyar was for many years a primary recipient of US aid.

Moscow Newspaper Criticizes Cuba

Moscow News (No. 10) carried an article criticizing Cuba, describing it as a discontented police state. Commentator Vladimir Orlov, who recently visited Havana, wrote: "From what I have seen there has been a switch from social apathy to a passive and still very hidden discontent." He said committees tracked down people listening to foreign radios or holding "politically immature conversations." Orlov said that, by attacking changes in Eastern Europe and the Soviet Union, Cuba aimed "to take on the role of a wise man who alone knows the true path."

Mixed Church Commission Begins Work in Ukraine

A mixed Catholic-Orthodox commission including representatives of the Vatican began work in Ukraine. The commission will try to settle disputes between the Orthodox Church and the Ukrainian Catholics. Many conflicts have arisen in connection with the question of ownership of church buildings that before 1946 were in the possession of the Ukrainian Catholics but after the forcible merger of that Church into the Russian Orthodox Church were taken over by the latter. TASS said the commission had appealed to believers to refrain from violence and had asked non-Church organizations not to interfere in Church affairs.

Soviet Envoy Calls for Unconditional Western Aid to Eastern Europe

The Soviet envoy to the European Community, Ambassador Vladimir Shemyatinkov, said the EC should not make democratization a condition for aid to Eastern Europe. The EC and some other institutions have called for countries receiving economic aid to meet certain levels of democratization. Shemyatinkov said in a speech in Brussels that the EC should either accept the current processes in Eastern Europe or reject them but not attach conditions to aid (*UPI*, March 7).

Estonian Popular Front Pickets KGB

The Estonian Popular Front conducted a picketing campaign of the KGB in Tallinn on March 6 and 7. The picketing was organized to demand a dialogue between the KGB and the front on the achievement of fundamental changes in the KGB's guiding principles and work methods and openness about its activities. Chairman of the Estonian Council of Ministers Indrek Toome, who happened to be at the scene, said negotiations with Moscow aimed at bringing the KGB under republican control were also planned (*Paevaleht*, March 7).

British Group Says Soviet Human-Rights Abuses Continue

A team of British journalists and members of parliament said the USSR had not yet met the conditions set by Britain for organizing a human-rights conference in Moscow in 1991. In London, the group reported on its recent trip to Moscow to monitor treatment of Soviet Jews. The team's report will help decide whether Britain will attend the proposed conference. A member of the group said it was still too early to pass a final decision. The team said the Soviet Union had met only one of Britain's six conditions—the freedom to monitor human rights (*RFE/RL Special*, March 7).

Thursday, March 8

Unrest in Georgia

According to Radio Moscow's World Service there has been "mass unrest" in Soviet Georgia, including the pulling down of statues of Lenin and calls for boycotts of the elections. The radio, broadcasting in English, said statues of Lenin had been pulled down in five cities and in a number of smaller settlements in the republic. It said informal parties and radical political movements were urging citizens to boycott the elections and were calling on candidates to withdraw. (Elections to the Georgian Supreme Soviet were scheduled for March 25 and to the local soviets for June 17.)

The same day, Reuters reported that a crowd had gathered at government headquarters in Tbilisi to protest against the plan to elect an executive president for the USSR. The rally was sponsored by the Georgian Popular Front. The same day, the Georgian Supreme Soviet held an emergency session to discuss the presidency plan. TASS said deputies adopted a resolution on how to maintain Georgian sovereignty under such a system.

Unsanctioned Meeting in Checheno-Ingush ASSR

Radio Moscow-1 (1900) reported that an unsanctioned meeting was going on for the second day in the city of Nazrani in the Checheno-Ingush ASSR. The main demand of the demonstrators, the number of which was estimated by the local MVD as 10,000, was the re-creation of the Ingush Autonomous Oblast with the borders of 1934. In 1934, the Ingush Autonomous Oblast was merged with the Chechen Autonomous Oblast. In 1944, when the Chechens and the Ingush were deported from their territories on Stalin's orders, what had earlier been part of the Ingush territory was transferred to North Ossetia. Last year, the Ingush started to voice claims to this territory. The radio said that despite the fact that passions were running high no violence had taken place.

The same day, *Sovetskaya Rossiya* reported that there had been a number of irregularities in the elections on March 4 in the Checheno-Ingush Autonomous Republic. In one district, for instance, voters who arrived late in the day but before the closing of the polling station were told that there were no ballots left and that they could not vote. In another district, an electoral commission violated constitutional norms by including close relatives of the district's candidate for the elections.On March 13, in response to continuing demonstrations, Mikhail Gorbachev proposed that the USSR Supreme Soviet and the Council of Nationalities set up a commission immediately to study the situation in the Checheno-Ingush ASSR.

Soviet Envoy Discusses Jewish Emigration

A Soviet envoy held talks in Saudi Arabia with the Saudi foreign minister on the issue of Soviet Jews emigrating to Israel. Vladimir Polyakov, head of the Middle East and

North African Countries Administration at the USSR Foreign Ministry, met in Riyadh with Prince Saud Al-Faysal. The Saudi press agency said Polyakov outlined the Soviet stance on the issue, but it did not elaborate. The Soviet Union has said it shares Arab opposition to the settlement of Soviet immigrants in occupied territories. Israel has said it has no policy of settling Soviet Jews in those territories (*Reuters*, *UPI*, *AP*, March 8).

Friday, March 9

USSR Applies for Observer Status at GATT

The Soviet Union formally applied for observer status at the General Agreement on Tariffs and Trade (GATT). The world free trade regulation body said in Geneva that the Soviet letter of application had been presented by Soviet Ambassador Evgenii Makeev with a request that the GATT council discuss the issue at its next monthly meeting on April 3. GATT spokesman David Woods said he expected no early decision on the matter, because members would probably need to consult further (*Reuters*, *UPI*, March 9). The agencies quoted GATT sources as saying that members were unlikely to oppose observer status but that there were differences over the timing. See RL 134/90.

Saturday, March 10

Prodemocracy Rally in Kiev

About 50,000 people gathered in Kiev for a prodemocracy election rally. In a telefax to Reuters, the Ukrainian reform movement "Rukh" said the rally also opposed the creation of a Soviet presidency with expanded powers. Speakers at the rally said that recent elections to the Ukrainian Supreme Soviet had been rigged but that non-Party candidates had still managed to win thirty-three contests and advance to runoffs in 120 others (*AP*, *Reuters*, March 10).

Hungary and USSR Sign Troop Withdrawal Agreement

Foreign Ministers Gyula Horn of Hungary and Eduard Shevardnadze of the USSR signed an agreement in Moscow calling for all 50,000 Soviet troops stationed in Hungary to be withdrawn by June 30, 1991. Horn called for the replacement of the Soviet-Hungarian Treaty of Friendship and Cooperation. Horn said that Hungary would remain in the Warsaw Pact but that the pact must be changed into a consultative body (*Reuters*, March 10). During their talks, Horn and Shevardnadze also discussed the situation along their common border. Horn said a very nearly untenable situation had evolved there. He said the black market was flourishing and public safety was endangered.On March 12, Radio Budapest reported the departure of the first train with 315 Soviet troops and forty armored personnel carriers.

First Jewish Newspaper Appears in Moldavia

TASS said the first Jewish newspaper to appear in Moldavia was published there today. TASS said *Unzer Kol* had a format of six pages in Russian and two in Yiddish. It appears in an edition of 7,000 copies. TASS said the paper would deal with the social and cultural life of Jews in Moldavia and would fight anti-Semitism.

Sunday, March 11

Lithuania Declares Itself Independent

The Lithuanian Supreme Soviet voted to reaffirm Lithuania's 1918 declaration of independence from the Soviet Union. The vote was 124 in favor and none against. There were six abstentions. After the vote was announced, deputies in the chamber joined hands and chanted "Lithuania." Outside, a crowd cheered wildly. Earlier the Lithuanian parliament had voted unanimously to change the name of the Baltic republic to "Republic of Lithuania," dropping the words "Soviet" and "Socialist" from its title. The parliament also changed the English translation of its name from Supreme Soviet to Supreme Council and elected Vytautas Landsbergis, the leader of "Sajudis," as its chairman. The other candidate for the post was Independent Lithuanian Communist Party First Secretary Algirdas Brazauskas (*Reuters*, *AFP*, *DPA*, *UPI*, *AP*, March 11).

On March 12, Landsbergis said Lithuanians now had the task of making a reality of the expectations raised by the declaration of independence. He was quoted as saying he was "not so naive" as to believe that the declaration had severed all ties with Moscow. Instead, he said, the act was intended to establish Lithuania's "legal position and popular will" together with its ability to write its own laws and conduct foreign policy. He said nearly all questions of economic relations with the Soviet central authorities would have to be resolved in future negotiations with Moscow. Lithuanians say any Soviet claims against the republic for compensation for factories and other infrastructure built during Soviet rule will be countered by a much higher Lithuanian claim for Soviet reparations (Western agencies, March 12). In a move reinforcing Lithuania's declaration of independence, the Lithuanian Supreme Council voted on March 13 to exempt Lithuanians from conscription into the Soviet Armed Forces. A Lithuanian deputy attending the opening of a new session of the USSR Congress of People's Deputies said he was only there as an observer. Vajdotas Antanajtis told the Congress that Soviet law was no longer valid in Lithuania. He called on the Soviet Union to recognize Lithuania's action and said his republic sought good relations with the Soviet Union (Western agencies, *TASS*, *Radio Moscow*, March 13).

Opening the session of the USSR Congress of People's Deputies on March 12, Mikhail Gorbachev described the Lithuanian action as "rather alarming." Politburo member Egor Ligachev said Moscow would not use force against Lithuania, but he urged the republic to "think long and hard" before finally seceding. Soviet Foreign Ministry spokesman Gennadii Gerasimov called the Lithuanian move unrealistic because—as he put it—the republic's economy "is incapable of standing on its own feet." He said the USSR Congress of People's Deputies had organized a commission to consider the consequences of the Lithuanian decision. On March 13, Gorbachev said there would be no negotiations with Lithuania, Latvia, or Estonia, because the Soviet Union negotiated only with foreign countries. He told the Congress that he considered Lithuania's reaffirmation of its independence from the USSR illegal and that he did not recognize it (*Reuters*, *UPI*, March 13). The same evening, Landsbergis made a television appeal to the Soviet people to show understanding and support for Lithuania's drive for independence (*AFP*, March 13).

On March 11, the United States called upon the Soviet Union to accept Lithuania's declaration of independence and to negotiate with its leaders to resolve the dispute over secession without violence. White House spokesman Marlin Fitzwater said, "The United States will urge the Soviet government to respect the will of the citizens of Lithuania as expressed through their freely elected representatives and expects the government of Lithuania to consider the rights of its minority population." Fitzwater did not say the United States accepted the declaration of independence but noted that Washington "has never recognized the forcible incorporation of the independent states of Estonia, Latvia, or Lithuania into the USSR." On March 13, US President George Bush said Lithuania must meet certain conditions to receive full United States diplomatic recognition, including demonstrated control over its territory (*Reuters*, *AP*, *UPI*,

March 11 and 13). Many other countries welcomed the Lithuanian declaration, including Canada, Australia, and Britain.

On March 15, the USSR Congress of People's Deputies declared Lithuania's decision to restore its independence invalid. The vote on the declaration was 1,463 in favor and 94 against, with 128 abstentions. The declaration said the sovereignty of the USSR and the Soviet Constitution were still in force in the Lithuanian Soviet Socialist Republic. Gorbachev, however, told the Congress that Moscow would hold "a mutually respectful dialogue" with Lithuania but said this dialogue should not be viewed as negotiations on the independence issue. He suggested that Lithuania could possibly secede from the Union after a lengthy process if its population voted to do so in a referendum. In an interview published in the Polish "Solidarity" daily *Gazeta Wyborcza*, Landsbergis said Lithuania was willing to face an economic blockade to achieve independence. He said Lithuania could now provide 30 percent of its energy needs (*TASS*, Western agencies, March 15).

On March 16, Gorbachev sent Landsbergis a telegram giving him three days to reply to the Congress of People's Deputies' resolution that declared Lithuania's resolution on independence illegal. Landsbergis said he would reply calmly to the telegram by March 19. He told RFE/RL he was astonished that Gorbachev's demand had come so quickly. He said he regarded the demand as the beginning of negotiations between Lithuania and Moscow.

On March 17, the Lithuanian parliament elected a new government. Kazimiera Prunskiene, a "Sajudis" deputy, was elected prime minister, and First Secretary of the Independent Lithuanian Communist Party Algirdas Brazauskas became deputy prime minister. Prunskiene said her most immediate goals were realizing independence and converting Lithuania to a market economy. Speaking at the parliamentary session, Brazauskas said he and Gorbachev had discussed Finnish-Soviet relations as a possible model for future Lithuanian relations with the Soviet Union (*Radio Vilnius*, March 17). AP, DPA, and AFP reported that independence supporters had rallied in Vilnius. Addressing the parliament, Landsbergis said holding a referendum on independence now would be a political mistake because it would be tantamount to saying that "the will of the people has not yet been expressed" (*Radio Vilnius*, March 17). The Lithuanian parliament also appealed to "democratic governments of the world" to recognize Lithuania's reaffirmation of independence and appointed a delegation for negotiations with Moscow. Radio Vilnius reported that Soviet military helicopters had dropped thousands of leaflets on the city urging people to attend an anti-independence rally on March 18.

On March 18, a Lithuanian delegation left Vilnius for Moscow to deliver a message to Gorbachev on Lithuania's reaffirmation of independence. The message said that Soviet interests would be taken into account in an independent Lithuania. Commenting on the message, Landsbergis said that these interests must be well defined and that this could only be done through negotiations. The same day, Soviet military forces began maneuvers in Lithuania. Western correspondents in Moscow quoted the Lithuanian authorities as saying that the maneuvers were routine. (On March 19, however, Landsbergis said that the military exercises were designed to increase tension in the republic [*Radio Vilnius*, March 19].) On March 20, Prunskiene sent a telegram to Moscow complaining about the military exercises and saying that the Lithuanian leadership had not been informed about the maneuvers in advance (*Reuters*, March 21). On March 18, an estimated 10,000 people joined a rally in Vilnius to express their opposition to Lithuanian independence (*AP*, *Radio Moscow*, March 18).

On March 19, the commander of the Soviet navy, Admiral Vladimir Chernavin, said an independent Lithuania would undermine Soviet strategic interests. Novosti quoted Chernavin as saying an independent Lithuanian army would be too weak to provide "a serious and reliable defense" against NATO forces. He also said an independent Lithuania would cut off the Soviet Baltic Fleet from its main base in Kaliningrad (*RFE/RL Special*, March 19). TASS reported that residents of Lithuania who opposed the republic's moves towards independence had appealed to Gorbachev to be included in talks about Lithuania's future. Meanwhile, the Soviet government issued a statement, signed by Nikolai Ryzhkov, informing Lithuania that severing economic and financial links with the USSR was illegal. The statement said that Soviet enterprises in Lithuania would continue to be administered directly by Moscow and that Moscow would significantly step up its vigilance over "vital objects," including nuclear plants. It also said that the police, the KGB, and customs officers had been charged with maintaining existing customs laws and that Moscow ministers had been told to administer directly air, rail, and sea transport links with Lithuania. On the evening of March 19, members of the Lithuanian delegation met with Gorbachev. Western agencies quoted them as saying both good and bad things were said.

Speaking before the Lithuanian parliament on March 20, Landsbergis said Lithuania might have to block the transmission of some Soviet television programs because some Soviet television coverage of the situation in Lithuania was provocative. Landsbergis was explaining why Lithuania's television and radio committee had interrupted transmission to the republic of a broadcast by Leningrad television on March 19 (*Radio Vilnius*, March 20). On March 20, the controversial broadcast was repeated. The same day, the Lithuanian parliament passed a resolution giving the Lithuanian public prosecutor the right to oversee laws on the republic's transport (*TASS*, March 20).

On March 21, several hundred USSR Supreme Soviet deputies urged Gorbachev to use his new powers as executive president to put Lithuania under his direct presidential control. The same day, Gorbachev ordered measures "to protect the rights of Soviet citizens and Soviet sovereignty in Lithuania." In a decree taking effect immediately, Gorbachev ordered the USSR Ministry of Internal Affairs to enforce the rights and legal interests of Soviet citizens in Lithuania. He also ordered Lithuanians to temporarily surrender all arms to the Soviet authorities and directed Soviet security forces to increase border checks and to introduce tougher visa restrictions (*TASS*, March 21). The decree accused the Lithuanian Supreme Council of continuing to "pass illegal acts." Landsbergis rejected the decree (*AP*, *Reuters*, *UPI*, March 21). He also called for more support from Western nations for Lithuania. Meanwhile, the Council of the Union of the USSR Supreme Soviet approved a law regulating the procedure for republics to secede from the USSR. But a Lithuanian deputy at the Moscow session said the law would not apply to Lithuania, because "we have already left."

On March 21, the Lithuanian government appealed to the International Red Cross to place under its protection Lithuanian soldiers who had left Soviet army units. Kazimieras Motieka, deputy chairman of the Lithuanian Supreme Council, told RFE/RL that more than 300 soldiers had already left their units. Motieka said soldiers who had deserted would be registered at the Supreme Council Presidium and housed together to ensure their safety (RFE Lithuanian service, March 22).

On March 22, Gorbachev sent a telegram to Landsbergis demanding an immediate stop to the setting up of organizations for the republic's defense. Gorbachev's telegram said reports coming from Lithuania showed that volunteers were being recruited in the republic to replace frontier troops and elements of internal security bodies.

The same day, it became known that in Kaunas Soviet army troops had forcibly seized practice weapons from the Voluntary Society for Cooperation with the Army, Navy, and Air Force (RFE Lithuanian service, March 22). The same day, the Lithuanian Supreme Council set up ministries of defense, energy, and the economy (*TASS*, March 22).

On March 22, Western countries expressed concern over Moscow's attitude towards the Lithuanian events (*Reuters*, March 22). US President George Bush urged Gorbachev to exercise restraint vis-à-vis Lithuania and to remember his promise not to use force (*RFE/RL Special*, March 22). Several East European countries expressed support for Lithuania. The Polish Sejm adopted a resolution welcoming Lithuania into the family of free nations. Radio Warsaw quoted the resolution as saying the Lithuanian parliament's affirmation of independence was a natural consequence of the recognition that the Molotov-Ribbentrop Pact was invalid. Czechoslovak President Vaclav Havel said he was convinced that Lithuania's dispute with Moscow over independence could be resolved "without bloodshed" (*Reuters*, March 22). The same day, Soviet Foreign Ministry spokesman Gennadii Gerasimov repeated that military force would not be used against Lithuania (*Reuters*, *AP*, March 22). The Lithuanian parliament announced that it had assumed control of the republic's radio and television services (*TASS*, March 22).

On March 22, the US Senate passed a resolution urging President Bush to "consider" recognizing an independent Lithuania (*UPI*, March 23). On March 23, Bush said any attempt by the USSR to "coerce or intimidate or forcibly intervene against the Lithuanian people is bound to backfire" (*RFE/RL Special*, March 23).

Speaking to the Lithuanian parliament on March 22, Landsbergis called for calm and the maintenance of public order in the republic's drive for independence. He said Moscow was using "psychological warfare" against Lithuania by deploying additional Soviet troops in the republic (*Radio Vilnius*, March 22; RFE Lithuanian service, March 23).

On March 23, the USSR ministries of foreign and internal affairs said they had begun to implement measures to "protect the sovereignty of the Soviet Union in Lithuania." TASS quoted a Foreign Ministry spokesman as saying Soviet diplomatic missions abroad had been told to issue visas to foreigners wishing to visit Lithuania on a case-by-case basis. He said this was to prevent access by people "inclined to engage in illegal activity." In addition, the Foreign Ministry ordered some Western diplomats in Lithuania to return to Moscow (*AP*, *Reuters*, March 23). The United States made a formal protest to the USSR about the expulsion from Lithuania of US diplomats (*Reuters*, March 23).

Meanwhile, the Lithuanian parliament continued to discuss the new government. TASS said the Supreme Council appointed ministers of finance, forest economy, health, internal affairs, justice, industry, and material resources. Of the seven newly named ministers, four had been members of the previous government.

On the morning of March 24, a column of about 100 Soviet military vehicles, including armor, entered Vilnius (*Reuters*, *AFP*, March 24). Landsbergis protested to Gorbachev over the move and also called on the United States to take a stronger stand over Lithuania (*AFP*, March 24). Addressing parliament, Landsbergis spoke of the psychological and political pressure being put on Lithuania, as a result of new security measures imposed by Moscow (*Reuters*, March 25). The Soviet Foreign Ministry informed Western reporters that they must cancel planned trips to Lithuania in view of the situation there (*AFP*, March 24).

Meanwhile, elections for local soviets took place in Lithuania (*TASS*, March 24). The candidates running for election represented the two Communist Parties, the Democratic, Social Democratic, Christian Democratic, and Green parties, as well as a number of public movements. Mikolas Burokjavicis, a representative of the pro-Moscow Lithuanian Communist Party, accused the republic's parliament and government of displaying an unserious attitude towards Gorbachev. In an interview with *Sovetskaya Rossiya*, Burokjavicis suggested that the Lithuanian parliament and government were deliberately moving towards confrontation and aggravation of the political situation (*AP*, March 24).

On March 25, several thousand people attended a rally in the Georgian capital, Tbilisi, to support Lithuania (*Radio Vilnius*, *Reuters*, March 25). The Ukrainian popular movement, "Rukh," also expressed solidarity with Lithuania and scheduled a pro-Lithuanian demonstration for the following weekend, despite the official ban (RL Ukrainian service, March 25 and 29). Pope John Paul II appealed for a peaceful solution to the dispute between the Soviet Union and Lithuania (*Reuters*, March 25). On March 25, popular front leaders from all the Baltic republics issued a statement calling on Moscow to open constructive negotiations with Lithuania (Western agencies, March 25).

On March 25, Lithuania's Bureau of Information said Lithuanian pro-Moscow Communists accompanied by Soviet troops had occupied two buildings belonging to the Independent Lithuanian Communist Party. The bureau also said the Vilnius city Communist Party headquarters and two other district Party headquarters had been taken over in the last two days (*AFP, UPI*, March 25). Radio Vilnius reported that the Presidium of the Supreme Council had issued a resolution protesting the takeover. Speaking on Radio Vilnius, Landsbergis appealed to Lithuanian citizens to remain calm in the face of the developments in the republic and of what he said was the possibility that the Lithuanian leadership could be removed.

On March 26, a member of the Lithuanian parliament, Algimantas Cekuolis, rejected charges by a senior Soviet military officer that "Sajudis" was trying to create an army in the Baltic republic. Cekuolis told *The Washington Post* that claims to this effect by Commander of Soviet Ground Forces General Valentin Varennikov were "outrageous lies." The same day, Lithuanian officials met Soviet army representatives in Vilnius to discuss the takeover of the Communist Party buildings (*AP, AFP*, March 26). Reuters said that military chiefs had refused to withdraw paratroopers from the key Lithuanian centers. Meanwhile, military helicopters flew over Vilnius again, dropping leaflets urging people to attend an anti-independence rally on March 27 (Western agencies, March 26 and 27).

Other countries commented on the situation in Lithuania. The White House issued a statement saying that US-Soviet relations could be damaged by further action by the Soviet Union in Lithuania (*Reuters*, March 26). The Polish government sent a delegation of "Solidarity" parliamentarians to Vilnius for talks with Lithuanian leaders (*AP*, March 26). (On March 27, the "Solidarity" group and the Lithuanians signed a communiqué warning that any attempt by Moscow to use force to oppose independence would meet with worldwide condemnation [*RFE/RL Special*, March 28].) Czechoslovakia said it was most interested in a peaceful solution of the present disagreements between Lithuania and the Soviet Union (*Czechoslovak Television*, March 26). (On March 29, President Vaclav Havel sent telegrams to Gorbachev and Landsbergis offering to mediate in their dispute [*Reuters*, March 29].) Gorbachev reiterated his pledge not to use force to solve the Lithuanian independence dispute. He implied, however, that force could be used "if civilian lives were in danger." Gorbachev's comment was made in a meeting with US Senator Edward Kennedy in the Kremlin (*TASS*, March 26). Landsbergis commented on Gorbachev's statement, saying that "in other words, force will be used" because Moscow could easily create the justification for it (Western agencies, March 27).

On March 27, it was reported that during the previous night Soviet troops had entered hospitals to seize Lithuanians who had taken refuge there rather than rejoin their Soviet army units. They were being supervised by the Lithuanian Red Cross. The Soviet army considers the men deserters and has demanded that they return to their units. Lithuania said the men could not be forced to serve in what it calls "an occupation army" (*AP*, March 27). Landsbergis condemned the Soviet troop actions as "open acts of aggression." Brazauskas also condemned the action. The Lithuanian Supreme Council and the government issued a formal protest against it (RFE Lithuanian service, March 27). Soviet Defense Minister Dmitrii Yazov denied that Soviet troops had carried out armed action in Lithuania. On March 27, a planned pro-Soviet rally took place in Vilnius, with a crowd estimated at between 2,000 and 10,000 attending. The Soviet Union ordered all foreign citizens to leave Lithuania (*UPI*, *Reuters*, March 27).

Western leaders continued to express their reaction to the events in Lithuania. British Prime Minister Margaret Thatcher urged Moscow and Lithuania's leaders to show restraint and to settle differences through dialogue. Thatcher reiterated her appeal for restraint in a telephone conversation with Gorbachev on March 28 (*TASS*, March 28). Commenting on the Western reaction, Landsbergis said he felt Lithuania was being abandoned by the West (*Reuters*, March 28). Andrei Sakharov's widow, Elena Bonner, sent a telegram to President Bush urging him to extend immediate diplomatic recognition to Lithuania (*RFE/RL Special*, March 28). On March 28, the Lithuanian authorities said they had been assured that the young Lithuanians seized as deserters would not be punished (*Reuters*, March 28). Landsbergis urged the Lithuanian parliament to pass an alternative service law to head off Soviet military conscription of Lithuanians (*Radio Vilnius*, March 28). A meeting of the Lithuanian Supreme Council was attended by several officials from Kaliningrad Oblast and several newly elected deputies from Leningrad. Seventy-five Moscow City Soviet members sent a telegram to Landsbergis expressing their support for Lithuanian independence.

On March 29, the USSR for the first time referred to international law as a basis for USSR-Lithuanian relations. (Until now Soviet officials have only referred to Lithuanian commitments under the USSR Constitution.) In an interview with *Izvestia*, the chief of the Soviet Foreign Ministry's International Humanitarian Cooperation and

Human-Rights Administration, Yurii Reshetov, referred to the Vienna convention of 1978. He said it required Lithuania to follow USSR laws on secession "even if it dislikes them." The same day, Landsbergis sent a message to the US Congress urging it to pass a resolution supporting US diplomatic recognition of Lithuania (RFE Lithuanian service, March 29). TASS reported that the USSR Defense Ministry had announced an amnesty for Lithuanian soldiers who turned themselves in after having left their units without permission. In the meantime, the leadership of the US Helsinki Commission criticized the USSR for what it called violence against Lithuanians who refused to serve in the Soviet Armed Forces (*RFE/RL Special*, March 29). The same day, TASS quoted the second secretary of the pro-Moscow Lithuanian Communist Party, Vladislav Shved, as suggesting that Moscow make use of Gorbachev's new powers as president to impose direct rule in Lithuania.

The same day, "Solidarity" Chairman Lech Walesa said in Gdansk that all governments should recognize Lithuania as an independent country. On the morning of March 30, French Foreign Minister Roland Dumas said he would urge the USSR to open talks with Lithuania when he meets his Soviet counterpart, Eduard Shevardnadze. Dumas gave an interview to a French radio station shortly before leaving Paris on a one-day visit to Moscow (*Reuters*, March 30). On March 30, President Bush made a direct appeal to Gorbachev for a peaceful solution to the crisis in a letter to the Soviet leader (*AP*, March 30). Several US senators have sent telegrams to Gorbachev protesting against the USSR's actions in Lithuania (*RFE/RL Special*, March 31).

Meanwhile, in an interview with the French newspaper *Libération*, Deputy Chairman of the Lithuanian Supreme Council Kazimieras Motieka said silence was the only response Lithuania had received to its repeated offers to negotiate with Moscow. In another French newspaper, *Le Figaro*, Soviet Defense Minister Dmitrii Yazov said that a formula for Lithuania's secession from the USSR must be worked out. He asserted that only 26 percent of the population of Lithuania supported the proindependence movement "Sajudis" and added that most of the people of Lithuania did not want to leave the USSR. Yazov did not reveal the basis for his assertions.

On the evening of March 30, Soviet troops occupied the premises of the Lithuanian Prosecutor's Office. The troops moved in after Moscow had ordered the sacking of the prosecutor, Arturas Palauskas, and had appointed Antanas Petrauskas as his replacement. Radio Vilnius said, however, that Palauskas did not intend to give up his duties. He was appointed last week by Lithuania's new government (*Reuters*, *AP*, March 30). The Belorussian Supreme Soviet said on March 30 that Belorussia would demand the return of territory given to Lithuania fifty years ago if Lithuania left the Soviet Union. The Presidium of the Belorussian parliament said six districts ceded to Lithuania under various agreements in 1939 and 1949 were ancient Belorussian lands (*AP*, *AFP*, March 30).

Meanwhile, there were demonstrations in Moscow and Ukraine in support of Lithuanian independence. Several hundred people gathered in Gorky Park in Moscow, a move that TASS overtly condemned. A press spokesman for the Ukrainian Popular Front, "Rukh," said at least 30,000 people had gathered in Kiev and Ivano-Frankovsk. Rallies were also held in Lvov, Ternopol, and other Ukrainian cities (RL Ukrainian service, March 31).

On March 31, Gorbachev warned Lithuanian leaders that failure to heed his call to retract their moves towards independence could have grave consequences (*TASS*, March 31). Gorbachev said that negotiations with Lithuania could be held, but only if the Lithuanian parliament reversed its proindependence policies (*UPI*, *AFP*, March 31). The Soviet military prosecutor, Aleksandr Katusev, said the Defense Ministry's announcement of an amnesty for Lithuanian soldiers who returned to their units had been incorrectly reported by the Soviet media. He said only the Prosecutor's Office and the courts could decide to drop charges against offenders. He said that criminal proceedings had begun in every case of desertion, which now numbered over 1,000 (*Central Television*, March 31). On April 3, the Lithuanian government halted all assistance to Soviet military conscription boards (*Radio Vilnius*, April 3).

Congress Convenes in Estonia

In Tallinn, 499 delegates elected in the first non-Soviet democratic elections in Estonia since 1940 convened for a two-day session of the Congress of Estonia—in effect an alternative parliament—to take the first steps towards re-establishing Estonian independence. The Congress of Estonia counts among its members virtually all major political figures in Estonia with the exception of the senior leadership of the Communist Party. The congress represents the most serious challenge yet to Soviet authority in Estonia. During the two-day session, the congress passed a number of resolutions. The most notable were demands for the USSR Congress of People's Deputies to end the illegal annexation of Estonia and calls for the immediate withdrawal of occupying Soviet forces under international supervision and the restoration of prewar borders. The congress also appealed to the UN General Assembly, the Conference on Security and Cooperation in Europe, and the European Parliament to consider Estonia's drive for independence (*RFE/RL Special*, March 12 and 13). See RL 141 and 142/90.

Central Committee Plenum

A plenum of the CPSU Central Committee, which reconvened after adjourning in February, discussed the Party's future and the prospect of giving up its constitutionally guaranteed leading role. TASS said the plenum decided to submit a draft law to the Congress of People's Deputies that would exclude the Party's leading role from the constitution. Party General Secretary Mikhail Gorbachev told the plenum the Party's vanguard role should be turned from a formal declaration into a political reality. He rejected, however, proposals to change the Party's name. He said dropping the word "Communist" would be a serious blow to the Party's ideological foundation. He also rejected proposals to allow the republican Party organizations to secede from the all-Union Party (*TASS*, in English, *Radio Moscow*, March 11).

The plenum ended on March 16. It approved new draft statutes that will democratize the Party, including one to replace the strictly controlled promotion system with competitive elections at all levels. In an interview published by the Novosti press agency, Gorbachev's aide Georgii Shakhnazarov said the CPSU could split in two and would in future probably have to compete with hundreds of other political parties. The leader of the Party's Democratic Platform reformists told the plenum that the Party could split into several groups unless it abandoned the principle of control from the center. Politburo member Vadim Medvedev said the Party would try to encompass different viewpoints but could not maintain unity at all costs (*APN*, in English, Western agencies, March 16). For the text of speeches made at the plenum, see *Pravda*, March 17.

***Pravda* Marks Five Years of Gorbachev**

Gorbachev came to power as CPSU General Secretary five years ago today. In an editorial marking the anniversary, *Pravda* said the past five years had changed the Soviet Union beyond recognition. It said it would have been hard to predict five years ago "the ups and downs" that were to come. It said people had come to feel free and had also suffered the bitterness of interethnic strife, economic adversity, and instability. *Pravda* said, however, that *perestroika* remained the correct path and that critics who complained that there was no step-by-step plan for reform were naive.

Moscow News Publishes Report on Poverty in USSR

Moscow News (No. 10) featured a hard-hitting article giving statistics on the numbers of people living below the poverty line across the USSR and describing a number of individual fates. The report noted that 41 million people—14.5 percent of the Soviet population—lived below the official poverty line of 78 rubles per month in 1988. Marel Amanova, who chairs the USSR Supreme Soviet Subcommittee on Quality of Life, disputed this figure, arguing that the official poverty level defined by Gosplan did not reflect today's realities—inflation and a lack of low-cost goods. The subcommittee has set the poverty line at 120 rubles. Amanova said that officials estimate that 95 million Soviet citizens are in need of some form of governmental support today. Accompanying the article was a table giving the percentage of the population of each Union republic that had incomes of below 75 rubles per month in 1988. As might be expected, the percentage was highest in Central Asia and lowest in the Baltic.

Soviet Union and Chile Reestablish Diplomatic Ties

The Soviet Union and Chile have officially restored diplomatic ties. TASS said the two countries agreed to restore full relations at embassy level as of today, the day Chile's new president takes office. The USSR withdrew its ambassador from Chile in 1973 during the coup in which Marxist President Salvador Allende died.

Vatican Delegation Celebrates Liturgy with Ukrainian Bishops

A Vatican delegation celebrated Liturgy with Ukrainian Catholic Bishops in the Church of the Transfiguration in Lvov. The Ukrainian Catholic Synod press service issued a statement in Rome, saying the service was the first of its kind in forty-four years. It said the ceremony was attended by about 30,000 people, inside the church and outside. A delegation of the Moscow Patriarchate was also present (RL Ukrainian service, March 12).

Monday, March 12

Dozens Hurt at Moscow Demonstration Marking February Revolution

Thirty-one people were detained and dozens injured when police broke up a demonstration in Moscow commemorating the February Revolution of 1917. The demonstration was organized by the Democratic Union, which regards itself as the only genuinely non-Communist opposition party. According to Aleksandr Molchanov, a spokesman for the group, demonstrators unfurled banners saying: "Down with the presidency," "Down with the KGB," and "Down with Gorbachev." They were swiftly dispersed by police and chased into sidestreets, where, according to one witness, they were beaten up (*The Times*, *TASS*, March 13).

USSR Complains about US Handling of KGB Defector

The USSR lodged a protest with the US over the handling of Viktor Sheimov, a KGB defector who recently surfaced after nearly a decade of hiding in the United States. Sergei Chetverikov, minister-counselor at the Soviet embassy in Washington, accused US intelligence agencies of violating international law in smuggling Sheimov and his family out of the Soviet Union in 1980. Chetverikov said he was particularly concerned about allegations Sheimov made at a press conference on March 2. On that occasion, Sheimov said that in the late 1970s the USSR had had two sources in the State Department who were able to deliver secret information on US policy and negotiating positions. Sheimov also said he was present in the Warsaw KGB station in 1979 when a cable arrived from Moscow ordering what he believed to be the first stages of a plot to kill Pope John Paul II. He also said the KGB probably had been involved in the death of Pakistani President Zia Ul-Haq in 1988. Chetverikov denied the claims about the pope and Zia (*AP*, *Reuters*, *UPI*, *AFP*, March 13). The US State Department rejected the protest, on March 13, saying that Sheimov was a US citizen and that he had spoken to the press on his own initiative (*RFE/RL Special*, March 13).

International Economic Conference Opens in Moscow

Businessmen from forty countries in Europe, Asia, and the Americas arrived in Moscow to attend a three-day economic conference. TASS said the meeting was sponsored by the Soviet Chamber of Commerce and Industry, the West German Deutsche Bank, and S.R.I. TASS quoted Chairman of the USSR Chamber of Commerce Vladislav Malkevich as saying the major aim of the conference was to learn about Western business views on economic cooperation and to discuss Soviet economic reforms.

Addressing the conference on March 14, Chairman of the USSR State Committee on Prices Vyacheslav Senchagov said the Soviet economy could benefit from wide-ranging price reforms. Senchagov said that price reforms would involve changes in the structure and composition of prices, which would "contain the cost of resources, entail more equal profit levels on key products, and [establish] a different balance between state-fixed and market prices." He went on to say that prices of fuel and energy, as well as of metals, raw materials, and large machinery would remain controlled, while prices on other goods "will shed their subsidies." What Senchagov has in mind is a revision of relative prices and not a real reform of the price mechanism. But even this should not be counted on in the near future; Senchagov went on to say that, without public support for such measures, the prospects for price reform are hopeless (*TASS*, March 14).

El'tsin Book Gives Gorbachev Critical Support

Reuters reported the publication in the West of Boris El'tsin's book, *Against the Grain*, in which he charts his often tormented relationship with Gorbachev, a man he calls "my perpetual opponent, the lover of half-measures and half-steps." But, despite flaying Gorbachev for alleged timidity in reforming the Soviet Union and rooting out corruption, El'tsin says he will continue to support him because "he is the only man who can stop the ultimate collapse of the Party." El'tsin's book is the first to give a penetrating glance into the innermost corridors of Kremlin power by someone who is still on the Soviet political scene (*Reuters*, March 12).

Tuesday, March 13

Congress Abolishes Party's Leading Role, Creates Strong Presidency

The USSR Congress of People's Deputies overwhelmingly approved the creation of a strong new presidency and formally abolished the leading role of the CPSU. The vote for the executive presidency came despite criticism from many deputies. They argued, among other things, that it would give the new president too much power. The ballot on the issue was 1,817 in favor of the new presidency and 133 against, with 61 abstentions. Among those who opposed the move was reformist deputy Yurii Afanas'ev, who spoke for the Interregional Group of Deputies. He also criticized Lenin—saying he had laid the foundations for a state policy of violence and terror—and urged the USSR to abandon communism (*Pravda*, March 14).

Yakovlev Says Power Sometimes a Burden to Gorbachev

In an interview with *Komsomol'skaya pravda*, Politburo member Aleksandr Yakovlev said that Gorbachev was not hungry for power and that, in fact, power was sometimes a burden to him. Yakovlev said that Gorbachev was sometimes hesitant because he did not like to decide individuals' fates or the fates of peoples. He also said that Gorbachev had for a long time argued against increased powers for an executive president while he, Yakovlev, had argued for them. He said Gorbachev had gradually come to the conclusion that a consolidating force was needed in the Soviet Union.

Large Majority of Soviet Citizens Want Direct Presidential Elections

According to a public opinion poll taken in various Soviet cities by the sociological service "Mnenie," over 60 percent of Soviet citizens approve of the new presidential system. Only about 20 percent of the respondents are against it. Of those who approve of the new system, 84 percent want direct election of the president. Only 8 percent of the respondents favor election of the president by the Congress of People's Deputies, while 3 percent say the president should be elected by the USSR Supreme Soviet. Seventy-two percent of the respondents favor Gorbachev for the first president of the USSR, 11 percent prefer Boris El'tsin, 8 percent name progressive Leningrad deputy Anatolii Sobchak, and 3 percent want Prime Minister Nikolai Ryzhkov (*Central Television*, "Vremya," March 13).

347 Law-Enforcement Officers Reported Killed in 1989

At a press conference, the USSR Ministry of Internal Affairs (MVD) revealed that 347 law-enforcement officers had been killed in the Soviet Union last year (*TASS*, March 13). The MVD said there had been frequent attacks on law-enforcement officers recently, some involving the use of firearms. For an interesting comparison, in 1987, 147 police officers in the US were killed in the line of duty, although the overall number of crimes reported in the United States is about five times that in the USSR. To improve the protection of law-enforcement officers, the Supreme Soviet is considering a bill that would stiffen criminal liability for attacking an officer, while increasing the rights of officers to defend themselves.

Tanai Says USSR Helped Najibullah during Coup Attempt

Defeated Afghan coup leader and former Afghan Minister of Defense Shahnawaz Tanai accused the Soviet Union of aiding Afghan President Najibullah during last week's coup attempt. Tanai's charges were broadcast by the Afghan News Agency (ANA), which is controlled by the fundamentalist resistance leader Gulbaddin Hekmatyar. Tanai claimed that Najibullah had taken refuge in the

Soviet embassy during the attempted coup and that Soviet planes had bombed Tanai's headquarters in Kabul, as well as the Bagram Air Base, which was controlled by Tanai's forces (*Reuters*, *AFP*, March 13).

South Korean Firm to Take Part in Soviet Chemical Project

South Korea's Hyundai company said it had agreed in principle to participate in the construction of a big Soviet petrochemical complex in Tobolsk in Western Siberia. Hyundai officials also said a US firm—Combustion Engineering—would be another participant in the project, estimated to cost 4–5 billion dollars. Work is expected to begin next year (*AP*, *AFP*, March 13).

***Izvestia* Reports Clashes in Kazakhstan**

Izvestia reported clashes in Alma-Ata on March 11 in which KGB border guard cadets, most of them Russians, brawled with Kazakh students from the Alma-Ata veterinary institute. The newspaper said up to 400 people were involved. *Izvestia* quoted a Kazakh deputy minister of internal affairs as saying that the situation was under control but that "passions" had not died down completely. The daily also reported clashes between Kazakh and Azerbaijani youths at a sovkhoz in Chimkent Raion on March 8 and a brawl between Kazakh youths and Caucasians in the city of Atbasar the following day.

On March 14, *Izvestia* reported that some of the border guard cadets faced criminal proceedings for their part in the clash. *Izvestia* also said that the official assessment of the clash was that it had not been an ethnic matter. It quoted the Alma-Ata military prosecutor as saying the cadets faced charges of violating public order and military discipline.

Mercury Contaminates Water Supply in Siberian City

Traces of mercury have been found in the water supply of the Soviet city of Barnaul on the Ob River south of Novosibirsk. *Pravda* said the metal had been discovered in the water in five apartments so far. It did not say whether anyone had been harmed. *Pravda* said investigators had been unable so far to trace the source of the poison. It said the police and the KGB were working on the case and had not ruled out the theory that someone had added mercury to the water supply on purpose.

Polish Military Wants Immediate Talks on Soviet Pullout

Poland's National Defense Committee called for immediate talks with the USSR on the withdrawal of Soviet troops from Poland. After meeting in Warsaw, the committee said the Soviet pullout should be made "in accordance with the development of the international situation." There are about 40,000 Soviet troops in Poland. About 5,000 are to leave by the end of this year, in accordance with cuts already announced by Gorbachev (*AFP*, RFE Polish service, March 13).

United States Suggests Joint US-Soviet Effort on Ethiopia

US Secretary of State James Baker has asked the Soviet Union to join the United States in an effort to end civil strife and starvation in Ethiopia. State Department spokeswoman Margaret Tutwiler said the United States wanted a cease-fire between the Soviet-backed Marxist government and the Eritrean rebels, so that food supplies could be moved in to relieve the suffering of millions of civilians (*RFE/RL Special*, March 13).

Wednesday, March 14

Ryzhkov Accused of Involvement in Tank Scandal

Radical Leningrad people's deputy Anatolii Sobchak implicated Prime Minister Nikolai Ryzhkov and his cabinet in a foiled scheme to sell a dozen Soviet tanks to the West. Ryzhkov furiously denied the charge and threatened to resign. The tank scandal, which involved an attempt by a private cooperative, ANT, to export twelve T-72 tanks as well as strategic metals in exchange for consumer goods, erupted during a session of the USSR Congress of People's Deputies when Sobchak took the floor to defend his support for cooperatives. But the defense turned into an attack on Ryzhkov and his government for approving the cooperative. Sobchak said ANT was technically a subsidiary of a government agency and that Ryzhkov himself had signed its organizational papers (*AP*, *Reuters*, *DPA*, March 14; *Central Television*, March 14).

"Edinstvo" Protests against Estonia's Attempts to Secede

Estonia's Russian-dominated "Edinstvo" organization staged meetings and demonstrations throughout the republic to protest against Estonia's attempts to secede from the Soviet Union. Swedish radio reported a 50,000-strong demonstration of Russians in Tallinn. TASS said the meetings were organized by the group's Committee for the Defense of Civil Rights and Soviet Rule. The committee was founded last month when Estonia declared its economic sovereignty and its intention to start talks with Moscow on independence.

Georgian Informal Groups Call for Election Boycott

Informal groups in Georgia called for a boycott of this month's republican-level Supreme Soviet elections. TASS quoted the groups as saying they were demanding a boycott because Georgia was "a state deprived of sovereignty." The call was made at a conference in Tbilisi, which was attended by all Georgian informal groups. The conference also approved a statement that declared Georgia's existing law-making and law-enforcement structures illegal. On March 16, the conference decided to elect an opposition congress to monitor the actions of the new republican Supreme Soviet.

USSR Heading for Energy Crisis, US Expert Says

A US energy expert said an energy crisis was looming in the USSR. Robert Ebel, vice president of Enserch Corp., predicted that Soviet oil output over the next five years would drop by about 2 million barrels a day to 10 million. At the same time, he said, the Soviet Union is falling far short of its nuclear power goals. While the Soviet Union plans to supply 20 percent of its energy needs through nuclear power, Ebel said it would be lucky to supply 13 percent. Ebel also said Soviet coal output was down and natural gas production was rising only slowly (*The Journal of Commerce*, March 15).

Pavlov and Baker Discuss US-Soviet Economic Cooperation

Soviet Finance Minister Valentin Pavlov met US Secretary of State James Baker in Washington to discuss US-Soviet economic cooperation. Chairman of the USSR State Bank Viktor Gerashchenko also attended the meeting. US Energy Department official Henson Moore says the United States is compiling a full list of technological equipment that the Soviet Union needs for its economic modernization. US Treasury Secretary Nicholas Brady says, however, that the United States will not join the proposed European Development Bank if too much of its money is loaned to Moscow. US President George Bush has said the United States can best help the Soviet Union by sending it technical knowledge. He says he does not support the idea of direct loans to the Soviet Union (*RFE/RL Special*, March 15).

Britain Says It Sold Baltic Gold

Britain said that the Baltic states had deposited nearly 13 tons of gold with the Bank of England before World War II but that Britain had sold it more than twenty years ago. A Foreign Office spokesman said the gold would be worth about 180 million dollars today—twenty times what it brought in 1967. The spokesman said Britain had sold the gold to compensate British investors for assets they lost when the Soviet Union annexed Lithuania, Latvia, and Estonia in 1940. The spokesman said he could not speculate on how the British government would react if Lithuania, which declared its independence on March 11, asked for the return of the gold. The Bank of France says it is still holding 2.2 tons of prewar Lithuanian gold and will return it once the French government recognizes an independent Lithuania (*RFE/RL Special*, *AFP*, March 14).

Thursday, March 15

Gorbachev Elected Executive President of the USSR

The USSR Congress of People's Deputies elected Mikhail Gorbachev the Soviet Union's first president with executive powers. He was elected by a vote of 1,329 to 495 (see *Pravda*, March 15 and 16). About 350 deputies did not take part in the voting. Gorbachev took an oath of office to serve the Soviet people for the next five years, to obey the Soviet Constitution, and to guarantee the rights and freedoms of Soviet citizens. The oath did not mention the Communist Party. On assuming office Gorbachev gave up the post of chairman of the USSR Supreme Soviet. Anatolii Luk'yanov, until now first deputy chairman of the Supreme Soviet, was elected to succeed him. Gorbachev ran unopposed for the presidency. He was nominated by the Central Committee at a plenum held on March 14 during a break in the Congress proceedings. Despite the fact that there is opposition to Gorbachev within the Central Committee, his nomination was supported "unanimously." Gorbachev was also nominated by the "Soyuz" group of USSR people's deputies, which put forward the nominations of Chairman of the Council of Ministers Nikolai Ryzhkov and of USSR Minister of Internal Affairs Vadim Bakatin as well. Both Ryzhkov and Bakatin withdrew their candidacies in favor of Gorbachev.

Also at issue was whether the president should be elected by the Congress or directly by the Soviet people. Many deputies took the podium during the discussion to report that their constituents were in favor of direct election of the president. But Academician Dmitrii Likhachev told the Congress that to hold a direct election now would lead to civil war. The deputies eventually voted 1,542 to 368 with 76 abstentions in favor of the Congress's electing the first president. Subsequent presidential elections will be by direct popular vote.

Gorbachev was not, however, elected to precisely the presidency he proposed. In order to get the motion through the Congress he was forced to agree to the introduction of several amendments limiting the president's powers. First, the president cannot unilaterally declare a state of emergency in any region of the USSR. He must advise the relevant republican Supreme Soviet or its chairman and wait until approval is given. If the declaration of a state of emergency is not approved, the president can ask the USSR Supreme Soviet to support the measure; two-thirds of the members must vote in favor. Second, the president cannot override a Supreme Soviet veto of legislation by appealing to the Congress. Third, the president will not appoint the chairman of the Constitutional Compliance Committee, whose job it is to check presidential actions for constitutionality and legality. The president is, however, still permitted to issue decrees binding throughout the Soviet Union.

In his inaugural speech to the USSR Congress of People's Deputies, Gorbachev said being president did not mean he would renounce his personal political convictions. But he promised to be objective and take into account the entire spectrum of views in Soviet society. Gorbachev said he would continue, at least for the time being, in his role as general secretary of the CPSU. He said this was "dictated by the interests of *perestroika*." Gorbachev said his most important task as president would be to continue *perestroika*. He also promised to use the full power of the law and public opinion against "nationalistic, chauvinistic, and even racist slogans" that are appearing in the USSR. He said he would never use the Soviet Armed Forces outside the country without the consent of the Congress or the Supreme Soviet unless there were a surprise attack on the USSR. In his first news conference as president, Gorbachev called for more radical economic reform and for a strengthening of the principles of the federation. Gorbachev also called for a restructuring of the armed forces, saying they must be distinguished by well-trained soldiers and up-to-date, effective weaponry (*Pravda*, March 16). See RL 132/90 and RL 133/90.

Gorbachev's Remarks on the Nationalities Question

In his speech accepting the presidency, Gorbachev reiterated his commitment to preserving the integrity of the Soviet Union, thus serving notice yet again that he does not intend to let the Baltic or any other republics secede without putting up a fight. Among his tasks as president he listed initiating work on drawing up a new Union treaty that will reflect present-day realities. On the subject of refugees from interethnic violence, he said that the republics should adopt laws on the matter and that once they were fully sovereign they would be held accountable for guaranteeing the political, legal, and material rights of all their inhabitants. Gorbachev said that as president he would work closely with the new Federative Council on all matters concerning strengthening republican sovereignty, raising the status of the autonomous formation, and drawing up legislation on the mechanics of secession (*Pravda*, March 16).

Estonian Supreme Soviet Session

The Estonian Supreme Soviet began a session at which the major topic is whether the republic should declare independence. In a vote this morning, 131 delegates favored putting an independence declaration on the agenda, but that was 11 votes too few. The delegates did, however, approve a motion to enlarge the powers of the Presidium of the Estonian Supreme Soviet (*The New York Times*, RFE Estonian service, March 15). Later in the day, the Supreme Soviet voted to start alternative service for conscientious objectors to the military draft. TASS said the alternative service would last three years, one year longer than military service.

Vatican and USSR Establish Official Ties

The USSR and the Vatican established official ties for the first time since the 1917 Bolshevik Revolution. A formal announcement was made in Moscow and Rome. Vatican spokesman Joaquin Navarro-Valls described the ties as "prediplomatic." The two envoys will not be resident in Rome and Moscow immediately but will exchange visits shortly. The Vatican representative to the USSR is the pope's roving envoy to Eastern Europe, Francesco Colasuonno. On March 29, the Presidium of the USSR Supreme Soviet appointed Yurii Karlov the USSR's representative to the Vatican. TASS said Karlov would hold ambassadorial rank, even though the two states have yet to exchange ambassadors. TASS said Karlov had been a diplomat at the Soviet embassy in Rome for several years. He was also a member of the UNESCO Executive Council from 1987 to 1989.

Gorbachev Asks Military Deputies for Calm

During a Kremlin meeting with representatives of the armed forces, including Defense Minister Dmitrii Yazov, Gorbachev appealed to them to keep calm in the face of defense spending cuts and public criticism of the armed forces. Gorbachev said the armed forces should listen to public opinion but take criticism calmly because calm in the army meant calm in the country. He assured them that scientific military research would continue and said the government planned to improve the social welfare of military personnel and their families (*TASS*, March 15).

Soviet Union Tells UN Jewish Emigration Will Continue

The Soviet ambassador to the United Nations, Aleksandr Belonogov, renewed attacks on the settlement of Soviet immigrants in occupied Arab lands but said Moscow had no intention of stopping Jewish emigration. Belonogov said Israeli moves to settle Soviet immigrants in the West Bank and the Gaza Strip threatened human rights, violated international law, and promoted confrontation and extremism. He said appeals for Moscow to stop Jews from leaving for Israel were not the answer, because this would "violate rights and freedoms." Israel says that it has no official policy of settling Soviet Jews in the occupied territories and that so far only a few hundred have done so (*Reuters*, *AP*, March 15).

Friday, March 16

New Party Leader Elected in Volgograd Oblast

Aleksandr Anipkin was elected to replace Vladimir Kalashnikov as Party first secretary in Volgograd Oblast. Kalashnikov resigned in January along with other oblast Party leaders following public demonstrations and protests. Anipkin was formerly first secretary of the Volgograd City Party Committee (*TASS*, March 16).

East Germany's Robotron Signs Computer Deal with USSR

The East German electronics concern VEB Robotron will provide the Soviet Union with six large computers, ADN reported. ADN said the 21-million-ruble deal had been signed between the state-owned Robotron and the Soviet foreign-trade organization Vneshtekhnika at the Leipzig international trade fair. The six computers will be able to run 620 different remote computer stations simultaneously (*Reuters*, March 16).

Four New Clinics for Radiation Victims to Be Set Up in Ukraine

The Ukrainian government has decided to set up four more medical centers to treat people affected by fallout from the Chernobyl' nuclear accident. Radio Kiev said the new clinics will be in Kiev, Dnepropetrovsk, Kharkov, and Lugansk, formerly called Voroshilovgrad (*Radio Kiev*, 1900, March 16). See RL 118/90.

Marshal Ogarkov Gets New Assignment

Soviet television said Marshal Nikolai Ogarkov had been elected chairman of the All-Union Army and Labor Veterans' Organization. He replaces former Politburo member Kirill Mazurov, who died recently. Ogarkov was ousted in 1984 from his post as chief of the General Staff of the USSR Armed Forces. The All-Union Army and Labor Veterans' Organization has gained political strength in recent months. As a public organization entitled to seats in the Congress of People's Deputies, it was able to ensure the election of several military commanders who would not have been elected otherwise.

Saturday, March 17

Shevardnadze Attends Warsaw Pact Meeting in Prague

Eduard Shevardnadze left Moscow for Czechoslovakia to attend a meeting of Warsaw Pact foreign ministers. Speaking on Soviet television after the Warsaw Pact meeting in Prague, Shevardnadze said the main issue regarding a united Germany would be its level of armament. Shevardnadze said Warsaw Pact foreign ministers agreed that all countries, including a united Germany, should have only the weapons and troops necessary for defense. He said the ministers also agreed that their main concerns were the building of European security and rapprochement between the two Germanies (*Pravda*, March 18).

Luk'yanov Meets with Central Asian Mufti

The life of Muslims in the Soviet Union and their relations with Muslims in other parts of the world was the subject of a high-level meeting in Moscow between Chairman of the USSR Supreme Soviet Anatolii Luk'yanov and the chairman of the Presidium of the Religious Board of Muslims of Central Asia and Kazakhstan, Mufti Mukhammad-Sadiq Mukhammad-Yusuf. TASS said the mufti had told Luk'yanov that Muslim religious leaders supported *perestroika* and that they were engaged in efforts to obtain the release of Soviet soldiers captured by the Afghan resistance.

Sunday, March 18

Elections in Estonia and Latvia

On March 18, voters in Latvia and Estonia elected new republican Supreme Soviets (*TASS*, *AP*, March 18). On March 19, the Latvian Popular Front said candidates it supported had won a majority of the seats in the Latvian Supreme Soviet (RFE Latvian service, March 19). See RL 154/90.

On March 23, the Tallinn daily *Paevaleht* published the final results of the elections in Estonia. According to the newspaper, Estonian Popular Front candidates won forty-nine of the 105 seats in the Estonian Supreme Soviet. The Communist-dominated Free Estonia Coalition won twenty-nine seats, and a bloc dominated by non-Estonians won twenty-seven seats. See RL 164/90.

Shevardnadze Visits Africa

Eduard Shevardnadze arrived in Angola, at the start of a nine-day visit to Sub-Saharan Africa, the first ever by a Soviet foreign minister. On March 20, Shevardnadze arrived in Namibia to attend independence celebrations there. He met with US Secretary of State James Baker. The situation in the Baltic republics was the main topic of their discussion. Other topics included German reunification and the Angolan civil war. Before meeting with Baker, Shevardnadze told reporters that Moscow would not use force to quash independence movements in the Baltic republics (*Reuters*, March 20). Shevardnadze also pledged continued Soviet support for the black nationalist South African movement in its fight against apartheid (*Reuters*, March 20).

On March 21, Shevardnadze had a meeting with South African black leader Nelson Mandela. Shevardnadze also met with South African President Frederik De Klerk. Correspondents called the Shevardnadze–De Klerk meeting the highest-level face-to-face contact between the Soviet Union and South Africa since the USSR broke off relations three decades ago. Both men said the talks were constructive (*AP*, March 21).

On March 22, Shevardnadze met in Windhoek with his West German counterpart Hans-Dietrich Genscher. Shevardnadze told reporters after the meeting that remaining obstacles to German unity could be overcome (Western agencies, March 22). The same day, Shevardnadze left Namibia for Mozambique (*TASS*, March 22).

On March 23, Shevardnadze arrived in Zimbabwe, where he met President Robert Mugabe. A Soviet embassy spokesman said the Angolan fighting and the guerrilla war in Mozambique were among the subjects discussed (*AP*, *Reuters*, March 23).

Shevardnadze concluded his tour on March 25 with a one-day visit to Nigeria. This followed talks in Tanzania with Foreign Minister Benjamin Mkapa on the situation in southern Africa and the prospects for peace there. In

Zimbabwe, Shevardnadze said the Soviet Union would do all it could to further peace in southern Africa. He said US Secretary of State James Baker had told him the United States would do the same (*AP*, March 24;, *Reuters*, March 25).

Estonian KGB Chief Replaced

Chairman of the Estonian Committee for State Security Karl Kortelainen has been replaced by Rein Sillar, *Rahva Haal* reported on March 18. Kortelainen, of Karelian background, was appointed KGB chief in June, 1982, after a career as a border guard officer. Rein Sillar is an ethnic Estonian jurist of about fifty years of age.

Soviet Citizens Take a Dim View of the Future

Soviet citizens have little faith in the future and even less in the Communist Party, a new poll showed. The poll of 2,696 people, conducted by the All-Union Center for the Study of Public Opinion and published in *Moscow News* (No. 11), showed that 55 percent of respondents had no concrete vision of the future and 10 percent believed nothing in their lives would ever change, despite Gorbachev's reforms. The poll also showed that the CPSU had lost virtually all popular support. Only 4 percent of those polled said the Party was acting in the best interests of the people. When asked if they believed it was possible to have a society where there were no poor and suffering—long a stated goal of the Soviet Union—67 percent answered no. The survey also suggested Soviet citizens were loath to rush headlong into capitalism. Fifty-five percent said they preferred a small salary in exchange for easy work and only 37 percent said they would like to be rewarded for hard work.

Monday, March 19

Gorbachev Meets Estonian Leaders

Gorbachev met with Estonian leaders in Moscow. TASS said opinions were polarized over republican sovereignty and over independence for the Estonian Communist Party. The Estonian group included the republic's president, Arnold Ruutel, and its prime minister, Indrek Toome, as well as leading Communist Party officials (*Reuters*, *UPI*, March 19; *Pravda*, March 20). USSR Supreme Soviet deputy Marju Lauristin, who is a member of the Estonian delegation, said the delegation would support a Lithuanian message being delivered to Gorbachev on March 19 (RFE Estonian service, March 19).

Frolov Calls for Afanas'ev's Resignation

CPSU Central Committee Secretary Ivan Frolov said the reformist people's deputy Professor Yurii Afanas'ev should resign from the CPSU for his remarks about Lenin (*TASS*, March 19). Afanas'ev told the USSR Congress of People's Deputies on March 13 that Lenin had laid the foundations for a state policy of violence and terror. Afanas'ev's harsh criticism of the USSR's past and present has provoked angry reactions by the Soviet leadership on more than one occasion in the past. In a speech on October 13, 1989, for instance, Gorbachev suggested that Afanas'ev's views were incompatible with his membership of the CPSU.

Soviet Comment on East German Elections, Reunification

Soviet Foreign Ministry spokesman Gennadii Gerasimov announced that the Soviet Union respected the voters' choice in the elections in East Germany on March 18, but he warned that Moscow also expected East Germany to respect its obligations to the Soviet Union and to the maintenance of stability in Europe (*TASS*, March 19). Other Soviet commentators were less pleased with the outcome of the elections. According to AFP, Nikolai Portugalov, the Central Committee specialist on Germany, admitted that the Soviet Union had expected the East German Social Democrats to do better. He also criticized what he called West German interference in the East German elections and predicted that, while East Germans "voted with their bellies" on this occasion, the Left would fare better in future elections. According to UPI, the Novosti news agency also deplored "the massive interference" of West German political parties in the East German elections. Gerasimov also warned against accelerating the German unification process and reiterated Soviet opposition to the inclusion of a united Germany in NATO. In contrast, Soviet military historian Vyacheslav Dashichev told *Die Welt* (March 20) that a united Germany should be a member of NATO and warned that the Four Powers (the World War II victors) should not tread on German national feelings, as was done in the Treaty of Versailles, because this might lead to revanchism.

USSR Requests Satellite Information

In a briefing at the Ministry of Foreign Affairs, spokesman Gennadii Gerasimov expressed Soviet concern over debris from a malfunctioning US satellite expected to fall back to earth soon. The satellite is expected to reenter the atmosphere by mid-April, and reports indicate that some fragments could land on Soviet territory. Gerasimov called for the United States to be more forthcoming in providing information on the satellite (*TASS*, March 19).

Tajik Officials Dismissed for Role in Dushanbe Events

TASS reported that the chairman of Tajikistan's Gosplan, Buri Karimov, and republican Minister of Culture Nur Tabarov had been dismissed by the Presidium of the republican Supreme Soviet for having "compromised themselves" during the disturbances in Dushanbe on February 12–14. The two officials were charged with an unconstitutional attempt to dislodge the chairman of the Council of Ministers during the disturbances. Both were expelled from the CPSU on March 3. Demonstrators demanding the resignation of the republic's top leaders elected Karimov to head a "Provisional Citizen's Committee" to negotiate with the authorities. Karimov, who has subsequently been accused of political careerism, has argued that he did not seek the role for himself. He recently told a *Literaturnaya gazeta* correspondent that the republican Party authorities, including First Secretary Kakhar Makhkamov, had told him to meet with the demonstrators to whom he had said "nothing in particular" other than reciting *rubais* in Tajik (*Literaturnaya gazeta*, March 14). Karimov argued that the objective of the "Provisional Citizens' Committee" was simply the normalization of the situation in Dushanbe, and he complained that he had been victimized.

Ukrainian Orthodox–Catholic Reconciliation Talks Break Down

The Ukrainian Catholic Church said differences with the Russian Orthodox Church had caused reconciliation talks to break down. The information came in a statement from Ukrainian Catholic bishops issued by the Church's press office in Rome. The talks, which are taking place in Lvov, are being attended by representatives of the Ukrainian Catholic Church, the Russian Orthodox Church, and the Vatican. The statement said the head of the Ukrainian Church delegation Archbishop Volodymyr Sternyuk had left in protest. He did so because the Moscow Patriarchate refused to admit that its forced takeover of the Ukrainian Catholic Church in 1946 had been illegal. On March 21, TASS reported that the Orthodox Church in Ukraine had set up a committee to defend its believers in conflicts with Ukrainian Catholics. TASS said the committee would resist the Catholic takeover of Orthodox churches and protect Orthodox believers "from persecution by Catholic extremists, especially in Western Ukraine."

Government to Clear Space Debris from Kazakhstan Fields

The Soviet government was reported to have promised to clear the metallic debris from space launches from the fields of Kazakhstan. Radio Moscow World Service said that 3,500 tons of metal had been falling on Kazakhstan every year and that this had caused a great deal of damage to Kazakhstan's agriculture. The main Soviet space launch facility is at Baikonur in central southern Kazakhstan.

Tuesday, March 20

Gorbachev Meets Latvian Leaders

Gorbachev received five members of a Latvian delegation formed in accordance with a decision of the Latvian Supreme Soviet to raise the issue of Latvia's political and economic independence from Moscow. According to Radio Riga, the delegation consisted of twelve members. The five with whom Gorbachev talked were: Anatolijs Gorbunovs, chairman of the Presidium of the previous Latvian Supreme Soviet; Vilnis Bresis, chairman of the Council of Ministers; Ilmars Bisers, a legal scholar and a deputy chairman of the USSR Council of Nationalities; Mavriks Vulfsons, professor of history and media commentator on foreign affairs; and Janis Vagris, first secretary of the Central Committee of the Latvian Communist Party (*Pravda*, March 21).

Elections to Georgian Supreme Soviet Postponed

The Georgian Popular Front called for the postponement of republican-level Supreme Soviet elections scheduled for this month. The popular front said the Georgian Supreme Soviet should first convene a special meeting to remove Article Six from the republican constitution and should also work out a new electoral law (*TASS*, March 20). On March 21, TASS reported that the Georgian Supreme Soviet, meeting in special session, had complied with the popular front's demands and postponed the Supreme Soviet elections until the fall.

Several Thousand Demonstrate in Kishinev

There was a rally sponsored by the "Unita" movement of non-Moldavians in the Moldavian capital, Kishinev. TASS said several thousand Kishinev residents took part in the rally, which was sanctioned by the Kishinev authorities. The agency said the rally was devoted to discussing the results of the elections to the Moldavian Supreme Soviet, in which deputies who support the movement's goals were reported to have won more than 30 percent of the seats. According to TASS, the rally also passed a resolution condemning Lithuania's reaffirmation of its independence.

Poland and USSR Sign Trade Protocol Following Deadlock

Poland and the Soviet Union signed a trade protocol in Warsaw. Radio Warsaw said it was signed after Polish Prime Minister Tadeusz Mazowiecki met the Soviet delegation to break a deadlock in negotiations. The protocol is for this year and provides for Polish deliveries of equipment and machinery to the Soviet Union to the value of 16 billion rubles.

Wednesday, March 21

RSFSR Gets Its Own Trade-Union Federation

Fifteen hundred delegates met in Moscow to found an all-Russian (*vserossiisky*) trade-union federation. Until now, the RSFSR was the only Soviet republic without its own trade-union organization. The new body will act as an umbrella organization for all official trade unions in the RSFSR; until now, these were subordinated directly to the All-Union Central Council of Trade Unions (*TASS*, March 21).

"Democratic Russia" Alliance Discusses Strategy

Candidates backed by the "Democratic Russia" alliance of informal groups won fifty-five of the sixty-five seats alloted to the Moscow area in the RSFSR Congress of People's Deputies and 263 of the 465 seats in the Moscow City Soviet. Gavriil Popov chaired a meeting of some 150 of the new deputies. The group was uncertain over whether to remain united (some felt this was the only way they could defeat the Party apparatus) or to split (*AP*, March 21).

Shevardnadze Gives Outspoken Interview to *Ogonek*

An unusually outspoken interview with Foreign Minister Eduard Shevardnadze in *Ogonek* (No. 11) provided a rare insight into squabbles in the Kremlin. Shevardnadze also sought to rebuff charges that he is "one of those responsible for the collapse of the Socialist camp," explaining that the end of communism in Eastern Europe was preferable from the point of view of Soviet security to the Soviet Union's former policy of supporting unpopular regimes in the region by force. Shevardnadze described previous Soviet behavior toward the peoples of the Warsaw Pact countries as "violence to history, democracy, traditions, [these peoples'] way of life, and to common sense."

In the interview, Shevardnadze also gave a detailed description of the controversy over the violent breaking up of a nationalist demonstration in Tbilisi on April 9,

1989. Shevardnadze was dispatched to his native Georgia together with Politburo candidate member Georgii Razumovsky immediately after the event. He described to the interviewer how the military commanders and USSR Military Prosecutor Aleksandr Katusev had persistently misinformed him and Razumovsky, denying that shovels and poison gas had been used against the demonstrators. Shevardnadze said that, because he and Razumovsky had acted on the basis of false information, they had undermined public trust in the Party leadership.

Moscow News Carries New Information on Katyn

A study of the KGB archives confirms that the Soviet Union was responsible for the murder of thousands of Polish army officers in Katyn Forest during World War II, according to *Moscow News* (No. 12). An article based on research by Soviet historian Natalya Lebedeva reported that Stalin had ordered the Poles killed because he feared they would stage an uprising and upset the secret provisions of his 1939 treaties with Hitler. Another reason for the massacre, Lebedeva said, was that Stalin needed the space the Poles were occupying in the prison camps in order to incarcerate Estonians, Latvians, and Lithuanians he was deporting from the Baltic. (For the second part of Lebedeva's article, see *Moscow News*, No. 18; for more details of her survey, see *Mezhdunarodnaya zhizn'*, No. 5.) On March 22, the Polish Sejm adopted a resolution urging the USSR to officially admit Soviet responsibility for the Katyn massacre (*Radio Warsaw*, March 22).

On March 30, USSR Supreme Soviet Chairman Anatolii Luk'yanov told a Polish Senate delegation that the Soviet Union was prepared to say who was responsible for the massacre of Polish officers at Katyn (*Radio Warsaw*, March 29). The same day, the Polish Katyn Committee held a protest in front of the Soviet embassy in Warsaw and gave diplomats a letter for Gorbachev. Radio Warsaw said the committee had asked the Soviet Union to officially reveal all the circumstances of the massacre before the fiftieth anniversary of the crime in April.

Soviet-Iranian Border Crossing Opened

Radio Teheran reported that, to mark the Muslim New Year, a border crossing in the city of Dzhulfa on the Soviet-Iranian border had been opened for the first time in seventy-three years. The crossing will remain open for three days; busloads of Soviet Azerbaijanis were welcomed with gifts by their conationals in Iran.

Pravda Criticizes Conservatives and Radicals

Pravda criticized both conservatives and radicals within the Party. The newspaper said there were some Party workers who saw attempts to reform the Party as threatening their Party positions and political influence. It said there were also some Party members who rejected the Party and had reduced its history to "the mistakes and distortions" of the Brezhnev and Stalin eras. In a front-page report, *Pravda* said there was a need to say a decisive "no" to both groups.

Yakovlev Denies USSR Surrounded by Enemies

Aleksandr Yakovlev said changes in Eastern Europe did not mean that the USSR had to rearm itself against hostile neighbors. In an interview with Novosti, Yakovlev said that Poland, Czechoslovakia, and Romania sincerely wanted to preserve friendly relations with the USSR and that "there are no symptoms of aggravation." Yakovlev noted that Comecon and the Warsaw Pact were intact.

Another Mass Grave of Stalin's Victims Found

Radio Kiev said a mass grave of Stalin's victims had been found near the East Ukrainian city of Lugansk, formerly called Voroshilovgrad. It was not clear from the broadcast when the grave had been discovered or how many bodies it holds. But the radio said the number of people killed in the region under Stalin is estimated at several tens of thousands. (Lugansk was named Voroshilovgrad in 1935 in honor of Stalin's associate Kliment Voroshilov. It regained its former name last November.)

In an interview with *Trud* (March 4), an activist of "Memorial," archivist Dmitrii Yurasov, said an extraordinary government commission that was set up after World War II under the chairmanship of Nikolai Shvernik to investigate Nazi crimes on the territory of the USSR had been secretly instructed to blame the Germans for mass killings that had been carried out by the NKVD. Yurasov said that, during his work in various Soviet archives, he had seen documents that described mass graves of Soviet citizens as "NKVD special objects" and had later seen the same graves identified by the Shvernik commission as graves of Nazi victims.

Thursday, March 22

Latvian Popular Front Leader Says Latvia Will Follow Lithuania

Chairman of the Latvian Popular Front Dainis Ivans said his republic wanted to follow the same road to independence as Lithuania. In an interview with *Die Welt*, Ivans said he was convinced the Soviet government would negotiate with the Baltic republic. Ivans, who left the Communist Party in February, said the Soviet government must be convinced that Latvian freedom is also in its interest. He said Moscow had already imposed "a de facto economic blockade" of Latvia. He said the USSR was no longer sending large amounts of raw materials to Latvian factories "even though this is not an official blockade."

USSR and US Reach New Long-Term Grain Deal

The United States and the Soviet Union reached a new grain sales accord that guarantees US farmers thousands of millions of dollars worth of sales to the USSR. The accord was announced in Washington after negotiators worked it out in Vienna. The five-year pact calls for minimum Soviet purchases of 10 million tons of US wheat, corn, and soybeans or soymeal each year. Moscow has, however, bought much more in recent years (*UPI*, *Reuters*, March 22).

Radiation Information Service Set Up in Kazakhstan

TASS said a radiation information service had been set up in Kazakhstan. The agency said the service was for people living near the Semipalatinsk nuclear testing ground and a nuclear power plant in Shevchenko. TASS said the service would also inform residents about natural radiation in the republic.

"Soyuz" Says It Will Fight against Separatist Tendencies

The "Soyuz" group of USSR people's deputies said it would fight against separatist tendencies in the Soviet Union. A member of the group, Georgii Komarov, said in an interview in *Sovetskaya Rossiya* that separatist and nationalistic tendencies were growing in the USSR. He said destructive forces were trying, clearly with political aims of their own, to destabilize a situation already made difficult by economic problems. He said a good example of this was Lithuania. The "Soyuz" group, which was set up earlier this year, includes 300 deputies among whom are Evgenii Kogan, a leader of the Russian-speaking "Intermovement" in Estonia, and Lieutenant Colonel Viktor Alksnis of the Baltic Military District.

Plenum of the RSFSR Writers' Union Board

Izvestia carried a report on the proceedings of the seventh plenum of the Board of the RSFSR Writers' Union, which took place this week. The plenum discussed the union's new draft rules and scheduled the union's next congress for December of 1990. The newspaper made clear that, while they were more restrained than at the last plenum in November, 1989, the delegates at the latest gathering still put forth xenophobic statements, demanding that only people of Russian origin be regarded as Russian writers. (The previous plenum of the Board of the RSFSR Writers' Union attracted wide attention in the Soviet press because of the overt anti-Semitism expressed in the speeches of participants.) The main documents of the seventh plenum and the abridged texts of the speeches were published in *Literaturnaya Rossiya*, No. 12.

Friday, March 23

Estonian Party Congress Opens

The Estonian Communist Party said it supported the idea of an independent Estonia but said the road to independence required a legal, economic, and social base. This statement was contained in a draft program distributed to delegates at the opening of the Party congress in Tallinn. The draft said that in the future the Party would reject administrative socialism and utopian models. In another document distributed today, the Party admitted to having made serious mistakes in the past. It said this was because the Estonian Party had never acted as an independent political force (*TASS*, March 23).

On March 25, the Estonian Communist Party voted to end its subordination to the CPSU. Russian-speaking delegates did not vote. Reuters and AFP said the Estonian CP decision on independence would not become final until October. On March 26, Radio Moscow announced that Russian-speaking Communists, mainly from Tallinn, had formed their own party loyal to Moscow and had appealed to the CPSU to recognize it as the real Communist Party of Estonia. A similar situation emerged in Lithuania after its Communist Party announced independence last December.

Fedor Burlatsky Becomes Editor of *Literaturnaya gazeta*

It was reported that prominent reformist and political commentator Fedor Burlatsky had been made chief editor of *Literaturnaya gazeta*. Burlatsky told Soviet television that he would try to make *Literaturnaya gazeta* more interesting and progressive to help it regain some of the 1.5 million readers who canceled subscriptions last year (*Central Television*, "Vremya," March 23). Burlatsky replaced Yurii Voronov, who had been chief editor of the weekly since December, 1988.

Soviet Union and South Korea Hold Trade Talks

South Korean business leaders and Soviet government officials held discussions in Seoul on bilateral trade. The head of the Korea Institute for Economics and Technology said that South Korea and the USSR could jointly build plants in the Soviet Union to make soap, electronics goods, textiles, and other consumer products (*Reuters*, *AFP*, March 23).

Saturday, March 24

Composition of Presidential Council Announced

Mikhail Gorbachev issued a decree on the composition of the Presidential Council. The task of this new body was to advise the Soviet president on foreign, domestic, and security policy. TASS said the new body would also be involved in the formulation of economic policy. The names of fifteen appointees were announced. They included some of the USSR's most important decision-makers and represented a wide range of opinion, from conservative writer Valentin Rasputin and a leader of the United Front of Workers of Russia Veniamin Yarin to reformist Politburo members Aleksandr Yakovlev, Eduard Shevardnadze, and Academician Stanislav Shatalin. Under the constitution, Prime Minister Nikolai Ryzhkov was granted *ex officio* membership. KGB Chairman Vladimir Kryuchkov, Defense Minister Dmitrii Yazov, Minister of Internal Affairs Vadim Bakatin, and Chairman of Gosplan Yurii Maslyukov were also appointed members of the council (*Izvestia*, March 29).

The Presidential Council held its first meeting on March 27. Chaired by Gorbachev, with Prime Minister Ryzhkov in attendance, the meeting was covered at length by Soviet television. In a televised interview, Gorbachev said that after "sharp discussion" the council had agreed that the economy was the country's number one problem and that urgent steps must be taken to "radicalize" the economic reform process. In an opening address to the council that was also read on Soviet television, Gorbachev said the country faced its "biggest turning point" and that "what we are talking about is a controlled transfer to market relations." Gorbachev said the council had agreed that the food problem was particularly acute. Calling for "a new agrarian policy," Gorbachev promised that state ownership of the means of production would remain "predominant" in the USSR. But, he said, ways must also be found to encourage small-scale private enterprise, cooperatives, family businesses, and joint ventures with foreign firms. The Presidential

Council, Gorbachev went on, is concerned about the rise in crime and "extremism." It set up a working group to coordinate the activities of all law-enforcement agencies. Politburo member Aleksandr Yakovlev was appointed to chair it. See RL 156/90.

Uzbekistan Elects President

Following the introduction of the new post of president at the all-Union level, the Uzbekistan Supreme Soviet elected republican Party First Secretary Islam Karimov president of the republic. Karimov was nominated (he apparently ran unopposed) by a plenum of the Uzbek Communist Party Central Committee that preceded the legislative session; the plenum also voted to restore Central Committee membership to former Samarkand Oblast Party First Secretary Nazir Radzhabov, who was arrested on corruption charges that were dropped recently.

On March 26, a new Supreme Soviet chairman was elected in Uzbekistan. He is Mirzaolim Ibragimov, who had been chairman of the Presidium of the Uzbek Supreme Soviet since last year (*TASS*, March 26). The same day, a new prime minister was elected at a session of the Uzbek Supreme Soviet. He is Shukrulla Mirsaidov, who had served for five years as mayor of the Uzbek capital, Tashkent, and last year was made the republic's deputy prime minister for planning (*TASS*, March 26). On March 27, Mirsaidov delivered a speech to the Uzbek parliament, calling for radical changes in relations with the central authorities. He said the proposed changes should ensure real political and economic sovereignty for Uzbekistan (*Radio Moscow-1*, 1900, March 27).

Uzbek Popular Front Activist Quits CPSU

Uzbek poet Gulchehra Nurullaeva, a leading activist in the Uzbek Popular Front, "Birlik," told RFE/RL she had resigned from the CPSU in early March because she was bitterly disappointed that the reform process had brought so little real change. Nurullaeva said that she had joined the Party out of idealism but that after twenty years of membership she was tired of "false slogans."

Sunday, March 25

"Rukh" Meets to Decide on Political Role

Some 800 delegates representing branches of the Ukrainian popular movement "Rukh" met in Khust, in the Western Ukraine, to decide the political future of "Rukh."

The participants decided that "Rukh" would not become a political party but would remain an umbrella organization for various informal groups. The creation of a political party was proposed on March 8 in a statement signed by twenty-two "Rukh" leaders (RL Ukrainian service, March 25).

Social Unrest Works against Economic Reforms

According to *Trud*, the incidence of strikes and ethnic unrest is much higher this year than last. *Trud* put the number of man-days lost due to all causes at 9.1 million for January and February alone. That stands in grim contrast to the 7.3 million man-days lost during all of 1989, which saw unprecedented labor stoppages and ethnic disturbances. The increase in work disruptions contributed to a drop of 1 percent in Soviet GNP for the first two months of the year as compared with the same period last year. Wages continued to grow in January and February and increased 15.5 percent over last year's figures. This is 1.2 times the growth of retail trade and much faster than the growth of consumer goods production as well.

New Violence in Transcaucasus

TASS reported on March 25 that nine people, including a family of five, had been killed in separate incidents on March 24 when armed Armenian militants attacked three villages in the Kazakh Raion of Azerbaijan. In addition, TASS stated that two Armenians had been killed on March 22 while attempting to shell an Azerbaijani village. Reuters quoted Armenian sources as claiming that two Armenians were killed that day in an artillery attack from Azerbaijani territory; it was not clear whether the reports referred to the same incident.

TASS further reported that there had been gunfire along the border between the two republics on the nights of March 22 and 23, that a time bomb had exploded in a gas station in the Azerbaijani-populated town of Shusha in Nagorno-Karabakh, and that a passenger train bound for Baku had been derailed in Armenia as the result of an explosion. An earlier TASS dispatch on March 23 reported that the Azerbaijani law-enforcement organs had launched an appeal to the population to surrender all weapons in the interests of expediting the lifting of the state of emergency imposed in the republic two months ago. The appeal noted that "irresponsible people are inciting citizens to unlawful actions."

On March 25, the Azerbaijani Council of Ministers asked the Soviet authorities to take measures to guarantee security along the Azerbaijani-Armenian border (*Radio*

Baku, March 25; *Komsomol'skaya pravda*, March 28). On March 26, one Azerbaijani was killed and four others wounded in a gun attack on a bus in Nagorno-Karabakh.

On March 29, the head of the troops department of the USSR Ministry of Internal Affairs Colonel General Yurii Shatalin, was sent to the Transcaucasus to help restore order (*TASS*, March 29). Meanwhile, Radio Baku said Azerbaijan was temporarily closing its border with Armenia.

On March 31, a plenum of the Azerbaijani Communist Party Central Committee appealed to Gorbachev, calling for all necessary measures to be taken to ensure Azerbaijani rights. In Tbilisi, government delegates from Azerbaijan and Armenia met to discuss the restoration of rail, road, and air links between their two republics.

Results of Kazakhstan Elections Reported

On March 26, TASS reported some results of the republican Supreme Soviet elections in Kazakhstan, which took place on March 25. Owing to the large number of candidates (up to four per seat), deputies were elected in only 131 districts out of 270. Republican Party leader Nursultan Nazarbaev had insisted that the members of the republican buro (with the exception of "token worker" Valentina Kuz'menko) run for ordinary, rather than "reserved" seats. According to TASS, Nazarbaev won 92 percent of the vote in his district, running against a kolkhoz chairman, and Chairman of the Council of Ministers Uzakbai Karamanov won 82 percent of the vote, but several Central Committee department heads, oblast Party secretaries, and local soviet chairmen did not advance to the second round of voting.

Monday, March 26

***Pravda* Condemns Opposition**

Pravda said an organized opposition to existing state structures was emerging in the USSR. It said destructive forces had tried to seize power by antidemocratic methods, "through . . . strong-arm pressure and calls to make use of the so-called round table." The article called for measures to reinforce public order and the rule of law.

Deteriorating Situation in Moldavia

Radio Moscow-1 (2330) said that the political and social situation in Moldavia was deteriorating. It said there had been an unsanctioned demonstration, blocking of transport, and picketing of government buildings, but the report did not say when these actions had taken place.

It did say that, at a recent plenum of the republican Central Committee, the head of the Moldavian Popular Front had attacked the local Communist Party and announced that he was leaving it. The report also said that many thousands of people had attended a meeting on March 25 at which popular front leaders and Supreme Soviet deputies hailed the results of the republican election on February 25 as a major victory for national democratic forces. On March 28, the Presidium of the Moldavian Supreme Soviet warned that the authorities might introduce a state of emergency in some parts of the republic unless people started respecting the law (*Radio Moscow*, March 28).

Green Party Formed

A conference of representatives from environmental organizations around the USSR gathered in Moscow on March 24–25 and announced the formation of a Green Party (*Radio Moscow-1*, 2200, March 26). A declaration passed at the conference stated that the party would work for "a radical transformation of society on the basis of the primacy of ecology, civil self-rule, and direct democracy." Acknowledging the strongly nationalist orientation of the ecological movement and the formation of Green parties in several republics, the resolution also stressed that the new party would not limit its activities to regional issues.

Gromov Denies Military Coup Rumors

Radio Moscow World Service broadcast an interview with Lieutenant General Boris Gromov in which the former commander of the Soviet forces in Afghanistan denied rumors that the armed forces were planning a coup against the present government. Gromov called such rumors "unfounded nonsense" and speculated that they might be part of "a policy being pursued by certain circles for whom the army, in these days of *perestroika*, is a thorn in the flesh." Gromov, currently commander of the Kiev Military District, is one of the most popular and best known military figures in the Soviet Union. His name has been linked in the past to rumors of a military coup allegedly arising from the High Command's opposition to the foreign and domestic policies of Mikhail Gorbachev.

Tuesday, March 27

Situation in Georgia

A second major Georgian political organization decided to boycott this fall's Supreme Soviet elections in Georgia. The Party for National Independence made the decision at a congress in Tbilisi. The party's spokesman, Georgi Popkhadze, told RFE/RL the party was boycotting the vote because it did not recognize the authority of the Georgian Supreme Soviet. On March 28, *Trud* quoted high-ranking Georgian and central officials as saying the situation in Georgia was "extremely tense." The newspaper complained that a power vacuum existed in the republic.

Orthodox Church in Lvov Occupies Deputy Mayor 's Office

The Orthodox Church in the Western Ukrainian city of Lvov occupied the office of the deputy mayor. An Orthodox official said on the radio that the Catholics had issued so many claims over church property that the Orthodox Church could not carry out its work or provide religious and pastoral services. The official said the Orthodox Church had taken over the state office to attract the attention of the authorities, whose duty it was to protect Orthodox people, first as citizens and second as believers. A government representative in Lvov also interviewed on the radio said the government had begun legal proceedings to regain control of the offices. He said no force would be used.

Cancellation of Volga-Don Canal Project Recommended

According to *Izvestia*, a commission of the USSR State Planning Committee has recommended the cancellation of the highly controversial project to build a Volga-Don irrigation canal. The sixty-five-kilometer-long canal, which was to have originated to the north of Volgograd, was conceived over ten years ago as a means of expanding agricultural production in the region. Water supplies from the Volga were to be diverted towards the Don, whose water supplies have been almost completely exhausted by other uses. Construction of the canal officially began in 1985 and has cost over 100 million rubles to date. The commission said the canal would cause excessive damage to the environment and would cost too much. Instead, it said, farm output could be increased by improving farms and irrigation systems that already exist in the region. The canal is just one of several grandiose projects of the Ministry of Water Resources located in that region of the USSR to fall under the axe in the past few years.

Yarin to Defend Army's Interests

Immediately after his appointment to the Presidential Council, Veniamin Yarin told *Krasnaya zvezda* that he would do his best to defend the interests of the armed forces in that new policy consulting body. Yarin said he himself had served in the army during the 1962 Cuba crisis and thus understood the need to have a strong army. He also said he did not exclude an internal threat to Gorbachev's reform policy and wanted to draw the president's attention to the problem of growing destabilization in Soviet society.

Abalkin on Soviet Economic Situation

Deputy Prime Minister Leonid Abalkin said the Soviet economy had been in a slump for three months and radical changes should be made quickly. Abalkin said overall production had fallen during the three months ending in February and that output of oil and coal, trucks, buses, and some consumer goods had fallen. Abalkin was interviewed by the official government periodical *Pravitel'stvennyi vestnik* (*TASS*, March 27).

Wednesday, March 28

Military Service Amendment Passed by Supreme Soviet

TASS reported that the USSR Supreme Soviet had passed an amendment to the law on military service, which transfers responsibility for ordering the military draft from the Ministry of Defense to the government. According to the chief of the General Staff of the Soviet Armed Forces, Army General Mikhail Moiseev, the change was needed because not all draftees fall under the purview of the Ministry of Defense and "it is the government that allocates human resources for the army." The amendment represents a victory for the military leadership. Last December Moiseev disclosed that the General Staff had proposed transferring responsibility for ordering the draft from the Ministry of Defense to the Presidium of the Supreme Soviet (*Kommunist vooruzhennykh sil*, No. 2, 1990). It seems likely that the growth of opposition to the draft in the non-Russian republics was a major reason for the General Staff's proposal. It apparently hoped that such a move would give the draft a firmer legal basis and compel state and local governmental organs to enforce existing draft regulations.

Multiparty System Starts Working in Moscow Soviet

"Democratic Russia," the bloc of liberal and radical deputies in the Moscow Soviet, won an important victory. Having gained 54 percent of the vote in elections to the Moscow City Soviet on March 4, the bloc's representatives successfully countered a proposal made by the city Party apparatus concerning the formation of the organizational committee that will prepare the soviet's first session (*TASS*, March 28). The apparatus said the committee should be formed on the traditional principle of territorial representation, but the bloc successfully argued that it be composed on the basis of the political composition of the soviet itself. As a result, it now holds 28 of 46 seats on the committee. After that, the meeting was interrupted and other deputies were invited to form their own factions to fill the remaining 18 seats. This victory was doubly significant: it was the first time that elected representatives had defeated the apparatus, and it represented the beginning of a working multiparty system in the Soviet Union. See RL 160/90.

Miners Declare Independence

Angered that the government has not honored the promises made to them after the strikes in the summer of 1989, and that the All-Union Central Council of Trade Unions has not protected their interests, Soviet coal miners held an extraordinary congress of their trade union in Moscow and declared their union's independence from the central union body (*Central Television*, "Vremya," March 28). Speakers demanded full financial independence for their pits; one said that the miners wanted veto power over ministerial decisions.

Reorganization of Soviet Press Politically Motivated

A desire by Party and government officials to get rid of some outspoken newspapers was behind the Soviet leadership's decision in 1989 to drastically reorganize several central publications, *Ogonek* (No. 12) said. Several newspapers were merged and given new names. *Sotsialisticheskaya industriya*, for example, was combined with *Stroitel'naya gazeta* to form *Rabochaya tribuna*. The editorial board of the new newspaper retained very few of the outspoken journalists who had worked on *Sotsialisticheskaya industriya*. *Ogonek* revealed that the management of *Sotsialisticheskaya industriya* had been told by a Council of Ministers official the newspaper was being closed because it had published too many critical articles on the Soviet economy. Your newspaper, he said, "has not passed any decision of the government without strong criticism." "Things can't go on like that," the official added.

Leaders Questioned in Supreme Soviet

The USSR Supreme Soviet's two chambers met in joint session to question government leaders. TASS said this form of "government accountability" would become a permanent fixture. It said question-and-answer sessions were expected to take place on the last Saturday of every month. Today's session focused on the course of implementation of the government's economic recovery program.

Thursday, March 29

Parliament Approves Bill on Nationalities Committee

The Soviet parliament has approved a bill creating a State Committee on Nationalities Issues. TASS said the committee's main goal was to prevent interethnic conflicts. A Soviet nationalities expert, Georgii Tarazevich, said the new committee's role would also include restoring the rights of people subjected to Stalin's repressions. Tarazevich is chairman of the Commission on Nationalities Policy and Interethnic Relations within the Council of Nationalities of the USSR Supreme Soviet.

Two Soviet Ministers Released

Soviet television reported that two ministers had been released from their duties. The released ministers are Health Minister Evgenii Chazov and Civil Aviation Minister Aleksandr Volkov. The report said the two had been transferred to other jobs at their own request. Both ministers were appointed to their posts in 1987.

Friday, March 30

Estonian Supreme Soviet Declares Continuing De Jure Existence of Republic of Estonia

The Estonian Supreme Soviet took a significant step towards the reestablishment of Estonian independence by declaring the continuing de jure existence of the Republic of Estonia. On the basis of this, it also declared the beginning of "a transitional period" to last until the creation of the Republic of Estonia's constitutional organs of state authority and stated that it would adopt "a temporary form of government." See RL 176/90.

Chernobyl' Victims on Hunger Strike

About 120 radiation victims of the Chernobyl' nuclear disaster are continuing their hunger strike in Moscow, *Trud* reported. The newspaper said the group was striking in front of the Kharkov Institute of Medical Radiology. It did not say when the strike began. The newspaper said the protesters were demanding special social benefits and better medical treatment. They said they would continue their strike until they received guarantees from the Soviet leadership

Independent Party Formed in Tataria

A political party has been formed in Tataria with the goal of establishing an independent state for Tatars. The party, which is called "Ittifak" (Unity), was formed by a committee headed by Mukhamed Dinov at a meeting a week ago in Kazan, the capital of the Tatar Autonomous Republic. Dinov is a philosopher and a lecturer at Kazan State University (RL Tatar-Bashkir service, March 30). The Tatar ASSR has the most active unofficial political movement among autonomous republics of the RSFSR.

Kazakh Informals Decide to Create Political Party

Sixteen informal groups have decided to form an independent political party in Kazakhstan. Poet Kial Sabdalin told RFE/RL the decision had been made at a meeting of the groups in Alma-Ata three days ago. He said the details still had to be worked out. Sabdalin also told Radio Liberty's Kazakh service that the sixteen groups had decided to call a rally in support of Lithuanian independence and that he had been named to the organizing committee.

Oil and Gas Workers Threaten to Strike

On March 30, *Izvestia* reported that emergency talks with representatives of Siberian oil and gas industry workers had been held on March 28 in Moscow. The report spoke of "social tension" in the industry and of a call by those attending the meeting for "urgent measures" but it did not mention the threat of a strike. Meanwhile, *Moscow News* (No. 13) carried an open letter to Soviet Prime Minister Nikolai Ryzhkov from the Tyumen regional trade-union leader, Nikolai Trifonov, threatening a strike starting April 1 if the government failed to respond to demands from the oil and gas workers for better living and working conditions. Among these was a demand that part of the hard currency generated by the export of oil be returned to the producing regions to help "resolve many social issues." The *Financial Times* on March 31 reported that emergency measures had been ordered by the government to deal with the complaints and that union leaders had therefore postponed the strike deadline until April 7.

Three Options for Price Reform

The chairman of the USSR State Price Committee, Vyacheslav Senchagov, told TASS on March 30 that the government had yet to select one of three options for wholesale and retail price reform. The first would eliminate state subsidies, retain some price regulation, and devalue the ruble by at least 50 percent. The second would follow "the Polish pattern" of a quick transition to a market economy, with prices of oil and coal rising by as much as 500 percent, closures of unprofitable enterprises, and increased unemployment. The third option would combine elements of the first two, fixing retail prices of some staple goods but freeing the prices of up to 30 percent of nonessential items. Senchagov said that he believed the government was leaning towards the third option but that "the Polish pattern" was probably inevitable in the long run. (A radical reform package has been promised for May 1 to go into effect by July 1.)

Saturday, March 31

Liberal Democratic Party Holds Founding Congress

The Liberal Democratic Party of the USSR held its founding congress in Moscow, TASS and Central Television reported. In an interview broadcast on the television news program "Vremya," the leaders of the new party said that their group had not yet adopted a program but that it adhered to the principles of the supremacy of law, political pluralism, and a market economy. Membership of the new party was declared open to all, and the group said it hoped to enter into a partnership with the CPSU. Its leaders claimed that the party had some 3,000 members and that its constituent congress was the first such gathering of a non-Communist party at the all-Union level.

Estonian Government Resigns

Izvestia reported that the Estonian Supreme Soviet had accepted the resignation of the Estonian government on March 30. On April 3, Estonian Popular Front activist Edgar Savisaar was elected by the Estonian Supreme Soviet as the republic's new prime minister. Savisaar resigned from the Communist Party at the beginning of 1990. He had been chairman of the republic's planning committee and helped to write Estonia's plan for economic autonomy (RFE Estonian service, April 3).

Soviet Press on Military Draft

In the face of widespread opposition to military service throughout the non-Russian Soviet republics, the USSR Council of Ministers announced that this year's spring call-up would begin on April 1. USSR Defense Ministry officials continued to voice displeasure over opposition to the draft, claiming that in many areas "a campaign of wrecking" had been launched to undermine what defense spokesmen called "an important, stirring, and festive event." In an interview with *Pravda* (April 2), Soviet First Deputy Defense Minister Mikhail Moiseev said some local and republican authorities had adopted an attitude of "connivance or even approval" towards draft evaders. *Krasnaya zvezda* (April 3) said there had been antiarmy campaigns in several republics encouraging young men to evade the draft. On March 31, the Uzbek Supreme Soviet discussed a proposal for altering the terms of military service to allow Uzbek recruits to serve near their homes. Uzbekistan thus joins a growing number of non-Russian republics whose elected officials have proposed or passed legislation contrary to the draft and service regulations mandated by Moscow (*TASS*, March 31). The fact that the draft decree was issued by the Council of Ministers was itself a first, indicating Moscow's efforts to invest the draft order with greater legitimacy. Previously, the order to begin the draft was given by the Ministry of Defense.

Georgia's Trade Unions Go Independent

The Georgian Council of Trade Unions has voted to become independent of the Soviet trade-union movement. In a report on a meeting in Tbilisi, TASS said the trade unions had admitted to having made mistakes in the past that had resulted in a drop in workers' standards of living. TASS said the Georgian trade unions would hold a congress in June to discuss organizational issues.

Another Alternative Draft Party Platform Published

A draft Party platform, differing from the official draft platform of the CPSU Central Committee, appeared in *Moskovskaya pravda*. The alternative draft was written by the Federation of Marxist Party Clubs. The draft criticized the leadership of the CPSU for attempting to preserve an unnatural unity in the Communist Party. It also condemned the CPSU leadership for "gradually transforming [the CPSU] into a social-democratic party." The alternative draft emphasized that only a Socialist system based on Marxist ideology "responds to the interests" of the USSR.

The Month of April

Sunday, April 1

Confrontation between Moscow and Lithuania Continues

On April 1, commenting on Gorbachev's warning that failure to retract the independence declaration could have grave consequences, President of the Lithuanian Supreme Council Vytautas Landsbergis said Gorbachev was threatening the safety of the Lithuanian nation. He said Gorbachev was asking Lithuanians to give up what they had cherished in their hearts for decades (*Radio Vilnius*, April 1). The same day, there were more Soviet troop movements in Vilnius and reports of tanks among the Soviet military vehicles (*Reuters*, *AP*, April 1).

On April 2, the Presidium of the Lithuanian Supreme Council called on Moscow to agree to talks with the Lithuanian government on a wide range of issues, including the restoration of Lithuanian independence. The Presidium noted that "overt Soviet military pressure" on Lithuania was increasing (*Reuters*, April 2). Radio Vilnius reported that Soviet troops had moved into the Lithuanian Party Central Committee press building in the capital. On April 3, four proindependence newspapers in Lithuania were told they could no longer publish at the Central Committee's plant (*TASS*, *Reuters*, April 3).

On April 3, the Estonian Supreme Soviet expressed its complete support for the aspirations of the Lithuanian people and their right to independence (RFE Estonian service April 3). On April 5, Lithuanian Television quoted a deputy of the Latvian Supreme Soviet, Danis Dansbergios, as saying his republic fully supported Lithuania.

On April 4, the Lithuanian parliament issued a statement saying the USSR was responsible for the political consequences of its actions towards Lithuania (*Radio Vilnius*, April 4).

The Belorussian Popular Front, "Adradzhen'ne," said Belorussian claims on Lithuanian territory should be settled by negotiations between "Adradzhen'ne" and "Sajudis." A spokesman for "Adradzhen'ne" said the movement was not in full agreement with claims put forward last month by the Belorussian Supreme Soviet that, in the event of Lithuania's gaining independence, Belorussia could claim the city of Vilnius and other Lithuanian lands (RL Belorussian service, April 4). See RL 175/90.

Meanwhile, the US House of Representatives approved a resolution urging President Bush to take steps "at the earliest possible time" to normalize diplomatic relations with the new government of Lithuania (*Reuters*, April 5).

Soviet officials continued to comment on the situation in Lithuania. Foreign Ministry spokesman Gennadii Gerasimov said Lithuania had the right to secede from the Soviet Union but must observe Soviet law if it was to do so (*RFE/RL Special*, April 4), and another Foreign Ministry spokesman, Yurii Gremitskikh, condemned the Lithuanian-Polish communiqué signed in March as an interference in the internal affairs of the Soviet Union. Gremitskikh told reporters in Moscow that the communiqué was an attempt to conduct relations with Lithuania as if it were a separate state (*Radio Warsaw*, *TASS*, April 4).

On the evening of April 4, Lithuanian television showed pictures of both pro- and anti-independence rallies in the republic. (The central Soviet press had accused the Lithuanian media of not giving anti-independence forces the opportunity to express their views.)

On April 5, the Lithuanian parliament adopted the final version of a reply to Gorbachev's demand that the republic rescind its decision to reaffirm its independence. The message said that the parliament proposed to hold, without delay, "initial, bilateral consultations" with Moscow (*Radio Vilnius*, *TASS*, April 5). The same day, the archbishop of the Russian Orthodox Church in Vilnius appealed to Gorbachev not to use military force in Lithuania. In his message, the archbishop said many Russian-speaking people in Lithuania were "very upset" that the republic's Moscow-allied Communist Party had "asked Soviet soldiers to help defend their material interests" (RFE Lithuanian service, April 5). TASS quoted Lithuania's permanent representative in Moscow, Egidijus Bickauskas, as saying the republic was ready for compromise on the issue of independence, and he did not rule out the possibility of a referendum. The same day, the Lithuanian parliament said about fifty armed Soviet troops had forced their way into the Lithuanian Prosecutor General's Office and had taken over the entire building (*Reuters*, April 5). A protest demonstration against this action took place on April 6 (*Radio Vilnius*, April 7)

On April 5, Radio Vilnius said about 300 mainly Russian-speaking people had demonstrated outside the Lithuanian radio and television headquarters, demanding that the broadcast services stop what the demonstrators called anti-Soviet and anti-Socialist propaganda.

On April 6, "Soyuz," the parliamentary faction within the USSR Congress of People's Deputies that favors the unity of the USSR, called for the introduction of presidential rule in Lithuania (*TASS*, April 6).

Another proindependence rally took place on April 7 in Vilnius. Those present, estimated to number hundreds of thousands, were addressed by Landsbergis and Chairman of the Council of Ministers Kazimiera Prunskiene, who urged the crowd to give its support to Lithuanian independence.

On April 8, USSR Foreign Ministry spokesman Gennadii Gerasimov complained that Lithuania could have given Gorbachev more time in his new office as executive president before pressing for independence (*Reuters*, April 8). In an interview with the ABC television network, USSR Foreign Ministry spokesman Vitalii Churkin said Lithuania was a Soviet issue, not a US-Soviet one. In contrast, USSR Foreign Minister Eduard Shevardnadze was quoted by Novosti on April 10 as saying US concern over Lithuania was understandable (*AFP*, *Reuters*, April 8). Another demonstration took place that day; crowds were reported to have gathered outside the main printing works in Vilnius after the arrival there of more Soviet security forces (*AFP*, *DPA*, April 8).

On April 9, the USSR Presidential Council described Lithuania's reply to Gorbachev concerning independence as unconstructive. TASS and Soviet television said the council had agreed on new political and economic measures designed to protect the USSR Constitution and the interests of Lithuanians. No details were given. The same day, the Lithuanian Supreme Council followed the republican Council of Ministers in ordering the Lithuanian authorities not to cooperate with this year's Soviet military draft (*TASS*, April 9). (The Lithuanian Council of Ministers issued a decree on the draft on April 6.)

On April 10, Gorbachev said presidential rule could be introduced in Lithuania "in an extreme case, if the situation develops into a civil conflict or hostile confrontation" (*TASS*, April 10). He reiterated the USSR's insistence that Lithuania rescind its decision on independence. Landsbergis sent Gorbachev a message urging him not to listen to extremist plans for Lithuania (*Reuters*, April 10).

On April 11, Bush told Baltic-American leaders that the United States must avoid taking any action in the Lithuanian secession crisis that would inflame the situation there (*AP*, April 11). *Pravda* published a commentary saying US congressmen were using confrontational language to encourage the White House to take a tougher stand on Lithuania.

On April 13, Gorbachev threatened to impose an economic blockade on Lithuania if it refused to rescind its declaration of independence within two days. Gorbachev and Prime Minister Nikolai Ryzhkov sent the ultimatum in a telegram to Lithuanian leaders. It said Moscow would order other republics to cut off deliveries of goods to Lithuania that could otherwise be sold for hard currency. Prunskiene, who read out the message on television, said the Soviet government could not expect Lithuania to continue exporting goods while receiving no imports (RFE Lithuanian service, *Reuters*, *UPI*, *TASS*, April 13).

On April 14, some 5,000 people gathered in Leningrad to call for a strike in support of Lithuania if Gorbachev imposed a blockade there (*AP*, April 14). The Soviet media apparently did not cover this demonstration. TASS did report, however, on a smaller anti-Lithuanian protest held the same day in Minsk.

On April 15, *Pravda* said, "There . . . cannot be a Lithuanian problem for the United States. It is really an internal matter for the Soviet Union." The newspaper's commentator Tomas Kolesnichenko, however, praised US President Bush for showing restraint on the issue and expressed hope that Lithuanian developments would do nothing to upset the superpower summit at the end of May.

On April 16, Lithuanian leaders called for urgent talks with Soviet leaders about Moscow's threat to impose economic sanctions. A telegram on the matter, signed by Prunskiene, was sent to Gorbachev and Ryzhkov (Western agencies, *Radio Vilnius*, April 17). RFE/RL was told that Lithuania and Estonia had agreed to exchange diplomatic representatives.

On April 17, the Frankfurt-based International Society for Human Rights reported that twenty-one Lithuanian conscripts seized by Soviet troops from a clinic in Vilnius several weeks ago had been sent to the Soviet Far East. According to the report, the youths are now stationed in two garrisons on the Chukot Peninsula, an area adjacent to the Bering Strait and approximately 9,000 kilometers east of Lithuania.

The same day, a speaker of the Lithuanian parliament announced the first Soviet economic sanction against Lithuania. Aleksandras Abisalas read out a message from a Soviet agency saying it was "sharply" reducing gas deliveries to Lithuania starting April 17 (*Radio Vilnius*, *AP*, April 17). (In fact, the sharp reduction in gas supplies started on April 19 [*Radio Vilnius*, April 19].) The supply of oil was cut off on the evening of April 18. In an interview with *Moscow News* (No. 16), Prunskiene said an economic boycott of Lithuania would harm the Soviet Union because Lithuania was one of the leading producers of oil-industry equipment, television screens, integrated circuits, and electricity meters for the Soviet Union. She also said that the first victims of the boycott would be Lithuanian factories that employed mainly Russian-speaking workers. Landsbergis said the oil cutoff would also affect Latvia, Estonia, and the Kaliningrad Oblast of the RSFSR. The USSR State Committee for Material and Technical Supply said, however, that, despite the cutoff of oil to the Lithuanian refinery, the supply of oil products to consumers in the neighboring regions would not change (*TASS*, April 19). On April 18, Prunskiene went to Oslo to hold talks with firms that had offered help if Moscow introduced economic sanctions against Lithuania (*AFP*, April 18). On April 19, Prunskiene discussed possible oil purchases with Norwegian Prime Minister Jan Syse (*UPI*, April 19). On April 19, residents of Lithuania were urged to conserve energy (*Radio Vilnius*, April 19). The same day, the Lithuanian Council of Ministers held a special session to discuss the energy situation (*TASS*, April 19). On April 19, Lithuania set up a commission to direct the distribution and rationing of products hit by the reduction in the fuel supply (*TASS*, April 19). See RL 190/90.

On April 18, Landsbergis urged the United States to take a stronger position in support of Lithuania. On April 19, he was quoted as saying the Soviet Union was drawing "a new iron curtain" around his country (*Reuters*, April 19).

On April 18, the Lithuanian parliament formally rejected Moscow's demand to revoke laws relating to independence but offered a two-week moratorium on new acts if Moscow agreed to talks (*Radio Vilnius*, April 18).

On April 19, President Bush and French President François Mitterrand discussed possible Western retaliation for Soviet economic sanctions against Lithuania (Western agencies, April 19). Concern at the Soviet imposition of economic sanctions was also expressed by Britain, Japan, and Poland (*UPI*, April 19). In Moscow, Foreign Ministry spokesman Vadim Perfil'ev sharply condemned US media coverage of Soviet policy towards Lithuania (*TASS*, April 19). Perfil'ev also warned that the Soviet Union may order more curbs on supplies to Lithuania (*TASS*, April 19).

The same day, a Polish deputy of the Lithuanian Supreme Council, Czeslaw Okinczyk, addressed the "Solidarity" Congress in Gdansk. He read a letter from Landsbergis thanking the union for support (*Radio Warsaw*, April 19). Speaking the same day in Vilnius, Landsbergis stressed that there was no question of Lithuania's going back on its declaration of independence (*Reuters*, April 19).

The second secretary of the pro-Moscow Lithuanian Communist Party, Vladislav Shved, said the situation in the Party had become very difficult on the eve of its congress. Shved said reporters from newspapers that "slander" the pro-Moscow Communist Party would not get accreditation (*TASS*, April 19). The same day, TASS said the Soviet leadership was still waiting for "a concrete reply" to questions raised by Gorbachev and Ryzhkov in their message to the Lithuanian government.

On April 19, President Bush said he was reluctant to take action against Moscow for its economic sanctions against Lithuania because of the effect this could have on US-Soviet relations, Eastern Europe, and many other countries. But Bush said there were limits beyond which Moscow should not go in dealing with Lithuania (Western agencies, April 19).

On April 20, Lithuanian Deputy Prime Minister Algirdas Brazauskas urged the Lithuanian Supreme Council to reach a compromise with Moscow over the republic's reaffirmation of independence. He told the deputies there was a limit to how long Lithuania could survive under economic sanctions (*AFP*, April 20). (On April 20, Moscow also started to cut deliveries of food and industrial products to the republic [*Reuters*, April 20].) The same day, reports from Vilnius said Soviet troops had occupied another key publishing facility (RFE Lithuanian service, April 20). A number of people protesting against the occupation were reported to have been hurt in the course of the troops' action.

The same day, AP reported that foreign correspondents were being allowed back into Lithuania, but only for a weekend trip organized by the USSR Foreign Ministry.

On April 21, "Sajudis" opened a congress in Vilnius. Addressing the congress, Landsbergis said Lithuanians had "a long and difficult path" ahead of them (*Reuters*, April 21). He said "Sajudis" had a new role but remained an essential organization. The congress adopted an appeal to the republic's government and citizens that said Lithuania was "breaking away from an empire that is economically impoverished and gripped by chaos." In a separate appeal, the Lithuanian national movement called on foreign governments to "resist by all possible means" the Soviet actions being taken against Lithuania (*Reuters*, April 21). The same day, a congress of Lithuania's pro-Moscow Communist Party also began. The congress delegates called on Gorbachev to declare direct presidential rule in the republic, and also for the resignations of Landsbergis and Prunskiene (*TASS*, April 21) The same day, *Pravda* carried a signed article attacking the leaders of the independent Lithuanian Communist Party. It said: "Instead of launching an active political struggle against the ideology of 'Sajudis' and its extremist wing, [the Party] has begun to adapt to the changing situation and has embarked on the road of a strange compromise that has strengthened the position of 'Sajudis' and weakened that of the Party." As a result, the article said, "Sajudis" had been able to take over the leading positions in the Party.

Meanwhile, the European Community issued a statement in Dublin criticizing Soviet economic sanctions against Lithuania. The statement fell short, however, of what Prunskiene wanted. She had appealed to the EC to recognize Lithuanian independence as a way of putting pressure on Moscow to end its economic sanctions (Western agencies, April 21). Reuters quoted Lithuanian Deputy Prime Minister Romualdas Ozolas as saying Moscow had now started an economic blockade of Lithuania. He told reporters that Moscow was also blocking financial transactions involving the republic's industry (*Reuters*, April 21). The same day, a top-level delegation from Lithuania, including Prunskiene, arrived in Copenhagen for talks with members of the Danish government and parliament (*AP*, April 21). On April 23, Prunskiene said she was satisfied with her Scandinavian trip, during which supplies of oil and natural gas to Lithuania were the main issue discussed (*Reuters*, April 23).

On April 22, the disinformation campaign against Lithuania continued. Moscow television reported that it had received information that the republic might delay its bid for independence for two years. Landsbergis flatly denied the assertion. On April 23, Landsbergis was quoted as saying Lithuanians should respond with civil disobedience if Moscow imposed presidential rule in the republic. He was also quoted as saying the Soviet economic blockade of Lithuania might be intended to cause mass unrest in order to provide a pretext for direct rule from Moscow (*UPI*, *Reuters*, April 23). The same day, "Vremya" devoted a lot of air time to Lithuania. It interviewed Russian-speaking workers, who said Lithuania's independence declaration had been a mistake. See RL 167/90.

On April 23, Reuters said Lithuania had begun closing down its only oil refinery owing to a lack of supplies from the USSR. Three thousand workers at that enterprise were affected. The same day, Landsbergis asked the republic's

Supreme Council to draw up an emergency plan to deal with possible mass unemployment resulting from Moscow's economic sanctions. Landsbergis also criticized comments about the possibility of use of force in Lithuania made by a close military adviser to Gorbachev. Marshal Sergei Akhromeev was quoted as saying the USSR could use force if necessary (*AP*, *Reuters*, April 23).

On April 24, a KGB spokesman in Moscow said border troops had tightened controls around Lithuania with the main aim of keeping out arms and ammunition (*TASS*, April 24). He said the checks also involved more extensive controls of persons, vehicles, and freight crossing Lithuania's borders. (*TASS*, April 24). Landsbergis sharply condemned the position of Western countries towards Lithuania. He compared the current position of the United States to British and French appeasement of Nazi Germany on the eve of World War II (*Reuters*, April 24). US leaders defended their policy against Landsbergis's criticism. President Bush said the political decisions he had taken on Lithuania had strong support from the American people (*Reuters*, April 25). US Secretary of State James Baker said both he and Bush thought the United States should follow "a balanced and measured" course with regard to Lithuania (*AP*, April 25).

On April 25, Prunskiene said Lithuania wanted to use its relative abundance of food to overcome the Soviet economic blockade of the republic. She told RFE/RL the republic was already in touch with Leningrad and Lvov about trading food for oil and other embargoed goods. Both the radical Leningrad City Soviet and the Lvov Oblast Soviet sympathize with Lithuania. She said another possible source of help was Tyumen, where oil and gas workers are in conflict with Moscow over local conditions. The Moscow City Soviet, headed by Gavriil Popov, would also be contacted by Lithuania, she said.

On April 25, West German Chancellor Helmut Kohl said the West should refrain from taking any action that would aggravate the situation in Lithuania and hamper *perestroika* in the USSR (*AFP*, April 25). French Foreign Minister Roland Dumas ruled out sanctions against the Soviet Union for the blockade (*UPI*, April 25).

On April 26, Gorbachev said in Sverdlovsk that he stood firmly by the demand that Lithuania must rescind its decision on independence before Moscow will consider the issue (*TASS*, *Radio Vilnius*, April 26).

On April 28, TASS said Moscow had cut coal supplies to Lithuania. It quoted Vladimir Kostyukhin, deputy chairman of the USSR State Committee for Material and Technical Supply, as saying, "There are large reserves of coal in Lithuania, for which it has so far not paid." Kostyukhin also said Lithuania was receiving only 30 percent of its former quota of natural gas, "which should fully meet communal needs if not used for industry." The same day, Denmark offered emergency medical aid to Lithuania to help people whose lives were threatened by shortages resulting from the Soviet economic blockade (*Reuters*, April 28). The Lithuanian government decided to start rationing some food items beginning May 1 (*Radio Vilnius*, April 29).

Commenting on the possibility of a dialogue between Moscow and Vilnius, presidential spokesman Arkadii Maslennikov said Moscow would not insist that Lithuania rescind its March 11 reaffirmation of independence, but nor should Lithuania insist on implementing it. He told Western reporters in Moscow that Lithuania should find a way to freeze or put a moratorium on its stand on independence and return to the Soviet constitution (Western agencies, April 28). Maslennikov also welcomed the Kohl-Mitterrand letter to Landsbergis, saying the main ideas expressed in it were not far from Gorbachev's own plans for a Lithuanian settlement. (The letter appealed to Lithuania to seek negotiations with Moscow and to "suspend" its independence efforts for a while.) On April 27, Prunskiene had also spoken positively about the letter, saying it might serve as a basis for a compromise.

On April 30, Lithuanian Deputy Prime Minister Romualdas Ozolas said in Copenhagen that Lithuania was ready to freeze implementation of its reaffirmation of independence in order to bring Moscow to the negotiating table (*Berlingske Tidende*, April 30). Landsbergis denied Ozolas's statement, however. He said he believed Ozolas had been misquoted by the Danish newspaper (RFE Lithuanian service, April 30). In her turn, Prunskiene also said the suspension or revocation of Lithuania's declaration of independence "is not even the remotest of possibilities."

On April 28, an organization of pro-Soviet Lithuanians who favor keeping Lithuania within the USSR was founded in Vilnius. Radio Vilnius quoted the organizers as saying more than 500 people attended the initial meeting.

On April 30, thousands of Lithuanians attended a memorial service in Vilnius for Stanislovas Zemaitis, who burned himself to death in Moscow last week (*Reuters*, April 30).

Developments in the Transcaucasus

On April 1, the newly appointed military commander of Baku, Major General Anatolii Kapliev, published a statement in the Azerbaijani press informing the population that "a reliable protective system" had been created to obstruct attacks by "armed Armenian extremists" in border areas. Kapliev also reported that thirty-five armed Armenians had been arrested over the past week.

On April 2, TASS reported that a two-month-old strike had ended in Stepanakert, the capital of the Nagorno-Karabakh Autonomous Oblast. The TASS report said the strike had affected factories, state institutions, and public transport in the city.

Kryuchkov Meets with Progressive Deputies

Central Television carried a fifty-minute report on a meeting that took place on March 23 between KGB Chairman Vladimir Kryuchkov and a group of liberal parliamentarians at KGB headquarters. Among the deputies were the chief editor of *Moscow News*, Egor Yakovlev; the playwright Aleksandr Gel'man; the Belorussian writer Ales Adamovich; the philologist Vyacheslav Ivanov; and, most notably, Sergei Kovalev, who was a political prisoner in the 1970s and was recently elected an RSFSR people's deputy.

The meeting highlighted growing KGB concern about public distrust of its work and about media criticism of the committee as an institution. Although Kryuchkov tried to sound as liberal as possible, he noted that he was not on speaking terms with *Ogonek*'s editor, Vitalii Korotich, because of two articles criticizing the KGB that were published in the journal earlier this year. The range of topics discussed at today's meeting included KGB relations with the anti-Semitic society "Pamyat'" and the fate of the KGB's archives.

KGB Military Intelligence Reduced

General Vasilii Sergeev of the KGB's Third Directorate, which is responsible for military counterintelligence, told a round-table discussion published in *Krasnaya zvezda* that more than thirty subdivisions of that directorate had been abolished. In all, the apparatus of the KGB's military counterintelligence has been reduced by 10 percent. Sergeev said one of its major tasks was the struggle against nuclear terrorism.

Gorbachev Calls for Better Conditions for Women and Children

Pravda featured a message from Mikhail Gorbachev to the USSR Supreme Soviet urging legislators to pass new laws to improve conditions for women and children. Gorbachev said that the matter "must take precedence over all else." He urged the legislature to pass emergency measures immediately to aid destitute families and called for new restrictions on the employment of women and juveniles in jobs entailing dangerous or heavy work, restrictions on night shifts for women, increased benefits for women and children, and more hard-currency expenditure on health care. Gorbachev cited the need for more flexible working hours and part-time positions (something almost completely absent from the Soviet economy) to help parents manage both work and child-raising. The most notable aspect of Gorbachev's statement, however, was that he said these rights should be extended to fathers and guardians—a progressive step in a society that has relegated child care almost exclusively to women.

On April 10, the USSR Supreme Soviet adopted a resolution on measures to improve the well-being of women and children. TASS said the measures included increasing allowances for children up to the age of eighteen months from thirty-five rubles to seventy rubles a month. TASS said similar allowances for nonworking women and for children in state or private care would be introduced. (For the text of the resolution, see *Izvestia*, April 13.)

Greens Consider Themselves a Political Party

Leaders of the Green Party in Leningrad said they now considered their organization to be a political party. TASS said the Green Party had been registered in the Moskovsky Raion Soviet in Leningrad as a new public organization. The report said, however, that members of the group considered themselves "a party with an ecological program," not a public organization.

***Moscow News* Condemns Military Action in Lithuania**

Moscow News (No. 13) strongly condemned the actions of Soviet troops in Lithuania. Specifically, it criticized the suggestion made by General Valentin Varennikov in an interview with *Sovetskaya Rossiya* that the army be used in Lithuania in the same way as it was employed in Baku in January. The weekly noted that people's deputies rather than generals should make such decisions. Another article in the same issue, signed by Novosti commentator Igor Sedukh, was even more critical. It condemned the pro-Moscow Communist Party in Lithuania, saying its appeal to the army to occupy buildings of the Independent Lithuanian Communist Party had only exacerbated the situation. Sedukh argued that such steps and the willingness of the military establishment to take orders from the pro-Moscow Lithuanian Communist Party had highlighted the need to depoliticize the armed forces. On April 6, the Soviet television program "Vzglyad" also let the voices of those demanding Lithuanian independence be heard and criticized "Vremya" for providing unbalanced coverage of the situation in Lithuania.

The same issue of *Moscow News* also carried an article sharply criticizing a leader of the Russian-speaking anti-independence movement in Estonia, people's deputy Evgenii Kogan. The weekly said that, in speaking about discrimination against non-Balts in the Baltic republics, Kogan had employed outright lies.

Union of Democratic Afghan War Veterans Speaks Out

Moscow News (No. 13) featured an interview with Vladimir Kovalevsky, the head of the unofficial Union of Democratic Afghan War Veterans. A lecturer at the Frunze military academy, Colonel Kovalevsky was expelled from the CPSU and stripped of his military rank in February, 1986, because he dared to compare the Soviet Union's invasion of Afghanistan with the US involvement in Vietnam. Besides helping veterans of the Afghan war, the Union of Democratic Afghan War Veterans is engaged in "the defense of democratic activities." Its members provide bodyguards for members of the anti-Stalinist "Memorial" society; they also offered to protect members of the "April" group of progressive writers following the attack on that group by "Pamyat'" on January 18. Right-wing extremist groups in the USSR, such as "Pamyat'" and "Lyubery," have already set up similar defense groups.

Oil Floods Village

The village of Syzran, on the Volga River, was flooded with 7,000 tons of oil from the ruptured "Druzhba" oil pipeline (*Izvestia*, *Radio Moscow-1*, April 4). It was reported that the oil formed two lakes, which inundated houses and gardens in the village. Residents were evacuated and gas and electricity to the area cut off to prevent fire. An earthen dam prevented the oil from reaching the Volga River nearby. *Izvestia* said this was the second pipeline accident in the region in the past few months and it complained that it was impossible for people living near pipelines to make operators improve safety.

Monday, April 2

New Law on National Equality, Territorial Integrity

Both chambers of the USSR Supreme Soviet passed a law "On Increasing Liability for Encroachments on the National Equality of Citizens and for Forcible Violation of the

Territorial Integrity of the USSR." An important feature of the new legislation is that for the first time it makes associations, not just individuals, liable to prosecution for activities aimed at propagating hostility and violence on an ethnic, racial, or religious basis and also for forcible violation of the territorial integrity of the Soviet Union. An organization found guilty will be disbanded and its property confiscated. For a summary of the law, see *Izvestia*, April 2.

New Law on Use of MVD Troops

The Supreme Soviet endorsed a new law "On the Duties and Rights of the Forces of the USSR Ministry of Internal Affairs in Safeguarding Order in Society." The MVD troops, which formerly could have been mobilized by order of the minister of internal affairs, can now be deployed only by presidential decree at the request of the Council of Ministers of a given republic or autonomous republic, or with the agreement of the USSR Council of Ministers. The head of the MVD troops, Colonel General Yurii Shatalin, told TASS that the new law also regulates the kinds of weapons and chemical substances that the special forces may use. He also said that experiments in forming special troops on a professional basis will be conducted over the next two years, although the costs of maintaining a professional interior force will be five times as high. Shatalin noted that, during the discussion of the law in the Supreme Soviet, there was a proposal to compose the special forces along ethnic lines. He said that, in many regions, indigenous soldiers already comprise 15 percent or more of special units, but he added that in some areas—presumably the Transcaucasus—such recruitment of indigenous soldiers "is not possible." For a summary of the law, see *Izvestia*, April 2.

On April 3, in *Krasnaya zvezda*, Shatalin elaborated on plans to man the MVD forces with volunteers on an experimental basis. Shatalin said switching to an all-volunteer force was "the behest of the times." The general said that the ministry had become aware of the need for a better-trained force when ten of its men were killed and four others deserted after internal troops were sent into Azerbaijan earlier this year.

***Pravda* Cautions against Anticommunism in Eastern Europe**

Pravda sharply criticized what it called "the dangerous trend" of anticommunism in some East European countries. *Pravda* said an anti-Communist wave was seeking to discredit Communist Parties and to call Party members to collective account. Urging a consolidation of "healthy forces," the paper said that unity based on understanding rather than hatred was needed in the creation of democratic societies. This article contains Moscow's harshest words yet on developments in Eastern Europe.

Psychiatric Abuse Said to Continue in USSR

The International Association on the Use of Psychiatry for Political Purposes said that the political abuse of psychiatry was continuing in the Soviet Union and that those responsible remained in their positions (*Reuters*, *AFP*, April 2). The group's general secretary, Robert Van Voren, told a Geneva press conference that affiliated Soviet groups had information on some thirty to forty political prisoners in psychiatric hospitals. This compares with about 1,000 such inmates five years ago.

Big Tax Break for Small Ethnic Groups

Cooperatives dominated by small ethnic groups in Siberia and the Soviet Far East will no longer have to pay state taxes, TASS said. The decision, apparently taken on local initiative, was announced following the end of the first all-Union conference of such ethnic groups. The Soviet news service also reported that land was being given back to these small nationalities in Khabarovsk Krai.

Belorussian Independence Party Calls for Sovereignty

The new Party of Belorussian Independence issued a call for the republic's political, economic, and cultural sovereignty, activists told RFE/RL. The party said it "reserves the right to be extreme" in pursuit of its goals. It called for the legalization of the white-red-white Belorussian national flag and the widespread use of the knight-on-horseback symbol of ancient Belorussia.

Personnel Changes in Ukrainian Party Leadership

Following his appointment to Mikhail Gorbachev's new Presidential Council, Grigorii Revenko was relieved of his duties as first secretary of Kiev Oblast Party Committee and as an alternate member of the republican Party buro, TASS reported. Former Second Secretary Anatolii Kikot replaces him in the Kiev post. In other moves, Vitalii Sologub was released from the republican buro at his own request, First Secretary of the Crimean Oblast Party Committee Nikolai Bagrov was named an alternate member of the buro, and Zaporozh'e Oblast Party leader Grigorii Kharchenko was promoted to full membership.

Tuesday, April 3

Shevardnadze in Washington

Upon his arrival in Washington for talks with US Secretary of State James Baker, Soviet Foreign Minister Eduard Shevardnadze told reporters that Moscow hoped to resolve the Lithuanian issue through dialogue with the people and the Lithuanian leadership (*AP*, April 3).

On April 4, it was reported that Shevardnadze had brought a response from Mikhail Gorbachev to US concerns over Lithuania. President George Bush wrote to Gorbachev recently urging a peaceful solution to the Lithuanian situation. The same day, Baker, who had started his talks with Shevardnadze, said Shevardnadze had again assured him that Moscow would not use force in Lithuania.

On April 6, Bush met with Shevardnadze. He was quoted as telling him that the way Moscow was dealing with Lithuania could impede progress in US-Soviet relations. Baker also had more talks with Shevardnadze. Baker confirmed that the Soviet foreign minister had suggested that his country might be willing to consider permitting direct flights for Soviet Jewish émigrés to Israel if Israel promised not to settle the émigrés in the occupied territories. Baker also said that the Soviet Union was dropping its demand that a unified Germany be neutral but that it would continue to resist its inclusion in NATO (*Reuters*, April 6).

Developments in Latvia

On April 3, the results of runoff elections in Latvia showed that candidates supported by the Latvian Popular Front had won only three of twelve contests held on April 1 for seats in the republic's Supreme Soviet (RFE Latvian service, April 3).

On April 5, Mikhail Gorbachev met leaders of the Communist Party of Latvia in Moscow. TASS said the meeting focused on ways to increase both Latvian sovereignty and the role of the Latvian Communist Party (*Reuters*, April 5). On April 5, deputies affiliated with the Latvian Popular Front formed a faction in the Latvian Supreme Soviet with the aim of proposing that Latvia declare its independence (RFE Latvian service, April 5). The same day, it was reported that the Latvian Communist Party had attempted to tighten control over the press in Latvia. Latvian Supreme Soviet deputy Eduards Berklavs said the Riga City Party Committee had halted publication of the Party newspaper *Rigas Balss* (Voice of Riga) because it had criticized the Communists. Opening the

Latvian Party Congress on April 6, Janis Vagris reiterated his warning against the republic's secession from the USSR (*Radio Riga*, 1217, April 6).

Poland Calls for Explanation of Border Restrictions

The Polish Foreign Ministry called on Moscow to explain its decision to restrict private and tourist traffic along Lithuania's border with Poland (*Reuters*, April 3). A ministry spokesman said "free border traffic is regulated by international agreements, which should be respected"; other officials said they had been advised that the restrictions were to remain in effect indefinitely. Border guards said that commercial traffic could proceed across the border but that Soviet visas were required for anyone else. Moscow imposed these restrictions in order to prevent people traveling to Lithuania from circumventing the Soviet Union's visa laws.

Laptev Elected Chairman of Council of Union

After several false starts, Ivan Laptev, the chief editor of *Izvestia*, was elected chairman of the Council of the Union (*TASS*, April 3). Laptev received 141 votes; his opponent, Konstantin Lubenchenko, 59.

Law on State of Emergency Approved

The USSR Supreme Soviet finally approved a law on a state of emergency. The bill establishes that a state of emergency can be imposed by the USSR Supreme Soviet or by the Soviet president if the lives of many people are endangered by natural calamities or mass disorders. It also says that any declaration of a state of emergency should include a statement about the grounds for the declaration, the exact area in which it is to be imposed, and for how long. USSR Justice Minister Veniamin Yakovlev said that the absence of such a law up to now had led to inaction on the part of the authorities and to the adoption of inadequate measures. For the text of the law, see *Izvestia*, April 9; *Pravda*, April 10. See also RL 197/90.

Gorbachev Appoints New Press Secretary

Gorbachev has appointed Arkadii Maslennikov, a former *Pravda* correspondent in Great Britain whom Gorbachev met in 1984, as his press secretary (*TASS*, April 3). Maslennikov is an experienced Soviet journalist who has spent his entire journalistic career with *Pravda*. Under Brezhnev, Maslennikov distinguished himself as one of the Party's top foreign propagandists and he has written numerous anti-Western articles. In 1989, he was appointed head of the Press Center of the new USSR Supreme Soviet.

Municipal Police Department Established in Dushanbe

TASS reported that Tajik parliamentarians had established an alternative force to preserve public order. Funded by local enterprises and individual contributions, the municipal police will defend law and order in outlying districts of the city. TASS said the need for such a body became evident during the February rioting. At that time the state police stayed primarily in the center of the city to defend Party and government institutions. People on the periphery were forced to defend themselves, which exacerbated the situation.

Ukrainian Party Backs Sovereignty

A plenum of the Ukrainian Communist Party passed a resolution proposing wide-ranging republican powers but rejecting the calls of "extremist elements" for Ukraine to secede from the Soviet Union. As summarized by Radio Kiev-3, the resolution calls for the full authority of the Ukrainian nation over its territory, the precedence of republican over federal legislation, and Ukraine's right to decide which powers it will delegate to federal organs. It also supports strengthening links between Ukrainian law and international law.

Meanwhile, Party leader Vladimir Ivashko endorsed the idea of transforming the Ukrainian Communist Party into a self-managing and independent organization within the ranks of the CPSU (*Radio Kiev-3*, April 3).

More Than 7,000 Soviet Jews Go to Israel in March

All but twenty of the 7,300 Jews who left the Soviet Union last month went to Israel, according to the Washington-based National Conference on Soviet Jewry. This is the highest monthly figure ever (*The New York Times*, April 3).

Wednesday, April 4

Law on Economic Relations between Moscow and Republics Adopted

The two chambers of the USSR Supreme Soviet finally adopted a law stipulating the basis for economic relations between the USSR and the Union and autonomous republics. The law comes into force on January 1, 1991. Under the new law the center retains control of the legislative bases of economic activity and the all-Union market, the organization of the tax system, overall pricing policy, the organization of a unitary finance and credit system and a single currency, and power systems. Two late changes would limit the powers of the republics: the independence of enterprises is to be guaranteed by their relations with republican and local organs of power on a contractual basis; and republics are banned from restricting imports and exports and introducing transit charges without the agreement of other republics. For the text of the law, see *Izvestia*, April 16.

Law on Mechanics of Secession Passed

Both chambers of the Supreme Soviet passed a law "On the Procedure for Dealing with Matters Connected with the Secession of a Union Republic from the USSR." The bill was adopted at the second reading with only thirteen dissenting votes in each chamber. The Baltic deputies declined to take part in the debate on the grounds that their republics cannot secede, since they were never legally part of the Soviet Union. Georgian deputy Tengiz Buachidze criticized the law as too tough and said the entire Georgian delegation would vote against it. See RL 187/90. For the text of the law, see *Pravda*, April 7.

Conservative Reelected to Head Leningrad Oblast Soviet

While democrats won elections to the Leningrad City Soviet, they failed to establish a majority in the Leningrad Oblast Soviet, where the previous head of the oblast soviet, Yurii Yarov, was reelected (*TASS*, April 4). Yarov is a member of the Leningrad Party *nomenklatura*. He studied together with Boris Gidaspov—the present Leningrad Party leader—at the Leningrad Technological Institute and became a candidate member of the Buro of the Leningrad Oblast Party Committee in 1986. In 1989, after having finished correspondence courses at the Leningrad Higher Party School, he was elevated by Gidaspov to the post of head of the Leningrad Oblast Soviet.

Solov'ev Back in Party

Former Leningrad Party First Secretary Yurii Solov'ev, expelled from the CPSU in February for illegally obtaining a foreign car, has been reinstated in the Party. After retiring, Solov'ev had bought an old Mercedes that was no longer being used to drive local Party leaders. Radio Moscow reported that the Buro of the Leningrad Party Oblast and City Committees admitted that a mistake had been made. The decision to expel Solov'ev seems to have been a tactical move by the local leadership to win electoral support; after the Party lost, Solov'ev could be readmitted.

Construction of Controversial Radar to Be Stopped

A government commission headed by Academician Evgenii Velikhov has decided to halt the construction of a phased array radar tracking station located in the Western Ukrainian village of Pestryalovo (*Radio Moscow-1*, 1700). The local inhabitants, concerned about the effects of the radar's electromagnetic radiation and heavy consumption of water, had protested strongly against the construction of the station. The radio said these concerns were justified and announced that the station would be put to economic use. This is the second radar station to be abandoned in as many months; in February, citizens in Kazakhstan forced the closure of a station there.

Foreign Ministry Disowns Dashichev

According to TASS, Soviet Foreign Ministry spokesman Yurii Gremitskikh said: "Professor [Vyacheslav] Dashichev and his political allies are not among the circle of experts who participate in the formation of Soviet policy." Gremitskikh's dismissal of the well-known Soviet foreign policy specialist came after Dashichev told a West German newspaper that Moscow's opposition to membership in NATO of a united Germany was only a negotiating ploy. Dashichev, a scholar at the Institute of Economics of the World Socialist System, said that the Soviet authorities would ultimately agree to such a proposal. Dashichev was thought in the past to reflect Gorbachev's own views. See RL 211/90.

Moscow to Investigate East German Mass Graves

The Soviet Foreign Ministry has begun a search through its archives for information about the mass graves recently found in East Germany, TASS said. The mass burial sites, apparently containing the bodies of victims who died in camps run by Stalin's secret police after World War II, have attracted much anti-Soviet comment in the East German media. A Soviet Foreign Ministry spokesman said, however, that the Soviet Union was not the only country to intern Germans after the war and that deaths from hunger, exhaustion, and disease were common in East Germany at that time.

More Ukrainian National Democrats Leave Party

Representatives of the national democratic movement in Ukraine are continuing to leave the Communist Party. This week, over twenty newly elected deputies to the Ukrainian Supreme Soviet from Lvov city and oblast issued a statement announcing their resignations from the Party. They denounced Marxism-Leninism in the USSR as a costly failure, condemned the principle of rule by a single party, and welcomed the formation of new political parties in Ukraine. Last week, four prominent leaders of "Rukh"—Ivan Drach, Dmytro Pavlychko, Volodymyr

Yavorivs'kyi, and Voleslav Heychenko—also left the Party, while three others were expelled (RL Ukrainian service, April 4).

Gorbachev's Reaction to Estonian Independence Resolution

Mikhail Gorbachev demanded that Estonia rescind a resolution declaring "a transitional period" leading to independence that was passed last week. Chairman of the Estonian Supreme Soviet Arnold Ruutel said Gorbachev expressed anger at the Estonian Supreme Soviet's actions in a telephone call on April 3. Ruutel said Gorbachev had called the resolution "invalid" and demanded that it be declared "null and void" (*Reuters*, *UPI*, April 4). Ruutel also disclosed that Gorbachev had summoned him to Moscow to discuss the independence resolution (*AP*, April 4). According to Western agencies, Radio Tallinn reported that the Estonian parliament had decided to send a message of protest to Gorbachev in response to the comments he made to Ruutel. On April 6, Ruutel said he would not go to Moscow (RFE Estonian service, April 6).

Tajik Deputies Protest about Distorted Reporting on Riots

In a letter to *Literaturnaya gazeta*, twenty-one Tajik people's deputies strongly objected to a report on the riots in Dushanbe on February 12–13 published in the newspaper on February 28. They described it as full of lies, malice, and half-concealed hatred of the Tajiks. A special correspondent for *Literaturnaya gazeta*, A. Kruzhilin, had alleged that, as a result of the riots, 260 Russian doctors had handed in their notice at two city hospitals. In fact, the deputies wrote, between January 1 and March 6, 1990, only twenty-six doctors from the city's fourteen medical institutions resigned in order to leave the republic. Kruzhilin also alleged that the vast majority of those injured in the riots and all those raped were Russians. The official figures are 565 casualties, of whom 226 were Tajik, 202 Russian, 22 Uzbek, 17 Tatar, 6 Ukrainian, 6 German, and 85 of other nationalities (including one Armenian). Of the 23 who died, 17 were Tajik (including a policeman), 4 Russian, and 2 Tatar. There have been no independent reports of rape.

Interview with Rasputin

Literaturnaya gazeta carried an interview with writer Valentin Rasputin, who was recently appointed a member of the new Presidential Council. The appointment of Rasputin aroused controversy because of his anti-Western and extreme Russian nationalist views. In the interview, Rasputin said he would use his new position to concentrate mainly on ecological issues. Asked about the appearance of his signature under the infamous letter of "seventy-four Russian writers," which in strong words blamed Zionists and other "evil forces" for the misfortunes of the Russians, Rasputin initially tried to evade the question. Later, however, he was pressed by the interviewer and finally said some of the statements in the letter "were unfortunate."

Thursday, April 5

Baltic Republics to Create Joint Wire Service

AP and AFP reported that the news agencies of Estonia, Latvia, and Lithuania had agreed to create a joint wire service called "Baltija." The reports said the Estonian ETA agency, Latvia's LETA agency, and Lithuania's ELTA agency had signed the agreement.

Consequences of Chernobyl' Still Felt

A USSR Supreme Soviet deputy said that 4 million people were still living in areas contaminated by fallout from the 1986 Chernobyl' nuclear disaster and that 118 villages should be evacuated immediately. Yurii Shcherbak said in Geneva that, four years after the accident, radioactivity remained at "seriously elevated" levels in parts of Ukraine, Belorussia, and the RSFSR. A Ukrainian hydrologist, Nikolai Kuz'menko, also said that water in the Dnieper reservoir was still heavily contaminated with radiation from the Chernobyl' disaster (*TASS*, April 5).

Friday, April 6

Armenian Party First Secretary Replaced

The Armenian Communist Party Central Committee replaced First Secretary Suren Arutyunyan with Vladimir Movsisyan, first deputy prime minister and chairman of Armenia's Agroindustrial Committee. TASS said Arutyunyan had requested a transfer to another position. Arutyunyan was appointed first secretary in May, 1988, following the first wave of ethnic violence concerning Nagorno-Karabakh. See RL 184/90.

Cathedral to Be Returned to Ukrainian Catholics

Ukrainian Catholic Church officials in Rome said the authorities in Lvov had decided to return to Ukrainian Catholics their main cathedral. A spokesman said the Ukrainian Catholics could have use of the cathedral of

St. George in Lvov starting next week. The cathedral is currently used by the Russian Orthodox Church (*AP*, April 7).

On April 11, the Russian Orthodox Church protested against the decision, saying it exacerbated the conflict between the two Churches (*Central Television*, April 11).

Shevardnadze Says He Intended to Resign over Tbilisi Affair

In the course of an interview on the popular television show "Vzglyad," Eduard Shevardnadze said that only the intervention of Mikhail Gorbachev had prevented him from resigning his posts as foreign minister and member of the Politburo in December, 1989. Shevardnadze was deeply upset after USSR Military Prosecutor Aleksandr Katusev told the USSR Congress of People's Deputies that Georgian demonstrators had provoked the military intervention in Tbilisi on April 9, 1989, and were therefore responsible for the resulting deaths. Shevardnadze, who was sent to Tbilisi immediately after the massacre, said he had promised that the truth about the incident would be made public and that he therefore found Katusev's misinformation intolerable.

Katusev has turned the investigation of the Tbilisi affair over to the State Prosecutor's Office, according to a report in *Literaturnaya gazeta* (No. 14), which explained that, although Katusev is supposedly independent of the Ministry of Defense, both his military rank and his working conditions depend on the military establishment.

Saturday, April 7

Leningrad TV Chief Attacked for Refusing to Air Ivanov Interview

The reformist-led Leningrad City Soviet attempted to fire the director of the city's television station for refusing to broadcast an interview with controversial former investigator Nikolai Ivanov. The members of the soviet ordered that Ivanov be given air time, but the director of Leningrad Television, Boris Petrov, refused to broadcast the interview as scheduled on April 5. The soviet then voted to fire Petrov. The State Committee for Television and Radio Broadcasting, to which Petrov is directly subordinate, overruled the decision, however. The interview with Ivanov was broadcast on April 6 (*Reuters*, April 7).

Belorussia Has New Prime Minister

The Presidium of the Belorussian Supreme Soviet appointed Vyacheslav Kebich the republic's new prime minister. Kebich replaces Mikhail Kovalev, who had asked to be released from the post in connection with his retirement. TASS said Kebich was fifty-four and had served as head of the republican planning committee since December, 1985. The agency said Kebich was popular in Belorussia for his role in guiding the republic's transition to self-management and self-financing.

Lizichev on Ethnic Problems in Soviet Armed Forces

According to reports carried by Radio Moscow and Central Television's "Vremya" newscast, a delegation of generals and officers from the USSR Ministry of Defense met in Tashkent with a group of Uzbek officials to discuss this spring's military call-up. Included in the group were staff members of military commissariats, leaders of republican ministries and departments, and various representatives of the public. Following the meeting, the head of the Main Political Administration of the Soviet Army and Navy, Army General Aleksei Lizichev, said in an interview that the Defense Ministry had been forced to reject hundreds of conscripts on the grounds that they were unfit for military service. He claimed that the number of conscripts suffering from nervous and psychological disorders had increased and that this was now a serious problem. Lizichev complained that the number of conscripts with religious beliefs was also increasing, as was the number of those who could not speak Russian. He warned that the rise in ethnic tensions throughout the Soviet Union was politicizing Soviet society and causing problems for the armed forces. He criticized groups who, in his words, were "deliberately trying to sever ties between the people and the army" and who were "slanderously attacking the Party, the army, and the organs of the KGB and the Ministry of Internal Affairs." See RL 224/90.

Medvedev on Gdlyan and Ivanov

Central Television broadcast an interview with Roy Medvedev, cochairman of the commission investigating charges of malfeasance against the investigators Tel'man Gdlyan and Nikolai Ivanov. Medvedev said that Gdlyan and Ivanov had indeed been involved in gross legal violations but that the USSR Prosecutor's Office, which was now prosecuting them, shared responsibility for their mistakes. (The USSR prosecutor-general today asked the USSR Supreme Soviet to deprive Gdlyan and Ivanov of their parliamentary immunity so that proceedings could be opened against them.)

New Measures to Help Chernobyl' Victims

The USSR Council of Ministers and the All-Union Central Council of Trade Unions adopted measures to improve medical care for people who took part in the cleanup after the Chernobyl' nuclear accident. TASS said the measures would include additional medical examinations and the creation of rehabilitation centers. On April 9, the Ukrainian government again appealed for international help to deal with the consequences of the Chernobyl' disaster. The appeal described the situation in the contaminated areas as still very serious (*TASS*, *Radio Kiev*, April 9).

On April 13, committees of the USSR Supreme Soviet on ecology and health care concluded two days of joint hearings on the effects of the Chernobyl' nuclear accident. TASS said the hearings had shown that people in contaminated areas were angry about the delay in implementing measures to eliminate the consequences of the accident. It was pointed out at the hearings that thousands of people had not yet been resettled or provided with uncontaminated food. TASS said people were especially upset because agricultural production was continuing in areas contaminated by radiation.

Latvian Communists Warned Not to Follow Lithuanian Example

A member of the Politburo warned Latvian Communists not to follow the path of Lithuania, saying their future would be bleak if they broke with the CPSU. Boriss Pugo, a former Latvian Party leader, said that the Lithuanian Party had been hurt by its split with Moscow and that such a break would be even more damaging for the Latvian Party (*Reuters*, *AFP*, April 7).

Demonstration in North Ossetia against Ingush Demands

According to "Vremya," several thousand people attended a rally in Ordzhonikidze, the capital of the North Ossetian ASSR. The rally was organized by various informal groups, ostensibly in support of the new law "On Increasing Accountability for Encroachments on the National Equality of Citizens and for Forcible Violation of the Territorial Integrity of the USSR." In early March, thousands of Ingush demonstrated for several days for the return to them of the Prigorodnyi Raion, which was given to North Ossetia when they were deported in 1944. The USSR Supreme Soviet recently set up a commission to look into their demands. According to "Vremya," among those taking part in the rally in Ordzhonikidze were representatives of the Greek, Armenian, and Cossack national cultural societies—i.e., traditionally Christian groups who would probably not look favorably on the prospect of being transferred to the jurisdiction of the Ingush, a traditionally Muslim group.

Sunday, April 8

Split in Latvian Communist Party

TASS announced a split in the Latvian Communist Party and the creation of a proindependence Party. This followed a walkout from the Party Congress in Riga by Party members favoring independence from Moscow. The walkout, which involved roughly 250 people, or about one-third of the members present, was staged to protest against a proposal by conservatives to defer the congress until midyear. The radicals viewed this as a bid to delay discussion of Latvian independence. The congress also elected a new Party first secretary, Alfreds Rubiks. Rubiks replaced Janis Vagris, who had held the post since October, 1988. Radio Moscow-1 (1400) reported that the congress adopted a resolution expressing support for those Estonian and Lithuanian Communists who had not broken ties with the CPSU. See RL 191/90.

Demonstration in Leningrad

A mass demonstration was held in Leningrad to mark the anniversary of the killings in Tbilisi in 1989 and to demand that similar events not occur in Lithuania. The demonstration was organized by the city soviet (*Central Television*, "Vremya," April 8). On April 10, *Sovetskaya Rossiya* criticized the Leningrad demonstration for being pro-Lithuanian and complained that the Leningrad City Soviet had permitted it despite the ban on pro-Lithuanian rallies. The newspaper alleged that speakers at the demonstration had incited interethnic hatred, and it complained that some speakers had sought to "impose their image of the USSR as a prison of nations."

Ligachev Advocates Party Purge

In separate interviews published in *Pravda* and *Sel'skaya zhizn'*, Politburo member Egor Ligachev said the CPSU must purge itself of revisionist and separatist elements that are weakening the Party from within. Those Party members who want to transform the CPSU into a parliamentary party with factions are, according to Ligachev, nothing but revisionists. Ligachev also said he favored coexistence and cooperation between states but not at the cost of abandoning socialism. If Eastern

Europe continued on its present course, he said, the Soviet Union might soon be the only Socialist state left in Europe.

Christian Democratic Party Created

Soviet television reported that a group of newly elected RSFSR people's deputies had set up a Christian Democratic Party in opposition to the CPSU. Cofounders of the new party were Viktor Aksyuchits, a religious writer and publisher, and Father Gleb Yakunin, a former political prisoner and leader of the informal group "Church and *Perestroika*." The party's draft program includes proposals put forward by other newly created democratic organizations, such as the establishment of a market economy and Western-style parliamentary government, and also stresses the growing role of the Church in society.

Soviet Foreign-Trade Deficit in 1989

Reuters cited the latest issue of *Ekonomika i zhizn'* as reporting a Soviet foreign-trade deficit in 1989 of 3.3 billion rubles. The agency did not, however, provide a breakdown of this figure between Socialist and non-Socialist nations. The preliminary data for 1989, given in the Goskomstat report (*Pravda*, January 28), had shown an overall visible trade deficit of 2 billion rubles, of which 800 million rubles were attributable to trade with non-Socialist countries. This, the first deficit in fourteen years, together with an estimated 8-billion-dollar increase in the Soviet Union's net hard-currency debt in 1989 and the evidence of a recession in 1989 and 1990, will hardly improve the Soviet Union's credit worthiness at a time when it is reported to be seeking major new credits. The same day, *Izvestia* said efforts to stabilize the market and improve the economy in the USSR had not brought the expected results in the first three months of this year.

Shatalin Interviewed

Academician Stanislav Shatalin, a liberal member of the Presidential Council, openly questioned the Party's insistence that the Soviet people chose socialism once and for all in 1917. In an interview with *Moscow News* (No. 14), he called for a referendum on the legitimacy of the October Revolution. Shatalin emphasized that he believed in many of the ideas of social democracy and said he thought he had influenced Gorbachev on that score, pointing to the latest draft Party program as evidence.

Pressure for Military Reform Builds Up

Komsomol'skaya pravda reported that the Armed Forces Subcommittee of the Supreme Soviet Committee on Questions of Defense and State Security had recently approved a draft plan for military reform. The draft plan calls for a gradual transition to a professional, volunteer army; civilian leadership of the Ministry of Defense; the introduction of alternative service; and a reduction in the number of political workers, officers, and generals and their replacement by increased numbers of sergeants and civilians. It also recommends the elimination of military construction detachments and seeks legal guarantees for the rights of military personnel. The commission that formulated the reform program was reported to be headed by Major Vladimir Lopatin, who also advocated the creation of national military formations in the republics and full accountability of the Defense Ministry to the Supreme Soviet and state organs. According to the *Komsomol'skaya pravda* account, seven institutes of the Academy of Sciences took part in the preparation of the draft, as did three military academies and four other institutes. That the Ministry of Defense opposes the plan was revealed, however, by the refusal of the Military Medical Academy, the Frunze Military Academy, and the General Staff Academy to take part in the work.

On April 13, *Izvestia* reported that the USSR Ministry of Defense had written to the USSR Supreme Soviet and the Council of Ministers proposing that the length of military service be cut from three to two years. It said the ministry also wants to create more posts for naval specialists, who would hold senior noncommissioned ranks. It also quoted Deputy Chief of the General Staff Grigorii Krivosheev as saying this would be a first step towards creating a professional army. Krivosheev said specialists would sign a three-year contract with the ministry and earn 200–380 rubles a month. See RL 171/90.

New Association for Independence Founded in Ukraine

A new association seeking independence for Ukraine held its founding congress in Lvov. Radio Liberty's Ukrainian service was told that the congress had elected Ivan Kandyba, a Helsinki monitor and former political prisoner, as leader of the association, which is called State Independence of Ukraine. Members of the Organization of Ukrainian Nationalists and of the Ukrainian Insurgent Army attended the congress. The congress issued a statement supporting Lithuania's campaign for independence.

Thousands Protest about Toxic Spill in Bashkiria

Thousands of protesters demanded that chemical plants near the city of Ufa be closed in the aftermath of a toxic spill that contaminated the city's water supply. Most of the population of Ufa has been without normal water since the Ufimka River was contaminated with a herbicide nine days ago. Another rally protesting about contamination of the water supply was held in the city on April 11. Radio Moscow said more than 900 people had signed a petition urging Gorbachev and Ryzhkov to declare part of Ufa an ecological disaster area (*Radio Moscow-1*, 1700, April 11).

Democrats Form Majority in New Moscow City Soviet

According to *Moscow News* (No. 14), the newly elected Moscow City Soviet consists of four independent blocs of deputies: the liberal bloc "Democratic Russia" (281 deputies); the Party apparatchiks' bloc "Moskva" (94 deputies); the bloc of independent deputies (35 deputies); and the national-Bolshevik bloc "Otechestvo" (10 deputies). Forty-three deputies have not yet decided which bloc to join.

Monday, April 9

Georgians Commemorate Victims of Tbilisi Massacre

Thousands of Georgians took to the streets to commemorate those killed a year ago when soldiers broke up a peaceful proindependence rally in Tbilisi (*UPI*, April 9). Mourners also demanded independence for the republic. Radio Moscow quoted Gorbachev as expressing sympathy for Georgians and for the families of those killed.

Soviet Germans Offered "New Kind of Autonomy"

Five representatives of the Soviet Germans were told by CPSU Central Committee Secretary Andrei Girenko in mid-March that it was impossible to restore their autonomous republic on the Volga, because of opposition from the local population in Saratov and Volgograd Oblasts. Girenko told them that instead the Party was offering them "a new kind of autonomy." They should remain where they are, set up national raions and village soviets, and then elect a government that would govern the 2 million Soviet Germans spread over the length and breadth of the Soviet Union "within the framework of the Soviet constitution" (*Frankfurter Allgemeine*, April 9).

Agreement on European Bank for Reconstruction

High-level officials from forty-two countries reached final agreement on the European Bank for Reconstruction and Development, according to Reuters. French President

François Mitterrand launched the idea for the bank last year, seeing it as the best way of directing international economic financial support to the battered economies of Eastern Europe. The bank's capital base will total some 12 billion dollars, and the countries of the European Community will hold 51 percent of this. The United States will have 10 percent of the bank's capital and the Soviet Union 6 percent. Moscow has agreed not to borrow more than its capital contribution for a period of three years. (Some countries had voiced concern that the Soviet Union's major economic problems could drain the bank's capital, leaving little or no money for the smaller countries.)

Tuesday, April 10

Shevardnadze and Hurd Sign Cooperation Agreements

The Soviet and British foreign ministers, Eduard Shevardnadze and Douglas Hurd, signed agreements providing for prompt notification of nuclear accidents and for expanded cultural, scientific, and educational exchanges, TASS reported. The agreement came after the first round of talks between Hurd and Shevardnadze. Hurd raised the issue of Lithuania, saying that Britain would like to see urgent and purposeful negotiations to resolve the issue of Lithuanian independence. Later in the day, Hurd met with Gorbachev and expressed satisfaction with his talks.

Politburo's Role Declining

Meetings of the CPSU Central Committee Politburo, which at the beginning of Gorbachev's incumbency were being reported as taking place on an almost weekly basis, are now occurring less than once a month. Since the beginning of this year, only three have been reported. In addition, the range of topics discussed by the Politburo has narrowed. On April 10, a TASS report of the Politburo's latest meeting indicated that it was restricted entirely to Party affairs.

El'tsin Again Criticizes Gorbachev

In the opinion of Boris El'tsin, the USSR should have introduced a presidential system only after the Supreme Soviet had passed a law regulating relations between the republics and Moscow. He told *Argumenty i fakty* (No. 9) that the republics should have decided themselves which functions to grant to the president. In other comments, El'tsin named Egor Ligachev and Mikhail Solomentsev as the initiators of the failed antialcohol campaign and criticized Gorbachev for relying on the ideas of a single economist—Leonid Abalkin.

Portrait of Boris Gidaspov

Sobesednik (No. 14) published a portrait of Leningrad Party leader Boris Gidaspov, whom it described as a capable industrial manager who is being manipulated by Party apparatchiks. According to the article's author, Mikhail Sokolov, Gidaspov's personality and his belief in a strong Socialist state were shaped by a long career in the military-industrial complex. Sokolov said that Gidaspov had become popular among hard-liners throughout the country last November after he managed to stage a workers' demonstration against reform. According to Sokolov, Gidaspov is a man of patriarchic-Bolshevik convictions who belongs to the generation that "missed the thaw [under Khrushchev] and ran fully into the period of stagnation."

Kirgizia Copies All-Union Model

Kirgizia became the latest republic to have its Party leader simultaneously serve as chairman of the legislature. According to TASS, Kirgiz Party First Secretary Absamat Masaliev has been elected chairman of the republican Supreme Soviet. That body also reelected Apas Dzhumagulov as prime minister.

Fund for Children Affected by Nuclear Tests

TASS reported that a private philanthropic fund had been set up to provide medical assistance for children affected by nuclear weapons testing in Semipalatinsk. The fund, which is headed by Kazakh writer Rollan Seisenbaev, is sponsored by Kazakhstan's antinuclear movement "Nevada-Semipalatinsk," the Soviet Literary and Children's Funds, and the Soviet Peace Committee, as well as by enterprises and educational institutions in Semipalatinsk Oblast and local newspapers. The TASS report said contributions had also come from firms in Japan, Finland, Hungary, and West Germany.

Soviet Praise for Radio Liberty

Argumenty i fakty (No. 10) said Radio Liberty's coverage of the RSFSR parliamentary elections was "well informed and professional." The weekly complained that Soviet coverage, in contrast, was poor. Soviet television interviewed a representative of the electoral committee who said no results would be available for a week. Meanwhile, Radio Liberty was carrying results and making predictions that later proved to be correct.

Party Reformers Denounced

In an open letter to Party members, the CPSU Central Committee sharply attacked the Democratic Platform, a group of reformists within the CPSU (*Pravda*, April 11). The letter, which was read on Soviet television, accused members of the Democratic Platform of trying "to split and even dismantle" the Party. The letter said the group wanted to turn the CPSU into "a shapeless association" and that the result would be the Party's removal from the political arena. On April 11, one of the founders of the Democratic Platform, Igor Chubais, urged CPSU members to leave the Party and join a new social democratic party. Chubais told Reuters that there was no longer any chance of the Party's transforming itself and that "those of us who have no illusions must act energetically and quickly."

On April 29, radical deputies and members of the Democratic Platform criticized the letter. A reply to the CPSU Central Committee, signed by Gavriil Popov, Yurii Chernichenko, Vladimir Tikhonov, Boris El'tsin, Igor Chubais, Vyacheslav Shostakovsky, and others, appeared in *Argumenty i fakty* (No. 15). The writers condemned the CPSU Central Committee for attempting yet again to speak in the name of millions of Party members and called for a referendum of Communists "on major issues concerning the development of the Party and the country." *Moscow News* (No. 16) carried an article in which Len Karpinsky also criticized the Central Committee letter, describing it as "the revenge of the Party apparatus" for the abolition of Article 6 of the USSR Constitution.

Thousands Rally in Moscow in Support of Gdlyan and Ivanov

Several thousand people held an unsanctioned rally in Moscow to support the former investigators Tel'man Gdlyan and Nikolai Ivanov. TASS said some participants in the rally accused the commission of the USSR Congress of People's Deputies dealing with the investigators' case of bias and demanded that its members resign. The rally's organizers called for a political strike and other nonviolent civil disobedience to support Gdlyan and Ivanov (*TASS*, April 11).

Tajik Party Requests Abolition of Leading Role

The Tajik Party Central Committee will ask the republican parliament to abolish the constitutional guarantee of the Party's leading role, TASS reported. TASS said the Central Committee had decided at a plenum to propose that and other changes in the republican constitution.

USSR Offers Troops for UN Peacekeeping

The Soviet Union said the time had come to involve troops from the major world powers in UN peacekeeping operations. Moscow said it was ready to provide such forces if asked. The Soviet Union was answering a request by the UN General Assembly for UN members to suggest how to make UN peacekeeping operations more effective (*RFE/RL Special*, April 11).

One Person Killed in Armenian Attack

TASS said one person was killed on April 9 when Armenians attacked an Azerbaijani village near the Armenian border. Several people were reported injured in the attack. TASS also said the situation in Nagorno-Karabakh had become aggravated again. The same day, the deputy head of the Erevan branch of the railway network, Al'bert Aroyan, said trains to Armenia were still being blocked in Azerbaijan (*TASS*, April 11).

On April 12, the Soviet media said Armenian militants had abducted five soldiers of the USSR Ministry of Internal Affairs from a checkpoint in an Armenian village. Radio Moscow said the abduction took place early that morning in the village of Aigipard in Armenia's Shamshadinsky Raion. On April 13, TASS reported that the soldiers had been found unharmed but without their guns and ammunition. It said that they had returned to their units and that a search was being conducted for the kidnappers.

NATO and US Reject Soviet Proposal on Germany

NATO and the United States rejected a Soviet proposal that a united Germany be a member of both NATO and the Warsaw Pact. Eduard Shevardnadze had told a Brussels magazine that dual membership should be seriously considered. A White House spokesman called the proposal "another formula for neutrality" (*Reuters*, *AFP*, April 11).

Estonia Rules Military Service Voluntary

The Estonian Supreme Soviet approved a law abolishing criminal penalties for Estonians who refused to serve in the Soviet army. The law also makes service in the Soviet army purely voluntary (*Radio Tallinn*, April 11).

Some Moldavians Refuse to Serve in Soviet Army

TASS quoted the military commissar of Moldavia, Major General Viktor Nazarov, as saying that some people in Moldavia had recently refused to serve in the Soviet army, citing political reasons. Nazarov said refusal to serve on political grounds had occurred for the first time during this year's spring draft. Previously, he said, there had been "isolated" cases of people refusing to serve in the army on religious grounds.

New Informal Organization Set Up in Donbass Region

A new unofficial association, called "Edinenie," has been set up in the Donbass region of Ukraine, TASS reported. The agency said the new association included representatives from several other organizations in the area, including the Taras Shevchenko Society, "Rukh," and the Jewish Cultural Society. It said its aim was to create an atmosphere of trust and friendship in the multinational region and help to solve ethnic problems.

Thursday, April 12

Economist Predicts Unemployment and Big Price Rises

The deputy chairman of the USSR Supreme Soviet Economics Commission, Pavel Bunich, said about 10 million people could become unemployed during the Soviet Union's transition to a market economy. He also said about 70 percent of the goods sold in the Soviet Union could double in price in 1991 under austerity measures being considered in parliament (*TASS*, in English, *AFP*, April 12). In an interview with *Pravda* on April 13, Chairman of the State Price Committee Vyacheslav Senchagov said Soviet goods were to be grouped into three categories with varying degrees of state control over prices. Senchagov said the state would continue to set prices for key commodities, such as oil, gas, coal, and ferrous metals, but in so doing would take account of world market prices. He said a second group of goods would be subject to "regulated prices," which would rise and fall within prescribed limits. The prices in the third group would be set by the market. He did not specify which goods the second and third groups would cover.

Agreement Reached on Baltic Common Market

The prime ministers of the Baltic republics signed an agreement in the Lithuanian capital of Vilnius creating a Baltic common market. A joint statement was issued saying the three republics had agreed to eliminate restrictions on the free flow of goods and services and to establish direct trade links between individual enterprises. The statement said that each of the three Baltic republics had pledged to create its own currency (*Reuters*, April 12).

USSR Proposes Provisional Government for Afghanistan

The Soviet Union proposed a provisional government for Afghanistan whose sole task would be to organize general elections. A spokesman at the Soviet embassy in Islamabad said the provisional administration would include Afghan factions from Afghanistan, Pakistan, Iran, and elsewhere. TASS said a political solution to the conflict was discussed today when Afghan President Najibullah met a UN envoy to Afghanistan (*TASS*, *AP*, *Reuters*, April 12).

USSR Seeks Japanese Cooperation in Raw Material Production

Officials at the Soviet embassy in Tokyo said Moscow was seeking Japanese participation in a major coal, oil, and natural-gas production deal in the Soviet Far East. USSR Minister of the Coal Industry Mikhail Shchadov, who was visiting Tokyo, met Japanese power and trading company representatives and proposed that his ministry supply 3 million tons of Siberian coal a year for ten years in exchange for Japanese capital goods, including drilling, sorting, and transport equipment (*Reuters*, April 12).

One Dead in Chemical Accident in Kazakhstan

TASS said a child had died after inhaling toxic hydrogen sulfide fumes in a chemical spill in the town of Ural'sk in northwestern Kazakhstan. TASS said the fumes were produced by a chemical reaction that took place after workers dumped sulfuric acid in the town's sewage system. TASS said the fumes spread through a populated area, and the concentration of hydrogen sulfide in the air there was reported to have been sixty times the permissible level. TASS did not say when the incident took place.

Tajik Supreme Soviet Elects New Chairman

Kakhar Makhkamov was elected chairman of the Supreme Soviet of Tajikistan. Makhkamov, who was the republic's Communist Party first secretary, defeated the incumbent chairman, Gaibnazar Pallaev, by 162–62 in a secret ballot (*TASS*, April 12). On April 13, the Supreme Soviet reelected Izatullo Khaeev as the republican prime minister (*TASS*, April 13).

Moscow Welcomes Havel's Proposal on European Security Commission

Soviet Foreign Ministry spokesman Yurii Gremitskikh has welcomed Czechoslovak President Vaclav Havel's proposal to set up an all-European security commission. TASS quoted Gremitskikh as saying the proposal corresponds with "our common efforts" to create a new European security structure.

Friday, April 13

USSR Issues Official Apology for Katyn Massacre

The Soviet Union formally apologized for the Katyn massacre and called it "one of the gravest crimes of Stalinism." The official admission of Soviet guilt—issued by TASS—reverses more than forty-five years of Soviet assertions that the Nazis were responsible for the crime. The Soviet statement came during a visit to Moscow by Polish President Wojciech Jaruzelski. Polish reaction was mixed. Polish deputy government spokesman Henryk Wozniakowski said the government was "very satisfied," adding that the issue had been a burden to Soviet-Polish relations. "Solidarity" Chairman Lech Walesa said the USSR must compensate the victims' families and punish those responsible (*Reuters*, *PAP*, in English, April 13). At a dinner for Jaruzelski on April 13, Mikhail Gorbachev said that it was not easy to talk about the massacre of the Polish officers but that telling the truth was the only way to reach real mutual understanding. Gorbachev also gave Jaruzelski a number of archive documents concerning the massacre. Jaruzelski visited Katyn on April 14 (*TASS*, Western agencies, April 13).

Saturday, April 14

Armenians Storm KGB Headquarters

A crowd of some 1,000 people tried to storm and burn the Armenian KGB headquarters in Erevan, TASS and Western agencies reported. One protester was killed. The KGB said the death occurred when a homemade bomb went off; Armenian activists claimed that a device had been thrown at the crowd from within the KGB building. The 1,000 protesters had broken away from a larger rally demonstrating against the release of poisonous gas from a chemical plant in Erevan.

Number of Soviet Advisers in Afghanistan Increased

Novosti press agency quoted Western diplomats in Pakistan as saying the Soviet Union had raised the number of its advisers in Afghanistan from approximately 300 to 500. The increase was reported to have begun in December, 1989, following growing internal troubles in the Afghan army. The diplomats said the advisers were being used primarily for training and defense. They also said the Soviet Union had increased deliveries of weapons, food, and fuel to Afghanistan. The diplomats estimated that the Soviet Union was currently spending 350 to 400 million dollars per month on supplies for Afghanistan, up from approximately 300 million last year. Arms and ammunition were said to account for about 80 percent of the supplies.

Komsomol Congress Condemns Central Committee Statement

The Twenty-first Congress of the All-Union Komsomol passed a resolution condemning the attack on the Democratic Platform by the CPSU Central Committee on April 11. Despite an attempt by the Party ideologist Vadim Medvedev to persuade the congress to withdraw the resolution, it was confirmed on April 16. The resolution of the Komsomol Congress called the Central Committee statement "a serious political error of judgment" and a return to the pre-*perestroika* era. It also called on the Party to refrain from using administrative methods against dissidents and on the leaders of the Democratic Platform not to form factions within the CPSU before the Party Congress (*Central Television*, April 16).

On April 18, the All-Union Komsomol elected Vladimir Zyukin first secretary of its Central Committee. TASS said Zyukin was a member of the CPSU and a mechanical engineer. He had served as a Komsomol Central Committee secretary since 1989.

Latvia's Independent Communists Elect Leader

Latvia's newly formed independent Communist Party elected Ivars Kezbers as its leader at the independent Latvian Communist Party's founding congress, Radio Moscow reported. From 1985 to 1987 Kezbers was chairman of Latvia's State Committee for Radio and Television, and in 1988 he became the ideological secretary of the Latvian Communist Party. As recently as last month Kezbers went on record as saying that he would not consider joining an independent Latvian Communist Party.

Sunday, April 15

Shakeout of Party "Extremists" Proposed

In an editorial, *Pravda* repeated the call of the CPSU Central Committee made on April 11 for the leaders of the Democratic Platform to be expelled from the CPSU. *Pravda* said that, "unfortunately," the Central Committee's letter had been seen by some as a signal for "reprisals" against independent-minded Communists. While ruling out "a return to the methods of the 1920s and 1930s" and denying that a Party purge was in the offing, *Pravda* said that the Party nonetheless needed "purification."

Interviewed on Soviet television on April 15, Politburo member Egor Ligachev said it was already too late to prevent a split in the Party's ranks. Citing the upheavals in the Baltic republics, Ligachev said, "There is no longer a united Communist Party." He said it would be futile to try to delay a split in the Party until the Party Congress.

Republics to Pay for Refugees

Radio Moscow announced that republican governments in Armenia and Azerbaijan would have to pay the costs of the more than 500,000 refugees from that area. The radio said Moscow would assume the costs of other refugees, who now include more than 600,000 Soviet citizens. By shifting the burden to the republics, Moscow may hope to make republican leaders think twice before backing popular agitation for change.

Marxist Platform in CPSU Holds Constituent Congress

A group of Party members calling themselves the Marxist Platform held a constituent congress in the town of Bykovo near Moscow over the weekend. The group—which published its platform in *Pravda* on April 16—called for a return to "classic Marxism" and denounced private ownership of the means of production. Although the Marxist Platform clearly intends to stand in opposition to the Democratic Platform, in an interview on Soviet television on April 14, the leaders of the Marxist Platform condemned the CPSU Central Committee statement of April 11, which attacked the Democratic Platform. They said the Central Committee statement had been motivated by material rather than ideological considerations, in particular by the fear that, in the event of a split in the Party, the Democratic Platform would demand a share of the Party's assets. Pointing out that members of the Democratic Platform had paid the same Party dues as anyone else, the Marxist Platform said such a demand would be fully justified.

Nina Andreeva Plans to Set Up New Bolshevik Party

Interviewed on Radio Budapest on April 15, Nina Andreeva said the "Edinstvo" (Unity) group she heads would hold its "second national congress" later this month. She said the group may decide to turn itself into a party. To be called "The New Bolshevik Party," it would dedicate itself to fighting what Andreeva called "the petty bourgeois, social-democratic, revisionist distortions" of "the right-wing opportunist group of Gorbachev, Yakovlev, and Shevardnadze."

Shift in Antidrug Policy Reported

Speaking on Radio Moscow (0300), Deputy Prime Minister Aleksandra Biryukova acknowledged that the Soviet antidrug program had not achieved "decisive successes." She said a new program was being formulated that would concentrate on reducing the demand for drugs rather than on interdiction of the drug trade. She said the government plan would be aimed at identifying the causes of drug use and would focus on schools and families. She said the help of cultural figures and the mass media would be enlisted. According to Biryukova, the policy shift received wide support at an international meeting on fighting drugs that she attended in London last week.

Monday, April 16

Meeting of Moscow City Soviet

Moscow's newly elected city soviet, in which the progressive "Democratic Russia" bloc holds 281 of the 465 seats, convened for the first time (*Central Television*, April 16). The progressives won an early victory in ensuring television coverage of the session and made a splash when they proposed donating the sturgeon in the private buffet to the poor. They also proposed the housing of homeless Muscovites in vacant buildings. To preempt such a move, a few weeks ago the Moscow city Party authorities quietly took possession of a number of buildings from the outgoing city soviet. In addition, on April 14 the Party announced that it was taking over Moscow's two local newspapers, *Moskovskaya pravda* and *Vechernyaya Moskva*, which have until now been jointly published by the Party and the city soviet. The move was clearly intended to curtail the access of the progressives to the mass media.

One of the soviet's first moves was the adoption of an appeal to the USSR Supreme Soviet, which met in the Kremlin on April 16, to consider carefully whether to lift the parliamentary immunity of the two former prosecutors Gdlyan and Ivanov. Deputies to the Moscow City Soviet criticized the findings of the official commission looking into the affair.

Azerbaijani Blockade of Armenia Continues

Radio Moscow said that the Azerbaijani rail blockade of Armenia was continuing, harming production elsewhere. The radio said Azerbaijanis had blocked the railroads into Armenia for 60 of the first 100 days of this year, stranding 180 trains elsewhere because there were no engines to move them. It added that the shortage of freight cars inside Armenia was now so acute that officials there had stopped loading cars destined for outside the republic.

Takeover of Lvov Cathedral by Catholics Delayed

Although the Lvov City Soviet had ordered the Russian Orthodox Church to turn over St. George's Cathedral to the Ukrainian Catholics in time for Easter, local officials decided not to press the matter following protests by Russian and Ukrainian Orthodox officials last week. The new chairman of the oblast soviet, Vyacheslav Chornovil, said the transfer had been delayed to "avoid a confrontation" (RL Ukrainian service, April 16).

No Change in Moscow's Position on Kurile Islands

Soviet Deputy Foreign Minister Vladimir Petrovsky told a Tokyo news conference that Shevardnadze's proposal on the Kurile Islands on April 12 did not represent any change in Moscow's position on Soviet sovereignty there, according to AFP. Shevardnadze had proposed that the two countries conduct joint ecological experiments on the disputed islands. The proposal and the denial came as Soviet officials sought to elicit Japanese participation in coal, oil, and natural gas production in the Soviet Far East. Japan has long maintained that it will not make major investments in the USSR until the disputed Kurile Islands are returned.

Deficiencies in Chernobyl' Cleanup Investigated

Major deficiencies and neglect in the effort to clean up after the Chernobyl' disaster were reported at a meeting of the Collegium of the USSR Prosecutor's Office. According to TASS, the USSR Prosecutor's Office has uncovered repeated violations of radiation safety rules, distortion of medical reports, poor medical treatment and observation, theft, and improper compensation of victims. The report did not cite specific violations, but it did say that they had been stopped and were under criminal investigation. The meeting also sharply criticized the Belorussian and Ukrainian Prosecutors' Offices for not reacting to such violations. In response, the collegium decided to set up special offices of the USSR Prosecutor-General in the region and to create a commission to coordinate the cleanup work.

Work on Ivanovo Nuclear Plant Halted

Radio Moscow (0330) reported that the USSR Ministry of Atomic Energy and Industry had decided to cancel plans to build a nuclear power plant located on the Volga River in Ivanovo Oblast, northeast of Moscow. Saying that "a calamity has been averted on the Volga," the radio added that the decision had been made at the request of the Ivanovo Oblast Executive Committee and that the ministry had also decided to halt construction on a nuclear-powered heating plant located in the oblast. This is the fourth time work on a nuclear power station has been halted this year. The other plants affected are near the cities of Arkhangel'sk and Rostov-on-Don, and in Karelia, near the Finnish border.

Soviet Television Provides Data on Pollution Problems

The USSR State Committee for the Protection of the Environment said 40 million Soviet citizens lived in regions where there was "a catastrophic level" of air pollution. The committee also said 15 percent of Soviet towns and 47 percent of villages had no sewage system. It said 70 percent of the water used in the Soviet Union was returned to nature without complete purification (*Central Television*, April 16).

Tuesday, April 17

Gdlyan-Ivanov Affair Discussed in Parliament

The USSR Supreme Soviet began discussion of a request by the USSR Prosecutor's Office to revoke the immunity of two people's deputies, the investigators Tel'man Gdlyan and Nikolai Ivanov, so that they could be brought to trial. Gdlyan and Ivanov have accused virtually the entire Soviet establishment, including Egor Ligachev, of involvement in organized crime (*Izvestia*, April 18). The two investigators did not attend the debate. They were reported to be in Armenia, where they have been nominated for election to the Armenian Supreme Soviet. Roy Medvedev, a cochairman of the commission set up by the Congress of People's Deputies to investigate the Gdlyan-Ivanov affair, told the Supreme Soviet that the USSR Prosecutor's Office was no less guilty than the two investigators of violations of the law in this case. Anatolii Denisov, the chairman of the Supreme Soviet's Ethics Commission, spoke after Medvedev. He said Gdlyan and Ivanov had violated the principles of parliamentary ethics. USSR Prosecutor-General Aleksandr Sukharev and KGB Chairman Vladimir Kryuchkov also addressed the Supreme Soviet on the issue.

On April 17, the deputies had still not decided whether to lift the parliamentary immunity of Gdlyan and Ivanov. In the course of the debates, many deputies, including those who favor the prosecution of Gdlyan and Ivanov, demanded the removal of Sukharev and his entire collegium.

The same day, an estimated 50,000 Muscovites rallied at the Kremlin Wall in support of Gdlyan and Ivanov. Many of the banners shown on television carried anti-Gorbachev slogans, accusing the Soviet president of having patronized the "mafia" that Gdlyan and Ivanov were investigating before their dismissal. Two hundred deputies of the Moscow City Soviet—almost half that body—attended the demonstration (*Central Television*, "Vremya," April 17). The earlier edition of "Vremya" showed a demonstration in Leningrad in support of Gdlyan and Ivanov. That demonstration was called by the Leningrad City Soviet, which, however, rejected a motion calling for a general strike in Leningrad in support of Gdlyan and Ivanov.

On April 18, the USSR Supreme Soviet adopted a resolution saying that Gdlyan and Ivanov had grossly violated the law. It did not, however, lift the investigators' parliamentary immunity, which would have allowed criminal proceedings against them (*TASS*, April 18). The resolution instructed Gdlyan and Ivanov to stop making insinuations about present members of the Party leadership—Egor Ligachev in particular—or risk losing their immunity in the future. The Supreme Soviet did agree to allow Gdlyan and Ivanov to be formally fired from their jobs in the USSR Prosecutor's Office. Perhaps the most important provision of the resolution was a suggestion that all investigations now being conducted by the Prosecutor's Office, the MVD, and the KGB be concentrated in a single body directly subordinate to the Supreme Soviet and thus independent of Party bodies (*Central Television*, April 18; *Izvestia*, April 19).

Shalaev Replaced as Trade-Union Chief

Stepan Shalaev retired from his post as chairman of the All-Union Central Council of Trade Unions (AUCCTU), TASS reported. He had held the post since 1982. Shalaev was replaced by fifty-two-year-old Gennadii Yanaev, who had been a secretary of the AUCCTU since 1986 and deputy chairman since 1989. His appointment—which was overseen by CPSU Central Committee Secretary Georgii Razumovsky—came at a time when the official unions were trying hard to improve their public image. Their track record as defenders of working-class interests was badly tarnished during the miners' strikes in the summer of 1989, when Shalaev negotiated not on behalf of the strike committees but as a member of the government team.

May Day Slogans Published

The CPSU Central Committee published its official slogans for May Day. The 1990 slogans reflected recent political developments. Gorbachev figured for the first time, but was mentioned not by name but in his new capacity as president. Also making their debut were cooperative workers: they were enjoined to "provide the population with goods and services." The CPSU's new-found goal of "humane, democratic socialism" found favorable mention, as did "the state based on the rule of law" and "common human values." Members of the CPSU were exhorted to "establish the Party's vanguard role through concrete actions" and to "consolidate the Party's ranks on a principled basis." Any hint of class struggle was banished, as were "imperialism," "neocolonialism," "hegemonism," and "fascism." Foreigners, insofar as they were referred to at all, were warmly commended as "fighters for social progress" and "democratic forces." Condemnation was reserved exclusively for "nationalist and separatist forces" inside the Soviet Union's own borders (*Pravda*, April 17).

Difficulties in Disposing of Chemical Weapons

Sergei Batsanov, who heads the Soviet negotiating team at the US-Soviet talks on chemical weapons, told Radio Moscow the USSR would be unable to conclude a chemical weapons treaty with the United States, because it does not have the facilities to destroy its stockpiles.

In January, 1989, Foreign Minister Eduard Shevardnadze told an international conference in Paris that the Soviet Union would soon complete construction of a facility to destroy chemical weapons in the town of Chapaevsk and would start destroying its weapons stockpiles there as soon as the facility was ready. Operations never commenced, however, and the facility, which is located in a densely populated area near the Volga, became the target of numerous protests by local residents. Last August, a special government commission reviewing the public's concerns recommended that the facility not be used for the destruction of chemical weapons but be converted to other uses. Batsanov said that the Soviet Union was now looking for new sites; a US offer to help construct a new facility that would not endanger the environment is now under discussion.

Head of Soviet Military Intelligence Interviewed

The Daily Telegraph published an unusual interview with Colonel General Vladlen Mikhailov, the chief of Soviet military intelligence (GRU). Mikhailov contrasted the GRU's duties with those of the KGB, stating that the GRU is responsible purely for military intelligence, including radio reconnaissance from Soviet territory, air reconnaissance, and monitoring foreign radio broadcasts. He also said that methods for acquiring information from the West had changed in recent times and he claimed that theft had been replaced by open sources and by sending people directly to exhibitions, conferences, and air shows. Mikhailov also said that the recent deemphasis on military capability had enhanced the role of intelligence gathering in both East and West.

Palestinian Delegation in Moscow to Protest against Jewish Emigration

A Palestinian delegation arrived in Moscow to protest against the mass emigration of Soviet Jews to Israel, according to Reuters. Faisal Al-Husseini, a leading Palestinian nationalist on the West Bank, told a news conference, "We do not demand that Jews should not emigrate, but we call on other countries to open their doors, and then we would know who wants to go to Israel and who would rather go somewhere else." The delegation participated in a round-table discussion with US embassy officials, Soviet Foreign Ministry representatives, and Soviet Jewish organizations.

Independence Rallies in Georgia

More demonstrations took place in Georgia to demand that Tbilisi take action over South Ossetia and that a referendum be held on Georgian independence, Radio Moscow reported. The radio's Interfax news service said that the protesters had given the Georgian leadership a week to act or face strikes, a blockade of South Ossetia, and the picketing of state and Party offices in Tbilisi itself. One of the rallies took place outside the offices of the Tbilisi military commandant to protest against the detention of Georgians who have sought to evade the draft.

Interethnic Clashes in Nagorno-Karabakh Increase Again

Radio Moscow reported that there had been an increase in clashes between Armenians and Azerbaijanis in Nagorno-Karabakh. Shooting incidents and the stoning of vehicles have become more frequent and there have been an unspecified number of casualties. The radio said that there had been continual exchanges of gunfire in an outlying district of Stepanakert and that Soviet patrols there had come under fire.

Ukrainian Party and Government Denounce Nationalism

The Ukrainian Party and government issued a statement denouncing "an unbridled nationalist campaign" in Lvov, Ivano-Frankovsk, and Ternopol Oblasts in Western

Ukraine, Radio Moscow reported. The statement said there had been active calls for secession from the USSR and for the creation of an independent Ukrainian state. It added that the conflict between Uniates (Eastern-rite Caatholics) and Orthodox believers was being deliberately stirred up, and it claimed that "Rukh," the Ukrainian Helsinki Union, and other groups were calling for young people to refuse to serve in the Soviet Armed Forces. In conclusion, the statement said decisive measures would be taken to enforce Soviet laws and the USSR Constitution. This was the harshest official statement yet from Kiev on the growth of nationalism in Ukraine. On April 18, the Lvov Oblast Soviet condemned the statement on nationalism (RL Ukrainian service, April 19). Radio Kiev complained that the election of former political prisoner and Ukrainian Helsinki Union leader Vyacheslav Chornovil as chairman of the Lvov Oblast Soviet had "aggravated tensions" in the region (*Radio Kiev-3*, 2100, April 19).

Members of Democratic Platform Leave CPSU

Nikolai Medvedev, a secretary of the Party committee at an instrument-making works in Mordovia who was recently elected to the RSFSR Supreme Soviet, was expelled from the Party. According to Radio Moscow, Medvedev was charged with "breaking the Party rules, factional activity, and membership in the Democratic Platform." Last week, the expulsion was announced of Democratic Platform leader Igor Chubais (on Chubais' expulsion see *Moscow News*, No. 16). On April 19, Yurii Afanas'ev was reported to have left the CPSU of his own accord. He told Reuters the Party was beyond redemption and that to remain a member was "equal to spreading illusions" that it can reform.

Latvian Popular Front Appeals to World

The Latvian Popular Front issued an appeal to all governments of the world "not to leave the Baltic states at the mercy" of the USSR. The appeal called on governments to exert diplomatic and economic pressure to persuade the USSR to start immediate negotiations with Lithuania and "to support Estonia and Latvia in the same way." The appeal said the Latvian Popular Front was not pleading for sympathy but "asking for concrete and effective help" (RFE Latvian service, April 17).

Leningrad Party and City Soviet Divide Control of Press

The conservative Leningrad Party organizations and the liberal Leningrad City Soviet divided responsibility for newspapers there. In the past, *Leningradskaya pravda* was a joint organ of the Leningrad Party Committee and the Leningrad City and Oblast Soviets, and *Vechernii Leningrad* was a joint newspaper of the Leningrad Oblast Party Committee and the city soviet. From now on, *Leningradskaya pravda* will be solely a Party newspaper, while *Vechernii Leningrad* will be issued by the Leningrad City Soviet (*Radio Moscow-1*, 2200, April 17).

Wednesday, April 18

Latsis on Latvian Independence

Izvestia featured an article by Otto Latsis, economics editor of *Kommunist*, on the economic consequences of independence for Latvia. It is noteworthy that this antiseparatist piece was written by someone whose reformist credentials are strong and who has a Latvian family background. In the article, Latsis reiterated the familiar point that any Baltic republic that secedes from the Soviet Union would face severe economic damage if it had to trade with Moscow at world market prices and with settlement in hard currency.

New Ministers Appointed

President Gorbachev appointed Igor Denisov, who is forty-nine, as Minister of Health, and Boris Panyukov, who is sixty, as Minister of Civil Aviation, TASS reported. They replaced Evgenii Chazov and Aleksandr Volkov, who both resigned at the end of March. Denisov, a practicing surgeon for almost twenty-five years, is the rector of the Ryazan Medical Institute and the author of over 100 scientific papers. He came to the Ministry of Health in 1987, heading the department of medical schools; in June, 1988, he was promoted to the position of first deputy minister. Panyukov has worked in civil aviation for his entire career, serving in various management positions, including the management of Vnukovo Airport. Since 1972, he has been at the Ministry of Civil Aviation and was elevated to the position of first deputy minister in 1982.

Abalkin on Economic Reforms

Deputy Prime Minister Leonid Abalkin said in Havana, where he was on an official visit, that Moscow did not yet have the social consensus it needed to introduce a modern market economy. He predicted that, as a result, the formation of a modern, developed, efficient market would take at least ten years. He blamed the absence of consensus on ethnic and regional conflicts, the growing number of popular movements, and the trade unions. But he warned that any delay in implementing reforms would only increase the possibility of serious social conflict. On April 17, Abalkin signed a series of agreements with Cuban officials that call for an 8.7-percent increase in trade between the two countries in 1990 (*Reuters*, *AP*, April 18).

Fight for *Izvestia*

The editorial staff of *Izvestia* were reported to be worried about their paper's future in connection with the departure of its chief editor, Ivan Laptev. On April 3, Laptev became chairman of the Council of the Union of the USSR Supreme Soviet. Soviet television quoted the trade-union chairman of *Izvestia*, Vyacheslav Shchepotkin, as saying that his paper's staff were worried about rumors that one of the disgraced Party conservatives would be named to head the paper. Shchepotkin said the employees of *Izvestia* had unanimously elected Igor Golembiovsky, first deputy chief editor of the newspaper, to be their chief editor. They appealed to the Soviet leadership for help in getting Golembiovsky confirmed. Their appeal was rejected, however.

Uzbekistan Limits Exports

TASS reported that the Council of Ministers of Uzbekistan had issued a resolution limiting the export from the republic of certain categories of goods, including nearly all food products and a number of consumer goods. The resolution also set standards for those goods that may be exported. The official reason for the limitations, which went into effect on April 20, was "stabilization of the internal market." The measures were supposed to be temporary. Uzbekistan was the third Central Asian republic to issue restrictions on the export of consumer items: Kazakhstan had earlier prohibited the export of certain manufactured items (to the dissatisfaction of some enterprise directors and workers' committees, who saw the move as a limitation on their new independence), and Kirgizia had prohibited all exports.

Shevardnadze Says Domestic Needs Determine Foreign Policy

Speaking to a Foreign Ministry Party conference, Eduard Shevardnadze said "the main goal" of Soviet foreign policy now was "the establishment of the most favorable conditions for domestic transformations in the country," TASS reported. He added that Moscow would be devoting increasing attention to developing countries.

South Koreans to Build Siberian Petrochemical Plant

South Korea's Hyundai Corporation announced plans to participate in the construction of a 600-million-dollar petrochemical plant in northwestern Siberia. Reuters said construction of the massive complex would involve US firms as well and was scheduled to begin in June.

More Graves of Polish Officers May Be Found

Polish historians studying recently released Soviet documents may be able to locate the burial places of more than 11,000 Polish officers missing since they were captured by the Soviet army during World War II, TASS reported. More than 4,000 of them were found buried in the Katyn Forest near Smolensk. TASS quoted Polish historians as saying the documents seemed to indicate that nearly 7,000 of the missing prisoners may be buried in Kalinin near Lake Seliger. TASS said the documents may also provide clues about the location of the graves of the final group.

Thursday, April 19

Gorbachev Offers Estonia and Latvia Special Status

Reports said Mikhail Gorbachev had offered Estonia and Latvia special status within the Soviet Union if they abandoned their moves towards independence. Gorbachev held separate meetings in Moscow with delegations from the two Baltic republics. Estonian Supreme Soviet Chairman Arnold Ruutel said Gorbachev had also threatened to impose economic sanctions and direct presidential rule on Estonia if it did not rescind its statements on independence. Gorbachev also expressed willingness to hold talks on the conditions of Latvian independence, but he added that he would not continue talks if Latvia went ahead with its plan to declare independence (*AP*, *Reuters*, *AFP*, April 19).

Soviet Nuclear Expert Says Nuclear Accidents Now Ruled Out

A Soviet nuclear expert said new precautions had been taken that ruled out a repetition of the Chernobyl' nuclear accident. Yurii Tsoglin, chief of nuclear safety at the Ukrainian Academy of Sciences Institute of Nuclear Research, told TASS that the Chernobyl' nuclear power station was now much safer than four years ago. Tsoglin said the design of safety rods had been changed and a more enriched fuel was being used. He said that the safety system worked twice as fast and that an additional back-up system had been installed (*TASS*, April 19).

Another Uzbek Official Sentenced for Corruption

TASS reported that the RSFSR Supreme Court had sentenced former Khorezm Oblast Party First Secretary Mad'yar Khudaibergenov to six years in an ordinary labor camp. Khudaibergenov had admitted taking 72,800 rubles in bribes. The report said much of the material incriminating Khudaibergenov could not be confirmed. In handing down a sentence that is less than the law requires, the court took account of his poor health and of his service in World War II, and also of the fact that he had returned money and valuables worth 6 million rubles.

New Independence Party in Uzbekistan

The Uzbek youth paper *Yash leninchi* reported that a new political party had been formed in Uzbekistan. The "Erk" (Free) Democratic Party seeks independence for Uzbekistan. It was formed at an extraordinary meeting of the "Erk Popular Front" on April 11 in Tashkent.

Friday, April 20

Gorbachev Delivers Lenin Anniversary Speech

Mikhail Gorbachev delivered an hour-long speech in Moscow to mark the anniversary of Lenin's birth, taking as his theme Lenin's willingness to change course when his international, economic, and nationality policies turned out to have been mistaken. The speech was obviously intended to draw parallels between Lenin's period in power and the USSR today. Gorbachev criticized what he said were attempts to represent the revolution of October, 1917, as "a mistake" and he denounced "vulgar slandering" of Lenin. He also criticized "separatist and extremist" actions in several regions of the USSR (*TASS*, April 20; *Pravda*, April 21).

Opinion Polls Show Pessimism

Ogonek (No. 15) published the results of an opinion poll showing increasing pessimism among the Soviet population about the future. In 1989, 34 percent of those polled said they expected the coming year to be better than the previous one, but in 1990 the optimists constituted only 4 percent of those polled. Those who thought things would stay much the same went up from 13 percent last year to 22 percent this year, while those who thought things would get worse went up from 6 percent last year to 14 percent this year. *Moscow News* (No. 15) published the results of another opinion poll showing a further decrease in the standing of the CPSU.

Gorbachev Undermines New Moscow City Soviet

Gorbachev used his presidential authority to issue a decree undermining the power of the Moscow City Soviet shortly after it had elected radical economist Gavriil Popov as mayor. According to TASS, the decree stripped the soviet of control over street demonstrations and protest rallies in the center of Moscow, transferring the regulation of such gatherings to the USSR Council of Ministers. Popov's election strongly displeased Soviet conservatives. The Russian nationalist newspaper *Literaturnaya Rossiya* carried an article attacking Popov in its latest issue. Signed by an employee of Moscow State University, where Popov used to be dean of the Department of Economics, the article accused Popov of accepting bribes for admissions and of attempting to bribe the USSR Academy of Sciences to secure election to it.

Environmental Activism in Kazakhstan

A delegation of Semipalatinsk citizens arrived in Moscow to press their campaign for the nuclear weapons testing site in Semipalatinsk Oblast to be shut down. On April 20, they presented the USSR Supreme Soviet with an appeal to permanently close the site (*TASS*, April 20). The head of the delegation later told a press conference that the Central Committee of the Miners' Union had decided to call a nationwide two-hour strike after the next test at Semipalatinsk and a twenty-four-hour strike after the following one.

The same day an international "round table" began a discussion of ways to save the rapidly desiccating Aral Sea (*TASS*, April 20).

Most Soviet Citizens Favor German Unification

An all-Union opinion poll published in *Argumenty i fakty* (No. 16) showed some 60 percent of the Soviet population in favor of the unification of the two Germanies. Those against comprised 24 percent of respondents. However, 67 percent of the sample was against the inclusion of a united Germany in any military bloc. Forty-five percent said they would favor a withdrawal of all Soviet troops as long as all NATO forces were pulled out as well.

Saturday, April 21

Popov Outlines Plans for Moscow

Moscow's new mayor, Gavriil Popov, said he wanted to introduce elements of a market economy in the Soviet capital to resolve acute social, economic, and ecological problems. TASS quoted Popov, who was elected on

April 20 to head the Moscow City Soviet, as telling reporters that the new city leadership intended to reject out-of-date, command-administrative methods of economic management. TASS did not say how Popov intended to implement this plan in practice. On April 22, Popov told *Rabochaya tribuna* he considered it necessary to establish immediately thirty to fifty free soup kitchens and clothing stores in Moscow to help protect the city's population from the hardships of a transition to a market-based economy (*Reuters*, April 22).

Supreme Soviet Approves Bill on Military Pensions

Supreme Soviet deputies approved at the first reading a draft bill on pensions for the military. The bill provides for an average 15- to 20-percent increase in benefits, while the pensions of war invalids and of families of soldiers killed on duty will be increased by 30–40 percent (*TASS*, April 21).

Links between Iran and Nakhichevan Expanded

The official Iranian news agency IRNA reported that work on bridges and roads between the Nakhichevan ASSR and Iran had begun, following the first-ever visit by an Iranian delegation to that autonomous republic. IRNA said that the visit had been arranged by the prime minister of Nakhichevan, Ismail Aliev, and that one result of it would be expanded cross-border visits.

Soviet Forces to Leave Vietnam by 1992

Vietnamese officials told a visiting US Congressional delegation that all Soviet troops, including those stationed at the Cam Ranh Bay naval base, would withdraw from Vietnam by 1992 (*AP*, April 21). Soviet forces first moved into Cam Ranh Bay, built by US forces during the Vietnam War, in 1975. Congresswoman Patricia Schroeder, who headed the US delegation, said the USSR was no longer making the departure of its troops contingent on the departure of US troops from the Subic Bay naval base in the Philippines.

Sakharov Collection Published

The "Sovetsky pisatel'" publishing house was reported to have issued a collection of the publicistic writings of the late Academician Andrei Sakharov (*Radio Moscow-2*, 1100, April 21). This was the first volume of Sakharov's writings to be published in the Soviet Union. It included his Nobel Prize lecture, his letters to the Soviet leadership, and his speeches to the USSR Congress of People's Deputies.

Karelians in Finland Press for Change in Soviet Border

Die Welt reported that organizations representing the nearly 400,000 ethnic Karelians living in Finland had called on Finnish President Mauno Koivisto to press for a redrawing of the Soviet-Finnish border. A large portion of traditionally Karelian land was transferred to Moscow as a result of the 1939–40 Winter War between the Soviet Union and Finland.

Sunday, April 22

Mass Protest in Ukraine to Mark Chernobyl' Anniversary

More than 50,000 people marched through Kiev to mark the fourth anniversary of the Chernobyl' nuclear disaster, Reuters reported. Speakers included people's deputies Yurii Shcherbak, Borys Oliinyk, and Volodymyr Yavorivs'kyi, and also the former political prisoner Leonid Plyushch, who now lives in Paris. They demanded that the power station be closed and that former Ukrainian officials be put on trial for failing to inform people of the seriousness of the accident. According to a press spokesman for the Ukrainian Helsinki Union in Kiev, demonstrations also took place in Kharkov, Kanev, Odessa, and other cities.

New Program to Assist Chernobyl' Victims Proposed

A special session of the Presidium of the USSR Council of Ministers approved a new, 16-billion-ruble plan of "urgent measures" to assist the victims of the Chernobyl' accident over the next three years (*Reuters*, *Central Television*, April 22). The plan provided for the resettlement of 180,000 to 200,000 people living in contaminated areas, for an improvement in medical aid to those affected by radiation, for the supply of "clean" food to the affected regions, and for an increase in social services, especially for children and the elderly. The Presidium also called for foreign scientists and specialists to be consulted on the program's formulation. Finally, the Presidium created a special department under the State Commission for Emergencies to monitor the implementation of the program. The program was approved by the USSR Supreme Soviet on April 25. See *Pravda*, April 26.

Controversy over Kuriles Continues

Speaking in Tokyo, radical historian Yurii Afanas'ev reiterated that Moscow should return the Kurile Islands to Japan, AP reported. He said, "Many people . . . have a negative view [on this issue] because they do not know their history." The same day, however, *Pravda* warned that Moscow "will not capitulate" to Japan on this issue. It accused the Japanese of taking "a regrettable, short-term view" of the situation. Earlier this year, the Soviet press attacked Afanas'ev for his position on the Kuriles.

Monday, April 23

Soviet Leaders Discuss Oil Workers' Grievances

Prime Minister Nikolai Ryzhkov told senior officials they had been too slow in improving working and living conditions in the Tyumen oil- and gas-producing regions. The meeting took place as the strike deadline the workers there had set passed without any report of work stoppages. Among those attending the session were Politburo member Egor Ligachev, Gosplan Chairman Yurii Maslyukov, RSFSR Prime Minister Aleksandr Vlasov, three Soviet deputy prime ministers, and representatives from Tyumen (*Reuters*, April 23).

Marchuk Reelected President of Academy of Sciences

Gurii Marchuk was reelected president of the USSR Academy of Sciences (*TASS*, April 23). Although his lack of credentials and conservative stance have made him unpopular with many academicians, he has support from above. His reelection seems to have been prearranged: the five other candidates in the first multicandidate presidential elections in the academy withdrew before the vote. A month ago, Marchuk's assistant, Nikolai Kaprakov, said the current backlog of problems at the academy would make any change in leadership impossible.

Chinese Leader Visits the Soviet Union

Carrying placards reading "Bloody Butcher Li Go Away," several hundred Muscovites protested against the visit of the Chinese premier, Li Peng, to the Soviet capital. The protest was sponsored by the "Memorial" society. Leaders of the newly elected Moscow City Soviet addressed the demonstrators (*Reuters*, RL Russian service, April 23).

Li was returning a visit Gorbachev made to Beijing in 1989. At an official dinner in Moscow hosted by Nikolai Ryzhkov, Li said China stood ready to expand friendly ties with the USSR (*TASS*, April 23). On April 24, Li and Ryzhkov signed an agreement providing for additional troop cuts along their 7,000-kilometer border. According to an article in *The Washington Post* (April 25), the agreement called for a mutual scaling down of troop levels along the border "to a minimum corresponding to normal good-neighborly relations."

On April 24, Li met with Gorbachev. A further cut in border troops was reported to be the main issue on the agenda. Apart from the agreement on border troops, TASS said an agreement was signed on economic matters and joint space exploration. Speaking in Moscow the next day, Li acknowledged the collapse of the Communist regimes in Eastern Europe but said it was too early to tell whether the countries concerned would also abandon socialism (*UPI*, April 25). On April 26, Li went to Leningrad. In the meantime, six Soviet parliamentarians issued a statement condemning Li's visit to the Soviet Union as "immoral." They said he was personally responsible for bloody repressions in China (*Reuters*, April 25).

Baku Adopts New Laws on Ethnic Conflicts

Drawing on the laws governing states of emergency and combating ethnic hostility recently adopted at all-Union level, the Presidium of the Azerbaijani Supreme Soviet has modified that republic's legal code, Radio Moscow reported. The broadcast suggested that the new republican legislation may be even more sweeping than the all-Union laws, allowing the authorities in Azerbaijan to crack down even without declaring a state of emergency.

Antinuclear Group Formed in Far North

TASS announced the formation of a new group—"Novaya Zemlya-Nevada"—to protest against plans to transfer Moscow's nuclear testing to a site on Novaya Zemlya. Moscow had planned to shift tests there after the expected closure in the next few years of its main testing site at Semipalatinsk.

Gorbachev Asks Aeroflot for Flights for Muslim Pilgrims

Mikhail Gorbachev asked Aeroflot to organize special flights to carry Soviet Muslims on the hajj to Mecca, TASS said. The flights are to depart from Moscow, Kazan, Baku, and other cities. The Soviet Union and Saudi Arabia do not have diplomatic relations, but Moscow officials said this would not affect the special flights. The announcement did not say how many Soviet Muslims would be allowed to go, but it will certainly be a far larger number than at any time since the revolution.

Supreme Soviet Approves New Tax Legislation

The USSR Supreme Soviet approved new income tax bills. TASS said the two chambers of the Soviet parliament approved bills progressively raising taxes for high earners and lowering taxes for low-income families. The bills also give tax relief to families with many children, to war veterans, and to students. TASS said both chambers also approved a bill abolishing a special tax for unmarried and single people as well as for childless families. The law will take effect in stages, coming into full effect on January 1, 1993. See *Pravda*, May 6, for the text of the law.

Tuesday, April 24

Soviet Economists Say CIA Figures Too Generous

A group of senior Soviet economists told CIA analysts and US academics that the CIA had overestimated the size of the Soviet economy. The group, which included Oleg Bogomolov, Vladimir Tikhonov, and Grigorii Khanin, spoke at the end of a four-day conference in Washington. They argued that the Soviet economy was in reality only 14–28 percent as large as the US economy, not half as large, as the CIA says. They added that defense costs totaled up to 200 billion rubles per year, not the 135–165 billion per year estimated by the CIA, and far more than the 77 billion that is the USSR's official defense budget figure.

Moscow Ready for Arms-Control Agreements, Chervov Says

Colonel General Nikolai Chervov, who is chief of the Arms-Control Directorate of the Soviet General Staff, told TASS that the Soviet Union was prepared to initial a treaty on strategic arms. He said recent accusations of Soviet intransigence were a product of Western negotiating tactics. He also denied that there was friction between civilian and military leaders on arms-control issues. He said that the political leadership had always listened to the Soviet High Command and that defense officials participated in all disarmament talks. "Neither the Foreign Ministry nor the Defense Ministry has ever made unilateral decisions," he added.

New All-Union Language Law

Both chambers of the USSR Supreme Soviet passed a law on language. TASS reported that the law granted Union and autonomous republics the right to determine independently the legal status of languages on their territories, while requiring that Russian continue to be recognized as the official language of the Soviet Union. In a related development, both chambers considered a bill that would allow ethnic minorities to set up special districts of their own. (This idea has been pushed by Academician Yulian Bromlei since 1985.) This measure drew heated debate in the Council of the Union, with some deputies arguing that it could provoke territorial conflicts. For the text of the law, see *Izvestia*, May 6.

Moscow Tightens Trade Controls

TASS reported that, beginning May 1, Soviet enterprises and other organizations would need an export license to sell seed grain abroad. This step continues the trend towards a reimposition of product-by-product central controls over exports. The foreign-trade reforms of 1987 transferred the right to engage in foreign transactions to an increasing number of Soviet production organizations. Initially, the center's detailed control was through currency allocations, affecting imports only. In early 1989, both exports and imports began to be subject to centralized control by licensing.

KGB to Reinforce Moldavian-Romanian Border

The chief of staff of KGB Border Troops said the Soviet-Romanian border would be reinforced in response to an increase in the number of violations there recently, TASS reported. Anatolii Parakhin said nationalists on both sides had been trying to dismantle frontier markings. He added that a Romanian group called "Bessarabia" and the Moldavian Popular Front were planning mass rallies at the border early next month. On April 23, AFP quoted Politburo member Aleksandr Yakovlev as telling Moldavian intellectuals in Kishinev that "anything is possible, except a change in borders."

Armenians Mark Genocide Anniversary

More than 200,000 Armenians assembled in Erevan to mark the seventy-fifth anniversary of the genocide that devastated their people under the Ottoman Empire. Coverage of the meeting was sparse; Moscow had prevented foreign reporters from travelling there "at the request of the local authorities," UPI said. A commemoration service also took place in Moscow at the Armenian Apostolic Church.

Kazakhstan Elects President

TASS reported that the Kazakh Supreme Soviet had elected republican Communist Party First Secretary Nursultan Nazarbaev to the newly created post of president of the republic. The post, modeled on that of the USSR president, carries extensive powers. The TASS report indicated that deputies saw the new post as a further assertion of republican sovereignty. Nazarbaev has been an active proponent of greater autonomy for Kazakhstan.

Lushev Rules Out Interference in Eastern Europe

Army General Petr Lushev said the Soviet Union must maintain its principle of noninterference in Eastern Europe. The commander in chief of Warsaw Pact Forces told TASS that relations among Warsaw Pact nations should be built in the spirit of mutual confidence and that the pact would remain a stabilizing factor in European security. Lushev also said German unification should proceed in tandem with the development of a new European security system that would eventually replace the current military alliances.

Meeting on Katyn, Commemoration in Kuropaty

A meeting on the Katyn executions of Polish officers under Stalin opened in Moscow. Organized by the "Memorial" society, it was attended by both Soviet and Polish historians, Radio Warsaw said. Also on April 24, officials attended a ceremony in the Kuropaty woods near Minsk to commemorate victims of Stalinism buried there. The Soviet media reported that Minsk planned to erect a monument to the victims on the burial site.

US-Soviet Talks Open

The United States went ahead with scheduled trade talks with the Soviet Union. There had been reports that negotiations might be postponed to protest against the Soviet economic blockade of Lithuania. The two sides met in Paris (*UPI*, April 24). The same day, Soviet Foreign Ministry spokesman Vadim Perfil'ev told reporters in Moscow that US economic sanctions over the Lithuanian dispute would have been counterproductive (*Reuters*, April 24).

Wednesday, April 25

Gorbachev Visits the Urals

Mikhail Gorbachev went to the Urals city of Sverdlovsk "to discuss local economic problems caused by central government policies," Radio Moscow said. He told workers at the city's giant "Uralmash" machine-building plant that he had come to sound out public opinion about planned economic reforms. He promised that the USSR would not follow the Polish example of "shock-therapy," involving sudden, steep price rises. Instead, Gorbachev said, a debate lasting at least six months would be held before market reforms were introduced, and he invited the workers to make their views heard. Accompanying Gorbachev is Veniamin Yarin, the leader of the conservative United Workers' Front who sits on Gorbachev's Presidential Council. Gorbachev is scheduled to go on from Sverdlovsk to Nizhnii Tagil, the Urals metallurgy center from which Yarin comes.

On April 26, Gorbachev met with young people at a housing project and toured a trading enterprise. He also met with workers at an electrical factory that has converted its production from defense to medical equipment and talked with regional Party officials. During Gorbachev's unexpected visit to a department store, many people expressed heated reservations about the Soviet economic situation, Radio Moscow said.

On April 27, Gorbachev left Sverdlovsk for Nizhnii Tagil. Speaking to workers there, he reiterated that some Soviet military production facilities must be retooled to mass-produce consumer goods (*TASS*, *Central Television*, April 27). See *Pravda*, April 26–29.

Mufti Criticizes Moscow on Soviet Television

Central Soviet television carried a special program on "Islam and Interethnic Relations" after the "Vremya" newscast. The chairman of the Religious Board of Muslims of Central Asia and Kazakhstan, Mufti Mukhammad-Sadiq Mukhammad-Yusuf, was interviewed. He complained that Moscow was holding up the shipment of foreign Korans to Soviet believers. He added that the Soviet media should balance their increased attention to Russian Orthodoxy with similarly expanded coverage of Islam. See RL 195/90.

Ryzhkov Says Chernobyl' Cover-Up Unintentional

Responding to a reporter's question about why there had been no criminal proceedings against officials of the Ministry of Health for failing to tell the truth about conditions after the Chernobyl' accident, Prime Minister Ryzhkov asserted that there had been no malicious intent on the part of anyone to mislead the people (*Radio Moscow*, April 25). Taking a defensive stand, Ryzhkov noted that he was not the sole person coordinating the government's response to the accident but a member of a commission. Any oversights, he said, were due to the fact that "we did not understand very much. We had no experience whatsoever."

Cooperatives under Attack

The "chief ideologist" of Veniamin Yarin's United Workers' Front, Aleksei Sergeev, laid out in *Nash sovremennik* (No. 4) his proposals for dealing with "the shadow economy." Sergeev wants a return to the policies of the 1920s when, "on the initiative of F. E. Dzerzhinsky, a commission was set up to investigate and halt the activities of underground capitalists and false cooperators." Sergeev won 16 percent of the vote when he stood for election to the RSFSR Congress of People's Deputies in March.

Expelled Academicians Reinstated

The USSR Academy of Sciences reinstated more than forty scientists, many posthumously, who were expelled under Stalin, TASS reported. A majority of the newly reinstated had emigrated after the revolution. The 1928 rules of the academy required their automatic expulsion. (Those expelled in connection with their arrests during Stalin's purges were reinstated after Stalin's death.) Also reinstated were foreign members, some of whom had left the academy of their own accord in protest over Stalin's purges, especially in connection with the crackdown on geneticists.

Demonstration in Alma-Ata

Protesters picketed the Kazakh Supreme Soviet building to press for the release of four people still imprisoned for their involvement in the riots in December, 1986, local sources told RFE/RL. Those riots were sparked when Gennadii Kolbin, an ethnic Russian, replaced Dinmukhamed Kunaev, a Kazakh, as republican Party chief. Today's demonstrators also called for Kolbin and former Politburo member Mikhail Solomentsev to be brought to justice for abuse of power.

Moscow Acknowledges Authenticity of Lenin's Letter on Famine

In another blow to the traditional image of Lenin, the Institute of Marxism-Leninism finally admitted the authenticity of Lenin's letter of March, 1922, calling for the suppression of the Church in the most brutal way. The letter also shows that Lenin intended to use confiscated Church property not to combat the famine—as Moscow has always claimed—but to fill the state coffers and build up the Red Army. The youth journal *Sobesednik* (No. 16) said that the letter would appear in *Izvestiya TsK KPSS* (No. 4). Soviet officials earlier had denied the authenticity of the letter, which was first published in the West. See RL 194/90.

KGB Official Says 3.5 Million Executed under Stalin

Major General of the KGB Aleksandr Karbainov was quoted by the Japanese newspaper *Sankei Shimbun* as saying 3.5 million people were executed under Stalin. He said about half the executions were during the purges of 1937 and 1938. The figure cited by Karbainov is higher than that given by the official KGB commission on rehabilitations. The commission has maintained that not more than one million people suffered some form of repression (not necessarily execution) at the end of the 1930s.

Thursday, April 26

Chernobyl' Anniversary

Soviet television broadcast a nonstop twenty-four-hour program to raise funds for Chernobyl' victims. US and British television stations also joined the Soviet appeal. In an interview with *Moskovskaya pravda*, Prime Minister Nikolai Ryzhkov said he wanted the world's best experts to help with the Soviet Union's new Chernobyl' program. In some parts of the contaminated areas, the Chernobyl' anniversary was marked with strikes. In the Belorussian city of Gomel, for instance, a day-long work stoppage was observed (*AP*, April 26). The strikers were calling for better medical care and the punishment of officials who misinformed the population following the disaster. Similar calls were made at a mass demonstration in Kiev (*Reuters*, April 26). See RL 180/90.

Nuclear Plant to Be Built Near Kharkov Despite Protests

Radio Kiev said the Soviet nuclear energy ministry planned to build a nuclear power plant near the city of Kharkov in Ukraine despite citizens' protests. According to the radio, the project had been stopped after demonstrations, but not for good. The radio said the project had been merely relocated to a site slightly farther from Kharkov.

Supreme Soviet Defines Federal and Republican Powers

The USSR Supreme Soviet adopted a law saying the powers of the central government may not be broadened without republican consent. It also gave the republics the right to suspend acts of the federal authorities if they contradicted republican laws. TASS said the republics would have any powers that the law does not expressly assign to the central government. Moscow would have the exclusive right to settle disputes between republics and to define and administer borders. It would adopt and implement the federal budget, set up national banks and a monetary system, set taxes, and make agreements on federal credits and loans. Moscow would be responsible for transport, communications, energy, defense, and foreign policy. TASS also said some powers would be shared between Moscow and the republics, including the setting up of a framework for autonomy and local self-government. For the text of the law, see *Izvestia*, May 3.

Soviet Citizens Fear "Islamic Holy War"

Soviet citizens now fear a war with "the Muslim East" more than with NATO, according to the results of a telephone poll of 3,000 Soviet citizens, *Novoe vremya* (No. 16) reported. The weekly noted that *glasnost'* in the news media had produced some "unexpected" results regarding the way Soviet citizens view the world. Thus, the country seen by Soviet citizens as "best able to help *perestroika*" is the US, followed by Japan, Israel, and Western Europe. Asked whether the USSR faced the threat of war, 73 percent said they saw no such threat from the United States. While 61 percent saw no threat of war from Western Europe, 60 percent said they thought the USSR faced the danger of "an Islamic holy war." Speculating that these fears had been aroused by events in the Transcaucasus, Central Asia, and the Middle East, *Novoe vremya* added, "No small role is played by Radio Liberty's broadcasts concerning the threat from the countries of the Muslim East."

KGB Briefing

Continuing efforts to burnish its public image, the KGB Moscow directorate held an unusual press briefing to announce the seizure of a large batch of contraband. KGB officials told foreign and Soviet journalists, as well as deputies from the new Moscow City Soviet, how a recent KGB operation at a Moscow customs checkpoint had led to the seizure by "astonished" agents of a cache of works of art and religious and other objects intended for illegal export as well as over half a million rubles (*TASS*, April 26).

Baku Calls Off Opening of Iranian Border

Reuters quoted Radio Teheran as saying the Azerbaijani authorities had called off the announced opening of a new border crossing point. The Iranian broadcast said Azerbaijan was "not prepared" for the opening.

Friday, April 27

Nuclear Reactor Shut Down in Georgia

The Georgian Academy of Sciences shut down its experimental nuclear reactor and began dismantling the equipment. TASS said the reactor had been working for thirty years in a densely populated region near the ancient capital of Georgia, Mtskheta. TASS said the shutdown had been demanded by the Georgian public. The same day, TASS reported that the Supreme Soviet of the Tatar Autonomous Republic had ordered a halt to the construction of a nuclear power plant there. See RL 182/90.

Five Soldiers Hurt in Clash with Crowd in Stepanakert

Casualties were reported to have occurred in an incident on April 26 in Stepanakert, the capital of Nagorno-Karabakh. TASS said up to 1,000 people marched to the local military commander's headquarters to demand the release of two ethnic Armenians detained after addressing an unsanctioned rally on April 24. MVD troops who tried to move the crowd away from the building were pelted with stones. TASS said the soldiers fired warning shots after three of their number were hurt. Altogether, five soldiers, two local policemen, and a Stepanakert resident were injured, the agency said.

Conservative Party Officials Reelected

TASS reported that Boris Gidaspov had been reelected Party leader in Leningrad, defeating four competitors in a secret ballot at a joint session of the oblast and city Party committees. On April 28, Ligachev associate Aleksandr Mel'nikov was reelected to head the oblast Party organization in Kemerovo. The West Siberian region was one of the centers of last year's coal miners' strikes. In his speech, the conservative Mel'nikov took a swipe at those who, he said, have "replaced creative work aimed at improving people's lives with a prolonged contest of political platforms, programs, and resolutions" (*TASS*, April 28).

Saturday, April 28

Supreme Soviet Lowers Quorum

The USSR Supreme Soviet adopted a decree allowing it to reduce the number of deputies needed to form a quorum for the adoption of legislation. (On April 27, lack of a quorum had forced the Supreme Soviet to postpone a vote on taxes and pensions until the following day.) TASS said that, under this decree, deputies who are unwilling or unable to attend a session may be excluded when the number needed for a quorum is calculated. The action is necessitated, TASS explained, because many deputies hold both state and Party posts and are therefore often absent from Supreme Soviet sessions. The situation has been further exacerbated by Lithuania's reaffirmation of independence on March 11. Since then, Lithuanian deputies have attended the USSR Supreme Soviet sessions only as observers. On April 28, however, the Lithuanian deputies said that they were withdrawing from the USSR Supreme Soviet entirely. In their turn, Estonian deputies to the Soviet parliament said on April 28 that they would not attend legislative sessions until formal negotiations on independence began (*Central Television*, "Vremya," April 28).

Snegur Elected Chairman of Moldavian Supreme Soviet

Proreform Communist Mircea Snegur was elected chairman of the Moldavian Supreme Soviet, TASS reported. He won by a vote of 196 to 164; his only opponent, republican Party leader Petru Lucinschi, received 160 votes in his favor and 200 against. Snegur, who was formerly chairman of the Presidium of the Moldavian Supreme Soviet, has called for the drafting of a new Moldavian constitution. At the same session, the legislature voted to revive the traditional Moldavian tricolor flag, which resembles the flag of neighboring Romania. The Moldavian flag was immediately hoisted over Moldavian official buildings.

Yakovlev Spells Out His Position on the Baltic Republics

Presidential Council member Aleksandr Yakovlev said Moscow was ready to meet Latvian and Estonian delegations to deal with those republics' moves towards independence by legal means. Radio Moscow quoted Yakovlev in an interview with *Moskovsky komsomolets* as saying he hoped a settlement would also be reached with Lithuania. Yakovlev said he did not know whether the solution would be a confederation or an economic alliance, "but we'll arrive at something," he said. He blamed the lack of dialogue with Lithuania on officials in Vilnius and again called upon Lithuania to suspend its reaffirmation of independence and laws implementing it. AP quoted the Estonian news service as saying an Estonian delegation had met with Yakovlev on April 27. The Estonian agency said Yakovlev had suggested Estonia suspend its drive for independence and hold a referendum on the issue.

Yazov Promoted to Rank of Marshal

TASS announced that USSR Defense Minister Dmitrii Yazov had been promoted to the rank of marshal. Appointed defense minister by Gorbachev in the summer of 1987 to oversee the restructuring of the Soviet Armed Forces, Yazov has been much criticized by both civilian and military officials. His promotion—making him one of only seven living marshals in the Soviet Union—comes on the eve of celebrations marking the forty-fifth anniversary of the Soviet Union's victory in World War II and represents another effort by Gorbachev to placate his disgruntled High Command.

Anomalies in First-Quarter Economic Figures

A report on first-quarter economic results, issued by the USSR State Committee for Statistics (Goskomstat) and published by TASS, contained the usual crop of statistical puzzles. Money incomes of the population were said to be 13.3 percent up on the same period in 1989, while the Goskomstat inflation figure, which is supposed somehow to incorporate a measure of worsening shortages as well as price rises, is up by only 8 percent. On the face of it, therefore, real incomes rose 4.9 percent. But the Soviet measure of real GNP growth is negative: a 2-percent fall. The implication is that output of investment goods fell enough to make room for a substantial increase in the output of consumer goods and therefore for improved consumption levels, despite an overall fall in output and worsening terms of trade.

Assad in Moscow

Soviet President Mikhail Gorbachev discussed emigration of Soviet Jews to Israel with Syrian President Hafez Assad, who was on a two-day visit to Moscow. Gorbachev denied reports of a secret deal between the USSR and the US to settle Jews in Israel. Gorbachev linked the increasing emigration from the USSR to "internal processes" in the Soviet Union (*TASS*, April 28; *UPI*, April 29). The two officials called for an international conference on the Middle East and cited problems created by the US as obstacles to the holding of such a conference (*TASS*, April 29).

Sunday, April 29

Kryuchkov Says KGB under Government Control

KGB Chairman Vladimir Kryuchkov told TASS his organization received constant guidance from Gorbachev and the Soviet government to keep its activities within the law. He said that this situation was very different from the days when the Party guided the KGB. Kryuchkov added that the Supreme Soviet would soon pass a law regulating KGB activities.

Military Reformer Expelled from CPSU

Radio Moscow reported that Major Vladimir Lopatin, a leading critic of the Ministry of Defense in the USSR Congress of People's Deputies, had been expelled from the CPSU on April 26. Lopatin has spoken out many times against the privileges enjoyed by the High Command and has emerged as the leading proponent of a draft bill on military reform opposed by the Ministry of Defense. His expulsion—on trumped-up charges initiated by the central military authorities—appears aimed at precluding his election as a delegate to the upcoming Party Congress. Another of the progressive soldier-deputies, Lieutenant Nikolai Tutov, was expelled from the Party in February.

On May 2, *Pravda* defended Major Lopatin. *Pravda* said the military authorities had put pressure on Lopatin's local Party committee to expel him, commenting that "this whole story looks more like a case of swift revenge than an objective Party investigation." *Komsomol'skaya pravda* (May 2) also reported that the authorities in the northern city of Vologda, where Lopatin is a people's deputy, had tried to prevent him from addressing the May Day parade but were forced by the crowd to relent. See RL 222/90.

Defense Law Endorsed

According to TASS, the Collegium of the USSR Defense Ministry recently endorsed the USSR Law on Defense. TASS said the main provisions of the bill were set out in the April 29 issue of *Krasnaya zvezda*. The TASS account gave few details, saying that the bill covered all spheres of defense activity for the first time in Soviet history.

Crackdown in Ukraine

"Rukh" activists told Reuters that the Ukrainian Communist Party had launched a secret campaign to crack down on "Rukh" members who won election last month. They said the secret plan called for "Rukh" members to be fired from influential jobs, for the republican government to deprive local authorities of certain powers, and for the disbandment of disloyal Party organizations.

Holy Synod Demands More Rights for Church

In a statement published in *Moskovsky tserkovnyi vestnik*, the Holy Synod of the Russian Orthodox Church called for the restoration of the rights it has lost since 1917. It demanded both full juridical rights for the Church and an end to political interference in its affairs. The Church also sought the right to provide religious instruction both in schools and elsewhere, the right to publish theological and religious literature in its own publishing houses, and free access to the mass media. The statement also demanded that the Church be allowed to own property and to carry out charitable activities in all forms.

Clergy in Georgia Exempt from State Taxes

Moscow News (No. 16) reported that the Georgian Council of Ministers had decreed that, from now on, clergymen, monasteries, and ecclesiastical institutions will be exempt from state taxes. The heavy tax burden imposed on the clergy has been repeatedly discussed in the Soviet press.

Solzhenitsyn Contributes to Solovki Restoration

Radio Moscow reported that exiled writer Aleksandr Solzhenitsyn had decided to give nearly 2 million rubles in Soviet honoraria for the reconstruction of the Solovki Monastery. This ancient Orthodox site was used as a concentration camp between 1922 and the end of the 1930s. A special chapter in Solzhenitsyn's *Gulag Archipelago* is devoted to the Solovki camp.

Details on Soviet Pilot Killed in 1960

Krasnaya zvezda said a Soviet pilot had been killed during the shooting down of an American U-2 spy plane over the USSR in 1960. The paper said that two MiG-19s sent to shoot down the plane were unable to reach it and that an unarmed SU-9 ordered to ram the U-2 could not locate it. The report said that ground crews fired two anti-aircraft missiles at the US craft while the Soviet planes were still in the air. The first damaged the U-2, but the second mistakenly struck one of the Soviet MiG-19s, killing the pilot, Sergei Safronov.

Situation in the Transcaucasus

During a special session of the Armenian Supreme Soviet, deputies voiced serious concern over Azerbaijan's changes in the administrative and territorial division of some of the districts in Nagorno-Karabakh. TASS said the Armenian deputies believed the changes, passed on April 21 by the Azerbaijani Supreme Soviet, infringed the rights of Armenians in the region. The changes were introduced in four districts and in the capital, Stepanakert. Radio Moscow quoted the head of the Secretariat of the Presidium of the Azerbaijani Supreme Soviet, Nizami Tagi ogly Sadykhov, as saying the decree attempted to rectify problems caused by previous measures that had illegally divided some settlements along ethnic lines. According to Radio Moscow, demonstrations against the Azerbaijani decree were held in Erevan on April 28 and 29. The protesters said the measures were aimed at decentralizing control of the region and at upsetting the established ethnic distribution in order to rule out Armenian success in referendums.

On April 29, Radio Moscow reported on the continuing Azerbaijani blockade of Nagorno-Karabakh and Armenia. The radio said a shortage of paper had prevented the printing of newspapers in Armenia, including the central dailies, *Pravda* and *Izvestia*.

On April 30, after a month-long interruption, passenger rail traffic resumed from Azerbaijan through Armenia to the Azerbaijani Autonomous Republic of Nakhichevan (*Central Television*, "Vremya," April 30).

Monday, April 30

Latvian Citizens' Congress for Independence

Over 260 delegates, representing almost 900,000 citizens and candidates for citizenship of the independent Republic of Latvia, met in Riga on April 30 and May 1 to push for the restoration of the independent and democratic Republic of Latvia that existed from 1918 until 1940. Some émigré Latvians were also able to attend the convention, though Egils Levits, an international law specialist from West Germany, was turned back by the Soviet authorities at Riga airport (*Reuters*, RFE Latvian service, April 30 and May 1). The congress called for the prompt withdrawal of Soviet troops from Latvia and the start of negotiations with Moscow on the speedy restoration of Latvian independence. Participants in the congress indicated willingness to work together for the time being with the Latvian SSR Supreme Soviet if that body supports Latvia's independence. A forty-nine-member Committee of Latvia was elected to work for the implementation of the congress resolutions.

Congress of Independent Workers' Organizations in Siberia

TASS reported that a three-day congress of independent workers' organizations had opened in the Western Siberian city of Novokuznetsk. The 140 delegates, who came from several Soviet republics, represented strike committees, workers' clubs, and independent democratic organizations. A spokesman told Reuters that the aim of the congress was to mount an alternative to the official state-run labor movement. On May 2, the delegates at the congress voted to unite the groups in a joint council, whose aim would be to "guarantee the rights of working people in this difficult economic situation" (*Reuters*, May 2).

Independence Party Formed in Ukraine

Ukrainian activists with dissident backgrounds decided to form a new political party with a program calling for secession from the USSR. A congress of the Ukrainian Helsinki Union voted on April 20 to rename itself the Ukrainian Republican Party. It adopted a program calling for the creation of an independent Ukrainian state as the party's first goal. It also called for political pluralism but said parties controlled from Moscow should be banned (*Reuters*, April 30). Radio Kiev reported that a former long-term Ukrainian political prisoner, Levko Luk'yanenko, had been elected head of the Ukrainian Republican Party (*Radio Kiev-3*, April 30).

The Month of May

Tuesday, May 1

Situation in Lithuania

On May 1, the Latvian Popular Front canceled a rally in support of Lithuania and Estonia. Radio Riga said it had heard warnings of possible provocations and wanted to avoid any gathering that could help opponents of the Baltic cause. The same day, President of the Lithuanian Supreme Council Vytautas Landsbergis cabled Gorbachev to offer his May Day congratulations and to express hope for improved relations (*Radio Moscow*, May 1). The Interregional Group of Deputies in Moscow called for an end to the Soviet blockade of Lithuania (*Radio Vilnius*, May 1).

In an interview in Ottawa, Lithuanian Prime Minister Kazimiera Prunskiene said Lithuania wanted international guarantees regarding its drive for independence before it considered suspending new laws and starting negotiations with Moscow. Prunskiene arrived in Canada on April 29. She said there were two laws that could be negotiated with Moscow. One concerns the exemption of Lithuanians from Soviet military service; the other deals with the certification of Lithuanian citizenship. Canadian Minister of Foreign Affairs Joe Clark said Canada could support the international guarantees Prunskiene mentioned. He said Canada was prepared to give Vilnius financial and legal advice, among other things (*UPI*, May 1). The same day, the US Senate adopted a resolution urging President Bush to delay improving trade relations with the Soviet Union because of its actions against Lithuania (Western agencies, May 1).

On May 3, Prunskiene arrived in Washington from Canada. She told members of the US Congress that Lithuania was willing to consider compromises with Moscow in order to get talks under way. She said a US-Soviet summit could make a decisive contribution to solving the Lithuanian crisis. Speaking at a press conference before meeting with Prunskiene, President Bush said he did not think he had to choose between support for Gorbachev and support for Lithuanian independence. He said he was in sympathy with Lithuania's drive for freedom but stressed that the dispute between Moscow and Vilnius was "enormously complicated" and that there was much at stake besides Lithuania (*AP*, May 3).

On May 5, Prunskiene said the Soviet Union would ultimately be forced to recognize an independent Lithuania. In his turn, Landsbergis said he wanted Moscow to show more flexibility and constructiveness in the dispute over Lithuanian independence (*AP*, May 5). The same day, Radio Vilnius quoted a spokesman for Lithuania's Bank for Economic Relations with Foreign Countries as saying it would not comply with a request to halt the issue of currency to Lithuanians traveling privately abroad. The request came in a message from the USSR Foreign Trade Bank. The radio called it another step in the Soviet economic embargo against Lithuania. Meanwhile, the Soviet authorities allowed a shipment of foreign aid from Austria to enter Lithuania from Poland (*UPI*, May 5).

On May 8, Lithuanian Agriculture Minister Vytautas Knacys said the republic was planning to cut meat and milk supplies to the USSR by a further 10 percent as a countermeasure to Moscow's blockade of Lithuania (*Reuters*, May 8). The same day, the Supreme Soviet of the Tatar Autonomous Republic said it was prepared to sell oil to Lithuania and to buy Lithuanian goods (RL Tatar service, May 8).

On May 8, Prunskiene arrived in London (*Reuters*, May 8). On May 9, she met with British Prime Minister Margaret Thatcher, who said she supported Lithuania's drive for independence (*AP*, May 9).

Lieutenant Colonel Valerii Shorupov, deputy commander of the Soviet army garrison in Vilnius, said that "to avoid bloodshed in Lithuania it would be better to introduce presidential rule" (*Reuters*, May 8).

On May 9, few Lithuanians took part in military parades in the republic marking the anniversary of the Soviet victory in World War II. Radio Vilnius said armed paratroopers and military vehicles blocked all entries to the main street in Vilnius, where war veterans and Lithuanian Communists loyal to Moscow joined the festivities.

On May 10, Prunskiene went to Paris, where she met with President François Mitterrand. During the meeting, the French president again urged formal talks between Moscow and Vilnius (*Reuters*, May 10). Speaking the same day in Switzerland, Deputy Chairman of the Lithuanian Supreme Soviet Algirdas Brazauskas said Soviet troops posed no immediate threat to the republic's independence drive. He stressed, however, that Lithuania could hold out against Moscow's economic blockade only for another four or five weeks (*Reuters*, May 10).

On May 11, Prunskiene held talks in Bonn with West German Chancellor Helmut Kohl and Foreign Minister Hans-Dietrich Genscher (*AFP*, May 11). At a press conference after the talks, Prunskiene reiterated that Lithuania was preparing to suspend the implementation of parts of its laws adopted after the proclamation of independence in order to start negotiations with Moscow (Western agencies, May 11).

Landsbergis said on May 12 that up to 300,000 people in Lithuania would soon be without a job if Moscow continued its economic blockade of the Baltic republic (*Radio Vilnius*, May 12). Meanwhile, Radio Warsaw said trucks carrying supplies for Lithuania from Poland and other countries were arriving at the Polish-Lithuanian border. On May 13, ending her tour of the US and Western Europe, Prunskiene expressed satisfaction with her meetings with Western leaders, saying that all the officials she had talked to had told her they regarded Lithuania's striving for independence as justified (*DPA*, May 13). She said she believed she had gained "de facto recognition" of her republic's independence from Western governments.

On May 13, Lithuanian Minister of Industry Rimvidas Jasimavicius said on Lithuanian television that Lithuanians in the West had purchased 80,000 tons of crude oil for about 1.4 million dollars. He said the oil was to arrive at the port of Klaipeda sometime soon. On May 15, the Lithuanian committee dealing with the economic blockade met in Vilnius. Radio Vilnius said it noted that the power crisis was getting worse and that gasoline was running out.

On May 14, Landsbergis told Lithuanian television he hoped a new proposal for the three Baltic republics to negotiate their independence jointly with Moscow would be received positively by the Kremlin. He said the republics had proposed four-state negotiations with a two-sided format—with Moscow on one side and the three Baltic republics on the other. On May 15, Landsbergis told Radio Vilnius that Lithuania might modify its approach to independence. He said, "Maybe we should ask for less now in order to get more later."

On May 15, a delegation of Lithuanian parliamentarians visiting the European parliament in Strasbourg called on the West to do more to help Lithuania (*AFP*, May 15). The same day, anti-independence demonstrations took place in Vilnius. The demonstrators expressed solidarity with anti-independence protesters in Latvia (*TASS*, May 15).

On May 16, the Lithuanian parliament met to discuss the independence dispute. Parliamentary spokesman Rita Dapkus said whatever concessions Lithuanian leaders offered, they would not freeze the independence declaration itself (*Reuters*, May 16).

On May 17, Prunskiene arrived in Moscow for a meeting with Mikhail Gorbachev at which she proposed for the first time that Lithuania go through a transitional period before achieving full independence (*Radio Moscow*, May 17). TASS quoted Gorbachev as telling Prunskiene that her republic must rescind or at least suspend its March 11 declaration of independence. TASS said the proposals brought to Moscow by Prunskiene showed some movement towards normalizing the situation but did not go far enough.

Speaking to reporters before his meeting with James Baker on May 18, Gorbachev said Moscow was prepared to examine any possible way to resolve the dispute over Lithuania's independence provided the Soviet Constitution was observed (*AP*, May 18). Gorbachev's comments came in response to a question about his meeting with Prunskiene. Commenting, in his turn, on the meeting, Landsbergis said it was "an important step forward." But he told RFE/RL in a telephone interview that the offer put forward by Prunskiene had not been enough to convince Moscow to halt its economic blockade. The same day, Prunskiene held a meeting with Baker (*AP*, *AFP*, May 18).

On May 19, UPI and Reuters reported that many Lithuanian deputies had told the Lithuanian Supreme Council they opposed suspending Lithuania's reaffirmation of independence to clear the way for dialogue with Moscow. Addressing a special meeting of the Supreme Council, Prunskiene urged deputies to agree to a compromise with Moscow over independence (*AFP*, May 19).

On May 20, Landsbergis told the RFE Lithuanian service that the Lithuanian Parliamentary Commission for Legal Reform would review only those legal acts relating to the March 11 reaffirmation of independence that were approved after that date. He said the majority of deputies were firmly of the opinion that the question of independence was not negotiable. On May 20, the Lithuanian Supreme Council appealed to the Ukrainian Supreme Soviet for Ukraine's help in overcoming Moscow's economic blockade of Lithuania (RL Ukrainian service, May 20).

On May 22, the Lithuanian parliament again discussed ways to break the deadlock with Moscow (*Reuters*, *DPA*, May 22). The same day, Lithuanian officials provided details of the effects on the republic of Moscow's economic blockade. A member of the blockade committee, Aleksandras Ambrazevicius, told Reuters that supplies of hot water to homes would have to end on May 25 because of power shortages. An unnamed spokesman for the Lithuanian parliament said that fuel supplies for public transport would be cut within two or three days and that the machine-building, defense, and construction industries would have to stop work (*TASS, Reuters, AP*, May 22). Deputy Chairman of the Lithuanian Supreme Council Ceslovas Stankevicius said Lithuanians living in cities might be evacuated to the countryside to conserve energy and food supplies (*Reuters*, May 22). Deputy Chairman of the Lithuanian Supreme Council Algirdas Brazauskas said that most foodstuffs were still available in Lithuania but that there were shortages of sugar and vegetable oil (RFE Lithuanian service, May 23). The same day, a number of USSR people's deputies from Lithuania attended a session of the USSR Supreme Soviet to raise the issue of the blockade. Lithuanian deputies have generally boycotted this parliamentary session because of the independence dispute (*Radio Moscow*, May 22). One of the deputies, Eduardas Vilkas, told the USSR Supreme Soviet that the blockade was "not only immoral but illegal" (*Radio Vilnius*, May 22).

On May 22, Assistant US Commerce Secretary Thomas Duesterberg said US trade relations with the USSR could be imperiled if Moscow continued its blockade of Lithuania (*Reuters*, May 22).

On May 23, the Lithuanian parliament passed a resolution that offered to suspend some laws implementing the Baltic republic's declaration of independence if Moscow opened negotiations. The resolution called for the suspension to take effect when negotiations on independence began (*AP, Reuters, Central Television*, May 23). On May 24, Soviet Prime Minister Nikolai Ryzhkov said Lithuania's offer was not sufficient to bring Moscow to the negotiating table (*Reuters*, May 24). In turn, Mikhail Gorbachev threatened to impose presidential rule in the republic unless it rescinded or suspended the declaration of independence entirely. He said that, if Lithuania agreed to this, then eventually, in two or three years, it could become independent (*Reuters*, May 24). He also said that, if the declaration were rescinded, the economic blockade of the republic would end. On May 25, however, senior Lithuanian officials said that Lithuania could make no further concessions. On May 25, Gorbachev called Lithuanian leaders "adventurists" and again suggested they rescind or suspend their independence declaration (*AP, Reuters*, May 25).

On May 23, Radio Vilnius reported that *Pravda* could not be published in Lithuania because of a paper shortage there.

On May 24, Lithuanian officials who had just met with Mikhail Gorbachev said they suspected his conciliatory line was designed to "score points" ahead of his summit in Washington. Their biggest surprise was Gorbachev's assertion that he did not oppose future Lithuanian independence if Lithuania "froze" its independence affirmation during negotiations (*Radio Vilnius*, May 26). The same day, in an interview with West German radio (Saarländischer Rundfunk), Prunskiene said the republic's future was closely bound up with the future of Eastern Europe (*AFP*, *DPA*, May 26). Speaking the same day at the Catholic Conference in West Berlin, Prunskiene said Lithuania could survive the Soviet economic blockade for a long time. She said that the blockade might destroy the Lithuanian economy but that the people of Lithuania were calm and determined. TASS reported the same day that practically all fuel reserves in the republic had been exhausted and that unemployment was growing.

In another development, TASS quoted Major General V. Kreminsky (deputy chief of an unspecified administration of the Main Staff of Soviet Ground Forces) as saying in Lithuania that many obstacles had been encountered in carrying out this year's spring military call-up (*TASS*, May 26). Meanwhile, the pro-Moscow Lithuanian Communist Party opened a plenum in Vilnius.

In an interview with *Time* magazine, Mikhail Gorbachev said there were "new and encouraging signs" in Moscow's dispute with Lithuania. He said the problem of the Baltic republics was "a truly historic one." He said that a political solution could be found and that there was already movement in this direction (*Reuters*, May 27).

In an interview with DPA released on May 29, Prunskiene rejected accusations of irresponsibility leveled by Gorbachev at Lithuanian leaders last week. She said, "It is unbelievable that a statesman who wants to build a common European house is making such remarks about an independent nation." On May 29, Radio Vilnius broadcast the text of a letter from Prunskiene to Gorbachev and Ryzhkov. The letter said the economic blockade could lead to an accident at the Ignalina nuclear power plant. She said the plant would be closed. The Ignalina plant is controlled by Moscow-based ministries, not the local authorities. Prunskiene said a shutdown of the Ignalina plant would harm production in Lithuania and in Kaliningrad Oblast, an enclave of the RSFSR situated between Poland and Lithuania (*AP*, May 29).

The same day, the Leningrad City Soviet passed a resolution urging Gorbachev to lift the economic blockade and to begin talks with Vilnius (*Radio Vilnius*, May 30). The resolution stressed that the blockade "is doing great harm to the economy of Leningrad and has increased tensions in various regions of the Soviet Union."

On May 30, Lithuanian leaders also called on Gorbachev to stop the blockade (*Reuters*, May 30). In a communiqué, the Lithuanian government said that, once negotiations were under way with Moscow, Lithuania would suspend "decisions and actions" arising from its March 11 reaffirmation of independence (*Radio Vilnius*, May 30).

On May 30, Landsbergis arrived in Prague. He praised Czechoslovakia for paying attention to Lithuania's problems (*AP*, *Reuters*, May 30). The same day, Landsbergis met with Czechoslovak President Vaclav Havel. Talking to reporters in Prague on May 31, Landsbergis said he did not expect the current US-Soviet summit to decide the fate of the Baltic republics (*AP*, May 31). He also said that, if the USSR intervened militarily in Lithuania, as it had in the past in Hungary and Czechoslovakia, Lithuania would achieve its independence much more quickly than did those two countries. Landsbergis's remarks came in response to Gorbachev's statement in Ottawa on May 30 that, in handling the Lithuanian independence issue, Moscow did not exclude "the most severe measures" (*Radio Prague*, May 31). Gorbachev's remarks were carried by Reuters on May 30.

On May 31, Radio Vilnius said Poland had started supplying Lithuania with goods that were in short supply owing to the blockade. The same day, TASS reported that the Moldavian Supreme Soviet had recognized Lithuania's right to self-determination and to the creation of an independent state (*Reuters*, May 31). The same day, Radio Vilnius revealed that Moscow Mayor Gavriil Popov had expressed interest in establishing direct trade relations with Lithuania in order to obtain more food for the Soviet capital. Meanwhile, a communiqué from the Lithuanian blockade committee said that in June the price of meat on sale in Lithuania would be increased by 15 percent.

Gorbachev Jeered by May Day Protesters

Soviet leaders were jeered by demonstrators during the May Day parade in Moscow's Red Square. The unofficial demonstration followed the official May Day parade organized by the state-run trade unions. This year, the authorities proclaimed the parade open to all. Demonstrators shouted "Shame, shame" and chanted slogans denouncing Communist power and Soviet actions against Lithuania as they passed the mausoleum where Mikhail Gorbachev and other leaders were standing. With Gorbachev on the stand was Gavriil Popov, the newly elected mayor of Moscow. Some demonstrators carried Soviet flags with the hammer and sickle torn out. After the Red Square demonstration, protests continued in Moscow's

Gorky Park. No May Day parade was held this year in Leningrad, but in the Western Ukrainian city of Lvov demonstrators called for Ukrainian independence and criticized Soviet influence in the region (Western agencies, May 1).

On May 5, Gorbachev sharply criticized the antigovernment protests that took place on May Day. Speaking at a festival for *Pravda*, the Soviet leader said the demonstrators were on "a dangerous path" if they thought they could carry out *perestroika* by whistling and stamping their feet (*TASS*, May 5). He added that his latest proposals should soon produce a sharp change for the better in the country's economy. (See also *Pravda*, May 14.) A day earlier, similar criticism of the demonstrators was expressed by the Soviet media and by officials. Writing in *Pravda*, Moscow Party leader Yurii Prokof'ev said "extremists" on the left and the right had taken to the streets because they knew that *perestroika* would put an end to their political ambitions. *Izvestia* said the unofficial slogans had been irresponsible and could have set in motion "an avalanche of unforeseeable consequences." Speaking on Soviet television on May 4, USSR Minister of Internal Affairs Vadim Bakatin said no political organization could permit excesses like those that had been displayed on Red Square. Aleksandr Yakovlev was less alarmist, however. He said that in any civilized country such slogans would be regarded as insulting to the authorities, but he emphasized that the incident "should not be exaggerated."

Best Officers Seeking Discharge

According to *Argumenty i fakty* (No. 15), a survey conducted by the Lenin Military-Political Academy indicates that young and capable officers constitute the majority of those seeking discharge from the armed forces. According to the survey, in 1989, 27 percent of those applying for discharge were younger than twenty-three; 43 percent were between twenty-three and twenty-five; and 21 percent were between twenty-five and thirty. Approximately 77 percent were described as efficient, conscientious, and having initiative; 90 percent had completed studies at a military academy with a "good" or "excellent" rating. These officers were said to be demoralized over living conditions in the army and pessimistic about the future.

"Patriots" Found New Party in Leningrad

Literaturnaya Rossiya reported that a new Republican National Party of Russia had been set up in Leningrad with the aim of uniting the various Russian nationalist organizations. The newspaper said "patriots" had decided that the time had come to create such a party, in view of the sympathy shown by "the major part of the CPSU towards social democratic ideas and towards a union with left-wing groups, who hate [the idea of] a great Russian state and want to undermine its integrity." According to reports received from Leningrad by RL's Russian service, speakers at the inaugural meeting of the new party attacked Gorbachev's reforms and called on nationalist parties around the world to unite.

On April 24, *Sovetskaya molodezh'* published information on another newly created Russian nationalist group, the Orthodox Constitutional-Monarchist Party of Russia. Its members believe that Russia is not yet ready for democracy and that therefore authoritarian monarchical rule would be the best political arrangement for it.

Officials Sign Chernobyl' Memorandum with WHO

Representatives from the USSR Ministry of Health and the World Health Organization (WHO) signed a memorandum on international cooperation to alleviate the consequences of the Chernobyl' accident. Under the agreement, WHO will supervise a comprehensive program to protect the health of those living in areas contaminated by radiation and of those who took part in the cleanup. In addition, an international center for the study of radiation problems will be set up in the city of Obninsk (*TASS*, May 1).

Wednesday, May 2

Soviet Official on Chernobyl' Statistics

Ukraine's ambassador to the United Nations told RFE/RL the official death toll of thirty-one from the Chernobyl' accident has never been revised because "nobody really knows the exact count." (The figure is based on the number of people killed during the explosion or immediately afterwards.) Gennadii Udovenko said that, while officials acknowledged that more people had died since then as a result of radiation, they were reluctant to define what constituted "a direct consequence" of the accident. A figure of 300 deaths has been cited in *Pravda* and elsewhere in the Soviet press recently. Udovenko said the government was not challenging these new estimates. Seen in this light, the Soviet government's reticence may be more an attempt to avoid a protracted battle over the compensation of victims and their families than to understate the consequences of the disaster.

Thursday, May 3

Armenian Supreme Soviet Session

The Armenian Supreme Soviet supported a proposal that Armenian youth drafted in the spring call-up should do reconstruction work in the zone damaged by the earthquake instead of serving in the armed forces. The situation in Nagorno-Karabakh was also discussed by deputies. TASS said they pointed out "serious deficiencies" in the work of the Armenian Ministry of Internal Affairs, especially in its efforts to stop "provocative activities" in Armenian-Azerbaijani border areas.

Patriarch Pimen Dies

The head of the Russian Orthodox Church, Patriarch Pimen, died in Moscow at the age of seventy-nine (*TASS*, May 3). Pimen, who had long been in frail health, had been head of the Church since 1971. In the past few years, he had come under criticism from reform elements in the Church for failing to introduce necessary changes. On May 4, Metropolitan Filaret of Kiev and Galicia was temporarily named acting patriarch of the Russian Orthodox Church by the Holy Synod (*TASS*, May 4). He will serve until a new patriarch is elected by the highest organ of the Church, the *pomestnyi sobor*. Filaret has a reputation as a hard-liner, having sharply attacked the Ukrainian Catholic Church.

Soviet Official Offers Energy for Technology

USSR Deputy Energy Minister Boris Takaev was quoted by AFP as telling a Brussels news conference that the USSR was willing to offer energy to Western companies in return for technology needed to produce that energy. Takaev said Moscow was looking for Western help to exploit gas in the Barents Sea, hydrocarbon resources in the Caspian Sea, and coal in the Kansk-Achinsk Basin. He said Moscow also needed help to build pipelines linking the Yamal Peninsula with Scandinavia and the Benelux countries.

Friday, May 4

Latvian Supreme Council Declares Independence

On May 4, the Latvian Supreme Council adopted a declaration reasserting Latvia's independence from the Soviet Union. The declaration stressed that Latvia's incorporation into the USSR had been illegal. It called for an unspecified period of transition "until the renewal of the

Latvian Republic's government." It said that, until that happened, the Latvian Supreme Council was the highest authority in the land (*Central Television*, "Vremya," May 4). At the opening of the Supreme Council session a day earlier, Anatolijs Gorbunovs was elected chairman of the Latvian Supreme Council. He had previously been chairman of the Presidium of the Latvian Supreme Council. Latvian radio reported that, during the discussions prior to the vote, Gorbunovs said relations between Latvia and Moscow should be placed on a new foundation of mutual respect and equal rights. On April 30, *Izvestia* had reported that 92 percent of the Latvians and 45 percent of the non-Latvians residing in Latvia wanted an independent Latvia outside the confines of the USSR. The figures apparently come from the results of a public opinion poll, involving 24,600 respondents, that was taken in Latvia earlier in April and first published in the Latvian Komsomol newspaper *Latvijas Jaunatne* on April 20.

President of the Lithuanian Supreme Council Vytautas Landsbergis sent a message of congratulations to the Latvian parliament following its decision to reaffirm Latvian independence (*Radio Vilnius*, *AFP*, May 5). The same day, the Latvian parliament sent a message to Mikhail Gorbachev urging a period of "close dialogue" during Latvia's transition to independence (*TASS*, May 5). Gorbachev's response was negative, however. He said he would take "retaliatory measures of a political, economic, and administrative nature" if Latvia "ignores the Constitution of the USSR." TASS said Gorbachev's statement was conveyed to the Latvian people on republican television by Alfreds Rubiks, first secretary of the pro-Moscow Latvian Communist Party, who had spoken to Gorbachev by telephone.

On May 7, Gorbunovs proposed Ivars Godmanis as the new Latvian prime minister. Godmanis, whose appointment was approved, is a senior lecturer in physics at the University of Latvia. The new deputy prime minister, also chosen on May 7, is Ilmars Bisers, a professor of law (*Radio Riga*, May 7). Reuters reported that Soviet tanks drove through the center of Riga before the Latvian parliament opened its session on May 7. The report said the troop movements were officially declared to be part of preparations for a Victory Day parade on May 9.

On May 8, Godmanis said in an interview with UPI that the new Latvian government had considered the possibility that the USSR might impose an economic blockade. He said such a blockade would be very hard for Latvia. The same day, an anti-independence group, "Edinstvo," appealed to Gorbachev not to take economic measures against the republic. The group argued that the Latvian parliament's stand on independence had been taken without considering the will of the majority of the population of the republic and that therefore ordinary people who did not bear responsibility for the decision should not suffer (*TASS*, May 8). Another anti-independence organization, the Latvian branch of the United Council of Work Collectives, called on Gorbachev to annul Latvia's decision to reaffirm its independence (*TASS*, May 8).

On May 9, an anti-independence rally reported to have been attended by thousands of people was held in Riga (*AP*, May 9). The rally followed a military parade.

On May 10, Dainis Ivans, the leader of the Latvian Popular Front, was quoted by *Izvestia* as saying Latvian members of the USSR Congress of People's Deputies should retain their posts until the republic was completely independent. He said that, by maintaining their mandates, Latvian people's deputies could "open the door" to talks with Moscow.

On May 14, about 200 Soviet army soldiers and officers scuffled with volunteer guards outside the Latvian Supreme Council as they tried to gain entry to the building. They were calling on the parliament to renounce the republic's declaration of independence. Gorbunovs came out and persuaded most of the soldiers to leave. Radio Riga, AFP, and Reuters said a helicopter flew over Riga dropping leaflets signed by "Interfront," an anti-independence group.

On May 15, "workers' collectives" staged protest meetings in many Latvian cities against independence. In Riga, at least 2,000 soldiers and cadets tried to break into the Supreme Council building (*TASS*, Western agencies, May 15). There was also a proindependence demonstration in Riga. TASS said that the Latvian anti-independence parliamentary group "Equality" had proposed to declare the Latvian independence declaration invalid until a referendum could be held on Latvia's status. The same day, the Latvian parliament agreed to demands by anti-independence protesters for a special parliamentary committee to be formed to discuss the situation in Latvia. In a separate vote, the parliament rejected the protesters' demands for an end to the debate on a new law on alternatives to military service.

On May 18, Latvian Minister of Internal Affairs Bruno Steinbriks urged all citizens of Latvia to keep calm and resist provocations leading to interethnic strife. He was speaking to the Latvian parliament (*Radio Riga*, May 18).

RSFSR Social Democratic Party Opens Congress

The constituent congress of the RSFSR's Social Democratic Party opened in Moscow. TASS said 300 delegates from social democratic organizations in various Soviet cities as well as social democrats from the United States, East Germany, and other foreign countries participated. The congress, which ended on May 7, did not make as much progress as its organizers had anticipated. Although some delegates hailed the congress as "a major political undertaking," others complained that the proceedings were dominated by marginal organizational issues. Debates on the new party's rules, which were adopted at the end of the congress, occupied most of the meeting, and by the end of the congress the party's program still seemed to be unclear even to its members. Radio Moscow reported that the congress had elected three cochairmen: people's deputies Aleksandr Obolensky and Oleg Ryazantsev and Moscow historian and unorthodox Socialist Pavel Kudyukin. All three have been prominent in the informal movement.

Yakovlev Denies That Gorbachev Faced Challenge from Military

A top associate of Mikhail Gorbachev, Aleksandr Yakovlev, denied reports that the Soviet leader had faced a challenge from the military. Yakovlev told reporters in Moscow that there had been no troop movements and no pressure on Gorbachev. Yakovlev's remarks came in response to Western news reports that elements of the military had put on a show of force in February to put pressure on Gorbachev to make policy changes. In a wide-ranging news conference, Yakovlev also said Gorbachev and other leaders had left the May Day reviewing stand for "political reasons." He said they disagreed with the ultraconservative positions being expressed by protesters who joined the parade on Red Square (*Radio Moscow*, *Reuters*, May 4). See RL 221/90.

Saturday, May 5

Armed Demonstration in Erevan

Radio Moscow reported that a group of 200 armed men had surrounded the building of the Erevan City Party Committee on May 4. Among their demands were the postponement of the Armenian Supreme Soviet elections scheduled for May 20 and the introduction of a multiparty system. The incident ended peacefully. On May 5, a plenum of the Armenian Communist Party Central Committee discussed the incident and set November 22 as the date for the next republican Party Congress.

Komsomol Restructures Top Bodies

The All-Union Komsomol restructured some of its top bodies. TASS said the number of Central Committee secretaries had been cut from ten to seven and that changes had been made in the organization's buro. The changes were made at a plenum of the Komsomol Central Committee. TASS said a number of resolutions were passed, including one on ecology. Two-thirds of the new Komsomol buro consists of republican Komsomol first secretaries and representatives of the army, the KGB, and the USSR Ministry of Internal Affairs. The former head of the Moscow Komsomol, Stanislav Smirnov, was elected second secretary of the All-Union Komsomol, a post that had not officially existed previously. Three new councils were created: for working with students; for supervising youth work in the army; and for dealing with young workers.

Ukrainian and Polish Parliamentarians Seek Closer Ties

A meeting of Ukrainian-Polish parliamentarians to discuss Ukrainian-Polish relations was held near Warsaw on May 4–5. Among those attending from the Ukrainian side were: Ivan Drach, the leader of the Ukrainian restructuring movement "Rukh"; Mykhailo and Bohdan Horyn; Dmytro Pavlychko; Vyacheslav Chornovil; and Myroslav Popovych. On the Polish side were Jacek Kuron, Adam Michnik, Bronislaw Geremek, Zbigniew Bujak, and Janusz Onyszkewicz. The two main themes discussed were "The Polish Route to Democracy" and "Ukrainian-Polish Relations in the Past and Present" (RL Ukrainian service, May 6).

Sunday, May 6

Ogarkov Attacks Media

In an interview with *Sovetskaya Rossiya*, Marshal Nikolai Ogarkov denounced what he called "a campaign" in the Soviet media aimed at blackening the name of the Soviet army. He said Soviet veterans were not Stalinists, and Ogarkov warned that veterans would not passively watch the development of "negative phenomena" in the Soviet Union and "in neighboring countries." The controversial former chief of General Staff and current head of the conservative Veterans' Union also blamed Stalin for the Red Army's losses in 1941 and disputed contentions that Berlin could have been taken earlier in 1945. Elsewhere in the same interview he called for improved living standards for the veterans of the Soviet Union.

Moldavian-Romanian "Bridge of Flowers"

Reuters reported that more than 300,000 Romanians surged across a bridge between Romania and Moldavia, forcing Soviet border guards to give way. The Soviet authorities had opened eight border crossing points for what organizers on both sides called "a bridge of flowers." Some participants chanted "Greater Romania," highlighting growing Moldavian interest in uniting with Romania. Gheorghe Ghimpu, secretary of the council of the Moldavian Popular Front, told AP that the tragedy of the Romanian people had begun with the Hitler-Stalin pact. Moldavian Culture Minister Ion Unguryanu told Reuters that the border would be permanently opened "when reason prevails."

KGB Opens Its Files

The KGB revealed some of its past secret operations, particularly during World War II. *Krasnaya zvezda* said the organization had published a new book on this topic. The newspaper said it was the first publication of its kind in the Soviet Union; in fact, a similar volume was published by the Cheka in the early 1920s.

More Information about Central Committee Attack on Democratic Platform

Not everyone in the CPSU Central Committee supported the open letter of April 11 attacking the Democratic Platform of nonconformist Communists. Writing in *Moscow News* (No. 18), Georgii Khatsenkov, a former consultant to the CPSU Central Committee Department of Organizational Party Work, said there had been at least two drafts of the open letter. The first, which was prepared under the direct supervision of Egor Ligachev, attacked nonconformists in the Party in the harshest terms. When some Central Committee members refused to go along with this version, a second, more moderate draft was prepared. But Khatsenkov objected to that version as well, so he resigned his post and quit the Party.

Moscow Court Dismisses Charges against Demonstrators

Moscow News (No. 18) reported that a Moscow raion court had dismissed charges against six members of "Memorial" who staged a silent protest during Chinese Prime Minister Li Peng's recent visit to Moscow. The "Memorial" group displayed banners protesting Li's role in the events in Tiananmen Square last year; after five minutes a special police unit (OMON) arrived and took away the group's banners. A lawyer argued that "Memorial" had the right to express its views about any such visit; the court agreed.

Monday, May 7

Ligachev Interviewed on Soviet Television

Egor Ligachev put himself in clear opposition to Gorbachev when he criticized reform in an interview on "Vremya." He called for the creation, prior to the Twenty-eighth Party Congress, of a Russian Communist Party with its own apparatus. (Gorbachev favored discussion of the membership of the leading organs of the Russian Party at the CPSU Congress.) Ligachev asserted that the present leadership had made a number of "serious mistakes" in the implementation of economic and political reform, and he criticized Gorbachev indirectly for having underestimated the danger of nationalism and having weakened the leading role of the Party. Ligachev said that for the past year he had fought to strengthen the organizational and ideological role of the Party but that Gorbachev had not supported his endeavor. Ligachev rejected radical reform on the ground that it would lead to mass unemployment, which he said was unacceptable for the Soviet Union.

Victory Day Celebrations

A meeting of World War II veterans was held in the Kremlin, TASS and Radio Moscow reported. Many veterans who spoke attacked the Soviet Union's reform policies. Gorbachev himself opened and closed the meeting, which formed part of the Soviet Victory Day celebrations, by praising veterans for their wartime sacrifices and telling them that their efforts had created a powerful Soviet Union capable of influencing world events. Gorbachev also discussed the Soviet Union's ethnic problems, denouncing so-called separatist forces for their "irresponsible policies" and "dead-end" approaches and criticizing "extremists" who demonstrated at the May Day parade.

Both Defense Minister Dmitrii Yazov, who addressed the meeting, and Warsaw Pact Commander Petr Lushev, who was interviewed by TASS, reopened the issue of Soviet losses in World War II, using it as a basis for attacking liberals for their alleged denigration of the Soviet performance in the war. Yazov accused critics of unjustly attributing the victory to attrition ("blocking the Germans with corpses"), while Lushev claimed that Soviet losses "testified to the unparalleled courage and heroism of the Soviet people and its army."

On May 8, Gorbachev addressed senior officers and veterans in the Bolshoi Theater. The Soviet president lauded the armed forces and the Soviet people for their heroism in World War II, restated his vision of a common

European home, and reemphasized the need for further military reform. His speech contrasted sharply with calls for a return to pre-*perestroika* values issued by representatives of the Soviet veterans on May 7. According to news agency accounts, Gorbachev told the stone-faced officers that "we are far from satisfied with the current situation in the army" (*TASS*, Western agencies, May 8).

On May 9, Soviet troops and World War II veterans paraded in Red Square to mark the World War II anniversary. Yazov addressed the crowd and pledged to pursue military reform. In his speech, Yazov repeated Moscow's denial that the Soviet Union had forcibly occupied the Baltic republics. He asserted that the will of the Baltic peoples had led the three republics to join the USSR and said "we were met with flowers" (*Reuters*, May 9).

Confederation of Labor Set Up in Novokuznetsk

At a congress in Novokuznetsk, 340 delegates from unofficial workers' movements of the USSR set up an independent umbrella trade-union organization, the Confederation of Labor. The Novosti press agency reported that the majority of delegates had rejected the idea of proclaiming the organization a political party. The main goal of the new group is to help introduce a market economy along with social programs that will protect the rights of working people. Novosti was somewhat skeptical that this goal was realistic, given the condition of the Soviet economy. Although representatives of unofficial workers' movements have often been highly critical of the official Soviet trade unions, the All-Union Central Council of Trade Unions supported the creation of the Confederation of Labor—an indication that the leaders of the official unions realize that they must cooperate with the new independent workers' movements to ensure the future of their own organizations.

Government Boosts Purchase Price of Grain

The USSR Council of Ministers passed a resolution effective immediately raising procurement prices for several types of grain by an average of 50 percent (*Radio Moscow-1, AP*, May 7). In addition, the government will pay a premium for grain grown without using pesticides. The measure was designed to stimulate production and is also part of the government's latest price reform effort. It runs counter to the stated goals of the reform, however, because the government is not proposing to raise the price it charges consumers for grain. It thereby increases subsidies to the agricultural sector and exacerbates the huge budget deficit.

Petrovsky in Iran

Deputy Foreign Minister Vladimir Petrovsky visited Teheran to help revive the deadlocked Iran-Iraq peace talks. Other regional issues discussed during Petrovsky's visit included the emigration of Soviet Jews to Israel and the future of Afghanistan (*Reuters*, May 7).

Soviet Officials on German Unification

Soviet Foreign Ministry spokesman Gennadii Gerasimov said the USSR was "generally satisfied" with the "Two-plus-Four" talks on German unification that have just finished in Bonn. Gerasimov said in Moscow that agreement had been reached at the talks to synchronize the German unification process with the creation of a European security system. He repeated that the USSR opposed German membership in NATO (*DPA*, May 7).

On May 8, in his speech to Soviet army officials, Mikhail Gorbachev said a united Germany would have an obligation to sign a peace treaty, but he made no reference to previous Soviet demands that it remain outside NATO. In an interview published in *Rabochaya gazeta*, Defense Minister Dmitrii Yazov reiterated Soviet opposition to NATO membership for a united Germany. The Soviet ambassador to East Germany, Vyacheslav Kochemasov, echoed that line; he told the press there that a united Germany in NATO would upset the political-military equilibrium in Europe. On May 8, Bonn rejected Gorbachev's demand for a peace treaty (*AFP*, May 7).

Tuesday, May 8

Estonia Adopts New Name

Estonia has adopted a new name for itself, dropping the words "Socialist" and "Soviet." The Estonian Supreme Soviet voted overwhelmingly to adopt the name "Republic of Estonia" (*AFP*, May 8). It also voted to change the English translation of the name of its parliament from Supreme Soviet to Supreme Council. Speaking on May 8 in Washington, Marju Lauristin, a deputy of the Estonian Supreme Council, said the Baltic independence issue should be taken up by an international forum such as the Conference on Security and Cooperation in Europe (*RFE/RL Special*, May 8).

Soviet Ambassador Says US Should Withdraw from Asian Pacific

Moscow's ambassador to Manila said that Moscow planned to reduce its military strength in the Pacific region—including withdrawing from Cam Ranh Bay—and that the United States should do the same, TASS reported. Oleg

Sokolov's statement comes on the eve of negotiations between the United States and the Philippines on the future of US bases there.

Three Mines Closed after Gas Poisoning

Rabochaya tribuna reported that three coal mines in the Donbass had been closed after an unexplained outbreak of gas poisoning. According to the newspaper, several dozen miners have fallen ill at the Uglegorskaya mine, and cases of poisoning have been reported at two others nearby. It said, however, that the gas may not be coming from the mines themselves but from a nearby defense industry chemical plant. Suspicion has focused on the plant because an earlier leak of chlorobenzene from the site resulted in the death of three miners. On May 11, about 10,000 coal miners at the Uglegorskaya mine walked off the job in protest against the health hazards to which they were exposed from pollution (*Radio Moscow*-2, 1830, May 11).

On May 15, Radio Moscow said that workers at two Donbass mines had returned to work after "thorough tests" had shown the mines were safe. Nevertheless, the radio reported that meetings and demonstrations were continuing at other mines and enterprises in the region. USSR Deputy Prime Minister Vitalii Doguzhiev arrived in Gorlovka and told TASS that rectification of the situation required "the most extraordinary measures." He compared the situation to the pollution problems of the Aral Sea and Chernobyl'.

On May 22, a government commission assigned to investigate the case said the chemical poisoning came from a formaldehyde leak at a nearby factory. Part of that facility will be closed down July 1 because of low standards.

Floods in Bashkiria Kill Fourteen

Recent floods in Bashkiria killed fourteen people and caused extensive damage. Radio Moscow said rivers swollen by heavy rain and melting snow had swept away bridges, buildings, and power lines. About 20,000 people were evacuated from the flood area, but 60,000 have remained there.

Wednesday, May 9

Arbatov Says Coup Unlikely

Soviet presidential adviser Georgii Arbatov said in London that he did not view the Soviet Armed Forces as an enemy of *perestroika* and that he did not expect a military coup in the Soviet Union. He rejected the suggestion that the threat of a coup was obliging Gorbachev to placate conservative military leaders (*Reuters*, May 9).

Afanas'ev Criticizes Reformers as Disorganized

Radical historian Yurii Afanas'ev said that reform movements in the Soviet Union were too disorganized to be effective and lacked the fresh ideas needed to win mass support, according to Reuters. Speaking at the Sakharov Hearings in Amsterdam, he suggested that the Soviet leadership was attempting to do everything it could to divide the various groups while trying to keep the Party as monolithic as possible. The Party apparatus clearly keeps a close eye on the activities of unofficial groups, as a study of these groups prepared for the Central Committee makes clear (see *Izvestiya TsK KPSS*, No. 4).

Thursday, May 10

Leningrad Branch of Russian Academy of Sciences Formed

TASS said a Leningrad branch of the Russian Academy of Sciences had already been formed, although the Russian Academy itself will not officially come into being until its inaugural congress. (This in fact failed to take place in 1990.) Like the Russian Academy, the creation of the Leningrad branch is in the hands of the most conservative elements of the all-Union academy. Indeed, its cochairman, Andrei Iezuitov, who for a long time was director of the Institute of Russian Literature (Pushkin House), is known for his lack of scholarship and for advancing his career through his connections with the Leningrad Oblast Party Committee.

Yakovlev and Afanas'ev on Future of Socialism

In an article written for the Novosti press agency, member of the Presidential Council Aleksandr Yakovlev spoke about the crisis in the dogmatic model of socialism and said a new model should be worked out. He said, "The modern idea of socialism must embrace the Western practices of social security, the positive heritage of social democracy . . . the new phenomena of capitalism." From Yakovlev's description of the new model of socialism, it is not clear how it differs from systems existing in many West European countries.

Professor Yurii Afanas'ev had expressed similar thoughts in a more direct form in the newspaper *Sovetskaya molodezh'* (April 25). He stressed that "the Bolshevik model of socialism" cannot be reformed, because it is completely dead and was utopian from the very start. He said that the Soviet Union should, therefore, follow the West in its political development.

First Session of USSR-EC Joint Commission

The Joint Commission of the Soviet Union and the European Community began its first session in Moscow. TASS said the meeting was opened by Eduard Shevardnadze and EC External Affairs Commissioner Frans Andriessen. The joint commission was set up in line with the recently signed USSR-EC agreement on trade and economic cooperation. Opening the session, Andriessen said the EC and the USSR could use their trade and cooperation agreement to help reshape Europe (*Reuters*, May 10). On May 11, the talks ended with the announcement that the USSR and the EC planned to expand their bilateral trade and investment (*TASS*, May 11).

Moldavia Abolishes Leading Role of Communist Party

The Moldavian Supreme Soviet voted to abolish the leading role of the republican Communist Party. TASS said that, from now on, all political parties, public organizations, and mass movements in Moldavia would be able to participate equally in state administration through their elected representatives. The agency said all Moldavians now had the right to join political and public organizations that adhered to the republic's constitution and laws. The Moldavian move follows that of a number of other Union republics.

Deputies from Three Republics Form Informal Trade Group

A group of Belorussian, Ukrainian, and Lithuanian parliamentary deputies have formed an informal group to promote trade links between the three republics. Sources in Belorussia told RFE/RL that the deputies had met in Minsk in late April. All the deputies belong to their respective republican popular fronts (RL Belorussian service, May 10). The sources said the deputies had signed a declaration expressing their intent to overcome the effects of the Soviet economic blockade of Lithuania.

New Tax Laws for Foreigners Living in USSR

Radio Moscow-2 (2230) reported that a new Soviet law would increase the tax burden on some foreigners living in the USSR. Tax officials at the USSR Ministry of Finance explained the new regulations at a news conference in Moscow. Foreigners who reside in the USSR for more than 183 days in a calendar year will be regarded as permanent residents for tax purposes. This means they will be liable for taxation on all income, regardless of whether it has been earned in the USSR or abroad. The officials said the amount of tax a foreign citizen had paid in other countries would be taken into consideration when calculating Soviet taxes. Foreigners who reside in the USSR for less than half the year will not be subject to taxation.

New AIDS Law Published

Residents of the USSR can be forced to undergo an AIDS test if the government suspects they may be carriers of the virus, according to the new AIDS law published in *Izvestia*. Diplomats will not be subject to the new regulation, but the Foreign Ministry must be informed if they are suffering from the disease. The law forbids discrimination against AIDS sufferers, including dismissal from work and denial of housing. It also guarantees medical treatment for all AIDS sufferers, but Soviet capability to treat AIDS remains rudimentary at best, and many health workers refuse to go near patients.

Protection for AIDS sufferers is clearly needed. In interviews carried by *Ogonek* (No. 16), several AIDS patients complained that promises of anonymous testing had not been kept and that the police had spied on visitors to testing clinics. Moreover, anyone known to carry the virus has been fired. The article portrayed homosexuals (an estimated 30 percent of Soviet AIDS carriers) as victims—an unprecedented perspective in the Soviet media—and called for an end to their persecution.

Friday, May 11

Gorbachev Speaks to Moscow Party Workers

Speaking to Party activists in Moscow's Frunze Raion, Gorbachev strongly criticized the antigovernment demonstration that took place in Red Square on May Day. (Soviet television broadcast Gorbachev's remarks on May 12.) He was also critical of the Democratic Platform faction of the Party. While claiming that many of the proposals of the reformists coincided with those put forward by the leadership, Gorbachev acknowledged "serious differences" over the Party's role. The Democratic Platform has called for "a parliamentary role" for the Party, while Gorbachev insisted in today's speech that the Party should play "a vanguard role" in all fields of Soviet life.

Gorbachev also said that *perestroika* could not be carried out in accordance with any concrete schedule. The session formally elected him a delegate to the Twenty-eighth Party Congress.

Shakhnazarov Says Communism Utopian

Presidential adviser Georgii Shakhnazarov is the author of an important article in *Kommunist* (No. 4), in which he said the Soviet Union should forget about building communism and concentrate instead on improving the Socialist system the country already has. Shakhnazarov said no one has ever proved that communism is a practical possibility, and he argued that Marx's ideas on the subject were "utopian." Western Marxists are accustomed to drawing a sharp distinction between the ideas of the young and the mature Marx, but their arguments were for a long time dismissed by Soviet theoreticians. Gorbachev has rejected proposals that the CPSU, in imitation of the East European parties, change its name from Communist to Socialist. Shakhnazarov's article seems, however, to pave the way for such a change. See RL 246/90.

Soviet High Command Defends Warsaw Pact

Marking the thirty-fifth anniversary of the Warsaw Pact alliance, Soviet military leaders reaffirmed the organization's continuing importance. Warsaw Pact Commander in Chief Petr Lushev told TASS that Western assertions that the alliance was in decline were "untenable." He argued that there was no alternative to the Warsaw Pact in Eastern Europe capable of guaranteeing stability in Europe. He also rejected the inclusion of a united Germany in NATO. Defense Minister Dmitrii Yazov expressed similar sentiments in an interview with *Izvestia* on May 10.

Effects of Chernobyl' in Western Russia Outlined

RSFSR First Deputy Minister of Health Viktor Panov said radioactive contamination in some parts of the Russian Federation was as bad as in areas closer to Chernobyl'. Panov said the contamination affected 8,130 square kilometers of Russian territory where 647,000 people live (*Sovetskaya Rossiya*, May 11).

Some Residents in Moldavia Reject New Flag

Izvestia reported that residents of Tiraspol, Bendery, and other predominantly Russian and Ukrainian areas of Moldavia had refused to recognize the republic's new flag. The newspaper said that residents there and their representatives in the republican legislature did not believe the Moldavian Supreme Soviet "had the right to copy the flag of foreign states." The new Moldavian flag, approved on April 27, is similar to the flag of Romania. The same day, the Moldavian Supreme Soviet elected the chairman of the republic's popular front, Ion Hadirca, as its first deputy chairman. TASS noted that the popular front holds a majority in the Moldavian Supreme Soviet.

Saturday, May 12

Ryzhkov on Economic Reforms

Speaking on Soviet television, Soviet Prime Minister Nikolai Ryzhkov said progress towards "a regulated market economy" must be gradual and accompanied by improvements in the country's social security system. Noting that there were differences within the leadership on the question of reform, Ryzhkov said he was opposed to unemployment as an instrument of change and believed that the shift to higher market prices should take place next year rather than this year. His comments came at a time of worsening economic and social news. On May 11, *Izvestia* reported that Soviet industrial production during the first four months of 1990 was 2 billion rubles less than in the same period last year.

Joint Council of Baltic Republics Established

The chairmen of the Supreme Councils of Lithuania, Latvia, and Estonia signed a declaration establishing a joint council to coordinate their republics' moves towards independence from the USSR. The declaration, signed in Tallinn, renews the Treaty on Unity and Cooperation of 1934. The new council will meet from time to time to discuss political and economic issues of mutual concern (*Reuters*, *AFP*, May 12). The Baltic leaders sent a telegram to Mikhail Gorbachev asking him to begin talks promptly on independence for the Baltic republics. They also issued a statement calling on the thirty-five signatory states of the Helsinki accords to meet to hear the arguments of the Baltic republics in their campaign for independence. See RL 233/90.

Moscow Rejects Estonian Law on Alternative Military Service

According to Estonian Prime Minister Edgar Savisaar, Moscow has said it will not recognize an Estonian law allowing young men to perform community service as an alternative to military service. Savisaar told RFE/RL the Soviet position had been conveyed to him during talks in Moscow on May 11 with Soviet Defense Minister Dmitrii Yazov.

Niyazov Reelected Head of Turkmen Party

A congress of the Turkmen Communist Party reelected Saparmurad Niyazov first secretary of the Central Committee. TASS said Niyazov was first elected to the position in December, 1985. The congress—which ended in Ashkhabad on May 12—adopted a declaration in favor of strengthening the Soviet federation.

Air Force Unit Attacked in Leninakan

Krasnaya zvezda said about forty armed men had attacked a Soviet Air Force unit in the Armenian city of Leninakan. The attackers were reported to have seized the unit duty officer and disconnected the alarm system. The newspaper said the attackers then entered the installation in a vehicle and opened fire on the barracks. The daily quoted a military spokesman as saying the increasing use of violence in Armenia and the spate of unlawful actions had reached "an extremely dangerous" level.

Moscow Considers Allowing Jewish Emigrants Back

Soviet Ambassador at Large Igor Andropov told the Jordanian news service that Moscow was considering a PLO request for Jewish émigrés to be allowed to return to the USSR if they were unhappy in Israel (*Reuters*, May 12). Andropov's statement is the latest in a series of efforts by Moscow to defuse Arab anger at Jewish emigration to Israel, which is now running at more than 10,000 people a month.

New Party to Be Formed in Leningrad

About 170 people met in Leningrad to prepare the founding congress of the Democratic Party of Russia. TASS quoted a deputy of the RSFSR Congress of People's Deputies, Marina Sal'e, as saying the main task of the congress was to find a way of consolidating the democratic movement.

Pollution Threatens Water Supply of Nine Ukrainian Cities

Trud said ground water pollution was a serious threat to drinking water supplies in nine Ukrainian cities. The newspaper said progress had been slow in establishing alternative sources of drinking water in the affected areas of the Donetsk and Lugansk Oblasts.

Sunday, May 13

Yazov Says Warsaw Pact Intact

Defense Minister Dmitrii Yazov said democratization in Eastern Europe had opened possibilities for discussion of a new European security structure, but he added that speculation about the collapse of the Warsaw Pact was unjustified. He said all pact members had reaffirmed their support for the alliance. Yazov made his comments in an interview with *Izvestia*. In an article appearing the same day in *Krasnaya zvezda*, the commander in chief of the Warsaw Pact, General Petr Lushev, also said the alliance should not be disbanded. The comments of the two military leaders were published to mark the thirty-fifth anniversary of the Warsaw Pact on May 14.

Proindependence Rally in Kiev

More than 20,000 people held a proindependence demonstration in Kiev, according to news agency reports. Among the slogans were "Power to the People, Communism for the Communists." Participants told RFE/RL that speakers had called for the resignation of republican Party leader Vladimir Ivashko and for support for the Lithuanian drive for independence. On May 14, Ukrainian Prime Minister Vitalii Masol complained about what he called widespread proindependence sentiments in the republic. Speaking to TASS, he said those calling for Ukrainian independence were more concerned with their own political ambitions than with their compatriots' future.

Azerbaijani Popular Front Headquarters to Reopen

Officials of the Azerbaijani Popular Front told RFE/RL that the republican authorities had given permission for the front's Baku headquarters to reopen and for the resumption of publication of its newspaper, banned since January under the state of emergency. A meeting between popular front representatives and republican leaders last week resulted in an agreement to set up a consultative council that would consider commemorating the declaration of Azerbaijan's independence on May 28, 1918, and introducing the Latin alphabet in place of the Cyrillic.

Plan for Return of Crimean Tatars

A government plan has been drawn up for the return of the Crimean Tatars to the Crimea. The chairman of the government commission for the problems of the Crimean Tatars, Vitalii Doguzhiev, told TASS that the plan calls for the organized return to begin in 1991 and to be completed by 1996. The program will be financed from all-Union funds and also from the resources of those republics from which the Crimean Tatars will be returning. Some will come back under government schemes, some on their own initiative, and some as groups, such as cooperatives.

Protest against Pollution in Bashkiria

Radio Moscow reported that citizens in the Bashkir capital of Ufa had formed a forty-kilometer-long human chain to protest about the government's failure to combat pollution problems in the autonomous republic. At the end of March, over half a million residents of Ufa went without drinking water for a fortnight after the water supply was contaminated with phenol from a local chemical plant. A huge demonstration was held on April 8 to demand the closure of chemical plants in the city, but the local government has not acceded to the public's demands.

Moscow Students Protest about Suppression of Chinese Democracy Movement

TASS said several dozen Moscow university students had started a hunger strike marking the first anniversary of the crushing of the prodemocracy movement in China. The agency said the strike had begun on May 12, and students had set up tents in front of the main university building.

Mongolian Party Leader Arrives in Moscow

Mongolian Communist Party General Secretary Gombojavyn Ochirbat and Mongolian President Punsalmaagiyn Ochirbat arrived in Moscow for an official visit (*Pravda*, May 13). On May 14, Gorbachev met the Mongolian leaders for discussions on regional problems and bilateral relations (*TASS*, May 14; *Izvestia*, May 15). (Recently, the Mongolian Communist Party, like the CPSU, was forced to give up its guaranteed leading role in society.) The Mongolian officials also held talks with Foreign Minister Eduard Shevardnadze. They left Moscow for home on May 16 (*TASS*, May 16). The same day, Radio Moscow confirmed that a new phase of the Soviet troop withdrawal from Mongolia was under way.

Monday, May 14

Gorbachev Declares Estonian and Latvian Independence Moves Illegal

Mikhail Gorbachev issued two decrees declaring the moves towards independence by Estonia and Latvia illegal. He said the two republics had violated the constitution and the law on secession when they declared the start of a transition period on the way to independence (*Central Television* and *TASS*, May 14; *Pravda*, May 15).

On May 15, Radio Moscow broadcast a commentary urging dialogue between Moscow and the Baltic republics. The radio said it was quite possible that economic sanctions similar to those applied against Lithuania would also be applied against Estonia and Latvia. The same day, Eduard Shevardnadze said in an interview with the US television network CBS that the Baltic republics had made a mistake in first issuing declarations of independence and only then seeking dialogue with Moscow.

USSR Supreme Soviet Finally Approves Slander Bill

After lengthy debates, the USSR Supreme Soviet approved a law that will make it a crime to insult the Soviet president. The bill calls for prison or labor camp terms of up to six years or a fine of up to 25,000 rubles to be imposed on people convicted of making public statements that insult or slander the president (*TASS*, May 14). Public criticism of presidential activity or of his policies do not constitute a violation of the law.

The law was proposed by Vladimir Foteev, chairman of the Supreme Soviet's Committee on *Glasnost'* and the Rights and Appeals of Citizens. Foteev, a former senior Party official who seems to be close to Gorbachev, justified his proposal on the grounds that the number of "slanderous fabrications against the Soviet president" has been on the increase in public statements and some periodicals. Last year the Soviet legislature abolished the Brezhnev-era law that banned "slandering the Soviet state and public order" and amended the old criminal law prohibiting "anti-Soviet agitation and propaganda" to apply only to appeals for the violent overthrow of the state. Even under Stalin there was no official ban on criticism of individual leaders in the Soviet Union.

RSFSR Election Campaign

Boris El'tsin, who is running for the post of chairman of the RSFSR Supreme Soviet, said in Moscow that Gorbachev had convened an unannounced meeting of Party loyalists among RSFSR deputies to promote RSFSR Prime Minister Aleksandr Vlasov for the post, AP reported. According to El'tsin, Gorbachev claimed that he—El'tsin—was "plotting a counterrevolution." El'tsin also complained that, while an interview with Vlasov was shown on Soviet television, his was canceled by the authorities. He promised that he would fight for full autonomy for the RSFSR, eliminate all republican ministries, and merge the KGB with the police. On May 5, *Sovetskaya Rossiya* published a letter attacking El'tsin's outspokenness and alleged drinking while abroad. The author, a Party veteran from Krasnodar, argued that El'tsin should thus be rejected on moral grounds.

One short interview with El'tsin did appear on Soviet television in the late night news on May 14. The interview focused on a documentary film entitled "Boris El'tsin: A Portrait against the Background of Struggle." Directed by Gennadii Popov, this film had been shown at the Central House of Cinema in Moscow on May 13. It was the second Soviet documentary devoted to the CPSU maverick. The first, "A Soviet Elegy," by director Aleksandr Sokurov, was shown throughout the USSR in 1989.

Grim Future for Joint Ventures

The *Financial Times* said joint ventures in the USSR were facing a grim future. The newspaper reported that only 40 percent of the 1,476 joint ventures in the Soviet Union involved investments of more than 1 million rubles. At a seminar in Frankfurt, West German businessmen who, with 16 percent, have the largest single share of the joint ventures, said they thought the lack of a legal framework, problems with the quality and reliability of Soviet suppliers, and a shortage of qualified Soviet administrators had hindered progress in this area. They also complained that the Soviet Armed Forces had resisted the idea of a special economic zone around Kaliningrad.

Brezhnev's Preinvasion Letter Published in Czechoslovakia

Rude pravo, the newspaper of the Czechoslovak Communist Party, published the text of a letter sent by Leonid Brezhnev to Alexander Dubcek four days before the Warsaw Pact invasion of Czechoslovakia in 1968. The letter contained no direct warning of military action, but it accused the Czechoslovak Party authorities of insufficient resolve in resisting "counterrevolutionary elements." Although the letter is not known to have been published before, its existence was no secret. Its appearance thus provides a missing document but no major revelation.

Georgian Communist Party Opens Congress

The Twenty-eighth Congress of the Georgian Communist Party opened in Tbilisi. During 1989, the Party had lost influence to radical groups campaigning for Georgian independence and secession from the USSR. In a *Pravda* interview on May 14, Georgian Party leader Givi Gumbaridze argued for greater political and economic autonomy for Georgia within the USSR. His assertion that the Georgian Party had not suffered a massive decline in membership was rejected by a spokesman for one of the radical parties as incorrect, according to AP. On May 15, in his opening speech to the congress, Gumbaridze denied that the Party would split into two factions. He further claimed that it was still a leading political force in the republic (*TASS*, May 15).

Mubarak Meets Gorbachev

Egyptian President Hosni Mubarak opened talks with Mikhail Gorbachev after arriving in Moscow for the first visit by an Egyptian leader in eighteen years (*AFP*, May 14). On May 15, Gorbachev and Mubarak signed a declaration criticizing the emigration of Soviet Jews to Israel's occupied territories (*Reuters*, May 15).

Gorbachev Meets Papal Envoy

Gorbachev met in the Kremlin with special papal envoy Archbishop Francesco Colasuonno. This was the first visit to the Soviet Union by a papal envoy. The Vatican and the USSR established "permanent official relations" in March—a status that falls short of full diplomatic ties (*TASS*, May 14).

Adamishin Becomes Soviet Ambassador to Italy

TASS said Anatolii Adamishin had been released from his job as Soviet deputy foreign minister to take up a new post as Soviet ambassador to Italy. It said he was replacing Nikolai Lun'kov, who has retired.

Alcohol Prices to Remain Steady

The chairman of the State Committee for Prices reported in *Pravda* that alcohol prices would not increase as part of a general price reform now being considered by Moscow. In fact, Vyacheslav Senchagov admitted that alcohol prices may be lowered in the future in an effort to thwart illegal *samogon* production and to ease shortages of sugar. The price of a half-liter bottle of vodka now averages about 10 rubles.

Moscow TV to Broadcast Children's Bible Stories

Moscow radio and television will broadcast cartoon-style Bible stories twice a week, beginning May 26, a Finnish religious leader told AP. Hannu Haukka said Estonian, Latvian, and Leningrad television stations had already begun to broadcast the Finnish-produced programs.

Russian Writer Venedikt Erofeev Dies

The Russian writer Venedikt Erofeev died on May 11. Erofeev, who was fifty-two years old at the time of his death, was the author of the novel *Moskva-Petushki*, which had won wide acclaim in the West but was not published in the USSR until 1989. *Moscow News* (No. 20) carried an obituary of Erofeev by the writer Evgenii Popov.

Dashichev on German Unification

In *Komsomol'skaya pravda*, outspoken military historian Vyacheslav Dashichev said the Soviet Union was wrong to insist that a united Germany remain outside NATO and that it sign a peace treaty with Moscow. Long viewed as a major Soviet spokesman for Gorbachev's "new thinking" in foreign policy, Dashichev was recently disowned by a Soviet Foreign Ministry spokesman who said Dashichev did not speak for Moscow and played no role in the formation of Soviet foreign policy.

Tuesday, May 15

Gorbachev Receives Only 61 Percent of Party Vote

Gorbachev was elected a delegate to the Twenty-eighth Party Congress this week, but he received only 61 percent of the votes in Moscow's Frunze Raion. Thirty-six percent of the electorate voted for Valerii Baranov, a factory worker. Local officials told Reuters that, a year ago, no one would have dared to vote against Gorbachev but that now this result reflects the situation in both the Party and the country. It is the first time, however, that Gorbachev has faced competition in an election.

Baker in Moscow

US Secretary of State James Baker arrived in Moscow for talks with Soviet Foreign Minister Eduard Shevardnadze expected to focus on problems standing in the way of a US-Soviet strategic arms treaty (Western agencies, May 15).

On May 16, Baker opened talks with Shevardnadze. The same day, Estonian Prime Minister Edgar Savisaar urged Baker to discuss the latest developments in the Baltic republics with the Soviet foreign minister (*Reuters*, May 16).

On May 17, Shevardnadze showed Baker a typical Russian village, Radonezh, which lies about sixty kilometers north of Moscow. Local residents complained to Baker about their low standard of living and about the fact that they did not have a church (*Reuters*, May 17).

On May 19, Marshal Sergei Akhromeev told reporters that most of the major issues regarding a strategic arms treaty had been resolved. US officials were optimistic, too, saying that some problems remained, but none that were "unbridgeable" (*Reuters*, May 19). The two officials also discussed regional issues. Speaking to reporters after the meeting, Baker said that substantial progress towards a Middle East peace settlement was unlikely under the present conditions in Israel. Baker also said the positions of the USSR and the US on Afghanistan were slowly moving closer. At a separate press conference, Shevardnadze said he had raised the question of Soviet Jewish emigration to Israel in his discussions with Baker (*AFP*, May 19).

On May 23, talking at the White House about his visit to the USSR, James Baker said there was too much at stake in US-Soviet relations to imperil further progress because of the crisis in the Baltics (*RFE/RL Special*, May 23). He also reiterated that the Soviet Union must codify more liberal emigration policies before the US would grant it most-favored-nation trade status.

Anti-Independence Forces Attack Estonian Parliamentary Building

In Tallinn, anti-independence demonstrators broke through a gate and occupied the courtyard of the Estonian Supreme Soviet building. Estonian Prime Minister Edgar Savisaar went on Estonian radio three times during the incident to call upon "all Estonians" for help. He called the incident "an attempted putsch" (*Reuters*, May 15). Estonian Foreign Minister Lennart Meri told Reuters that the demonstrators had thrown stones and overturned a vehicle while occupying the courtyard.

On May 17, the Estonian authorities announced a temporary ban on political strikes in the republic and on the activities of the anti-independence United Council of Work Collectives, which had helped organize the anti-independence protest outside the Estonian parliament (RFE Estonian service, May 17).

On May 18, the Estonian Supreme Council decided to remove the statue of Lenin from the Supreme Council hall (*TASS*, *Central Television*, "Vremya," May 18).

Supreme Soviet Passes Pensions Law

After weeks of debate over the fine print, the Supreme Soviet finally passed a law on pensions. The law contains over 130 articles, will affect 60 million Soviet pensioners, and will cost almost 100 million rubles annually. While discussion of the law lasted over six months, its basic tenets were not debated. Major changes under the new law will be the establishment of periodic cost-of-living adjustments, the provision of pensions for those without employment records, and an increase in the differential between the minimum and maximum pensions by tying benefits more closely to an individual's work history. The text of the law was published in *Izvestia* on May 30.

Warning Strike in Northern Fleet

Soviet television reported that sailors on board the Soviet Northern Fleet's nuclear-powered icebreakers had staged a two-hour warning strike to protest against poor salaries and deteriorating safety conditions. The captain of one of the ships was quoted as saying, "We have reached that invisible point where nuclear safety can only start to deteriorate." Turnover of personnel on board these vessels is said to be increasing, and the technical qualifications of the ships' operators are therefore suffering a decline.

Moscow's Economic Situation Examined

The Executive Committee of the Moscow City Soviet examined the economic situation in the Soviet capital and proposed measures to address pressing economic problems there, according to TASS. The chairman of the committee, Yurii Lyzhkov, noted that the economic situation in the capital had reached a crisis point, with a city budget deficit totaling some 265 million rubles. He said the first priority in Moscow was to stabilize the consumer sector.

Social Democratic Party Established in Moldavia

TASS reported that a Social Democratic Party had been established in Moldavia. According to the agency, the party wants Moldavia to be a sovereign state but does not necessarily want the republic to leave the USSR.

New Call to Bury Lenin

Ogonek (No. 18) published a letter repeating earlier calls to bury Lenin's body instead of keeping it in the mausoleum. Muscovite Yu. Zhbanov pointed out that this was what the Bulgarians had recently decided to do with the body of Georgii Dimitrov. It too had been put in a mausoleum, following the Soviet example.

Lenin Said to Be Responsible for Expulsion of Scholars

Literaturnaya gazeta (No. 19) said that Lenin had worked out the entire scenario for the expulsion of leading Russian philosophers and scholars in 1922. Although the expulsion of Semen Frank, Father Sergei Bulgakov, Nikolai Berdyaev, and others has already been discussed in the Soviet press, *Literaturnaya gazeta* is the first Soviet publication to draw attention to Lenin's role in the action.

Wednesday, May 16

***Pravda* Defends Gorbachev**

Pravda said Gorbachev had fallen out of favor with the population because his reforms had not improved their lives fast enough. It defended the Soviet president, however, saying that his critics were ungrateful for the reforms. The article was published alongside extracts from a letter from a long-time Communist who had expressed her disillusion with the Party leader.

RSFSR Congress of People's Deputies Starts Work

On May 16, a session of the RSFSR Congress of People's Deputies opened in Moscow, with Mikhail Gorbachev attending the opening. Supporters of Boris El'tsin won an important victory when the RSFSR Congress voted to include a report on the outgoing Russian government in the agenda of the Congress, Radio Mayak reported.

Aleksandr Vlasov, El'tsin's rival in his contest for the post of chairman of the RSFSR Supreme Soviet, was prime minister of this government, and radical deputies hoped that evidence of his role in bringing about the current disastrous state of affairs in the RSFSR would help El'tsin's candidacy for the post of chairman of the RSFSR Supreme Soviet. Many deputies went further, questioning Vlasov's right to be a deputy in view of the fact that he was a member of three soviets—the USSR Congress of People's Deputies, the RSFSR Congress of People's Deputies, and a local soviet—concurrently. Soviet law stipulates that no one may be a member of more than two soviets at once.

The Congress also excluded Valentin Chikin, chief editor of the conservative newspaper *Sovetskaya Rossiya*, from the prestigious editorial commission. He was the only one of fifty candidates for membership of this commission who was rejected by the Congress.

On May 17, Mikhail Gorbachev addressed the RSFSR Congress. He warned against confrontation among the various pro-*perestroika* forces in the Russian Federation. He also warned against attempts to lead the Russian Congress astray and urged deputies to speak less but do more (*TASS*, May 17). Speaking during a break in the Congress proceedings, Gorbachev added that a conservative public was holding back his reform efforts (*Reuters*, May 17).

On May 18, some fifty progressive deputies walked out of the RSFSR Congress to protest against conservative efforts to adopt a resolution condemning Lithuania's declaration of independence. The measure had been proposed by fifty-five deputies with military and KGB backgrounds. It condemned the Lithuanian declaration of independence as "destructive and one-sided" and said that the Lithuanian authorities were violating the rights of Russians and soldiers. Put to a vote without discussion by conservative chairman Vasilii Kazakov, the measure was passed in principle by a vote of 522 to 203 with 23 abstentions. (Constitutionally, the measure should not have passed; the RSFSR basic law says that such a resolution requires the support of more than half of the deputies—in this case, no fewer than 530 votes.) The final version of the resolution, which was formulated by the Congress Editorial Commission and passed without a recorded vote, expressed the hope that Lithuania could achieve complete sovereignty within a renewed Soviet federation. The editorial commission is headed by liberal Leningrad scholar Mikhail Tolstoi (*Radio Mayak*, May 18).

On May 18, Aleksandr Vlasov addressed the Congress, saying the RSFSR needed "fully-fledged economic and political sovereignty" for a radical solution to its problems. Vlasov also said a sovereign Russia should have the right to conduct its own foreign policy (*TASS*, May 18).

On May 19, the RSFSR Congress of People's Deputies debated the republic's switch to a market economy. Radio Moscow said many deputies had criticized a report delivered by Vlasov on May 18 on the republic's economic situation. They said it did not match expectations and had "no original, bold ideas" (*TASS*, May 19). The same day, radical reformers proposed amending the constitution of the RSFSR to give its laws priority over the laws of the Soviet Union within the republic. The proposed draft declaration of "sovereignty" was similar to the ones that began the Baltic drive for independence eighteen months ago. In contrast, Vlasov said he supported economic, rather then full political sovereignty for Russia. He strongly criticized the radical proposal as a violation of the Soviet Constitution.

On May 21, the Congress resumed after a one-day break with discussion of the social and economic situation in the RSFSR. A lot of criticism of the authorities was heard. A deputy from the Kuzbass mining region in Siberia, where there were widespread miners' strikes last year, said that problems there were even worse now and that there was a danger of another strike (*Central Television*, May 21).

On May 23, the RSFSR Congress decided to adopt a declaration on the republic's sovereignty.

Constitutional Committee to Study Gorbachev Decree

The newly created Constitutional Oversight Committee met for the first time. One of its first tasks was to consider whether a decree issued in April by President Gorbachev on demonstrations in Moscow complied with the Soviet Constitution (*TASS*, May 16). The decree banned marches and demonstrations in the center of Moscow and transferred the authority for regulating such activities from the Moscow City Soviet to the USSR Council of Ministers. The committee has only an advisory function, however, and cannot itself overrule presidential decrees. In mid-September the Constitutional Oversight Committee ruled the decree unconstitutional (see *Izvestia*, September 15).

Soviet Rabbis Say Anti-Semitism Not Widespread in USSR

The chief rabbis of Moscow and Leningrad were quoted by AP as saying that anti-Semitism in the Soviet Union was limited to a small section of the population. They made this claim at a conference of European rabbis in Brussels. Also on May 16, a Helsinki newspaper reported that plans were being made to send thousands of Soviet Jews to Israel via a small town in eastern Finland. Soviet Foreign Minister Eduard Shevardnadze told the Egyptian news agency MENA the same day that he would press the United States to open its doors to more Soviet Jewish emigrants.

Soviet Union Gets GATT Observer Status

The USSR was granted observer status in the General Agreement on Tariffs and Trade, giving it its first formal link with the global trade organization. The United States and Japan had wanted to delay this move until after the current round of GATT talks but withdrew their objections earlier this week (*Reuters*, May 16).

Controversy over Soviet Submarines

A Dutch consortium won a Soviet contract to raise the Soviet submarine *Komsomolets*, according to news agency reports. The Dutch group was scheduled to sign a contract in June in Moscow worth between 200 and 250 million dollars to raise the "Mike"-class submarine, which sank off the coast of Norway in April, 1989. It was also reported that the Swedish navy had dropped depth charges on a submarine intruder in its territorial waters. The Swedish navy said that there was no indication a target had been hit; it is continuing the search.

New Chairman of Moscow Oblast Soviet Executive Committee Elected

TASS reported that engineer Anatolii Tyazhlov, aged forty-seven, had been elected chairman of the Moscow Oblast Soviet Executive Committee.

Referendum Votes against Nuclear Power

The "Vremya" television news program announced the results of a referendum held on May 15 in the central Russian city of Voronezh. The referendum, in which local inhabitants expressed their views on the building of a new atomic power station, was organized by the oblast soviet. Voronezh already has one nuclear power station located some distance from the city in Novyi Voronezh, but the local authorities are planning to build another, much closer to the city. In the wake of the Chernobyl' nuclear accident, local inhabitants have felt this was unsafe. Eighty-two percent of those eligible to vote took part in the referendum; of those, 96 percent voted against the construction of the power station. There have been other, unofficial referendums on the subject of nuclear power in the Soviet Union, but this was the first held under official auspices.

Public Opinion Mixed on Cooperatives

Public opinion on the Soviet cooperative movement continues to be mixed. An opinion poll published in *Ekonomika i zhizn'* (No. 20) showed that cooperatives received the most favorable ratings from people in higher income brackets who patronized them. The lowest ratings came from pensioners on low, fixed incomes.

Paper Shortage Affects *Novyi mir*

The journal with the Soviet rights to Solzhenitsyn's writings has been effectively closed by the authorities. In the current issue of *Knizhnoe obozrenie*, readers complained that subscribers to *Novyi mir* had not even received the March issue. The official explanation for the situation was a shortage of paper. Since 1985, the monthly has trebled its circulation to more than 2 million. Publication eventually resumed, but every issue came out with a considerable delay.

Thursday, May 17

Prosecutors Ordered to Supervise Constitutional Compliance in Estonia and Latvia

The USSR Prosecutor's Office ordered prosecutors in Estonia and Latvia to strictly supervise the observance of the USSR Constitution and laws in those republics. The prosecutors were also ordered to "defend the rights of citizens and labor collectives there" and to protest immediately against actions and decisions taken by the Estonian and Latvian authorities on the basis of resolutions of the republican parliaments that contradicted the USSR Constitution. The USSR Prosecutor's Office said it would "firmly put a halt" to any actions that infringed on the territorial integrity of the USSR or on the national equality and rights of its citizens.

US Congressmen Write to Gorbachev on Armenia and Nagorno-Karabakh

Three US congressmen wrote a letter to Mikhail Gorbachev deploring what they said were human-rights violations in Nagorno-Karabakh and Armenia. The congressmen said the situation was "explosive" and "was bound to have serious repercussions unless immediate corrective measures were taken." The congressmen urged that the state of emergency be lifted so that the oblast soviet could assume control. They also requested that the military command in the region protect the people and they urged Gorbachev to take steps to lift the economic blockade of the enclave by Azerbaijan (*RFE/RL Special*, May 17).

Mutalibov on Strikes and Refugee Problem in Azerbaijan

Azerbaijani Party First Secretary Ayaz Mutalibov said in a *Pravda* interview that the organizational committee set up in December, 1989, to administer Nagorno-Karabakh was managing to stabilize the situation there, "despite ferocious resistance." (Armenians argue that the committee, composed exclusively of Azerbaijanis, is colluding with the military to oppress the Armenian population.) Mutalibov said strikes had cost the republic's economy nearly 1,400 million rubles in the last two years. He added that Azerbaijan's most serious problem was lack of housing and employment for the 165,000 refugees from Armenia and the 40,000 Meskhetian refugees from Uzbekistan.

Friday, May 18

Novosti Says Gorbachev Lacks Support

In an unusual commentary, Novosti press agency said Mikhail Gorbachev had delayed implementing radical economic reforms because he lacked popular support. The agency criticized Gorbachev for failing to prepare Soviet citizens adequately for the economic reforms that were scheduled to be announced on May 10 but that have not been unveiled amid reports that they are on hold at least through this year. The agency also criticized Gorbachev and his Presidential Council for issuing "a vaguely worded communiqué" to cloud their true intentions in putting off the economic reforms.

Trade-Union Leader Gives Warning on Soviet Reforms

The new leader of the official Soviet trade-union movement, Gennadii Yanaev, demanded that the Soviet government agree to index wages and guarantee full employment; otherwise, Yanaev said in an interview in *Pravda*, the trade unions would resort to the strike weapon.

Altai Deputies Urge Statehood for Soviet Germans

The Altai Krai Soviet appealed to Gorbachev to quickly restore statehood to ethnic Germans living in the Soviet Union. The body said there could be no further delay. A Radio Moscow report said almost 128,000 Germans lived in the Altai Krai. More than 2,000 Germans emigrated from the territory in 1989, and the number of applications for exit permits has risen sharply this year.

Dubcek Returns to Moscow as Guest

Twenty-two years after being brought to the Soviet Union in disgrace, Czechoslovak reformer Alexander Dubcek returned to Moscow as an official guest. Now chairman of the Czechoslovak Federal Assembly, Dubcek was invited to Moscow by the USSR Supreme Soviet. During talks with Dubcek, Mikhail Gorbachev denounced the Soviet invasion of Czechoslovakia in 1968. TASS said Gorbachev told Dubcek the invasion had had a bad effect not only on Czechoslovakia but also on the USSR, by causing a freeze on reforms and pushing the country into "the blind alley of stagnation." Dubcek told reporters he was very impressed by Gorbachev (*Radio Prague*, *TASS*, May 21).

United States Panning for Soviet Gold Statistics

US experts estimate that gold production in Uzbekistan amounts to between 1.9 and 2.6 million troy ounces a year (*Reuters*, May 18). The estimate, made by the US Bureau of Mines, was based on statements made by Shukrulla Mirsaidov, the chairman of the Uzbek Council of Ministers, and reported in *Pravda Vostoka* on March 29. Mirsaidov said that the republic's gold output was worth 790 to 910 million dollars annually, adding: "It is time to lift the curtain of secrecy and be open about what allows us to call Uzbekistan one of the main sources of hard-currency earnings for the country."

Falin Criticizes German Treaty

The head of the CPSU Central Committee International Department, Valentin Falin, criticized the new German economic accord, saying it did not treat the two Germanies as equal partners. In an interview with East German radio, Falin said the treaty "is hardly an example of how two sovereign states can represent their interests and positions with equal rights" (*Reuters*, May 18).

Crimean Tatars Mark Deportation Anniversary

In the Crimea, many Crimean Tatars marked the anniversary of their deportation during World War II. TASS said flags of mourning flew over the houses of many Tatars who had recently returned to the Crimea. Meetings were held to pay homage to the victims of the deportation. In the Ukrainian capital, Kiev, the republic's Supreme Soviet observed a minute of silence in memory of the victims of the deportation.

Deputies Propose Scientific-Industrial Union

In a letter carried by *Izvestia*, a group of Soviet scientists who are also people's deputies proposed the creation of a Scientific-Industrial Union of the USSR, which would include workers, engineers, and scientists among its members. The aim of the union would be to improve the scientific basis of Soviet industry. The authors of the letter, who include Academicians Zhores Alferov and Evgenii Velikhov, economists Pavel Bunich and Nikolai Shmelev, as well as a member of the Presidential Council, Veniamin Yarin, complained that Soviet industry is at present not ready for serious economic reforms. They propose that the union should help find financial support for industrial and engineering projects, improve the Soviet Union's economic contacts with the West, and defend the rights of workers, engineers, and scientists against bureaucrats.

Saturday, May 19

Moldavian Party Congress Opposes Secession

The Moldavian Communist Party Congress, which ended in Kishinev on May 18, decided to oppose any move by Moldavia to secede from the USSR. TASS said a congress resolution instead supported a course of economic and political sovereignty for Moldavia within "a renewed Soviet federation." The resolution said all required changes must be achieved through talks and laid down in "a new Union treaty." It asserted Moldavia's right to independent political and economic ties with foreign countries, including diplomatic exchanges.

Gorbachev Declares Estonian "Provisional Rule" Illegal

Mikhail Gorbachev declared illegal a law on "provisional rule" adopted by the Estonian parliament on May 16 to guide that republic's transition to independence. The law stipulated that all Estonian state and judicial organs should no longer be subordinate to their counterparts in Moscow and should from now on only obey laws adopted by the Estonian authorities. In a decree published in Moscow, Gorbachev called the measure "unlawful" and said any actions based on it were also illegal. He said the law violated the Soviet Constitution and the provisions of the law regulating the secession of a republic from the Soviet Union (*TASS*, May 19; *Pravda*, May 20).

Presidential Decree Lifts Restrictions on Housing

Mikhail Gorbachev directed the Soviet government to prepare legislation allowing the purchase of existing housing from the state, individual bank loans for new housing construction, the construction of apartments for immediate sale, and a sharp increase in the availability of construction materials (*TASS*, May 19; *Izvestia*, May 20). His decree did not make it clear whether housing would be "sold" privately in the future, though it did warn against "speculation." This step is intended to alleviate the chronic housing shortage in the USSR and to help cope with the huge monetary overhang.

On May 21, a member of the Presidential Council, Evgenii Primakov, said Gorbachev's decree on housing was one of the main acts of his presidency (*Central Television*, "Vremya," May 21).

Monarchists Hold Congress

The first all-Russian congress of monarchists ended today, Moscow television reported. One delegate told a television journalist that the congress had proclaimed another monarchist party, the Orthodox Monarchist Order. It seeks to restore the monarchy, to preserve the empire, and to return land to the peasants. According to this spokesman, all members of the new party must be Orthodox Christians but they do not have to be ethnic Russians. No information was given about the party's size, nor about the number of delegates who participated in the congress, but it is unlikely to be a mass movement.

Exodus from Party in Karelian Republic

Radio Moscow reported that last year and in the first quarter of this year a total of 1,380 Communists had handed in their Party cards in Karelia. It said many of those who quit the Party were "respected Party members of long standing." Radio Moscow said the exodus was prompted by reports that some Karelian Party leaders had abused their positions. This is the latest in a string of reports indicating that Party membership throughout the USSR is falling; 44 percent of those handing in their resignations are said to have been Party members for over twenty years.

Association of Soviet Koreans Created

Soviet Koreans now have their own association, TASS reported. Some 300 representatives at a Moscow congress elected orientalist Mikhail Pak president of the Association of Soviet Koreans. The new group can be expected to put pressure on the authorities to allow the Koreans to return from Central Asia to the Soviet Far East, from where many of them were deported by Stalin.

More Violence in Armenia

The Armenian Ministry of Internal Affairs said armed groups had stolen twenty-one tanks in the republic on May 18 but had given them up after a brief exchange of gunfire with security forces. Radio Erevan quoted a ministry statement as saying the attackers had issued threats at gunpoint and had taken the tank drivers hostage. The ministry said there were no casualties and added that criminal proceedings had been started in connection with the incident.

On May 21, the Interfax Service of Radio Moscow reported that a Soviet officer had been killed in Azerbaijan on May 19 by gunfire from the neighboring Shamshadinsky Raion in Armenia. Three similar incidents of armed violence against Soviet troops in the area that night were also reported.

Belorussian Front Candidate Loses

The chairman of the Presidium of the Belorussian Supreme Soviet defeated a candidate of the local popular front in elections for the post of chairman of the Supreme Soviet. Nikolai Dementei, who is also a Communist Party Central Committee secretary, won 51 percent of the vote, thus defeating popular front candidate Stanislav Shushkevich, who in fact came very close to Dementei in the number of votes he received. The results were reported by TASS. TASS did not report that the majority of the legislators had voted against Dementei in the first round.

Republican Parliament Fails to Register Belorussian Popular Front

TASS reported that the Belorussian legislature had again refused to register the Belorussian Popular Front. The news agency did not tell the whole story, however. It failed to report that the proposal to register the front had actually been approved by a vote of 151 in favor, 150 against, with 7 abstentions, but that the results of the voting were judged inconclusive (RL Belorussian service, May 19).

Sunday, May 20

"Home Guard" Formed in Estonia

Several thousand Estonians took on oath of allegiance to the republic as they were sworn in as members of a volunteer "home guard" that would protect government buildings and other facilities. In remarks to guard members, Estonian Prime Minister Edgar Savisaar said the unarmed force should guarantee that Estonia could continue its struggle for freedom despite "whatever hostile acts are carried out against us." The guard was formed after an attempt on May 16 by anti-independence protesters to storm the Estonian parliament (*Reuters*, May 20).

Constitutional Democrats Hold Congress

The Party of Constitutional Democrats, which announced its creation in 1989, concluded its first congress on May 20. Soviet television gave relatively extensive and sympathetic coverage to the meeting, apparently believing that the Constitutional Democrats so far pose no threat to the CPSU. Like another new group, the Party of Liberal Democrats, the Party of Constitutional Democrats claims to be continuing the traditions of the Kadets, the largest non-Socialist party in Russia before 1917.

Armenian Supreme Soviet Elections

Elections were held in Armenia for the republican and local soviets. TASS and Radio Moscow predicted that because of the large number of candidates—an average of six for each of 260 seats in the republican Supreme Soviet—runoff elections would be necessary in many districts. Initial voter turnout was low: polls conducted in Erevan in February indicated that up to 30 percent of those questioned intended to boycott the elections.

On May 23, Soviet reports said residents of Nagorno-Karabakh had secretly voted in the Armenian republic's parliamentary elections. *Krasnaya zvezda* said polling was conducted in apartments and entry ways in the most ethnically Armenian oblast of Azerbaijan. Reports said efforts were made to confiscate ballots and that the airport in Stepanakert was closed for two days. Some people were detained while transporting ballots between Nagorno-Karabakh and Armenia.

New Uzbek Party Founded

A new political party was reported to have been founded in Uzbekistan. It is called the "Uzbekistan National Progress Party." The party will publish a newspaper called *Tiklanish* (Progress). This is the second political party to be founded in Uzbekistan in the past two months. On April 11, the "Erk [Will] Democratic Party" was established. The authorities have yet to register either party (RL Uzbek service, June 1).

Monday, May 21

Party's Authority Failing

Pravda said, based on its poll of 5,000 Party members in eighteen regions of the USSR, that a crisis was developing in the CPSU as its authority declined. The news agency said there was no unity of opinion among Communists, especially on how to deal with socioeconomic problems.

More on Gorbachev's Salary

The USSR Supreme Soviet set the salary for the office of president at 4,000 rubles a month; after taxation, this should leave 2,300 rubles a month (*TASS*, May 21). The Supreme Soviet also agreed that the president should be provided with dachas near Moscow and in the Crimea, a service flat in Moscow, and special planes, helicopters, and cars. On retirement, the president will receive a monthly pension of 1,500 rubles and be provided with a state-owned country house with service, guards, and transport. Many of these non-monetary benefits have long been provided for Soviet leaders but they have not previously been publicly accounted for.

Fight for *Glasnost'* Goes On

On May 18, the USSR Supreme Soviet Committee on *Glasnost'* refused to take action against Vitalii Korotich, the chief editor of the outspoken weekly *Ogonek*. Some Soviet generals had attacked him for publishing materials discrediting the army, but the legislative committee concluded that Korotich's publication of such materials "deserves all possible support," according to its chairman, Vladimir Foteev. The timing of the hearing, however, prevented Korotich from attending a meeting in Copenhagen of the International Federation of Newspaper Publishers (*Central Television*, May 21). In a related case, Egor Yakovlev of *Moscow News*, which has been the target of similar attacks, appeared to have found a way to overcome the problems editors face as a result of state control of the publishing industry. He decided to go private, and his newspaper's issue for May 20 invited readers to become shareholders.

Papal Envoy in Lvov

Archbishop Francesco Colasuonno, the special Papal envoy to the USSR, made an unofficial visit to Lvov to discuss tensions between Uniate Catholics and Russian Orthodox faithful there, Radio Kiev said. Colasuonno had met with the ranking prelate of the Ukrainian Catholic Church (Uniates), Archbishop Volodymyr Sternyuk, and with Uniate activist and Deputy Chairman of the Lvov Oblast Soviet Ivan Hel'.

Tallinn Meeting Supports Baltic CSCE Participation

Legislators from the Baltic republics, Poland, and Czechoslovakia recommended that Estonia, Lithuania, and Latvia take part in the Conference on Security and Cooperation in Europe. The recommendation was made at a meeting organized by the Estonian Popular Front in Tallinn. It was a continuation of a meeting that was held two weeks ago for the purpose of discussing the political transformation of Europe (RFE Estonian service, May 21).

Gorbachev Addresses Agricultural Experts

Mikhail Gorbachev said the speed with which the Soviet Union solved its acute food problems depended on how fast changes took place in agriculture. Speaking to a meeting of agricultural experts in the Kremlin, he called for open discussion of the problems of introducing new forms of farming. Gorbachev said he wanted to know why people in rural areas feared leasing land and having their own family farms. Gorbachev asked whether the problem lay in resistance to new forms of ownership by managers, in a lack of legal guarantees of equal treatment for private farms, or in a shortage of farming equipment (*Radio Moscow*, World Service, May 21). He said the Soviet leadership wanted to have answers to these questions.

The same day, *Pravda* said grain imports were a major factor in the country's dire financial situation. It said the Soviet Union had spent nearly a third of its hard currency earnings last year importing 6 billion dollars' worth of grain and pulses.

Tuesday, May 22

USSR Supreme Soviet Passes Law on USSR Citizenship

Both chambers of the USSR Supreme Soviet adopted a new law on USSR citizenship. The law retains the provision that every citizen of a Union republic is simultaneously a citizen of the USSR and in this capacity enjoys equal rights with the citizens of a republic on the territory of that republic. This provision is anathema to the Baltic republics, which have tried to restrict citizenship so as to deny the vote to immigrants. An innovation is the article stipulating that persons can only be deprived of their Soviet citizenship if they are living outside the country. In the past the authorities have deprived individuals of their citizenship prior to their expulsion from the Soviet Union. The text of the law was published in *Izvestia* on June 1.

Estonian and Latvian Leaders Meet Gorbachev

The leaders of Estonia and Latvia, Arnold Ruutel and Anatolijs Gorbunovs, discussed the issue of Baltic independence with Mikhail Gorbachev. Ruutel said the meeting was "unpleasant for both sides." He said Gorbachev had restated his demand for Estonia and Latvia, as well as Lithuania, to rescind their recent reaffirmations of independence (*AP*, May 22).

The same day, the leaders of Estonia and Latvia also met with members of the Federation Council to discuss their independence resolutions. The council is Gorbachev's advisory body on matters concerning republics and nationalities (*AP*, *AFP*, May 22).

Changes in Foreign Ministry Announced

TASS announced a number of personnel changes in the Soviet Foreign Ministry. Yulii Vorontsov became ambassador to the United Nations. He replaced Aleksandr Belonogov, who has been named a deputy foreign minister. Vladislav Terekhov has been appointed ambassador to Bonn. He will replace Yulii Kvitsinsky, who has been named a deputy foreign minister. Aleksei Obukhov has also been appointed a deputy foreign minister, and Yurii Kashlev has been named ambassador to Poland.

***World Marxist Review* to Close**

The Prague-based monthly of the world Communist movement is to cease publication. The journal was set up in 1958 in an attempt to deal with ideological differences within the bloc. In its heyday it was published in over thirty languages, and representatives of ninety Communist Parties sat on its editorial board. An official liquidating the journal told Reuters that, by the middle of 1989, only the USSR and Czechoslovakia still supported the journal. Citing the crumbling of communism in Eastern Europe, he said "there did not seem to be any reason to continue publication."

Journalists Lose Fight for *Izvestia*

"Vremya" reported that the Presidium of the USSR Supreme Soviet had appointed Nikolai Efimov editor of *Izvestia*. The staff of the government daily had unanimously elected Deputy Chief Editor Igor Golembiovsky to this post. Golembiovsky was, however, made first deputy chief editor, the post held by Efimov until his appointment to head the USSR State Committee for Book Publishing, Printing Plants, and the Book Trade in July, 1989. In this job Efimov gained notoriety as an incompetent and reactionary *apparatchik*, particularly following his unsuccessful attempt to fire Evgenii Averin, editor of the progressive weekly *Knizhnoe obozrenie*, who had criticized the anti-Semitism of the leadership of the RSFSR Writers' Union.

KGB to Erect New Building

The KGB will erect a new building in the Tainitsky Garden of the Kremlin, according to *Moskovsky komsomolets*. The newspaper remarked that, since the creation of the Presidential Council, Mikhail Gorbachev had transferred his office to the Kremlin, while the offices of other members of the Politburo remain in the Central Committee building on Staraya Ploshchad'.

Soviet Jews Arriving in East Germany

According to Reuters, East Germany has quietly opened its doors to Soviet Jewish immigrants. During the past two weeks, sixty-one people have arrived at a reception camp on the outskirts of East Berlin. Reuters saw the move as part of East Germany's desire to atone for the Holocaust and improve ties with Israel. The agency quoted an East Berlin city official as saying that the authorities would support Soviet Jewish immigrants but could offer them no priority as regards employment.

Democratic Youth Organization in Moldavia

A new youth organization has been formed in Moldavia, one of the main goals of which is the withdrawal of Soviet troops from the republic. The organization also favors the establishment of a Moldavian national army. The new movement, called Free Dacia, seems to be small; TASS said that about forty delegates attended its founding congress in Kishinev. Radio Moscow's Interfax news agency reported on May 21 that a clash between Russian speakers and members of the Moldavian Popular Front had occurred on May 20.

Party Delegation in China

A CPSU delegation headed by candidate Politburo member Boriss Pugo was in Beijing to study the Chinese Communist Party's control and discipline bodies under the conditions of reform and expanding foreign relations. According to the press agency Xinhua, this was the highest-ranking CPSU delegation to visit China since the two parties restored relations last year.

Congress of Alternative Political Parties in Tbilisi

A congress of the National Forum, the umbrella organization that was created in March in order to unite the diverse alternative political groups that have sprung up in Georgia, opened in Tbilisi. Representatives of both moderate and radical parties and of the Georgian Supreme Soviet and the republic's Union of Writers attended. The congress debated a law on holding elections to a National Congress, a body intended as an alternative to the Georgian Supreme Soviet (*Reuters*, May 22). See RL 243/90.

New Proindependence Party Formed in Kazakhstan

A new political party has been formed in Kazakhstan. The main aim of the new group, which is called the Jeltoqsan National Democratic Party, is to achieve full sovereignty for the republic. A Kazakh journalist told RFE/RL that the group had been founded at a meeting in Alma-Ata on May 20. He said most of the unofficial groups and organizations in the republic had sent representatives to the meeting.

USSR Calls for German Pledges

The Soviet Union called on West Germany to give concrete pledges on the fulfilment of East Germany's delivery commitments. Soviet Deputy Prime Minister Ivan Silaev submitted to West German Economics Minister Helmut Haussmann an urgent list of goods and projects that he said the USSR could not forego when the two Germanies merge their economic, monetary, and social systems on July 1. He submitted the list at the eighteenth session of the German-Soviet Economic Commission, which ended today in Moscow. According to the list, the USSR wants East German–Soviet operated mining projects in the Soviet Union and the joint uranium production in Wismut, East Germany, to be continued. The USSR also insists that deliveries continue of spare parts from East Germany for its plant and machine construction (*DPA*, May 22).

Wednesday, May 23

Prominent Reformist Elected Mayor of Leningrad

Leningrad's new city soviet elected as its chairman Anatolii Sobchak, who is considered one of the Soviet Union's most radical advocates of reform. TASS said Sobchak defeated two opponents. Sobchak, a lawyer by training, is a USSR Supreme Soviet deputy and a member of the Interregional Group of Deputies. The Leningrad City Soviet is now dominated by reformists.

Bessmertnykh Becomes New Soviet Ambassador to United States

Aleksandr Bessmertnykh became Soviet ambassador to the United States (*RFE/RL Special*, May 23). Bessmertnykh, formerly the Soviet Union's first deputy foreign minister, is an expert on relations with the United States and has participated in most top level US Soviet negotiations for the past seven years. He replaces Yurii Dubinin, who has been chief Soviet diplomat in Washington since 1986 and is now to become Soviet ambassador to France.

Gorbachev Accuses El'tsin of Seeking to Split USSR

President Mikhail Gorbachev accused Boris El'tsin of trying to split the Soviet Union. Radio Moscow said Gorbachev made the accusation in answer to questions from delegates to the meeting of the RSFSR Congress in Moscow. El'tsin told the Congress on May 22 that the Russian Federation needed "real sovereignty." To this Gorbachev said E'ltsin sought to divorce the Russian Federation from socialism and engage it in confrontation with the rest of the USSR (*Radio Moscow*, May 23).

Hearst and *Izvestia* to Publish Joint Weekly

The US-based Hearst Corporation, one of the world's largest media groups, and the Soviet government newspaper *Izvestia* said they had agreed to explore joint publication of the first uncensored weekly Soviet-American newspaper. The planned newspaper is to be called *My* (Us). The paper is to be distributed in both countries in their respective languages (*Reuters*, May 23).

Kazakh Parliament Approves Closure of Semipalatinsk Site

The Kazakh Supreme Soviet approved a resolution to close down the USSR's main nuclear testing site at Semipalatinsk. TASS said the resolution also included measures to protect the environment and the health of the local population in the area. The parliament also called on Uzbekistan, Kirgizia, Tajikistan, and Turkmenia to join in efforts to save the Aral Sea.

Thursday, May 24

Details of Economic Reform Plan Revealed

Prime Minister Nikolai Ryzhkov presented the government's economic reform plan to the USSR Supreme Soviet. He told the parliament that the plan envisaged "a decisive transition to a regulated market economy." According to TASS, the program foresees a rise in food prices by an average of 100 percent. Radio Moscow said, however, that it also includes measures to protect the public from the shock of price rises. This will be done through compensation payments and social security measures so as to maintain living standards. The program contains a series of options to reshape the centralized system into a regulated market economy.

After Ryzhkov had outlined the plan, radical deputies in the parliament called for a vote of no confidence in the government. They warned of potential unrest if the proposed price hikes took effect. Leningrad deputy Aleksei Levashov said the government was not offering a market economy, "just price increases" (*Reuters*, *AP*, May 24). Meanwhile, Radio Moscow reported that the USSR was experiencing a new wave of panic buying, which was obviously provoked by reports of planned price rises. See RL 228/90.

Gorbachev Threatens to Impose Presidential Rule in Latvia

Mikhail Gorbachev threatened to impose presidential rule in Latvia unless it rescinded or suspended its reaffirmation of independence. Gorbachev's comments were reported by Longinas Vasilauskas, a spokesman for Latvia's permanent mission in Moscow. His remarks came after talks between the Soviet president and Latvian members of the USSR Congress of People's Deputies (RFE Latvian service, May 24).

Moldavian Prime Minister Resigns

Moldavia's Prime Minister Peter Paskar resigned, citing "a negative attitude" towards his government. Paskar told TASS it was his decision to resign. He said it was up to other members of his government to decide whether to stay in their posts.

British Princess Meets Gorbachev

Princess Anne, Queen Elizabeth's daughter, met with Mikhail Gorbachev in Moscow. She is on the first official visit to the Soviet Union by a member of the British royal family since the 1917 October Revolution. TASS said Gorbachev told Princess Anne that her visit "corresponded well with the fruitful contacts between the two countries" and that there was good progress in British-Soviet relations.

Latvian Cardinal Dies

The head of Latvia's Roman Catholic Church, Cardinal Julijans Vaivods, died at the age of ninety-four, Radio Riga announced. Vaivods was elevated to the rank of cardinal by Pope John Paul in early 1983, making him the first cardinal to be physically based in the USSR since 1917.

Ukrainian Parliament to Discuss Sovereignty, Party Clause

The Ukrainian Supreme Soviet agreed on an agenda for its current session that included drafting a resolution on Ukrainian sovereignty and economic independence. TASS said deputies would also discuss changing Article 6 of the Ukrainian Constitution, which deals with the leading role of the Communist Party. The analogous similar article of the Soviet Constitution was repealed in March by the USSR Congress of People's Deputies. Several other republics have done the same since.

Friday, May 25

Gorbachev Meets Mitterand

French President François Mitterrand arrived in Moscow for talks with Soviet President Mikhail Gorbachev. The talks were expected to focus on the future of Europe, NATO, and the Warsaw Pact. Mitterrand was accompanied by French Foreign Minister Roland Dumas (*TASS*, May 25). Speaking at a joint press conference in Moscow, Gorbachev said Western insistence that a united Germany should be a member of NATO could lead the Soviet Union to reconsider its attitude towards the entire European security process. Gorbachev said placing Germany in NATO would "upset the balance, sow discord and distrust, and thus prejudice the entire positive process that has been launched on a global scale" (*Reuters*, *AP*, May 25).

Turkmenistan Decides against Introduction of Presidency

Turkmenistan decided not to create a presidential post but instead to expand the powers of the chairman of the republican Supreme Soviet. Radio Moscow said the decision was taken at a session of the Turkmen Supreme Soviet that ended today. The radio said the Supreme Soviet also amended constitutional articles concerning the leading role of the Communist Party and adopted laws on the status of people's deputies.

Kapitsa Says Killings Hurt Relations with Israel

Mikhail Kapitsa, a former Soviet deputy foreign minister, said the killing of Arabs by a deranged Jewish gunman and the subsequent deaths of Palestinian protesters had seriously hurt Soviet-Israeli relations. Kapitsa was heading a five-member delegation to Israel. Talking to reporters in Jerusalem, Kapitsa said: "During the last week, Israel has badly damaged—I should have said sabotaged—relations with the Soviet Union." The Soviet delegation is from the Soviet Afro-Asian Solidarity Committee. The group's visit was arranged with Palestinian leftists well before the recent killings (*Reuters*, May 25).

Pro-Moscow Communists Revamp Latvian-Language Daily

The pro-Moscow Communist Party of Latvia decided to end publication of its Latvian-language daily, *Cina* in its present form. Radio Riga said the Party's Central Committee had decided to replace *Cina* by a Latvian translation of the Party's Russian-language daily, *Sovetskaya Latviya*. The radio also said the chairman of Latvia's independent Communist Party, Ivars Kezbers, had received permission to publish a newspaper and would hire the staff of *Cina* to do the job (RFE Latvian service, May 25).

Association of Independent Trade Unions Set Up in Latvia

A congress of Latvian trade unions said it would create "an association of independent trade unions." According to TASS, the decision, which does away with the Latvian republic's Council of Trade Unions, was made at the opening session of the congress in Riga (*TASS*, May 25).

Bonner Announces Formation of Andrei Sakharov Foundation

Elena Bonner, the widow of Andrei Sakharov, announced the creation of an international foundation in her husband's name. Bonner said in Rome that the Andrei Sakharov Foundation would hold an international conference in Moscow in 1991 devoted to the democratic process in Eastern Europe and to the effects of the Chernobyl' nuclear disaster. She added that the foundation was still in the process of being organized and that it was in search of funding (*AP*, May 25).

Lack of Housing Blamed for Delay in Soviet Pullout

The Soviet Union said the reason for the halt in its troop withdrawal from East Germany was the housing shortage in the Soviet Union. At a news conference in East Berlin, Mikhail Logvinov, spokesman for the Soviet embassy, said: "The housing shortage is a problem that will take years to solve. The army barracks are still filled with refugees from the earthquake area of Armenia and from Azerbaijan, where there has been unrest." Before the suspension of the troop withdrawal, the West German authorities said the Soviet Union had pulled out about 12,000 of the more than 30,000 military personnel expected to be withdrawn from East Germany (*AP*, *AFP*, May 25).

Liquidation of Party Monopoly on Publishing Proposed

Ogonek (No. 20) carried a letter from a deputy to a local soviet, V. Goreninsky, saying that the Soviet press could not be free as long as the majority of periodicals continued to be published by publishing houses belonging to Party organizations. This point was also made by the chairman of the Moscow journalists' organization, Mikhail Poltoranin, in an interview with *Tyumensky komsomolets* on May 19. Poltoranin pointed out that provisions of the press law allowing informal groups and individuals to set up their own press organs would continue to exist only on paper if the press law were not complemented by a law stipulating the demonopolization of the USSR's polygraphic base. He also suggested that, because the law on the press provides for the courts to resolve conflicts arising in connection with the publication of press materials, the Soviet legal system should also be removed from Party control.

Two Opposing Views on Whether the USSR Needs Ideology

In an article in *Kommunist* (No. 7), historian Roy Medvedev asserted that the current crisis in traditional Soviet ideology did not mean that the USSR should abandon altogether ideological justification of its leadership's policies. He suggested that it was quite natural that the inhabitants of the Russian Empire should have chosen socialism in 1917 and that therefore there was no need to abandon it now. He proposed instead that the Soviet Union should revitalize Marxism and said that the ideas behind "the new political thinking" were steps in this direction. Medvedev also stressed that the CPSU "should not lose its leading role and become an opposition party, since this would mean the disintegration of the country and the creation instead of several states with various ideologies."

In an interview with *Sovetskaya kul'tura*, Aleksandr Tsipko, deputy director of the Institute of Economics of the World Socialist System and a former consultant to the CPSU Central Committee, urged that ideology be removed completely from Soviet political and economic life. Tsipko argued that "the current crisis of *perestroika*" resulted from the naïveté of the initial concepts underlying Gorbachev's policies. Tsipko stressed that Soviet leaders were mistaken if, in initiating reforms, they hoped that they could merely renew the facade of Soviet society without completely abandoning the Soviet system. The same day, *Izvestia* published an article by Tsipko in which he argued that talk of Russia's leaving the Soviet Union and becoming a sovereign state was not serious. He stressed that the situation of Russia was different from that of the Baltic republics, which were incorporated into the USSR involuntarily. Tsipko said Russia had created the empire and therefore bore responsibility for its future. See also Tsipko's articles in *Komsomol'skaya pravda* (May 24) and *Sobesednik* (No. 20) and RL 247/90.

Saturday, May 26

Gorbachev Interviewed by *Time* Magazine

In an interview with *Time* magazine, Mikhail Gorbachev said that he remained a Communist and that the West should not "panic" over this. He added that, according to his beliefs, to be a Communist means "to put universal human values above everything else." He argued that Lenin, Marx, and Engels bore no responsibility for the distortions that had occurred when communism was put into practice. He said the magnitude of the changes now going on in the USSR were on a par with the October Revolution. He said that the USSR would remain Socialist but that it would become an entirely different society. Gorbachev also said he supported the concept of real sovereignty for all Soviet republics in all spheres. Regarding international events, Gorbachev advocated the scrapping of NATO and the Warsaw Pact in favor of pan-European unity.

Ligachev Elected Delegate to Party Congress

Conservative Politburo member and Central Committee Secretary Egor Ligachev was elected a delegate to the Twenty-eighth Party Congress scheduled to start on July 2. TASS said Ligachev received nearly 80 percent of the vote in a race with two other candidates in Belgorod Oblast. By contrast, Mikhail Gorbachev received only 61 percent of the vote in Moscow last week.

Makhkamov Reelected Tajik Party First Secretary

Kakhar Makhkamov was reelected first secretary of the Tajik Communist Party at the close of the Party's three-day congress in Dushanbe. He was the only candidate. TASS said the congress also passed a package of laws to prepare for a multiparty system.

KGB Denies Involvement in El'tsin's Plane Accident

TASS reported that the KGB had issued an official statement denying allegations that it had tried to murder Boris El'tsin during the latter's trip to Spain. The statement referred to an article by V. Mezentsev in the May 19 issue of *Leningradskaya smena*, which indirectly blamed the KGB for the airplane accident in which El'tsin was injured. The KGB also stated that it was asking the USSR prosecutor general to investigate the allegations.

Pro-Soviet Deputies Form Council in Estonia

A group of Estonian deputies met in Tallinn to form a pro-Soviet council called the Interregional Council of People's Deputies and Workers of the Estonian SSR. TASS said the group was committed to a Soviet federation, and it quoted speakers at the founding congress as saying that the deepening social, political, and economic crisis in Estonia had been triggered by the Estonian Supreme Council's attempts to change the state system and destroy the Soviet federation. Estonian television quoted anti-independence activist Mikhail Lysenko as saying the group had voted not to abide by the laws passed by the Estonian Supreme Council and to obey only Moscow.

Arbatov Criticizes Military Establishment

Ogonek (No. 22) carried an article in which Soviet foreign policy adviser Georgii Arbatov accused Marshal Sergei Akhromeev of lying about Soviet defense needs and of taking part in "disastrous" military decisions in the 1970s and 1980s. Akhromeev, a former chief of the Soviet General Staff and currently a military adviser to Gorbachev, has been a staunch defender of the military establishment. He and other members of the High Command have been engaged in a long-running media battle with civilian critics—led by the chief editor of *Ogonek*, Vitalii Korotich—over Soviet defense policy.

Georgians Rally to Mark 1918 Independence Anniversary

Thousands of people rallied in Tbilisi to mark the seventy-second anniversary of Georgia's brief independence from the Soviet Union (*AP*, May 27). AFP said marches and rallies also took place in other Georgian cities.

Democratic Party of Russia Holds Constituent Congress

The constituent congress of a new center-left party—the Democratic Party of Russia—took place in Moscow over the weekend (*Central Television*, "Vremya," May 26). The initiative for the creation of the new group, which describes itself as a parliamentary party dedicated to the restoration of Russian statehood, comes from disaffected former members of the CPSU, including radical parliamentarians Nikolai Travkin and Gennadii Burbulis, world chess champion Gary Kasparov, and former Central Committee official Georgii Khatsenkov. A leader of the Leningrad Popular Front, Marina Sal'e, is also a strong supporter of this party, and it was she who first put forward ideas for its program. The "Vremya" report said that the conference saw "many quarrels" but that delegates were united in the idea that "the party must be based on a platform of anticommunism." Its aim, the report went on, "is to dismantle in Russia the power structures set up seventy-three years ago." In an interview with Reuters (May 27), Khatsenkov confirmed that the group's primary aim "is to get rid of the CPSU." He said he thought the new party would be "in a position to rival" the ruling Party by October.

Sunday, May 27

Gorbachev and Bush on Soviet Television

Mikhail Gorbachev addressed the Soviet Union via Central Television in an attempt to calm some of the unrest that erupted following Prime Minister Nikolai Ryzhkov's announcement of price rises for many consumer staples last week. Gorbachev said that the Soviet people had learned many painful but important economic lessons over the past five years and that the practical situation in the country meant that there was no choice but to press ahead with a regulated market economy. He stressed that this could not be done without the support of the population, and he called on the Soviet people to extend their trust to the government's new program.

Soviet television followed up Gorbachev's address with a ten-minute interview with US President George Bush, who expressed support for Gorbachev's reforms but said that Baltic problems might slow down the pace of progress in East-West relations. Bush said the United States saw the success of *perestroika* as being in the interests not only of the USSR but also of the rest of the world.

More Pressure to Close Semipalatinsk Testing Site

Thousands of people took part in an antinuclear demonstration in the town of Karaul, near the nuclear testing site at Semipalatinsk (*TASS*, May 27). The occasion for the protest was the laying of a foundation stone for a monument to the victims of the atomic bombs dropped on Hiroshima and Nagasaki. Participants in last week's international antinuclear congress in Alma-Ata were also in attendance.

Gorbachev Awarded Peace Prize

Coretta Scott King will present the Martin Luther King Nonviolent Peace Prize (including a cash award of 1,000 dollars) to Mikhail Gorbachev in a Washington ceremony on June 1 (*AP*, May 26; *TASS*, May 27). The award, given by the Friends' World College, has in the past been given to South African Archbishop Desmond Tutu and President of the Philippines Corazon Aquino.

Twenty-four Killed in Renewed Violence in Armenia

At least twenty-four people were killed in two separate clashes between troops and civilians in Erevan. TASS and local Armenian sources differed in their accounts of the first incident, which took place at the main railway station in Erevan. TASS claimed that armed Armenians had opened fire on USSR MVD troops, who returned their fire; six Armenians were killed and ten soldiers and some bystanders were wounded. Armenpress said that the troops had opened fire thinking they were about to be attacked by civilians who in fact wished only to persuade them to leave the city. In the second incident, in the southern suburb of Sovetashen, five people were killed when troops opened fire after their convoy was halted by barricades.

On May 28, the commander of the USSR Internal Security Forces, Colonel General Yurii Shatalin, urged Armenian leaders to authorize the use of MVD troops to put an end to violence in the republic (*TASS*, May 28).

Western reports from Moscow said that about 100,000 people rallied in Erevan on May 28 to mark the anniversary of Armenia's brief period of independence and to mourn those killed in the clashes on May 27. On May 28, Armenian Communist Party First Secretary Vladimir Movsisyan went on local television to appeal for calm.

On May 30, a crowd of thousands gathered in Erevan again to mourn those who had died in the clashes (*DPA*, May 30). The same day, USSR people's deputy Galina Starovoitova said an Armenian activist, Arkadii Manucharov, had been released from prison in Moscow on May 29. He had been jailed since late 1988, when he was detained together with eleven other members of the Karabakh Committee (*Reuters*, May 30). The Interfax news agency said that charges against Manucharov had not been dropped, however, and that he was still under investigation. See RL 252/90.

Kortunov Says Aid to Cuba Will End

Andrei Kortunov of the USA and Canada Institute told ABC television he believed the USSR's aid to Cuba—estimated at an annual 4 billion dollars for economic aid alone—would gradually come to an end and that economic ties between the two countries would be switched to a commercial basis. He did not offer a specific timetable but noted that "this change will take some time, of course." Kortunov's statements come in contrast to those of Yurii Pavlov, a Latin American specialist at the Soviet Foreign Ministry. According to AP, Pavlov reaffirmed support for Cuban leader Fidel Castro at a "Moscow-

Miami" conference on May 26. Pavlov also said, "We are giving aid not to the Cuban government but to the Cuban people."

Soviet General Calls for Changes in Border Policing

The head of the Soviet Union's border guards said there must be a thorough review of border policing. The official, Lieutenant General Il'ya Kalinichenko, said events in the Baltic republics, the Transcaucasus, and Moldavia had shown the need for serious changes in the Soviet Union's approach to protecting its territory. In an interview with *Krasnaya zvezda*, he said Soviet frontiers with East European states posed the most complex problem. He cited an example of tourists in Poland who strayed inadvertently over the Soviet frontier. Kalinichenko said there were also problems on the Afghan frontier, where he said some Afghan groups had been trying to extend their activities onto Soviet territory.

Estonian Popular Front Holds Second Congress

The Estonian Popular Front held its second national congress in Tallinn. TASS said the congress adopted a new general program and charter and elected leading bodies. It said the congress set up "a chamber of deputies" as a new subdivision within the front's leadership. The new body includes some Estonian Supreme Council deputies, some Estonian members of the USSR Supreme Soviet, and some members of the Congress of Estonia—a group made up of citizens of prewar Estonia and their descendants.

Monday, May 28

Ban on Food Sales to Nonresidents of Moscow Imposed after Panic Buying

A ban on food sales to nonresidents of Moscow came into effect after news of planned price rises prompted a wave of panic buying. The ban, originally scheduled to take effect on May 27, was postponed until today to allow nonresidents who had already arrived in Moscow for shopping over the weekend to make their purchases.

On May 27, Presidential Council member Aleksandr Yakovlev said the economic situation in the Soviet Union was "very serious, critical." He said the panic buying was "a normal reaction in a society in which shortages are a regular feature" (*Reuters*, May 27). On May 31, Boris El'tsin announced at a session of the RSFSR Congress of People's Deputies that Moscow had lifted restrictions on the sale of food to nonresidents (*Moscow Television*,

May 31). Meanwhile, three Soviet oblasts limited their shipments of goods to Moscow in retaliation for the ban. TASS said Vladimir and Kalinin Oblasts had declared a total food blockade of Moscow and Kaluga Oblast had cut off deliveries of meat and dairy products effective June 1.

Ukrainian Communist Party Chief Opposes Economic Plan

Ukrainian Communist Party First Secretary Vladimir Ivashko joined Prime Minister Vitalii Masol in criticizing the Soviet government's radical economic package. During a session of the Ukrainian Supreme Soviet, Ivashko said Moscow should first consult with the republics over the economic plan and then hold a referendum.

RSFSR Komsomol Splits

The RSFSR Komsomol, which became an autonomous organization last February, has split. TASS reported that an independent social democratic faction had been formed at the RSFSR Komsomol Congress. The leader of this faction, Aleksandr Bek, said that it would project ideals other than Marxist ones and would espouse political pluralism. The faction consists of sixty of the 900 RSFSR Komsomol delegates. The first secretary of the All-Union Komsomol, Vladimir Zyukin, did not denounce this split in his organization; rather, in order to avoid losing control of the social democratic faction, he offered it financial and material support.

Negotiators Reach Civil Aviation Accord

US and Soviet negotiators reached an agreement to dramatically increase air traffic between the two countries, according to *The New York Times*. The agreement will give six US passenger or cargo airlines the right to fly to Kiev, Tbilisi, Minsk, Riga, Magadan, and Khabarovsk. Aeroflot and any other potential Soviet competitor will gain access to Chicago, Miami, San Francisco, and Anchorage. The agreement will open the first regular flights between the two countries over the Pacific. According to the terms finally agreed to, 8.75 percent of the tickets on the US airlines will be sold to Soviet citizens for rubles, but the US airlines will have to convert the rubles to hard currency when paying for services in the Soviet Union.

Social Democratic Party Founded in Kazakhstan

TASS reported that a Social Democratic Party had been founded in Kazakhstan. The report said the new party espoused the ideals of liberal democratic socialism and called for a market economy, for private ownership of land, and for ridding the state of ideology. This is the second opposition party to be founded in Kazakhstan in the past month.

Pyongyang Expels TASS Correspondent

In another hint that relations between the Soviet Union and North Korea are souring, Aleksandr Shebin, a Korean-speaking veteran correspondent for TASS who had been based in Pyongyang for seven years, was sent back to Moscow. Shebin left on May 12 after North Korea asked the Soviet embassy to have him recalled. Shebin had written articles critical of President Kim Il-Sung's regime and about the difficulties of being a correspondent in Pyongyang. According to one AFP source, Shebin had written those kinds of articles before, but TASS had not published them.

Ukrainian Enterprises Stage Warning Strike over Nuclear Plant

A number of industrial enterprises in Khmelnitsky Oblast in Ukraine announced a two-hour warning strike for today. The purpose of the strike was to draw attention to demands to stop construction of the Khmelnitsky nuclear power station. Radio Kiev said a coordinating strike committee had been set up and a plan of action made.

Former Uzbek Oblast Party Secretary Sentenced

TASS reported that former first secretary of the Surkhandarya Oblast Party Committee in Uzbekistan, Abdukhalik Karimov, had been sentenced to six years in a strict-regime corrective-labor institution. TASS said Karimov had been found guilty of receiving and giving bribes.

Russian-Speakers Demonstrate for Estonian Independence

A group that included some Russian-speakers staged a demonstration in the Estonian capital, Tallinn, to express their support for the republic's independence. Estonian radio said the demonstration took place in the city's main square, but it did not say how many people took part. The radio said that some of the groups represented at the rally had proclaimed a week of solidarity between democratic-minded Russian-speakers and proponents of Estonian independence. The radio said representatives of democratic Russian-speaking groups in Estonia would meet on May 31 to discuss establishing a forum to coordinate support for the republic's independence.

Tuesday, May 29

El'tsin Elected Chairman of RSFSR Supreme Soviet

After a third round of voting, Boris El'tsin finally won the chairmanship of the RSFSR Supreme Soviet with 535 votes. Conservative candidate Ivan Polozkov withdrew his candidacy, but the present chairman of the RSFSR Council of Ministers, Aleksandr Vlasov, who on May 25 decided to leave the race, returned to challenge El'tsin. Vlasov received 467 votes—six fewer than Polozkov had received during the first round. Immediately after his election, El'tsin called for a coalition government and set up "a conciliation commission" representing all factions in the parliament to discuss the composition of the new Russian government (*TASS*, *Reuters*, *UPI*, May 29).

While El'tsin supporters were reported to be dancing in the streets after the announcement of his election, the official Soviet line, as expressed by Foreign Ministry spokesmen Vitalii Churkin and Gennadii Gerasimov, was that El'tsin's victory would strengthen reform in the Soviet Union. Churkin said El'tsin's election "might actually help Gorbachev, because Gorbachev is for radical reform and he needs more popular support for that." Gerasimov called it "a blessing in disguise" and said it was better that a critic from the left had been elected than one from the right.

President Gorbachev told reporters in Ottawa that he was "somewhat worried" about the situation in the RSFSR Congress—i.e., the confrontational attitude between conservative and reformist deputies that manifested itself during the first session of the Congress. His interview was broadcast in full on Soviet television on May 29.

On May 30, Baltic officials said the election of El'tsin was extremely positive for Estonia, Latvia, and Lithuania (*DPA*, May 30).

On May 30, El'tsin gave a press conference in his new capacity as chairman of the RSFSR Supreme Soviet. He said that his election had reduced social tensions and prevented a rebellion against the government from below. At the conference, carried live by Radio Mayak, El'tsin indicated that he wanted to move faster than Gorbachev on major political decisions. The RSFSR, he said, would have a new constitution before the USSR did; the question of the sovereignty of the RSFSR would be sorted out in the next hundred days; and, when the RSFSR introduced a presidential system, the powers of the USSR and RSFSR presidents would be equal. El'tsin also warned that, without the support of Russia, Gorbachev was powerless, and he criticized Gorbachev's foreign policy as being too heavily oriented towards the West. El'tsin urged Ryzhkov's government to resign because, he said, its reform program had failed. He argued that neither the president of the USSR nor the head of the RSFSR parliament should remain members of the CPSU in a multiparty system, and he called for the educational role of the Russian Orthodox Church to be restored.

On May 31, El'tsin said that as Supreme Soviet chairman he now represented all the people of the Russian Federation and not just the Democratic Russia political faction. TASS quoted several RSFSR deputies as strongly criticizing El'tsin's remarks at the press conference.

Gorbachev in Canada

Mikhail Gorbachev arrived in Canada at the start of his North American visit. He called on Canada and other nations to join in building a new international order in Europe. He said in an arrival speech, "We want to be partners with Canada and other Western nations in building a new European home." During his twenty-nine-hour stay, Gorbachev met several Canadian officials (Western agencies, May 29). After talking to Canadian Prime Minister Brian Mulroney, Gorbachev told reporters he was confident there would be a summit agreement on a formula for German reunification without upsetting the balance of power in Europe (*Reuters*, *AP*, May 29). On May 30, supporters of independence for the Baltic republics in Ottawa jeered Gorbachev. The same day, Gorbachev left Canada for the United States (*AP*, May 30).

Baltic Republics Say Gorbachev Has No Right to Represent Them

The three Baltic republics said Gorbachev had no legal right to represent them at the US-Soviet summit meeting. Addressing reporters in Stockholm, Estonian Prime Minister Edgar Savisaar read a statement from the three republican foreign ministries to the effect that the republics did not want anything signed behind their backs in Washington (*RFE/RL Special*, May 29). The same day, officials of the parliaments of Latvia and Estonia spoke in Vilnius and urged the Baltic republics to cooperate closely in their struggle for independence (RFE Lithuanian service, May 29).

Refugee Problem in USSR

Assistance to the January wave of refugees from the Transcaucasus alone has cost the state over 1 billion rubles, and providing them with permanent accommodation and jobs in other areas will cost at least as much again. Petr Rudev, chairman of the Coordinating Committee for

Refugee Affairs of the USSR State Committee for Labor and Social Questions, told TASS that the problem of providing jobs for the 600,000 or so Armenian, Azerbaijani, Meskhetian, and Russian refugees from the Transscaucasus and Central Asia was very acute. There is also an urgent need for a law defining a refugee. At present, anyone leaving his or her permanent place of residence can claim to be a refugee and demand compensation.

Nishanov Interviewed in *Pravda*

In an interview in *Pravda*, Rafik Nishanov, chairman of the Council of Nationalities of the USSR Supreme Soviet, said that the newly created USSR State Committee for Nationality Affairs would include among its members the permanent representatives of the Union republics in Moscow and representatives of the autonomous republics and other autonomous formations, thus resembling a lower-level Federation Council. To supply the necessary scholarly support for solving ethnic problems, Nishanov urged the creation of an all-Union scientific research institute of nationality relations attached to the Council of Nationalities. He also advocated the publication of a journal of the Council of Nationalities.

Shatalin Emphasizes Need for Western Aid

Presidential Council member Academician Stanislav Shatalin told the *Financial Times* that "we should make it very clear that without big credits from the West we will not be able to build a market economy." The Council of Ministers, he said, "has no clear position on whether credits are needed or when they are needed." Shatalin conceded that the Soviet Union's creditworthiness had declined, but added that "the country is not asking for charity but for a dynamic process to start, the West should help us."

Dismantling of Krasnoyarsk Radar Station Begins

Reuters and *The Washington Post* reported that the Soviet Union had begun to dismantle the Krasnoyarsk radar station in Siberia to clear the way for a strategic arms treaty with the United States. The United States has charged that the radar station is a violation of the Antiballistic Missile Treaty of 1972, and the last two US administrations have said they will not sign a new strategic arms reduction treaty until it has been dismantled. Last fall, the Soviet Union admitted that the radar station violated the treaty and said that it would be dismantled without conditions.

Chervov Criticizes US Position on Arms Control

Head of the Treaty and Legal Directorate of the General Staff of the Soviet Armed Forces Colonel General Nikolai Chervov, who is overseeing arms control negotiations, charged in *The New York Times* that the United States was still trying to achieve military superiority over the Soviet Union. Chervov criticized the United States for refusing to discuss reductions in naval power; for maintaining military bases around the periphery of the USSR; for developing new strategic weapons systems; for continuing nuclear testing; for attempting to integrate a united Germany into NATO; and for maintaining an aggressive military doctrine that includes first use of nuclear weapons. His comments reflect positions taken consistently by the Soviet High Command and are clearly aimed at publicly buttressing Soviet arms control positions in advance of the forthcoming summit.

Wednesday, May 30

Shevardnadze Proposes New European Security Structure

Soviet Foreign Minister Eduard Shevardnadze called for a new set of all-European security structures and proposed the creation of "a council of greater Europe." The council would be made up of senior leaders of all the states participating in the Helsinki process and would meet at least once every two years to discuss and decide major policy issues. Shevardnadze also suggested the formation of a committee of foreign ministers, which would prepare issues for examination by the council and would monitor the implementation of the council's decisions (*Izvestia*, May 30).

Ligachev Says Party Excluded from Decision-Making

Hard-line Politburo member Egor Ligachev complained in an interview with Radio Moscow that the CPSU Central Committee had not been a party to the momentous political decision to introduce a market economy in the USSR. He called for a plenum to be convened to discuss the reorientation of the economic system and demanded that the Party be included immediately in the planning and implementation of the process. He said it was an illusion to think that the Party could be ignored. Ligachev rejected the idea of a free market economy, saying that he favored a Socialist market system in which the plan controls economic stimulation and the volume of production. Ligachev's interview was broadcast on Radio Moscow-1 at the same time that Mayak was broadcasting El'tsin's press conference.

Jehovah's Witnesses Rehabilitated

Keston College reported that a request by the state prosecutor of Khabarovsk Krai for eight leaders of the Jehovah's Witnesses to be rehabilitated had been approved by the presidium of the krai court. The eight were sentenced in November, 1984, to terms of between three and five years in strict-regime labor camps.

Thursday, May 31

US-Soviet Summit

Mikhail Gorbachev arrived in Washington to begin summit talks with US President George Bush. Welcoming Gorbachev to the White House, Bush said the two sides had made progress since their last summit six months ago, but he said no one should lose sight of US-Soviet differences. Here he cited the Lithuanian independence dispute. In his turn, Gorbachev said he had come to Washington primarily to make progress towards a strategic arms agreement. In commenting on Bush's remarks concerning Lithuania, Gorbachev's press spokesman, Arkadii Maslennikov, insisted that the Lithuanian dispute was an internal Soviet problem. Gorbachev and Bush then started their first round of talks, covering all major issues facing the two countries. The same day, Gorbachev addressed a group of prominent US business, cultural, and academic figures. He stressed that he needed to introduce radical economic reforms in the USSR (Western agencies, May 31).

In an address to US Congressmen at the Soviet embassy broadcast on US television, Gorbachev said the time had come for the US Congress and the USSR Congress of People's Deputies to begin considering the proposed nuclear arms reduction treaty. On the issue of a united Germany's membership of the NATO alliance, Gorbachev said Soviet opposition to that idea was not based on fear of Germany. He said Moscow was concerned about the possibility of an imbalance of military forces in Europe. Commenting on speculation that his political position had been weakened, Gorbachev said he had not come to the summit to beg for anything. He said, however, that "a favorable gesture on trade" from the US side would be "very helpful politically" in his efforts to introduce economic reform in the USSR. Gorbachev said the USSR was now like a ship that had "lost its anchor," because the country's old economic system was being dismantled while the new market system was not yet in place. During his speech, Gorbachev also alleged that Israel was purposely using the dispute over Soviet Jewish émigrés to make Moscow's relations with Arab countries difficult.

Gorbachev said Soviet Jews were being settled in the Israeli-occupied territories, where they provoked clashes (*AP*, *Reuters*, June 1).

Meanwhile, on May 31, about fifty Jewish refusedniks rallied in Moscow to demand that their struggle to emigrate not be forgotten (*AP*, May 31).

On June 1, Bush and Gorbachev signed agreements on a framework for a strategic arms treaty and on normalizing trade between the United States and the USSR. The signing of the latter agreement was in doubt until the last moment because of Moscow's blockade of Lithuania (*Reuters*, *AP*, June 1). Meanwhile, about 1,000 people rallied in front of the Capitol in Washington in support of Baltic independence. Addressing the crowd, Senator Alfonse D'Amato and AFL-CIO President Lane Kirkland said there should be no trade benefits for the Soviet Union until it ended economic sanctions against Lithuania (*RFE/RL Special*, June 1). Commenting on the signing of the US-Soviet trade agreement, US Secretary of State James Baker said, however, that the United States had made no direct linkage between the agreement and the Soviet leadership's handling of the Baltic dispute (*Reuters*, June 1).

Latvian Supreme Council Wants Direct Contacts with Russia

The Latvian Supreme Council proposed the establishment of direct contacts between it and the Supreme Soviet of the RSFSR. The offer came in a telegram sent by the Latvian parliament to Boris El'tsin congratulating him on his election as chairman of the RSFSR Supreme Soviet. The telegram also called El'tsin's election "the beginning of the spiritual, economic, and legal rebirth of Russia" (RFE Latvian service, May 31).

Daily Protests outside Belorussian Supreme Soviet

Continuing protests were reported outside the building in Minsk where the Belorussian Supreme Soviet was meeting. Journalist Kamila Malevich told RFE/RL that the demonstrators included both local residents and people who arrived in buses from the areas of Belorussia contaminated by the 1986 Chernobyl' nuclear power plant explosion. Malevich said the people from the contaminated areas were demanding help, while other demonstrators called for the resignation of the newly elected chairman of the Belorussian Supreme Soviet, Nikolai Dementei.

Yakovlev Proposes New Federal Constitution

Aleksandr Yakovlev, a member of the Presidential Council, proposed the drafting of a new federal constitution. The *Financial Times* said Yakovlev's proposal would allow each Soviet republic to reach individual treaties with the central government in Moscow. The newspaper quoted Yakovlev as saying "the Union treaty should not be a dogma." He said some republics could "delegate a few of their powers to the Union" while others could delegate "a major proportion of their functions." Yakovlev's remarks were made at the opening of a *Financial Times* conference in Moscow (*AP*, May 31).

Tajikistan Imposes Restrictions on Export of Goods

The government of Tajikistan ruled that food and most consumer goods could not be taken out of the republic. TASS said the government had also imposed restrictions on sending parcels out of the republic containing goods in short supply. It said surplus farm products would be sold only to the local population. On May 29, Radio Moscow reported that the Uzbek Council of Ministers had temporarily restricted some food supplies to citizens of Uzbekistan.

Increase in Gold Sales

A Soviet banker said the USSR planned to increase its sales of gold and other goods to pay outstanding bills from Western countries. Viktor Gerashchenko, the head of the USSR State Bank, announced this move at a business conference in Moscow. He also told Reuters that the ruble proceeds from the sales would equal some 2 billion dollars. Gerashchenko said one reason for late payments was that Soviet state trade organizations had overestimated exports while increasing purchases of Western consumer goods—a situation that led to a hard-currency shortage. Other officials cited the decline in world market prices for Soviet oil, gas, and gold exports. They said Moscow must pay the bills to maintain its credit standing (*Reuters*, May 31).

Opposition to USSR Economic Reform Plan

The RSFSR Congress of People's Deputies adopted a statement on the economic reform package proposed by the Ryzhkov government. The statement expressed serious concern about the reform plan and said it was to be hoped that its implementation would not lead to a decline in the standard of living. While declaring the RSFSR's readiness for constructive cooperation on the government's plan, it instructed the new RSFSR Supreme Soviet to develop alternative programs for economic reform (*Moscow Television*, June 1). On June 1, Radio Moscow reported that the Presidium of the Federation of Independent Trade Unions of Russia had rejected the government's economic reform program and proposed a round-table discussion on the issue. In its turn, the Belorussian Supreme Soviet said it opposed any economic reform that involved price increases for consumer goods (*TASS*, June 1).

Latvian Parliament Nationalizes Printing Plant

The Latvian parliament decided to transfer control of Riga's only printing plant to the republican government. The plant had previously been controlled by the faction of the Latvian Communist Party loyal to Moscow. The parliament's move was prompted by the recent decision of the pro-Moscow Communists to change the editorial boards of the Latvian-language daily *Cina* and the Russian-language daily *Sovetskaya Latviya* (*TASS*, RFE Latvian service, May 31).

The Month of June

Friday, June 1

Elections of Deputy Chairmen of the RSFSR Supreme Soviet

Only two candidates garnered enough votes on the first ballot to be elected to the posts of deputy chairmen of the RSFSR Supreme Soviet. They were Boris Isaev, the chairman of the Executive Committee of the Chelyabinsk Oblast Soviet, and Svetlana Goryacheva, a lawyer from Vladivostok. (*TASS*, June 1).

***Pravda* Publishes First Advertisement for US Company**

Pravda printed its first advertisement in almost eighty years of publishing. The half-page advertisement, from a US company based in Minnesota, welcomed Gorbachev to that state. *Pravda* called attention to the advertisement in a front-page announcement that included the name of a Soviet advertising agency that will handle advertisements for the Party daily.

Saturday, June 2

US-Soviet Summit

On June 2, the US-Soviet summit moved to the presidential retreat at Camp David outside Washington. Presidents George Bush and Mikhail Gorbachev held private and informal talks there (*Reuters*, *AP*, June 2). The major topics were regional issues and German reunification. In Washington, Soviet Presidential Council member Evgenii Primakov said this summit was the most fruitful in the history of US-Soviet relations (*AP*, June 2). He said Bush and Gorbachev had succeeded in clearing obstacles from the agenda that in the past had prevented relations from moving foward.

The same day, US and Soviet negotiators signed three new agreements. The State Department said that, under a new customs cooperation agreement, Washington and Moscow would share intelligence information, primarily in order to combat international drug trafficking. Another agreement provided for the two countries to open cultural centers in each other's capitals. The third document signed was a memorandum of understanding to increase the circulation of the government-published magazines *America* and *Soviet Life* (*UPI*, June 2).

Commenting on the Bush-Gorbachev talks, Vitalii Churkin, an adviser to Eduard Shevardnadze, said the US and Soviet leaders were not deadlocked over the issue of German unification. He said that Bush and Gorbachev were discussing "creative approaches" to a united Germany's membership in NATO. He also told a CNN interviewer that the agreements signed at the summit would enhance Gorbachev's standing in the Soviet Union. He dismissed doubts about Gorbachev's political future, saying he was "enormously popular" at home as well as abroad. Interviews conducted by Western correspondents in Moscow with Soviet citizens showed, however, that Churkin's comments on Gorbachev's popularity at home were something of an exaggeration. For instance, on June 2, AP quoted people in Moscow as complaining that *perestroika* had resulted in a further decline in Soviet living standards and suggesting that instead of going to Washington Gorbachev should have stayed in Moscow to deal with domestic problems. Some of those interviewed said Gorbachev should not have been given humanitarian awards. (On June 1, Gorbachev was presented with a humanitarian award named after US President Franklin Roosevelt. Gorbachev also received the Albert Einstein International Peace Prize and the Martin Luther King Peace Prize.)

Also on June 2, an estimated 1,000 US supporters of Baltic independence rallied again on the steps of the Capitol in Washington (*RFE/RL Special*, June 3). Senator Alfonse D'Amato told the demonstrators that Moscow's sanctions against Lithuania should be lifted and that Lithuanian-Soviet negotiations should begin; otherwise, he said, there would be "a serious battle" in Congress over approval of the trade agreement signed by Bush and Gorbachev on June 1.

On June 3, Gorbachev and Bush gave a joint press conference. The two leaders did not indicate any narrowing of differences on two key issues of the summit—the role of a united Germany and the future of the Baltic republics. But Bush said the spirit in which both sides discussed their disagreements was a mark of how far the US-Soviet relationship had come. Bush and Gorbachev also pledged to expand US-Soviet cooperation to preserve the environment. On June 3, Soviet Central Television also broadcast an interview with Gorbachev on the summit.

Commenting on the US-Soviet summit in an NBC interview, US Secretary of State James Baker said the United States was not risking anything in trying to support Gorbachev's endeavors to introduce openness and democracy in the Soviet Union. What the United States was doing, Baker said, was trying to lock in agreements that were to the mutual advantage of the Soviet Union and the United States while Gorbachev was still in power (*Reuters*, *DPA*, June 3).

The same day, the Israeli minister for immigrant absorption, Yitzhak Peretz, said that Gorbachev and Bush could come to see for themselves that Israel was not settling Soviet Jews on the West Bank and the Gaza Strip. Peretz was responding to a warning given by Gorbachev at his press conference that he might halt further emigration of Soviet Jews if Israel continued to settle them in the occupied territories (*AP*, *Reuters*, June 3). On June 4, the National Conference on Soviet Jewry sent a telegram to Gorbachev warning the Soviet leader against imposing restrictions on Jewish emigration (*RFE/RL Special*, June 4). On June 5, Soviet Foreign Minister Eduard Shevardnadze told US Secretary of State James Baker in Copenhagen that the Soviet Union would not curb Jewish emigration (Western agencies, June 5).

Also on June 3, Gorbachev went to Minnesota, a region of successful farming and industry. That day, he met with Minnesota's governor, Rudy Perpich. Among guests at the luncheon hosted by Perpich was the British publisher Robert Maxwell, who, together with Perpich, announced the formation of a 100-million-dollar Gorbachev-Maxwell Institute of Technology (Western agencies, June 3). Afterwards, Gorbachev left Minnesota for San Francisco to meet with South Korean President Roh Tae Woo and former US President Ronald Reagan. Gorbachev told reporters after the meeting with President Roh that it had been agreed that the two countries would establish relations in the near future. He also said he was convinced that the eventual reunification of South and North Korea was "inevitable." In San Francisco, Gorbachev also held a meeting with a large group of US corporate executives. He told them he would speed up plans to make the ruble a convertible currency in order to help foreign companies take their profits out of the Soviet Union. In an address delivered at Stanford University, Gorbachev presented his vision of a world in which old alliances based on hostility would give way to peaceful cooperation in combating such problems as hunger, disease, drug addiction, and ignorance (*Reuters*, *AFP*, *AP*, June 4). Gorbachev returned to the Soviet Union on June 5. For Soviet press reporting on the summit, see *Pravda*, June 3–5.

Situation in Lithuania

On June 1, the first deputy chairman of the Belorussian Supreme Soviet, Stanislav Shushkevich, said he fully supported Lithuanian independence because it had been declared by an elected parliament. Shushkevich also told RFE/RL that he opposed the blockade of Lithuania.

The same day, Lech Walesa nominated the Baltic republics for a Nobel Peace Prize for "rare courage" in struggling for independence despite Soviet pressure (*Reuters*, June 1). Meanwhile, speaking in Washington, Mikhail Gorbachev defended his actions in Lithuania. He called Lithuania's proclamation of independence "nothing but an adventurist and separatist action" (*RFE/RL Special*, June 1).

TASS reported the same day that the Soviet authorities had set up a new Lithuanian radio station. The radio, broadcasting in Lithuanian, Russian, and Polish, went on the air for the first time on June 2 with live coverage of the congress of Lithuania's pro-Moscow Communist Party.

On June 2, Lithuania's pro-Moscow Communist Party resumed its congress after having adjourned in April (*TASS*, June 2). On June 3, DPA reported that speakers at the congress had criticized Gorbachev for introducing reforms that had destabilized the USSR economically and politically.

On June 2, President of the Lithuanian Supreme Council Vytautas Landsbergis said criticism of the Baltic republics expressed by Gorbachev in Ottawa and Washington was baseless and undiplomatic (*Radio Vilnius*, June 2). The same day, TASS reported that Poles living in the region of Vilnius were demanding autonomy for traditionally Polish areas.

On June 4, in an interview with the Voice of America, Landsbergis criticized President Bush for signing a provisional trade agreement with Gorbachev. He said Bush had thus given Gorbachev a free hand to continue the blockade against Lithuania (*AP*, June 4). The same day, Prime Minister Kazimiera Prunskiene told the VOA that a delegation from the RSFSR had come to Lithuania to discuss possible direct agreements. (On June 3, Soviet Foreign Ministry spokesman Vitalii Churkin warned the Russian Federation not to make trade deals with Lithuania as an independent nation [*Reuters*, *AFP*, June 3].)

On June 6, Lithuanian Foreign Minister Algirdas Saudargas told the East German daily *Junge Welt* that closer ties to other Soviet republics were vital to Lithuania's independence drive. He noted: "We will stick to our independence campaign but we are in no way interested in a confrontation with Gorbachev." He added that "democratic forces" in the Siberian oil field in Tyumen Oblast had offered to supply 300,000 tons of oil in exchange for meat. Radio Vilnius reported the same day that three oil wells near the city of Vilkaviskis in southern Lithuania would be activated to produce 80 tons of oil a day.

On June 7, Prunskiene said Latvia and Estonia were trying to help Lithuania overcome the effect of Moscow's economic blockade. Radio Vilnius quoted her as saying a proposal had been made by Latvia and Estonia to share some resources with Lithuania. Prunskiene said Latvia and Estonia were trying to find jobs for the unemployed from Lithuania. On June 8, the Lithuanian authorities said the Soviet Union had eased its blockade of shipments of oil and natural gas to Lithuania (RFE Lithuanian service, June 8).

On June 8, Mikhail Gorbachev issued a decree that declared a partial amnesty announced by Lithuania a month ago unconstitutional (*Pravda*, June 9). The amnesty covered first-time offenders convicted of minor crimes before Lithuania reaffirmed its independence in March. Gorbachev's decree ordered the USSR Ministry of Internal Affairs and the USSR prosecutor-general to ensure that the Lithuanian amnesty was not implemented (*TASS*, June 8).

On June 16, the Lithuanian Council of Ministers met to discuss a response to Moscow's stand on talks about Lithuanian independence (*Radio Vilnius*, June 16). The Lithuanian government proposed a temporary moratorium on the March 11 declaration of independence, but "Sajudis" criticized this proposal and said the Lithuanian parliament should not approve it (*Reuters*, June 19). In defending the proposal, Prunskiene said her government had followed the advice of US, French, and West German leaders (*AFP*, June 19).

On June 21, sixteen Communist deputies in the Lithuanian parliament announced that they had formed a centrist faction. They said they wanted to take a middle line between the official policy of the independent Lithuanian Communist Party and the views of what they called the "radical" wing of "Sajudis." Deputy Audrius Rudys said the centrist faction was made up of independent Communists who had the backing of "Sajudis." One of its members was Egidijus Bickauskas, Lithuania's official representative in Moscow.

On June 24, in an interview with Radio Vilnius, Lithuanian Finance Minister Romualdas Sikorskis said Moscow's economic blockade had resulted in a loss of more than 100 million rubles from the republic's budget. Sikorskis said Lithuania would eventually seek to recover the money it had contributed so far this year to the Soviet budget.

On June 26, the Lithuanian Supreme Council began debate on the issue of a moratorium on its declaration of independence. In this connection, Prime Minister Kazimiera Prunskiene said that too many conditions placed on a proposed moratorium on independence would make it "meaningless" (*Radio Vilnius*, *TASS*, June 26). Many deputies in the Lithuanian parliament, however, spoke against the moratorium, and a decision was, therefore, taken to postpone voting on it (*DPA*, *TASS*, June 26).

The same day, Landsbergis held talks with Gorbachev in Moscow. Gorbachev also spoke to Prunskiene by telephone. On June 27, Gorbachev again met with Lithuanian leaders. (Prunskiene also arrived in Moscow for this meeting.) Both meetings indicated that the central leadership wanted the moratorium to be approved, although Gorbachev was careful not to give any assurance to the Lithuanians that Lithuanian independence would then automatically be granted (*AFP*, *AP*, June 26 and 27). A spokesman for Landsbergis called Moscow's stand confused and quoted him as saying there was no point in debating the moratorium on independence until matters were clarified.

On June 28, the Lithuanian parliament resumed discussion of the moratorium. In her address to the session, Prunskiene strongly advocated the move, insisting that it would not represent a retreat but would, on the contrary, be a step towards independence (*Radio Vilnius*, June 28).

On June 29, the Lithuanian Supreme Council voted to approve a 100-day moratorium on the republic's declaration of independence to go into effect as soon as Lithuania and Moscow began talks on Lithuanian independence (*TASS*, Western agencies, June 29). See RL 305/90.

On June 30, Moscow lifted the economic blockade against Lithuania (*Radio Vilnius*, *AP*, June 30); see RL 286/90. The same day, about 5,000 ethnic Russians and Poles gathered on a hill outside Vilnius to demonstrate against the Lithuanian drive for independence. The meeting was organized by the anti-independence group "Interdvizhenie" (*Reuters*, June 30).

Moscow Opens Commodity Exchange

Moscow officials announced the formation of a rudimentary commodity exchange in the hope of overcoming the severe inefficiencies in the Soviet wholesale distribution system. Reuters quoted Chairman of the Moscow City Soviet Gavriil Popov as saying: "We have two enemies to creating a market economy: one is the shadow economy, and the other is the administrative system that rules our centralized economy. A commodity exchange will strike a blow at both." He said the exchange would act as a middleman and accommodate trade in a variety of goods ranging from construction materials to high-technology equipment.

Demonstration against Nuclear Power Plant

About 1,500 people formed a human chain through the streets of Balakovo in Saratov Oblast in the RSFSR to protest against the construction of a new reactor at the Balakovo nuclear power station, TASS reported. Local citizens had earlier called on Moscow to shut the station down.

Gromov Says Military Coup Impossible

Army General Boris Gromov told a West German military delegation that the Soviet army's officer corps was divided over a united Germany's membership in NATO. According to *Die Welt*, Gromov said older military leaders still regarded NATO as a threat, while the younger ones had grown up in a different atmosphere and therefore had "a totally different attitude." Gromov also said that Soviet generals would never stage a coup, even if the country's situation deteriorated further.

Demonstrators Claim 15,000 Conscripts Killed over Past Four Years

Central Television reported that Moscow demonstrators had accused the USSR Defense Ministry of covering up the deaths of some 15,000 conscripts. The largest demonstration took place in Gorky Park, where the mothers of dead recruits called for the ouster of Defense Minister Dmitrii Yazov and the elimination of conscription. UPI reported that the demonstration had been organized by the renegade military union "Shield." A demonstration also took place outside the Main Military Prosecutor's Office. The demonstrators also mourned the deaths of Soviet soldiers in Afghanistan. UPI reported that a former major, crippled in Afghanistan, had charged that most of those killed in the war had died because they had not received proper combat training. Soviet television said Yazov met with a group of mothers of soldiers killed in Afghanistan and expressed his regrets to them.

Proindependence Groups Boycott Latvian Round Table

Proindependence organizations in Latvia boycotted a meeting organized by the republic's pro-Moscow Communist Party. TASS said on June 2 that the meeting held in Riga the previous day was intended to be "a round table" bringing together groups with widely differing views. It quoted pro-Moscow Party leader Alfreds Rubiks as saying the aim of the session was to find common approaches to Latvia's urgent problems and to find points of unity rather than disagreement. But TASS said only six of the sixteen organizations invited attended. Among those that stayed away were the Latvian Popular Front, the Social Democratic Party, and trade unions. TASS said leaders of the Independent Communist Party of Latvia had attended the opening of the meeting but had walked out after deciding that dialogue with the pro-Moscow group was not possible.

Situation in Armenia

The Soviet media reported increased thefts of arms in Armenia and an attack on a military hospital in Erevan in the wake of clashes between Armenian militants and Soviet troops. The buro of the Armenian Communist Party Central Committee condemned the incidents as "a crude provocation" intended to arouse feelings against the army (*TASS*, *Reuters*, June 2). On June 3, the International Service of Radio Erevan criticized Radio Mayak for allegedly reporting on May 25 that a coup d'état was scheduled in Armenia for May 28—the anniversary of the declaration of Armenian independence in 1918. Runoff elections took place on June 3 in eighty-two districts of Armenia where no single candidate had won a clear majority in the first round of elections to the new Armenian Supreme Soviet on May 20 (*TASS*, June 3).

Events of 1962 Commemorated in Novocherkassk

The city of Novocherkassk commemorated the killing of more than twenty people during a demonstration twenty-eight years ago. Soviet television said on June 3 that participants in a memorial rally held on June 2 had appealed to the Soviet and Russian governments to investigate the incident, which had begun when local workers struck over reduced wages and higher prices and marched to local Party headquarters. The authorities called out the troops, who met the marchers with tanks and heavy arms. Gunfire then broke out, leaving more than twenty people dead and thirty wounded.

Sunday, June 3

Yazov on Military Reform

Krasnaya zvezda carried an article in which Soviet Defense Minister Dmitrii Yazov gave details of military reforms planned for next year. In the article, Yazov mentioned the possibility of increasing voluntary service in the armed forces. He also said reform should lead to a 20-percent cut in personnel in the High Command and to large reductions among the ranks of senior officers. The defense minister added that more housing would be set aside for army personnel and that pensions would be increased by up to 20 percent. But he ruled out the idea of Soviet republics' forming their own armies.

More Discussion of Privileges for Generals

Ogonek (No. 21) published a letter from a thirty-five-year-old veteran lambasting the High Command for maintaining luxurious dachas at a time when veterans like himself were struggling to keep a roof over their heads. The letter gave details of the sizes of the dachas and of the large tracts of land on which they were located. The generals singled out for criticism include Yazov, Akhromeev, Lushev, and former Defense Minister Sergei Sokolov. This letter is the latest salvo in the long battle between the liberal journal and the military top brass.

Officers Resent Performing Police Functions

Moscow News (No. 22) said that Soviet army officers were increasingly opposed to performing domestic policing operations. The weekly implied that such sentiments were behind the desire of some 30,000 officers to leave the armed forces. The article outlined the case of Major Viktor Trofimov, who refused to "volunteer" for service in Baku.

In the same issue of the weekly, a letter was published in which it was revealed that two officers had been discharged from the Soviet Armed Forces for suggesting that the CPSU make its financial situation public. According to the letter, "the gravest sin" of the two officers was their support for the Democratic Platform within the CPSU.

Arbatov Criticizes Economic Reform

Academician Georgii Arbatov, head of the USA and Canada Institute, told *The Los Angeles Times* that Nikolai Ryzhkov's plans for economic reform were "a very serious mistake" because they raised prices without increasing production. Arbatov suggested that Ryzhkov could not remain prime minister, because "his team has failed." Arbatov acknowledged that there had been "tremendously costly" mistakes in economic policy.

Monday, June 4

Human-Rights Conference in Copenhagen

Senior officials from thirty-five states opened a conference in the Danish capital, Copenhagen, with a plea for the resolution of the problems of national and regional minorities in Europe. The conference was part of the follow-up process to the 1975 Helsinki Accords.

In his address to the conference on June 5, Soviet Foreign Minister Eduard Shevardnadze announced additional cuts in the Soviet nuclear arsenal in central Europe and said they were intended to create better conditions for East-West arms talks. He also said he believed compromise was possible on differences between East and West over German unification. Shevardnadze also proposed an international seminar to discuss ethnic tensions and conflicts in Europe. The same day, Shevardnadze held talks with US Secretary of State James Baker to discuss German unification and arms control. At a meeting of NATO foreign ministers on June 7, Baker said Moscow's attitude to a unified Germany had become "much more encouraging" since the Washington summit (Western agencies, June 5, 6, and 7).

On June 8, the three Baltic republics formally applied to the conference in Copenhagen for observer status. Asked to comment, Soviet Deputy Foreign Minister Vladimir Petrovsky said the Baltic republics had "no legal ground" for such a request, since they were still part of the USSR (*RFE/RL Special*, June 8).

Latvian Supreme Council Confirms Appointment of Interior Minister

The Latvian Supreme Soviet confirmed the appointment of a career police officer, Aloizs Vaznis, as the republic's new minister of internal affairs. Vaznis promised to work for "an independent Latvia" and said he would carry out the orders of the Latvian government and obey laws approved by the Latvian parliament (RFE Latvian service, June 4).

Supreme Soviet Approves Law on Enterprises

The USSR Supreme Soviet passed a Law on Enterprises that gives more independence to Soviet businesses and puts all businesses—whether cooperatives or state enterprises—on an equal legal footing (*TASS*, June 4; *Izvestia*, June 5. For the text of the law on enterprises, see *Izvestia*, June 12). While the law should in theory simplify the maze of special rules and regulations on various types of businesses, it is unclear what authority other laws such as the Law on Cooperatives will have. On June 5, the Supreme Soviet approved at the first reading a draft law that will set a uniform tax rate of 45 percent for businesses. TASS said the vote was a compromise between two draft laws, one calling for a 55-percent rate on business profits and the other stipulating a 35-percent rate (see also *Izvestia*, June 5 and 6).

RSFSR Bureaucracy Being Reduced

New statistics published in *Argumenty i fakty* (No. 20) showed that the government bureaucracy in the Russian republic had been cut by 28.5 percent since 1985. It revealed that the staffs of the republican ministries had been reduced by 34.6 percent and oblast staff by 32 percent. At the start of 1990, the RSFSR had fifty-four ministries and state committees. Most of the people released were reemployed as managers of industrial enterprises. The number of employees at that level increased by 7 percent (500,000 people).

Ivashko Elected Chairman of Ukrainian Supreme Soviet

Ukrainian Party First Secretary Vladimir Ivashko was elected chairman of the Ukrainian Supreme Soviet after more than 100 radical deputies walked out to protest against the Party first secretary's holding this post. The vote was 278 in favor, 61 against, with no abstentions. Eleven candidates were originally nominated for the post, including representatives of both "Rukh" and the Republican National Party. TASS described the debate over combining the top Party and state offices as "stormy," and Reuters (June 4) reported that about 10,000 demonstrators outside the hall carried placards denouncing Ivashko and waving the yellow-and-blue Ukrainian national flag. On June 5, reports from Kiev and Lvov said demonstrations were continuing in protest over Ivashko's holding both posts. According to TASS, Ivashko, speaking after his election, agreed that no individual could combine the two offices but said that he could not abandon Party work only fifteen days before the Ukrainian Party Congress.

Election Officials Sentenced for Forgery

Radio Moscow reported that two electoral commission officials in Kazakhstan's Karaganda Oblast found guilty of forging election results had been sentenced to two years in labor camps. The officials—the head of the Nurinsk Raion Electoral Commission and the second secretary of the raion Komsomol Committee—went on trial in May for having altered vote tallies so that the raion Party chief would get a seat on the raion soviet. This is the first known sentence for election fraud in the Soviet Union.

US-Soviet Petroleum Development Plans

Western agencies reported that Chevron and Tengizneftegaz, the enterprise responsible for developing the Tengiz oil field in western Kazakhstan, had signed a letter of intent calling for a feasibility study for joint development of the field. *The Los Angeles Times* reported that representatives of the Kazakhstan government had also signed the agreement. See RL 273/90.

New Commercial Satellite Telecommunications System

Soviet Communications Minister Erlen Pervyshin announced the creation of the first Soviet satellite data system designated for commercial use, according to Western agency accounts. Called "Marafon," the new system will provide telephone, telegraph, telex, and telefax links among the regions of the Soviet Union and worldwide beginning in 1991. The new system will double Moscow's information link capacity with the outside world.

Ukrainians Protest against Radar Station and Nuclear Plant

Protests were again held in Ukraine against the construction of a radar station and the operation of a nuclear power station. The radar station was to be built near Mukachevo, while the power station was located at Khmelnitsky, both towns in Western Ukraine. Radio Kiev said that a one-day protest strike had been held in Mukachevo and that thousands of people had turned out for protest meetings. It also said a majority of people living around the Khmelnitsky nuclear plant opposed its operation; people attended protest meetings there and also picketed the plant (*Radio Kiev*, June 4).

Draft Laws on Political Parties and Freedom of Conscience Published

Pravda published the draft of the USSR Law on Public Associations, discussion of which started in the USSR Supreme Soviet on June 1. The public associations discussed in the draft include political parties, popular fronts, and other new movements. According to the draft law, organizations must register with the Ministry of Justice, but registration may be refused only if the organization's aims conflict with the USSR Constitution. The Law on Public Associations does not cover the activities of religious groups, which come under the jurisdiction of the Law on Freedom of Conscience, the draft of which appeared in *Izvestia* on June 5 and in *Pravda* on June 6. The draft allows religious organizations and churches to own property and legalizes the Church's charitable activities.

Tuesday, June 5

Unrest in Kirgizia

The Supreme Soviet of Kirgizia declared a state of emergency and imposed a night curfew in the city of Osh, located in the Kirgiz part of the Fergana Valley, after fighting broke out between Kirgiz and Uzbeks in the wake of a land dispute. A spokesman for the USSR Ministry of Internal Affairs told Reuters that the death toll in the Osh region was thirty-six, with more than 350 people injured, including some members of the security forces. A local journalist said that the center of Osh was quiet, with troops blocking roads into the city to prevent rival groups from entering, but that unrest was spreading in the nearby countryside. *Komsomol'skaya pravda* said the dispute had taken on a political character, with Uzbeks, who make up about a third of the population of Osh Oblast, demanding more regional autonomy and Kirgiz demanding equal treatment with the Uzbek majority in the city of Osh.

On June 6, the rioting spread to the Kirgiz capital, Frunze, where several Uzbeks were beaten in the marketplace. Radio Moscow said troops from the USSR Ministry of Internal Affairs had been sent to restore order. USSR Presidential Council member and writer Chingiz Aitmatov appealed for calm in the republic and urged his fellow Kirgiz "not to raise their hands against their Uzbek brothers" (*Komsomol'skaya pravda*, *AP*, RL Kirgiz service, June 6).

On June 7, USSR Minister of Internal Affairs Vadim Bakatin said the ethnic violence in Kirgizia had spread to neighboring Uzbekistan and that the death toll had risen to forty-eight. Bakatin said 900 MVD troops, 1,500 army troops, and another 450 border guards had been deployed to the republic. Bakatin said that the situation in Osh had stabilized somewhat but that thousands of people armed with sharpened sticks, stones, and other weapons had gathered at the border of the two republics between Osh and Andizhan (*TASS*, Western agencies, June 7).

On June 8, TASS reported a big increase in the number of casualties that resulted from the clashes between Kirgiz and Uzbeks: the figure was at least seventy-eight people dead and another 330 injured. There was a sanctioned public meeting in Frunze on June 8 to mourn the victims. The same day, a state of emergency was declared in areas of Uzbekistan that bordered on Osh Oblast in Kirgizia (*TASS*, June 8). Meanwhile, the USSR Supreme Soviet called for calm and restraint in Kirgizia and Uzbekistan.

On June 9, the commandant of Frunze gave security forces permission to open fire in the event of any serious incident, but the city was reported to have remained quiet (*TASS*, June 9). The following day, Radio Moscow reported that a rally called by the democratic movement "Kyrgyzstan," an informal group founded three weeks previously to press for radical reforms, had been banned by the military authorities in Frunze. Central Television reported that militants were continuing to fight with troops in Osh Oblast and had attacked truck convoys on the Osh-Khorog highway. June 11 was a day of mourning in Kirgizia for those who died in the interethnic clashes. An army unit was reported to be in control in the town of Uzgen, where six people had died the previous week (*Radio Moscow*, June 11).

On June 12, Radio Moscow said the situation in the oblast and in neighboring areas of Uzbekistan was returning to normal, though troops were continuing to block access to towns to prevent "terrorist groups" from renewing the fighting. TASS reported on June 12 that the chairman of the Uzbek Council of Ministers, Shukrulla Mirsaidov, had categorically rejected the demand of some Uzbeks in Osh Oblast that an autonomous area be established for the Uzbek population of Osh.

On June 15, *Pravda* said a group of investigators had arrived in Osh to "establish the causes of the bloody events."

Mirsaidov told the Uzbek Supreme Soviet on June 18 that the majority of the dead in the violence in Osh Oblast were Uzbeks. The same day, "Vremya" reported that the deputies were demanding the immediate establishment of a USSR commission to investigate what happened in Osh. A correspondent for *Izvestia* in Frunze wrote that the office of his newspaper had received anonymous telephone threats, with callers accusing the daily of inflaming interethnic antagonism (*Izvestia*, June 11). The correspondent noted that functionaries of various ranks and "newly hatched democrats" wanted to muzzle the press: a photojournalist was beaten up at an unsanctioned meeting in Frunze, and Central Television journalists were "advised" by the republican leadership not to film events.

On June 19, TASS gave a figure of 186 dead in the clashes in Osh. The agency said that "a fragile peace" had been established in Osh Oblast but that tensions remained high in the town of Uzgen, where Uzbeks and Kirgiz were not disposed towards reconciliation. Further bloodshed was reportedly being prevented by the presence of troops.

On June 20, Radio Moscow reported that more than 500 people had been registered with the police as missing after the ethnic clashes. See RL 262/90.

Baltic Leaders Appeal to Gorbachev to Open Talks

In Jurmala, the chairmen of the three Baltic Supreme Councils reached agreement on a common negotiating stance with Moscow. They pledged that nonnative residents of the republics would be guaranteed full human rights, and they sent a telegram to Gorbachev asking him "to call a joint meeting without delay to define the issues and order of full negotiations," according to Radio Riga.

El'tsin Deputy Wins Election at RSFSR Congress

Boris El'tsin's choice for his first deputy, Ruslan Khasbulatov, was elected by the RSFSR Congress of People's Deputies. The vote was 604 to 378. El'tsin secured Khasbulatov's election only after reading out a letter from two conservative deputies who came out in support of him (*TASS*, June 5).

KGB Spy in Brussels Had Contacts in EEC Commission

A KGB spy in Brussels was reported to have defected to the United States, where he revealed that he had had top-level contacts inside the EEC Commission, the Belgian Defense and Interior Ministries, and possibly NATO as well. The Belgian daily *La Libre Belgique* said that among the contacts was an aide to the president of the EEC Commission, Jacques Delors, who was in charge of negotiating trade agreements with East European countries. The report said the spy had also used several Belgian journalists as "agents of influence" to publish articles opposing German unification (*AFP*, June 5).

Moscow Said to Be Reducing Pacific Fleet Forces

Japanese Defense Agency officials said the Soviet Union had reduced the number of naval vessels and military aircraft deployed in the Far East by scrapping old ships (*AP*, June 5). On June 4, a Japanese newspaper quoted an internal report of Japan's Self-Defense Force, which forecast that the number of Soviet submarines and major surface ships was likely to fall by 27 percent by the end of the century.

Moscow and Seoul to Set Up Joint Economic Committee

Concrete results of Gorbachev's meeting with South Korean President Roh Tae Woo in San Francisco included an agreement to set up a joint committee to boost trade and other exchanges. Noh Da Rey, the deputy director of South Korea's Economic Planning Board, forecast that the agreement would be signed "in the second half of this year when the two governments establish diplomatic ties." The agreement came on the heels of a visit to Seoul by a Soviet delegation, which made offers on 100 projects for joint technological and industrial cooperation. Bilateral trade has been steadily growing over the past two years and totaled 599 million dollars in 1989 (*Reuters*, June 5).

On June 1, North Korea warned that Gorbachev's meeting with Roh could have serious consequences for the future of the Korean Peninsula (*Reuters*, June 1).

On June 19, Presidential Council member Evgenii Primakov told *Pravda* that no political deals had been made at the June 4 meeting between Roh and Gorbachev. As reported by TASS, Primakov explicitly denied that Moscow had offered political contacts in exchange for loans, equipment, and consumer goods. See RL 259/90.

Churches the Most Trusted Institutions in Soviet Society

According to two opinion surveys published by *Moscow News* (Nos. 22 and 23), religious organizations now enjoy more trust from the Soviet public than any other institution. Since March, 1989, Churches have moved from being the least trusted institutions (enjoying the full trust of only 13 percent of respondents) to being the most trusted (enjoying the full trust of 37 percent of respondents). Trust in the Communist Party slumped over the same period from 38 percent to 16 percent. All other public institutions covered by the survey also showed a decline in public confidence, with the exception of the law-enforcement agencies. They now enjoy the full trust of 18 percent of respondents compared with 15 percent in 1989.

Wednesday, June 6

RSFSR Congress Enlarges Legislature

The RSFSR Congress of People's Deputies provisionally agreed to enlarge the two Supreme Soviet chambers to 163 members each. TASS said representatives of autonomous entities had opposed enlarging the Supreme Soviet from its current size of 126 members in each chamber. It said they feared that a larger system could not ensure the rights of small ethnic groups and nationalities.

Ter-Petrossyan Says Armenians Will Talk with Russia Directly

The leader of the Armenian Pan-National Movement, Levon Ter-Petrossyan, told the Paris daily *Libération* that his group had proposed to Boris El'tsin, the chairman of the RSFSR Supreme Soviet, that the two republics establish direct relations "without passing through the Kremlin." Ter-Petrossyan also said his movement and the Armenian Communist Party had reached an agreement in principle on a coalition government. He said the newly elected government would overhaul the constitution (*RFE/RL Special*, June 6).

Detentions and Arms Seizures Continue in Nagorno-Karabakh

TASS said 445 people had been detained in Nagorno-Karabakh since Moscow imposed a state of emergency in the region earlier in the year after renewed ethnic violence. It said they had been detained for failing to present documents or for not having residence permits. TASS also said that during this period 225 firearms had been confiscated, as well as grenades, mines, and more than 9,000 rounds of ammunition.

Ukrainian Democratic Bloc Goes into Opposition

The Ukrainian Democratic Bloc announced that it now stood in formal opposition to the Communist Party in the Ukrainian Supreme Soviet. The bloc informed the Supreme Soviet that it would not propose candidates for Supreme Soviet posts as long as the parliament was under the present Communist leadership. Bloc deputies decided to create a "people's council" to draft alternative laws and other proposals for consideration by the Supreme Soviet (RL Ukrainian service, June 6). On June 8, TASS quoted the bloc as saying Ukrainian law should have priority over all-Union law.

Gorbachev Seeks to End US-UK Special Relationship

According to *The Guardian*, during the summit, the Soviet side demanded an end to the transfer of US nuclear technology to Britain. Any follow-up strategic arms reduction treaty would be inconceivable as long as the Anglo-American relationship continued, Soviet officials said. The US side refused bluntly, however, saying its commitment to Britain was not negotiable.

USSR Denies Plans for Nuclear Testing in the Arctic

Rafik Nishanov, chairman of the Council of Nationalities of the USSR Supreme Soviet, told Canadian parliamentarians in Ottawa that the USSR had no plans to carry out nuclear tests in the Arctic. Nishanov's comment was apparently in response to a statement by Canadian Foreign Minister Joe Clark that Eduard Shevardnadze had told him last week that nuclear testing was to be shifted from Kazakhstan to Novaya Zemlya because of public protests. Nishanov added that the Soviet Union would like to see all nuclear testing stopped (*RFE/RL Special*, June 6).

Chernobyl' Reactor Lacked Proper Safety System, Medvedev Says

A new book written by exiled Soviet biologist Zhores Medvedev said the Number 4 nuclear reactor at Chernobyl' ran for more than two years with an important element in its emergency safety system faulty or missing. He also said Soviet officials had covered up the omission. Medvedev made the allegations in *The Legacy of Chernobyl'*. He said he was skeptical about some aspects of the official, now almost universally accepted Soviet account of the accident. While Soviet officials say the accident occurred during an experiment to improve the reactor's safety system, Medvedev claimed that engineers were not trying to improve the system but to install it, something that should have been done before the reactor went into operation (*RFE/RL Special*, June 6).

Washington Blocks Export of Fiber Optics to USSR

Fearing that the technology involved had military applications, the US Department of Commerce announced that it intended to block the shipment of fiber-optics equipment to the Soviet Union, according to *The Los Angeles Times*. While the equipment is five to seven years behind state-of-the-art communications technology, its export is still forbidden by the seventeen-nation Coordinating Committee for Multilateral Export Controls (CoCom).

Supreme Soviet Amends Law on Cooperatives

TASS reported that the USSR Supreme Soviet had endorsed amendments to the Law on Cooperatives of 1988. The amendments were to go into effect on October 1 and were intended to tighten control on the activities of cooperatives and, in particular, to prevent price-gouging by trade cooperatives acting as middlemen between producer and consumer.

Vorotnikov Interviewed by Radio Liberty

Vitalii Vorotnikov became the first Politburo member to be interviewed by Radio Liberty. Speaking to the editors of Radio Liberty's news show "In the Country and the World," he firmly rejected the idea that the Party apparatus was trying to manipulate the decisions of the RSFSR Congress of People's Deputies.

Beria Ordered Testing of Poisons on People

Moscow News (No. 23) reported that Stalin's secret police chief Lavrentii Beria had ordered his subordinates to test poisonous compounds on human subjects during World War II. The newspaper published documents showing that this was one of the official charges made against Beria after he was arrested in 1953. Beria, who was tried secretly and executed later that year, apparently admitted that several people had died as a result of the tests.

Uzbek Party Congress Calls for Sovereignty

A congress of the Uzbek Communist Party ended with a call for genuine political sovereignty for the republic inside a renewed Soviet federation. TASS said the congress also adopted a resolution on the transition of the republic to a market economy. The resolution said that any national economic reform plan must take into account the conditions specific to each republic so that its people would be protected. During the congress, Islam Karimov was reelected Party first secretary by secret ballot.

Thursday, June 7

Gorbachev Calls for Reform of Warsaw Pact

At a one-day summit of the Warsaw Pact member states in Moscow, Soviet President Mikhail Gorbachev told fellow leaders that the organization must be radically changed but not disbanded. A Polish government spokesman quoted him as saying that dissolution of the pact would be "premature" because of the continuing changes in Eastern Europe. At the end of the meeting, the Warsaw Pact states adopted a communiqué calling for a review of the character and functions of the treaty that established the organization. The communiqué said the treaty review would lead to the transformation of the Warsaw Pact into a democratically formed group of sovereign states, each enjoying equal rights (*TASS*, Western agencies, June 7).

On June 18, Warsaw Pact Chief of Staff General Vladimir Lobov argued that the pact needed to retain a military function as well as a political one. He cautioned that NATO remained committed to the use of military force, drawing an analogy between the pre–World War II German army and the NATO alliance (*APN*, June 18).

Soviet Press Plays Up Bush-Gorbachev Personal Ties

In the wake of the Washington summit, the Soviet press highlighted the close personal relationship established there between Presidents Bush and Gorbachev. *Pravda* said the importance of good personal relations between the US and Soviet presidents could hardly be overestimated and it cited Gorbachev's description of Bush as someone "with whom he could do business." *Izvestia* praised the new, relaxed tone of what it called "superpower diplomacy without neckties."

***Izvestia* Says Kremlin Commission Has Rehabilitated 2 Million Purge Victims**

Izvestia quoted Soviet Politburo member Aleksandr Yakovlev as saying the rehabilitation of the victims of Stalin's purges was nearing its end. Yakovlev, who headed the Politburo Commission on Rehabilitation, said some 2 million victims had been rehabilitated since that body was established in September, 1987.

Moldavia Adopts Romanian-Language Name

The Moldavian Supreme Soviet decided to rename the republic "the Soviet Socialist Republic of Moldova." That is the Romanian-language name for the area. Deputies from predominantly Russian areas of the republic boycotted the session and demanded the right to form an autonomous republic. The chairman of the Supreme Soviet, Mircea Snegur, told Soviet television that their request could not be granted, because the republic was too small to be divided.

United States to Help Improve Soviet Food Supplies

Representatives from fifty US food production companies met with Soviet officials in Washington to discuss joint efforts to improve Soviet food supplies. US firms, such as Heinz, are seeking creative ways to enter the Soviet market while avoiding difficulties in repatriating profits. Since as much as half of all food grown in the Soviet Union spoils before it reaches the shelves, Soviet officials are urgently seeking assistance in the area of food packaging and processing. The same day, US Commerce Secretary Robert Mosbacher and Soviet Agriculture Minister Vladilen Nikitin signed an agreement providing for a team of US and Soviet government officials to study the food-processing systems of the two countries and determine how US technology and methods could be incorporated into the Soviet system (*AP*, June 7).

New Russian Orthodox Patriarch Chosen

TASS reported that, at a meeting in Moscow, the Holy Synod of the Russian Orthodox Church had elected Metropolitan Aleksii of Leningrad and Novgorod as the new patriarch of Moscow and all Russia. Aleksii, an ethnic German, was born in Tallinn in 1929. He replaced Patriarch Pimen, who died in March. Aleksii is the first patriarch of the Russian Orthodox Church not of Russian origin. On June 10, Aleksii was enthroned as patriarch in Moscow, and Gorbachev sent him a message congratulating him on his election (*TASS*, June 10). See RI 270/90.

On June 12, Aleksii met with Gorbachev and also with Soviet and foreign journalists. During the meeting, the patriarch complained about "attempts by the Russian Orthodox Church Abroad to split Russian Orthodox believers in the USSR." He said the Church Abroad was attempting to take under its jurisdiction some religious communities on the territory of the USSR (*Radio Moscow-1*, 1900, June 12). (According to reports in the West, several religious communities in Siberia have recently announced their break with the Moscow Patriarchate and requested that the Russian Orthodox Church Abroad take them under its jurisdiction.)

Fresh Inquiry into Evidence Concerning Wallenberg's Fate

The International Raoul Wallenberg Organization said it had asked deputies of the USSR Supreme Soviet to help find out what happened to Wallenberg—the Swedish diplomat who saved hundreds of Hungarian Jews from the Nazis during World War II. Wallenberg was arrested by Soviet troops in Budapest in 1945, and the USSR maintains he died in prison two years later, but there have been several reports that he was seen alive in Soviet camps years later (*RFE/RL Special*, June 7).

On June 8, the chief Soviet delegate at the Copenhagen human-rights conference, Yurii Reshetov, said the USSR would continue to search for evidence concerning the fate of Wallenberg. Talking to reporters in Copenhagen, Reshetov said the Soviet Union was aware that the documents it had produced were insufficient to convince Wallenberg's relatives and organizations concerned with his fate (*RFE/RL Special*, June 8).

El'tsin Supports Human-Rights Center for Moscow

A former Soviet political prisoner said he planned to set up a human-rights center in Moscow with the support of Boris El'tsin, chairman of the RSFSR Supreme Soviet. Yurii Orlov, who teaches at Cornell University in the United States, outlined his plan at a news conference in Copenhagen. Orlov said El'tsin supported the idea of starting an independent center to distribute information about human rights in the Soviet Union. Orlov is a founder of the Soviet Helsinki Committee monitoring the implementation of the Helsinki agreement on human rights (*AFP, DPA*, June 7).

Kazakh Party Congress Opens

At the opening session of the Seventeenth Congress of the Kazakh Communist Party in Alma-Ata, Kazakh Party First Secretary Nursultan Nazarbaev called for real sovereignty for the republic within a renewed Soviet federation. He also called for more independence for the republic's Party within the framework of the CPSU. Later, during debates, some congress delegates said that attempts to capitalize on the republic's vast economic opportunities were hampered by restrictions imposed by the federal authorities. Some delegates also said relations between Kazakhstan and other USSR republics should be based on equal treaties (*TASS*, June 7).

Pope Meets with Soviet Vatican Representative

Pope John Paul II met with the Soviet Union's new official representative to the Vatican, Yurii Karlov, to mark the formal beginning of the Soviet diplomat's mission. The Vatican gave no details of the audience. The Vatican and the Kremlin announced the establishment of "official permanent relations" in March. They fall short of full diplomatic relations but are the first formal ties since the 1917 October Revolution (*RFE/RL Special*, June 7).

Siberian Oil Workers Impose "Economic Sanctions"

Disgruntled oil workers in Siberia held back deliveries to a Moscow refinery. TASS said that, for the third straight day, oil workers in Tyumen had failed to send the expected delivery of 10,000 tons of oil to the capital. Radio Moscow (June 8) said the oilmen's action was a response to "the reduction in housing construction by the [Moscow companies] in Nizhnevartovsk." Reports of mass discontent in Tyumen have been emerging for several months, and the government has sent representatives to the region to try to mollify the miners and ward off a potentially crippling strike. Gorbachev has visited the region twice (*UPI*, June 7).

US and Soviet Automakers Sign Joint Agreement

The US car manufacturer General Motors and the USSR's Volga auto works signed a deal worth 1 billion dollars. General Motors announced the deal in the United States, saying it involved the purchase of GM-designed engine parts for two of Volga's cars sold under the Lada trade name. GM said shipment to Volga could begin in early 1992. It said the two automakers would also discuss the formation of a joint venture to manufacture parts in the Soviet Union. Initially, components will be made in General Motors' plants in the United States and Europe (*Reuters*, *AP*, June 7).

Brezhnev's Senior Deputy Dies

Vasilii Kuznetsov, who served as first deputy to three Soviet presidents, died in Moscow at the age of eighty-nine. He became first deputy chairman of the Presidium of the USSR Supreme Soviet in 1977 under Leonid Brezhnev and retired from the post in 1986, when Andrei Gromyko became president. He also served under Yurii Andropov and Konstantin Chernenko. Gorbachev and other top Soviet officials signed Kuznetsov's obituary, which appeared in *Pravda*.

Help Ordered for Pensioners, Veterans, Children in Azerbaijan

The Azerbaijani government decided to supplement the social benefits the USSR offers veterans and children in the republic. *Pravda* said the increased benefits had been decreed by Azerbaijan's new president, Ayaz Mutabilov. The newspaper quoted Mutabilov as saying some 35,000 invalids from World War II and the families of dead servicemen would no longer have to pay rent for their apartments. The paper said additional money had been provided to reduce the rents of World War II veterans and "internationalist servicemen"—i.e., those who fought in Afghanistan. *Pravda* also said the veterans were exempt from paying taxes on private automobiles and had better opportunities now to use rest homes and sanatoria.

Friday, June 8

Gorbachev Speaks on BBC Television

Mikhail Gorbachev said he was "optimistic" about the possibility of reaching a settlement with Lithuania, Estonia, and Latvia. Gorbachev said during an interview in Moscow televised by the British Broadcasting Corporation that "evolutionary processes are prevailing all over the world" and that assertions that the USSR was breaking up were "superfluous." On *perestroika*, the Soviet president said the reform program was his life, destiny, and "predicament, as a person and as a politician." He said that he was not going to "deviate from this path, whatever the pressure applied." Regarding the election of Boris El'tsin as the chairman of the RSFSR Supreme Soviet, Gorbachev said "there is no room for personal emotions"—his attitude towards El'tsin would be decided by El'tsin's future actions (*UPI*, *AFP*, June 8).

Gorbachev Meets with Thatcher

Mikhail Gorbachev met in Moscow with British Prime Minister Margaret Thatcher, who arrived in the Soviet capital on June 7. Speaking at a press conference after the meeting, Gorbachev said that the reforms under way in the Soviet Union were the most important of the century and that they made Moscow "the center of world politics." He said that negative public reaction to his government's economic reform program was understandable but that the reforms were needed. Concerning German reunification, Gorbachev said this issue had been a main topic of discussion in his talks with Thatcher. At a dinner hosted by Gorbachev, Thatcher said no country was more entitled to assurance on the question of a united Germany than the USSR. The same day, Thatcher and her Soviet counterpart, Nikolai Ryzhkov, signed documents on economic and cultural cooperation between the USSR and Britain (*Reuters*, *AFP*, June 8).

On June 9, Thatcher addressed the Ukrainian Supreme Soviet in Kiev. She declined a proposal to open a British embassy in Ukraine (*TASS*, June 9). On June 10, she went to Armenia and was greeted by tens of thousands of Armenians in Leninakan, where she dedicated a British-built school (*TASS*, June 10). The same day, Thatcher left the USSR for home.

Supreme Soviet Disagrees on Telecommunications Interception Law

The two chambers of the USSR Supreme Soviet split on a government proposal to allow surveillance of telephone conversations in the Soviet Union. TASS said the Council of Nationalities had rejected the proposal on June 8, while the Council of the Union approved it without reservation. TASS said this meant that a conciliation commission made up of representatives of both chambers would have to seek consensus. The agency said the government proposal would allow tapping of telephones and subsequent use of the recordings in court. It said the bill would also allow the use of voice and video recordings in court. TASS said the minister of internal affairs, Vadim Bakatin, defended the bill by saying that telephone tapping would only be used in major criminal cases and only with the approval of a court or prosecutor.

"Genuine Sovereignty" for Azerbaijan Urged by Party

TASS said a plan for "genuine sovereignty" for Azerbaijan was on the agenda of the Azerbaijani Communist Party Congress, which opened today in Baku. According to the agency, the plan envisages national statehood and economic and political independence. TASS said the plan was prepared by the Azerbaijani Party Central Committee and included a program for "the renovation" of the Azerbaijani Communist Party.

Moscow Urges Soviet-US Talks on Asia-Pacific Security

Soviet Deputy Foreign Minister Igor Rogachev said the USSR wanted talks with Washington on reducing military tension in the Asia-Pacific region. Rogachev said in Kuala Lumpur that the talks would be "devoted solely to one question—reducing military confrontation and tension in Asia and the Pacific." He was speaking at the end of a two-day visit to Malaysia. Rogachev said the USSR was worried by "the rapid modernization of naval and nuclear weapons" in the region (*Reuters*, June 8).

Saturday, June 9

El'tsin Interviewed on Soviet Television

The chairman of the RSFSR Supreme Soviet, Boris El'tsin, urged his countrymen to be calm and promised in return to improve their lives within three years. In an interview broadcast by Soviet television, El'tsin also called on coal miners to refrain from striking again. El'tsin's political and economic program for the RSFSR was also laid out in detail in his interview with *Moscow News* (No. 23).

El'tsin's television interview was initially scheduled to be broadcast on June 8 but was postponed on the grounds that the reporting on British Prime Minister Margaret Thatcher's visit to Moscow was more extensive than expected. El'tsin, however, said he believed the broadcast had been postponed on purpose by the Soviet leadership in order to insult him. On June 9, the incident was discussed in the RSFSR Congress of People's Deputies, with many deputies supporting El'tsin. The Congress summoned Mikhail Nenashev, the chairman of the USSR State Committee for Television and Radio Broadcasting, whose attempts to justify the postponement were not accepted by the deputies, and it was suggested that television broadcasting be put under the control of the Russian legislature. The debate was broadcast in full by "Mayak" on June 9.

On June 11, a letter from Mikhail Gorbachev was read out to the Congress in which the USSR president denied being behind the failure of Central Television to broadcast El'tsin's interview on June 8 (*Central Television*, "Vremya," June 11).

Elections to RSFSR Supreme Soviet

The RSFSR Congress of People's Deputies held elections to fill most of the 252 seats in the republican Supreme Soviet (*TASS*, June 9).

On June 13, TASS said El'tsin had nominated the secretary of the Arkhangelsk City Party Committee, Aleksandr Veshnyakov, for the deputy chairmanship of the Council of the Republic. Ramazan Abdulatipov was elected chairman of the Council of Nationalities.

On June 17, a group of RSFSR deputies expressed dissatisfaction with the composition of the new RSFSR Supreme Soviet. TASS said the group had issued a statement saying the Supreme Soviet had a large majority of members who made a practice of voting against all democratic proposals. They called for the Congress to take a vote of no confidence in the new body. They also said they had no intention of taking a position of "passive consent" and were ready to go into opposition.

Stalin Victims Set Up Association in Moldavia

More than 500 delegates attended the founding conference of the Association of the Repressed of Moldavia, TASS reported. Some of the delegates represented the Chernovtsy and Odessa regions of Ukraine. According to

TASS, approximately 100,000 people were deported from Moldavia under Stalin, and hundreds were killed.

Spate of Hijackings of Soviet Planes

A Soviet airliner with 135 people on board was hijacked while flying from Minsk to Murmansk and forced to land in Sweden. No one was hurt in the hijacking, which Swedish police said was carried out by a seventeen-year-old using a fake hand grenade (*AP*, *Reuters*, June 9). Dmitrii Semenov told Swedish radio he was desperate to seek asylum in a Western country after his parents kicked him out. Sweden returned the plane to the USSR, and TASS reported that measures were being taken to extradite the hijacker. On June 14, Swedish police said the hijacker would not receive political asylum in Sweden (*Reuters*, June 14).

On June 18, a Soviet civilian pilot asked for political asylum in Turkey after flying a small plane to the Kocaeli province, east of Istanbul, according to the Turkish Anatolia News Agency (*Reuters*, June 18). On June 20, Reuters reported that the Turkish authorities intended to file border violation charges against the Soviet pilot.

On June 19, AP and UPI reported that a twenty-year-old Soviet man had hijacked a plane flying from Riga to Murmansk and forced it to land in Helsinki. He then surrendered to the Finnish authorities. On June 20, the aircraft was returned to Riga. Finnish authorities were quoted as saying the hijacker would not be extradited until his request for political asylum had been considered (*Reuters*, June 20).

On June 24, a Soviet man claiming to have a bomb in his luggage hijacked a plane flying from Tallinn to Lvov and forced the pilot to fly the plane to Helsinki (*Reuters*, *AP*, June 24).

On June 25, "Vremya" interviewed USSR Deputy Minister of Civil Aviation Mikhail Timofeev on the hijackings. He dismissed the notion that they were politically motivated, attributing the actions to the recent rise in crime.

On June 28, a hijacking attempt was foiled. TASS said a man on a passenger flight from Krasnodar to Krasnoyarsk had demanded that the plane's pilot divert the plane to Turkey. The agency said the pilot landed the plane at the southern Siberian city of Orenburg. There, a special force seized the hijacker.

On June 30, correspondents in Stockholm quoted airport officials as saying a hijacked Soviet airliner had landed in the Swedish capital (*AFP*, June 3).

On June 30, *Rabochaya tribuna* carried a report on the history of hijackings in the USSR since 1958. The newspaper quoted KGB figures as saying that 120 people had been killed and more than 200 injured in hijackings or attempted hijackings of Soviet aircraft over the past thirty-two years. The newspaper said there had been sixty-three hijackings or attempted hijackings, involving some 500 conspirators.

Soviet Troops Ask Supreme Soviet for Action on Armenia

Members of the Soviet armed forces and internal and border troops deployed in Armenia issued an appeal to the USSR Supreme Soviet for help. *Pravda* quoted the appeal as saying extremists in Armenia "are slinging mud at us, trying to discredit us in the eyes of the people and to provoke clashes, and they have recently started committing terrorist acts." The appeal said local Armenian authorities had been "practically paralyzed" and that "no action has been taken regarding the terrorists' criminal actions against servicemen." It went on to say: "We are appealing to you to make a political assessment of the events in Armenia and do everything possible to stabilize the situation in an area where blood is being spilled." On June 11, Lieutenant General Vyacheslav Eremin told TASS that attacks on Soviet soldiers were increasing in the Transcaucasus and complained that the local authorities were doing little to prevent them.

Sunday, June 10

Statistics on Draft Evasion

A program on draft evasion broadcast by Central Television revealed that vast numbers of potential Soviet draftees were avoiding the spring call-up. According to figures supplied by the General Staff, the following percentages of eligible draftees had actually been conscripted in the various republics as of June 1: Lithuania—19 percent; Latvia—13 percent; Estonia—8 percent; Georgia—33 percent; Armenia—0 percent; and the country as a whole—26 percent.

A short item in *Kommunist vooruzhennykh sil* (No. 4) reported that in 1989 there were 7,500 draft evaders in the Soviet Union—a higher figure than had previously been reported. The item also revealed that legal proceedings had been instituted against 1,482 of the accused draft evaders.

"Associate Status" for Republics That Want to Secede

A leading Soviet specialist on nationality problems argued that republics that did not want to remain in the USSR could be granted "associate" status. Writing in *Kommunist* (No. 6), E. Tadevosyan suggested that this would allow them the opportunity to return to the fold once they saw how difficult total independence would be.

Radioactive Waste Found in Izmailovsky Park

Radio Moscow reported that radioactive waste had been discovered buried in Izmailovsky Park during a regular survey of radiation levels in the area at the beginning of June. A local government official revealed that the park, a popular recreation area for Muscovites, had been used as a dump for industrial and household wastes during the 1950s, but he assured listeners that the radiation did not present "a great health hazard." The area was cordoned off, and signs posted to indicate that operations to clean up the area were under way.

Monday, June 11

Coal Miners' Meeting in Donetsk

Miners from all the USSR's main coal-producing regions met in Donetsk. Angry about the government's failure to honor the pledges made at the end of strikes in summer, 1989, the miners met to discuss the formation of a new trade union that would represent underground workers only. The miners also threatened to call a general coal strike on July 1 if their demands for financial independence for their pits were not met (*TASS*, June 11). On June 12, the participants in the meeting criticized the government's proposals for food price rises and called for the government's resignation (*AFP*, June 12). The meeting also heard that more than 650 miners had died last year in accidents at work. That very day, five miners were killed and several others hurt in an explosion in a Donetsk mine. On June 13, the miners approved a vote of no confidence in Ryzhkov's government. Deputy Chairman of the Vorkuta City Soviet Valentin Kopysov told RFE/RL that the miners had appealed to the entire Soviet Union to endorse their vote of no confidence.

On June 15, the miners' meeting voted to create an independent union and distance themselves from the Communist Party. Politburo member Yurii Maslyukov called this "an alarming and serious signal." The miners passed a resolution saying the CPSU no longer protected or represented the interests of Soviet workers (*AP*, June 15).

1990 Production Figures Poor

Izvestia reported that Soviet economic statistics for the first five months of the year reflected a dismal state of affairs. It reported that overall production was down 1.1 percent from the same period last year, while oil production saw a 5-percent drop. Since the rate of increase in the money supply practically doubled over this period, store shelves were emptier than one year ago, even in areas of increased production. The output of meat and canned vegetables was reported down 3–5 percent.

Interview with Lopatin

In a wide-ranging interview appearing in *Nedelya* (No. 22), USSR people's deputy Major Vladimir Lopatin addressed a number of the issues that have earned him the enmity of the Soviet military leadership. Among his observations were that 45 percent of conscripts suffered psychological disorders; that 15 percent had been convicted of a crime (in 1989 the Supreme Soviet examined seventy cases of soldiers stripped of their decorations because they had committed crimes); and that one-third of all conscripts could not speak Russian. Lopatin was highly critical of the defense industries, claiming that they were failing to implement conversion to production of civilian goods. He also tackled the Defense Ministry for its failure to address the army's housing shortage.

Azerbaijani Supreme Soviet Discusses State of Emergency on Border

The Azerbaijani Supreme Soviet discussed a proposal for the declaration of a state of emergency along the border with Armenia. Radio Moscow said the parliament had set up a special commission to deal with the issue. The radio said members of "The Armenian National Army" had for a long time been carrying out attacks on settlements in Azerbaijan. It said the Azerbaijani leadership had recently proposed to the Armenian government the creation of a ten-kilometer zone on both sides of the border from which illegally armed groups would be removed. The radio said Armenia had not yet responded to the proposal.

Tuesday, June 12

Gorbachev Meets Representatives of Baltic Republics

Mikhail Gorbachev met in Moscow with leaders of the three Baltic republics to talk about their drive for independence. Western agencies quoted Latvian Supreme Council President Anatolijs Gorbunovs as saying he had proposed to Gorbachev that negotiations begin on forming a legal basis for a transitional period to independence. He said Gorbachev had again suggested that such negotiations could begin if the Baltic republics were to freeze their independence declarations. Gorbunovs said such a formulation amounted to recognition in principle of the Baltic independence declarations. Lithuanian Supreme

Council President Vytautas Landsbergis was quoted as telling Gorbachev that there could be no normal dialogue between Moscow and Vilnius until the economic blockade against Lithuania was lifted (*Reuters*, June 12). The US government welcomed Gorbachev's talks with the Baltic leaders as a step in the right direction. The same day, US Secretary of State James Baker said that the US Congress would not approve a US-Soviet trade accord until Moscow ended the "deadlock" over Lithuania (Western agencies, June 12).

RSFSR Congress in Favor of Sovereignty Declaration

The RSFSR Congress of People's Deputies voted overwhelmingly in favor of adopting a declaration of sovereignty. The declaration had no binding legal authority; it was simply a statement of intent that "expressed the mood" of the Congress, according to Vyacheslav Maslennikov (*AP*, June 12; *Izvestia*, June 12). The deputies voted against dropping the words "Soviet" and "Socialist" from the RSFSR's official name.

Press Law Adopted

The USSR Supreme Soviet adopted a law on the press and other mass media, TASS reported. The law, preparation of which has taken several years, is the first of its kind in Soviet history. It is a liberal law, banning censorship of the mass media and allowing newly created political parties as well as individuals to set up press or other information organs (conservative CPSU officials attempted to prevent the inclusion of the latter provision). The press law has some obvious shortcomings, however, the most serious of which is its failure to address the fact that most of the USSR's publishing base still belongs to the CPSU. See RL 291/90. For the text of the law, see *Izvestia*, June 20.

Novosti Round Table on Multiparty System

Representatives of four political movements that have been created in Moscow—the Party of Liberal Democrats, the Social Democrats, the Democratic Platform, and the Christian Democratic Movement—took part in a round-table discussion on prospects for the development of a multiparty system in the Soviet Union. The participants in the discussion, which was organized by Novosti press agency, spoke about their parties' programs for overcoming the current economic and political crisis in the USSR and about their attitudes to the present Soviet leadership and to the October Revolution of 1917. The participants concluded that a coalition of new political movements should be established and that this should evolve into a formal opposition to the current leadership.

EC-CMEA Discussion of Environmental Cooperation

Negotiations on environmental cooperation began in Moscow between representatives of the European Community (EC) and the Council for Mutual Economic Assistance (CMEA), according to TASS. It was the fourth such meeting since official relations between the EC and CMEA began in June, 1988. During the two-day meeting, delegates discussed such topics as cooperation in the areas of statistics and standards and the exchange of information and materials.

The same day, Finland and the Soviet Union agreed to set up a telephone link to warn each other of impending hazards to the environment (*Reuters*, June 12). The agreement came at the end of a visit to Finland by Environment Minister Nikolai Vorontsov.

Reaction to Gorbachev's Proposal on Germany

Gorbachev's June 12 proposal that Germany remain in both military alliances was rejected by Western leaders. According to agency reports, US President George Bush said: "Our position is well known to him, which is that a unified Germany should be in NATO with no conditions." West German Chancellor Helmut Kohl dismissed the idea, saying: "This is a proposal we cannot consider realistic. We reject it." British Prime Minister Margaret Thatcher said: "I doubt very much whether one country can be a member of two different pacts."

New Burial Place of Polish Officers Found

Warsaw Television said the remains of more Polish officers killed by the NKVD in 1940 had been found. It called the discovery "a second Katyn," in a reference to the known burial site of some 4,000 murdered Poles. The broadcast said that a mass grave containing the bodies of thousands of Soviet and Polish citizens had been found in a park in the Ukrainian city of Kharkov. It said the discovery was described in a message sent to *Moscow News* by a deputy chief of the Kharkov Oblast KGB administration. An estimated 15,000 Polish officers were killed by the NKVD in 1940. On June 18, the Soviet authorities gave Warsaw documents about the graves. On June 19, the Polish media said the Soviet authorities were providing information about a third grave containing the bodies of Polish officers killed in 1940. The third grave is said to lie near the town of Mednoe. For further articles on NKVD responsibility for Katyn, see *Smena* (May 23, 24, and 25) and *Sovetsky tsirk* (No. 16).

Wednesday, June 13

El'tsin Meets Gorbachev

The chairman of the RSFSR Supreme Soviet, Boris El'tsin, said he and Mikhail Gorbachev had decided to work together. TASS said they had agreed at a meeting on June 12 that neither Russia nor the USSR could survive without the other. El'tsin was also quoted as saying Gorbachev had not reproached him for declaring Russian sovereignty.

On June 14, the RSFSR Supreme Soviet approved a resolution on the protection of its chairman, stipulating that El'tsin should no longer be guarded by the KGB but by a special subunit of the parliament's secretariat. TASS announced the creation of the subunit on June 15.

El'tsin's Autobiography Published in His Hometown

Boris El'tsin's autobiography, already published in several Western countries, was reported to have been published in El'tsin's hometown, Sverdlovsk. TASS said 300,000 copies of the book had been printed. El'tsin donated the entire proceeds from the book to a fund to fight AIDS in the USSR.

Ryzhkov on Market Economy

Nikolai Ryzhkov said a market economy was the only way for the Soviet Union to get ahead, whether under his government or another. He spoke after the USSR Supreme Soviet had failed to approve his controversial economic reform plan (*Reuters*, June 13). Deputies voted to give the government until September 1 to rework its plan. The USSR Supreme Soviet also called on Gorbachev to issue a series of decrees effective from July 1 to speed up key aspects of the reform. Ryzhkov said that, while he knew price increases would be hard on consumers, he thought society "was more prepared" to accept them. On June 14, the USSR Supreme Soviet voted overwhelmingly to postpone a plan to sharply increase bread prices (*TASS*, June 14; *Pravda*, June 16).

Registration Begins for Latvian Paramilitary Group

Registration began in Riga to reactivate the Latvian paramilitary organization "Ayzsarg" (Defenders). TASS quoted the Latvian Popular Front newspaper *Atmoda* as saying the organization was needed to deal with "the unstable situation" and increasing breaches of public order in the republic. It said members must pledge "to spare neither effort nor life for the restoration of the Latvian republic and for the defense of its independence." TASS said "Ayzsarg" existed in Latvia from 1919 until 1940. Organizers said that the majority of personnel in the republic's existing militia groups were not indigenous

Latvians and that Latvia must have its own self-defense groups made up of native Latvians.

Peasants' Union Formed

Egor Ligachev said he was certain the agriculture sector would continue to rely on state and collective ventures integrated with private farms. Ligachev spoke on June 12 at the inaugural congress of the Soviet Peasants' Union (for the text of his speech, see *Izvestia*, June 14). He said that farmers needed support from the state but that they should be free to choose how to work. According to a Radio Moscow broadcast of June 13, congress delegates criticized Ligachev's speech, saying he offered no plan for the future of the countryside. The radio said there were no delegates from the Baltic republics, Moldavia, or Georgia. Radio Moscow reported that the head of a kolkhoz, Vasilii Starodubtsev, had been elected chairman of the Peasants' Union. Under Brezhnev and Chernenko, Starodubtsev encountered problems when he wanted to reform the operation of his kolkhoz. Lately, however, he has been branded a conservative by the Soviet press for wanting to preserve kolkhozes as the main form of Soviet agricultural organization.

Ban on Food Sales to Nonresidents of Moscow and Leningrad Extended

The Moscow City Soviet extended its ban on food sales to nonresidents. *Trud* said Moscow residents would be issued special cards allowing them to purchase foodstuffs. The daily said the same measures would be taken in Leningrad. The ban began in late May in an effort to end panic buying, which was sparked by the government's proposed economic reforms calling for major price increases on basic food items.

New Journal for Muslims Comes Out in Uzbekistan

The first official Uzbek-language journal for Muslims was reported to have been published in the Uzbek capital, Tashkent. The biweekly journal, an organ of the Religious Board of Muslims of Central Asia, is called *The Light of Islam*. It will have a print run of 40,000 copies in the Uzbek language with editions in both the Arabic and Cyrillic scripts. *Moscow News* (No. 23) said the journal would focus on Muslim dogma, rites, and rituals, print excerpts from the Koran, and report on religious rights.

USSR Announces Details of Tactical Nuclear Reduction

Soviet Foreign Ministry spokesman Gennadii Gerasimov told reporters that the Soviet Union would cut sixty short-range nuclear-missile launchers from arsenals in East Germany, Czechoslovakia, Poland, and Hungary in 1990.

Gerasimov also said 1,500 assorted "nuclear charges" would be eliminated.

Thursday, June 14

Defense Ministry Announces Troop Reduction Statistics

The USSR Defense Ministry said troop reductions made so far had cut the size of the armed forces by nearly 300,000 men. Gorbachev announced in December, 1988, that the Soviet Union intended to make major, unilateral reductions in its armed forces. The Defense Ministry issued a statement on June 14 outlining some of the reductions (*TASS*, June 14).

Millions of Soviet Migrant Workers May Seek Western Jobs

Soviet Labor Minister Vladimir Shcherbakov said 2–3 million Soviet migrant workers might soon be seeking temporary jobs in the West. Shcherbakov said a law would go into effect by September that would give Soviet citizens "the freedom to leave and to return." He said allowing Soviet workers to take temporary jobs abroad could alleviate the high unemployment expected to accompany the transition to a market economy (*Reuters*, *UPI*, June 14). See RI 330/90.

Deportations under Stalin Commemorated in Baltic Republics

Lithuania, Latvia, and Estonia commemorated the beginning of the mass deportations of Baltic citizens under Stalin in 1941. It was a day of mourning in all three Baltic republics, coinciding with the Catholic holiday Corpus Christi. TASS reported that church services were conducted to commemorate those who perished during the deportations.

Uzbek Decrees on Strengthening of Economic Independence

Two new Uzbek presidential decrees were published on strengthening the republic's economic independence. Radio Moscow said one decree was on the defense of Uzbekistan's interests regarding the production of cotton and other fibers. The other decree provided for the creation of a state committee for trade and foreign ties to develop new forms of cooperation with other nations (*Radio Moscow-1*, 1000, June 14).

Friday, June 15

Election of RSFSR Prime Minister

The RSFSR Supreme Soviet elected Ivan Silaev as prime minister, giving him 70 percent of its votes. He defeated

Mikhail Bocharov. A third candidate, Rector of the Moscow Aviation Institute Yurii Ryzhov, withdrew from the race before the voting started (*TASS*, in English, June 15).

Chernobyl' Union Opens First Congress

The newly created Chernobyl' Union opened its first congress in Kiev. TASS said that Chairman Georgii Lepin and other delegates expressed concern about the fact that the Chernobyl' nuclear disaster was continuing to affect the lives of many people. They referred to people who had participated in the cleanup operation or stayed in the contaminated zone (*TASS*, June 15).

Moscow Tells Finland about Nuclear Accident in 1975

The Soviet Union informed Finland that there had been a nuclear accident at the Leningrad power plant in 1975. An official at the Finnish center for radiation and nuclear safety said the center was provisionally regarding the accident as "a class three event." This means "classing it as a serious incident." The official said the plant was back in use two weeks later. He added that the reactor was similar to the type used at Chernobyl' (*Reuters*, *AP*, June 15).

Troops Act to Stop Prison Riots

MVD troops moved in to stop prison rioting in Ukraine. Reports from the scene in Dnepropetrovsk said one prisoner had been killed and one injured in the violence, which began on June 14. *Izvestia* said more than 1,000 prisoners had started fires during a rampage through prison buildings. It said inmates had demanded better conditions during negotiations with authorities. The newspaper said the situation on June 15 was still not stable, although some prisoners had returned to their cells.

On June 18, TASS reported that inmates at a prison in Chelyabinsk had rioted, seizing six guards as hostages and allowing some 1,000 prisoners out of their cells. The inmates demanded a meeting with churchmen and representatives of the USSR Ministry of Internal Affairs and the USSR Prosecutor's Office to complain about prison conditions. Although a meeting was held, the inmates refused to release their hostages. MVD troops then stormed the facility. On June 19, TASS reported that several people had died in the Dnepropetrovsk prison mutiny.

Saturday, June 16

RSFSR Abolishes One-Party System

The RSFSR Congress of People's Deputies removed from the RSFSR Constitution the provision proclaiming the

Communist Party "the leading and guiding force" in Soviet society. TASS said that, in doing this, the Russian parliament was providing "a legal basis" for the multiparty system that already existed in the RSFSR. In its original form, the draft constitutional revision stated that other political parties, trade unions, and public and youth organizations would be able to take part in political activity alongside the CPSU. Mention of the CPSU was dropped after the draft came under fire from deputies who objected to the CPSU's being singled out for mention. Deputy Anatolii Shabat was applauded when he said the CPSU "should be put on trial for genocide, not mentioned in the constitution" (*Central Television*, June 16).

RSFSR Abolishes "People's Control"

The RSFSR Congress of People's Deputies voted to abolish the institution of "people's control" from enterprises in the RSFSR. Notoriously inefficient and corrupt, "people's control" dates back to the Workers' and Peasants' Inspectorate, which existed under Lenin and was run by Stalin. Its officers were supposed to root out and expose instances of economic mismanagement and crime. The RSFSR Congress also elected a commission to draft a new constitution for the republic (*TASS*, June 16).

Former KGB General Says KGB Needs Reform

A meeting of the Democratic Platform was addressed by a former general of the KGB, Oleg Kalugin, who had quit the organization several months previously. In his address, Kalugin suggested that the KGB did not know how to respond to the interethnic clashes that had taken place in various parts of the USSR (*AFP*, June 16). On June 20, *Komsomol'skaya pravda* carried an interview with Kalugin in which he criticized the KGB and called for it to be radically reformed. On June 22, the KGB issued a statement attacking Kalugin and dismissing his criticism of the organization as unfounded (*TASS*, June 22).

On June 23, Kalugin told Soviet television that no one could return Soviet society to where it was ten years ago but that the KGB could turn the clock back some way if a conservative prevailed in the leadership. He urged that KGB directorates involved in political surveillance and disinformation be disbanded. Kalugin said he had received numerous messages of support from his colleagues for his earlier statements about the Soviet security service. *Moscow News* (No. 25) also carried an interview with Kalugin and details of his biography.

On June 28, the KGB accused Kalugin of embarking on the road to treachery by publicly criticizing the organization. A sharply worded article in *Pravda* said: "It is a very bitter thing for [KGB] operatives when one in their ranks sets out on the path of unlawful actions, does not behave correctly and morally, and even embarks on treachery." The same day, the KGB's chief public relations officer, Aleksandr Karbainov, told *The Baltimore Sun* that the KGB had strictly followed the law since Stalin's death, although it might be argued that the law was bad. General Karbainov told the newspaper he disapproved of what had been done to dissidents in the 1960s, 1970s, and early 1980s, but said that the KGB had always acted within the law and had followed the will of the political leadership.

On June 30, Gorbachev issued a presidential decree stripping Kalugin of his rank, awards, and privileges (*TASS*, June 30).

On July 2, Kalugin said Gorbachev's decree demonstrated that the KGB was still all-powerful in the Soviet Union. He said that Gorbachev's decision was based entirely on the KGB version of the conflict between himself and the organization and that he had not been given a chance to present his side of the story to Gorbachev (RL Russian service, June 30).

On July 3, a group of deputies from the USSR Congress of People's Deputies called for an independent inquiry into Kalugin's allegations that the KGB was still using Stalinist methods (*TASS*, July 3).

On July 4, the Moscow City Soviet asked Gorbachev to restore Kalugin's rank and awards. It also demanded the resignation of the KGB chief, Vladimir Kryuchkov (*Radio Moscow-1*, 2200, July 5).

Pravda Holds Discussion on Military Reforms

A group of high-ranking military officers gathered in the editorial office of *Pravda* to discuss Soviet military reforms. The meeting also focused on the role of the political organs in the armed forces and on the social welfare of servicemen and their families.

Union of Poles Established in Belorussia

The Union of Poles in Belorussia held its constituent congress in Grodno, TASS reported. The new group unites the various regional organizations of the 420,000 Poles living in Belorussia. Polish Senate Speaker Andrzej Stelmachowski led a delegation from Warsaw. TASS said the new group would promote the cultural revival of the Polish community. One activist said that it might also publish a newspaper and nominate candidates for public office.

Party Congress Ends in Kirgizia

A two-day congress of the Communist Party of Kirgizia concluded with the reelection of Absamat Masaliev to head the republican Party organization. According to TASS, discussion of the recent disturbances in Osh Oblast occupied a prominent place in the congress proceedings. The independent "Postfactum" news agency reported on June 14 that, in his report to the congress, Masaliev had accused the secretary of the board of the republican Writers' Union, Kazat Akmatov, and the Party secretary of the Frunze Pedagogical Institute, Topchubek Turgunaliev—both leading figures in the new "Kyrgyzstan" democratic movement and both delegates to the Party Congress—of inciting interethnic conflict. Most speakers, according to "Postfactum," demanded that the two be expelled from the CPSU. Turgunaliev rejected the charges and complained of a disinformation campaign against "Kyrgyzstan." Presidential Council member and writer Chingiz Aitmatov intervened in support of Turgunaliev and warned the republican Party leadership that it was unwise to enter into a confrontation with a 3,000-member movement. He said they would do better to cooperate with it. TASS reported that a resolution adopted by the congress had attributed the outbreak of violence to unresolved socioeconomic problems, personnel irregularities, a bureaucratic and indifferent attitude to people's fates, and the failure of Party and government organs to keep pace with the changes taking place in society.

Uzbek and Kazakh Leaders Oppose Party Split

TASS said the leaders of Uzbekistan and Kazakhstan, Islam Karimov and Nursultan Nazarbaev, had met in the Uzbek capital, Tashkent, on June 15 to discuss ways to develop cooperation between their two republics. It said they had also agreed on the need for ideological and organizational unity within the CPSU and were opposed to any moves to split the Party.

Sunday, June 17

Belorussia Calls for Return of MVD Troops

Izvestia reported that the Belorussian Supreme Soviet had demanded the return of Belorussian MVD troops from Central Asia and the Transcaucasus, claiming that a shortage of personnel was impeding the fight against crime in Belorussia. The republic's Supreme Soviet also said MVD troops should be sent to other regions "only by mutual consent between sovereign republics," and it urged the USSR Supreme Soviet and Gorbachev to insure that violence in Central Asia and the Transcaucasus was handled by forces from those republics.

Nenashev Defends Central Television

Mikhail Nenashev, the chairman of the USSR State Committee for Radio and Television Broadcasting, said at a press conference in Moscow that Central Television was not prepared to make room for an independent Russian republican network. Existing programs served the entire country, he said. He added, however, that measures would be undertaken to make Soviet television and radio stations more independent from local authorities. On June 17, Nenashev suggested that Central Television be governed by a board consisting of the directors of the five channels.

El'tsin Praises Church

Boris El'tsin praised the Russian Orthodox Church for its contribution to public life in the Soviet Union. El'tsin made his remarks after attending a service at St. Isaac's Cathedral in Leningrad (*TASS*, June 17). The service—the first conducted in the cathedral in more than seventy years—featured the first sermon by Aleksii in his new capacity as Russian Orthodox patriarch.

Meanwhile, the Soviet press carried discussion of problems faced by the Moscow Patriarchate in connection with the growing popularity among believers in the USSR of the Ukrainian Autocephalous Orthodox Church, the Ukrainian Catholic Church, and the Russian Orthodox Church Abroad (see, for instance, *Komsomol'skaya pravda*, June 13).

Demand for Autonomy for Crimea

A group of deputies from the Crimean Oblast Soviet suggested that a meeting should be called of local soviets in the Crimea and representatives of the population to discuss reestablishing the autonomous status of the oblast, which was abolished after the Crimean Tatars were deported in 1944 (*TASS*, June 17). After the adoption by the Ukrainian Supreme Soviet of a law making Ukrainian the state language of Ukraine, there were demands for the return of the Crimea to the RSFSR, to which it belonged until 1954. The deputies also suggested that, once autonomy was reestablished, the population should decide to which republic the Crimea should belong.

On June 27, the oblast soviet in Simferopol in the Crimea asked Crimean Tatars to stop picketing the oblast soviet building and to give back lands they had seized. Radio Moscow said the parliament had criticized delays in reaching a decision on the resettlement of the Tatars in the Crimea. It said the deputies had urged the state commission examining the problems of the Crimean Tatars to speed up its work. A plan has been announced to start their repatriation in 1991, but the

Tatars started resettlement ahead of the plan. On June 28, "Vremya" reported that 85,000 Crimean Tatars had already returned to their homeland.

Monday, June 18

Ligachev Calls for Referendum

Conservative Politburo member Egor Ligachev called for a nationwide referendum to decide the Soviet Union's social and economic future. Interviewed in *Pravda*, Ligachev said the Soviet people should be asked "which path we should take—the Socialist or the Capitalist one." Ligachev made it clear that he was against the idea of switching to a market economy, because it would lead to massive unemployment. He also said he was opposed to any form of private ownership of the means of production.

Controversy over Decree on Power in Russian Congress

The RSFSR Congress of People's Deputies adopted in principle a Decree on Power proclaiming that democratically elected soviets, not the CPSU, were the legitimate authorities in that republic. The draft decree, prepared by Leningrad deputy Vladimir Varov, was more radical than that suggested by the former republican leadership (*Radio Mayak*, June 18).

On June 19, despite demands by radical deputies, the Congress did not give its final approval to the Decree on Power. Instead, the meeting decided to pass the draft to the relevant commissions of the RSFSR Supreme Soviet (*Radio Mayak*, June 20; *Izvestia*, June 21).

New Russian Prime Minister on Economic Reforms

The new prime minister of the RSFSR, Ivan Silaev, said he wanted Russia to be an economically independent, sovereign state within the Soviet Union. TASS said Silaev made this comment in a speech outlining his program to the RSFSR Congress of People's Deputies. Silaev said the present unequal trade between Soviet republics meant that Russia was essentially covertly financing other republics. He said that the Russian Federation contributed more than 100 billion rubles to the USSR's federal budget every year but that the central government only spent about 30 billion of it on Russia.

Infant Mortality Said to Have Fallen

On USSR Medical Workers' Day, "Vremya" featured an interview with USSR First Deputy Minister of Health Aleksandr Baranov. Baranov said infant mortality in the

Soviet Union had fallen 9 percent between 1988 and 1989, and he noted that there had been 26,000 fewer deaths among children under the age of two. (*Sem'ya* [No. 22] puts the Soviet infant mortality rate in 1989 at 22.6 per 1,000. These figures are based on the Soviet method of calculation and must be adjusted upwards to be comparable with world standards.) Baranov said that Moscow was preparing a law to establish a state insurance program to cover medical costs. Asked about rural health problems, Baranov acknowledged that infant mortality in rural areas was 30 percent higher than in urban locations and that life expectancy was two years less.

Ukrainian Party Congress Opens

The Twenty-eighth Congress of the Communist Party of Ukraine opened in Kiev. The most important topic on the agenda was whether the republican Party organization should seek greater independence from the CPSU by adopting its own statutes and "programmatic principles of activity" (*TASS*, June 18).

On June 19, Ukrainian Party First Secretary Vladimir Ivashko told the congress that he favored a new Union treaty that would enable Ukraine to assert its sovereignty vis-à-vis the center. Ivashko's call was the latest in a series of moves by Kiev to appease rising public demands for Ukrainian autonomy (*TASS*, June 19).

On June 22, Stanislav Hurenko was elected the new first secretary of the Ukrainian Communist Party. Hurenko was previously second secretary of the republican Party. He replaced Ivashko, who had been elected chairman of the Ukrainian Supreme Soviet (*TASS*, June 22).

Moldavian Parliament to Establish Republican Television Center

The Moldavian Supreme Soviet recently voted to establish a radio and television center free of politics and ideology, TASS reported on June 18. No party or social organization will be allowed to influence the information broadcast. In a related action, the republican legislature voted to establish its own newspaper. To be called *Sfatul Tsarii* ("Council of the Country"), the paper will appear six times a week in both Russian and Moldavian. The legislature will also issue an official monthly periodical.

Campaign against Ethnic Germans Reported

An independent Moscow weekly, *Megapolis-express*, was told by an employee of the KGB that the local authorities were conducting a hate campaign against Germans living on the territory of the former Volga German ASSR. Since April, 1989, he said, the Saratov Oblast Party Committee had forbidden any discussion in the press of autonomy for the Germans. He warned that the situation could turn into a new Nagorno-Karabakh, with armed groups trying to force the Germans to leave the area.

Shevardnadze Meets Genscher

Eduard Shevardnadze and his West German counterpart, Hans-Dietrich Genscher, held "constructive and useful" talks in Münster, according to press accounts. They agreed on the four most important areas for negotiation regarding the unification of Germany: institutionalizing the Helsinki process; the relationship between members of the two alliances; conventional disarmament; and the Polish border.

Commenting on his meeting with Genscher on Moscow television on June 19, Shevardnadze said that Moscow had not asked for aid from Germany but that Bonn had offered it. This followed reports in the Western media saying that the USSR had asked Germany for financial compensation for agreeing to the membership of a united Germany in NATO.

On June 21, West German officials said the Bonn government was willing to guarantee DM 5 billion in bank credits for the Soviet Union. They also said Chancellor Helmut Kohl had suggested to his partners in the European Community and at the World Economic Summit Conference that the West should provide economic aid to the Soviet Union. The credit deal was signed by Soviet officials and West German bankers on June 27.

Shevardnadze Accuses Moscow of Chemical Arms Buildup

Soviet Foreign Minister Eduard Shevardnadze told *New Times* that Moscow officials had fueled a chemical arms buildup in order "to win an honor banner of Socialist competition," AP reported. Shevardnadze pointed to Soviet advantages in chemical weapons stockpiles, saying that the Soviet Union had continued manufacturing these weapons after the rest of the world had stopped. He called for officials behind the effort to be brought to account. His comments came in the wake of a chemical arms agreement signed at the summit.

New Jewish Publication Launched in Moscow

The first issue of *Menora*, a publication of the Jewish community of Moscow, appeared this week, DPA reported. Printed in color, the first issue featured an interview with V. Fedorovsky, a leader of that community.

Meanwhile, TASS reported that "unknown hooligans" had drawn swastikas on Jewish tombstones in Moscow and in Tashkent. Police officials said that they had arrested several youths in Tashkent but that they were still investigating the Moscow incident.

Tuesday, June 19

RSFSR Communist Party Created

The first conference of Russia's Communists in sixty-five years opened in the Kremlin. Mikhail Gorbachev was in the chair, and the opening ceremonies were shown on nationwide television. In his opening speech, Gorbachev spoke about the situation in the CPSU and in the Soviet Union. The main item on the agenda, which was approved by an overwhelming majority, was the creation of a Communist Party of the RSFSR. The Russian Federation had been the only Soviet republic without its own Party organization.

Commenting on the speeches delivered at the conference, TASS said that the leadership of the CPSU and its general secretary had perhaps never been subjected in a Party forum to criticism sharper than that thrown at the Gorbachev leadership. Speakers at the opening of the conference accused the Gorbachev leadership of obstructing the creation of a Russian Communist Party. The Party leader in Kemerovo Oblast, Aleksandr Mel'nikov, for instance, said Gorbachev was gradually removing the Central Committee and the Party from the decision-making process. Accusing Gorbachev of "sliding towards a personality cult," Mel'nikov said Kemerovo's Communists had demanded the resignation of the Central Committee and the Politburo. Gorbachev came under attack from the armed forces too, with Army General Al'bert Makashov, commander of the Volga-Urals Military District, accusing him of leaving the country vulnerable to attack. See RL 298/90.

On June 19, the Russian Party Conference transformed itself into the founding congress of the RSFSR Communist Party.

On June 20, addressing the assembly, Gorbachev raised the prospect that he might soon cease to be CPSU general secretary. Gorbachev's statement came in the course of sharp criticism of his policies by the delegates. One of the critics on June 20 was Egor Ligachev, who told the meeting that Gorbachev had failed to consult Party colleagues on key questions of foreign and economic policy. Ligachev complained that Gorbachev had allowed the initiative in such matters to slip out of the Party's hands altogether. Saying that "the main danger" was the destruction of the Party from within, Ligachev attacked Social Democrats in the Presidential Council, revisionist currents in the Party, and, in particular, the Democratic Platform, which he alleged was planning a purge of conservative Party leaders at every level. He also called for the introduction of quotas in the soviets and in Party bodies to guarantee the proper representation of workers and peasants (*Central Television*, June 20).

On June 21, Gorbachev rejected charges that he had ignored the Communist Party in planning his radical economic reforms. He told the congress that "it is wrong to think the idea of a market economy was hit upon by chance—conceived by someone and offered as an overnight coup to push the country off the right course." Gorbachev said his reform plan had been set out after numerous discussions at Party meetings and with various sectors of the population (*TASS*, in English, *Reuters*, June 21).

The same day, candidates were nominated for the post of first secretary of the Russian Communist Party. The two leading conservative candidates for the post were the first secretaries of Kemerovo Oblast and Krasnodar Krai, Aleksandr Mel'nikov and Ivan Polozkov. The other candidates were: Valentin Kuptsov, Oleg Shenin, Oleg Lobov, Vladimir Lysenko, and Nikolai Polovodov.

On June 21, the RSFSR Communist Party Congress adopted a declaration. Among its points were: (1) to establish "genuine state, political, and economic sovereignty" in the RSFSR on the basis of a new Union treaty; (2) to abide by the rules and programmatic aims of the CPSU and not to seek "a special role" for the Communist Party of the RSFSR; (3) to adhere to the "time-tested" ideas of Marx, Engels, and Lenin, and (4) to overcome the crisis situation in the economy and work out the best way towards "a regulated market economy" (*TASS*, June 21).

On June 23, "Vremya" devoted its entire evening broadcast to Gorbachev's ninety-minute question-and-answer session at the close of the founding congress of the Communist Party of the RSFSR. The most interesting answers given by Gorbachev concerned why he had agreed to the formation of the RSFSR Communist Party organization, his avowal to remain general secretary of the CPSU (contrary to his earlier statement), and his defense of the Party leadership, *perestroika*, and his military policies. See *Pravda* and *Izvestia*, June 26.

The same day, Ivan Polozkov was elected first secretary of the Russian Communist Party. Upon his election, Polozkov said he would work to hold the CPSU together. He also set a conciliatory tone and promised to cooperate with Mikhail Gorbachev and Boris El'tsin. Polozkov, who won by only a narrow majority against

Oleg Lobov—a former El'tsin associate from Sverdlovsk—obviously felt that his power base was too small to challenge Gorbachev directly. Although he criticized Gorbachev's cautiousness in handling the country's problems, he rejected Ligachev's proposal that Gorbachev should step down as Party general secretary (*TASS*, *Central Television*, June 23; *Izvestia*, June 24).

On June 24, Polozkov gave an interview to *Pravda* in which he denied that he was a conservative. At the same time, however, he said he was "no radical" and took a cautious attitude towards radical changes. He said the retrograde views of Party conservatives were capable of destroying the new RSFSR Party.

On June 25, Polozkov spoke to the Novosti press agency. He said that he had supervised the work of the Stavropol Party organization in the 1970s and had thus in effect been Gorbachev's boss. In yet another attempt to cast off his image as an opponent of reform, Polozkov told Novosti he and Gorbachev had introduced several innovations in Party organizational and ideological work in Stavropol Krai. See RL 288/90 and 289/90.

Military Casualties in Transcaucasus

TASS reported that between January 19 and June 18, 1990, thirty-seven Soviet servicemen had died as a result of interethnic conflicts in the Transcaucasus. The figure, published in *Krasnaya zvezda*, included eight officers, three warrant officers, and twenty-six soldiers and sergeants. A warrant officer's wife also died. Twenty-eight of those killed were said to be Russian, five Ukrainian, two Azerbaijani, one Belorussian, one Kazakh, and one Estonian. Eleven of these deaths were accidental. A further 153 military personnel were said to have been wounded.

Moscow Rehabilitates Polish Opposition Leaders

The Soviet Union formally rehabilitated sixteen leaders of Poland's postwar anti-Communist opposition who were jailed for up to ten years, Polish sources said (*Reuters*, June 19). The sixteen, who supported the Polish government-in-exile, were arrested after being lured to Moscow in 1945 on Stalin's orders. The sources said the Soviet Union had told the Polish embassy in Moscow that the USSR Supreme Court had annulled the jail sentences and formally rehabilitated the sixteen.

New Chairman for Leningrad City Executive Committee

USSR People's Deputy Aleksandr Shchelkanov was elected chairman of the Leningrad City Soviet Executive Committee in a multicandidate election, "Vremya" reported.

Shchelkanov's most recent occupation was as a warehouse employee in a Leningrad "Beriozka" store.

Demonstrators Demand Upgrading in Status of South Ossetia

The unofficial Georgian news agency Iveria reported from Tbilisi that a mass demonstration organized by the separatist organization "Ademon Nykhas" had been held in Tskhinvali, the capital of the South Ossetian Autonomous Oblast. The demonstrators were demanding that a session of the oblast soviet be convened to discuss upgrading the oblast's status to that of an autonomous republic. A session of the oblast soviet scheduled for June 16 was postponed because it failed to reach a quorum.

USSR Signs Agreement with Libya

The USSR and Libya reached agreement on bilateral cooperation, including how they would pay for each other's goods (*TASS*, June 19). Soviet Minister of Foreign Economic Relations Konstantin Katushev signed the agreement for the Soviet side in Libya on June 18. He also met with Libyan leader Moammar Gaddafi and delivered a message from Soviet President Mikhail Gorbachev.

Wednesday, June 20

El'tsin Defends Gorbachev

Boris El'tsin came out in defense of Gorbachev against attacks by hard-liners at the Russian Party Conference. He told *Pravda* that the conference "had featured too much criticism of the leadership's policy of *perestroika*." El'tsin added that Gorbachev was not the only one who deserved blame.

First Meeting of Working Group on New Union Treaty

The first meeting of the working group drawing up a new Union treaty was held in the Kremlin (*TASS*, June 20). The group, set up the previous week by the Federation Council, was made up of "roughly" two representatives from each of the Union republics, together with a large group of experts. The Lithuanian Supreme Soviet told Gorbachev that under present conditions it could not delegate representatives to the working group but might send experts or observers. The meeting decided to let the experts continue their work and report back to subsequent sessions of the group.

Moscow Authorizes Joint Stock Companies

TASS said the Soviet government had approved documents allowing the creation of publicly held companies.

Both Soviet citizens and foreign nationals will be able to purchase shares. These documents were authorized to speed up the transition to a market economy. They represent a necessary prerequisite for the creation of a stock market.

Uzbekistan Declares Sovereignty

The Uzbek Supreme Soviet adopted a declaration of republican sovereignty. According to TASS, the declaration stated that republican laws would be supreme within Uzbekistan and that the republic would have authority over questions of domestic and foreign policy.

Slavic Deputies Return to Moldavian Parliament

Following a month-long boycott of the Moldavian Supreme Soviet, Russian-speaking deputies returned to the hall after the Moldavian parliament promised some concessions to non-Moldavians in the republic, Radio Moscow reported. The deputies had walked out in protest against the parliament's moves to increase Moldavian autonomy.

Georgian Parliament Convenes

In response to public pressure, the Georgian Supreme Soviet convened one month earlier than originally planned and adopted a declaration recognizing the right of all Soviet republics to self-determination. The session also passed a law on the foundations for creating economic autonomy for Georgia and set up a commission to create a legal mechanism for the restoration of Georgia's state sovereignty. It also called on the RSFSR Supreme Soviet to give a legal and political evaluation of the invasion and annexation of the independent Georgian Republic in February, 1921, in violation of the nonaggression treaty signed the previous year (*TASS*, June 20). On June 21, the parliament voted to ignore Moscow's blockade of Lithuania and to begin trading with the breakaway republic directly (*AP*, *TASS*, June 21).

***Izvestia* Says General Should Be Asked to Retire**

Izvestia said General Al'bert Makashov, commander of the Volga-Urals Military District, should be asked to retire because of his criticism of foreign and domestic policies. In a front-page report, *Izvestia* commentator Vladimir Nadein said President Mikhail Gorbachev should act in his capacity as commander in chief and ask Makashov to resign. In a speech at the Russian Party Conference on June 19, Makashov complained that the Soviet army, the KGB, and the Ministry of Internal Affairs were being defamed and that NATO was being allowed to gain strength, while the Warsaw Pact "no longer exists." The general also complained that "the Soviet army is being driven without a fight out of countries that our fathers liberated from fascism."

Thursday, June 21

Gidaspov Defends Gorbachev

Leningrad Communist Party First Secretary Boris Gidaspov said critics of Mikhail Gorbachev should modify their attacks and remember that Gorbachev has done a lot for their country. Gidaspov also told reporters in Moscow that he hoped Gorbachev would remain general secretary of the CPSU because if he left the post "it would be a big loss for the Party." Boris El'tsin, however, told reporters in Moscow that he has advised Gorbachev to give up the Party post. El'tsin said he could imagine that doing both jobs was too much for Gorbachev (*Reuters*, *DPA*, *AFP*, June 21).

Lithuanian and Polish Prime Ministers Meet

Lithuanian Prime Minister Kazimiera Prunskiene arrived in Warsaw on an unannounced visit to Poland and held talks with Polish Prime Minister Tadeusz Mazowiecki and Foreign Minister Krzysztof Skubiszewski. Emerging from talks with Mazowiecki that she described as "sincere and penetrating," Prunskiene said she and the Polish government leader had discussed steps each side could take to build ties across the Polish-Lithuanian border. She also said both sides had agreed that neither Poland nor Lithuania had any outstanding territorial claims against each other (*RFE/RL Special*, June 21).

Big Fire on Oil Pipeline in Tyumen

TASS said lightening had struck an oil pipeline station at Nefteyugansk in Tyumen Oblast, starting a fire that spread to four oil storage tanks. It said firefighters had been flown in from other districts to help combat the blaze, control of which was being hampered by high winds.

Popular Front Stages Rally and Fast in Nakhichevan

Members of the Azerbaijani Popular Front were reported to be demonstrating in front of the Supreme Soviet building in the capital of the Azerbaijani region of Nakhichevan. Two popular front activists told RFE/RL that the demonstration had begun with a rally of about 20,000 people in Nakhichevan. Following this, five local activists began a fast and were subsequently joined by others. Activist Alibey Ismailov said the rally and fast were in support of demands for secure borders with Armenia and the release of all political prisoners held since January 19. That was the date Soviet troops established military control of Baku. Ismailov said the front also sought to prevent the rebuilding of the border fence between Azerbaijan and Iran, portions of which were torn down by Azerbaijanis last January (RL Azerbaijani service, June 21).

RSFSR Congress Calls for Independent Republican Media

The RSFSR Congress of People's Deputies called for the creation of republican-controlled mass media independent of the Party. Several journalists speaking in the Congress said the republican media should be independent of the Supreme Soviet and of its chairman as well. Meanwhile, speakers at the congress of the RSFSR Communist Party indicated that the Party was not inclined to give up its ideological monopoly. On June 20, for example, the editor of *Sovetskaya Rossiya* asked the Party Congress to ignore the request of the RSFSR Congress that the republic's Supreme Soviet and Council of Ministers become the sole publishers of his newspaper and said the Party should take control of it (*Radio Mayak*, June 20 and 21).

Friday, June 22

Shevardnadze Proposes Withdrawal of Allied Troops from Berlin

At the start of the second round of the "Two-plus-Four" talks in Berlin, Soviet Foreign Minister Eduard Shevardnadze proposed the withdrawal of all allied troops from Berlin six months after German unification (*AP*, June 22).

Soviet Hard-liner Predicts Comeback for Socialism

Politburo member Egor Ligachev predicted that socialism would make a comeback in Eastern Europe after its defeats in multiparty elections. "We must say clearly and distinctly that socialism in this region [Eastern Europe] has suffered a defeat," Ligachev said in an interview with *Sel'skaya zhizn'*. "The Socialist community, unfortunately, has collapsed, and the forces of imperialism have undeniably strengthened on the continent," Ligachev complained. But, he added, "I am sure that this is a temporary situation. In the end, the Socialist idea will gain the upper hand."

Newspaper Predicts Rise in Emigration

Rabochaya tribuna said 1.5 million people were expected to emigrate from the USSR annually for the next three or four years. The newspaper said 235,000 people had left the USSR in 1989. Most of the emigrants were Germans, Jews, or Armenians. The paper said many were professionals who had left for better jobs and wages. It said others had left to avoid growing political instability and interethnic conflicts in the Soviet Union.

Saturday, June 23

Yakovlev Tells *Pravda* the CPSU Must Renew Itself

On June 23, *Pravda* interviewed Politburo and Presidential Council member Aleksandr Yakovlev. Yakovlev told *Pravda* that if the CPSU did not begin to work "in a new way" it would be "unable to meet the challenge of the times." "The Party," he continued, "is being swept by a wave of reaction from bad to worse. If the Party does not find enough courage and strength for a real renewal, in the spirit of *perestroika*, then . . . life will pass it by."

Assault on State Monopolies

The *Financial Times* said the Soviet government planned to follow up the legislation of June 20 that allows for the creation of joint-stock companies with a series of reforms, including an assault on state monopolies and a restructuring of the banking system. Gennadii Melikian, a member of the government's reform team, said that a commission for the management of state property would be set up by July 1. He said the commission would help determine the value of state enterprises in order to allow for their sale to Soviet and foreign investors. Melikian said the state would receive the proceeds from the initial sales of state enterprises but would forego dividend payments from denationalized enterprises on condition that the money be spent on capital improvements.

Soviet Television Interviews Moscow Soviet Leaders

Central Television featured an hour-long program on the new leadership of the Moscow City Soviet—the mayor, Gavriil Popov, his deputy, Sergei Stankevich, and the chairman of the Executive Committee, Yurii Lyzhkov. Popov said that the stage at which *perestroika* was controlled by the Party and government apparatus had ended and that power now belonged to the people and their representatives. The time was ripe, he continued, for reformist politicians to form an alliance with the progressive wing of the leadership (the term usually applied to Gorbachev, Yakovlev, and Shevardnadze). Popov added that he did not believe that conservatives could pose a real threat to the process of democratization in Russia.

New Peasants' Party Created

The Party of Free Labor, uniting peasants who oppose the kolkhoz system and want free ownership and inheritance of land, was reported to have been established (*Radio Moscow-2*, June 23). The party stands in opposition to the newly created Union of Peasants, whose inaugural congress earlier this month was attended by kolkhoz chairmen and addressed by Politburo member Egor Ligachev.

Central Asian Leaders Conclude Cooperation Agreement

Following a two-day meeting in Alma-Ata, leaders of the five Central Asian republics concluded an agreement on economic, scientific, and cultural cooperation. The agreement, which is to run until 1996, must be ratified by the parliaments of the republics involved. Other republics were invited to join the accord. The agreement envisaged joint efforts to save the Aral Sea (*TASS*, June 23). See RL 303/90.

Moldavia Declares Sovereignty

Moldavia became the latest Soviet republic to declare sovereignty and to state that its laws had precedence over Moscow ones, TASS reported. After a stormy debate, the Moldavian parliament also declared its territory a demilitarized zone and said its natural resources were "the exclusive property" of the republic. The parliament stated further that all residents of the republic were Moldavian citizens and it outlawed dual citizenship, implicitly rejecting the notion that its citizens were also Soviet citizens. It also said Moldavia would seek admission to the United Nations.

On June 24, tens of thousands of Romanians and Moldavians united across the river Prut, pushing past frontier controls in a display of emotion dubbed "operation open borders" (*UPI*, *AP*, June 24). The gathering was held to mark the fiftieth anniversary of the Soviet Union's annexation of Bessarabia. Soviet and Romanian border guards abandoned any attempt to control the crowd, but at midday Soviet MVD troops arrived and shepherded the Romanians back across the border.

New Party Emerges in Belorussia

Radio Moscow-1 reported that the founding congress of the National Democratic Party of Belorussia was under way in Minsk. The Party advocates national rebirth and political and economic independence for Belorussia.

Soviet Oil Exports Decline Sharply

According to a CIA report, the Soviet Union's oil exports dropped nearly 10 percent in 1989 (*AP*, June 26). The

USSR exported 3.69 million barrels of oil a day in 1989—down from 4.08 million barrels in 1988. US experts said the decline in oil exports was almost equal to the decline in domestic oil production. They attributed the lower output to aging oil fields, to a lack of funds for new exploration, and to labor and ethnic unrest.

Opinions of Muscovites

On June 23, *The Economist* published a roundup of recent polls taken in Moscow. In one survey, the Institute for Sociology asked people to rank their principal worries. Those polled named pollution first, followed by crime, food shortages, AIDS, and ethnic violence. In April, the Center for Sociological Research conducted a poll showing that only two-thirds of ordinary Communist Party members wanted to stay in the Party after the Twenty-eighth Party Congress. The same poll indicated that only 10 percent of the 5,300 people questioned believed the economy was improving.

On June 25, *Pravda* published another opinion poll demonstrating a further decline in the public standing of the CPSU. According to the poll, conducted by the CPSU's own Center for Sociological Research, more than half of the 1,500 Soviet citizens questioned—53 percent—no longer consider the CPSU the leading force in Soviet society.

Sunday, June 24

Tsipko Predicts Gloomy Future for Social Democrats

The most articulate Soviet critic of Marxism-Leninism, philosopher and former CPSU Central Committee consultant Aleksandr Tsipko, said in *Moscow News* (No. 24) that citizens of the Russian empire had not chosen the Socialist system in 1917. Speaking about the future of Russia, he said Social Democrats were unlikely to play a significant role in its politics. He also predicted a further decrease in popularity for Social Democrats in the West. Tsipko argued that in the past Social Democrats had gained popularity through favorable comparison with Communist parties but that now the collapse of the Communists would also reflect negatively on the Social Democrats. In a lengthy article in *Rodina* (Nos. 2 and 3), Tsipko argued that the complete failure of attempts to build a society according to Marxist concepts should be apparent to everyone by now.

Liberal Communists Refuse to Join Russian CP

Vladimir Lysenko told *Komsomol'skaya pravda* that Russian Communists who supported the Democratic

Platform might refuse to join the RSFSR Communist Party. *Moskovskaya pravda* reported that 116 delegates to the founding congress of the RSFSR Communist Party from Moscow, Leningrad, Sverdlovsk, Gorky, and Kuibyshev had issued a declaration charging that the congress "had ignored the real political situation in the country." One hundred fifty-one delegates from Moscow Oblast filed a written protest objecting to the haste with which the RSFSR CP Central Committee was elected and the fact that the candidacies had not been discussed by primary Party organizations.

On June 26, the alternative Soviet television news service, "TSN," reported that the entire crew of the Leningrad television show "The Fifth Wheel" had resigned from the CPSU to protest against the formation of the RSFSR Communist Party. The crew said the Russian Communist Party was now "the Party of Nina Andreeva."

In a later broadcast, TSN reported that, in protest against the formation of the Russian Communist Party, editorial staffers at *Literaturnaya gazeta* were refusing to pay their Party dues and/or suspending their membership. The same day, Reuters reported that employees of two Academy of Sciences institutes—the Institute of Economics and the Institute of the Economics of the World Socialist System (recently renamed the Institute of Eastern Europe)—were refusing to join the Russian Communist Party.

On June 27, "Vremya" also reported that the conservative nature of the congress of the Russian Communist Party had outraged many Communists in the Russian Federation.

Bulgarians and Gagauz Rally for Autonomy

TASS reported that thousands of Soviet Bulgarians and Gagauz had staged a demonstration near Odessa to press their demands for autonomy. The protesters were concerned that new language laws in Ukraine and Moldavia would adversely affect them.

***Moscow News* Interviews Baltic Leaders**

Moscow News (No. 25) carried interviews with the presidents of the Supreme Councils of Estonia, Latvia, and Lithuania in which they discussed the proposed overhaul of the Soviet federation, the future of economic relations between the Baltic republics and Russia, and Baltic reaction to the economic blockade of Lithuania. All three chairmen, Arnold Ruutel, Anatolijs Gorbunovs, and Vytautas Landsbergis, were allowed to express their opinions at length.

Ukrainian Bishops Meet

The bishops of the Ukrainian Catholic Church held a meeting for the first time since the Church was forced underground in 1946. Church officials said ten bishops from the Ukraine and eighteen other bishops from around the world celebrated mass at Rome's Ukrainian Catholic Cathedral of St. Sophia (*Reuters*, June 24). On June 25, the bishops began a two-day meeting with Pope John Paul II to discuss the legalization of the Ukrainian Catholic Church under a proposed Soviet law on freedom of conscience (*Reuters*, June 25). The pope called on the bishops to build "a bridge of unity" with the Russian Orthodox Church through forgiveness and reconciliation, but he also emphasized his support for the full legalization of the once persecuted Church. This two-pronged approach was echoed in remarks by Cardinal Myroslav Lyubachivs'kyi, who said that his Church was willing "to forgive, forget, and begin a new way of living together" with the Orthodox Church. A Vatican official noted the Kremlin's view that reaching accord with the Russian Orthodox Church was essential for the resolution of the Ukrainian Catholic issue (*RFE/RL Special*, June 26).

Monday, June 25

TASS on EC Aid to Moscow

Two days of meetings of the leaders of the European Community countries began in Dublin. Economic assistance to the Soviet Union was the main topic under discussion. West German Chancellor Helmut Kohl and French President François Mitterand called for immediate support in order to help the USSR overcome its economic difficulties. The other members of the EC responded positively to this suggestion, TASS said. The TASS report, however, failed to mention that there was some disagreement among EC members regarding aid to the USSR: according to AP, Britain insisted that calls for immediate large-scale aid were premature.

On June 26, the EC leaders decided to postpone a decision on giving financial aid to the Soviet Union. Their communiqué said that the EC supported Soviet President Mikhail Gorbachev's reform programs, but it added that a final decision on aid would have to wait until October, when a study of Soviet economic problems was due for completion (Western agencies, June 26). The same day, Soviet Foreign Ministry spokesman Gennadii Gerasimov said that, if the USSR received financial assistance from the European Community, it would use it to pay off Soviet foreign debts. The Soviet Union has a current account deficit of 2 billion dollars. Reuters quoted Gerasimov as saying: "Our previously immaculate record of debt repayment on the external market is now in question."

El'tsin Announces His Plans for the RSFSR

RSFSR Supreme Soviet Chairman Boris El'tsin told "Vremya" that the new Russian bank would be separated from the national finance system and that Russia would stop pumping money routinely into the national budget. The RSFSR would contribute funds to only six all-Union ministries, among them the Defense Ministry and the KGB. El'tsin announced severe cuts in the Russian bureaucracy, saying that republican ministries would be cut by 50 percent and the number of personnel in the remaining ministries halved. He added that all ministers would be replaced by younger and more radical officials.

Following his attendance at the graduation ceremonies of the Moscow Higher Combined Arms Command School, El'tsin told a Radio Moscow interviewer on June 23 that reform must continue in the army and that the armed forces should not be used to put down domestic disorders. Defense Minister Dmitrii Yazov also appeared at the ceremony, and El'tsin claimed to have conferred with him on the issue of military reform.

On June 26, El'tsin told *Krasnaya zvezda* that he favored radical reform of the armed forces, including significant reductions in military personnel and improved social welfare for all servicemen. El'tsin said that the appointment of an RSFSR minister without portfolio to oversee defense in the RSFSR—as decreed by the recent RSFSR Congress of People's Deputies—was a means of demarcating republican and all-Union functions. The new minister would be a civilian with some twenty military experts on his staff. They would monitor the combat readiness of troops deployed in the RSFSR, the draft, and the administration of exercises there.

The same day, El'tsin gave a press conference in Moscow that was televised live. El'tsin said his cabinet would include both Communists and members of other political parties; he added that the mayors of Moscow and Leningrad (Gavriil Popov and Anatolii Sobchak) would be members. He also said that the RSFSR had begun talks with several other Soviet republics on how to go about drafting a new Union treaty. He identified those republics as Latvia, Lithuania, Estonia, Belorussia, Ukraine, Moldavia, and Kazakhstan.

Ivashko Calls for Ukrainian Conscripts to Serve at Home

Saying "our children have nothing to die for in Azerbaijan," Chairman of the Ukrainian Supreme Soviet and former Communist Party First Secretary Vladimir

Ivashko told the Ukrainian parliament that Ukrainian conscripts should be allowed to perform military service in the republic. Ivashko's statements, reported by the news agency "Rukh" Press International, came in the wake of similar declarations concerning military service in the Baltic and Transcaucasus and demonstrate the extent to which opposition to the current military draft is spreading not only geographically but also through official circles.

Founding Congress of Socialist Party

Fifty delegates from twelve cities elected a committee to form a Socialist Party, the Novosti press agency reported. Boris Kagarlitsky, organizer of the informal Club of Socialist Initiatives and a member of the new committee, said that the Socialist Party supported "social forms of ownership, control over distribution, and a role for workers in management" and was opposed to a market economy. The Socialist Party's congress was attended by representatives from Britain, France, and Italy.

Masol Reelected Ukrainian Prime Minister on Fourth Ballot

Vitalii Masol, Ukraine's incumbent prime minister, failed to be reelected to his post by the republican Supreme Soviet on the first ballot. Though he was the sole candidate and the favorite of Vladimir Ivashko, Masol fell eleven votes short, according to Reuters.

On June 26, Vitol'd Fokin, the chairman of the Ukrainian State Planning Committee, was also rejected by the republican Supreme Soviet for the post of Ukrainian prime minister, Radio Kiev-3 announced. Like Masol, Fokin was also Ivashko's nominee.

On June 27, a third attempt to elect a Ukrainian prime minister also failed. At the parliamentary session in Kiev, Ivashko proposed two candidates: Masol again, and Volodymyr Chernyak—an economist and people's deputy. But Central Television ("Vremya") said both rounds of voting were declared invalid—the first because of unspecified violations of rules, and the second for lack of a quorum.

On June 28, however, Masol was finally reelected the republic's prime minister. In the final vote, Masol received 229 votes, TASS reported.

Slyun'kov on Market Economy

CPSU Central Committee Secretary Nikolai Slyun'kov said the country must create a legal basis for the transition to a market economy. In an interview with *Pravda*, he was quoted as saying that a market economy would lead to higher living standards. He said the system of economic management by decree had failed but that the country's production potential was still huge. He said it could saturate the market in the next few years.

Abalkin Expresses Worry about Republican Trade Wars

Deputy Prime Minister Leonid Abalkin was quoted by Radio Moscow as expressing concern about future trade wars within the Soviet Union. Speaking at a meeting of the State Commission for Economic Reform, which Abalkin heads, the deputy prime minister said his concern stemmed from the declarations of economic sovereignty of some republics. Abalkin said his commission was working on a draft decree to restructure economic relations between the republics and the USSR. It said the commission had decided to require "compulsory participation" by representatives of all fifteen republics in this work.

Tuesday, June 26

Gorbachev Insists There Is No Retreat from Reforms

The Soviet Union has "arrived at a critically important threshold of change, probably the most important [one] since October, 1917," Gorbachev told military graduates. "A modern civil society and a law-governed state are being created," he said. Gorbachev emphasized that the past held no answers and that, despite "the costs and losses," the only solution to the numerous problems facing the country lay in "stepping up our forward movement."

In other remarks to the newly commissioned officers, the Soviet president stressed the achievements of his foreign policy initiatives, but tipped his cap to military leaders by noting that the world still awaited positive, concrete responses from NATO. Gorbachev also hit back pointedly at his domestic critics, saying that the political leadership was doing everything necessary to maintain the strength of the Soviet Armed Forces (*TASS*, June 26).

International Club of Gorbachev's Supporters Formed

A new public organization, the International Club of Gorbachev's Supporters, met in Moscow, "Vremya" reported. While Soviet television did not identify any foreigners present, it did provide an extensive list of Soviet cultural figures. Its chairman, playwright Mikhail Shatrov, told Soviet television that Gorbachev's policies must be defended against those who, like many delegates to the recent congress of the Russian Communist Party, opposed democratization.

Sverdlovsk Oblast Soviet Chairman Ousted

TASS reported that Vladimir Vlasov had resigned from his post as chairman of the Sverdlovsk Oblast Soviet following a vote of no confidence in him by that body. Members of the soviet criticized him for failing to fulfill his mandate as an RSFSR people's deputy—namely, for his failure to support El'tsin in his candidacy for chairman of the RSFSR Supreme Soviet. El'tsin is from Sverdlovsk and is immensely popular there.

Sobchak Plans Free Economic Zone for Leningrad

Chairman of the Leningrad City Soviet Anatolii Sobchak told TASS that he planned to turn Leningrad into a free economic zone "as soon as they grant us the right to create one." He said he planned to transfer industries from ministerial to municipal control and to expand the use of contracts between the soviet and local industry. Sobchak also revealed plans to include the city in "the Baltic Market" by establishing direct economic ties with the Baltic republics.

China and USSR on Border Force Reductions

A round of talks between China and the Soviet Union on reducing military forces along the Sino-Soviet border ended on June 26, the official New China News Agency reported. The two sides discussed implementation of an accord on demilitarization reached during Chinese Prime Minister Li Peng's visit to Moscow in April. The Soviet delegation was headed by Foreign Ministry official Genrikh Kireev, while the Chinese were led by Kireev's counterpart, Liu Guangzhi.

Church Opposes All-Russian Orthodox Conference

Writing in *Moskovsky tserkovnyi vestnik* (No. 12), officials of the Russian Orthodox Church said that the "Coordinating Group for the Preparation of the All-Russian Orthodox Conference" consisted of only five priests and fifteen laymen. The group called earlier this month for an Orthodox conference in order to bring together representatives of the Moscow Patriarchate, the Russian Orthodox Church Abroad, and the Underground (Catacomb) Russian Orthodox Church (see *Moscow News*, No. 23). The article said the group was acting without the blessing of the Moscow Patriarchate's hierarchy and without the participation of representatives of the Church.

Meanwhile, *Moscow News* (No. 24) published an interview with Father Sergii Popov, one of the initiators of the All-Russia Orthodox Conference. Father Sergii said the Church must finally face up to the truth about its past and present. He called for a return to Church traditions and for the restoration of the canons of the All-Russia

Council of 1917–18, at which Patriarch Tikhon spoke out against the inhumane policies of the new Soviet leaders. Calling for recognition for the Orthodox martyrs of the Soviet period, Father Sergii criticized the Church leaders of today, who, he said, lived so well that they saw no need for further reforms.

Death and Casualty Figures from Afghan War

Officials organizing aid for Afghan veterans and their families were told that 50,000 Soviet troops had been wounded in Afghanistan—previous Soviet reports had put the number at 37,000—and that some 11,500 of them were invalids, Radio Moscow reported. It was also reported that 14,500 Soviet troops had died during the war, a figure slightly higher than earlier estimates.

USSR Denies Unscheduled Moves of Nuclear Weapons

Soviet Foreign Ministry spokesman Gennadii Gerasimov denied that nuclear weapons had been moved out of certain areas of the Soviet Union because of concerns about civil unrest. He said there was no need to move troops equipped with nuclear weapons around Soviet territory. He cited the USSR Defense Ministry for this information. Unofficial reports circulated in the West last week saying that nuclear warheads were being moved out of some politically volatile republics for fear they could fall into the hands of extremists (*TASS*, June 26).

Green Party Created

APN reported that a Green Party had been created in the USSR. Delegates of ecological movements from the RSFSR, Ukraine, Belorussia, and Kazakhstan attended the inaugural congress of the new party in Moscow. APN said that the preparatory work for the creation of the party had been going on for a year and a half.

Wednesday, June 27

Draft Declaration for Forthcoming Congress Published

Pravda published the draft of a declaration to be debated at the forthcoming Party Congress. The document outlined various items of legislation that the Party would like to see put through. According to the declaration, the Party pledges itself to socialism but sees communism only as "a perspective" for some later date. While the Party forswears "democratic centralism" as it evolved under Stalin, it reaffirms its loyalty to Lenin and its determination to retain political organs in the Soviet Armed Forces and police.

The section devoted to national security generally embraced Gorbachev's foreign and domestic defense initiatives. It declared that, while the danger of armed conflict still confronted the USSR and necessitated the maintenance of "a reliable defense," military reform should continue on the basis of "the new defensive doctrine" and the principle of "reasonable sufficiency."

The document also contained several statements on nationalities relations that seemed particularly concerned with the rights of the smaller nationalities and those without a national territory as well as with the priority of human rights over the rights of nations.

Mini-Strike of Performing Artists

Soviet actors, dancers, and musicians decided to stop their performances for five minutes in protest at the shortage of cultural facilities in the USSR. The USSR minister of culture had approved the gesture; TASS quoted him as saying the state of Soviet culture was "tragic."

Measures to Defend Believers' Rights

Moskovsky tserkovnyi vestnik (No. 12) reported that a new Commission for Freedom of Conscience and Confessions, Charity, and Welfare had been set up by the Moscow City Soviet. The commission consists of twenty-seven deputies, both believers and nonbelievers, and aims to defend the interests and rights of members of all faiths and creeds.

Hunger Strike in Chernovtsy

A correspondent for RFE/RL in Moscow reported that residents of the Western Ukrainian city of Chernovtsy had been staging hunger strikes since June 7 to demand better medical care for children afflicted by the mysterious "Chernovtsy disease," a condition that leads to alopecia and nervous disorders among the young. The illness first made world headlines in November, 1988, but until now, Soviet and international efforts to find the cause of it have been fruitless. Meanwhile, some 2,000 signatures were collected on a petition to express no confidence in all deputies to the Ukrainian Supreme Soviet from the Bukovina area (RL Ukrainian service, June 27).

Compensation for Germans Who Served in "Labor Army"

TASS said Soviet Germans who, after their deportation in 1941, were put in labor camps would receive compensation from the state. The decision, which was made by the official Commission on the Problems of the Soviet Germans, was justified on the grounds that the Germans had contributed to victory in World War II by their hard work in labor colonies and camps. For some time now the

Germans had been arguing that those who served in the so-called "Labor Army" should be treated the same way as war veterans.

Fuel Shortage Threatens Harvest

Pravda said shortages of petrol and diesel fuel were disrupting the harvest, causing officials to consider cutting back on fuel exports. The reports blamed economic decentralization, which has given the republics greater control over distribution channels. Falling petroleum production and lack of conservation were also blamed for the shortfall.

Mass Poisoning in Kuibyshev

For the second time in a month, there was an outbreak of mass food poisoning caused by contaminated ice cream. Earlier in June, 400 people became ill after eating at an ice-cream parlor in Beregovo, in Western Ukraine. On June 27, Radio Moscow reported that 325 people, including 224 children, had been hospitalized after eating bad ice cream in the Kuibyshev Oblast. This incident has been blamed on the failure of a dairy to properly treat a shipment of milk, some of which then went on to an ice-cream factory. According to the report, the dairy needs new equipment, which is almost impossible to obtain.

Silaev Promises to Obey El'tsin

The RSFSR's newly elected prime minister, Ivan Silaev, said that, should he receive conflicting instructions from RSFSR Supreme Soviet Chairman Boris El'tsin and USSR Prime Minister Nikolai Ryzhkov, he would "observe the laws of the RSFSR" and obey El'tsin. Silaev said this would be the logical consequence of the Decree on Power approved in principle by the RSFSR parliament on June 18. The decree gave priority to republican laws over national ones. Silaev added that, although the transition to a market economy was the RSFSR's first priority, "the population of Russia can sleep peacefully knowing that it is not threatened by any surprises, such as totally unexpected increases in bread prices." Silaev also noted his intention to remain in the Party unless new legislation made it impossible for him to do so while holding the post of RSFSR prime minister.

Estonia Votes to Cut Off Funds for KGB

The Estonian parliament voted to cut off funds for the republican KGB. TASS said it had also cut off cash for literary censors and local military offices. TASS said the move was largely symbolic because Moscow supplies most of the funding anyway.

Talks between Leningrad and Estonia

The Estonian government and the Leningrad City Soviet agreed to start talks on political and economic cooperation. The Estonian news agency ETA said the agreement was included in a joint communiqué signed in Leningrad on June 26 by Estonian Prime Minister Edgar Savisaar and Chairman of the Leningrad City Soviet Anatolii Sobchak.

Georgian Popular Front Opens Second Congress

TASS reported that the Georgian Popular Front had opened its second congress. TASS said the organization would review its work since its foundation a year ago, elect leaders, and make amendments to its statutes and program. The agency quoted representatives of the front as saying their organization's aim was the sovereignty of the republic and the establishment of a democratic system.

On June 30, the Georgian Popular Front told its Communist members to leave the Party or resign from the front. The ultimatum came during the front's second congress in Tbilisi. TASS said 1,500 delegates attended, as well as guests from popular movements in other Union republics.

Estonia Passes Immigration Law

The Estonian parliament passed an immigration law setting an immigration quota, introducing rules on temporary and permanent residence, and regulating other issues connected with immigration and the residence of foreigners. The law did not impose any limits on the immigration of those who had Estonian citizenship before June, 1940, when Estonia was annexed by the Soviet Union, or on their descendants. A group of Russian-speaking deputies called the law discriminatory and did not take part in the voting (*TASS*, June 27).

Radio Moscow Criticizes Hungarian Move on Warsaw Pact

A commentary by Radio Moscow said Hungary's decision to leave the Warsaw Pact appeared rash and was causing negative reaction in the USSR. The commentary said the decision had been made more on the basis of emotion than of political wisdom. The Hungarian parliament voted 232–0 with four abstentions on June 25 to support government efforts to leave the Warsaw Pact.

Alliance of Democratic Parties Formed

Demonstrating understanding of the need for consolidation, Moscow's newly formed democratic parties decided to form an alliance, Radio Moscow World Service reported on June 27. The alliance, which is the result of negotiations held in the Soviet capital, unites the Party of Constitutional Democrats, the Social Democratic Party of Russia, the organizing committee of the Free Labor Party (which includes cooperative workers and those advocating individual farming in agriculture) and the Democratic Party of Russia. These are the major parties with liberal democratic programs set up in Moscow this year.

Thursday, June 28

TASS Reports Severe Criticism of Gidaspov

TASS said Leningrad Party leader Boris Gidaspov had been "severely criticized" by the Leningrad Oblast Party Committee. The report said a committee meeting on June 27 had attacked Gidaspov for not making clear his stand on events at the inaugural congress of the RSFSR Communist Party. TASS said delegates at the Leningrad meeting spoke of the need for Communists to support *perestroika* and to work with soviets at all levels. It said the delegates had also approved an appeal for unity in the CPSU.

Friday, June 29

RSFSR to Seek Independent Ties with Japan

RSFSR President Boris El'tsin said Russia hoped to conclude a treaty with Japan on trade, social, and cultural relations. He said Russia could do this without approval from the central authorities (*Reuters*, June 29). The same day, RSFSR Foreign Minister Vladimir Vinogradov said Russia might build on its newly declared sovereignty by establishing links with foreign countries and international organizations (*Reuters*, June 29).

Soviet Trade-Union Leader Demands Referendum on Reform

A Soviet trade-union leader demanded a public referendum on the government's plan to convert the economy to a regulated market system. Gennadii Yanaev, chairman of the All-Union Central Council of Trade Unions, told a Moscow news conference that, although the unions acknowledged the need for a market economy, they disagreed with the government's approach and felt they should become "a constructive opponent" in the process. He said more thought should be given to guarantees of social welfare in order to ease the adverse effects of a transition period. Yanaev said that 12 million people could become unemployed nationwide in the first year of transition (*TASS*, June 29).

Comecon May Be Replaced

A senior Comecon official said the trading group might be replaced by another organization. Hungarian minister Bela Kadar said this was being considered by a Comecon restructuring committee that he heads. The Hungarian MTI news agency quoted Kadar as saying the committee had decided that each Comecon member country should create its own market system and switch its trade to world market prices. Kadar said the committee had also decided that prices for all trade between Comecon states should be conducted in hard currency.

CPSU Central Committee Plenum

The CPSU Central Committee met in Moscow to discuss the forthcoming Party Congress. TASS said the plenum focused on Gorbachev's report for the congress. TASS said the congress was taking place at a difficult time for the CPSU, when its prestige was sharply declining and its membership decreasing.

TASS also said that ousting Gorbachev as head of the CPSU could spell "disaster." Commentator Andrei Orlov suggested that the only way to help the CPSU to overcome its crisis would be to reelect Gorbachev as its head and allow him to speed up democratic reforms in the country.

Planned Soviet Law to Declassify Stalin-Era Documents

Eduard Shevardnadze was quoted as saying the USSR planned to declassify some secret documents from the Stalin era, enabling historians to better study the origins of the Cold War. As the source of this information, Western agencies cited Western scholars who had come to Moscow for a seminar with Soviet historians to examine documents relating to US-Soviet relations after World War II.

Saturday, June 30

Ligachev Interviewed on Eve of Congress

Interviewed in *Pravda* on June 30, Egor Ligachev denied that he was "the leader of the Party's conservative wing," preferring to describe himself as "a realist." Ligachev went on to complain that these days anyone who wanted to "strengthen socialism and the Party" was branded a conservative. He defended his role in the campaign against alcohol but admitted that mistakes had been made in its implementation.

Meeting of Baltic Leaders

At a meeting in Tallinn, the leaders of Estonia, Latvia, and Lithuania called for joint negotiations with Moscow on their demands for independence (*Reuters*, June 30). A spokesman for the Lithuanian parliament told RFE/RL by telephone that the three leaders had issued a communiqué calling for "Three-plus-One" talks that would involve the three Baltic republics and the Soviet authorities.

USSR Restores Citizenship to Three Noted Figures

Gorbachev ratified the recommendations of the USSR Citizenship Commission and restored Soviet citizenship to scientist Zhores Medvedev and writers Vladimir Maksimov and Aleksandr Zinov'ev, Radio Moscow reported. Medvedev, twin brother of the historian Roy Medvedev, was stripped of his citizenship in 1973 and lives in London. Zinov'ev, a satirist, left the Soviet Union in 1978 and lives in Munich. Maksimov was stripped of his Soviet citizenship in 1975 while living in France.

Branch of Social Democratic Party Holds Congress

The branch of the Social Democratic Party covering western regions of the Russian Federation held its inaugural meeting in Kaliningrad, Radio Moscow-1 reported. (The Social Democratic Party of the RSFSR held its inaugural congress in May.) The coordinator of the Kaliningrad meeting attributed the high attendance to the fact that many people had turned away from the CPSU following the conservative tenor of the congress of the Russian Communist Party.

On June 27, *Vechernyaya Moskva* provided details about the Russian Social Democratic Party. The newspaper quoted leaders of the new party as saying that they rejected Marxism, although some of the new party's members felt they had a connection with the Menshevik wing of the prerevolutionary Russian Social Democratic Workers' Party. The newspaper also said that the new Russian Social Democratic Party had more than 4,000 supporters in 100 cities of the RSFSR.

Moldavian Front Seeks Unified, Independent Moldova

The leader of the Moldavian Popular Front told its second congress that the front's ultimate goal must be "the reunification of Romanian territories east of the Prut in an independent state—the Romanian Republic of Moldova." TASS said that Ion Hadirca had appealed to Moldavians to be aware of their national links with Romania. On July 2, the congress called for the establishment of a self-governing Romanian Orthodox Church of Bessarabia, Transylvania, and Northern Bukovina (*TASS*, July 2).

Baku Suspends People's Control Committee in Nagorno-Karabakh

Radio Erevan reported that the Azerbaijani government had suspended the mandate of the Nagorno-Karabakh People's Control Committee. Having earlier suspended the power of the oblast soviet and the local government in Gadrutsky Raion, Baku now has virtual direct rule over the disputed territory.

Rostov Oblast Stops Work on Atomic Plant

Radio Moscow reported that the Rostov Oblast Soviet had decided to stop construction of the Rostov nuclear power station. As has been the case with other abandoned projects for nuclear power stations, the decision was the result of public protest.

The Month of July

Sunday, July 1

Council of Ministers Adopts Measures to Improve Harvest

The USSR Council of Ministers adopted measures to improve this year's harvest. Radio Moscow reported directives had been issued to radically increase supplies of fuel, spare parts, and other equipment needed to bring in a timely harvest. Moscow was also reported to be trying to encourage kolkhoz workers to produce and harvest more by allocating more cars, televisions, refrigerators, and other consumer goods to them in the first quarter of 1991.

Frolov Urges Radical Restructuring of Party Press

The chief editor of *Pravda*, Ivan Frolov, said there must be radical restructuring of the country's Party press. In an interview with his own newspaper he said the Party press was lagging behind other sections of the media in promoting *glasnost'*.

***Pravda* Proposes UN Trusteeship of Disputed Kurile Islands**

Pravda suggested a compromise solution to the territorial dispute with Japan over some of the Kurile Islands. The newspaper said the islands could become a special economic zone owned jointly by Japan and the Soviet Union under United Nations trusteeship.

Cossacks Form Association

Cossacks from various parts of the USSR ended a three-day meeting in Moscow. The delegates from the Don, the Kuban, the Urals, Siberia, Transbaikal, and other areas established a leading body for the Association of Cossacks. TASS said the first issue of the association's newspaper, *Kazachie vedomosti*, appeared during the meeting.

***Vekhi* to Be Republished in Moscow**

Moscow News (No. 26) reported that *Vekhi*, the famous collection of works by leading Russian liberal democratic thinkers first published in 1909, would be republished in Moscow. The collection contains warnings by the most prominent Russian intellectuals about the possible consequences of a Marxist revolution in Russia. Philosopher Aleksandr Tsipko, who is preparing the new edition of *Vekhi*, stressed in *Moscow News* that the authors in fact predicted the October Revolution, Lenin's and Stalin's terror, and the horrors of collectivization long before these events actually happened.

Socialist Party Sticks to Marxism

Moscow News (No. 26) said the Socialist Party, set up in Moscow at the end of June, had a membership of more than 1,000 people from Russia, Ukraine, and Kazakhstan who regard themselves as Marxists. *Moscow News* quoted the leader of the party, Boris Kagarlitsky, as saying that, while it advocated a Socialist system, his party did not deny the need for a market economy or for various forms of ownership.

Polozkov Interviewed by *Sovetskaya Rossiya*

The leader of the conservative Russian Communist Party, Ivan Polozkov, called for the consolidation of "sound forces" in the CPSU. In an interview published in *Sovetskaya Rossiya* before the Twenty-eighth Party Congress, Polozkov said that consolidation was what rank-and-file members of the Party wanted. He also said he supported the transfer of political power to the soviets as long as they were dominated by Communists. He named the Church as a natural ally of the CPSU in the struggle for moral values and against interethnic conflicts. He offered to cooperate with Boris El'tsin but warned him not to be influenced by forces urging him to quit the Party. Polozkov also said he welcomed the shift towards a market economy but feared negative social consequences.

Enterprise Refuses to Pay for Party

Moscow News (No. 26) reported that the management and work collective of a Vladivostok mining enterprise had submitted a bill for 46,000 rubles to its local Party committee, saying that this was what it cost the enterprise annually to fund its Party officials. (The whole bill comes to 200,000 rubles, but the bulk is paid by the CPSU Central Committee in Moscow.) With the USSR switching to a multiparty system, the enterprise said it no longer felt obliged to foot the bill. The local Party organization, however, said it had no money of its own and could not pay.

Monday, July 2

Twenty-eighth Congress of the CPSU

On the morning of July 2, Mikhail Gorbachev welcomed the 4,683 delegates and several hundred guests to the Twenty-eighth Congress of the CPSU. The congress began by electing its Presidium, Secretariat, and Editorial and Mandate Commissions and voting on its agenda. The proposal by a delegate from Leningrad, Yurii Boldyrev, to devote a special session of the congress to discussion of the CPSU's guilt before the people and to the issue of the CPSU's control over a large amount of the country's property was turned down. Gorbachev also managed to sidestep the proposal of a delegate from Magadan, who suggested that the entire CPSU Central Committee and its Politburo should resign. Gorbachev suggested instead that, in contrast to the practice at previous congresses, each member of the Politburo and Secretariat should present a twenty-minute report on his or her activities.

Before starting his major address to the congress, Gorbachev stated that coverage of the proceedings would be limited. The congress approved Gorbachev's suggestion to establish a special team to control media coverage of the congress, particularly live television relays.

Gorbachev started his speech by defending *perestroika.* He criticized those who blamed all the current problems of the country on his reform drive.

Gorbachev laid out a vision of economic reform that indicated that he had not given in to conservative pressure to retreat from market-oriented reforms. Among Gorbachev's proposals were the creation of a healthy environment for smaller enterprises with the aim of generating competition among producers. Gorbachev also called for the creation of conditions that would attract more foreign investment—namely, a move to world market prices both at home and in foreign trade with Comecon partners.

Gorbachev had nothing new to say in the passage of his report devoted to the nationalities question. He repeated that the leadership had initially underestimated the seriousness of the problems in this area, which had given free rein to separatist forces. In his speech, he referred to the fundamental reorganization of the Soviet Union into a real union of sovereign states and the drawing up of a new Union treaty. He appealed for calm and cooperation while this process was taking place.

Regarding the USSR's foreign policy, Gorbachev said it was now based on new principles—namely, that no country could seek to ensure its own security at the expense of others. He said East European countries had the freedom to choose their own way.

The concluding part of Gorbachev's speech was devoted to the situation of the CPSU under the new conditions. He said that, unless the CPSU worked out realistic and attractive policies, people would transfer their support to other, competing parties.

Subsequently, Aleksandr Yakovlev, Vadim Medvedev, and Nikolai Ryzhkov addressed the congress. Yakovlev said that only a renewed Party that leaned more to the left could lead the country towards radical reforms. In his speech, Yakovlev also justified his activities as one of the architects of the policy of *glasnost'* and of the development of "new thinking" in Soviet foreign policy.

In his turn, Medvedev said it was particularly important to regain people's trust in *perestroika*. He claimed that achieving freedom of the press was one of his main goals as chief Party ideologist. (In fact, Medvedev attempted to drop some of the more liberal provisions of the law on the press.)

Ryzhkov complained that people had responded very negatively to all the reform projects put forward by the government (*TASS*; *Central Television*, "Vremya," July 2).

On July 3, four senior Party officials, Politburo members Nikolai Slyun'kov and Vitalii Vorotnikov, candidate Politburo member Aleksandra Biryukova, and Central Committee Secretary Gumer Usmanov submitted their resignations. Gorbachev said Slyun'kov and Usmanov had resigned for health reasons. TASS said Biryukova and Vorotnikov had reached retirement age.

The same day, the congress was addressed by Egor Ligachev. In a speech greeted by loud applause, Ligachev attacked *perestroika*, telling the congress that "thoughtless radicalism, improvisation, and swinging from side to side had yielded little good during the past five years" (*Reuters*, *Radio Moscow*, July 3). Ligachev also attacked the Soviet media for allegedly destabilizing the USSR.

Foreign Minister Eduard Shevardnadze delivered a very frank speech, defending the USSR's policy towards Eastern Europe and calling for more cuts in military spending.

Confirming his responsibility for defense matters but neglecting to mention his tenure as Moscow Party first secretary, Lev Zaikov told the Party Congress on July 3 that all security problems had previously been strictly controlled by the Politburo. Zaikov referred to a secret Politburo "special commission"—chaired by himself and including Yakovlev, Shevardnadze, the heads of the Defense Ministry, KGB, and other departments—charged with working out "military-technical" questions, including preparations for arms control talks. The commission's main achievements, Zaikov said, had been ending the war in Afghanistan, easing international tensions, bringing about unilateral troop reductions, and shedding the USSR's image as an aggressor (*TASS*, *Central Television*, July 3).

Two other important speakers on July 3 were Defense Minister Dmitrii Yazov and KGB Chairman Vladimir Kryuchkov. Though he is a critic of Gorbachev's security policies, Yazov told the congress he supported the new defensive doctrine and the easing of international tensions that had resulted from it. Yazov gave mixed reviews to domestic military reform. He noted the social problems that still confronted the armed forces, but spoke positively about troop reductions, the conversion of defense industries, and reductions in defense spending. He sharply condemned increasing draft evasion and desertion in the non-Russian republics, however, and criticized local authorities for failing to support the armed forces on these issues. In his turn, Kryuchkov emphasized his commitment to reform in domestic and foreign policy but said that the security organs should act more resolutely to safeguard public order.

A speech by a delegate, Nikolai Kruchina, also attracted attention. Kruchina told the congress on July 3 that the Party's property was worth 4.9 billion rubles. This figure included printing presses, schools, office buildings, and vacation retreats but not the special dachas or stores of the leadership. He noted that the Party would no longer pay for officials' dachas. The new law on property, Kruchina said, guaranteed that only the owner of a piece of property could dispose of it. Kruchina maintained that the Party was the owner of all its assets, which, he insisted, had been purchased with Party dues (*TASS*, July 3).

On July 4, speaking to reporters between sessions, Gorbachev said the Party leadership should resign if the population's living standards did not improve within two years. He did not say whether that would include himself, and he rejected allegations that the Party leadership had launched *perestroika* in an attempt to cling to power.

On July 3 and 4, the delegates formed a number of commissions and elected chairmen. Gorbachev was elected by a 2,000-vote margin to head the Party Rules Committee. Commissions charged with drafting resolutions "On the Policies of the CPSU in Conducting Economic Reform and Adopting Urgent Measures for Stabilizing the Socioeconomic Situation in the Country" and "On the CPSU's Youth Policy" were also formed.

The name of the commission dealing with economic policy was changed from "The Commission on the Transition to a Market Economy" to "The Commission on Urgent Measures to Stabilize the Socioeconomic Situation in the USSR." Other commissions were charged with working on the Party's "programmatic statement" and with drafting a document on the work of the Central

Control Commission. Egor Ligachev was elected by a vote of 2,233 to 1,963 to chair the commission drafting a resolution on agricultural policy "under the conditions of a radicalization of economic reform." The commission responsible for drafting the resolution on nationalities policy was headed by the writer Chingiz Aitmatov. Conservative Army General Aleksei Lizichev was chosen to head the commission formulating "the basic directions of the CPSU's military policy at the present stage." Aleksei Kamai, the second secretary of the Belorussian Communist Party, was chosen to head a special commission charged with preparing a political evaluation of the Chernobyl' nuclear accident.

On July 4, the congress was addressed by Deputy Prime Minister Leonid Abalkin. He called for a more resolute approach to economic reform. Moreover, he denounced such shibboleths as democratic centralism and managed economies as dogma and myth. He said that the forces of history signaled the need for a multiparty system and that any party that did not heed those forces would be swept aside.

Another speaker was Leningrad Party leader Boris Gidaspov, who gave one of the strongest endorsements yet of Gorbachev's policies. Speaking to the congress, he said that the powers of the presidency should be increased. He urged Gorbachev to post presidential envoys around the country to prevent the USSR from slipping into anarchy. Gidaspov, generally regarded as leader of the hard-line faction in the Party, also said that giving government by the soviets priority over Party rule was "unquestionable" and that his appeals to the Party to support the soviets should not be seen as a tactical move. (*TASS*; *Central Television*, "Vremya," July 4). Transcaucasian and Central Asian Party leaders also addressed the congress on July 4 (*TASS*, July 4).

On July 5, the delegates broke up into groups, each of which was given a specific subject to consider. These included the renewal of the Party, ideology, sociopolitical organizations and movements, socioeconomic policy, nationalities policy, international affairs, and agrarian policy.

On July 5, delegates to the congress discussed the restructuring of the Party in meetings held behind closed doors. TASS said most of the speakers endorsed communism as the Party's continuing goal, but military historian Dmitrii Volkogonov said communism was "an ephemeral goal" and "a grand Utopia." Volkogonov proposed changing the name of the CPSU to "the Party of Democratic Socialism." He said that to preserve the name of Communist Party of the USSR was to underline the Party's connection with Stalinism, since the current name was given to the Party in 1952 at Stalin's suggestion. Volkogonov spoke at a meeting of a working group on Party renewal. Another speaker at the same meeting was the candidate Politburo member and member of a special committee set up to rehabilitate victims of Stalin-era repressions Boriss Pugo, who said the committee had uncovered "an abyss of horrors" (*Central Television*, "Vremya," July 5).

On July 5, both Gorbachev and Ryzhkov addressed a lengthy meeting of the working group on agrarian policy, headed by Ligachev. They were told by the delegates that the agricultural sector was not yet ready to switch to a market economy. Ryzhkov said that a market economy would help the agricultural sphere, but in the same breath he expressed his support for the creation of a Ministry of Agriculture. Gorbachev said that, if food shortages could be eliminated, two-thirds of the country's other socioeconomic problems would be solved. He also talked about the necessity of "revealing the potential of kolkhozes."

Discussion held the same day in the section on international affairs focused on the increasingly acrimonious debate over whether Gorbachev's "new thinking" constituted a victory or defeat for Soviet foreign policy. An unexpected argument broke out between two representatives of the Soviet Armed Forces. Chief of General Staff Mikhail Moiseev, who in the past has been a forceful critic of Gorbachev's security initiatives, warned the diplomatic community that maintenance of strategic parity was imperative but he nonetheless appeared to endorse current Soviet foreign policy. Moiseev's evaluation was rejected by the newly appointed chief of the Southern Group of Forces Political Directorate, however. Major General Ivan Mikulin claimed that the Soviet Union was being pushed out of Europe, and he said that "the new political thinking" was to blame.

On July 6, TASS carried a report by Stanislav Hurenko, chairman of the group discussing socioeconomics. About ten delegates expressed concern about the "critical" state of the economy. The majority of the speakers were in favor of a transition to a market economy, not as an end in itself, but as a means of solving current economic difficulties and establishing a connection between producers and consumers. According to TASS, the speakers expressed fear that "certain forces" were trying to use the market economy to lead Soviet society to capitalism.

The same day, Andrei Girenko, one of the two CPSU Central Committee secretaries responsible for nationality matters, reported on the work of the section on the Party's nationalities policy. Girenko said that speakers had sharply criticized the central Party bodies and Central Committee secretaries for inconsistency and dilatoriness in implementing their own decisions. A subject of heated discussion, Girenko continued, was the thesis in the draft program issued on the eve of the congress that human rights should have priority over the rights of nations.

On July 6, Boris El'tsin addressed the congress, delivering a frank and realistic assessment of the Party's position and a warning about what the Party could expect in the future if it failed to alter radically its political and social role. Among the highlights were his predictions that the people would confiscate the Party's property if the Party did not willingly give it up and that they would put Party officials on trial "for the damage they personally had caused." El'tsin set four tasks before the congress and the Party as a whole: (1) legalizing internal factions; (2) changing the Party's name; (3) postponing the adoption of a new platform and rules; and (4) relinquishing all state functions and disbanding Party cells in the armed forces, the police, and the KGB.

The same day, the congress was also addressed by the leaders of three independent platforms. Aleksandr Bryzgalov of the Marxist Platform supported the idea of workers' self-management and called for the abolition of the Party's present bureaucratic structure. Bryzgalov was seconded by Vyacheslav Shostakovsky, the director of the Moscow Higher Party School and a leader of the Democratic Platform, who argued for the abolition of Party cells in the armed forces, the KGB, the police, and the workplace. Shostakovsky also suggested that the Party should apologize to the people for the mess it had made of the country since 1917. The third speaker was economist Aleksei Sergeev, of the retrograde United Workers' Front, who argued against the introduction of a market economy.

The same day, "Vremya" criticized the Party Congress. The program's presenter even went so far as to complain that it was very difficult for journalists to cover the event because the speeches delivered at the congress contained no new ideas.

In a televised question-and-answer session at the CPSU congress on July 7, Egor Ligachev advocated a return to the discipline campaign initiated by Yurii Andropov in 1983 in order to stabilize the Soviet economy. Ligachev said he had felt comfortable in the Politburo only during the first three years of *perestroika*, when he was running the day-to-day work of the Party Secretariat. He added that he had been transferred to agricultural affairs against his will.

The same day, Prime Minister Nikolai Ryzhkov fielded a series of tough questions on his economic program; his answers served only to provide further evidence that the leadership was in disarray. Specifically, he was asked to reconcile his statements on the necessity of quick price reforms with those of General Secretary Gorbachev, who had said that it would be absurd to begin the transition to a market economy with price increases. Ryzhkov answered that he had discussed this with Gorbachev and was now in agreement with the general secretary. Ryzhkov also announced that he planned to take some 7 million tons of oil out of the Soviet export quota (including some oil targeted for Eastern Europe) in order to provide more fuel for this year's harvest.

Politburo member Aleksandr Yakovlev also answered questions, and his answers were televised in an abridged form. Yakovlev was attacked among other things for "having encouraged the Baltic popular independence movements during his visit to Latvia and Lithuania in the summer of 1988." Speakers also criticized Yakovlev for his role as chairman of the commission set up to investigate the Molotov-Ribbentrop Pact of 1939, whose secret protocols Yakovlev had denounced as illegal. A number of questions dealt with Yakovlev's alleged responsibility for the fall of the Communist regimes in Eastern Europe and for the reunification of Germany. Yakovlev replied that the local Communist Parties had lost the elections because they had lost the trust of the people, and he cited the numerous attempts to suppress popular uprisings in these countries by force: in East Germany in 1953; in Hungary in 1956; in Czechoslovakia in 1968; and in Poland in 1980.

The same day, the chief of the CPSU Central Committee Department for Work with Sociopolitical Organizations, Valentin Kuptsov, said that delegates were united in the belief that Communist Party organizations must work jointly with other movements and parties, especially those of a Socialist inclination. A multiparty system was a fact, he noted, and the CPSU would have to learn to cooperate with new political parties.

In his own question-and-answer session with delegates, Foreign Minister Eduard Shevardnadze defended Soviet support for German unification and Soviet policy in Eastern Europe, and he lauded the NATO declaration of July 6. Obviously responding to conservative criticism, Shevardnadze denied that the Soviet Union had cut "a deal" on the German question by agreeing to "make a gift" of the GDR to Bonn. "The fate of the GDR was decided by the German people themselves," he said, according to the TASS account. In his turn, Ligachev complained that it was not a question of unification but of West Germany's "swallowing" East Germany.

Commenting on the congress on July 7, *Pravda* said its delegates were still "a long way from consensus" on the Party's future.

On July 9, the congress approved major changes in the composition of the Party Politburo but rejected proposals to rename it the "Presidium." The plan provided for a doubling in size of the Politburo and the inclusion among its members of the Party leaders of the USSR's fifteen Union republics.

On July 9, the congress adopted several resolutions. Declaring that "the military threat to the USSR continues" and that "there are no guarantees of the irreversibility of positive changes" in the international environment, the congress adopted a strongly conservative resolution on defense policy. Reuters and TASS reported that delegates had rejected two amendments that would have softened the wording of the resolution, which was proposed by Army General Aleksei Lizichev, head of the Main Political Administration of the Soviet Army and Navy. The resolution, which made no mention of the previous week's NATO summit, stressed the role of the armed forces in defending Soviet borders and repelling aggression. See *Pravda*, July 11.

Vladimir Ivashko, chairman of the congress's editorial commission, put a draft resolution "In Defense of the Democratic Rights of Communists and against the Persecution of Communists" before the delegates. The resolution was adopted by the congress "almost without discussion." According to TASS, the resolution expresses "the solidarity of Communists with all those who, because of their beliefs, are subjected to political persecution and moral terror." See *Pravda*, July 11.

On July 9, the congress set up a commission to investigate an alleged forgery defaming Politburo member Aleksandr Yakovlev. An anonymous leaflet distributed at the congress contained a false account of Yakovlev's meeting with a group of 500 members of "Democratic Unity," a coalition of supporters of the Democratic and Marxist Platforms and a group of young Communists. On July 13, the commission confirmed that the leaflet had falsified Yakovlev's statements, but it failed to identify who wrote the leaflet (*TASS*, July 13).

On July 9, the congress decided to establish a special commission on privileges, and it elected Yu. A. Peskov, general director of the Rostov Agricultural Machine-Building Enterprise, as its chairman. Nikolai Kruchina, who heads the Administrative Affairs Department of the CPSU Central Committee, told delegates that, as of 1989, only the president of the USSR, the chairman of the USSR Supreme Soviet, and the chairman of the USSR Council of Ministers had their own dachas. The Central Committee, he asserted, no longer had special allocations, stores, or buffets.

On July 9, the congress was again addressed by KGB Chairman Vladimir Kryuchkov, who defended measures taken against former KGB General Oleg Kalugin, saying Kalugin had tried to blackmail the KGB. Kryuchkov again rejected Kalugin's criticism of the KGB. Meanwhile, writing in *Moscow News* (No. 27), retired KGB officer Mikhail Lyubimov said Kalugin had been speaking the truth when he said political surveillance, eavesdropping, and postal censorship were still being practiced by the KGB. Lyubimov, who, like Kalugin, used to work for KGB intelligence, said the present leadership of the KGB was responsible for the misdeeds of the organization under Brezhnev and that now the KGB chiefs were fighting for their political survival.

On July 10, congress delegates nominated eight people for the post of Party general secretary, six of whom subsequently withdrew, leaving the names of Gorbachev and Teimuraz Avalyani, the first secretary of the Kiselevsk City Party Committee, on the ballot. Gorbachev received 3,411 votes in favor and 1,116 against. Avalyani received 501 votes in favor and 4,026 against.

The six men who declined to run were Politburo and Presidential Council members Aleksandr Yakovlev and Eduard Shevardnadze; Minister of Internal Affairs Vadim Bakatin; Nikolai Stolyarov, a lecturer on Marxism-Leninism at the Gagarin Military Academy; the second secretary of the Armenian Communist Party, Oleg Lobov; and Oleg Sysoev, the chairman of the Kuibyshev Oblast Soviet.

The same day, Gorbachev addressed the congress, summing up the discussion of his own congress report and those of the other Politburo members. He passionately defended his policies and supporters and refuted criticism of both that had been expressed by many delegates.

The resolution adopted by the congress on Gorbachev's political address reflected the deep divisions between conservatives and reformers and offered a compromise rather than a new consensus (see *Pravda*, July 11). In support of the reformers, it linked the Party's fate to the realization of *perestroika*, backed the presidential system, said the Party would work in a competitive environment, and argued that the Party's values were universal as well as class-based. But it also denounced as "liquidationism" any call for removing Party organizations from the workplace. The resolution also called for basic improvements in the work of the Party Politburo and Central Committee.

On July 10, TASS released the full text of the resolution "In Defense of Democratic Rights, against the Persecution of Communists" adopted by the congress on July 9. Inter alia, it stated that it was "impossible" to hold Communists responsible for the actions of "regimes repudiated by time." In a reference to the fate of Communists in Eastern Europe, the resolution noted that "many thousands of honest and sincere people there are now victims of discrimination."

On July 11, Vladimir Ivashko, the former Party first secretary of Ukraine, was elected to the newly created position of deputy general secretary of the CPSU. In nominating Ivashko, Gorbachev said it was important that the two people at the top of the Party leadership be "close in their views" and that the Party not be divided (*TASS*, July 11). Egor Ligachev was the other candidate for the post, but he won only 776 votes against Ivashko's 3,109.

On July 11, candidate Politburo member Boriss Pugo, who was the Council of Delegates' nominee, was elected chairman of the CPSU Central Control Commission. Pugo had been chairman of the Party Control Committee since September, 1988. He defeated Vyacheslav Prokhorov, a Party committee secretary at a Moscow research institute.

The same day, the congress adopted a resolution on Party assets (see *Pravda*, July 12). The resolution said that the sale, transfer, or any other "alienation" of Party property was possible only in accordance with "the opinion of Communists," the Party Rules, and Soviet laws. It also called for a change in the way Party budgets were devised and for a rationalization of expenditures, spending cuts, and expanded rights for primary Party organizations with regard to raising and spending money. The chairman of the commission responsible for drafting this resolution, Ivashko, told the delegates that the commission had been given an alternative draft supported by the Democratic Platform and submitted by Vladimir Lysenko. The alternative draft called on the Party to relinquish all assets acquired "by illegal means." That draft was dismissed by the committee.

On July 12, Gorbachev outlined the new draft Party Rules, which gave greater power to republican Party organizations but rejected the principle of federalism. Under the draft rules, lower-ranking bodies were given broader rights in discussion and decision-making. Gorbachev also said members could unite in platforms as long as they did not contravene the Party Rules. He said he did not agree with calls to remove Party organizations from the armed forces. The delegates then began a lengthy discussion of the Party Rules (*Central Television*, July 12).

The same day, a small group of delegates belonging to the Democratic Platform announced the platform's decision to break with the CPSU. Its leader, Vyacheslav Shostakovsky, rector of the Moscow Higher Party School, said the platform had decided to dissociate itself from the CPSU and create a new party, because it was evident that the congress was not going to bring any radical change in the CPSU. In fact, only seventeen supporters of the Democratic Platform walked out following Shostakovsky's announcement. Some 100 other delegates belonging to the Democratic Platform circulated a declaration announcing their intention to remain in the CPSU and to fight for reform (RL Russian service, July 13). The same day, the dismissal of Shostakovsky as rector of the Higher Party School was announced (*Central Television*, July 13).

The same day, Boris El'tsin announced that he was resigning from the Party. He told the congress that, as chairman of the Supreme Soviet of the multiparty RSFSR, he felt he could not associate himself with one party (*Central Television*, "Vremya," July 12).

Gorbachev's evaluation of the Twenty-eighth Party Congress on July 13 had little in common with what actually occurred there. He told the delegates that the meeting had demonstrated the CPSU's determination to overcome "the alienation" of the Party from society and thereby maintain its vanguard role. And he maintained that the congress had shown the CPSU's readiness to expand ties with other sociopolitical movements and organizations and form "a broad coalition."

On July 13, the congress issued several more resolutions (see *Pravda*, July 14). The resolution on economic policy ruled out both a return to the administrative-command system and "an immediate denationalization" of the means of production. Acknowledging that the situation in the economy was getting worse and that the Soviet standard of living was falling, the resolution said that the Party's "most important task" was to explain to the people the need for a shift to a regulated market economy.

In the resolution on science and education, the congress called for the adoption of a Soviet law on the defense of morality, a key conservative demand. The resolution said that the low cultural and educational level of the population posed a threat to the renewal of socialism and that nationalism, nihilism, and the impact of "mass culture" on youth must be rebuffed.

In its resolution on youth policy, the congress said that it continued to see the Komsomol as its "political ally." At the same time, it stated that the Party would seek to "help" the youth organization become "a full and authoritative participant in the political process." And it called for the creation of bodies in both the legislative and executive branches of the government to handle youth questions.

In its resolution on the mass media, the congress complained that "the role of the Party press in the process of social renewal is decreasing." The resolution said that some Party periodicals did not yet reflect the policy of *glasnost'*, while others had gone too far and begun to defame the Party and its role in Soviet history. Both extremes, it said, were especially dangerous at a time when a multiparty system was emerging in the USSR. The resolution also said that non-Party publications should have access to CPSU-owned publishing facilities, but it rejected demands that the Party's publication industry be turned over to the state.

The resolution on the Chernobyl' disaster blamed the failure of the authorities to react promptly on "the administrative-command system of the former leadership of the country," but it did not let the current leadership off the hook entirely. The resolution charged that the Politburo, the USSR Council of Ministers, and the Party and government leaders of Ukraine and Belorussia had not responded in a timely fashion and had not yet taken sufficient or satisfactory measures to liquidate the consequences of the accident.

The resolution on nationality problems sharply criticized the Party leadership for failing to recognize the severity of nationality issues. Noting that ethnic problems represented "a real threat" to the Soviet Union's democratic processes, the resolution denounced "any form of violence" in dealing with such problems, and it called for the signing of a new Union treaty to create "a union of sovereign states" based on the true equality of all signatories. The adoption of the resolution was reported by TASS.

The Estonian delegation at the congress protested against a resolution that criticized the splits in the Baltic Communist Parties and condemned "separatist tendencies" in the USSR. Radio Moscow quoted an unidentified member of the delegation as saying the resolution was an insult to the Estonian people.

The same day, the congress adopted a much amended version of the Party Rules (*TASS*, July 13; the text of the new Party rules was published in *Pravda* on July 18). More than 100 delegates spoke prior to its adoption. TASS said that the sharpest debates centered on a proposal to require that republican Party organizations develop their programs and rules on the basis of the all-Union Party Program and Rules. Despite the objections of several republican delegations, this centralizing amendment was passed "with a small majority." TASS also reported that the congress had set up a commission headed by Gorbachev to draft the new Party Program. The congress concluded by electing a new Central Committee. The new body consisted of 412 people. This was larger than the old Central Committee, which had 300 members (*Central Television*, "Vremya," July 13). The congress also adopted a programmatic statement entitled "For A Humane and Democratic Socialism." On the Party Congress, see RL 301, 307, 308, 309, 311, 312, 320, and 322/90.

Protests in Moscow

Although access to Red Square was restricted while the Party Congress was in progress, on July 2 about 300 people held a peaceful demonstration on the edge of the square, according to Reuters. One banner read, "Bring the Communist Party to justice for crimes against the people." On July 3, several thousand people gathered in Moscow for another demonstration against the rise of antireform forces (*Central Television*, "Vremya," July 3).

***Izvestia* Criticizes El'tsin**

Izvestia devoted a long article to Boris El'tsin's policies and criticized him for telling the public that economic reforms would be carried out in the RSFSR without the population's feeling any negative effects. "Is El'tsin not," the newspaper asked, "making precisely the same mistakes Mikhail Gorbachev made three years ago when he said that price reforms would not affect living standards?" "Then," *Izvestia* said, "promises of the impossible paralyzed reform."

New Clashes in Erevan

AFP quoted the Interfax news service as saying Armenian militants had taken six Soviet troops and policemen hostage in Erevan on the weekend and surrounded the Armenian Ministry of Internal Affairs building in an attempt to bargain for the release of an arrested leader.

The hostages, some of whom suffered gunshot wounds, were released after negotiations between the militants and Armenian Minister of Internal Affairs Levon Galstyan. One person was reported to have been killed and two wounded on June 30 in a clash between rival Armenian military formations.

Military and Economic Backing for Cuba to Continue

The Soviet Union's ambassador to Cuba, Yurii Petrov, told foreign journalists that Moscow would back Cuba as long as the United States maintained its hostile stance. "The United States has exerted economic pressure on Cuba for thirty years, but the government of Fidel Castro is not about to fall," Cox newspapers quoted him as saying. Petrov denied that ties between Cuba and the Soviet Union were strained and said that Soviet imports of medical goods from Cuba were expected to triple next year.

USSR and Yugoslavia Conclude Trade Agreement

The USSR concluded an agreement with Yugoslavia on repayment of the Soviet Union's long-standing 2-billion-dollar trade debt. Soviet officials agreed to repay as much as possible in goods by the end of 1993 and then pay the remainder in cash, Reuters quoted the Belgrade daily *Politika* as saying. The Soviet Union is Yugoslavia's biggest trading partner, and the Soviet debt has hampered their trading relations. In 1988, Yugoslav President Raif Dizdarevic said that the debt was one of the factors contributing to Yugoslavia's inflation.

Patriarch Sees Broader Role for Church

TASS quoted Patriarch Aleksii as saying on a recent visit to Novgorod that the Russian Orthodox Church would engage in agricultural work, open small enterprises, and participate more actively in the economy. RSFSR Prime Minister Ivan Silaev recently proposed similar steps for the Church.

Alternative Parliament of Latvia

The Latvian Citizens' Congress declared itself the alternative parliament of Latvia and pledged to work in tandem with the Latvian Supreme Council. Riga journalist Iveta Medina told RFE/RL that the announcement had been made the previous weekend at the second session of the citizens' congress. Medina said the declaration was proposed by Valdis Steins, who told RFE/RL that the citizens' congress must broaden its role in Latvian politics.

Tuesday, July 3

More Soviet Hijackings

July saw a further spate of attempted hijackings of Soviet planes, but most of the attempts were thwarted. On July 3, Deputy Civil Aviation Minister Mikhail Timofeev told reporters in Moscow that air piracy was assuming a mass scale in the USSR. Timofeev called for measures to make clear to the hijackers the seriousness of their acts (*Reuters*, July 3).

Meanwhile, Sweden and Finland approved the extradition to the Soviet Union of a number of Soviet citizens who hijacked planes to the two countries in June. They included Dmitrii Semenov, Oleg Kozlov, and Anatolii Mikhailenko.

New Independent News Agency Set Up in USSR

TASS said a new independent news agency had been set up in the Soviet Union. It said the agency, Ninfa, would provide information about the Soviet Union and would be aimed at foreign readers. It said the new agency had been set up by the Center for International Contacts, a new Soviet association for establishing economic and cultural links with foreign countries.

Wednesday, July 4

Miners Urged Not to Strike

During the Party Congress, Gorbachev joined other delegates in appealing to Soviet miners to call off a one-day strike planned for July 11. Saying he agreed with the miners' criticism of the government's slow implementation of its promise to create better living conditions, Gorbachev expressed his confidence that the miners would respond to the appeal and call off their strike.

This discussion occurred one day after the Soviet government and the All-Union Central Council of Trade Unions had announced its decision to give the miners longer vacations, beginning in 1991. "Vremya" reported that vacations would be increased by twenty-one or twenty-two days, with those working underground in future being entitled to fifty-seven days of annual leave, while surface workers would receive forty-five days vacation each year. These benefits come in addition to extra vacation benefits established by other legislation for those working in the Far North or certain other regions.

On July 8, Gorbachev made a televised appeal to Soviet coal miners to call off their planned strike. Gorbachev said the strike threat had not originated with the miners but that "someone wants to incite the workers." He said it was "unacceptable" for the miners to resort to strikes to press their demands. He said he and Ryzhkov had held a meeting with workers and peasants present at the Party Congress and promised that the working class would play a larger role in the Party in future.

Theater Profits to Support Democratic Party of Russia

Moscow's Komsomol Theater has decided to give all the profits from its popular play *Yunona i Avos* to a fund to support the newly created Democratic Party of Russia. Radio Moscow quoted the theater's liberal director, Mark Zakharov, as saying the decision reflected the political views of the theater company.

Reformers' Letter Slams Military Leadership

A letter harshly attacking the Soviet military leadership was published in *Komsomol'skaya pravda.* Penned by forty-seven liberal Soviet politicians and academics, including Georgii Arbatov, Tat'yana Zaslavskaya, and three members of the USSR Supreme Soviet, the letter accused the military leadership of teaming up with conservatives to block army reforms and urged radical measures to bring the army under parliamentary control. The letter also called for banning activity by any political party within the army and other security bodies and for a purge of the Defense Ministry. It also charged that the armed forces were trying to use their problems to discredit Gorbachev.

On July 12, a group of top Soviet military officials accused reformers of inciting "antiarmy hysteria" to advance their political careers. A letter signed by seventy-seven military officials appeared in *Krasnaya zvezda.*

New Committees Established in RSFSR

Chairman of the RSFSR Supreme Soviet Boris El'tsin oversaw the appointments of people to head a number of new parliamentary committees, including reformist economist Sergei Krasavchenko to chair a committee on economic reform, of former political prisoner Sergei Kovalev to head a committee on human rights, of Russian Orthodox priest (and member of the Christian Democratic Party) Father Vyacheslav Polosin to head a subcommittee on charitable works, and of the leader of the Democratic Russia Party, Nikolai Travkin, to head the committee on local self-government (*Central Television,* July 4).

Former Envoy Says North Started Korean War

A former North Korean ambassador to Moscow said Kim Il-Song was responsible for the attack on South Korea in 1950, after consultations with Stalin (*Reuters*, July 4). The former envoy, currently a political exile in the Soviet Union, was reported to have told *Moscow News* that the invasion was a carefully executed affair and came about on the initiative of Kim himself. For four decades both North Korea and the Soviet Union have asserted that the South Koreans started the war. The interview came as Moscow appeared to be moving towards the establishment of diplomatic relations with South Korea.

Thursday, July 5

Ligachev Interviewed by Novosti

Egor Ligachev said he favored a planned market in the Soviet Union but not one that specified which articles should be produced and how many. Ligachev said that kind of planning was absurd. In an interview with the Novosti press agency, Ligachev said supply and demand should be allowed to determine what was produced and in what quantity. He said government planners should limit themselves to planning major scientific and technological programs and "maintaining proper economic proportions."

Estonian Veterans' Meeting Called Off

The organizers of a planned gathering of Estonian veterans of the German Army canceled the meeting after a Soviet military column arrived in the town of Tori, where the event was to take place. The commander of Soviet Armed Forces in the Baltic called the proposed meeting a gathering of fascists. The Estonian government sent a message to the Soviet commander, Colonel General Fedor Kuz'min, protesting against the deployment of troops in Tori (*AP*, *Reuters*, quoting the Estonian *ETA* news agency, July 5).

Moscow Mayor Refuses to Give Housing to Polozkov

The conservative first secretary of the new RSFSR Communist Party, Ivan Polozkov, was said to be having trouble locating a place to live in Moscow. Interfax quoted Polozkov as saying that Moscow Mayor Gavriil Popov had told him it was not possible to give him an apartment in the capital, where many people have to wait for years for proper housing. Polozkov is from Krasnodar Krai.

Friday, July 6

Gorbachev Accepts NATO Invitation

Mikhail Gorbachev said he accepted NATO's invitation to address a future meeting of the Western alliance. The NATO offer came at the end of a two-day NATO meeting in London that US President Bush called "a historic turning point." NATO leaders also agreed to offer the Warsaw Pact a nonaggression pact, to adopt a strategy treating nuclear weapons as a last resort, and to work towards deeper cuts in conventional forces. They also offered to limit the size of unified German armed forces (*AP*, July 6).

Commenting on the NATO proposals, Soviet Foreign Ministry spokesman Gennadii Gerasimov said they would help vindicate Gorbachev's foreign policy. Gerasimov said that Gorbachev's supporters "can tell those grumbling generals they were wrong." Some conservative delegates to the CPSU Congress (mostly from the Soviet Armed Forces) have attacked Gorbachev's foreign policy, saying it has weakened Soviet national security (*Reuters*, July 6).

USSR Admits and Apologizes for Mongolian Repressions

The USSR officially admitted that it had played a role in "repressions" carried out in Mongolia during the Stalin era. TASS said that several leading Mongolian Party, state, and military officials—including two prime ministers—had been "unlawfully repressed" in the USSR in 1937–39. TASS said that the repressions had darkened the history of relations between the USSR and Mongolia and that the Soviet Union "deeply regretted" them.

Saturday, July 7

Situation in the Baltic Republics

On July 7, USSR Prime Minister Nikolai Ryzhkov repeated the Soviet position that Lithuania must hold a referendum on independence. He was speaking to delegates at the Party Congress (*Reuters*, July 7).

On July 9, the Lithuanian government received a letter signed by Boris El'tsin and RSFSR Prime Minister Ivan Silaev proposing bilateral economic cooperation with the RSFSR in 1991 (*TASS*, July 9).

On July 9, Gorbachev chose members of a Soviet delegation to conduct talks on Lithuanian independence with Vilnius. Ryzhkov was appointed to head the delegation, which TASS said would include twenty-two members, among them the heads of several USSR ministries and departments and representatives of the Presidential Council, the USSR Supreme Soviet, and trade unions. On July 12, one of the members of the Soviet delegation, Army General Mikhail Moiseev, who is chief of the general staff, said Lithuania's secession from the Soviet Union would considerably decrease defense capability in the northwestern USSR (*TASS*, July 12).

On July 10, in Riga, the Latvian parliament approved a resolution calling for negotiations with the USSR. TASS quoted President of the Latvian Supreme Council Anatolijs Gorbunovs as saying that the approval of the resolution did not mean the talks would begin right away.

On July 11, *Sovetskaya Estonia*, the Estonian Party daily, published the text of a petition in which residents of the Urals city of Sverdlovsk expressed their support for Lithuanian independence. It said there was no freedom for people of Lithuania or Russia without solidarity.

On July 12, Lithuanian Foreign Minister Algirdas Saudargas said the talks with Moscow on Lithuanian independence had been delayed because the Soviet side had refused to treat the talks as discussions between independent states (*RFE/RL Special*, July 12). The foreign minister was in Washington for talks with US Secretary of State James Baker.

Meanwhile, a Russian delegation arrived in Lithuania to participate in the celebration of the seventieth anniversary of a peace treaty that laid the foundations for Lithuanian independence (*Radio Vilnius*, July 12).

Leningrad Free Democrats Hold Congress

The northwestern section of the Democratic Party of Russia opened its inaugural conference in Leningrad. The party is anti-Communist and is dedicated to the creation of a market economy based on private property. It also calls for the convocation of a constituent assembly that would establish a sovereign democratic republic of Russia. TASS quoted an organizer of the congress, Marina Sal'e, as calling for the unification of all democratic forces in Russia. (Those who organized the inaugural conference in Leningrad were not satisfied with the proceedings of the inaugural conference of the Democratic Party of Russia held in Moscow in May. The Leningrad delegates then refused to join the Moscow-based party.)

Congress of Stalin's Victims Meets in Moldavia

The newly created Association of Victims of Stalinist Repression held its first congress in the Moldavian capital, Kishinev. Congress delegates represented all cities and regions of Moldavia, plus the Western Ukrainian regions of Chernovtsy and Odessa. Speakers called for the rehabilitation of all citizens who were unlawfully repressed under Stalin and for compensation for those people.

Demonstration Held to Press Demands for Help for Chernobyl' Victims

There was a big demonstration on Red Square to back demands for more help in dealing with the consequences of the Chernobyl' accident. Soviet television showed crowds of people gathered outside the Kremlin, some of them carrying placards criticizing the Soviet authorities for their handling of the aftermath of the disaster.

Sunday, July 8

Gorbachev Appoints New Envoy to Sweden

TASS said Nikolai Uspensky had been appointed the USSR's new ambassador to Sweden. Uspensky held diplomatic posts in Canada and Britain in the 1970s and in the European Department of the Soviet Foreign Ministry in the 1980s.

Thirty-eight Dead in Soviet Train Accident

Thirty-eight people died when a train hit a bus crossing a railway in the northwestern RSFSR. TASS said the bus was crossing the track against a red light—as were other vehicles—because people wanted to get home to watch the World Cup final on television. The accident happened near Petrozavodsk, the capital of the Karelian Autonomous Republic.

Monday, July 9

Situation in Kirgizia Still Tense

On July 9, *Izvestia* said tensions remained high in Kirgizia's Osh Oblast, where fighting broke out last month between Kirgiz and Uzbeks. On July 8, MVD troops and police blocked access to the city of Dzhalal Abad, where some 5,000 Uzbeks were staging an officially sanctioned protest over the murder of an Uzbek youth. This rally provoked "a counterreaction from Kirgiz residents," the newspaper said. *Izvestia* complained that the local authorities were depending more on arms than on persuasion to deal with the tensions.

On July 10, *Komsomol'skaya pravda* reported that as many as 800 people may have died in the ethnic clashes in Kirgizia last month. Major General Aleksandr Kotlyarov of the USSR Ministry of Internal Affairs said that "the scale of the crimes and their cruelty surpass those committed in Fergana, Azerbaijan, and Armenia."

Sporadic fighting between Kirgiz and Uzbeks took place on July 14 and 15 in Osh, TASS reported. Sixteen people were hospitalized, and at least one death was registered.

On July 17, Soviet television said the town of Osh was virtually paralyzed after the latest outbreaks of violence. On July 18, TASS reported that four people had been killed in Osh in the previous twenty-four hours and that the chairman of the Osh Oblast Soviet Executive Committee and the police chief had been fired.

On July 19, *Rabochaya tribuna* devoted an article to the ethnic unrest in Kirgizia, saying it was mostly a result of severe economic problems in the republic. The same day, TASS, in English, reported that the commander of USSR MVD troops, Colonel General Yurii Shatalin, had gone to the Osh region to oversee law-enforcement units working to halt the ethnic fighting. TASS also updated the official death toll from the clashes, saying it had reached 212, including twelve killed this week.

On July 23, the TASS correspondent in Osh Oblast reported that the town of Osh was peaceful: there was no shooting, shops were open, and buses were running. But the commandant of the raions covered by the state of emergency lengthened the curfew. The town of Uzgen was reported to be still barricaded. Vehicles entering have military escorts, but stones were thrown at them. The same TASS report said that a commission of the USSR Supreme Soviet had finished its investigation of the causes of the strife. The USSR Council of Ministers has issued a resolution on assistance to Kirgizia, in particular for dealing with unemployment among Kirgiz young people.

On July 25, reports carried by Radio Moscow said increasing hooliganism, fighting, and unauthorized rallies were continuing to exacerbate the situation in southern Kirgizia. The reports said additional MVD troops had been sent to the area around Uzgen.

On July 26, *Krasnaya zvezda* questioned how long Soviet troops would have to remain in Kirgizia to maintain order. The newspaper said commanders of troops, the defense minister, and the country's leadership had been receiving appeals from servicemen in Kirgizia who consider the continued presence of troops in areas of mass uprisings and ethnic conflicts "to be inappropriate."

Radio Moscow said on July 28 that, as of July 27, eighty-eight people were missing in the Osh Oblast of Kirgizia. Radio Moscow said preliminary estimates indicated that material losses in the Kirgiz town of Uzgen amounted to about 30 million rubles and that efforts were being made to provide housing for residents.

Moscow City Soviet Announces New Plans

The reform-minded Moscow City Soviet announced plans to withhold from the all-Union ministries an additional 12.5 percent of the city's industrial production to help relieve the dire economic situation in the capital, according to Radio Moscow. The Executive Committee of the Moscow City Soviet said it intended to petition the central authorities for permission to retain certain items, such as television sets and industrial equipment, which are in short supply in Moscow. Some of the goods will be exchanged for foodstuffs that have become scarce in Moscow.

Strikes Related to Ethnic Disputes on the Rise

Data on the incidence of strikes in the USSR were published for the first time (*Nedelya*, No. 10; *Izvestiya TsK KPSS*, No. 5). Broken down by republic, they covered 1989 and indicated that work time lost through protests inspired by national grievances far exceeded the time lost as a result of economically motivated strikes. Thus, the republics of Azerbaijan, Moldavia, and Georgia each recorded man-day losses in 1989 greater than those in the RSFSR.

Ukrainian Opposition Wants Parliament Replaced

Ukrainian opposition groups launched a campaign to win public support for a national congress to replace the republic's parliament. Radio Kiev said the campaign was being led by the Assembly of Ukrainian Democratic Forces, an interparty organization that has set up a coordinating council of citizens' committees. The radio said the group had urged citizens who support restoration of an independent Ukrainian state to sign a statement backing the formation of citizens' committees and the convocation of a national congress to replace the current parliament.

Tajikistan's Ethnic Minorities Leave

There were reports of continuing tensions in Tajikistan. Radio Moscow, World Service, said a curfew and state of emergency were still in force in the republican capital, Dushanbe, following disorders there in February. The radio also said the republic's nonindigenous population was leaving and that as a result there were hundreds of vacant jobs in big industrial enterprises.

Situation in Soviet Psychiatry

Semen Gluzman, a Soviet psychiatrist and former political prisoner, told AFP that Soviet psychiatry was still "behind the iron curtain." Gluzman, who is a member of the Ukrainian movement "Rukh," was speaking in Paris. He said that, while dissidents had been released from Soviet psychiatric hospitals, those responsible for their incarceration remained in their posts. Gluzman said the USSR's readmission to the World Psychiatric Organization was "a mistake," because *glasnost'* had not reached the Soviet psychiatric community.

On July 11, Amnesty International named two Soviet citizens who it believed were still in psychiatric hospitals at the end of 1989 after being confined for political reasons. A spokeswoman for the London-based human-rights group told RFE/RL that Mstislav Vink, an ethnic German confined after trying to emigrate to West Germany in the late 1970s, was still in a maximum-security hospital in Dnepropetrovsk in December, 1989. A second man, Sergei Borsnikov, who was arrested near the Romanian border in September, 1987, was also believed to be in the same hospital at the end of last year. Amnesty International has made representations to the Soviet authorities about the men. No response has been forthcoming on Borsnikov and the chief psychiatrist in Ukraine wrote to Amnesty International in March of this year denying all knowledge of Vink.

Donetsk Miners Disband Party Cell

Workers at a coal mine in the Ukrainian Donetsk region disbanded their Communist Party cell and banned any Communist political activities in the workplace. TASS said the Workers' Council of the Kalinin mine also decided to refuse office space to all political groups. The disbanding of Party cells in the workplace and in the army and the KGB were among the demands made by miners when they staged strikes in 1989.

Tuesday, July 10

Demonstrations in Northern RSFSR

There were large rallies in some parts of the northern RSFSR organized by the Federation of Independent Trade Unions of Russia, TASS reported. The federation, set up in February of this year, claimed that the authorities had repeatedly ignored requests from the local population to deal with social and environmental problems. The protest action was scheduled to go on for ten days.

Government Writes Off Agricultural Enterprises' Debts

A TASS report of July 10 said the USSR Council of Ministers had passed a resolution to write off the debts of kolkhozes and sovkhozes and other agricultural enterprises. The debts amounted to 40.3 billion rubles. An additional 28 billion rubles owed by farms converted to leasing were said to have been written off over the previous two months. Vladilen Nikitin, first deputy chairman of the Council of Ministers, explained in an interview on the television news program "Vremya" on July 10 that the government had written off these debts in order to show moral support and respect for those who worked the land and fed the country.

Democrats Gain Strength in Belorussian Parliament

TASS reported that nearly a third of all members of the Belorussian parliament had joined the "Democratic Club of Deputies." Among them were six members of the Presidium, one of whom is First Deputy Chairman Stanislav Shushkevich. The club seeks genuine state sovereignty and economic independence for the republic, the defense of social guarantees and human rights, and a multiparty system. It plans to work through legislative action, coordinated voting, and contacts with other democratic movements in the USSR and abroad.

Moldavian Government Wants Direct Ties with Other Republics

Moldavian Supreme Soviet Chairman Mircea Snegur told TASS that his republic could not survive without direct economic ties with other republics. Snegur said that Kishinev had already concluded an intergovernmental agreement with Belorussia.

Wednesday, July 11

Soviet Miners Strike

Rallies and strikes were staged in all the USSR's major coal-mining regions. Ignoring Gorbachev's appeal to call off their one-day action, tens of thousands of miners downed tools to demand the resignation of the Soviet government following its failure to meet the pledges it had made to the miners after a massive strike in summer, 1989. Soviet television gave extensive and sympathetic coverage to the miners' protests, showing many posters and banners, including one reading "Leninism Is the Utopia of the Demons of Darkness." The miners also called for the removal of Party bodies from the workplace. In Moscow, an unauthorized meeting was held near the Kremlin to support the striking miners, TASS reported.

THE USSR IN JULY, 1990

On July 12, the coal miners began to return to work. Strike organizers in Ukraine's Donbass region, in the Kuzbass region in Siberia, and in Vorkuta in the far north said mining in their areas was back to normal (*AP*, *UPI*, July 12). The same day, Prime Minister Ryzhkov told the Party Congress that some miners who took part in the strike were threatening to stage further stoppages unless their demands were met (*TASS*, July 12). See RL 325/90.

West Agrees to Provide Technical Support for Soviet Economy

The seven leading industrial powers agreed at their summit in Houston to provide technical support for Soviet reforms but stopped short of providing financial assistance. While it implied that the success of *perestroika* and hence of further positive developments in East-West relations depended largely on the fate of Soviet leader Gorbachev, the sixteen-page communiqué issued by the group declared that a comprehensive and coordinated financial assistance program could only follow more radical steps towards economic liberalization, a further shift of resources away from the armed forces, and a cut in Soviet aid to nations supporting "regional conflict" (*Reuters*, July 11). In an immediate response, the Soviet government welcomed efforts by Western democracies to improve economic relations with the USSR (*AP*, July 11).

On July 12, US President George Bush said that the USSR would not get any cash assistance immediately but that Western leaders were united in a desire to help Gorbachev's reforms. Bush said that Gorbachev should view the outcome of the Houston summit as "positive." The final communiqué allowed Western nations to decide for themselves on aid to the USSR (*Reuters*, *AP*, July 12).

Reduction in Meat Production Reported

Rabochaya tribuna reported a "particularly alarming" decrease in meat production in the USSR during the first half of 1990. The article quoted an official of the State Committee for Statistics as saying initial figures on meat production showed a 4-percent drop compared with the same period in 1989. The official also noted a decrease in production of vegetable oil but an increase in margarine and bread and bakery products.

New Informal Movement in Kazakhstan, Coalition in Azerbaijan

TASS said that a new movement, "Azat" (Liberty), had held its founding conference in Alma-Ata. A cochairman of the group told TASS that its objective was to help transform Kazakhstan into a flourishing republic by pressing for reform without social dislocation. It hopes to unite "positive forces and groupings" without regard to party, national, or religious affiliation. "Azat" intends to put out its own publication in Kazakh and Russian. Representatives of informal groups in the RSFSR, Azerbaijan, Kirgizia, and Uzbekistan attended the conference.

The same day, reports came from Baku saying fifty-seven new Azerbaijani political, social, and cultural organizations had formed a coalition called the Democratic Forum to compete in the parliamentary elections in Azerbaijan on September 2 (RL Azerbaijani service, July 11).

1937 Census Data Published

Sotsiologicheskie issledovaniya (No. 6) began publishing the most important data from the 1937 census. This census, crucial in calculating the demographic losses in the USSR resulting from Stalin's repressions, was denounced and suppressed by Stalin. It was believed that the results of the census had been destroyed. In 1989, however, two Soviet scholars reported that in fact the results of the census had survived in a Soviet archive; but at the time these scholars divulged only the figure for the total Soviet population. The article in *Sotsiologicheskie issledovaniya* is the first detailed report on the other data provided by this census. It quoted items of secret correspondence between those in charge of conducting the census and Stalin, Molotov, and the NKVD, revealing the panic that arose among the Soviet authorities because of the unexpectedly low figure for the total population of the USSR, especially in those areas hit by the famine. See RL 343/90.

USSR Denies It Has Chemical Weapons in East Germany

Soviet officials denied charges that Moscow had large quantities of chemical weapons stored in East Germany. Foreign Ministry spokesman Gennadii Gerasimov described as "a provocative hoax" West German and Hungarian press reports that Soviet forces had stockpiled up to 30,000 tons of poison gas in East Germany (*Reuters*, *DPA*, July 11). On July 13, the USSR foreign and defense ministers issued statements saying the USSR had never had chemical weapons stationed outside its own national territory (*TASS*, July 13).

Thursday, July 12

Gorbachev Says Three Dead in Attack in Nagorno-Karabakh

Mikhail Gorbachev said three people had died and twenty-four others had been wounded when Armenian militants attacked a convoy in Nagorno-Karabakh. Gorbachev interrupted today's session of the Party Congress to announce the latest violence in the region. He said the attackers had opened fire on July 11 on a convoy of vehicles in the Mardakert area (*TASS*, *Reuters*, July 12).

On July 16, a bomb explosion at Stepanakert airport killed the manager of the airport and injured two other people, TASS reported. The Soviet news agency blamed the explosion on "those who do not want the situation in the region to improve."

On July 17, TASS reported that the police station in the town of Lachin in Nagorno-Karabakh had been attacked, but it provided no details of the incident. The news agency did say that troops had managed to disarm "a large group of terrorists" who had crossed into the enclave from Armenia. It said they were carrying mortars, grenade launchers, and machine guns. The agency said bluntly that its reports from the area now resembled wartime communiqués, with each one citing casualties and attacks on both security forces and civilians.

On July 18, the Soviet media reported that the situation in Armenia and neighboring regions of Azerbaijan remained extremely tense. Clashes and arms seizures continued to be reported.

Friday, July 13

Sobchak and Popov Leave CPSU

The chairmen of the Moscow and Leningrad City Soviets, Gavriil Popov and Anatolii Sobchak, announced that they were leaving the CPSU. According to a TASS report, they called on Soviet officials at all levels to show their independence by refusing to be members of any one party.

Lizichev Ousted; Replaced by Shlyaga

The Defense Ministry Press Center announced that Aleksei Lizichev, head of the Main Political Administration of the Soviet Army and Navy (MPA) since the spring of 1985, had resigned from his post for reasons of health. The sixty-two-year-old army general was said to have been reassigned to the Defense Ministry's Group of General Inspectors. His replacement, fifty-five-year-old Colonel General Nikolai Shlyaga, had been the first deputy head of the MPA since late 1989. See RL 333/90.

Latvian Official Speaks against Moratorium

A top Latvian official said his republic would not put a moratorium on its reaffirmation of independence as a condition for negotiations with Moscow. Andrejs Krastins, deputy chairman of the Latvian parliament, said such a moratorium would mean a loss of Latvia's legal status and of its equality in any talks with the USSR (RFE Latvian service, July 13).

Tatar Branch of Democratic Party of Russia

A branch of the Democratic Party of Russia has been created in the Tatar ASSR, Radio Moscow-1 reported. The Democratic Party is gradually becoming the most influential new political group in the Russian Federation and, of all the autonomous republics in the USSR, Tataria is the one with the most active unofficial political movement.

Poland Asks Moscow to Investigate Killings of Officers

Poland again asked the Soviet Union to initiate hearings on the killing of Polish officers interned in Soviet camps during World War II. Radio Warsaw said Polish First Deputy Prosecutor-General Aleksander Herzog had filed repeated requests with USSR Prosecutor-General Aleksandr Sukharev to investigate "the crime of genocide" committed against Polish officers who were interned in the camps of Kozelsk, Starobelsk, and Ostashkovo. Earlier this year, the Soviet Union for the first time acknowledged that the NKVD had murdered some 15,000 Polish officers from these camps in 1940.

Saturday, July 14

Situation in Lithuania

Lithuanian Prime Minister Prunskiene offered a program for economic reform in Lithuania that included almost total privatization. Her program called for payments to Lithuanians who had lost property because of the annexation of Lithuania by the USSR (*Radio Vilnius*, July 17).

On July 17, the Lithuanian Supreme Council passed a law setting up the republic's own army units and requiring all men over the age of nineteen to serve in the republican armed forces or to perform alternative service (*TASS*, July 17). On July 18, USSR Defense Minister Dmitrii Yazov accused Lithuania of disregarding Soviet laws on the military draft. Radio Moscow quoted Yazov as complaining that local Lithuanian authorities were blocking the work of Soviet draft boards.

On July 18, a Lithuanian commission responsible for preparing for the independence negotiations with Moscow held its first meeting. It decided to create working groups to develop positions on key aspects of Lithuanian independence (*Radio Vilnius*, July 19).

On July 25, Radio Vilnius reported that Lithuania had not reached the draftee levels set by military authorities for the spring call-up. A representative of the military commissariat, Konstantin Golubev, said 5,880 youths should have been drafted, but 60 percent of them had refused to serve in the Soviet army.

New Politburo Elected

The CPSU Central Committee elected seven people to the Politburo in addition to the fifteen republican Communist Party leaders who became ex officio members under the changes made at the Twenty-eighth Party Congress. Those elected were: the first secretary of the Moscow City Party Committee, Yurii Prokof'ev; the chairman of the All-Union Central Council of Trade Unions, Gennadii Yanaev; CPSU Central Committee Secretary Egor Stroev; *Pravda* editor Ivan Frolov; the chairman of the USSR Supreme Soviet Commission on International Affairs, Aleksandr Dzasokhov; the first secretary of the Krasnoyarsk Krai Party Committee, Oleg Shenin; and Galina Semenova, the editor of a weekly magazine for women. Mikhail Gorbachev and Deputy General Secretary Vladimir Ivashko are also members (*TASS*, in English, July 14; *Pravda*, July 15).

Frolov told reporters that the composition of the new Politburo "underscores the Party's break with former practice, under which it was organically included in the administrative-command system and was at the top of the hierarchy." The Party will now be "a force competing with other sociopolitical forces, asserting its advantages mostly in ideological and political struggles," he said (*TASS*, in English, *Reuters*, *AFP*, July 14).

On July 16, Prokof'ev said the Presidential Council rather than the Politburo would run the country and that the Politburo and the Central Committee Secretariat would concentrate purely on Party matters. He said the Politburo would in future meet once a month and the Secretariat once a week.

Composition of the New Secretariat

At its plenum, the CPSU Central Committee elected eleven secretaries and five "members" to serve on its Secretariat. Only four of the secretaries—Oleg Baklanov, Andrei Girenko, Yurii Manaenkov, and Egor Stroev—served on the previous Secretariat. Their responsibilities will be, respectively: the defense industry; nationality issues; supervision of the Russian Communist Party; and agriculture. The other new secretaries are Aleksandr Dzasokhov—ideology; Galina Semenova—women's issues; Oleg Shenin—Party organizational work; Gennadii Yanaev and Valentin Falin—foreign affairs; Valentin Kuptsov—chief of the CPSU Central Committee Department for Relations with Informal Groups and Sociopolitical Movements; and Boris Gidaspov—first secretary of the Leningrad Party organization.

The five members of the Secretariat are Viktor Aniskin, chairman of the Gorky kolkhoz outside Moscow; Valentin Gaivoronsky, a worker; Ivan Mel'nikov, secretary of Moscow State University Party Committee; Aleksandr Teplenichev, secretary of the Novolipetsk Metallurgical Combine Party Committee in Lipetsk; and Gulchakhra Turgunova, a farm worker. See RL 313/90.

Democratic Platform Announces Its Strategy

The Baltimore Sun said the Democratic Platform had appointed a special commission to plan its strategy. The Democratic Platform planned to begin legal proceedings to claim a portion of the CPSU's assets. In the meantime, Democratic Platform supporters were being asked to remain in the Party so as to maintain access to its resources and strengthen the Democratic Platform's legal claim to a share of them.

On July 15, Yurii Boldyrev, Vyacheslav Shostakovsky, Dmitrii Smirnov, Stepan Sulakshin, and Vladimir Lysenko, who were among the seventeen Democratic Platform members who left the CPSU at the Twenty-eighth Party Congress, held a press conference to announce their plans to form a new party (*Reuters*, July 15).

Republican Involvement in Foreign Policy

Chairman of the RSFSR Supreme Soviet Boris El'tsin said that the RSFSR would end the transfer of military hardware to Afghanistan in order to help secure the release of 300 Soviet prisoners of war, *Moskovsky komsomolets* reported. The Iranian news agency IRNA reported that Uzbekistan, Tajikistan, Azerbaijan, and Turkmenistan had signed trade pacts with Iran.

RSFSR Supreme Soviet Concludes Session

The RSFSR Supreme Soviet ended the inaugural session it began on June 13, after electing more republican ministers and adopting a number of resolutions. Radio Moscow said Nikolai Malyshev had been elected deputy chairman of the RSFSR Council of Ministers and chairman of the State Committee for Science and Education. Others elected were Igor Gavrilov as chairman of the Ecology Committee; Viktor Yaroshenko as minister of foreign economic relations; Vladimir Bulgak as minister of communications, automation, and space; and Valerii Grebennikov as the republic's chief arbiter. He pledged to uphold Russian laws and interests even if they conflicted with those of the Soviet Union as a whole (*Reuters*, July 15).

On July 9, two leading members of the Interregional Group of Deputies were appointed members of the RSFSR government. Mikhail Poltoranin, El'tsin's right-hand man who now writes for *Moscow News*, was appointed RSFSR minister for the press and mass media. Nikolai Fedorov, a young lawyer from Chuvashia, beccame the RSFSR minister of justice. Two of Fedorov's namesakes also became RSFSR ministers—Boris Fedorov became minister of finance and Dmitrii Fedorov became minister of natural resources and geology (*Central Television*, July 9).

Ivashko on Party Resignations

CPSU Deputy General Secretary Vladimir Ivashko told Radio Moscow that people who left the Party "should not be declared enemies," because the Party still needed to work with them. Ivashko said he saw nothing wrong with discussing things with people who were anti-Communist, and he called for "normal, full-blooded relations" between the CPSU and other political parties and groups in the Soviet Union.

Activists Denied Visas for Human-Rights Conference

The Soviet authorities denied exit visas to two activists invited to participate in a human-rights conference in the United States. The two were Helsinki Watch's Lev Timofeev and the Democratic Union's Sergei Skripnikov. The meeting, the Andrei Sakharov Memorial Goodwill Conference, took place at the end of July in Seattle (*Reuters*, July 14).

Sunday, July 15

Anti-Communist Rally Staged in Moscow

The largest anti-Communist, prodemocracy rally since February 25 took place in Moscow. Estimates of the number of participants varied from 25,000 to 400,000. The rally was organized by the Democratic Platform, the Moscow Voters' Club, "Democratic Russia," and the military reform group "Shield." Demonstrators carried banners reading "Every Communist to his own mausoleum" and "Throw the Communist Party on the trash heap of history." They marched from Gorky Park to Manezh Square—Red Square was blocked off by the police. RSFSR people's deputy Sergei Belozertsev told the crowd: "We are here to express our contempt for the Party Congress that has just ended" (*DPA*, *AFP*, *TASS*, July 15).

Gorbachev Issues Decree on Television Broadcasting

Gorbachev issued a decree stating that television must function independently of all political and public organizations, including the CPSU, and should provide impartial and all-round coverage of processes taking place in the country. The decree called on the USSR Supreme Soviet to prepare a law guaranteeing the right of local soviets, political parties, and local organizations to set up their own television centers using their own resources or to lease air time from official broadcasting centers. He said that, in accordance with international practice, "the operations of independent broadcasting centers should be regulated under a system of licenses." At the same time, however, Gorbachev's decree reaffirmed Moscow's control over television, stating that "all legal acts of republican and local authorities aimed at changing the legal and ownership status of television are invalid" (*Central Television*; *TASS*, in English, July 15).

On July 16, Mikhail Nenashev, the head of the USSR State Committee for Television and Radio Broadcasting, said he feared "an orgy of democracy" now that Gorbachev had moved to loosen the state broadcasting monopoly. He said in an interview with Soviet television that Gorbachev's decree would make "managing television much more complex than in the past" (*AP*, July 17).

KGB and Armed Forces Excluded from New Central Committee

KGB and many military officials were not reelected to the new Central Committee. The membership list did not include the KGB deputy chiefs or the deputy ministers of defense (*Pravda*, July 15). Also excluded from the Central Committee were senior diplomats, except for Aleksandr Bessmertnykh, Soviet ambassador in Washington.

Fear of AIDS Keeps Blood Donors Away

"Vremya" reported that the number of blood donors in the Soviet Union was declining as a result of fears of exposure to the AIDS virus. The report admitted that this was understandable, given past instances of patients' being infected through unsterile medical equipment. The report assured viewers that donated blood was always checked for AIDS and hepatitis B and that donors were fully guaranteed safety from infection when giving blood. The laboratory worker being interviewed urged more people to donate.

Monday, July 16

Gorbachev Says United Germany Can Be in NATO

Following talks with Chancellor Helmut Kohl, Gorbachev dropped his earlier objections to Germany's remaining in NATO after reunification, according to news agency reports. He told reporters that a united Germany could choose which alliance to be a member of. The two leaders also announced that the 350,000 Soviet troops stationed in East Germany would leave three to four years after the two sides signed a treaty to that effect. Kohl told Gorbachev that West German troop levels would be reduced and that no nuclear weapons or foreign troops would be stationed on the territory currently belonging to East Germany (*Reuters*, *DPA*, *AFP*, July 16). See RL 329/90.

Ukraine Declares Sovereignty

The Ukrainian Supreme Soviet declared Ukraine a sovereign state. By a vote of 355 in favor and only four against, with one abstention, the republican legislature declared among other things that "the Ukrainian SSR has the right to [maintain] its own armed forces" and will strive to become "a neutral state that does not participate in military blocs" and that rejects "the production, deployment, and use of nuclear weapons." Citizens of Ukraine are, as a rule, to do their military service on Ukrainian territory and may not be used for military purposes outside the republic's borders "without the consent of the Supreme Soviet of the Ukrainian SSR." The section on international relations empowered Ukraine to conduct its own affairs in this field. The declaration would also establish Ukrainian citizenship while recognizing the right of residents to retain USSR citizenship (RL Ukrainian service, July 16; see *Pravda Ukrainy*, July 17).

While hailing the declaration, radical Ukrainian parliamentarians were quick to point out that it did not go as far as some would have liked. Deputy Larysa Skoryk told RFE/RL that she wanted to see the elimination of the words "Soviet Socialist" from the republic's name, for instance. See RL 326/90.

Estonia Tells Moscow to Rein in the Troops

Tallinn protested about recent Soviet troop movements in the Baltic and called for a direct link with the armed forces, ETA reported. In a note delivered to the Soviet Foreign Ministry by Estonian Deputy Foreign Minister Toivo Kuldsepp, Estonia called on the Kremlin to rein in its troops to avoid a possible clash with the local population. The note also called for the establishment of a commission giving Estonia a direct link with the armed forces in order to avoid "confrontational situations . . . , examples of which could be observed in Tbilisi and Baku." Soviet Deputy Foreign Minister Valentin Nikiforov told Kuldsepp that the Soviet Foreign Ministry was willing to mediate in situations of conflict but said that Estonia's status had not yet reached a level that would allow communication via diplomatic notes.

Chernobyl' Victims from Latvia

According to Radio Riga, sixty-seven persons from Latvia are now listed as victims of the Chernobyl' disaster; thirty-eight have died and twenty-nine are classified as invalids. All the victims had participated in the cleanup effort after the explosion at the nuclear energy plant. Nearly 1,000 other Latvians were also involved in that effort.

More Crimes against Foreigners

Crimes against foreigners, especially theft, doubled in the first half of 1990 compared with the same period in 1989, USSR Minister of Internal Affairs Vadim Bakatin said. But he provided no precise number or breakdown of the increase. Bakatin also reported an overall 14.6 percent increase in the crime rate in the Soviet Union, with 1.26 million crimes registered from January to June of this year (*TASS*, July 16).

More Accidents in Siberian Oil Fields

Some 400,000 tons of oil were lost as the result of accidents in Siberian oil fields over the weekend, TASS reported. The accidents occurred in the Nizhnevartovsk and Novourengoi regions of Western Siberia. This brought the total loss of crude oil there due to accidents so far this year to 700,000 tons. TASS reported that sixty-five kilometers of pipeline had had to be closed down. According to local officials, there have already been more than 1,100 pipeline bursts and leaks in the region's oil fields this year. Faulty maintenance is to blame, the news service said.

Chief of General Staff Meets with Wörner

NATO Secretary General Manfred Wörner, in Moscow for talks with Gorbachev and Shevardnadze, met with Soviet Chief of the General Staff Mikhail Moiseev, TASS reported. Emphasizing that NATO is not seeking unilateral advantages over the Soviet Union, Wörner invited the Soviet army general to NATO headquarters in Brussels for further discussions. For his part, Moiseev called the meeting "historic, exceptionally useful, and promising." He outlined Soviet military reforms and changes in doctrine and did not rule out the possibility of developing unprecedented direct contacts between NATO and the Soviet military at the level of deputy chiefs of the General Staff.

Moscow Denies Italian Allegations of Spying

The Italian authorities arrested a Soviet Foreign Trade Ministry official and an Italian accomplice last week on charges of trying to steal a technical manual used to decipher NATO messages, according to Reuters. A Soviet Foreign Ministry spokesman today denied the charges, calling them "worthy of the Cold-War era." He added that the accusations were aimed at derailing Soviet-Italian trade.

Record Emigration Figures

Reuters reported that 196,000 people had left the Soviet Union in the first six months of 1990: 63,000 went to West Germany, 15,000 went to Greece, and 107,000 left with visas for Israel.

Thousands Leaving Moscow Party

Yurii Prokof'ev, first secretary of the Moscow City Party Committee, told TASS some 23,000 people had left the Moscow Party this year, with 8,000 leaving the Party in June alone. He said about half the new departees were workers. Only 12,000 people left the Moscow Party in 1989. Prokof'ev blamed the increase on the Party's losing sight of the working class, "which has benefited from *perestroika* least of all."

On July 18, Leningrad Party leader Boris Gidaspov told TASS that 23,000 of the roughly 600,000 CPSU members in Leningrad had left the CPSU; he did not say when the resignations occurred.

China to Acquire Soviet Military Technology

For the first time in three decades, China opened negotiations with the Soviet Union for the purchase of military technology, *The Washington Post* reported. The negotiations were the culmination of a series of high-level meetings between the two nations that began in May, 1989. A Western military analyst said that China wanted to gain access to Soviet technology in part because Western nations had suspended sales of military equipment to China following the Tiananmen Square massacre. The Chinese were reported to be especially interested in Soviet aviation technology and eager to barter their surplus of light industrial goods for Soviet military equipment.

Tuesday, July 17

Little Support for Communists, Poll Finds

An official Soviet poll said more than 80 percent of Soviet citizens did not support the CPSU within a multiparty system. According to the poll, the Communist Party still had more adherents that any other group, but it was supported by only 19 percent of the 1,500 people questioned. The Democratic Platform was second with almost 11 percent. Radio Moscow, World Service, said the poll, conducted by the All-Union Public Opinion Research Center, found support for social and liberal democrats as well as for workers' and ecology parties. The Christian Democrats and anarchists had the least support. Of those polled, 29 percent expressed no clear preference.

Medvedev Appointed to Presidential Council

Vadim Medvedev, who was not reelected to the Politburo or the CPSU Central Committee last week, was appointed by Mikhail Gorbachev to the Presidential Council. During a question-and-answer session before the Party Congress, Medvedev had signaled his willingness to relinquish his Politburo seat (*TASS*, July 17). See RL 323/90.

Further Dispute over Semipalatinsk Test Site

The commander of the Semipalatinsk nuclear weapons testing site said in *Krasnaya zvezda* that the site could be operated without any damage to local inhabitants or the environment and thus should not be closed. An official of the Semipalatinsk City Soviet, questioned on Radio Moscow, repeated local demands that the site be closed and a program instituted to deal with the effects of forty years of testing there. Head of the Kazakh Writers' Union and USSR people's deputy Olzhas Suleimenov, founder of the large antinuclear movement "Nevada-Semipalatinsk," told an interviewer from *Nedelya* (No. 23) that he believed not enough had been done internationally to eliminate nuclear weapons.

Moscow Scientists Claim Breakthrough on AIDS

A group of Soviet scientists claimed to have developed a drug that can prolong the lives of AIDS patients and might eventually cure some, the current issue of *Rabochaya tribuna* reported. Boris Mednikov, a geneticist at Moscow University, said the USSR Ministry of Health had hindered their work. He estimated it would take the Soviet Union about three years to start mass-producing the drug, a remarkable statement given current Soviet shortfalls in the production of other medicines.

Valentin Pikul Dies

TASS reported that novelist Valentin Pikul had died at the age of sixty-two. Pikul' was the author of controversial novels on Russian history, most of which were condemned by the intelligentsia as potboilers. But he was popular among the broader public. In several of his books, Pikul' elaborated on the idea of a Judeo-Masonic plot around Nicholas II.

Patriarch Interviewed in *Pravda*

Russian Orthodox Patriarch Aleksii told *Pravda* that not all Communists should be blamed for the sins of the past; instead, he said, blame attaches only to "those in power." He said that the Church blessed the recent moves of Gorbachev and El'tsin towards cooperation. The Patriarch also stressed that society must return to eternal values that stress a humanitarian attitude towards all mankind.

Commercial Television Channel Established in Odessa

A commercial television station began operations in the Ukrainian city of Odessa. Radio Moscow said the "Privoz" channel featured public service information, video clips, and some Leningrad television productions. (Leningrad television is regarded as the most outspoken in the Soviet Union.) The popularity of Leningrad television was discussed in detail in *Komsomol'skaya pravda* on July 12.

Wednesday, July 18

USSR People's Deputies Quit CPSU

AP reported that seven USSR people's deputies had resigned from the CPSU. They were Sergei Stankevich, the deputy chairman of the Moscow City Soviet, a leader of the Democratic Platform, and a member of the USSR Supreme Soviet; Vladimir Tikhonov, an economics professor; Aleksei Yablokov, biologist and deputy chairman of the USSR Supreme Soviet Ecology Committee; Valentin Logunov, deputy editor of *Moskovskaya pravda*; Academician Yurii Ryzhov, a member of the USSR Supreme Soviet; Aleksei Emel'yanov, a professor of agriculture at Moscow State University; and Mikhail Bocharov, a member of the USSR Supreme Soviet and a radical economist. Bocharov said the group had resigned "to facilitate the process of democratizing the country."

Gidaspov to Combine Two Posts

Leningrad Party leader Boris Gidaspov said he would combine the posts of head of the Leningrad Party organization and Central Committee secretary. Speaking at a press conference in Leningrad, he added that he wanted to concentrate on solving the economic problems of northwestern Russia, and he repeated his wish to cooperate with all constructive forces in society.

Shenin Gives Up Krasnoyarsk Post

Oleg Shenin, who was elected to the Politburo and Central Committee Secretariat last week, resigned from his post as first secretary of the Krasnoyarsk Krai Party Committee, Radio Moscow reported. It was also reported that his successor would be Veniamin Sokolov, formerly second secretary of the committee, and that Shenin, who would be responsible for Party organizational matters, was still chairman of the Krasnoyarsk Krai Soviet.

Ukrainian Parliament Accepts Ivashko's Resignation

The Ukrainian Supreme Soviet accepted the resignation of Vladimir Ivashko as its chairman and nominated candidates to replace him, TASS reported. Ivashko resigned last week during the Party Congress, citing a lack of support in the Ukrainian parliament for his reform proposals. He is now Gorbachev's deputy.

RSFSR Claims Control over Russian Banks

In an interview with Soviet television, Gosbank Chairman Viktor Gerashchenko said the recently published decree by the RSFSR Supreme Soviet "on the state bank of the RSFSR and banks on the territory of the republic" had created a conflict between the RSFSR Supreme Soviet and USSR Gosbank. The RSFSR decree basically claims that all banks on the territory of the RSFSR come under Russian subordination. Gerashchenko said he would go to Gorbachev to request an annullment of the Russian decree.

On July 30, TASS reported that Gorbachev had taken steps to reassert central control over the Soviet Union's ailing banking and financial system. In his decree, Gorbachev "recommended" that the Union republics refrain from taking any further legislative steps concerning the independence of their banking and financial systems pending the adoption of a new Union treaty. The decree also stated that a council consisting of the head of the USSR Gosbank and the heads of the Union-republican state banks would be formed to work out a common credit and monetary policy.

Food Delivery Problems Increase

Farmers in Kostroma Oblast, northeast of Moscow, threatened to stop deliveries of meat and milk products to the state and start selling them in their own villages, Radio

Moscow reported. The managers of kolkhozes in the region were reported to be organizing strike committees to present their demands to the local authorities. The farmers want immediate assistance with their crops, facilities to supply goods to the local population, and better communications links in the region. A second Radio Moscow report said the Rostov Oblast in the southern RSFSR had virtually stopped supplying Moscow and Leningrad with vegetables in protest against a halt in shipments of cars and other manufactured goods from those two cities.

Moscow Objects to US Support for Soviet Opposition

Gorbachev's press spokesman said that US "encouragement of or assistance for" opposition groups in the USSR would not be tolerated, TASS reported. Arkadii Maslennikov was responding to US Secretary of State James Baker's statement on July 17 that the United States intended to contact opposition groups in the USSR. In fact, Baker made no mention of providing support. He simply said that the purpose of contacts would be to exchange views (*AP*, July 18).

Mass Graves Sought in Moscow

TASS reported that the KGB was looking for mass graves of victims of Stalin-era repressions that were reported to be located in Moscow and the surrounding area, TASS reported. The agency quoted a KGB spokesman as saying the organization had general information about the possibility of the existence of mass graves at the Donskoe and Vagankovskoe cemeteries and in the Butovo area. Several mass graves have already been found in Moscow, and dozens have been discovered in other parts of the USSR, particularly in Siberia and Ukraine. The largest graves, containing tens of thousands of bodies, are at Kurapaty (Belorussia), Bykovnya (Ukraine), and Chelyabinsk (Siberia).

Soviet Visa Applications Flood South African Mission in Finland

Since February, more than 6,000 Soviet citizens from all over the Soviet Union have applied to emigrate to South Africa through its mission in Finland. This was reported by Johannes Lotter, South Africa's ambassador to Helsinki. He said that previously there had been no applications. Lotter said 90 percent of the applicants were unqualified and stood little chance of acceptance. He said most seemed to be applying for economic reasons. No applications have been approved so far (*Reuters*, July 18).

Thursday, July 19

RSFSR Abolishes Privileges

The RSFSR abolished a number of privileges for officials in the republic. The order was outlined in a resolution issued by the RSFSR Supreme Soviet Presidium. As reported by TASS, the order did not spell out which privileges were being lost. Senior Party officials in the Soviet Union have traditionally had access to limousines, country homes, and special shops, among other privileges.

Delors Meets Gorbachev and Ryzhkov

Mikhail Gorbachev called the visit to Moscow by European Commission President Jacques Delors a reflection of positive changes taking place in Europe. TASS quoted Gorbachev as making the statement at a meeting in the Kremlin with Delors. During the meeting Gorbachev also appealed to Delors for economic aid to help the Soviet Union's reform program. The agency said that, earlier the same day, Delors had discussed Soviet economic reforms with Prime Minister Nikolai Ryzhkov. TASS said Delors and Ryzhkov had also discussed ways of allowing the Soviet Union to form global economic ties and to expand its relations with the European Community. TASS also said that during talks between Delors and Deputy Prime Minister Leonid Abalkin, which took place in Moscow on July 18, an agreement had been reached "in principle" that the EC would help the process of economic restructuring in the Soviet Union.

Belorussia to Give More Aid to Chernobyl' Victims

The Belorussian Supreme Soviet approved additional funds to help people living in areas affected by nuclear fallout from the 1986 Chernobyl' disaster. From August 1, people living in the areas where radiation levels are high will receive an additional fifteen rubles each per month. The Belorussian parliament last week declared the republic an ecological disaster area (*TASS*, July 19).

Estonian Foreign Minister Meets Baker

Estonian Foreign Minister Lennart Meri held what he called "excellent" talks with US Secretary of State James Baker in Washington. One topic on the agenda was Estonia's views on possible independence talks with Moscow. Meri said he was optimistic about the future of the Baltic republics and believed that Estonia, Latvia, and Lithuania would all ultimately regain their independence (*RFE/RL Special*, July 19).

Ukrainian City to Dismantle Marx and Lenin Monuments

The soviet of the Western Ukrainian city of Ternopol decided to take down the city's monuments to Karl Marx and Vladimir Lenin. TASS said city residents had been demanding the removal of the monuments for a long time. The city soviet decided the monuments would not be destroyed but would be preserved for posterity. The city executive committee was instructed to find a fitting place for the monuments.

***Ogonek* Staff to Become Weekly's Sponsor**

The staff of the weekly *Ogonek* decided that the Communist Party would no longer be the magazine's sponsor. TASS quoted executive editor Aleksandr Shcherbakov as saying the staff had decided to list themselves as the sponsor when the weekly registers under the new press law on August 1. Until now, *Ogonek* had listed as its sponsor the Pravda publishing house of the CPSU Central Committee. The new press law ends the Party's monopoly on the mass media. It calls for all publications to register on August 1 and to state who sponsors them.

Frolov Warns of Civil War, Condemns Radicals

Bloodshed and civil war may result from *perestroika*'s upheavals and from the current "euphoria about democracy," the editor of *Pravda*, Ivan Frolov, told *la Repubblica*. Frolov called the political situation in the USSR "explosive" and strongly condemned "extremists" and "second-rate politickers" who turned "decent people" against the CPSU; he said "a more constructive attitude" was needed from the opposition. Frolov also suggested that USSR Minister of Internal Affairs Vadim Bakatin was allowing "political crime" to increase in order to bolster his own popularity. He accused Boris El'tsin and other reformers who had recently left the Party of being interested only in power. Frolov called Gorbachev "indispensable . . . to the Party and to the country" and said that the CPSU could avoid the fate of the East European Communists by renewing itself. He defended communism and Marxism as still valid ideas, depending on their interpretation.

Protests Continue at Khmelnitsky Nuclear Plant

It was reported that hundreds of people were continuing a two-week-old protest at the Khmelnitsky nuclear power plant in Western Ukraine. Soviet television said the protesters had put up a tent city where the third and fourth reactors are to be built. The protesters said they would stay until the Ukrainian parliament agreed to suspend the plant expansion (*Central Television*, "Vremya," July 19).

Ancient Russian City Gets Former Name Back

The ancient Russian city of Tver, renamed Kalinin in 1931, had had its old name restored in response to citizens' demands. Soviet television said the decision was made by the Presidium of the RSFSR Supreme Soviet. Tver, situated on the Volga River northwest of Moscow, was the center of a principality during the Middle Ages (*Central Television*, "Vremya," July 19).

USSR Welcomes US Move on Cambodia

The Soviet Union welcomed the United States' change of position regarding the Cambodian conflict, calling it "a step in the right direction." Washington today renounced its recognition of the Cambodian resistance coalition's seat at the United Nations and agreed to new talks with Vietnam on Cambodia (*AFP*, *DPA*, July 19).

Friday, July 20

RSFSR Draws Up Plan for Radical Economic Reform

The RSFSR government was reported to have drawn up a plan for radical economic reform that stands in sharp contrast to the more moderate project for all-Union economic reform designed by Soviet Prime Minister Nikolai Ryzhkov (*The Washington Post*, July 21.) The Russian plan called for a 500-day transition period, after which a large share of Russian industry would be privatized in some way.

The Russian plan was divided into four steps. The first would comprise the legalization of private property and an inventory of state assets. After the initial 100–250 days, the second stage would begin, during which state subsidies would be abolished and all unfinished construction projects sold off to the highest bidder, including foreigners. The third stage of reform would see the lifting of state control over prices. This would take place between days 250 and 400. The final stage would be reserved for fine-tuning the economy.

Food Shortages Worsen

Nikolai Ryzhkov delivered a grim report at a high-level government meeting, saying that, "At the rate things are going, we cannot expect an improvement in food supplies" (*Izvestia*, July 22). Ryzhkov warned that the government's supply of hard currency was insufficient to cover expected grain shortfalls. Soviet food production this year was barely enough to keep pace with population growth, and Ryzhkov said he expected the worsening food shortages to trigger social unrest.

The USSR in July, 1990

Moscow Asks Baltic Republics to Cooperate

The USSR Supreme Soviet called on the Baltic republics to "come together in a constructive social dialogue." The appeal, broadcast on Radio Moscow, said there was a great need for mutual understanding and respect, cooperation, and pooling of resources to overcome the difficulties of renewing society. The appeal also said the forthcoming signing of a new Union treaty would open the path to free national development within a union of sovereign states. It failed, however, to mention the declarations of independence that were passed in Lithuania, Latvia, and Estonia this spring.

Border Controls to Be Tightened

Increased smuggling and speculation on the Soviet Union's Western frontiers were reported to have prompted the government to impose tighter border controls. Soviet Prime Minister Nikolai Ryzhkov told Soviet television that illegal trading along the Western border had gotten out of control. Ryzhkov did not specify what kinds of new controls would be imposed. The Soviet Union eased cross-border travel in 1988 (*AP*, July 20).

Latvian Officials Meet with Baker

US Secretary of State James Baker met with Latvian Prime Minister Ivars Godmanis and Foreign Minister Janis Jurkans to talk about recent changes in Latvia, Baltic-Soviet relations, economic reforms, and aid. Baker reiterated the US policy of nonrecognition of the incorporation of the Baltic states into the USSR, adding that they had a special status vis-à-vis the Soviet Union.

Early Pay Raises for Workers in Health, Culture, and Education

Soviet Prime Minister Nikolai Ryzhkov announced on Central Television that about 7 million Soviet workers in the health service and in the culture and education sectors would get higher salaries beginning in 1991, and not in 1994 as had been planned. Health workers and teachers recently threatened to strike unless their living standards were improved.

Dukhobors Leave Georgia

Moscow News (No. 28) devoted a whole page to the Dukhobors, who have lived in Georgia for 150 years and are now returning to Russia. The Dukhobors, a Russian sect formed in the late eighteenth century, have preserved old Russian customs and rituals. They are leaving Georgia, the article says, because they are afraid that Georgia will secede from the Soviet Union.

Demonstration in Far East against Dumping Nuclear Submarines

Residents of the port town of Gavan in the Soviet Far East are protesting plans by the Soviet navy to disassemble and then dump obsolete nuclear-powered submarines in local waters. Protesters demonstrated today demanding that the area be declared a nuclear-free zone. On July 16, members of the Green Party picketed the checkpoint at the local naval base and prevented personnel from entering. There have been conflicting statements by naval officials about the planned submarine disposal, with the commander of the Pacific Fleet, Gennadii Khvatov, appearing to deny the plans (*Radio Moscow*, July 22).

Belorussia Cancels Leading Role of Communist Party

Belorussia became the latest Soviet republic to abolish the leading role of the Communist Party. The Belorussian Supreme Soviet amended Article 6 of the republic's constitution, which had guaranteed the Party's monopoly on political power. The constitution now allows various political parties, public organizations, and mass movements to take part in determining the republic's political, social, and economic development (*TASS*, July 20).

Saturday, July 21

Soviet Annexation of Baltic States Marked as Day of Tragedy

Contrary to the practice of recent decades, when the Soviet annexation of the Baltic states was observed as an official holiday, in 1990 the freely elected governments of Estonia, Latvia, and Lithuania denounced the takeover. The Presidium of the Latvian Supreme Council said that July 21, 1940, marked the beginning of "mass terror and genocide against the residents of Latvia"; the Lithuanian Presidium called it "a day of injury, humiliation, and tragedy" (*AP*, *UPI*, *AFP*, July 21).

Polish-Lithuanian Border Crossing Opened

The border crossing between Lazdijai, Lithuania and Ogrodniki, Poland—closed since early April—was reopened. Both sides will be able to cross without visas: a passport and an invitation from someone on the other side of the border will suffice. PAP quoted a Polish border guard as saying that he expected up to 10,000 Lithuanians and Poles to use the crossing every day.

Clashes Reported in Armenia

Krasnaya zvezda reported that a Soviet army unit had been attacked twenty kilometers southwest of Erevan. It said the attackers had seized thirty seven automatic rifles, ammunition, and a grenade launcher from troops. The report did not say whether there were any casualties. The same day, the Armenian Supreme Soviet placed limits on the actions of Soviet army and MVD troops on its territory, declaring that they could carry out punitive action only with the parliament's permission (*Central Television*, "Vremya," July 21).

Soviet Film-Maker Paradzhanov Dies

Armenian filmmaker Sergei Paradzhanov died in Erevan, following a long illness, TASS reported. He was sixty-six. Paradzhanov was jailed as a dissident several times and was barred from making feature-length films for fifteen years after the release of his film *Sayat Nova* (also known as *The Color of Pomegranates*). Among his best-known works are *Shadows of Our Forgotten Ancestors* (1964), *The Legend of Suram Fortress* (1984), and *Ashik Kerib* (1988).

Kumyks Demand Autonomous Territory

The Kumyks, a Turkic people living in Dagestan, have joined the long list of peoples asking for their own autonomous territory, Radio Moscow reported. The demand was made by the "Tenglik" (Equality) Committee at an unsanctioned meeting of over 2,000 Kumyks in the Dagestani capital, Makhachkala.

Ukrainian Parliament Wants Gold Back from England

The Ukrainian parliament was reported to be asking for the return of a barrel of gold sent to the Bank of England in the 18th century for safekeeping. Ukrainian military leader Colonel Pavel Polubotok sent the gold to the Bank of England before he set out for St. Petersburg for talks with the Russian imperial government. When Polubotok got to the city he was thrown in jail by Tsar Peter the Great and died there in 1723. TASS said Ukrainian deputy Roman Ivanychuk valued the gold at 16 trillion pounds sterling, or 29 trillion dollars (*AFP*, *Reuters*, July 21).

On July 23, the Bank of England said it had not yet found proof that the gold had been deposited. It also said that the claim probably could not be settled unless Britain recognized Ukraine as a sovereign state.

Sunday, July 22

Draft Debate Continues

The war of words between Marshal Sergei Akhromeev and civilian defense analyst Georgii Arbatov continues. On the television show "In the Service of the Fatherland,"

Akhromeev charged that separatist forces in the Baltic and Transcaucasus were undermining the military draft system and lowering the nation's military capabilities. He called for the government to enforce the draft laws in these republics and to prosecute draft evaders. More ominously, he said that the armed forces were the guarantors of the state's integrity and that they would act to prevent its dissolution. At the same time, however, he dismissed accusations voiced by liberals that the High Command was contemplating a military coup, calling it an insult to the officer corps. Akhromeev insisted, moreover, that the United States remained a military threat to the Soviet Union, pointing especially to US naval and air power.

Arbatov, in contrast, dismissed the military threat from abroad, saying that the greatest danger to Soviet security lay in dismal Soviet economic performance. He rejected any use of the armed forces for domestic policing duties, saying that such work should be left to the MVD troops. He called, finally, for faster military reform and argued that the current size and unwieldiness of the Soviet military machine made it vulnerable to attacks on the periphery. (See also *Izvestia*, July 20.)

A Betrayal behind Gorbachev's Victory over Ligachev

Writing in *Literaturnaya gazeta* (No. 29), its chief editor, Fedor Burlatsky, said that Gorbachev had "paid a high price" for his victory over conservatives at the Party congress—namely, that "the best representatives of the Party intelligentsia," such as Aleksandr Yakovlev, had had to quit the Central Committee. At the same time, Egor Yakovlev, the editor of *Moscow News,* revealed that Party officials had only agreed to part with Ligachev if Yakovlev went too. (In the election of Gorbachev's deputy, only 776 delegates voted for Ligachev, whereas at least 1,200 delegates regularly voted in favor of all other conservative proposals.)

In *Moscow News* (No. 29), Boris Reznik, a member of the commission set up by the congress to investigate the distribution of a forged account of Yakovlev's meeting with reformist political groups, revealed that the commission knew who had distributed the leaflets—namely, Igor Rodionov, the general responsible for breaking up the peaceful demonstration in Tbilisi on April 9, 1989.

El'tsin Says Western Aid Ought to Go to Russia

In an article in the Vienna newspaper *Kurier*, RSFSR leader Boris El'tsin argued that Western credit ought to go to the RSFSR and not to the Soviet Union. According to a

DPA account of his interview, El'tsin said this was the only way to ensure that the credits would go to a democratic movement and real economic reforms.

Soviet Muslim Delegation Seeks Release of Soviet POWs

A delegation of Soviet Muslim clergymen arrived in Islamabad on a mission to seek the release of Soviet soldiers held captive by the Afghan mujahidin, the Associated Press of Pakistan said. Grand Mufti Mukhammad-Sadiq Mukhammad-Yusuf, delegation leader and chairman of the Religious Board of Muslims of Central Asia, said that about 300 Soviet soldiers were believed to be held by the Afghan resistance. The five-man delegation was scheduled to hold talks with the leaders of the mujahidin government-in-exile in Peshawar. A Georgian POW was released on July 21.

On July 29, the delegation ended its visit to Pakistan having failed to win the release of any of the Soviet prisoners of war held by the Afghan resistance. The delegation leader said in Islamabad that talks with resistance officials had led only to an agreement to meet again, perhaps in October.

The same day, Afghan President Najibullah began a previously unannounced trip to the Soviet Union. Radio Kabul said it would be "a short visit" and that he would undergo a medical checkup during his stay (*AP*, *Reuters*, July 29).

Historian Warns of Growing Anti-Semitism

In an article in *Pravda*, historian Sergei Rogov said anti-Semitism in the Soviet Union had reached alarming proportions and threatened the process of political reform. The article, the most extensive official treatment of anti-Semitism in the *glasnost'* era, said hatred of Jews was no longer the preserve of extremists and had spread to some intellectuals. The article noted that 100,000 Soviet Jews had left the Soviet Union in 1989. It attacked publications openly espousing anti-Semitism and said current laws against racist propaganda should be enforced.

Kazakh President in United States

Nursultan Nazarbaev, president and Communist Party leader of Kazakhstan, was reported to be on a visit to the United States on a personal mission to explore opportunities for direct economic relations between US firms and his republic. According to a Radio Alma-Ata report, Nazarbaev has already met with a number of US government officials to promote his vision of Kazakhstan's economic and political sovereignty, which involves extensive connections with the outside world. In its issue for July 24, *Le Monde* noted that Kazakhstan's striving to realize economic independence had met with interested responses abroad. In addition to an Anglo-American consortium that wants to exploit the oil and gas fields of western Kazakhstan, a society called "Expan-Kazakhstan" has been set up in France to promote exchanges with the republic, and a direct air route between Paris and Alma-Ata is under consideration, which would give Western skiers access to the slopes near the Kazakh capital. Novosti noted on July 23 that a Kazakh-Indian joint construction venture had started to build a 400-bed hotel in the mountains near Alma-Ata.

Monday, July 23

Party Official Elected Chairman of Ukrainian Supreme Soviet

Leonid Kravchuk, second secretary of the Ukrainian Communist Party, was elected chairman of the Ukrainian Supreme Soviet after two rounds of voting. He replaces Vladimir Ivashko, who last week became deputy general secretary of the CPSU. The opposition group "Narodna Rada" withdrew from the second round of voting after issuing a statement saying: "Party interests have been given priority over the people's interests" (*Reuters*, *AP*, *TASS*, RL Ukrainian service, July 23).

CSCE Turns Down Baltic Republics Again

An appeal from Estonia, Latvia, and Lithuania for observer status in the CSCE process was turned down again. According to AFP, quoting the CSCE Secretariat, none of the thirty-five member states submitted the Baltic appeal—distributed to delegates on July 19—for consideration. The three Baltic republics last appealed for observer status in June at the CSCE human-rights conference in Copenhagen.

Galina Semenova Speaks Out on the Position of Women in the USSR

On the television program "Who Is Who" new Politburo member Galina Semenova spoke out strongly on the need for real action to improve the position of women in Soviet society. She said women were disadvantaged in the Soviet Union and felt like second-class citizens. She stated that, although existing women's associations had developed positive programs, these had not been followed up with practical measures. She said there was a need for real political force to support women and the family, and she added that the Party would not rely on slogans and empty promises since "the balance in the trust account is already zero." Semenova is responsible for a new Party portfolio on women's affairs, a sphere of activity that she defined as dealing with the problems of the family, women, and the women's movement.

Kaliningrad City Soviet Moves to Open City to Foreigners

In a move that appeared to violate Soviet law, the Kaliningrad City Soviet was reported to have agreed to allow foreign visitors from West Germany to visit the city (*Moscow News*, No. 28). Three groups of tourists traveling on a cruise liner were scheduled to visit the city on a trial basis. The oblast Party organization criticized the Kaliningrad City Soviet for overstepping its legal boundaries, pointing out that, according to Soviet law, Kaliningrad was still closed to foreigners.

New Newspapers and Radio for Moscow

TASS reported that the Moscow City Soviet had founded two new daily newspapers and a local radio station. Unlike previous organs of the city government, the two newspapers *Kuranty* and *Nezavisimaya gazeta* will not report to the Moscow City Soviet. A spokesman for the soviet stressed that it was "only a founder" and would not interfere in the operation of the newspapers. The radio station *Ekho Moskvy* was cofounded by the city soviet, the Journalism Faculty of Moscow State University, and the staff of *Ogonek*, which recently cut its ties with the Communist Party (see July 19).

Bryansk Goes Thirsty after Toxic Spill

TASS reported that a toxic chemical spill had forced the authorities in the city of Bryansk, in the western RSFSR, to shut off water supplies. Some forty tons of liquid tar from two damaged containers at a glass factory leaked into the soil, according to the report. Some of the tar was washed into the Ivotok and Desna Rivers, leading to high concentrations of formaldehyde and phenol.

Hungary Asks USSR to Condemn 1956 Intervention

The Hungarian parliament asked the Soviet Union to condemn the use of Soviet troops to crush the Hungarian revolution in 1956. The motion was introduced by a member of the Hungarian Democratic Forum, Gyorgy Csoti. He told parliament: "The Hungarian people have been waiting for decades to receive moral amends from the Soviet Union." On July 24, USSR Foreign Ministry spokesman Gennadii Gerasimov said in Prague that "the events of 1956 in Hungary, just like the events of 1968 in Czechoslovakia, must be considered inadmissible" (*AP*, July 25).

New Socioeconomic Program for Miners in Ukraine

Radio Moscow reported that a new socioeconomic program for mining towns in the Ukraine had been developed. The program foresees an increase in housing construction of 150 percent over the next five years. The report expressed hope that the miners would have to wait "not more than six years" for an apartment. Construction of hospitals, clinics, schools, and day-care centers will also be accelerated under the plan, and more attention will be given to food supplies and ecological questions.

Committee of Soldiers' Mothers Gives Figures on Deaths of Recruits

An article in *Moscow News* (No. 29) cited figures from the Committee of Soldier's Mothers on the peacetime deaths of army recruits. The committee claimed that 3,900 draftees had died in the past year alone and that, since the beginning of *perestroika*, 15,000 soldiers had died in irregular circumstances. The article cited letters from recruits and their parents detailing cases of brutality, and it printed the full text of a letter from the committee to the USSR Supreme Soviet and Mikhail Gorbachev, demanding that action be taken. The Soviet Armed Forces have so far not released their own figures on peacetime deaths of soldiers.

Soviet Union to Sell Rocket Engine to United States

Reuters reported that the Soviet Union was ready to sell its powerful RD-170 rocket engine to the United States in an effort to forge new ties with the US space program and earn hard currency. Reuters quoted the journal *Aviation Week and Space Technology* as saying that this was "the first time the engine is being made available as a stand-alone item together with Soviet technical support." The RD-170 is the largest rocket engine in the world and is fueled by kerosene and oxygen.

Soviet-Indian Summit

On the first day of their meeting in Moscow, Soviet President Mikhail Gorbachev and Indian Prime Minister Vishwanath Singh issued a statement reaffirming their commitment to building a nuclear-free and nonviolent world. Singh also met with Soviet Prime Minister Nikolai Ryzhkov, who assured him that trade between the two countries would not suffer as a result of Soviet economic reforms. In particular, India obtained an agreement from the Soviet Union to continue bilateral trade in rupees rather than in hard currency for at least five more years (*TASS*, *Reuters*, July 23).

Tuesday, July 24

USSR Announces Bold Policy on Foreign Currency

In an effort to soak up some of the foreign currency circulating in the Soviet economy, the government announced a new policy that will allow Soviet citizens to buy foreign and Soviet-made luxury items for hard currency. Commenting on the new policy, Deputy Prime Minister and Chief of the Foreign Economic Commission Stepan Sitaryan said that Soviet citizens held some 340 million dollars' worth of hard currency that they could not spend in the USSR. The new measures include the establishment of a network of special stores in which Soviet citizens can spend their hard currency and relaxed banking regulations that will allow Soviet citizens to deposit and withdraw their hard currency without special permission. Sitaryan said that the government would reconsider its interest-rate policy regarding these accounts in order to attract hard-currency savings.

At a press conference in Moscow on July 30, Chairman of the USSR State Bank Viktor Gerashchenko criticized the Soviet government's decision to lift the ban on Soviet citizens' holding foreign currency. Gerashchenko warned, AFP reported, that the decision would introduce a parallel currency, which the State Bank opposes. He added that "most people work for rubles and are unable to get foreign currency" and that legalization of the holding of foreign currency would be unjust to the vast majority.

Gorbachev Says Foreign Aid Tied to Capabilities

Gorbachev declared that the amount of Soviet foreign aid would in the future take into account "the real capabilities of our country" (*TASS*, July 24). Many observers noted that this could be Gorbachev's way of responding to Western pressure on the USSR to cut economic assistance to countries like Cuba, Libya, and Vietnam.

"Pamyat'" Leader on Trial

Konstantin Smirnov-Ostashvili, leader of a faction of the Russian nationalist movement "Pamyat'" called the "Union for Proportional National Representation," went on trial in Moscow (*TASS*, Western agencies, July 24). Ostashvili was accused of organizing an anti-Semitic protest in the Moscow Writers' Club in January, during which writers were beaten up, threatened, and told to leave Russia. His trial was adjourned for a day after the judge denied his request for "a lawyer from a democratic country." Ostashvili had told the court earlier that he did not trust his Moscow lawyer and that most Soviet lawyers were Jewish. He also denied being anti-Semitic but continued to accuse Soviet Jews of "holding the leading posts in our society." On the various factions of *Pamyat'*, see *Sobesednik*, No. 49.

On July 25, Ostashvili failed to appear in court for the second day of the trial. The judge ordered the police to find him.

Two New Parties Formed

Novosti Press Agency reported that two new parties had been created in the Soviet Union. The Information-Popular Party of Russia and the Information-Popular Party of the USSR were created to defend popular rights through the complete "*informatizatsiya*" (information saturation) of the population. According to their joint program, any citizen may join one or both parties to promote "the creation of an informed and law-abiding self-governing society of equal opportunity." Both parties were founded by governmental and cooperative news services, newspapers, and unions. The report did not mention where the parties were based or give the names of their members.

Latest on Soviet Emigration Law

A member of the USSR Supreme Soviet said the long-awaited law on emigration would "take into consideration the interests of Palestinians in the Israeli-occupied territories and Arabs in general." Speaking in Jordan, the legislator, a member of a parliamentary delegation, added that the new law would make it easier for Soviet emigrants to return to the Soviet Union and retain Soviet citizenship. Israel expects 150,000 Soviet immigrants this year, and Arab countries have expressed grave concern over the prospect that they will settle in the Israeli-occupied territories (*Reuters*, July 24).

The Guardian reported that for the first time a group of Soviet emigrants to Israel would depart from Finland on July 25 barring technical difficulties. Finland said it was allowing the flights on condition that the emigrants did not settle in the occupied territories. The Israeli government countered that it would not settle the immigrants on the West Bank but neither would it prevent them from moving there.

Kiev Transportation Workers Strike

Thousands of trolley-bus and tram drivers in Kiev went on strike, making hundreds of thousands of people late for work. By evening, the strike was over, after the Kiev City Soviet agreed to meet the strikers' demands, including higher pay, early retirement, compensation for work done during the Chernobyl' cleanup efforts, more housing, and spare parts for their vehicles. The transportation workers likened the intensity and nervous strain of their work to that of coal miners (*TASS*, *AP*, July 24).

Reports of Cholera and Bubonic Plague

TASS issued a report saying thirteen people on a camping trip had been hospitalized in Stavropol after contracting cholera from drinking spring water that was polluted with effluent. All those who had contact with the victims or who had drunk the water were also hospitalized. RSFSR First Deputy Minister of Health Viktor Panov said a group of doctors had been sent to Stavropol to take sanitary measures to prevent an epidemic.

On July 25, *Komsomol'skaya pravda* reported that a twenty-seven-year-old man had died of bubonic plague in the town of Makat in western Kazakhstan. The newspaper said rats carrying bubonic plague bacilli had been found along railway lines linking towns in Kazakhstan, Uzbekistan, and Turkmenistan. The director of the emergency epidemiological service in Tashkent, I. Akhmedov, called for "decisive and quick measures" to prevent an epidemic. According to the report, the first infected rat was found three weeks ago in the Karakalpak ASSR, and immediate measures were demanded.

These reports came just after the military commandant of Baku had warned about the possibility of an epidemic arising from unsanitary conditions in the city. Enormous piles of garbage were reported to have accumulated on the streets of Baku, and sewage and water purification systems were said to be in "a sorry state" (*Radio Moscow*, World Service, July 24).

On July 31, Soviet doctors said the source of the recent outbreak of cholera in Stavropol Krai was Syrian workers. TASS quoted USSR Surgeon-General Aleksandr Kondrusev as saying the Syrians were carrying cholera bacteria of a particularly resistant type. Kondrusev said forty-nine people had been infected with cholera in Stavropol Krai, including eleven Syrian workers.

Three Soviet Army Deserters Flee to West Germany

Three Soviet soldiers were reported to have deserted from their units in East Germany and gone to West Germany. Two soldiers crossed to West Germany on July 21 and asked for asylum, the Lower Saxony state government said. A third soldier went to the West on July 19 but did not request asylum and was in prison awaiting extradition, a spokesman said.

On July 26, a spokesman for the Lower Saxony government said the three soldiers would not be handed back to the Soviet authorities. He said the soldiers would be treated as asylum seekers (*Reuters*, July 26).

On July 30, five more Soviet soldiers crossed the open border between East and West Germany and asked for asylum in West Germany, DPA reported. Police said that the soldiers, wearing civilian clothing, arrived in a car with East German license plates.

Criminal Investigation Launched against Kalugin

Izvestia said the USSR's General Military Prosecutor had been ordered to start legal action against former KGB General Oleg Kalugin. Kalugin was accused of having disseminated state secrets in the mass media.

On July 27, Kalugin told *Komsomol'skaya pravda* that he did not believe he had revealed any state secrets in his publications. He said he had written only about illegal acts that must not be allowed in a state based on law.

Meanwhile, Kalugin continued his criticism of the KGB, saying that, as along as it remained in place, democracy would never be achieved in the Soviet Union. In an interview with *The Los Angeles Times*, Kalugin said the KGB was the institution that had changed the least under *perestroika* and that, although it had recently acquired a friendlier face, it could immediately revert to old practices if the political wind were to blow in that direction. Kalugin also said that *perestroika* was now at a deadlock and needed more energetic and vigorous people to move the process forward.

USSR Says 43,000 Died in Camps in Soviet Zone of Germany

The Soviet Foreign Ministry said that almost 43,000 Germans died in internment camps in the Soviet zone of Germany between 1945 and 1950. That is more than one-third of the 120,000 prisoners interned in the camps. The statement said that most had died of tuberculosis. The figures were compiled from Soviet archives at the request of East Germany, following the discovery of mass graves near the camps. Georgii Kenin, Deputy Director of the Foreign Ministry's Historic-Diplomatic Department, said that the archives did not show "deliberate mass physical annihilation" of the prisoners. But he did say that there were breaches of the rules on treatment of prisoners, "which at times recalled the monstrous crimes of the Nazis."

Flooding Causes Deaths and Damage Near Baikal

Severe flooding in Siberia west of Lake Baikal caused an undetermined number of deaths and left thousands of people homeless. TASS said heavy rains had resulted in widespread flooding, sweeping away more than 400 bridges and causing 400 million rubles' worth of damage. TASS said army and civil defense units had joined relief efforts.

Wednesday, July 25

Bush Pledges "Unflagging Support" for Balts

Speaking at a White House ceremony commemorating Captive Nations Week, US President George Bush renewed the United States' pledge of "unflagging support" for "the long quest for national self-determination" of the Baltic republics.

Gorbachev Cracks Down on Unofficial Armed Units

In the face of rising ethnic violence, President Mikhail Gorbachev issued a strongly worded decree ordering all illegally armed groups to disband and relinquish their weapons, ammunition, and explosives to MVD troops (*TASS*, Western agencies, July 25). Should these groups fail to comply, republican and local organs of power, as well as MVD and KGB troops, will be authorized by the decree to seize their arms. "If actions of these armed formations endanger the safety of the population and the state," the decree declared, "the USSR Minister of Internal Affairs has the right to use internal troops, and, under certain circumstances, the participation of Defense Ministry units is also authorized." The armed bands were given fifteen days to comply with the order. While TASS said the decree applied to all armed groups, it was clearly aimed at disarming militant forces in Armenia. Authorities there have reported increasing attacks on Soviet military personnel by Armenian nationalist groups.

On July 26, USSR Deputy Prosecutor-General Vladimir Kravtsev said militants in the Transcaucasian republics had seized thousands of firearms and explosives from security forces. Kravtsev described the situation following weapons thefts from security forces around the country as "exceptionally serious" (*TASS*, in English, July 26).

USSR Minister of Internal Affairs Vadim Bakatin stated on July 27 that military force would be used if the paramilitary groups in Armenia, whose strength he estimated at between 10,000 and 20,000 men, did not disband and surrender their arms. The head of the Armenian National Army, Razmik Vasilyan, was quoted as stating that his group would not comply with the decree but that he was ready for negotiations with Azerbaijan and Moscow to resolve tensions in the Transcaucasus (*AP, AFP, DPA, TASS*, in English, July 27).

On July 28, the Armenian Supreme Soviet voted by a wide margin to suspend Gorbachev's presidential decree of July 25 outlawing unauthorized military formations in the USSR, on the grounds that the decree violated Article 75 of the Armenian Constitution, which specifies that all-Union laws are effective in Armenia only after ratification by the republican parliament (*TASS*, July 28).

On July 30, the Armenian Supreme Soviet reiterated its ruling rejecting Gorbachev's decree but affirmed its readiness to negotiate with Gorbachev on the issue, according to a spokesman for the Armenian Pan-National Movement. Soviet television reported that the decree was being ignored in Armenia and that "armed attacks" were continuing.

On August 1, Radio Moscow's Interfax service reported that Armenian militants had attacked several police posts in the Erevan area over the previous two days in an attempt to seize additional weapons. On August 2, the Armenian Supreme Soviet reiterated that it was willing to negotiate over Gorbachev's decree (*TASS*, August 2). See RL 335/90.

Human-Rights Committee Created in RSFSR Parliament

The first-ever Soviet Committee on Human Rights was reported to have been created in the RSFSR Supreme Soviet. According to its chairman, human-rights activist Sergei Kovalev, the committee has a permanent staff of eighteen deputies and has already been contacted by over 1,000 people. Kovalev said that human rights could only be defended with the help of appropriate laws. He said he hoped that a human-rights institute of some kind would eventually be created but that for now his committee must help people who do not know where else to go. TASS noted that the committee was composed of members of other parties as well as Communists. Kovalev's deputy is Nikolai Arzhannikov, an organizer of the Leningrad Popular Front.

On July 29, TASS carried an interview with Kovalev. TASS, detailing the structure of the committee, said it consisted of thirty-six deputies, only half of whom would work full-time. Kovalev, who is also a member of the Presidium of the RSFSR Supreme Soviet, told TASS that the committee would work on the creation of separate Russian citizenship. Kovalev said that a special group of deputies had been set up to inspect conditions in Soviet labor camps and that a member of the group had just left for the North Caucasus to examine complaints from convicts in a labor camp near Rostov-on-Don.

Pravda Blames Liberal Media for Unrest

Pravda carried a front-page article accusing the liberal Soviet news media of inciting strikes and unrest. The *Pravda* article, which did not name any liberal news source in particular, warned that blaming the Party leadership and *perestroika* for the situation in the Soviet Union would lead to disorder and pogroms, which could bring down the Party and the country.

Soviet Banking Official on West German Loan

Reuters quoted Tomas Alibegov, a senior official at Vneshekonombank, as confirming that more than half the 5-billion-mark West German credit to the Soviet Union would be used to repay unpaid bills owed to German firms. Alibegov said he did not know the total figure of Soviet debts to Western firms.

De Beers to Market Soviet Diamonds

A subsidiary of South Africa's De Beers diamond cartel was reported to have signed an exclusive contract with the Soviet Union to export and sell the USSR's rough diamonds. Under the deal, the subsidiary pledged to advance 1 billion dollars to the Soviet Union against future diamond deliveries.

Kurds Ask Gorbachev for Area to Settle

Kurdish refugees inside the Soviet Union have asked Gorbachev to provide them with an area to settle in the southern part of the RSFSR. TASS said the association of Soviet Kurds had staged a rally in Moscow at which they called for a new homeland. It also quoted *Krasnaya zvezda* as saying that 18,000 Kurdish refugees from Armenia and 2,000 from Uzbekistan had gathered in the Krasnodar area.

Soviet General Sees Possibility of Soviet Union Joining NATO

In an interview with *Die Welt*, Major General Gelii Batenin said he could imagine a situation in which the Soviet Union would join NATO as a military partner. He said this could happen if a comprehensive system of stability and security could be created within Europe. He suggested this could be done within the Helsinki process.

Thursday, July 26

Gorbachev Asks West for Aid

Soviet President Mikhail Gorbachev joined other politicians in asking for foreign aid to help make Soviet economic reform work. He said aid was needed—some straight away—to produce more food and consumer goods so the reform process would not lose momentum. Gorbachev spoke at a Moscow press conference after meeting with Italian Prime Minister Giulio Andreotti, the current president of the European Community. Andreotti supported giving aid to Moscow. In particular, Gorbachev said the USSR needed help converting its defense industries to produce food and consumer goods. He added, however, that the USSR "cannot depend on foreign sponsors to fix its economy" but must depend mainly on itself. He said any aid would not be "a handout" but would be paid back. RSFSR Prime Minister Ivan Silaev said the republic's move to a market economy would also require foreign aid in order to avoid big price rises (*AP*, *Reuters*, *AFP*, *DPA*, July 26). See RL 337/90.

El'tsin Announces Measures to Help with the Harvest

Chairman of the RSFSR Supreme Soviet Boris El'tsin announced measures to boost harvesting in the RSFSR. In an article in *Sovetskaya Rossiya,* he said the Russian government would pay all those involved in the harvesting and transportation of crops in special "Harvest '90" coupons allowing them to buy goods in short supply. He also said farmers would be allowed to sell freely all produce in excess of quotas set for delivery to the government (*AFP*, July 26). The Soviet press reported earlier this week that the harvest was being threatened by a shortage of fuel for farming machinery and farmers' refusal to sell to the state.

Georgian Protesters Block Main Transcaucasus Rail Link

Approximately 800 representatives of Georgian unofficial organizations began a sit-down strike at the rail intersection in the west Georgian city of Samtredia. They were demanding that the Georgian SSR Supreme Soviet convene immediately to pass a law regulating a multiparty system so that those of the estimated 100 alternative parties in Georgia who wished to field candidates for the October 28 elections might do so.

On July 28, Radio Moscow said hundreds of people calling for a multiparty system in Georgia had virtually halted rail traffic on the main railway line through the Caucasus. The Georgian government urged the protesters to end their action (*Rabochaya tribuna*, July 29).

By July 29, more than thirty trains carrying 25,000 passengers had been halted by the protest, and measures were under way to evacuate passengers by air. The collegium of the USSR Ministry of Railways met in emergency session and called upon the Georgian leadership and the Georgian Popular Front to take "immediate measures" to restore normal rail traffic. A statement subsequently issued by Chairman of the Georgian Supreme Soviet and Party First Secretary Givi Gumbaridze warned that force might be used if the protesters did not disperse peacefully (*Radio Moscow*, July 29).

On July 30, TASS reported that Zviad Gamsakhurdia was behind the protest. Gamsakhurdia, head of the Georgian Helsinki Union and the Round Table coalition of informal groups, was campaigning for an immediate session of the republic's Supreme Soviet to be held in order to pass a law on multicandidate elections in preparation for the Supreme Soviet elections on October 28. Speaking on Georgian television on July 29, Gamsakhurdia said that the blockade would continue until his demands were met. The Soviet authorities responded by halting all rail shipments of goods to Georgia. Gumbaridze warned of "anarchy, chaos, and extreme, unpredictable consequences" if a compromise were not reached.

On July 31, Soviet television said that the rail blockade in Georgia had been extended from the junction at Samtredia to Tbilisi and that the situation had been exacerbated by a strike of engine drivers in Sukhumi. Some 40,000 passengers and 20,000 rail cars were stranded. The official Georgian news agency, Gruzinform, reported that talks between the authorities and members of the coalition of informal groups had broken down on July 30.

On August 1, the Georgian news agency Iberia said the blockade had ended after the Georgian Communist Party daily *Kommunist* published a draft law outlining changes in the election rules in Georgia. The same day, Gumbaridze said the republic would not comply for the time being with Gorbachev's order to disarm irregular military units. Gumbaridze said the decree would not be implemented in Georgia during the term of the current Georgian Supreme Soviet (*Radio Moscow*, August 1).

On August 2, Radio Moscow said criminal proceedings would be instituted against those responsible for losses caused by the Georgian railway blockade.

Ukrainian Deputies Leave Party

Twenty-eight Ukrainian Supreme Soviet deputies announced that they were leaving the Party. Kharkov deputy Sylenko told the Supreme Soviet that the deputies, all members of the Democratic Platform, had signed a declaration stating their intention to resign. Another member of the Democratic Platform, Stanislav Lylyk, told RFE/RL that the declaration said the Party had had a chance to reform itself at the Twenty-eighth Party Congress but had wasted the chance (*Radio Kiev*, RL Ukrainian service, July 26).

Finance Minister Says Budget Deficit Has Decreased

USSR Finance Minister Valentin Pavlov said the USSR's budget deficit had been significantly reduced in the first half of 1990. Pavlov told *Trud* that the deficit for this period was 24 billion rubles. The deficit for all of 1988 was 120 billion rubles, but it declined in 1989. Pavlov also said the transition to a market economy must not begin with retail price increases. He said that the central wholesale and agricultural purchase prices as well as the pricing system should be changed first.

Moldavia Says Its Parliament Must Approve USSR Laws

The Moldavian parliament ruled that it must approve any Soviet laws and presidential decrees before they can take effect in the republic. It also decided that it could restrict or suspend Soviet laws that it had already approved. The moves were amendments to the Moldavian Constitution. They were based on proposals outlined in the declaration of sovereignty that the parliament approved in June (*TASS*, July 26).

Soviet Censorship Agency to Remain in Business

The director of the main Soviet censorship agency Glavlit said his agency would not be abolished despite the new law on the press that forbids state censorship of the media. In an interview with *Izvestia*, Vladimir Boldyrev said his agency would continue to check foreign publications and audio and visual materials mailed to the USSR.

Friday, July 27

Baltic Republics Refuse to Participate in New Union Treaty

The three Baltic leaders signed a joint statement announcing that no representatives of their governments would take part in the drafting of the new USSR treaty of the Union. They also declared that, in drafting treaties with foreign countries or other republics, Baltic independence must be recognized; that the three-plus-one principle was favored in Baltic-Soviet talks; that the Baltic republics had no territorial, property, or other claims against one another; and that, if any of the other twelve Union republics had territorial, property, or other claims against the Baltic republics, they should make these known within one month.

Soviet Scientists to Monitor Baltic Sea Pollution

A team of Soviet scientists said it planned to collect data on pollution in the Baltic Sea. "We want to set up a computer station to monitor pollution in the area to prevent another Chernobyl'," said Academician Boris Laskorin. The Baltic Sea is one of the most polluted in the world, with the Soviet Union depositing between 10 and 15 percent of its waste in it. The project was expected to cost 500,000 rubles (*Reuters*, July 27).

Gromov Opposes Depoliticization

Colonel General Boris Gromov told Novosti Press Agency that he opposed the depoliticization of the Soviet army. The commander of the Kiev Military District said that political officers had played an important role in Afghanistan. While the military-political organs should be reformed, he said, they should not be eliminated. Gromov also said that the conservative views of Colonel General Al'bert Makashov were not representative of the army as a whole, and he denied that there was a split in the armed forces between the High Command and middle- and lower-level officers.

New Air Force Chief Named

Krasnaya zvezda reported that Evgenii Shaposhnikov had been appointed commander in chief of the Soviet Air Force and a USSR deputy minister of defense. The forty-eight-year-old Shaposhnikov had been first deputy commander in chief of the Air Force since 1988. He succeeded Marshal of Aviation Aleksandr Efimov, who had occupied the post since 1984.

Belorussia Declares Sovereignty

Belorussia became the latest Soviet republic to proclaim its sovereignty. Voting today, the republican Supreme Soviet approved a declaration of state sovereignty very similar to Ukraine's. In addition to asserting the supremacy of Belorussian laws and Belorussia's full jurisdiction over the resources located on its territory, the declaration stated that the republic had the right to maintain its own army and security forces, appoint its own procurator, and issue its own currency. The text also expressed Belorussia's wish to become a "neutral" state and asserted the republic's independence in external relations—Belorussia is already a member of the United Nations in its own right (*Radio Minsk*, July 27).

Peasants Send Complaint to Gorbachev

Radio Moscow reported that the Soviet Peasants' Union had sent a statement to Mikhail Gorbachev complaining about their poor social situation and threatening to take collective action unless their situation was improved. The statement was published by *Sel'skaya zhizn'*. The same day, *Pravda* reported that kolkhoz workers in the Kostroma region were threatening to withhold their produce unless they were given more fuel, machinery and spare parts, and extra labor at reasonable prices to bring in the harvest.

Rafsanjani Urges Soviet Cooperation with OPEC to Raise Oil Prices

Iranian President Ali Akbar Rafsanjani said the Soviet Union should cooperate with OPEC to raise the world price of crude oil. Speaking in Teheran, Rafsanjani suggested a price of 30 dollars a barrel. This would be an increase of 12 dollars a barrel over current prices charged by OPEC cartel countries. The Soviet Union, the world's biggest oil producer, is not a member of OPEC. Rafsanjani's comments came as OPEC oil ministers began their mid-year conference in Geneva (*AFP*, *Reuters*, July 27).

Saturday, July 28

Gorbachev Meets Economists and Journalists

Gorbachev met with leading Soviet journalists and economists who advocate a market economy. Among them were Nikolai Shmelev, Vasilii Selyunin, Larisa Piyasheva, Anatolii Strelyanyi, and Yurii Chernichenko. The meeting was also attended by Aleksandr Yakovlev and by Gorbachev's economic adviser, Nikolai Petrakov. The current economic and political situation in the USSR was discussed. During the meeting Gorbachev said foreign aid was crucial to give him room to maneuver while pursuing *perestroika*. Gorbachev said some people thought that the harder things got for the USSR without aid, the more radical reforms would become. But he said that in fact "a lack of room to maneuver could force us to interfere more in economic activities" (*TASS*, in English, July 28).

The same day, Prime Minister Ryzhkov and Foreign Minister Shevardnadze met in Moscow with the managing director of the International Monetary Fund, Michel Camdessus. TASS said they discussed economic reform, the introduction of the convertible ruble, and aid. After the meeting, Shevardnadze said the USSR was ready to begin discussions on membership in the IMF.

Reporter Says He Was Demoted for Covering Sensitive Stories

A Soviet broadcasting journalist, Aleksandr Zhetvin, told *Argumenty i fakty* (No. 30) that he had been demoted for reporting politically sensitive stories on state-run radio and television. Zhetvin said one such instance occurred in February, 1989, when he prepared a commentary for Radio Moscow about new Polish archival documents showing that the NKVD had been responsible for the massacre of Polish officers in Katyn. At the time, the Soviet Union was still denying NKVD involvement in the massacre, blaming it on the Nazis. Zhetvin told *Argumenty i fakty* that he had been suspended from work for three months as a punishment for his commentary. He also said he had been disciplined again in February and June of this year for covering a prodemocratic rally outside the Kremlin and for questioning Soviet leaders' travel privileges.

Vladivostok Reported Closed to Tourists

Opened to foreigners with much fanfare at the end of 1988, Vladivostok has now been closed to tourists until further notice, TASS reported. The news service said the local authorities had taken this step without providing any explanation, thus giving rise to "all kinds of stories and rumors about plague and cholera" there. On August 2, Moscow media reported that there was a threat to the water supply, which had been contaminated as a result of a recent typhoon. Vladivostok is the home port of the Soviet navy's Pacific Fleet.

Moldavian Parliament Rejects Gagauz Autonomy

The Moldavian Supreme Soviet rejected a declaration of autonomy by the republic's Gagauz population, TASS reported. The parliament also rejected the idea of forming any autonomous republics within the republic, noting that Moldavians were the only indigenous people. It described the republic's minorities as ethnic groups.

Gorky Street Gets Old Name Back

The Moscow City Soviet changed the name of Gorky Street back to its old name, Tverskaya Street, according to TASS. Called Tverskaya from the fifteenth century onwards, it was renamed in 1932 to honor Maxim Gorky, one of Stalin's favorite writers. *Izvestia* ridiculed Gorky Street as "a living classic of Socialist Realism" and praised the name change.

Press Invited to CPSU Secretariat Meetings

The press was allowed to cover a meeting of the CPSU Central Committee Secretariat. TASS said the decision to admit reporters was "unprecedented." The Secretariat oversees the Party's daily activities. TASS said the July 28 session, chaired by Gorbachev, discussed the work of Party bodies in implementing the decisions of the Twenty-eighth Party Congress.

Sunday, July 29

***Pravda* Reports Deepening Economic Crisis**

Midyear figures released in *Pravda* painted a gloomy picture of the Soviet economy: gross national product fell by 1 percent compared with the first six months of 1989. Labor productivity fell 1.5 percent, yet the average wage rose by nearly 9 percent. As a result, the buying power of the ruble dropped. There was a 7-percent increase in the prices of consumer goods and services in 1989. The balance of trade continued to worsen during the first half of the year: the value of exports dropped by about 10 percent, while the value of imports rose by nearly 3 percent, compared with the first half of 1989.

On July 20, *Izvestia* reported that gas extraction had increased by 3 percent, that oil extraction had decreased by 5 percent, and that coal extraction had fallen by 6 percent—in all, 2 percent less fuel was obtained during the first half of 1990 than during the same period in 1989.

Navy Day Marked

The Soviet media carried a number of interviews with the Naval High Command to mark Soviet Navy Day. On the television program "Na sluzhbe otechestvu," the commander of Soviet Naval Forces criticized liberal commentators who had called for the full professionalization of the Soviet Armed Forces. Admiral Vladimir Chernavin called for reform to take place within the confines of the present mixed system of professionals and conscripts. He also said that military professionals had to view "reasonable sufficiency" in more precise, concrete terms than did politicians. In the area of naval forces, he repeated the often-used argument that the West continues to enjoy clear superiority, and he said that the Soviet Union had to counter it. Chernavin also called for the retention of political officers in the navy.

The commander of the Baltic Fleet told TASS on July 28 that, while military tensions in Europe had decreased, the West had been unwilling to match Soviet cuts in naval forces. Admiral Vitalii Ivanov implied, in fact, that an obstacle to independence for the Baltic countries was Western intransigence in this area.

Arbatov Again Criticizes Military Conservatives

Academician Georgii Arbatov told Czechoslovak television that the conservative wing of the armed forces was endangering *perestroika.* Arbatov called for fully professional armed forces as a means of bringing the High Command directly under civilian control. He said that there were various conservative elements in the armed forces who "believe that they alone are a safeguard for the state's security." He said that only the president and the parliament should play that role, while "the army is here only to execute decisions." He added that the state's security was dependent on more than military power.

Tuva Becomes New Center of Ethnic Conflict

Radio Moscow said interethnic tensions in Tuva had led people to flee the area and generated many economic problems. Radio Moscow was citing the weekly *Ekonomika i zhizn'* (No. 29), which reminded the Tuvinians that their autonomous republic imported 80 percent of the goods it needed and that the total value of imports (330 million rubles annually) was eleven times the value of the republic's exports.

On July 3, *Izvestia* reported that hostility directed against the Russian-speaking population had resulted in eighty-eight deaths in recent months. After the murder of two fishermen and a schoolboy, thousands of inhabitants of the Tuvinian capital, Kyzyl, demanded the resignation of the oblast Party committee and the republican Council of Ministers and Ministry of Internal Affairs.

On August 3, RSFSR Prime Minister Ivan Silaev met with officials from the Tuva Autonomous Republic to discuss the tensions there. TASS said Silaev was planning to visit the republic to try to solve the problems personally.

Central Asian Muslims to Get Pakistani Help

The chairman of the Religious Board of Muslims of Central Asia, Mufti Mukhammad-Sadiq Mukhammad-Yusuf, signed an agreement with the Pakistani Ministry of Religious Affairs under which Pakistan will undertake to provide Islamic literature and help establish mosques and Islamic schools in Soviet Central Asia, Reuters and AP reported. The mufti praised *perestroika* to Western correspondents, noting that it had enabled those who had previously practiced Islam secretly to come out into the open.

Seven to Stand Trial for Urals Train Disaster

Izvestia said seven Soviet officials would go on trial in connection with the train disaster in the Urals that killed nearly 600 people. The accident occurred on June 3, 1989, when gas leaking from a pipeline caused an explosion and destroyed two trains that were passing each other on the line between Ufa and Chelyabinsk. *Izvestia* quoted investigator Vladimir Lysenko as saying there had been gross negligence in the construction of the pipeline.

Prunskiene Contradicts Landsbergis on Negotiations with USSR

On July 29, Lithuanian Prime Minister Kazimiera Prunskiene said negotiations with the Soviet leadership were more important for Lithuania's independence than talks with the Russian Federation. Lithuanian Supreme Council President Vytautas Landsbergis said earlier in July that talks with the RSFSR might be as important as talks with the USSR. Prunskiene emphasized, however, that it was the USSR, not the RSFSR, that controlled the army, the borders, and other important spheres. Her comments were carried by TASS.

Monday, July 30

Ukrainian Supreme Soviet Orders Conscripts Home

In the first important test of the power of sovereignty, the Ukrainian parliament voted to order all Ukrainian conscripts and police stationed outside the republic to return home by December. Troops serving in places of major ethnic unrest were ordered to return to Ukraine by October 1. The resolution also urged the parliaments of Armenia, Azerbaijan, and Kirgizia to use their own forces to maintain law and order on their territory.

The resolution, reasserting a major point contained in Ukraine's recently adopted declaration of sovereignty, stated that Ukrainian troops may not serve in other Soviet republics without the permission of the parliament (*Reuters*, July 30).

A USSR Defense Ministry spokesman said on July 31 that Ukraine's resolution could impair the Soviet Union's capacity to defend itself, AP reported. But Ukrainian Supreme Soviet Chairman Leonid Kravchuk defended Kiev's demand for the recall of Ukrainian troops from other republics (*Reuters*, July 31).

Yakutia Discusses Draft Sovereignty Declaration

Radio Moscow reported that a draft declaration of state sovereignty by the Yakut ASSR and a draft law delimiting powers between the Yakut ASSR, the USSR, and the RSFSR had been published in the Yakut ASSR press and were being widely discussed by the population, Radio Moscow reported. The purpose of the draft documents was to raise the status of the autonomous republic to that of "a sovereign state within the RSFSR." Under all-Union legislation, an autonomous republic has only recently been designated "a state" and is not considered sovereign. The draft law delimiting powers between the Yakut ASSR, the USSR, and the RSFSR appeared to be the first of its kind at the level of an autonomous republic.

The Yakut ASSR has more reason than most to want to lay claim to its immensely rich natural resources; it produces nearly all Soviet diamonds and large quantities of gold, tin, antimony, valuable furs, coking coal concentrate, and timber. Not only are the prices the republic receives for these products artificially low, but it sees little or none of the foreign currency they earn.

Belorussian First Secretary Stresses Need for Communist Party

Belorussian Party leader Efrem Sokolov told *Pravda* that the Belorussian Communist Party was the only political force capable of shouldering the burden of the republic's economic and social problems, TASS reported. Sokolov said that, if the Party were to leave the political arena, the result would be chaos. Sokolov made himself very unpopular in the republic in 1988 for suppressing the activities of unofficial groups.

Improving Rural Living Standards in Uzbekistan

Radio Moscow reported that Uzbek President Islam Karimov had signed a decree ordering that the installation of water mains be tripled and that of gas mains quadrupled in rural areas of Uzbekistan over the next two years. The report noted that only 20 percent of rural families had access to natural gas and that more than 5 million rural inhabitants did not have piped drinking water. Access to clean drinking water is a critical problem in rural areas of all the Central Asian republics. Karimov's decree seemed to represent a serious effort to relieve some of the economic and social problems that have fueled strife in the region.

Draft Law on Psychiatry Published

The draft law on psychiatry just published in the Soviet Union was reported to include provisions for jailing doctors who confine healthy people in psychiatric institutions, a practice that has long besmirched the reputation of the Soviet psychiatric community. TASS quoted Marat Vartanyan, director of the All-Union Center for Mental

Health, as saying the bill offered reliable protection against abuses of psychiatry. The bill also said that clinical psychiatric treatment must be voluntary and that patients had a right to be informed about the nature of their illness, to choose doctors, and to discuss treatment. Disputes must be settled in court.

Religious Educational Center Established

Ogonek (No. 29) reported that a new religious educational organization, "The Mother of God Center," had been established. Its members are currently giving religious instruction in eight Moscow schools. One of the organizers, Father Kiprian, noted that the center faced serious difficulties, owing to a lack of religious literature and money to pay teachers. He appealed to the public for support and cooperation.

Latvian Officials in Washington

Latvian Prime Minister Ivars Godmanis and Foreign Minister Janis Jurkans met US President George Bush and asked for greater support for Latvian independence. After the White House meeting, Godmanis said they had encouraged Bush to shift US policy from nonrecognition of the forced incorporation of the Baltic states into the USSR to full support for their independence (*AP*, *UPI*, July 30). On August 2, Godmanis was quoted by TASS as saying the visit to the United States had been a political success.

Tuesday, July 31

Shenin Wants to Change Party's Cadres Policy

Politburo member and Party Secretary for Cadres Oleg Shenin told *Pravda* he planned a major change in Party personnel policy. He said that leading posts should be occupied not by professional Party functionaries but by historians, political scientists, psychologists, sociologists, philosophers, and journalists. He also indicated that, in contrast to past practice, he, not the Party second secretary, would be in charge of Party cadres. Vladimir Ivashko, he added, would work on socioeconomic problems and run the Secretariat. In other comments, Shenin said the Party would not interfere in the economy, focusing instead on "concrete" questions such as social conditions and ecological problems. Shenin said the creation of the Russian Communist Party had had both positive and negative consequences, and he rejected the supposition that the conservative Ivan Polozkov would dominate the organization's policies.

Kalugin Files Suit against Gorbachev

Oleg Kalugin, formerly a general in the KGB, filed suit against Mikhail Gorbachev, Nikolai Ryzhkov, and Vladimir Kryuchkov, *Komsomol'skaya pravda* reported. In a statement to a Moscow court, Kalugin said that to deprive him of his military rank, decorations, and pension was illegal. Also on July 31, USSR people's deputy Sergei Belozertsev requested the Supreme Soviet's Constitutional Oversight Committee to look into this matter (*TASS*, July 31).

Volgograd Begins "500 Days" Program

Volgograd Oblast began implementing the RSFSR's "500 Days" economic program, which aims to create a market economy in the Russian Federation. "Vremya" reported that from September any person or group, including foreigners, would be permitted to buy a small store or factory, have the status of "a legal person," and open a bank account in Volgograd Oblast. Volgograd officials said they hoped such steps would both soak up the excess rubles in the economy and bring foreign currency into the government coffers. TASS also reported that the Volgograd Oblast Soviet had removed the prohibition on the import of goods into the region by cooperatives.

Shevardnadze-Baker Talks

The Soviet and US foreign ministers, Eduard Shevardnadze and James Baker, met in the Siberian city of Irkutsk for talks on a possible second summit, Afghanistan, regional conflicts, and the Helsinki process, Reuters and AP reported. Disarmament, cooperation in economic matters, and the joint exploration of space were also on the agenda.

On August 1, Baker and Shevardnadze ended their first round of talks and held a joint news conference (*Reuters*, *TASS*, August 1). At the conference, Shevardnadze said the USSR would stop production on January 1, 1991, of intercontinental ballistic missiles mounted on rail cars. Baker welcomed the announcement but said it would not immediately alter the US position on a treaty to reduce strategic weapons systems. The officials said they had not reached agreement on settling the Afghan conflict but had narrowed their differences (*Reuters*, *AP*, August 2).

USSR to Reduce Arms Exports to North Korea

The Japanese newspaper *Sankei Shimbun* quoted Valentin Falin as saying the Soviet Union would reduce arms exports to North Korea. Falin said the Soviet Union had had many difficulties with Pyongyang recently over various issues. He also confirmed that oil exports to North Korea had been cut back (*Reuters*, July 31).

Polluted Water in Yaroslavl

Radio Moscow reported that the drinking water of the city of Yaroslavl, northeast of Moscow, had been polluted by a chemical spill. Authorities shut off water supplies temporarily after large concentrations of phenol and petroleum products were found in the city's reservoir. Although they failed to identify the source of the pollutants, the authorities later resumed supplies.

Supreme Court Rehabilitates More Victims of Stalin

TASS said the USSR Supreme Court had rehabilitated 170 people who were repressed under Stalin. Among those rehabilitated were persons shot in September, 1941, in the Orel prison for alleged "defeatist agitation." TASS said they had been executed on Stalin's orders without trial.

***Moskovskie vedomosti* Is Back**

Radio Moscow reported that the newspaper *Moskovskie vedomosti*, published between 1756 and 1917, would resume publication under the auspices of a cooperative enterprise. Its chief editor, Leonid Krasner, said it would publish a chronology of current events in Moscow in addition to items about the city's history.

The Month of August

Wednesday, August 1

Gorbachev and El'tsin Cooperate on Economic Reforms

Gorbachev and El'tsin began to cooperate in designing an economic reform program for the USSR, according to TASS and Western agencies. This approach highlighted the increasing role of the RSFSR in driving *perestroika*. Gorbachev and El'tsin commissioned a group of experts to take primary responsibility for the drafting of a reform program to be ready in September. The group met for the first time on August 1. One of its members, Gorbachev's economic adviser Nikolai Petrakov, told AP that "the 500-day plan for economic reform" recently adopted for the RSFSR would serve as the general basis for Union-wide plans. E'ltsin attended a meeting of the new group on August 6. Its core members were listed by Radio Moscow on August 4 as: Stanislav Shatalin, Nikolai Petrakov, Leonid Abalkin, G. Yavlinsky, A. Vavilov, L. Grigor'ev, A. Zadornov, V. Martynov, V. Mashchits, A. Mikhailov, Boris Fedorov, Nikolai Shmelev, and Evgenii Yasin.

Problems with the Harvest

Prime Minister Nikolai Ryzhkov spoke on "Vremya" about problems with the harvest. Unless emergency measures were taken, he said, at least a quarter of this year's bumper grain crop could rot in the fields. Shortages of labor, fuel, and farming equipment were the main cause of the crisis.

On July 28, *Trud* reported that peasants in Perm Oblast had gone on strike and refused to deliver milk to the city's residents unless they helped bring in the harvest. A state of emergency was declared in Yaroslavl Oblast because of problems with the harvest (*TASS*, July 30).

On August 8, *Izvestia* said that the Moscow City Soviet had decided to send 40,000 residents of the capital to the countryside to help bring in the harvest, which was rotting in the fields. Radio Moscow reported that five oblasts—Chelyabinsk, Tver, Ivanovo, Yaroslavl, and Kuibyshev—had declared states of emergency due to harvest problems and that they soon would be joined by a sixth, Voronezh.

On August 9, Moscow announced that some state purchase prices for farm goods would rise by an average of 32 percent with effect from January 1, 1991 (*Radio Moscow*, August 10).

On August 15, Soviet newspapers appealed to readers to help bring in this year's harvest. *Komsoml'skaya pravda* said an enormous amount of grain was "sticking in the throat of our already gasping economy." *Krasnaya zvezda* said the USSR Ministry of Defense had sent troops and 10,000 trucks to the fields to help harvest and haul the grain. The Ukrainian government was said to have ordered students from vocational schools and universities to help out (*TASS*, *Radio Moscow*, August 15, 0600).

On August 20, *Pravda* reported that at least a million tons of grain was spoiling every day owing to a lack of proper storage and transportation facilities. The newspaper called for emergency measures to bring in the bumper crop. TASS said the Soviet government had allocated an additional 600,000 tons of fuel for gathering and transporting the harvest.

On August 25, *Izvestia* reported that half of the Soviet Union's crops were still awaiting transport to processing and storage facilities. The newspaper cited three main bottlenecks that were clogging the transportation system: a shortage of railroad cars; work stoppages that prevented full railroad cars from moving the crops; and the unwillingness of the authorities to unload railway cars that did make it to storage points, because it was cheaper to use the cars as silos than to organize the unloading.

Party Congress Delegates Name Their Favorites

Argumenty i fakty (No. 28) reported on a poll taken at the Twenty-eighth Party Congress, in which 2,066 delegates—about 40 percent of the total—agreed to name their favorite leader. Twenty-seven people were named by at least 1 percent of the respondents. Gorbachev topped the list, named by 54.4 percent of those polled; Aleksandr Yakovlev was second with 20.6 percent; Internal Affairs Minister Vadim Bakatin was third with 16.7 percent; and Prime Minister Nikolai Ryzhkov was fourth with 12.7 percent. Egor Ligachev landed in eighth place, having been named by 8.1 percent of the respondents.

Reduction in Number of Generals Recommended

The chief of the General Staff of the Soviet Armed Forces told TASS that the armed forces recommended reducing the present number of Soviet generals by at least 30 percent. Some of them would be replaced by more junior officers; other slots would be eliminated, General Mikhail Moiseev said. He added that the proposal was part of a broader plan to reduce armed forces personnel by half a million men and that the reduction of generals could begin this year. Moiseev also welcomed an earlier US announcement that the United States would be reducing the number of its generals.

Ukraine Declared Ecological Disaster Area

Following the example of Belorussia, the Ukrainian Supreme Soviet declared the whole of Ukraine an ecological disaster zone because of the Chernobyl' accident, Radio Moscow reported. The parliament also proposed a program costing 17 billion rubles to deal with the consequences of the accident and called for the evacuation of an unspecified number of people. The eleven-point resolution gave the Ukrainian government until December 1 to come up with a plan to shut down the Chernobyl' plant.

Another Memorial to Lenin Removed

Chervonograd, a mining center in Lvov Oblast, became the latest town in Western Ukraine to take down its statue of Lenin, Radio Moscow reported. On August 9, the Ukrainian Party Central Committee issued a strong protest against the dismantling of Lenin monuments in Chervonograd and Ternopol (*TASS*, August 9).

Poles Press Moscow to Question Katyn Officer

Polish Justice Minister Aleksander Bentkowski has asked the Soviet Union to question a former NKVD official said to be responsible for the massacre of Polish officers at Katyn, the *Financial Times* reported. The official concerned is General Petr Soprunenko, now eighty-two and living in Moscow, who, as an NKVD officer, signed the list of the Poles selected for execution in the spring of 1940. After Stalin's death, in the 1950s, several NKVD officials were arrested and sentenced to various terms in prison, but the majority have gone unpunished. Any move against Soprunenko could set a precedent.

Popular Front Becomes Formal Opposition

The thirty-five members of the Belorussian Popular Front in the Belorussian Supreme Sovier combined to create a formal opposition group. Popular Front Chairman Zyanon Paznyak said the opposition deputies would concentrate on drafting new laws on land use, private property, and Belorussian citizenship. Paznyak told RFE/RL the opposition also wanted action on a new constitution to incorporate provisions of the sovereignty declaration approved on July 27 (RL Belorussian service, August 1). On August 11, a Citizens' Council was reported to have been formed in Belorussia under the auspices of the Belorussian Popular Front, the independent Workers' Union, and various strike committees (*Central Television*, August 11).

Thursday, August 2

The Soviet Union and the Gulf Crisis

On August 2, the USSR called for the "swift and unconditional" withdrawal of Iraqi forces from Kuwait. In the first official Soviet response to the Iraqi invasion, USSR Foreign Ministry spokesman Yurii Gremitskikh said the territorial integrity of Kuwait must be restored and protected (*TASS*, August 2). Deputy Foreign Minister Aleksandr Belonogov met with Iraq's ambassador to the USSR, Ghafil Jassim Hussain, and called on Iraq to observe a UN Security Council resolution demanding the immediate withdrawal of Iraqi troops from Kuwait (*TASS*, August 2).

On August 3, in an unprecedented measure of cooperation regarding a regional conflict, the United States and the Soviet Union issued a joint statement condemning Iraq's invasion of Kuwait and calling on all countries to cut off arms shipments to Iraq. The statement also demanded that Iraq withdraw its troops from Kuwait immediately. The statement followed a meeting in Moscow between the US and Soviet foreign ministers (*Reuters*, August 3). The Soviet media also condemned Iraq's invasion of Kuwait. Al'bert Balebanov of TASS said that, as a result of the aggression, Iraq was becoming "a permanent source of tension." He said the invasion almost certainly reflected an attempt by Iraqi President Saddam Hussein to rescue the country's ailing economy and boost his own waning political prestige. Aleksandr Shumilin, writing in *Komsomol'skaya pravda*, said it was regrettable that the weapons used by the Iraqi army in its invasion had been supplied by the Soviet Union. Such outspoken comments marked a radical departure from decades of reticence by Soviet journalists and officials regarding criticism of any close ally.

On August 6, the Soviet representative in the United Nations Security Council voted in favor of a resolution establishing mandatory economic sanctions against Iraq.

On August 9, the Soviet Union condemned Iraq's annexation of Kuwait and called for a collective response under United Nations control. A Foreign Ministry spokesman said only a united response to Iraqi aggression would bear fruit. He said Moscow would consider military action if if were organized by the UN (*AFP*, *Reuters*, August 9). DPA quoted *Rabochaya tribuna* as saying that the Soviet

Foreign Ministry would prefer a political solution to the Gulf crisis. In their frequent discussions with US representatives, however, Soviet officials did not attempt to challenge US efforts to organize a multinational naval force in the Persian Gulf region or to stop the United States from deploying military forces in Saudi Arabia.

On August 11, the USSR welcomed Arab action to resolve the Gulf crisis. The Soviet Foreign Ministry issued a statement on the Arab League summit, which ended in Cairo on August 10, saying Moscow was satisfied with "the aim of the Arab leaders to make an energetic contribution to settling the dangerous crisis." The statement, published by TASS, coincided with the creation by Gorbachev of a special commission to handle the evacuation of 880 Soviet citizens from Kuwait (*Reuters*, August 11).

On August 13, Foreign Ministry spokesman Yurii Gremitskikh said Iraqi President Saddam Hussein's peace proposal would not resolve the present crisis. Hussein had said that his government might reconsider its occupation of Kuwait if, among other things, the US, Israeli, and Syrian governments removed their military forces from foreign territories in the Middle East (*Reuters*, August 13).

Gremitskikh also said that, as far as he was aware, none of the 8,000 Soviet advisers still in Iraq had been involved in the preparation of "concrete military plans." The USSR's new ambassador to Egypt, Vladimir Polyakov, told reporters in Cairo that "the several dozen" Soviet military advisers in Iraq "did not participate in military operations. Their work is basically training" (*AP*, August 13). The continuing presence of Soviet military advisers in Iraq was, however, reported to be causing friction between Moscow and Washington (*The Los Angeles Times*, August 12).

On August 15, Gremitskikh said the Iraqi authorities were refusing to allow male citizens of the Soviet Union to leave the country. He said the Iraqi authorities had given permission for the evacuation only of women, children, and invalids (*Reuters*, *AFP*, August 15).

On August 17, Gorbachev charged that, in invading Kuwait, the Iraqi authorities had violated their pledge to use Soviet-acquired weaponry only for defensive purposes. His comments came in a nationally televised hour-long address to participants in a military exercise in the Odessa Military District. He added that permitting Iraqi aggression would undermine international security. According to TASS, the Soviet president also called for a collective political solution to prevent "a full-scale military confrontation." Gorbachev's speech marked the end of his previous low-profile stance regarding the Gulf conflict.

After meeting with a senior Iraqi envoy in Moscow on August 20, Soviet Foreign Minister Eduard Shevardnadze said that some elements of Iraqi President Saddam Hussein's proposal of August 19 merited attention. He specifically listed Hussein's offer to permit the departure of the 13,000 Western nationals from Iraq in return for a withdrawal of foreign troops from Saudia Arabia and a cessation of the economic sanctions against Iraq. According to TASS, he stated that Soviet experts were studying the proposal, which was widely dismissed by Western officials.

Shevardnadze's remarks came after he had met for three hours at Iraq's request with Iraqi Deputy Prime Minister Saadoun Hammadi, who was on a two-day visit to Moscow (*TASS*, August 20).

On August 21, Hammadi met again with Soviet officials in Moscow. Prime Minister Nikolai Ryzhkov told Hammadi the Soviet Union would continue to implement economic sanctions against Iraq and urged Baghdad to withdraw its troops from Kuwait. Deputy Foreign Minister Igor Belousov also urged the Iraqi government to guarantee the safe departure of foreign nationals from Iraq and Kuwait. After these talks, Soviet Foreign Ministry spokesman Yurii Gremitskikh said that Iraq was "apparently disposed" towards a diplomatic solution to the Gulf crisis but had failed to address the cause of the crisis—Iraq's occupation of Kuwait (*TASS*, August 21).

On August 21, State Department spokesman Richard Boucher described the level of US-Soviet cooperation during the present crisis as "excellent." He also said that US officials were very satisfied with the Soviet Union's support for international measures against Iraq (*UPI*, August 21).

On August 24, TASS reported that Gorbachev had sent a personal message to Hussein warning him that the United Nations would be obliged to approve "additional measures" if he did not abide by the Security Council's resolution.

TASS reported on August 24 that the evacuation of Soviet citizens from Kuwait was complete. Soviet Foreign Ministry spokesman Yurii Gremitskikh said on August 25 that the Soviet embassy in Kuwait retained the status of a diplomatic mission. The Soviet evacuation from Iraq began on August 26. Soviet Prime Minister Nikolai Ryzhkov said on August 25 that the Soviet Union did not consider its citizens in Iraq to be hostages, AP reported. Iraq permitted Soviet citizens to fly out of Baghdad, whereas many other foreigners in Iraq were able to leave only by driving overland to Jordan or Turkey.

THE USSR IN AUGUST, 1990

US National Security Advisor Brent Scowcroft said on August 26 that the United States would welcome Soviet participation in collective military action to enforce UN sanctions against Iraq (*Reuters*, August 26), but Shevardnadze reiterated that Moscow had no plans to use force or take part in military operations of this kind (*TASS*, Western agencies, August 26).

The situation in the Gulf also became a central issue of the Soviet-French communiqué issued on August 26 at the end of the Dumas-Shevardnadze talks. In the communiqué the USSR and France appealed to Iraq to display realism and common sense and to heed the wishes of the international community for a peaceful end to the Gulf crisis.

On August 27, Soviet officials told UN Secretary-General Perez de Cuellar they would "observe the regime of sanctions" against Iraq until the Gulf crisis was over. In a letter to him, the Soviet leadership said that all its deliveries of goods to Iraq, including military supplies and equipment, had been halted, and that visits by economic delegations, contract talks, payments, and loans had also been put on hold. The USSR said no ships with goods for Iraq or Kuwait had left any Soviet port since the sanctions resolution was adopted (*TASS*, August 27).

On August 28, Soviet Foreign Ministry spokesman Gennadii Gerasimov said at a briefing that the USSR was not planning to require Iraqi diplomats in Moscow to leave (*TASS*, August 28). According to *The Los Angeles Times* (August 28), Gerasimov said, "Iraq's actions to close embassies in Kuwait are illegitimate . . . but, if you use a tit-for-tat policy in this question, you risk being caught in a spiral of escalation and aggravating the situation."

On August 30, TASS reported that members of the Supreme Soviet Foreign Affairs Committee had recommended that the government consider recalling Soviet military experts from Iraq. In its statement, the committee said the recall of the experts could begin after all Soviet women and children had been evacuated. The same day, in a message addressed to the Arab League and published by TASS, Eduard Shevardnadze said the avoidance of war in the Middle East depended on whether Arabs could unite. He called on the league to step up efforts to find a political solution to the Gulf crisis. Meanwhile, Warsaw Pact Chief of Staff General Vladimir Lobov expressed concern about the buildup of US military forces in the Gulf (*DPA*, August 30).

On August 31, Soviet Defense Minister Dmitrii Yazov repeated denials that the USSR had given secret information to the United States on Soviet-made missiles provi ously delivered to Iraq. Yazov was responding to published reports that a Soviet military attaché in Washington had given the missile information to the US Defense Department earlier in the month (*Radio Moscow*, World Service, August 31). See RL 348/90 and RL 430/90.

370,000 Quit CPSU in Six Months

TASS quoted the head of the Party Control Committee, Boriss Pugo, as saying 370,000 people quit the CPSU during the first six months of 1990. He said that another 150,000 Party members had stopped paying dues and ceased taking part in Party activities and that a further quarter of a million members had been expelled.

Meanwhile, the head of the CPSU Central Committee department in charge of cooperation with informal groups, Valentin Kuptsov, said many Party officials were psychologically unprepared to accept the USSR's new political situation. Speaking to TASS, he called for more cooperation between the CPSU and newly emerging Socialist parties.

Moldavia Bans Provocative Rallies

Moldavia's parliament banned for the rest of this year any rally or other demonstration that could be considered provocative. The parliament also said anyone who organized such demonstrations would be brought to account. The parliament said it had imposed the ban to help calm the social and political situation in the republic, which it described as tense (*Radio Moscow*, August 2).

The parliament also criticized some local soviets in the republic for failing to recognize the status of the Moldavian language and other republican symbols. The Presidium said in a resolution published on August 2 that the soviets in the cities of Tiraspol, Bendery, Rybnitsa, and adjacent rural areas were mainly to blame. Most of their populations are not ethnic Moldavians (*TASS*, August 2).

Bakatin Agrees to Give Estonian Government Control

USSR Minister of Internal Affairs Vadim Bakatin signed an agreement with Estonian Prime Minister Edgar Savisaar guaranteeing the Estonian government total control over law enforcement within Estonia (RFE Estonian service, August 2). Similar moves were being discussed for all the Union republics (*Izvestia*, July 31).

Uzbekistan Orders Measures to Enforce Gorbachev's Order

The Uzbek Council of Ministers issued directives designed to enforce Gorbachev's order to disband illegal armed groups. TASS said the directives were published in the Uzbek press. It said they set up special working teams at republican and local levels to enforce the order, but it gave no further details.

Friday, August 3

RSFSR-USSR Talks on Union Treaty

Talks began between the USSR and the RSFSR on a Union treaty. The RSFSR proposed a confederation of sovereign states with the central government controlling only two or three spheres, such as defense, internal security, and some monetary matters. RSFSR Supreme Soviet Chairman Boris El'tsin said that the Soviet army would have a specific status and a specific strength and that the KGB must be transformed into an organization protecting human rights. El'tsin's remarks were carried by Radio Riga and TASS.

CPSU Discloses Diamond Scandal

The CPSU disclosed a scandal inside the Soviet diamond industry that it said had cost the Soviet Union 22 million dollars in hard currency. Chairman of the Party Control Committee Boriss Pugo said Evgenii Bichkov, head of the state valuables depository, Goskhran, and several officials of the USSR Ministry of Finance were involved. He said they had sold Soviet diamonds directly on international markets in the fall of 1989 at lower prices than they would have obtained by selling through the state diamond monopoly, Glavalmazzoloto. According to the Party, the officials sold the diamonds in concert with the controversial cooperative ANT, which was caught selling Soviet T-72 tanks for Western currency in January, 1990. The report did not say why the officials chose to bypass the normal channels for selling Soviet diamonds (Western agencies, August 3).

Sweden Returns Soviet Hijacker

A young Soviet man who hijacked a Soviet passenger jet to Sweden in June was returned to the Soviet Union. Sweden agreed to extradite the man, Anatolii Mikhailenko, on condition that he be tried only for air piracy and not for illegally leaving the Soviet Union (*TASS*, August 3).

On August 16, the Swedish Supreme Court ruled that eighteen-year-old Mikhail Mokretsov, who hijacked a Soviet airliner to Sweden on July 5 in order to avoid military service, should not be sent back to the Soviet Union. The court said that he would not be able to stand Soviet prison conditions and should be tried in Sweden.

Mokretsov had told the court he would "rather die in Sweden than suffer in a Soviet jail" (Western agencies, August 16).

On August 20, the Finnish Justice Ministry decided to send back twenty-year-old Mikhail Varfolomeev, who hijacked an Aeroflot flight on June 24. The Ministry said Varfolomeev was being returned on condition that he be tried for air piracy charges only, TASS reported.

New Team Boards "Mir"

A Soviet "Soyuz" spacecraft with two fresh cosmonauts aboard reached the "Mir" space station and docked successfully. Cosmonauts Gennadii Manakov and Gennadii Strelakov relieved two other cosmonauts who had been aboard the station for six months. The new team planned to spend four-and-a-half months in orbit and to conduct some 250 experiments (*TASS*, *AP*, *UPI*, August 3).

Saturday, August 4

Armenian Parliament Elects New Chairman

After three rounds of voting, the Armenian parliament elected as its chairman Levon Ter-Petrossyan, a forty-five-year-old oriental philologist and member of the Karabakh Committee and the Armenian Pan-National Movement. Ter-Petrossyan polled 140 votes against Armenian Communist Party First Secretary Vladimir Movsisyan's eighty. Ter-Petrossyan subsequently told AFP that his first priority would be to resolve the crisis involving the informal military formations in the republic and the question of Armenian sovereignty.

Moldavian Supreme Soviet Chairman Suspends Own Membership in Communist Party

A Moldavian Party Central Committee plenum accepted the decision of the republican Supreme Soviet chairman, Mircea Snegur, to suspend his membership in the Communist Party for the duration of his term in office. Snegur took this step after the Moldavian Supreme Soviet's recent decision to separate Party and state and to ban all Party organizations from public institutions (*TASS*, August 4).

Sunday, August 5

Radio Moscow Blames Kremlin for Baltic Independence Drive

A Radio Moscow commentary blamed the Soviet government for the independence drives of the Baltic republics. The commentator, Vyacheslav Solov'ev, said Moscow had failed to "rectify historical injustice and errors" and had neglected the problems of interrepublican and nationality relations. "The result is that, fifty years after becoming members of the Soviet Union, the parliaments of the Baltic republics have proclaimed their intention to seek independence," Solov'ev said.

Baltic Leaders Agree to Work towards Common Market

Officials of the Baltic republics reached agreement to work towards a common economic market with Russia, Belorussia, Moldavia, and the cities of Leningrad and Moscow. They also agreed to resist Soviet efforts to dictate economic policy from Moscow and condemned what they called organizations of the "Integral" type. "Integral" is a conglomerate of all-Union enterprises that the USSR Council of Ministers created in Estonia in July. It will unite Estonian organizations in "an independent industrial-economic complex" that will deal directly with Moscow. A meeting in Tallinn called the creation of "Integral" an attempt to "perpetuate the *diktat* of departments" (*Central Television*, *Reuters*, *AFP*, August 10).

Lenin Monument Dismantled in Lithuania

The dismantling of a Lenin monument in Kaunas evoked protests by the pro-Moscow Lithuanian Communist Party and by the pro-Russian Citizens' Committee. TASS quoted the groups as saying it was an act of "vandalism" carried out with the knowledge of the mayor of Kaunas and the Lithuanian government. On August 9, TASS said Soviet army tanks were guarding two monuments in Vilnius—one to Lenin and one to the Soviet general who led the Red Army into Lithuania at the end of World War II. TASS quoted an official of the pro-Moscow Lithuanian Communist Party as saying the measures had been taken because "nationalists" were planning to remove the monuments.

Free Democratic Party Created in Russian Northwest

TASS reported that the Leningrad section of the Democratic Party of Russia had split from the main party and formed a separate Free Democratic Party. The new party was reported to have some 500 members in Leningrad, Pskov, and Novgorod; it aims to work for the removal of the CPSU from power and for the introduction of market relations. But according to Marina Sal'e, a leader of the new party and a former organizer of the Leningrad Popular Front, the Free Democrats will not be as single-mindedly anti-Communist as the Democratic Party of Russia and will uphold the right of any party to engage in constitutional activity.

Ryzhkov Supports Creation of Unemployment Fund

Prime Minister Nikolai Ryzhkov was quoted by Radio Moscow as supporting the creation of a public fund to deal with unemployment. The proposal, which is being championed by the newspaper *Rabochaya tribuna*, aims to channel money into retraining workers made redundant when loss-making factories are forced into liquidation.

Chernobyl'-Type Reactor to Go into Operation in Smolensk

TASS reported that a Chernobyl'-type nuclear reactor was ready to go into operation at a nuclear plant in Smolensk Oblast. The plant's director, Evgenii Safrygin, said that the one-megawatt reactor would operate under stricter safety conditions than the one at Chernobyl' and that previous design and construction flaws had been removed. TASS also reported that the Soviet nuclear power ministry was planning to dump nuclear waste in Smolensk Oblast but that the local authorities had refused to give their permission. Their reasoning is that the area is a watershed for rivers in the European half of the Soviet Union—a factor that should also have been considered in the placement of the nuclear plant.

Belorussia Monitoring Chernobyl' Victims

The head of Belorussia's only radiation medicine clinic said that she had 500,000 patients who needed systematic observation to determine the effects of radiation exposure from the Chernobyl' accident. She also said that the clinic did not have sufficient equipment to perform all the necessary ultrasonic examinations, thyroid tests, and blood tests. The doctor said she expected sharp increases in leukemia and cancer rates and feared that thyroid malfunctioning among children could lead to mental retardation. Officials say that more than 2 million people, including 600,000 children, still live in contaminated areas of Belorussia (*The Baltimore Sun*, August 5).

Chernobyl' Contamination in Romanian Border Area

Radio Kiev said abnormally high levels of radiation had been found in southern Bukovina, a region encompassing parts of Ukraine, Moldavia, and Romania. It said the contamination was attributed to fallout from the Chernobyl' nuclear accident. It quoted Ukrainian experts as saying the air, soil, and water were all contaminated. The report said the soil in the region was so contaminated that earth was being removed to make the land suitable for farming again.

Special Police Sent to Tuva

TASS said special police units had been sent to the Tuva Autonomous Republic on the Mongolian border. The move followed reports of increased tension in the area between the native population and Russian-speaking immigrants. TASS said there had been violent incidents involving the use of firearms, but it mentioned no casualties. It said many enterprises in Tuva were on the brink of collapse because so many people had left the republic. Over 3,000 people were reported to have left Tuva in the first half of 1990. See RL 381/90.

Islamic Democratic Party Formed

Muslim militants from southern republics of the Soviet Union announced the formation of an Islamic Democratic Party in the town of Namangan (*The Los Angeles Times*, August 6). The provisional leader of the new party, Uzbek singer Dadakhan Hasan, praised Ayatollah Khomeini, who "opened the windows for us." Hasan is a leader of the Uzbek Popular Front, "Birlik," and apparently remained with "Birlik" when moderate members broke away earlier in the year to form the "Erk" party. The Islamic Democratic Party, according to *The Los Angeles Times* report, does not insist on fundamentalist practices such as the veiling of women, but it aspires to make the Shariat the law of the land in traditionally Muslim regions. It also seeks the establishment of a completely sovereign Islamic state.

Demonstration in Estonia

Over 5,000 people staged a demonstration in Tallinn to mark the fiftieth anniversary of the Soviet Union's annexation of Estonia, ETA reported on August 6. The rally, organized by the Estonian Popular Front, circulated petitions calling for the Baltic republics to be allowed to participate in the Conference on Security and Cooperation in Europe and appealed for Baltic unity.

ABM Designer Says Many Soviet Defense Projects "Absurd"

The designer of the Soviet Union's first antiballistic missile defense system said many secret Soviet defense projects were absurd and a waste of money. Grigorii Kisunko said the Soviet system for early detection of US missile launches did not and could not work. He said Moscow's present missile-detection system left two directions uncovered. He also confirmed Western reports that more than fifty nuclear devices to explode incoming nuclear weapons had been placed along Moscow's perimeter highway despite the danger to the people of Moscow (*Sovetskaya Rossiya*, August 5).

Monday, August 6

El'tsin on Tour of RSFSR

Chairman of the RSFSR Supreme Soviet Boris El'tsin began a three-week tour of the RSFSR. On the first day of his tour, El'tsin visited the oil and gas works of Tataria, TASS and Moscow Radio reported. Commenting on the current discussion of state sovereignty in Tataria, El'tsin repeated his earlier statements that autonomous territories should have as much autonomy (*samostoyatel'nost'*) as they wanted and that power should emanate from the bottom up. However, he clearly envisaged that Tataria would remain part of the RSFSR when he said that the present Russian parliament would be "an earnest protector of those rights that Tataria delegates to Russia." *Pravda* reported on August 9 that El'tsin was facing repeated questions about the food supply in Tataria (*TASS*, August 9).

The next stop on El'tsin's tour was Bashkiria. Topics of discussion there included the catastrophic ecological situation in the autonomous republic—particularly in the chemical center of Sterlitamak—food shortages, and the construction of a nuclear power station, which is opposed by the local population. According to Soviet television, El'tsin proposed the drafting of a law on the status of indigenous nationalities. Such a law could play a significant role in many autonomous territories of the RSFSR where—as is the case in Bashkiria—the indigenous nationality is in the minority.

El'tsin began the second week of his three-week tour of the RSFSR with a visit to Vorkuta in northern Russia. In Vorkuta, El'tsin visited miners' settlements and met with members of the strike committees set up in 1989. Addressing the miners, El'tsin promised that the RSFSR government would lower taxation in order to allow the miners to run their pits themselves. (Financial independence was a key demand of the striking miners in 1989; the Soviet government agreed to the demand, but miners have complained that the authorities have defaulted on the pledge.) The miners complained to El'tsin that the fact that they were obliged to pay a tax of 45 percent on profits to the central authorities made a mockery of the idea of financial independence.

On August 15, El'tsin broke off his Russian tour and returned to Moscow for talks about economic reform. The Soviet media said he would meet the group of economists tasked by him and Mikhail Gorbachev with drafting a program for economic reform. Reuters quoted El'tsin as saying there was "some turmoil" in the group (*TASS*, *Central Television*, "Vremya," 1900, August 15).

On August 17, El'tsin resumed his tour of the RSFSR with a visit to the Kuzbass coal-mining region, birthplace of the strikes of summer, 1989. There he met representatives of the miners' strike committees, who expressed their confidence in El'tsin's government and said they were ready to extend their trust to El'tsin for 500 days, the time El'tsin wants to implement his economic reform program in the RSFSR. In return, El'tsin expressed his support for proposals to declare the whole of Kemerovo Oblast a special economic zone. He said that, at present, the central authorities took 70 billion rubles yearly from the Russian Republic "and we don't know where the money goes" (*TASS*, *Central Television*, August 17).

Radio Moscow said El'tsin's bus was stopped on the way to the West Siberian mining town of Novokuznetsk by people who wanted him to see the conditions they lived in. Seeing the barracks erected in the 1930s in which many miners live, El'tsin said that they could be described only as slums and that the local authorities should pay people to live there, instead of charging them rent.

"TSN," the "alternative" Soviet television news program, broadcast a short additional report on Boris El'tsin's meeting on August 19 with miners' representatives in Novokuznetsk. There El'tsin added his signature to a declaration of the miners' strike committee calling for full independence for the pits; the depoliticization of the KGB, police, army, and courts; and the establishment of "a government of national trust."

On August 20. El'tsin continued his tour with a visit to the Far Eastern ports of Vladivostok, Nakhodka, and Vostochnyi. Soviet television said he met members of the Soviet fishing fleet.

On August 21, at an open-air meeting in Vladivostok, El'tsin extolled the advantages that a free-enterprise zone could bring to the area. He also discussed the possibility of creating an autonomous Far Eastern Republic within the RSFSR (*TASS*, August 21).

On August 22, El'tsin arrived on the island of Sakhalin. He said it was time the region lost its "colonial" status and was rescued from "the thieving *diktat*" of the Moscow ministries (*TASS*, August 22). Talking to journalists upon his arrival, El'tsin said the law on property soon to be adopted by the parliament of the RSFSR would legalize private property. He also promised that the free-trade zones that were created in the RSFSR would offer favorable terms for foreign investment. From Sakhalin El'tsin traveled to the Kurile Islands. TASS said he was the highest-ranking Soviet official to visit the islands in the forty-five years that they have been part of the USSR. El'tsin described the attitude of past Soviet leaders to the Kuriles as being "to take as much as possible and to give as little as possible in return." El'tsin said many of the islands' social and economic problems could be solved if they joined with Sakhalin in a free-trade zone. On Japanese demands for the return of the Kuriles, El'tsin said he continued to believe in "the third way" he proposed after his trip to Tokyo earlier this year.

On August 23, El'tsin returned to Sakhalin. TASS quoted him as urging the involvement of foreign investors in exploiting oil deposits off the coast of the Soviet Far East.

On August 25, El'tsin arrived in Kamchatka, the last stop on his tour of the RSFSR. On his arrival, El'tsin restated his view that Gorbachev's decree nullifying the RSFSR's decision to assert republican control over its natural resources was a mistake. He said Gorbachev had no right to issue such a decree. In Kamchatka, El'tsin toured fish-processing and construction industry enterprises and addressed a meeting of local deputies. He also met with ethnic minorities from the area (*TASS*, August 25).

El'tsin Announces Contest for RSFSR Federal Treaty

El'tsin announced that a contest was being held for the best draft federal treaty for the RSFSR that would define the RSFSR's relationship with its constituent units, TASS and Moscow television reported. They said the first prize would be 5,000 rubles; entries must be submitted by October 15; and First Deputy Chairman of the RSFSR Supreme Soviet Ruslan Khasbulatov would head the jury.

Increase in Social Security Benefits Promised

At a press conference, the chairman of the State Committee for Labor, Vladimir Shcherbakov, said that the state had earmarked 45 billion rubles to cushion the impact of the transition to a market economy on the less well-off members of Soviet society. The bulk of the money will be spent on new child allowances (to be paid directly to parents instead of the present system of subsidized prices). From January 1, 1991, all families will receive a lump sum of three times the minimum wage on the birth of a child. In addition, a monthly benefit will be paid for each child between the ages of one-and-a-half and six years to families where income per family member is less than double the minimum wage. The plan also sets aside 6 billion rubles to help the unemployed, and pensions are to increase by 40–50 percent (*Reuters*, August 6).

Environmental Crimes Increasing

Soviet Deputy Prosecutor-General Vladimir Andreev said environmental crimes were on the rise in the USSR. TASS quoted him as saying these crimes included the dumping of raw sewage into the Volga River, the Azov Sea, and Lake Baikal. Andreev said that such incidents had been occurring more frequently over the past few years and that prosecutors had been ineffective in combating the problem, because the USSR had insufficient legislation in this area. He said that, unless measures were taken soon, the Soviet Union would be faced with irreparable damage. Sixty-eight Soviet cities are already considered environmental disaster areas.

Polozkov Interviewed

Russian Communist Party First Secretary Ivan Polozkov told *Pravda* that the market should be subordinated to the interests of the workers and not be allowed to become a playground for shady businessmen. Polozkov also said that under the new political conditions parliamentary work had become essential for the Russian Party. In his opinion, every republic, including the RSFSR, had to adopt a law protecting minority rights. If a person was forced to leave a republic, that person should be reimbursed for his losses by the republic's government.

Poll of Women Shows Dissatisfaction with *Perestroika*

The results of an opinion poll surveying women's attitudes to *perestroika* revealed widespread dissatisfaction. The Union-wide opinion poll, carried out by the Sociology Department of the Academy of Social Sciences, questioned 2,667 women in ten republics, including the RSFSR. Only 10 percent of the respondents said they thought *perestroika* was succeeding, while 38 percent had no confidence in it and 30 percent were undecided. Of the women dissatisfied with *perestroika*, one in three expressed lack of confidence in the leadership, one in five thought the timetable for reform was unrealistic, and one in six thought that there were insufficient resources to implement promised changes. The poll also revealed a lack of confidence in the Supreme Soviet and the CPSU. On the question of women's participation in public life since the beginning of *perestroika*, 62 percent believed that women were not playing a more active role, and half of these believed that women's participation had decreased.

Draft Sovereignty Declaration Published in Kirgizia

TASS reported that a draft declaration of republican sovereignty had been published in the Kirgiz press. The draft declared Kirgizia to be a sovereign, Socialist, multinational state that wished to remain part of the USSR on the basis of the free self-determination of the inhabitants of the republic. The draft envisaged the establishment of republican citizenship but guaranteed that every citizen retain Soviet citizenship. The draft stressed the links between the Kirgiz economy and that of the USSR as a whole, a point also made by republican Communist Party head Absamat Masaliev, who argued that those demanding full economic sovereignty did not realize what the effect would be of breaking ties built up over seventy years.

Kaliningrad Dissolves Raion Committees

The Communist Party organization in the city of Kaliningrad became the latest to dissolve Party committees at raion level. Similar moves have been made this year in other cities, such as Tambov and Stavropol.

USSR Calls for Further US Defense Cuts

Foreign Ministry spokesman Yurii Gremitskikh told reporters that recently announced US defense cuts were "an important milestone" but that the United States still seemed unready to cut other expensive programs. According to AP, Gremitskikh pointed especially to Pentagon programs for the B-2 bomber, trident submarine missile construction, and "Star Wars."

Sobchak Asks for US Aid for Leningrad

Speaking to a gathering of American Bar Association officials in Chicago, the former law professor and current chairman of the Leningrad City Soviet, Anatolii Sobchak, appealed to the United States for aid for his beleaguered city, according to the *Chicago Tribune.* He made his pitch for foreign investment in Leningrad by offering tax breaks and other incentives and urged the West to provide "logistical and organizational support" to help solve the economic crisis in the city. Sobchak noted that 60,000 new apartments in the city remained vacant owing to lack of plumbing, while 6 billion rubles' worth of unused products and materials are gathering dust in city warehouses. He also described plans to develop historic St. Petersburg as a tourism center and to handle customs duties and taxation on the local level.

USSR and South Korea Talk Trade

Kim Chong Whi, assistant for foreign and national security affairs to South Korean President Roh Tae Woo, said after trade talks in Moscow that "there are basically no more obstacles to opening formal relations" between the Soviet

Union and South Korea. South Korea presented six draft agreements to the Soviet Union on trade, investment, tax, aviation, fisheries, and scientific and technological cooperation. Kim said Soviet officials raised no objections to the draft agreements, AP reported.

Tobacco Shortage Prompts Calls for Ryzhkov to Resign

Soviet protesters complaining about the country's tobacco shortage called on the government of Nikolai Ryzhkov to resign. Radio Moscow's Interfax news agency said the protesters had sent their demands to the RSFSR and USSR parliaments. It said they also wanted Party property nationalized and the army and KGB freed from Party control. The news agency said the protests began with what it called the Perm tobacco rebellion of July 26, when protesters in the city of Perm demonstrated in front of the city hall against shortages of cigarettes.

On August 7, smokers blocked traffic for three hours outside a shop in Minsk after it ran out of cigarettes. The crowd then moved to the local police station nearby and refused to leave even after an official told them that six truckloads of cigarettes had just arrived in the city. Special police units were called in to maintain order, but no incidents were reported.

On August 25, Soviet television reported that a train packed with an emergency shipment of cigarettes was heading for Moscow. "Vremya" said that the heavily guarded train, with thirty railcars full of cigarettes, was on its way from the USSR's western borders. Nikolai Ryzhkov said on August 24 that the USSR was buying cigarettes from Yugoslavia, Turkey, Bulgaria, and elsewhere to cover a shortage that has caused unrest in some cities.

On August 28, the RSFSR Supreme Soviet Committee on Human Rights assembled a panel of experts to investigate the cigarette shortage, according to UPI. Meanwhile, the 2.2 million imported cigarettes distributed to Moscow kiosks on August 27 were sold out by noon, Reuters reported. On August 29, Gorbachev met with USSR and RSFSR ministers to discuss the cigarette shortage. TASS reported that he found their explanations "unconvincing and unjustified."

Tuesday, August 7

New Armenian Supreme Soviet Chairman Appeals for Calm

The newly elected Armenian Supreme Soviet chairman, Levon Ter-Petrossyan, appealed for calm in the republic, where militants were reported to be continuing to attack

Soviet soldiers in order to obtain weapons. Ter-Petrossyan told the Armenian Supreme Soviet that the only way out of the current "crisis" was for Armenians to unite behind the national parliament and the concept of Armenian statehood. Ter-Petrossyan later flew to Moscow for talks with Soviet Prime Minister Nikolai Ryzhkov and Minister of Internal Affairs Vadim Bakatin on the Armenian suspension of the presidential decree calling for the disarmament of illegal military groupings. Also today, the Armenian parliament began debating three alternative drafts of a declaration of sovereignty.

On August 10, Ter-Petrossyan again appealed to unauthorized armed groups in the republic to pledge their loyalty to the Armenian Supreme Soviet and asked them to enlist in the republic's police force. Soon after the appeal, men loyal to Ter-Petrossyan began armed patrols of the Supreme Soviet building (*Reuters*, August 10).

TASS said two rallies demanding secession had been held in Erevan on August 9. It said demonstrators also called for the creation of an Armenian national army, for Armenian control of the police and the KGB, and for the removal of Party cells from these bodies. The news agency also said that about 100 people attacked a police station in Armenia's Talin Raion and that gunmen had fired on a border village and a military unit in Nakhichevan.

On August 11, Gorbachev extended by two months the deadline by which unauthorized paramilitary groups in Armenia must surrender their arms. The same day, Ter-Petrossyan told a news conference in Erevan that many armed groups had already pledged their allegiance to the republican Supreme Soviet. He said these groups would be formed into military detachments to disarm unauthorized groups—a process he estimated would take three months (*TASS*, August 11).

On August 14, the situation in Nagorno-Karabakh was reported as still serious. The military commander of the region, Major General Vladislav Safonov, said attacks on Azerbaijani settlements and "provocations" against soldiers were continuing. He said groups of armed militants from Armenia continued to "destabilize the situation." Safonov said additional MVD forces were being sent to Azerbaijani districts that bordered Armenia to reinforce frontier units and to "disable" Armenian militants (*TASS*, August 14).

On August 15, Ter-Petrossyan said reestablishment of civilian control in Nagorno-Karabakh was a precondition for a compromise between Armenia and Azerbaijan. In an interview with *Moscow News*, Ter-Petrossyan said the

Soviet army had not only had a repressive function in Nagorno-Karabakh but had also been performing all political, administrative, and economic functions (*TASS*, August 15).

At a meeting of the Armenian Supreme Soviet on August 18, Ter-Petrossyan spoke about renewed clashes on the border between Armenia and Azerbaijan, which he said had been occasioned when armed Armenians attempted to free hostages taken by Azerbaijanis. He stated that negotiations with Azerbaijan on the return of the hostages were in progress, and he called on unofficial Armenian military formations to renounce violence. At least five people were killed on August 19 in clashes on the border between the two republics. The USSR MVD claimed that a missile had been fired at a bus in Azerbaijan and that militants also fired at military helicopters (*TASS*, August 20).

On August 21, Ter-Petrossyan traveled to Idzhevan for talks with the commander of the USSR MVD troops, Yurii Shatalin, and with the commander of the Transcaucasian Military District, Valerii Patrikeev. Clashes continued along the Armenian-Azerbaijani border, particularly in the Kazakh Raion of Azerbaijan, where local residents were blocking the railway link to Armenia (*TASS*, August 22).

On August 23, TASS reported a deterioration of the situation in the Kazakh Raion. The agency reported a battle between Soviet soldiers and armed Armenians there. On August 24, *Izvestia* said fifty people had been killed in the recent clashes in the Kazakh Raion. On August 23, a decision was taken during talks between Ter-Petrossyan and Shatalin to move MVD troops into three Armenian raions along the Azerbaijani border to stop bloodshed there (*TASS*, August 23).

In a television address on August 20, Azerbaijani President Ayaz Mutalibov demanded that the USSR impose "real political, legal, and other sanctions" against Armenia. His comments came following recent clashes on the Armenian-Azerbaijani border in which five people were killed. Mutalibov implied that Armenia had violated the USSR Constitution, and he stated that Azerbaijan might request international assistance to protect its sovereignty. He further criticized the decision to extend by two months the deadline for the surrender of arms and for the disbanding of illegal military formations in Armenia. Similar criticism was expressed last week by the Azerbaijani KGB.

A missile launcher was among weapons confiscated in two border villages in Azerbaijan on August 24, and the Armenian population of these villages was evacuated, according to the head of the republican KGB, Vagif

Guseinov (*TASS*, August 24). On August 25, "Vremya" estimated the damage caused by the recent shelling of Kazakh Raion by Armenian militants at approximately 2 million rubles.

MVD troops fired warning shots and used tear gas against a crowd of 3,500 demonstrators gathered in the mainly Armenian Shaumyan Raion in northwest Azerbaijan on August 26, TASS reported. The demonstrators were protesting about the removal of the raion's Armenian first secretary. The demonstrators subsequently dispersed peacefully. Armenian armed groups were likewise reported to have attacked Soviet troops in Armenia's Oktemberyan Raion and in the Nakhichevan ASSR in Azerbaijan.

On August 29, the Armenian parliament declared a state of emergency and imposed a curfew from 2200 to 0600. It also called for the disbanding of the Armenian National Army, following the killing by its members of Armenian Supreme Soviet deputy Viktor Aivazyan and of an officer of the military wing of the Armenian Pan-National Movement. According to *Izvestia*, three more people were killed in a further clash in Erevan later on August 29 (*Izvestia*, August 30).

Announcing the state of emergency in the Armenian Supreme Soviet, Chairman Levon Ter-Petrossyan accused the ANA of "flagrant terrorist activities" and blamed it for the recent escalation of tension along the Armenian-Azerbaijani border. He announced a deadline of 2000 by which members of the ANA were to surrender their arms and the vehicles they had hijacked and to vacate the premises they were occupying. Ter-Petrossyan subsequently dismissed Armenian Minister of Internal Affairs Levon Galstyan, who had occupied his post for less than three months. (His predecessor was fired under similar circumstances in April, following an attack on the Armenian Supreme Soviet building.)

On August 30, it was reported that the Armenian National Army had agreed to disband in line with the Supreme Soviet's order. TASS said the action was announced by two of the group's leaders.

Pravda Hails "Political Alliance"

In a front-page commentary, *Pravda* called the recent agreement between Mikhail Gorbachev and his former foe Boris El'tsin "a political alliance" that would lead to a radicalization of the Soviet Union's attempts to move towards a market economy. *Pravda* praised both men for their flexibility and responsibility. Meanwhile, in an interview published in *Moscow News* on August 5, Gorbachev's aide Georgii Shakhnazarov said the alternative to a move to the left was "political death."

RSFSR Official on Armed Forces

In a long interview broadcast by Central Television ("Na sluzhbe otechestvu"), the chairman of the RSFSR Supreme Soviet Committee for International Affairs called for a radical reevaluation of the role and size of the Soviet Armed Forces. Vladimir Lukin said that the present massive Soviet army was an outgrowth of Soviet imperialism and that the easing of international tensions should be reflected in significant conventional force reductions. He did call for the Soviet Union to maintain a reserve of strategic weapons, however. He supported the creation of an RSFSR Ministry of Defense and said it should be given the task of coordinating the activities of all-Union ministries in guaranteeing the welfare of armed forces personnel. Lukin also urged the creation of a Russian state organ to be responsible for retraining military officers.

Currency Exchange Market to Be Set Up

TASS reported that, as of January 1, 1991, all Soviet enterprises would have the right to buy and sell foreign currency in exchange for rubles. The Soviet government will open a central exchange in Moscow and other exchanges in the capital cities of the Union republics. The ruble is currently nonconvertible and subject to several different official exchange rates. *Izvestia* called the government's decision an important step towards turning the ruble into a convertible currency. Currently, both Soviet enterprises and foreign companies are prohibited from exchanging rubles for hard currency, and this has been a critical barrier to trade and economic growth in the USSR. Vneshekonombank, the Soviet bank for foreign economic relations, has held periodic hard currency auctions during the past year, but only a limited number of Soviet firms have been allowed to participate, and joint ventures with foreign companies have been excluded from such auctions.

Marchuk Accused of Defending Ecologically Dangerous Projects

In an article in *Izvestia*, a group of scientists and people's deputies accused Gurii Marchuk, president of the USSR Academy of Sciences, of defending ecologically dangerous projects. The subject of the controversy was the Leningrad dam, built in the Brezhnev era. An independent commission of forty-three highly qualified Soviet specialists came to the conclusion that the dam was a principal cause of the worsening environmental situation in Leningrad, and this verdict was approved by the academy's presidium. Nonetheless, Marchuk rejected this decision, informed Prime Minister Ryzhkov that no clear verdict had been reached, and called for an international commission to study the question. The scientists criticized Marchuk in their article for doubting the expert commission appointed by the academy leadership, including Marchuk himself. They added that over the past few years the staff of the academy had been "playing up to the authors of antiecological and wasteful projects" in a fashion suited to old-style politics—"serving the institution and not scientific truth."

Chief of General Staff on United Germany

Chief of the General Staff Army General Mikhail Moiseev told TASS that the inclusion of a unified Germany in NATO and the subsequent creation of a NATO border along the Oder River would complicate the Soviet Union's strategic position in Europe. Moiseev also said that the increased use of political means for settling international disputes did not absolve the armed forces of responsibility for Soviet security. He added that NATO concepts and doctrines continued to be based on the use of nuclear weapons and said that the danger posed by NATO for the Soviet Union had not disappeared.

Christian School to Open in Moscow

Novosti reported that a Christian lycée would open in Moscow in September. It said the courses would include languages, mathematics, and logic in addition to religious subjects, such as apologetics and religious philosophy. The teaching will not be limited to a single confession.

Radio Moscow Contradicts Ministry of Health

Radio Moscow reported that cholera had never been eliminated from the Soviet Union and that there had been periodic outbreaks in various regions. Therefore, it said, it was "wishful thinking" to say that a group of Syrian workers were responsible for the recent outbreak of the disease in Stavropol Krai, which infected forty-nine people. A deputy minister of health had blamed the Syrians for bringing in the disease.

New Press Law Takes Effect

TASS reported that the State Committee for Publishing had received applications from about 100 organizations and five private individuals to register new publications in accordance with the new press law. The report did not indicate whether any of these periodicals had actually been registered. Each applicant must indicate the language in which the periodical will be published, the number of copies to be produced, and the source of its financing. Registrations may be canceled if the periodicals contain "calls for the violent overthrow of the state system; propaganda in support of war; violence, cruelty, or racial or ethnic intolerance; or pornography." The registration fee for domestic periodicals is 2,000 rubles.

Wednesday, August 8

Savisaar in Moscow for Talks

Estonian Prime Minister Edgar Savisaar met with Soviet Prime Minister Nikolai Ryzhkov, ETA reported. The two leaders discussed the Tallinn-Moscow relationship, the Soviet conglomerate "Integral," and the Soviet troop presence in Estonia. Ryzhkov also expressed interest in the recent meeting of officials from the Baltic republics, Moscow, Leningrad, Belorussia, and Moldavia in Tallinn. Savisaar's visit to Moscow came a day after Estonia's Supreme Council set guidelines for independence negotiations and declared nonbinding the Soviet law incorporating Estonia into the Soviet Union in 1940. The guidelines for the negotiations were as follows: that the Soviet Constitution, with its secession clause, does not apply to Estonia; that Estonia will not participate in drafting a new Union treaty; that the Soviet military presence in Estonia is illegal without a Soviet-Estonian treaty; and that the basis of talks must be the Tartu Peace Treaty of 1920 and other subsequent treaties in effect until 1940, supplemented by Supreme Council laws passed between November, 1989, and May, 1990 (*Radio Estonia*, August 7).

On August 10, the USSR was reported to have agreed to Estonia's plan to establish its own customs controls on its border with the Russian Federation. A member of Savisaar's staff, Rein Koov, said the plan was a first step towards creating a true international border for Estonia, with Estonian officials controlling both people and goods (RFE Estonian service, August 10).

On August 12, Soviet President Gorbachev denounced the Estonian Supreme Council's resolution of August 7 rejecting the 1940 Soviet law annexing Estonia into the Soviet Union. In a declaration read on Soviet television, Gorbachev said the resolution was unlawful, adding that "such unconstitutional actions and demands in the form of ultimatums have no grounds and no future."

On August 15, the Estonian Foreign Ministry again said Estonia had never been legally part of the Soviet Union. It also said that the issue of Estonia's political status relates directly to the "Two-plus-Four" talks on German unification, in which the Soviet Union was taking part. The ministry said it was impossible to prepare a final document without the participation of the Baltic states, pointing out that, since the USSR and Germany had never signed a peace treaty ending World War II, the western border of the USSR had not been defined by international law (RFE Estonian service, August 15).

Effect of Afghan War on Soviet Central Asia

In *Moscow News* (No. 31), prominent Uzbek novelist and political commentator Timur Pulatov said that the Soviet intervention in Afghanistan had been motivated by the fear that the country would be taken over by Muslim fundamentalists who might then exert influence over the peoples of Soviet Central Asia. He added, however, that the intervention itself turned out to have much greater significance for the Islamic renaissance in the region. Pulatov described the effect on Soviet Central Asian soldiers of coming into contact with Afghans, Tajiks, and Uzbeks, many of whom are descendants of postrevolutionary refugees and might therefore have been unknown relatives.

El'tsin Gives Himself Three Years

Interviewed in *Komsomol'skaya pravda*, Boris El'tsin said he might step down if his economic reform program did not succeed in three years and if he lost the confidence of the people. El'tsin criticized Gorbachev's blockade of Lithuania as "a serious political mistake." The forthcoming treaty between the RSFSR and Latvia he described as "an equal agreement between two sovereign states." In other statements he said that the KGB administrations on Russian territory would soon become subordinate to the newly formed RSFSR Committee for Public Security. A chairman has not been found yet for the committee, but El'tsin revealed that the outspoken army officer and USSR people's deputy Vladimir Lopatin had been nominated as its deputy chairman. El'tsin denied that he had spoken to Oleg Kalugin about the possibility that he might become chairman of the committee.

New Measures to Encourage Small Businesses

In an effort to encourage output of consumer goods and services, the USSR Council of Ministers issued a decree that could help the development of small business ventures in the Soviet Union. Small businesses in the USSR are those with up to 200 people in industry and construction, 150 people in science and research and development, and fifteen people in retail trade (*TASS*, August 8). Most significantly, the decree acknowledged the legitimacy of all forms of ownership, including cooperative and joint ventures.

Free Economic Zone for Novgorod

Moscow News (No. 31) reported that the USSR's seventh free economic zone (following Leningrad, Vyborg, Nakhodka, Sakhalin, Kaliningrad, and Chita) would be established in Novgorod. Foreign investment will be sought to encourage tourism, clean up the environment, and develop the local electronics industry. The newspaper recalled that an earlier proposal to set up such a zone in Novgorod had been defeated in 1989 by an alliance of the conservative United Workers' Front and local ecological and patriotic groups. The local people were scared off by warnings that they would be sold into slavery to foreign businessmen and that their ancient Russian city would be destroyed by "prostitution, drug addiction, and AIDS." On August 11, Magadan Oblast in the RSFSR also declared itself a free economic zone (*Radio Moscow*, August 11).

Ministry of Health Drafts Law on Medical Insurance

TASS reported that the USSR Ministry of Health had completed the first draft of a law on the fundamentals of financing medical care with the help of an insurance system. The draft envisaged using insurance payments by enterprises, combined with continued state financing, to raise the total contributions to the health sector to 50–60 billion rubles per year. Soviet health care is currently financed entirely by the state, at a cost of 27.3 billion rubles this year. Although each republic would be expected to implement the plan differently, its basic elements would comprise enterprise insurance contributions for each worker, insurance policies that would entitle a citizen to receive care at any medical institution, and equal insurance for all citizens. Continued government contributions would pay for the care of nonworking citizens.

More Border Restrictions

Radio Kiev said the Ukrainian Supreme Soviet had issued a decree stipulating that citizens trying to take goods subject to export restrictions out of the country would be liable to have the goods confiscated. The decree was scheduled to come into force on August 10, the same day visa-free travel for Soviet citizens along the USSR's western border will be restricted again. These moves followed the USSR's closing of its entire western border on August 1 to curb smuggling. The measure was suspended when thousands of citizens, unaware of the closure, were left stranded at border crossings.

Belorussian Deputy Says Sovereignty Most Important Task

A member of the Belorussian parliament, Gennadii Grushevoi, said the most important task before the republican parliament was to help Belorussia achieve real sovereignty. Grushevoi, speaking at RFE/RL in Munich, said a sovereign Belorussia would be able to restore its national culture, improve its economy, and deal more effectively with the aftermath of the Chernobyl' nuclear disaster.

USSR Increases Natural Gas Supplies to Turkey

Lev Voronin, a first deputy chairman of the USSR Council of Ministers, said the Soviet Union would increase its natural gas supplies to Turkey to 4.5 billion cubic meters, TASS reported. Voronin concluded an official visit to Turkey on August 8. TASS said his talks with Turkish officials also focused on Soviet technical assistance in expanding and modernizing Turkish railways.

Russian Communist Party Urged to Move to the Left

At a press conference in Moscow, Deputy Head of the CPSU Central Committee's Ideology Department Viktor Ryabov said that, unless the newly created Russian Communist Party moved to the left, people would ignore it. His opinion was seconded by Central Committee members Otto Latsis and Vladimir Lyakishev, who also attended the press conference. Ryabov also accused the first secretary of the Russian Party, Ivan Polozkov, of being behind the times (*TASS*, August 8).

Thursday, August 9

Petrakov Calls for Legalization of Private Property

Economist Nikolai Petrakov, an adviser to Mikhail Gorbachev, said private property must be legalized in the USSR. In an interview with *Moscow News* (No. 32), Petrakov said it would be absurd to free prices without allowing the competition created by private ownership. He said the USSR needed to create the conditions for privatization and competition and end state monopolies

TASS Gives New Death Toll in Kirgiz-Uzbek Clashes

TASS reported that the official death toll in the clashes between Kirgiz and Uzbeks in recent months had risen to 230. Previous reports had put the figure at 213. The latest figures also indicated that 400 people were still missing and more than 4,000 injured and that 100 people who allegedly took part in the clashes had been arrested. On August 8, five Uzbeks began a hunger strike on Red Square in Moscow in protest against the failure of the official media to report the full extent of the violence against Uzbeks. The hunger strikers were said to want a UN commission to be set up to investigate interethnic conflicts in the USSR (*TASS*, August 8).

RSFSR Declares Some Foreign Economic Agreements Invalid

The Presidium of the RSFSR Supreme Soviet declared invalid any agreements signed since June, 1990, on the sale of the RSFSR's natural resources to foreign countries. The RSFSR Congress of People's Deputies in June adopted a declaration of sovereignty that proclaimed the republic's right of ownership over its resources. The Presidium proposed to instruct the Russian government to revise such agreements and to inform foreign partners that they were valid only if approved by Russian legislative and executive bodies (*TASS*, August 9).

On August 23, Mikhail Gorbachev issued a decree rejecting the RSFSR decree as illegal and said all foreign economic agreements signed by the Soviet Union would be observed (*TASS*, August 23).

On August 24, Boris El'tsin said Gorbachev had made "a mistake" by nullifying the RSFSR decision. El'tsin called Gorbachev's decree an attempt to infringe on Russian sovereignty (*Radio Moscow*, *TASS*, August 24). A member of the Presidium of the RSFSR Supreme Soviet, Vladimir Isakov, said Gorbachev had exceeded his competence by issuing the decree (*TASS*, August 24).

Weapons and Explosives Confiscated in Donetsk and Kuibyshev

The Soviet media said police had seized weapons and explosives in Donetsk in Ukraine and in Kuibyshev in the RSFSR. Radio Kiev said the quantity of arms confiscated in Donetsk would be enough for an infantry regiment. Radio Moscow reported from Kuibyshev that workers at a vehicle equipment plant had been jailed for illegal production and marketing of firearms.

Donetsk Miners Oust Party Committee from Enterprise

Arguing that "the mines are not the place for the expression of political disagreements under a multiparty system," miners at the Trudovskaya coal mine in Ukraine's

Donetsk region voted to oust the Communist Party committee from the enterprise. Central Television reported that more than 2,000 people had recently resigned from the Communist Party in the Donetsk region. In addition, many miners have withheld all or part of their Party dues and "the political enlightenment rooms are empty."

Friday, August 10

Lithuanian Officials Hold Preliminary Talks in Moscow

A Lithuanian delegation met with Soviet officials in Moscow to present proposals on procedures for the coming talks on independence. A member of the delegation, Lithuanian Deputy Prime Minister Romualdas Ozolas, later said he was satisfied with the meeting. Radio Vilnius said that the Lithuanian government had banned state enterprises and organizations in Lithuania from moving equipment or other property to the USSR or to "other foreign countries." The government also said it must approve any plans for Lithuanian enterprises to associate with USSR enterprises.

Factory Workers Stage Warning Strike in Kiev

Factory workers in Kiev staged a two-hour warning strike to press their demands for the closure of the Chernobyl' nuclear plant and for major improvements in health measures to protect people from the effects of radiation. The head of the strike committee said the strikers wanted Communist Party facilities turned into accommodations and schools for families evacuated from the danger zone after the Chernobyl' accident. He also said they wanted extra money for people still living in the contaminated zone (*The Independent*, August 10).

In a related development, experts from the International Atomic Energy Agency began an investigation in the Soviet Union into the effects of the Chernobyl' nuclear disaster. The group was reported to be working about 150 kilometers northwest of Chernobyl' in Gomel, one of the areas hardest hit by Chernobyl' radiation. The work will include taking soil and air samples. The group will also examine people with health problems caused by radiation (*TASS*, August 10).

Karelia Declares Sovereignty

Karelia became the first autonomous republic within the RSFSR to declare itself sovereign. Its laws will now take precedence over RSFSR and USSR laws except in those spheres in which Karelia has explicitly delegated powers to the higher authorities, according to TASS. The news service said this did not mean the autonomous republic was planning to secede from the federation.

New Party in Tajikistan

Radio Moscow reported the opening of the constituent conference of the Democratic Party of Tajikistan. A TASS report said that the founders of the new party had had difficulty in obtaining permission for the conference because of the state of emergency in effect in Tajikistan since February. Nonetheless, the new party already has some 4,000 members, mostly Tajik intellectuals, although some Russians, Uzbeks, and Tatars have joined as well.

Explosion in Azerbaijan Kills Seventeen

An explosion aboard a bus in Azerbaijan killed seventeen people. Sources at the newspaper *Bakinsky rabochii* said the explosion had been caused by a time bomb probably hidden in the luggage compartment. The newspaper's correspondent said the bomb exploded just as the bus, which had set out from Tbilisi, was about to enter the bus station in Agdam. He said most of the passengers were women and children.

Final Report on White Sea Disaster Published

Pravda featured the final report from the special interdepartmental commission on the White Sea disaster that killed millions of starfish in May. TASS reported that the commission had confirmed its preliminary conclusion that the source of the pollution was the release of a large quantity of a sulfuric compound from a passing ship. But the newspaper added that the commission had stressed that the current ecological situation in the White Sea was not satisfactory. Particularly worrying is Dvina Bay, which receives unpurified effluent from enterprises in Arkhangelsk and Severodvinsk. See RL 292/90.

Saturday, August 11

Radiation Cover-Up in Leningrad?

Komsomol'skaya pravda charged that a detailed map displaying more than 1,500 areas in Leningrad with higher than normal radiation levels was being withheld from the public. The newspaper said that radiation from local industries had already destroyed 150,000 cubic meters of land in the city and that the Leningrad authorities had rejected twenty-three out of twenty-four recommended sites for the disposal of radioactive material.

Prison Inmates Take Hostages in Sukhumi

Seven inmates overpowered prison guards at a temporary holding facility in Sukhumi, the capital of the Abkhaz SSR, and took three of them hostage (*TASS*, August 13). The inmates released about seventy other prisoners from their cells and seized guns that police had confiscated from arrested criminals. Some prisoners said they wanted representatives from informal associations to be brought in for negotiations; others refused to negotiate altogether and demanded a car so they could leave the city.

On August 15, KGB and MVD forces stormed the jail and released a number of hostages. TASS said the security forces exchanged gunfire with the prisoners. The leader of the hostage-takers was reported seriously wounded. Also wounded were two hostages and two members of the security forces.

KGB Members Prepare Alternative Draft Law on Security

A group of KGB staff members were reported to have prepared an alternative draft law on state security and the KGB. KGB Lieutenant Colonel Vladimir Morozov told *Komsomol'skaya pravda* that the draft called for giving the existing state security bodies fundamentally new functions. Morozov said security service employees should not belong to any party or engage in political activity during their period of service. He said he himself had quit the CPSU. He also said the staff of the KGB could be cut by more than half without damage to Soviet security.

Sunday, August 12

Soviet Commander on Cuts in Far East

The commander of the Soviet Pacific Fleet told Radio Moscow that the Soviet Union was continuing to withdraw men and ships from the region. Admiral Gennadii Khvatov, who was highly critical of Gorbachev's security policies at the recent Party Congress, said that 200,000 military personnel would be withdrawn from the Soviet Far East by July, 1991. He added that, over the past five years, fifty-seven ships had been withdrawn from the Pacific Feet and sixteen more would be withdrawn during 1990. He made no mention of the Soviet naval modernization program in the region. Khvatov, who was recently in the United States on a good-will mission, said US and Japanese forces had an overwhelming superiority in the region, although the USSR was superior in ground forces.

Preservation through Privatization

Aleksei Kovalev, the twenty-six-year-old chairman of the Leningrad City Soviet's Committee on Historic Preservation, told AP that the city government would consider following Moscow's lead by transferring control of the city's apartment stock to its residents. Kovalev said that "the preservation of our city is possible in only one instance: if we now start to transfer homes to individual owners."

Memorial Built to Millions Who Died in 1933 Famine

A monument to the millions of peasants who died in the 1933 famine engineered by Stalin to force them into collectivization was dedicated today. The simple memorial, called the Hill of Sorrow, is on the outskirts of Lubny in Ukraine. It takes the form of a burial mound topped by a cross surrounded by a row of sticks planted in the ground and crowned with small sheaves of rye. The monument was consecrated under Orthodox ritual in a public ceremony (*AP*, August 12).

Rallies in Ukraine Demand Aid for Chernobyl' Victims

Some 1,500 people rallied in Kiev to demand aid for victims of the Chernobyl' disaster, the abolition of Communist Party organizations in the workplace, and the removal of Lenin statues from enterprises, parks, and schools, TASS reported. Demonstrators in Ivano-Frankovsk voiced the same demands.

Monday, August 13

Armenian Government Resigns

The Armenian government headed by Prime Minister Vladimir Markaryants resigned. Chairman of the Armenian Supreme Soviet Levon Ter-Petrossyan named a fellow member of the Karabakh Committee, forty-four-year-old mathematics lecturer Vazgen Manukyan, to form a new government, which Ter-Petrossyan said would be "non-Party and non-coalition . . . a government of experts." Manukyan was quoted by Radio Moscow as affirming that he was a supporter of the denationalization of property and favored the independence of Armenia in all internal and external affairs. He said the primary task facing the republic was the struggle against armed criminals, brigandage, and corruption.

Gorbachev Denounces Crimes of Stalin Era

President Mikhail Gorbachev signed a decree restoring the rights of all victims of Stalinism, TASS reported. The decree singled out the rehabilitation of so-called kulaks, who were suppressed under mass collectivization, and condemned the brutal repression of religious and ethnic groups. The decree did not, however, pardon citizens who had "committed crimes against the fatherland"—i.e., those who fought against the regime in World War II. Unlike earlier decrees on this subject, Gorbachev's made no effort to justify Stalin's crimes by citing his alleged achievements (*Pravda*, August 14).

Speaking on "Vremya" on August 20, member of the Presidential Council Aleksandr Yakovlev praised Gorbachev's decrees on the rehabilitation of victims of Stalin's terror and on the restoration of Soviet citizenship to exiled dissidents. Yakovlev called the decrees an act of "repentance" on the part of the Soviet regime for its misdeeds. Yakovlev also said those who persecuted dissident writers and human-rights activists in the post-Stalin period should be exposed. He said that such people should not be put on trial, because that would only start "a new cycle of vengeance," but that society should know who they were and what they had done so that they could be subjected not to legal but to moral judgment.

Soviet-Ukrainian Talks on Union Treaty

A Ukrainian delegation met Soviet officials in Moscow to discuss the new Union treaty. The delegation was headed by Deputy Chairman of the Ukrainian Supreme Soviet Volodymyr Hryniv. TASS said Ukrainians wanted a substantial reduction in central control over their republic, leaving Moscow in control of only some sectors, such as defense. Hryn'ov told Soviet television that Ukraine would certainly remain in the Soviet Union.

In its talks in Moscow about the treaty on August 14, the Kazakh delegation said it wanted to preserve the Soviet Union. The leader of the Kazakh delegation, Kazakh First Deputy Prime Minister Kalyk Abdullaev, said Kazakhstan must work to help strengthen the Union (*TASS*, August 14).

Public Outcry Brings Down Radar

TASS reported that the USSR Council of Ministers had ordered a halt to construction at the Mukachevo radar station in Ukraine. This decision followed the approval of legislation by the Ukrainian Supreme Soviet declaring a five-year moratorium on high-power radar construction in Ukraine. The Moscow decision also requires the USSR Defense Ministry to recultivate land damaged during construction. TASS said the end of construction represented a victory for those who had raised their voices in protest.

Bush Lifts Limit on Soviet Businessmen Allowed in United States

US President George Bush was reported to have eliminated the restrictions on the number of Soviet business people allowed to live and work in the United States. Previously, only sixty-nine Soviet citizens had been allowed to live in the United States at any one time to pursue business activities (Western agencies, August 13).

State Housing Construction Drops

A senior Soviet housing official said only a little over 30 percent of the annual state plan for housing had been completed in the first six months of 1990, Radio Moscow reported. This was less than was completed by the same time in 1989. The official added that only 15 percent of the annual plan for school construction had been completed by the end of June.

Tuesday, August 14

***Kommunist* Calls for Statistics on Psychiatry**

The Soviet Party journal *Kommunist* (No. 12) said the time had come to publish statistics on people confined in psychiatric institutions in the Soviet Union. The article said that, in Moscow alone, psychiatrists confined 81,000 patients to institutions in 1987 and 71,000 in 1988. It said these figures did not include "a considerable number of people" sentenced to psychiatric treatment by the criminal courts. *Kommunist* urged support for poet Evgenii Evtushenko's proposals for a commission to examine the actions of psychiatrists whose diagnoses caused "enemies of the people" and "dissidents" to be hospitalized under Stalin and later Soviet leaders. *Kommunist* also said the Soviet Union must observe the provisions of the final document of the Vienna Conference on Security and Cooperation in Europe under which it committed itself to defend citizens against psychiatric abuses.

Many Moscow Communists Leave Party

The first secretary of the Moscow City Party organization, Yurii Prokof'ev, said some 46,000 Communists had left the Moscow Party between January and July, 1990. He said almost 20,000 had quit the Party following the Twenty-eighth Party Congress in July. Prokof'ev said half the people turning in their membership cards were workers and the rest were intellectuals or pensioners. He said the majority of those leaving had joined the Party to promote their careers (*TASS*, *Pravda*, August 14).

Prices of Periodicals and Books to Rise

Prices of periodicals and books will rise in the Soviet Union in 1991. TASS said the State Committee for Publishing and the Press had announced the price rises at a press conference in Moscow. It said prices of books would more than double and the cost of all national periodicals would go up by 50–100 percent. The annual subscription rate for *Izvestia*, for example, will rise from 9 to 22.56 rubles, while that for *Ogonek* will go up from 27.6 rubles to 46.8 (*The Times*, August 15).

Dashichev Says Eastern Europe Has Most to Gain from German Unity

In an interview with the East German daily *Der Morgen*, Vyacheslav Dashichev, chairman of the Foreign Relations Department of the Moscow Institute for the Economy of the World Socialist System, said the USSR and Eastern Europe had the most to gain from German unification. Dashichev said unification meant the end of the Cold War and therefore the end of the need for the Soviet Union and the other members of the Warsaw Pact to suffer the burden of the arms race. He said the arms race had caused the countries of Eastern Europe to put overwhelming emphasis on armaments and heavy industry while neglecting consumer goods production and agriculture (*DPA*, *AFP*, August 14).

Abalkin Says Economic Reform Plan Must Be Changed Drastically

Soviet Deputy Prime Minister Leonid Abalkin said the government's economic reform plan would be changed drastically, partly in order to take into account the sovereignty declarations adopted by many Soviet republics. Many of the sovereignty declarations say a republic's resources belong to it, not to the Soviet Union. Many also call for bilateral economic cooperation between one republic and another. Abalkin also said it was impossible to stabilize the consumer market and fill the shops at current prices (*Pravitel'stvennyi vestnik*, *Reuters*, *TASS*, August 14).

The same day, Prime Minister Nikolai Ryzhkov said a free pricing system should not be introduced in the USSR this year or next, because this would lead to rampant inflation. Ryzhkov said that inflation in the Soviet Union was currently running at 7.5 percent and that it would get out of hand unless the government regulated some prices, especially food prices (*Radio Moscow*, August 14, 1000).

Shevardnadze Calls for Restrictions on Weapons Sales

Soviet Foreign Minister Eduard Shevardnadze called for international restrictions on the sale and supply of conventional weapons. Shevardnadze outlined his proposal in a letter sent to United Nations Secretary-General Javier Perez de Cuellar. His letter said it was necessary for the United Nations to put the issue of conventional weapons sales on its agenda. Shevardnadze also said the USSR was ready to talk with the United States and other suppliers of conventional weapons about the proposed restrictions. He said countries that received such weapons could also join the talks (*TASS*, Western agencies, August 14).

Wednesday, August 15

Gorbachev Restores Citizenship to Soviet Exiles

Soviet President Gorbachev ordered Soviet citizenship to be restored to people exiled between 1966 and 1988. TASS said he had lifted government orders stripping a number of people now living abroad of their citizenship.

On August 16, TASS revealed that the list of people to whom citizenship would be restored included writer Aleksandr Solzhenitsyn. Other exiles covered by the decree were scientists Yurii Orlov and Valerii Chalidze, literary critic Lev Kopelev, chess grandmaster Viktor Korchnoi, poet Joseph Brodsky, and writers Vasilii Aksenov, Georgii Vladimov, and Vladimir Voinovich. *Izvestia* quoted Soviet parliamentary secretary Vladimir Cheremnykh as saying that Solzhenitsyn had had high-level contacts with the Soviet authorities and had agreed to reassume Soviet citizenship. In the United States, however, Solzhenitsyn's wife emphatically denied that her husband had accepted and said he had not been contacted (*Reuters*, *UPI*, *AP*; August 16).

In an interview with *Pravda* on August 18, Natalya Solzhenitsyna again denied published reports that her husband had been in contact with Soviet authorities concerning the restoration of his citizenship. She told *Pravda* that her husband believed Gorbachev's decree "does not apply to him." Having been charged with treason by the USSR Prosecutor's Office and stripped of his citizenship by the USSR Supreme Soviet, Solzhenitsyn believes that only these institutions can revoke their decisions. *Sovetskaya Rossiya* reported that RSFSR Prime Minister Ivan Silaev had invited Solzhenitsyn to visit the Soviet Union as his personal guest. Silaev praised the exiled writer as "a great son of the fatherland" whose arrival would be "as valuable as air for the country." He added that Solzhenitsyn could choose his own itinerary.

On August 23, TASS reported that Solzhenitsyn had turned down Silaev's invitation. In a letter to Silaev, Solzhenitsyn said that he could not imagine being a guest or a tourist in his own country. He said that, when he does return to the Soviet Union, it will be to live and die there.

Bilateral Trade Agreements Signed between Republics

A number of Soviet republics signed direct bilateral agreements that bypass the central Soviet government. In Vilnius, the RSFSR and Lithuania signed an agreement on bilateral trade for 1991. The leaders of Azerbaijan and Georgia also signed agreements on developing bilateral relations and cooperation. The signing followed talks in Tbilisi. On August 16, Azerbaijan and Belorussia were reported to have signed a bilateral agreement on political, economic, and cultural relations (*TASS*, August 15 and 16).

Another Mass Grave of Stalin's Victims Found near Moscow

Another mass grave of Stalin's victims was reported to have been found, this time on a sovkhoz near Moscow. TASS said the grave contained the remains of people killed during Stalin's purges, including former members of the Cheka. TASS did not say how many bodies the grave contained. It said the KGB found out about the grave after interviewing retired members of the NKVD. On August 16, TASS reported that another mass grave had been found in Grozny, the capital of the Chechen-Ingush ASSR. It gave no details.

Iranian-Soviet Border Opened for Visits

The Iranian news agency IRNA said the Iranian-Soviet border in Azerbaijan had been formally opened for visits. The report said a group of Iranians crossed a border bridge at Jolfa. The agency said Iranian and Soviet citizens living within 45 kilometers of the border could now visit the other side with a travel pass valid for fifteen days.

Texaco to Help Develop Soviet Oil Field

The US oil company Texaco said it had reached an agreement with the Soviet Union that could lead to the development of major Soviet oil reserves. Texaco said that, under the agreement, it would begin a study on oil production in the Timan-Pechora region near the Arctic Circle. The area is one of the world's major undeveloped oil fields (Western agencies, August 15).

Tajikistan Issues Draft Declaration of Sovereignty

Tajikistan became the latest Soviet republic to issue a draft declaration of sovereignty. The declaration said Tajikistan had the right to freely leave the USSR. It also guaranteed equal rights for all political parties and public organizations that operated within the framework of the republic's constitution. It did not, however, demand the right to set up its own army, as the Belorussian and Ukrainian declarations do (*TASS*, August 15). The declaration was adopted by the Tajik Supreme Soviet on August 24.

More Cholera Cases Reported

The local authorities banned the drinking of water from the Don River after seven people fell ill with cholera in Koluzaevo, near Rostov-on-Don. *Pravda* reported that 80,000 cubic meters of raw sewage were being pumped everyday into the Temernik River, a tributary of the Don, causing bacterial levels to reach up to 100 times the permitted level. Another outbreak of cholera was reported recently in Stavropol Krai.

Thursday, August 16

Cathedral Returned to Ukrainian Catholics

Officials of the Ukrainian Catholic Church said the cathedral of St. George in Lvov had been returned to the city's Catholics by the Russian Orthodox Church authorities. On August 19, the first Catholic service was held in the cathedral since 1946, when the Ukrainian Catholic Church was forcibly merged with the Russian Orthodox Church. The eighteenth-century cathedral is considered the seat of the Ukrainian Catholic Church (RL Ukrainian service, August 16).

On August 22, the Russian Orthodox bishop in Lvov said "a religious war" was under way between his Church and the Ukrainian Catholic Church. Meanwhile, in Moscow, Patriarch Aleksii expressed his concern about "the occupation of the cathedral in Lvov by Greek Catholics" (*TASS*, August 22).

On August 23, the Ukrainian Catholic Church said it wanted "coexistence" with the Russian Orthodox Church. The proposal came in a statement issued by the head of the Ukrainian Catholics, Cardinal Myroslav Lyubachivs'kyi (RL Ukrainian service, August 23).

Friday, August 17

Gorbachev on Military Reform

In an address to military personnel following an exercise near Odessa, Gorbachev said the Soviet government was considering plans for far-reaching military reform. According to TASS, Gorbachev said that the existing structure of the armed forces had been developed in response to the Cold War. The ending of the East-West conflict and the general easing of international tensions should now be reflected in a revised structuring of the Soviet Armed Forces, Gorbachev continued. He said that the government was working out a reform plan that would reexamine the following principles of military structuring: the need for five force branches; the benefits of moving to a professional, voluntary force; cuts in personnel and defense spending; and the possibility of establishing national territorial formations.

Ryzhkov Endorses Proposals for New Economic Reforms

Soviet Prime Minister Nikolai Rzhkov endorsed proposals for broad new economic reforms and said they should be included in the government's economic program. The proposals were outlined by Abel Aganbegyan, head of an expert commission working on ways to introduce a market economy. Among the proposals was a new law allowing foreigners to fully own companies they set up in the USSR; the introduction of private property; measures for financial stabilization; and increased production and importation of consumer goods (*Reuters*, *TASS*, *APN*, August 17).

Addressing military personnel in Odessa the same day, Mikhail Gorbachev said the USSR's top priority was to reform property relations through privatization and an end to state monopolies. He said there was a need to "encourage the spirit of enterprise in every way" and to promote "an atmosphere of respect for property" (*TASS*, in English, August 17).

Moscow Media on Anniversary of Trotsky Assassination

On the eve of the fiftieth anniversary of the assassination of Leon Trotsky, the Soviet media published several items on him. On August 17, *Izvestia* carried an article by General Dmitrii Volkogonov, the author of a biography of Trotsky, who asserted that Stalin had begun to plan the assassination as early as 1931. This followed the publication in *Trud* on August 15 of an interview with a brother of Ramon Mercader, Trotsky's assassin. In the past two years, Soviet writers have reappraised Trotsky's role, and some of his works have been republished in the USSR.

***Pravda* Unveils Soviet Space Research Program**

The director of the Soviet Academy of Sciences' Space Research Institute, Al'bert Galeev, told *Pravda* the Soviet Union planned to send astrophysical observatories into space during the next ten years. The goal of the program is to examine other planetary systems to provide scientists with detailed information on the composition and evolution of the universe. Galeev said the United States was investing 50 million dollars in the Soviet program.

Directory of Informal Groups Published

Moscow News (No. 32) reported that an official directory of informal groups and associations in the USSR had been published under the aegis of *Molodaya gvardiya*. The directory, called *Neformal'naya Rossiya*, came out in early 1990 and is the work of Vitalii Ponomarev, an organizer of the information center of the Moscow Popular Front.

Latvia to Redraw Borders, Set Up Customs Controls

It was reported that Latvia had decided to reestablish its 1940 borders with Belorussia, Russia, Lithuania, and Estonia and to set up customs control points on the borders with Belorussia and the Russian Federation. Latvian Prime Minister Ilmars Bisers told *Izvestia* that the borders would be restored in stages, first using archive material and then through talks with neighboring republics to sort out any disputes.

USSR Opens Foreign Ministry Archives

TASS said the Soviet government was opening the Foreign Ministry's archives to researchers. The agency said that, after thirty years, the "classified document" stamp would be removed from foreign policy documents. TASS said documents exempted from the order would be those that deal with "especially important national interests" or those whose publication could jeopardize basic human rights and freedoms.

Saturday, August 18

Gromov on Force Cuts

In comments appearing in *The European* of August 17–19, the commander of the Kiev Military District said he and his men backed reforms in the Soviet Union and the withdrawal of Soviet troops from Eastern Europe. "The Soviet army has to be cut to a size that fits the economic potential of the country," Colonel General Boris Gromov was quoted as saying. "But the immediate problem now is guaranteeing proper living conditions for our officers and NCOs and finding jobs and social protection for those who must leave the army."

Ryzhkov "Surprised" at El'tsin's Comments

Reacting to RSFSR Supreme Soviet Chairman Boris El'tsin's suggestion that he relinquish his responsibility for economic reform, USSR Prime Minister Nikolai Ryzhkov said he was "surprised" that El'tsin had made such a statement (*TASS*, August 18). El'tsin had said that Ryzhkov's efforts should be abandoned in favor of the proposals being worked out by the Gorbachev-El'tsin team because the country had lost faith in the Soviet government.

On August 20, First Deputy Chairman of the RSFSR Supreme Soviet Ruslan Khasbulatov asked the Ryzhkov government to resign, claiming that it was undermining Gorbachev's policies by blocking radical economic reform. According to TASS, Khasbulatov said that the Ryzkhov government was "extremely incompetent" and had led the country into "an economic and social impasse."

RSFSR Communist Party Continues to Lose Members

The recently established RSFSR Communist Party lost 162,750 of its 11 million members in July (about 1.5 percent), according to its first secretary, Ivan Polozkov (*Sovetskaya Rossiya*, August 18). Of those who quit, 90,000 were workers.

Georgian Parliament Convenes

The Georgian Supreme Soviet convened to debate three alternative drafts of a law establishing the conditions for multiparty elections, postponed from March 18 to October 28 (*TASS*, August 18). The Supreme Soviet passed a new electoral law stipulating that half of the 250 seats in the new parliament would be filled by candidates who polled the largest number of votes in their constituencies, with the remaining half distributed according to the proportion of the vote polled by each political party. The law stipulated that only persons who had been resident in Georgia for ten years or more were eligible to stand for election and it precluded the participation of political parties that advocated violence, ethnic hatred, or the violation of Georgia's territorial integrity. This last provision effectively barred the Abkhaz Popular Front and the Ossetian organization "Ademon Nykhas," which were campaigning for the secession of their respective autonomous formations from Georgia. Demonstrations were held in front of the Georgian government building during the Supreme Soviet session to demand the resignation of Chairman of the Georgian Supreme Soviet and Party First Secretary Givi Gumbaridze and of the chairman of the Georgian Council of Ministers, Nodar Chitanava (*Reuters*, August 20).

Protests in Checheno-Ingushetia

There was a wave of protests in the towns and villages of Checheno-Ingushetia against the undemocratic way business had been conducted in the local Supreme Soviet (*Radio Moscow*, *Central Television*, August 18 and 19). The parliament, which is dominated by the Party *nomenklatura*, decided not to discuss a declaration of sovereignty, apparently out of fear that deputies would vote in favor of declaring Checheno-Ingushetia a Union republic. To the dismay of some deputies, the parliament voted in favor of combining the post of Party first secretary and chairman of the Supreme Soviet. Moreover, the Supreme Soviet session was held behind closed doors, and the local press was forbidden to report on the proceedings.

Lvov Authorities Try to Close Down *Pravda* Office

The authorities in Lvov were said to be trying to close down the Lvov office of *Pravda* and take its correspondent to court. Vyacheslav Chornovil, chairman of the Lvov Oblast Soviet, wrote to the editor of *Pravda* urging that the office be moved out of the city. Radio Kiev quoted the letter as saying the Lvov government wanted the office removed because of an escalating campaign in *Pravda* against the Lvov authorities. Radio Moscow said that the Secretariat of the Soviet Journalists' Union had protested against Chornovil's demand; it said the action was illegal and in the interests of those who wanted to stifle *glasnost'*.

Two Oblasts Restored in Kazakhstan

Radio Moscow reported that two oblasts in Kazakhstan would be restored. The Turgai and Mangyshlak Oblasts were abolished in 1988 in a move aimed at reducing bureaucracy in the republic. There was an immediate outcry from the inhabitants of Arkalyk, the oblast center of Turgai, who feared that the level of services would fall when the town lost its status. In the aftermath of interethnic disturbances in summer, 1989, in what had been Mangyshlak Oblast, local officials suggested that the oblast should be restored because the authorities in Gurev Oblast, which had absorbed Mangyshlak, were neglecting the area. Turgai will take its old name back, but the former Mangyshlak Oblast will be known as Mangystau.

Sunday, August 19

Duties of Presidential Council Detailed

Moscow News (No. 33) carried a double-page spread describing the work of Gorbachev's Presidential Council. According to the article, each member of the council had a specific area of responsibility. Gennadii Boldin, once Gorbachev's aide, administered the staff of the Presidential Council and organized its work; Grigorii Revenko was responsible for the new Union treaty; and Aleksandr Yakovlev handled "political questions." The assignments of other council members bore less relation to their past experience. Former foreign policy adviser Evgenii Primakov liaised with the USSR's new parties and political movements and with the press, while Vadim Medvedev, the council's newest member, dealt with foreign economic relations; he was, *Moscow News* noted disapprovingly, the only council member whose responsibilities duplicated governmental ones. Ryzhkov and the other government ministers on the council prepared briefing documents for Gorbachev's consideration. *Moscow News* also reported that members of the Presidential Council received a monthly salary of 2,100 rubles, noting that, after Gorbachev's presidential salary of 4,000 rubles, these were the highest salaries in the Soviet Union.

Moldavian Gagauz Demand Own Republic

At a meeting on August 19 in Komrat, Gagauz deputies to the local and republican soviets called for the secession of Gagauz-inhabited territory from the Moldavian SSR and the formation of a Gagauz republic within the USSR (*TASS*, August 20). The gathering appealed to Gorbachev, the USSR Supreme Soviet, and the Supreme Soviets of all the Union republics to back the demand for a Gagauz republic.

In response, on August 20, the Moldavian Supreme Soviet Presidium ruled illegal the Gagauz call for the establishment of a separate republic. It said such calls reflected "ignorance of law and history," *Izvestia* reported.

On August 22, the Moldavian government banned the "Gagauz Khalky" (Gagauz People) movement, citing what the government termed violations of Moldavia's constitution and territorial integrity, TASS reported. The government had been directed by the Moldavian Supreme Soviet Presidium to look into the legality of the "Gagauz Khalky" movement following the assembly in Komrat on August 19.

Monday, August 20

Armenian Supreme Soviet Debates Draft Sovereignty Declaration

The Armenian Supreme Soviet began a debate on a draft declaration of Armenian sovereignty that called for renaming the republic "the Republic of Armenia" and for the formation of an Armenian army, embassies abroad, and a separate currency but did not advocate Armenia's secession from the USSR. The last, however, was the subject of heated debate. A preamble and ten articles, including those providing for the creation of security forces and a separate currency, were approved on August 21. Further articles on a new republican constitution and on the Turkish genocide of 1915 were discussed on August 22. The parliament failed to agree, however, on any of four alternative versions of an article condemning the Turkish genocide. This delayed the final vote on the declaration of sovereignty. On August 23, the Armenian Supreme Soviet finally passed the declaration of sovereignty (*Interfax*, *TASS*, August 23).

Army Deserters Killed in Ukraine

Two twenty-year-old Soviet servicemen were shot and killed after leaving their unit and resisting arrest, *Pravda* reported. The newspaper said that the servicemen, who were stationed in the Nikolaev Oblast in Ukraine, had tied up a duty officer and injured another soldier before fleeing their unit with arms and ammunition. They were found in a forest in Cherkassy Oblast, where they were killed in an exchange of gunfire.

Lopatin Quits CPSU

Major Vladimir Lopatin, the political officer who spearheaded the drive for radical military reform in the USSR Supreme Soviet, announced in *Argumenty i fakty* (No. 30) that he was leaving the Party. His announcement came on the heels of an unsuccessful effort launched by the military leadership prior to the Twenty-eighth Party Congress to expel the popular people's deputy from the CPSU. Lopatin said in *Argumenty i fakty* that his dissatisfaction with decisions taken at the Party Congress had prompted his decision to give up his Party membership. He reiterated his belief that political activities should be prohibited in the armed forces and said he would not join any other party.

Foreign Journalists Visit Army Base

Foreign reporters and television crews received an unusual opportunity to visit a Soviet army base outside Leningrad, AP reported. They were offered a mock tank and helicopter battle, a session with Soviet grenade launchers, and a look inside an armored personnel carrier. The tour, which began at the prerevolutionary Second Guards Artillery base outside Leningrad, provided a less than typical picture of the armed forces, however.

According to the report, it was carefully prearranged to present an idealized portrait of army life, with recently painted buildings and an "ordinary" soldiers' canteen complete with "white tablecloths, artfully arranged salad plates, and hovering waiters."

Military-Industrial Complex Attacked

Novoe vremya (No. 33) carried a long commentary by Aleksandr Pumnyansky lampooning the Soviet High Command and the military industries. Among the former, he singled out for criticism outspoken military conservatives Colonel General Al'bert Makashov and Colonel General Igor Rodionov. Furthermore, Pumnyansky pointed to the existence in the Soviet Union of "a military-industrial complex," which, he charged, had always existed beyond the reach of civilian control. Quoting former US President Dwight Eisenhower on the threat posed by military interests in the United States, he asserted that Soviet military officials too had long used calls for patriotism and warnings about an external threat as a pretext for maintaining their own privileged positions.

Tatar Intelligentsia on Sovereignty Declaration

A week before the Tatar ASSR Supreme Soviet was to adopt a declaration of sovereignty, a plenum of the republic's creative unions issued a statement calling for the people to be allowed to decide what the relations of Tatarstan with other republics should be. According to Radio Moscow, the statement recognized the need for close ties and "a firm union" with the RSFSR and other republics, since a large proportion of the Tatar people resided outside the autonomous republic. At the same time, it said that the declaration should proclaim the sovereignty of the republic without indicating its subordination, thus "enshrining the right of Tatarstan to a voluntary, equal union with all the republics of the country."

Soviet Hijacking Ordeal Ends

TASS said Pakistan would extradite eleven Soviet convicts who overpowered their guards and hijacked an Aeroflot flight to Karachi. Fifteen Soviet convicts, who were being transported from Neryungri to Yakutsk, seized two submachine guns and a pistol from their three guards. The hijackers then demanded that the plane return to Neryungri and released forty-one of the seventy passengers. Six of the convicts surrendered to the authorities, and two additional convicts boarded the plane. After refueling in Krasnoyarsk and landing in Tashkent for negotiations, the plane flew to New Delhi but changed course suddenly and landed in Karachi instead. USSR Deputy Minister of Internal Affairs Ivan Shilov told TASS on August 20 that "such a large group of prisoners should ideally be transported separately, of course. But chronic shortages of flights even for ordinary passengers prevented us from using a special plane."

Khrushchev's Chief Ideologist Dies

TASS announced the death of Leonid Il'ichev at the age of eighty-four. Il'ichev, who held the posts of chief editor of both *Izvestia* and *Pravda* during Stalin's last years, acted under Khrushchev as the Party's chief ideologist. A keynote speech in 1963, in which Il'ichev warned that "freedom to struggle against communism" would never be tolerated in the USSR, heralded a widespread campaign of persecution of liberal artists and writers.

Metropolitan Pitirim Visits Sakhalin

Metropolitan Pitirim of Volokolamsk and Yur'ev visited Sakhalin Island, according to Radio Moscow. This was the first time a religious figure of that rank had visited the island. Pitirim, who has helped to restore and reopen numerous Orthodox churches throughout Russia, consecrated the site of a new church in Yuzhno-Sakhalinsk.

Polozkov Visits Leningrad

First Secretary of the RSFSR Communist Party Ivan Polozkov arrived in Leningrad on what TASS described as "a working visit." There Polozkov spoke in favor of retaining Party organizations in the workplace. Workplace organizations have always been the backbone of the Communist Party's structure; in recent months, however, this method of organization has come under increasing attack from reformers, and calls have been heard from some parts of the country—notably, from coal miners in the Donbass—to ban the Communist Party from the workplace altogether.

Falin Claims He Was Demoted Because of Katyn Research

CPSU Central Committee Secretary Valentin Falin implied that he was demoted in 1983 because of his personal research on the Katyn massacre. Falin lost his job as first deputy head of the Central Committee Department for International Information in 1983. He was then appointed political observer of *Izvestia*. Falin indicated the reason for the demotion in an interview with *Pravda*. Falin's claim does not correspond with his traditionally conservative stand on historical issues. Even under *perestroika* he was one of those who continued to defend Stalinist versions of historical events, including the Katyn massacre and the Molotov-Ribbentrop pact, at a time when more open discussion of these subjects was already possible.

Tuesday, August 21

Trud Publishes Draft Law on Collective Labor Agreements

Trud published a draft law regulating the agreements covering such matters as working conditions signed annually in each enterprise by the management and the work force. The official trade unions were reported to be up in arms because the recently adopted USSR Law on the Enterprise allows bodies other than the official trade unions (conceivably, therefore, indepen-dent unions) to negotiate and sign the collective contract on behalf of the work force. In the past, this was the exclusive right of the official trade unions.

Interethnic Conflicts and the Prosecutor's Office

An expanded session of the collegium of the USSR Prosecutor's Office met to discuss strengthening legality and law and order in conditions of exacerbated interethnic relations, "Vremya" reported. Prosecutor-General Aleksandr Sukharev complained about the criticism the Prosecutor's Office had been subjected to as a result of republican declarations of sovereignty and of demands from areas of interethnic conflict that investigators and prosecutors be recalled. He reminded his audience that, until a new Union treaty was signed, it was their duty to defend the primacy of all-Union laws and that they should not give in to pressure. In an interview with Radio Moscow, Sukharev gave a figure of 900 for the victims of interethnic violence over the past two years.

Repercussions from Violence in Kirgizia

Tilektesh Ishemkulov, chief editor of *Sovettik Kyrgyzstan*, told RFE/RL that the longtime Party first secretary in Osh Oblast, Renat Kulmatov, who was elevated in April to the post of deputy chairman of the Kirgiz Supreme Soviet, had resigned from the latter post. Kulmatov was severely criticized at a Osh Oblast Party plenum for not having taken steps to prevent the tensions that exploded in June. Ishemkulov also said that Kambaraly Bektemirov, head of the Kirgiz informal group "Osh aymagi," was in jail awaiting trial, as were several leaders of "Adalat," an informal group of Osh Uzbeks. Both organizations were harshly criticized by the republican authorities for their role in the events that culminated in the clashes in June and July

Nuclear Reactor in Tomsk Shut Down

TASS said the authorities had shut down one reactor at the Tomsk nuclear power station and would soon shut down the second. The news agency said that these closures would reduce by half the flow of hazardous substances into the nearby Tom River.

Wednesday, August 22

Secretariat Meets

TASS reported on the latest meeting of the CPSU Secretariat. Secretaries gave their impressions after a series of trips around the country. Their findings were gloomy. They found the population to be highly critical of inactivity on the part of the CPSU and of the opinion that, in "the heat and dust of discussion," the real concerns of ordinary people were still being overlooked. Oleg Baklanov, back from a trip to defense industry establishments in Ukraine's Dnepropetrovsk Oblast, said the process of conversion of defense production to civilian use was creating numerous social problems.

Soviet Soldier Murdered in GDR

Citing Western press agencies, Soviet television reported that local authorities in East Germany were investigating the murder of a nineteen-year-old Soviet soldier. The report quoted Reuters as saying that this was the third such murder since the beginning of August.

Controversial Congress of RSFSR Journalists' Union

Journalists from Moscow and Leningrad refused to attend as delegates the inaugural congress of the RSFSR Journalists' Union, which opened in the Soviet capital on August 22. TASS explained that media representatives in those cities felt that the working group entrusted by the USSR Journalists' Union with setting up the RSFSR Union had been unfairly dominated by editors of conservative periodicals. The agency quoted RSFSR Minister of the Press and Mass Media Mikhail Poltoranin as saying the inaugural congress was in fact illegal.

Poltoranin Vows to End Party's Media Monopoly

RSFSR Minister of the Press and the Mass Media Mikhail Poltoranin told *Knizhnoe obozrenie* (No. 33) that his office had worked out a program to end Party control over the local media. He suggested that the newsprint shortage could be eased by cutting the number and print runs of Party publications, and he complained that it was inappropriate for the Party to start new publications when older journals like *Novyi mir* could not be published for lack of paper. Paper, Poltoranin added, was wasted "on books about Lenin, the leading role of the CPSU, Socialist competition, etc." He suggested a moratorium on such publications "for about three years." Poltoranin also said that the RSFSR State Committee on Publishing, Printing Houses, and the Book Trade had been abolished.

Budget Cuts Hit Tomsk Party Organization

Radio Moscow reported that the Tomsk City Party Committee would be abolished in connection with a 40-percent cut in the local Party apparatus. The decision was taken in response to a sharp drop in income resulting from declining membership and arrears in dues. More than 1,300 people have quit the Party in Tomsk since January; several thousand more have not paid their dues. The city's four district Party committees will continue to operate. The Tomsk decision was an unusual one—in the other cases reported, it was the district committees that were closed down.

Turkmenistan Adopts Sovereignty Declaration

Radio Moscow reported that the Turkmen Supreme Soviet had adopted a declaration of republican sovereignty in which the republic claimed the right to determine its own political and social system and to secede from the USSR. The declaration is to form the basis for a new republican constitution and for the conclusion of a Union treaty with the USSR. The report did not mention what changes were made by the Turkmen legislature in the draft of the declaration that appeared in the republican press on August 14. The draft described the Turkmen SSR as a sovereign national state governed by common human values and the norms of international law. Nowhere was Turkmenistan characterized as a Socialist state or as committed to a Socialist order. Rather, the draft stated that the Turkmen SSR was the protector of the national statehood of the Turkmen people and was to ensure their national and cultural renaissance. The draft also gave republican state organs the right to overrule all-Union laws that conflict with those of Turkmenistan and required republican authorities to ensure that the cultural and linguistic needs of Turkmen outside the republic were met (*Izvestia*, August 22).

Lithuanian CP Demands Party Archives

Deputy Chairman of the Lithuanian Supreme Council Kazimieras Motieka said members of the Communist Party of Lithuania still loyal to Moscow had demanded that the archives of the Lithuanian Communist Party be handed over to them. Motieka told RFE/RL that a number of Soviet soldiers had entered the archives building in Vilnius and that six armored vehicles had been stationed outside the building. Motieka told RFE/RL that the Vilnius authorities had contacted the MVD in Moscow and had been told that the action had not been approved by the central authorities. Hearing this, most of the soldiers left the archives building. Later the same day, Motieka went on television to appeal to residents of the city to gather at the archives building to prevent materials from being taken away by force. A thousand people were reported to have responded to the appeal.

Baltic Popular Fronts Honored

The Poul Lauritzen Foundation of Denmark awarded its 1990 Freedom Prizes to representatives of the popular movements of the three Baltic republics. The foundation is a private group dedicated to supporting persons and organizations who work for the realization of the UN Declaration of Human Rights (*AFP*, *AP*, August 22).

Thursday, August 23

Gorbachev's Decree on USSR Academy of Sciences

Apparently in response to numerous reports about the rapidly deteriorating level of research conducted by the Soviet Union's main scientific institution, the USSR Academy of Sciences, Mikhail Gorbachev issued a decree on the status of the academy. "Vremya" said the decree defined the academy as an all-Union self-governed organization and forbade any interference by the government or any other nonscientific bodies in its activities. Indeed, one of the main reasons for the gradual deterioration of the scientific level of the academy is believed to be constant interference by the Party apparatus in the process of selecting candidates for election to the body. Gorbachev's decree also stipulated that all the equipment of institutes and laboratories should be regarded as the academy's own property. The decree stipulated further that the Soviet government would continue to provide the academy with financial support, especially for fundamental research (*Pravda*, August 24).

Anniversary of Hitler-Stalin Pact Marked in Lithuania and Poland

Thousands of people gathered at checkpoints on both sides of the Lithuanian-Polish border to mark the anniversary of the Molotov-Ribbentrop Pact that led to the USSR's annexation of the Baltic states and to its invasion of Poland. The Soviet Foreign Ministry said that the gathering had "an illegitimate character" and that responsibility for any negative consequences lay with the Lithuanian leadership. Consequently, the planned mass crossing of the Lithuanian-Polish border was called off. A correspondent for the "Sajudis" information agency said the cancellation was due to the fact that the Lithuanian organizers and the Soviet border authorities could not agree on terms for the crossing (*Reuters*, *AP*, August 23).

Chemical Plant Explodes in Ufa, Residents Evacuated

An explosion and fire at a chemical plant in the Southern Urals city of Ufa was reported to have injured twenty-five people and forced the evacuation of a nearby village (Novye Cherkassy). Chemicals from the plant leaked into the Ufimka River, forcing the authorities to turn off the water supply in Ufa. TASS said dangerous substances from the fire had also polluted the atmosphere. Ecologically, Ufa is one of the worst places in the USSR. The explosion was the second major accident involving a chemical plant in the city.

Estonian-USSR Talks Begin in Moscow

The first formal political negotiations between a Baltic republic and the Soviet leadership opened in Moscow. TASS said the negotiations concerned relations between Estonia and the Soviet Union. It said the Soviet Union was represented by Nikolai Gritsenko, a member of the Presidium of the USSR Supreme Soviet and rector of the Moscow Higher School of the Trade-Union Movement. The head of the Estonian delegation was the republican Supreme Council speaker, Ulo Nugis. The negotiations continued on August 30. TASS said the two sides discussed historical and legal aspects of the Soviet Union's annexation of Estonia in 1940.

Friday, August 24

Clashes over Supermarket Supplies in Chelyabinsk

A number of people in the city of Chelyabinsk were hurt during clashes between police and citizens upset over the unavailability of goods in shops. TASS said the trouble began on August 22 when a salesman refused to sell alcoholic drinks in the biggest supermarket in the Urals city. It said eleven policemen and one civilian were hurt in the unrest that followed. It said thirteen police cars were damaged and fifty-eight people detained.

Charges Brought against Man Who Insulted Gorbachev

Criminal proceedings began against a man accused of insulting Mikhail Gorbachev (*Vechernyaya Moskva*, August 24). A law against insulting the Soviet president was passed in May by the USSR Supreme Soviet. *Vechernyaya Moskva* said that the accused, who is unemployed and has no known place of residence, had walked around Moscow with a portrait of Gorbachev covered with various insulting drawings and slogans.

Moscow Rations Cigarettes

Mayor Gavriil Popov announced the introduction of cigarette rationing in Moscow on local television. Every resident over the age of sixteen was entitled to five packs of twenty cigarettes a month. Since there was no time to print special coupons, Muscovites were instructed to use their December sugar coupons for cigarettes. Those who did not trade in their sugar coupons for cigarettes were entitled to extra sugar.

Saturday, August 25

US–Soviet Cooperation during Gulf Crisis

Soviet Foreign Minister Eduard Shevardnadze said the United States and the Soviet Union had used high-level telephone communications to coordinate their stances on the Gulf crisis (*TASS*, August 25). On August 26, *Izvestia* published an article denying that Moscow had provided Washington with sensitive information on Iraq's Soviet-supplied missile systems. "In accordance with treaty commitments to Iraq and established practice in this sphere of international relations, there was no talk either of the quantity or of the tactical and technical characteristics [of the weapons]," the newspaper said.

Moscow Grants Privileges to Stalin's Victims

Radio Moscow said the Moscow City Soviet had instituted a number of privileges for people persecuted under Stalin. They include priority access to food stores, free travel on urban transport, and priority in health care. The radio said the soviet planned to give them other privileges, including free medicines and a 50-percent reduction in rent. It said the privileges applied only to those rehabilitated persons registered as Moscow residents.

Statistics on Deaths in Ethnic Clashes

Moscow television reported that some 946 people had died and 8,652 had been injured in interethnic clashes over the previous thirty months. The broadcast also said property damage from ethnic conflicts had passed the 10-billion-ruble mark.

Buryatia Intelligentsia Demand Review of Frontiers

Representatives of the intelligentsia of the Buryat ASSR sent a letter to the USSR Supreme Soviet asking for the return to the republic of territorial units that belonged to it until 1937 and that are currently part of Irkutsk and Chita Oblasts, TASS reported. They also want the restoration of the republic's original name—the Buryat-Mongolian ASSR. Stalin's dismemberment of the republic was described as an unconstitutional act that had serious consequences. The appeal was published in the local press.

Tbilisi Annuls Abkhaz Sovereignty Declaration

The Abkhaz ASSR Supreme Soviet voted seventy to zero with two abstentions to restore to that territory the status of Union republic, which it enjoyed briefly in 1921, and to assert the supremacy of its laws over those of the USSR and the Georgian SSR (*TASS*, August 25). None of the Georgian deputies to the Abkhaz Supreme Soviet was present. The following day, the Georgian Supreme Soviet Presidium annulled the Abkhaz declaration on the grounds that it violated the Georgian Constitution (*TASS*, August 26). The sovereignty declaration followed two years of campaigning by the Abkhaz to have the status of their republic upgraded from that of an autonomous to that of a Union republic.

On August 31, the Abkhaz parliament annulled the declaration of sovereignty. TASS said the session of the parliament, which was attended by 71 of the 140 elected deputies, decided that the declaration was against the interests of the majority of the population. TASS said that, after the declaration of sovereignty had been passed on August 25, the republic's deputies had had a meeting at which criticism was leveled at "separatist forces" who wanted to pursue their own interests by means of an "open confrontation between Abkhaz, Georgians, and other nations, which for centuries have lived together."

Protests in Chelyabinsk

Rioters in the Urals city of Chelyabinsk rallied for the third night running to protest about food and other shortages. TASS said 1,500 people were involved. It said many threw stones and petrol bombs, blocked traffic, and damaged several cars. On August 26, the situation in the city calmed down (*TASS*, August 26).

Moldavia Discusses Cooperation with Romania

Romanian Foreign Minister Adrian Nastase said his ministry was discussing with both Moscow and Kishinev a number of projects that would involve Romanian-Moldavian cooperation, according to an RFE reporter in Bucharest. Nastase also expressed the hope that a time would come when there would be only "a spiritual border" between Romania and Moldavia and when the need for visas would no longer exist.

Moldavian Official Criticizes Gagauz

Deputy Chairman of the Moldavian Supreme Soviet Victor Puscasu complained on Soviet television that "conservative forces" in Moldavia and the USSR were working to destabilize the Kishinev government. He said they were encouraging "adventurist" Gagauz attempts to secede from Moldavia. Puscasu also complained that the Moscow media had "hastened" to publicize the Gagauz declaration of secession (promptly invalidated by Kishinev) without making known the Moldavian government's position.

Sunday, August 26

Antimilitary Protests in Lvov

A rally at the headquarters of the Carpathian Military District in Lvov called for the creation of Ukrainian national armed forces, Moscow television reported. Participants in the rally, which was organized by "Rukh," also called for recruits from Lvov Oblast to be recalled from units outside Ukraine and for a boycott of the fall military draft in Lvov Oblast (RL Ukrainian service, August 26).

Venereal Disease in the Soviet Army

Krasnaya zvezda reported that over the past two years the number of soldiers seeking medical treatment for venereal disease had risen significantly. The army newspaper said that among Air Defense troops alone the number of cases had doubled. The report added that preliminary statistics for 1990 indicated that the problem was worsening.

North Caucasian Islamic Party Created

The founding conference of the North Caucasian Islamic Party, "Rebirth," took place in the Dagestani capital, Makhachkala, Radio Moscow reported. Over 200 delegates from Dagestan, Checheno-Ingushetia, and Karachaevo-Cherkessia took part. The conference elected a council of seventeen people, with Adem Deniev of

Checheno-Ingushetia as chairman. It favors the restoration of the laws of the Shariat and the opening of medreses (religious schools). The creation of the new party followed the setting up of an Islamic party in Central Asia. Over the previous eighteen months, there had been considerable dissension among the Muslims of the Northern Caucasus, with those of Checheno-Ingushetia, Kabardino-Balkaria, and Karachaevo-Cherkessia insisting on breaking away from the Religious Board of Muslims of the Northern Caucasus.

Soviet Trade Unions Ask for Referendum on Market Economy

Soviet trade unions called for a national referendum on the introduction of a market economy. TASS said the call came in a declaration adopted at the final session of a Kremlin meeting of trade unionists from across the USSR. The declaration said the lack of a well-thought-out economic program over the past five years had brought about an economic crisis that was now reaching a critical point. It called on the government to make public a complete analysis and forecast of the economic conditions in the country and to announce a concrete deadline for solving the country's economic problems.

Former Intelligence Officer Urges Investigation of KGB Killings

Retired intelligence officer Mikhail Lyubimov told *Moscow News* (No. 34) that the KGB must acknowledge and condemn its practice of political killings and kidnappings. Lyubimov cited a long list of OGPU and KGB "wet affairs" from the 1920s to the 1950s, including the assassinations of Simon Petlura, Leon Trotsky, and Stepan Bendera. Naming the leaders of the White Russian emigration, Ukrainian nationalists, and KGB defectors killed by the organization, Lyubimov said that this practice was still praised by the KGB today. In this connection he mentioned a laudatory article about the White general and NKVD agent Nikolai Skoblin who played an active role in kidnapping the White Russian generals Aleksandr Kutepov and Evgenii Miller.

Monday, August 27

***Ogonek* Sues "Pravda" Publishing House**

The staff of *Ogonek* sued the "Pravda" publishing house for the right to be registered as the journal's "founder" in accordance with the new press law, its executive secretary, Aleksandr Shcherbakov, said on Soviet television. The staff of *Ogonek* apparently believed that the

CPSU Central Committee, owner of both the publishing house and the newspaper that bears the same name, planned to subsidize its publications at the expense of *Ogonek* and other *glasnost'*-minded journals, such as *Znamya*, that are also claimed by the house's management.

In addition, under the new press law, the founder of a given periodical is entitled to close the periodical down if it publishes material contrary to the founder's aims; the editor of *Znamya*, Grigorii Baklanov, told Soviet television the previous week that this was why he objected to working under the "Pravda" publishing house. In 1989, *Pravda* editor Ivan Frolov threw the journal *Rodina* out of the publishing house because it published articles critical of Lenin.

Leningrad Party Officials Say *Pravda* Must Be Saved

Leningrad Party officials appealed to the CPSU Central Committee to save *Pravda* (*AFP*, August 27). Anticipating the doubling of subscription prices in 1991, they called for a special subsidy, saying that otherwise the Party would "lose its influence over people and society."

Defense Chief on Arms Race, Conversion

Deputy Defense Minister Army General Vitalii Shabanov, who is responsible for armaments, told the Novosti press agency that Soviet modernization of defensive weapons systems would not result in a qualitative arms race with the West. Shabanov blamed US development of atomic weapons in the 1940s for the postwar arms race, and he warned that Washington's current attempts to develop "a third generation" of nuclear arms posed a threat of renewed competition. He lamented the halt to testing at Semipalatinsk, saying that, given continued US testing, this put Moscow at a disadvantage. Shabanov said conversion of military industry to civilian use was proceeding satisfactorily and agreed with proposals to concentrate defense spending in the Ministry of Defense.

Halt in Nuclear Weapons Testing Opposed

Deputy Minister for Atomic Energy Viktor Mikhailov told Radio Moscow that he was concerned about the halting of Soviet nuclear weapons testing at a time when Western countries were continuing to develop their nuclear weapons potential. The deputy minister said that Western countries were trying to improve the accuracy and survivability of their nuclear weapons systems, and he warned that the West still had not renounced the first use of nuclear weapons. Under these circumstances, Mikhailov said, a halt to Soviet testing should come only as part of a broader international ban on nuclear testing.

Fund to Save Leningrad Established

Anatolii Sobchak returned to Leningrad following a visit to the United States, where he addressed the annual session of the Association of American Lawyers. Interviewed by Radio Moscow, Sobchak reported the creation of an "International Fund for the Rescue and Development of Petersburg-Leningrad." Accounts have been opened in the United States and Soviet Union.

Armenian Communist Party Newspaper Changes Name

Following the previous week's declaration of sovereignty and the decision to rename the Armenian SSR "the Republic of Armenia," the Russian-language republican newspaper *Kommunist* changed its name to *Golos Armenii*, Radio Moscow reported. Daily radio and television programs were prefaced with the national anthem of the indepen-dent Armenian republic (1918–20); the tricolor flag has replaced the Armenian SSR flag on official buildings in Erevan.

Statue of Lenin in Tbilisi Dismantled

The unofficial Georgian news agency *Iveria* reported that the giant statue of Lenin in the center of Tbilisi had finally been dismantled. Earlier attempts by informal groups to do so were unsuccessful, and the statue had been placed under official guard for several months. Monuments have been dismantled in Moldavia, the Baltic republics, and some other areas of the USSR.

Moscow Promises to Open Files on Wallenberg

An international group investigating the fate of Raoul Wallenberg, the Swedish diplomat who was seized by the Soviet army at the end of World War II, announced that the KGB and other interested agencies had promised to open their files on the case. Neither this group nor the Wallenberg family has been satisfied with earlier Soviet information on the case (*UPI*, August 27).

On August 28, TASS reported that a group of Swedish forensic experts had already begun studying a Soviet death certificate for Wallenberg issued in 1947 and other documents relating to him. Soviet Foreign Ministry spokesman Gennadii Gerasimov said the Swedish experts had been working at the USSR Justice Ministry's forensic research institute since August 22. He said other experts had begun working at the Vladimir prison archives.

Tuesday, August 28

Sununu and Shevardnadze Meet

White House Chief of Staff John Sununu arrived in Moscow on a visit that comprised part of a US-Soviet exchange of information on presidential administration, TASS reported. Sununu and Soviet Foreign Minister Eduard Shevardnadze discussed superpower relations, *perestroika*, and the possibility of sharing information on organizing state agencies. In June, Mikhail Shkabardnya, head of the USSR Council of Ministers' Administrative Department, spent two days observing operations at the White House.

New Presidential Spokesman Appointed

Vitalii Ignatenko, the chief editor of *Novoe vremya*, was named assistant to the USSR president and head of the presidential press service, TASS reported. Ignatenko, who is forty-nine, had been the editor of *Novoe vremya* for four years; he has also worked for TASS, the CPSU Central Committee, and *Komsomol'skaya pravda*. He replaced Arkadii Maslennikov, who returned to his position as press aide to the chairman of the USSR Supreme Soviet, Anatolii Luk'yanov.

On August 29, Ignatenko told reporters at a briefing that his new job included providing information about members of the USSR Supreme Soviet and the Presidential Council, explaining how presidential decrees are formulated and how they work, and promoting a two-way relationship between the president and the people (*TASS*, August 29).

Thirteen Candidates for Polozkov's Former Post

Nikolai Kondratenko, previously chairman of the Krasnodar Krai Soviet Executive Committee, defeated twelve other contenders to be elected chairman of the Krasnodar Krai Soviet, Radio Moscow reported. That post was most recently held by Ivan Polozkov, now first secretary of the RSFSR Communist Party.

East Germany Returns Weapons to USSR

Reuters reported that the East German army had begun giving top-secret Soviet-made weapons back to Moscow. The East German Disarmament and Defense Industry said the weapons consisted mostly of air defense and communications equipment. The return of sensitive equipment is part of an agreement between the USSR and West Germany covering unification issues.

Belorussian Government Begins Paying Chernobyl' Victims

The Belorussian government began paying compensation to those exposed to radiation as a result of the Chernobyl' accident, Radio Moscow reported. They will receive fifteen rubles a month.

Albania and USSR to Resume Direct Trade Ties

The Soviet Union and Albania will resume direct trade starting January 1, 1991, TASS said. The agreement was reported during a visit to Moscow by an Albanian delegation led by Deputy Foreign Trade Minister Konstantin Hoxha—the first visit by an Albanian trade official since 1961—which resulted in the signing of a protocol on economic, technological, and trade cooperation (*AFP*, August 31).

234,000 Soviet Citizens Emigrate in First Half of 1990

TASS reported that 234,000 Soviet citizens had received exit visas for permanent emigration abroad in the first half of 1990. The head of the passport agency OVIR, Rudol'f Kuznetsov, said this number was 2.2 times higher than last year. Of those who emigrated, 132,000 went to Israel, almost 90,000 to Western Europe, and 5,000 to the United States. Only 0.2 percent of all applications for exit visas were rejected, Kuznetsov said. He also said that some 816,000 Soviet citizens had left the Soviet Union since 1945, 344,000 of them in 1988 and 1989 alone.

Tajikistan Officials Punished, Investigated for Bribery

A former official of Tajikistan's Ministry of Internal Affairs, Lieutenant Colonel Dzhunaid Ibodov, was given a six-year prison sentence for taking bribes. Ibodov worked in the department that issued emigration visas. TASS said he took advantage of his position to promise would-be emigrants that their requests would be dealt with quickly if they paid a sum of money. It said he was caught taking a 2,000-ruble bribe. Tajikistan Public Prosecutor Gennadii Mikhailin said a number of high-ranking officials had recently been charged with bribe-taking.

Wednesday, August 29

Gorbachev Meets with El'tsin

Mikhail Gorbachev and Boris El'tsin met in Moscow to discuss economic reform and relations between the RSFSR and the central government. "Vremya" led its evening news program with a joint interview with Gorbachev and El'tsin. The first question to Gorbachev concerned "the sharp confrontation between the positions of the president and the leadership of the Supreme Soviet of the Russian Federation." Gorbachev tried to take the high ground, referring to constitutional law and the importance of reaching an agreement on issues of republican-Union relations and emphasizing that the formal process for changing the constitution should be followed. Asked to comment, El'tsin spoke in more practical terms. He noted that the declaration of Russian sovereignty left behind an obsolete constitution. These processes, he said, would sometimes come into conflict with current legislation, but this must be tolerated, "otherwise we will simply lag behind society." On the subject of economic reform, El'tsin expressed his satisfaction with the work of the group that he and Gorbachev created about a month ago, noting that they had come up with some "radical" plans to move quickly towards a market economy. Gorbachev was at pains to emphasize that the reform program was not to be viewed as just the product of a small group working under the direction of Academician Stanislav Shatalin (a member of Gorbachev's Presidential Council) but that it involved the participation of specialists from all the republics as well. He was clearly eager to stress the cooperation of the republics in the reform process.

Secretariat Partially Abolishes Central Committee *Nomenklatura*

The CPSU Secretariat took further steps towards dismantling the *nomenklatura* system of personnel appointments, Radio Moscow reported. The move came at a meeting attended by a number of Party, government, and economic officials. The *nomenklatura* list attached to the CPSU Central Committee has been abolished in part. Henceforth, the Central Committee will approve the appointment of Party employees and of heads of press organs, scientific agencies, and academic institutions that are subordinate to the Central Committee itself. The Secretariat also "recommended" that republican Party organizations review their personnel policies, taking into account "new conditions."

Yazov Addresses Political Officers

Marshal Dmitrii Yazov told a gathering of political officers in Moscow that their work was critical in ensuring the success of radical military restructuring, TASS reported. The Defense Minister also said that political officers were needed to combat growing ethnic tensions in the army and in society. Politburo member Aleksandr Dzasokhov also attended the meeting.

Engineering Academy Created to Serve Business

Boris Gusev, president of the newly created private Academy of Engineering, said his organization would serve the needs of emerging Soviet businesses, TASS reported. The new group will work on a contract basis, pursuing research and development projects for all types of firms. While he said that the academy would seek to avoid politics, Gusev noted that, at a time when "centrifugal forces threaten the Union with collapse, scholars must become an integrating force."

Azerbaijan Supreme Soviet Demands Return of Village

The Azerbaijani Supreme Soviet approved a resolution demanding the return of a village in Nakhichevan that it said had been annexed by Armenia. Azerinform Director Azad Sharifov told RFE/RL that the resolution had been passed on August 29 at the urging of the chairman of the Supreme Soviet of Nakhichevan, Afiyaddin Dzhalilov (RL Azerbaijani service, August 30).

Thursday, August 30

Health Minister Says Drug Shortage Serious

USSR Minister of Health Igor Denisov told *Trud* that, in its present condition, the Soviet pharmaceutical industry would be able to meet only 30 percent of domestic demand next year. He added that if the industry continued its downward trend, the country could run out of drugs altogether as early as next February. He said the industry was deteriorating even more rapidly than the rest of the economy. The newspaper said that, of the nearly 4,500 essential medicines on the market, 1,200 were not produced domestically and that only 20–40 percent of the demand for another 1,900 products was met. *Trud* said that, unless the situation was resolved, "cigarette riots in the Soviet Union will be followed by aspirin riots."

Komi Supreme Soviet Issues Sovereignty Declaration

The Komi ASSR declared itself sovereign. The declaration said the republic now remained within the Russian Federation and the USSR by choice. It also said any decision to secede from the Russian Federation or the USSR must be approved by a referendum (*TASS*, August 30).

Tataria Declares Itself Sixteenth Union Republic

By 240 votes in favor, none against, and one abstention, the Tatar Supreme Soviet declared itself the sixteenth Union republic and said it was no longer part of the Russian Federation. Editor Rimzil Valiev of Kazan told

RFE/RL that the decision will serve as the basis for drafting a new constitution and for negotiating treaties with the RSFSR and the USSR. The Tatar Public Information Center had warned that protests would follow if this declaration was not made. Boris El'tsin recently traveled to Kazan to try to dissuade the Tatars from taking this step.

Severe Fuel Problems Reported in Tajikistan

Almost all the Tajik government's vehicles were reported to be at a standstill for lack of fuel. *Izvestia* said the chronic shortage of gasoline and other oil products was also affecting farms in Tajikistan, which, it said, were receiving only half the fuel they needed.

Moscow City Soviet to Register New Parties and Media

Moscow City Soviet and its executive committee decided to create a commission to register all new political parties, public associations, and organs of the media in the city, TASS reported. This means that such organizations will have legal standing, according to Leonid Abayushkin, a city official working with the new public associations. After registering with the Moscow City Soviet, public associations will be able to open their own bank accounts and newspapers, and also participate in foreign trade and possess foreign currency, Abayushkin said.

Friday, August 31

Gorbachev Finishes Talks with Economic Advisers

Mikhail Gorbachev said his two days of talks with top advisers and with leaders of the republics on the situation in the Soviet economy had been "dramatic and emotional." Also attending the meeting were members of the Presidential Council and the Council of the Federation, which comprises the leading officials of the fifteen Union republics. Gorbachev told reporters that it was necessary "to move resolutely forward" towards a market economy, and that it would not be possible "to just leap into the market" without stabilizing the economy (*TASS*, August 31).

Azerbaijan and Tajikistan Sign Cooperation Agreement

The Soviet republics of Azerbaijan and Tajikistan signed an agreement on economic, scientific, and cultural cooperation in Baku. TASS said the agreement provided for increased trade and exchange of raw materials and called for the establishment of reciprocal missions in Baku and Dushanbe. TASS said Tajikistan is the third republic with whose government Azerbaijan has signed an agreement; the other two republics are Belorussia and Georgia.

Moscow Police Guard Taxi Depots after Driver Killed

Moscow police stepped up patrols at taxi depots after hundreds of Moscow taxi drivers drove in procession through the capital earlier in the week. They were protesting at the attack by about twenty-five armed men at the main city taxi depot, during which one driver was killed and two were wounded. *Moskovskaya pravda* quoted Aleksandr Polozov, the director of the depot, as saying that the drivers were attacked almost daily.

Religion on Rise in USSR

Argumenty i fakty (No. 32) published a table indicating an increase in the number of religious congregations in the USSR between January 1, 1985, and July 1, 1990. The number of Russian Orthodox congregations rose from 6,806 in 1985 to 11,118 in 1990; Baptist and Pentecostal, from 2,537 to 2,841; Muslim, from 392 to 1,103; and Jewish, from 91 to 106. These include only officially registered congregations and therefore do not provide a complete picture of each confession's influence.

Uchitel'skaya gazeta (August 29) reported that there were 20–30 million Orthodox believers in the Soviet Union, and complained that the number of Orthodox churches in the country was too low.

The Month of September

Saturday, September 1

El'tsin Backs Directly Elected Supreme Soviet

Chairman of the RSFSR Supreme Soviet Boris El'tsin held a press conference in Moscow at which he talked about his recent meeting with USSR President Mikhail Gorbachev, TASS reported. El'tsin said he and Gorbachev had agreed that both the USSR and RSFSR Supreme Soviets should be directly elected next time around. He also said they had agreed that the USSR and the RSFSR Congresses of People's Deputies should be abolished at that time. In other comments, El'tsin proposed replacing the USSR Presidential Council with a council of Union republican presidents.

Creation of Alternative Russian Communist Party Proposed

Literaturnaya gazeta (No. 35) carried a front-page appeal to every Communist Party member in the RSFSR who is "unwilling to join the Party of [Ivan] Polozkov." The signatories, four members of the weekly's staff, suggested calling an All-Russian Conference of Communists, presumably to set up an alternative RSFSR Communist Party. Their proposal was echoed on the late night news on September 1 by the editor of *Moscow News*, Egor Yakovlev. Among the Russian Communist Party's shortcomings listed in the appeal were the reactionary character of its economic program and its "imperial mentality"—i.e., its failure to mention the right of Union republics to secede.

Defense Council Meets

Mikhail Gorbachev presided over a meeting of the USSR Defense Council at which Defense Minister Dmitrii Yazov spoke about plans for military reform and the withdrawal of Soviet troops from Eastern Europe and Mongolia. According to TASS and Central Television, the council discussed possible changes in the structure of the service branches and problems connected with military management and technological modernization. Council members agreed on the need to raise the level of professionalism in the officer corps, to increase the number of specialists serving on a contractual basis, and to consider shortening the term of active military service.

Commander on Redeployment of Troops

The commander of the Belorussian Military District told TASS that troops being withdrawn from Eastern Europe would be redeployed primarily in Belorussia, Ukraine, the RSFSR, and Uzbekistan. Colonel General Anatolii Kostenko said that Belorussia would receive troops from the Soviet Union's Central and Southern Groups of Forces and that the withdrawal would not weaken the Soviet Union's western frontiers. He added that none of the units redeployed to Belorussia had nuclear or chemical weapons or large radars. Kostenko also said that the decision to redeploy troops to Belorussia—a move that has been badly received in that republic—was taken a year ago, before the current government assumed power.

New Heads of KGB and MVD Appointed in Armenia

Reuters reported the appointment of Usik Surenovich Arutyunyan as chairman of the Armenian KGB. Arutyunyan was dismissed in April from the post of republican minister of internal affairs after a group of people described as hooligans raided the parliament building in Erevan and injured the Supreme Soviet chairman. Arutyunyan is a graduate of the USSR KGB Higher School and began work in the Armenian KGB in 1979. He was appointed a deputy chairman of that organization in 1985 and moved to the post of republican minister of internal affairs in June, 1988. Arutyunyan's new appointment was confirmed by TASS on September 4. The same TASS report also said that Karlos Kazaryan, former police chief in Erevan, had been appointed the new head of the Armenian MVD.

Shevardnadze Meets Chinese Foreign Minister

Soviet Foreign Minister Eduard Shevardnadze and Chinese Foreign Minister Qian Qichen met in Harbin, China, and stressed that Beijing and Moscow had "nearly identical" views on the Persian Gulf crisis (*The Los Angeles Times*, September 2).

TASS quoted Shevardnadze as saying that, as a result of his talks with Chinese officials, the two countries had decided to open new consulates in order to boost trade along their border. Moscow will set up a mission in the northeastern Chinese city of Shen-yang. Beijing will have a new consulate in Khabarovsk.

USSR and Czechoslovakia Sign New Trade Agreement

Czechoslovakia and the Soviet Union signed a new trade agreement. Soviet Foreign Trade Minister Konstantin Katushev signed the accord with Czechoslovak Deputy Prime Minister Vaclav Vales, TASS reported. The agreement called for the two countries to conduct their trade in convertible currencies and at world market prices, starting on January 1, 1991. Comecon members recently agreed to these trade conditions.

Sunday, September 2

Bread Shortages in Moscow and Other Cities

TASS and Radio Moscow reported that "for the past several days it has been practically impossible to buy bread" in Moscow. They said the problem was due mainly to a shortage of workers in bakeries and to poor production equipment.

On September 4, USSR President Mikhail Gorbachev accused some Soviet farmers of holding back grain deliveries to the state. Soviet television said he had sent a telegram to the country's principal regional leaders instructing them to act at once to make sure the grain was delivered. His telegram stressed that grain hoarding and transport problems had also contributed to bread shortages in several other parts of the USSR.

The same day, the Moscow City Soviet and Executive Committee, the Moscow Prosecutor's Office, and the city police formed a crisis committee, it was reported on Soviet television. Deputy Chairman of the Moscow City Soviet Sergei Stankevich said during the program that the committee's task was to forecast which items were likely to become scarce, the hope being that enough warning could be given to officials to permit preemptive action. After touring a bread factory, the chairman of the soviet, Gavriil Popov, authorized the release of 5 million rubles in order to raise bakery workers' wages to 400–450 rubles per month in an effort to attract more workers. Agreement was also reached with military officials on the release of military bakers and bakeries for hire by individuals or cooperatives.

According to *Pravda* and *Izvestia* (September 8), bread shortages spread from Moscow to Leningrad, Arkhangelsk, Tula, and Kiev as panic buying, sparked by reports of the shortage in Moscow, set in. In Ukraine, the government banned the sale of grain to other republics, despite their willingness to pay high prices.

The same day, *Krasnaya zvezda* said soldiers from military bakeries were ready to help alleviate the Moscow bread shortage. *Ogonek* (No. 35) published a letter ridiculing the fact that the Soviet Armed Forces had been ordered to help peasants bring in the harvest.

Goskomstat Says 65,000 Workers on Strike Every Day

The State Committee for Statistics said an average of 65,000 workers were on strike every day during the first half of 1990, Radio Moscow reported. It also said that almost 1,700 enterprises had been affected by strikes during this period.

Human-Rights Conference in Leningrad

The Second International Human-Rights Conference opened in Leningrad (*Radio Moscow*, September 1). The conference was originally scheduled to take place in Vilnius but was moved to Leningrad when the organizers were told that visas might not be issued by the Soviet authorities. On September 2, TASS reported that some 1,500 Soviet and 400 foreign representatives were taking part in the conference, including Lithuanian leader Vytautas Landsbergis. On September 2, there was also a meeting in Leningrad's Palace Square in support of the conference. Central Television, in a sympathetic report (September 3), stressed the moderate character of the rally and contrasted its mass character with the actions of solitary dissidents in the Brezhnev era. The conference ended on September 4 (*TASS*, September 4).

Western Observers Visit Soviet Troops in East Berlin

In an effort to counter Western reports of demoralization among Soviet troops in East Germany, the Soviet army invited Westerners to its Berlin Brigade Base for the first time, Reuters reported. Visitors saw well-kept dormitories, examined tanks, and watched Soviet soldiers drill. Soviet officers conceded, however, that the Berlin Brigade was composed of elite troops with the best living conditions to be found on bases in East Germany. A Western officer said: "I'm not sure this base reflects the wider reality of Soviet forces in East Germany."

***Pravda* Asks Solzhenitsyn to Return**

Pravda asked writer Aleksandr Solzhenitsyn to return to the Soviet Union, calling him "a gigantic talent." The same day, *Komsomol'skaya pravda* published Solzhenitsyn's essay "Live Not by the Lie" to mark the first day of the new academic year. "Solzhenitsyn's lesson is needed today," *Komsomol'skaya pravda* noted.

Belorussia and Kirgizia Sign Agreement

Representatives of Belorussia and Kirgizia signed an agreement calling for economic, scientific, and cultural cooperation, Radio Moscow reported. The two also agreed to consider setting up representations in each other's capitals. Belorussia had earlier signed such an agreement with Estonia.

More Separatist Tendencies within Moldavia

After the Gagauz demanded their own republic in southern Moldavia, non-Moldavians in the eastern part of the republic also called for secession from Moldavia. At a meeting on September 2 in Tiraspol, deputies from the republican and local soviets in the area of eastern Moldavia along the Dniester proclaimed secession from Moldavia and the formation of a new Soviet Socialist republic in that area, Reuters and TASS reported. Chairman of the Moldavian Supreme Soviet Mircea Snegur called for immediate measures to defend the integrity of the Moldavian republic and said that separatist leaders should face legal action.

The Moldavian Supreme Soviet went into emergency session on September 2 in response to the problem. The republican parliament declared the secession invalid, saying it was a violation of the republic's constitution, of its recent declaration of sovereignty, and of its territorial integrity (*TASS*, September 3). The legislature instituted presidential rule, to be carried out by Snegur, dissolved the soviets of the seceding cities and raions, resolved to seek the right for Moldavian citizens to perform military service in the republic, and decided to establish Moldavian "national military formations" to enforce the parliament's decisions.

On September 4, the Moldavian Supreme Soviet voted to suspend until further notice the obligation of the republic's citizens to serve in the Soviet Armed Forces, USSR Internal Affairs Ministry Troops, and other types of USSR forces (*TASS*, September 4). The parliament also instructed the republican government to start talks with the government of the USSR on bringing Moldavian servicemen stationed in other parts of the Soviet Union back to Moldavia to complete their term of service in their native republic.

In a related resolution, the Moldavian Supreme Soviet instructed the government to submit a program for organizing "units of a national army of the Moldavian SSR" and to begin creating "the material-technical conditions" for such a force. The Moldavian government also decided to create a Moldavian police force of 10,000 under the Moldavian Ministry of Internal Affairs. These steps were meant to enforce the decisions taken by the Moldavian parliament to counter demands for secession by non-Moldavian ethnic groups in the south and east of the republic. See RL 448/90.

On September 5, Snegur and Chairman of the Moldavian Council of Ministers Mircea Druc were received by Gorbachev in Moscow to discuss continuing attempts by non-Moldavian ethnic groups to secede from the republic. TASS cited the Moldavian leaders as telling

Gorbachev of their "conviction that the sovereign republic of Moldavia can develop successfully only as part of the USSR." Gorbachev was quoted as replying that he "stands firmly in favor of maintaining the integrity of the republic as part of a union of sovereign states." He also suggested that the solution to the conflict lay in "balanced decisions" that took all interests into account. Interviewed the same day on Central Television's news program "Vremya," Gorbachev criticized "separatist actions" in the republics, referring specifically to Moldavia, and he expressed the hope that the Moldavian leadership would be able, through dialogue, to "restore the normal functioning of the entire republic." Interviewed the same day by Radio Moscow, Snegur said the secessionist movements were preventing the Moldavian government from dealing with urgent economic problems that affected all groups in the republic equally.

Groups of Moldavian Supreme Soviet deputies visited the Gagauz and Dniester areas to begin face-to-face dialogue. They were, however, blocked from traveling into the area on the left bank of the Dniester by the mayor of Tiraspol, TASS reported. On September 5, TASS quoted Moldavian Minister of Internal Affairs Ion Costas as telling the republican Supreme Soviet session that "self-defense detachments" were being set up in some places in the secessionist areas.

On September 7, Costas said Moldavia's new military formations would be composed of both new recruits and Moldavian residents with prior military service (*TASS*, September 7).

On September 8, Gagauz leaders in southern Moldavia and Russian leaders in the eastern part of the republic continued to take steps to set up state structures in the two areas with a view to forming their own republics within the USSR, TASS and Central Television reported. Moldavian Supreme Soviet deputies completed a series of apparently unsuccessful meetings with officials in twelve raions of the two would-be republics. In a broadcast on Moldavian television, Snegur warned that, if the secessionist movements obtained recognition in Moscow or Kiev, "Moldavia would completely revise its position on the Union treaty." USSR Minister of Internal Affairs Vadim Bakatin turned down a request by leaders of the "Dniester republic" for approval of the establishment of their own MVD subordinate to the USSR MVD; Bakatin replied that the group's attempt to create a separate republic was "unconstitutional" (*TASS*, September 8).

On the same day, the Presidium of the Moldavian Supreme Soviet gave the leaders of the would-be Gagauz and Dniester republics until September 13 to renounce their declarations of secession (*TASS*, September 11). Spokesmen for the secessionists interviewed by TASS vowed to resist but also offered to negotiate "a compromise" with Moldavia. Members of soviets at all levels in the Dniester area who opposed secession held a congress (*TASS*, *Moldovapres*, September 11). The congress condemned all "attempts to dismember Moldavia," endorsed Kishinev's decisions to uphold the republic's integrity, and appealed to the USSR Supreme Soviet and the Union republics not to support the secessionist moves "undertaken against the provisions of the USSR and Moldavian Constitutions."

Interviewed by TASS on September 9, the second secretary of the Moldavian Communist Party, Eugen Sobor, called for "round-table talks" among all political forces in the republic with a view to achieving "reconciliation and civic accord."

On September 12, Radio Moscow reported that Gorbachev, Chairman of the USSR Supreme Soviet Anatolii Luk'yanov, USSR Prime Minister Nikolai Ryzhkov, and Chairman of the Council of Nationalities Rafik Nishanov had met with a group of non-Moldavian USSR people's deputies from Moldavia who criticized the Moldavian leadership for "errors" in its approach to interethnic relations and to relations with the Union. Arguing that the situation in the republic required "urgent measures," the deputies requested the Presidential Council and the USSR Supreme Soviet to form and dispatch to Moldavia a special commission to "assist" in normalizing the situation.

On September 16, a second congress of people's deputies from Gagauz-inhabited areas, held in Komrat, confirmed the decisions taken by the first congress on August 19 to secede from Moldavia and form a new Soviet republic. The assembly appealed to Gorbachev for support and resolved to send a delegation to Moscow for talks with USSR leaders. Members of the non-Moldavian movement from the left bank of the Dniester addressed the Gagauz assembly. Moldavian Supreme Soviet deputies who attempted to speak were denied the floor, TASS reported.

Interviewed the same day on "Vremya" during a mass rally "for the integrity of the republic," Snegur ruled out any negotiations with "separatist" Gagauz and left-bank leaders until they renounced not only secession but also "autonomist" demands.

Also that day, Moldavian prosecutors arrested Leonid Dobrov, leader of the Gagauz organization "Arkalyk" (Cooperation), TASS reported. A spokesman for the Prosecutor's Office said the group had planned to take Moldavian people's deputies hostage on September 16.

The Gagauz secession movement is led by the Gagauz People's Movement, which is separate from "Arkalyk."

On September 29, an ad hoc commission of the USSR Supreme Soviet was appointed by Gorbachev and dispatched to Moldavia on a fact-finding mission and "to contribute to the stabilization of the situation," TASS announced. The commission included Georgii Tarazevich, chairman of the Supreme Soviet's permanent Commission on Nationality Policy and Interethnic Relations, and Marshal Sergei Akhromeev, an adviser to Gorbachev.

The same day, Igor Smirnov, the leader of the "Dniester Soviet Republic," was expelled from the CPSU by a decision of the Moldavian Communist Party for "destructive actions directed against the Moldavian SSR's state order and territorial integrity," TASS reported. The measure followed Moldavian Communist Party First Secretary Petru Lucinschi's public warning two days earlier that Party sanctions would be imposed on secessionist leaders.

Meanwhile, Ivan Burgudji, cochairman of the Gagauz People's Movement and self-styled national security minister of the would-be Gagauz Soviet Republic, was detained by the Moldavian police for investigation, it was announced on September 30 in Kishinev (RFE Romanian service, October 1).

On September 25, the Moldavian Supreme Soviet Presidium made public a declaration of "firm protest against the insulting remarks" about Moldavia made by Gorbachev in his speech on September 21 to the USSR Supreme Soviet. Gorbachev deprecated Moldavia's declaration of sovereignty as "declarative euphoria," blamed the Moldavian leadership for the deterioration of interethnic relations in the republic, and demanded that Moldavia clarify whether it sought "membership in the [Soviet] community or just a concubinage" (the latter remark was deleted from the printed text of Gorbachev's speech, which was televised live). "Given such an attitude towards republican sovereignty, Mikhail Gorbachev's request for special powers poses obvious dangers and should not be granted," the Moldavian Supreme Soviet Presidium concluded. Its declaration was broadcast by Moldavian radio and television and by Radio Bucharest.

Kalugin Wins Seat in USSR Congress of People's Deputies

Former KGB Major General Oleg Kalugin won a seat in the USSR Congress of People's Deputies. He received more than half of the votes in the runoff election in Krasnodar on September 2 (*Radio Moscow*, September 3). Kalugin was stripped of his rank, pension, and medals last month by a presidential decree after publicly attacking the KGB.

On September 4, *Izvestia* published an interview with Kalugin in which he said he would like to report to the Supreme Soviet on KGB activities that are unknown to both the public and the leadership. Kalugin said he planned to work in the Supreme Soviet Committee on Defense and State Security and to campaign for the depoliticization of the KGB and for the disbanding of the part of the agency that conducts political surveillance.

Estonians Attempt to Restore Old Borders

Members of a recently revived Estonian home guard unit, "Kaitseliit," erected a border marker near Komarovka in Leningrad Oblast, TASS reported. When asked by Komarovka residents what their purpose in so doing was, members of "Kaitseliit" answered: "We want to demonstrate to the Russian and Estonian governments the will of the Estonian people to restore Estonia's old borders." "Kaitseliit" also tried to erect border markers in Pskov Oblast. The RSFSR government protested against the action. The Estonian government also condemned "Kaitseliit," whose action, it said, was not authorized (*Radio Tallinn*, September 3).

Monday, September 3

RSFSR Supreme Soviet Reconvenes

The RSFSR Supreme Soviet reconvened to hear a report from the chairman of the RSFSR Council of Ministers, Ivan Silaev, on the plan for the transition to a market economy (*TASS*, September 3). In his opening speech at the session, Boris El'tsin said that one of the main items on the agenda was the adoption of a new constitution for the Russian Republic but that priority must go to the early adoption of a program to set the RSFSR on the road to economic recovery. El'tsin said economic reforms were vital, since poverty and even destitution were widespread in Russia and living standards were falling.

On September 4, following Silaev's presentation of the economic plan, the Russian parliament broke up into various committees and commissions to discuss radical economic reform. The same day, the Moscow City Party first secretary, Yurii Prokof'ev, said there was a danger that the Soviet Union was heading towards chaos and dictatorship. He said that to rectify the situation the Party must take control of events (*TASS*, September 4). A Soviet deputy prime minister, Leonid Abalkin, said the USSR's economy had never been in a worse condition, the war years excepted (*TASS*, September 4).

On September 8, the RSFSR Supreme Soviet confirmed the appointment of six republican ministers and rejected one. It voted against Mikhail Chizhevsky as chairman of the State Committee for Architecture and Construction. Radio Moscow reported that Vasilii Machuga had been confirmed as chairman of the State Committee for Sports, Aleksandr Khlystov as trade minister, Vitalii Efimov as transport minister, and Leonid Cheshinsky as minister for bakery products. Also confirmed were Valerii Shubin as minister for forestry and Viktor Barannikov as minister of internal affairs.

Gerasimov Defends US Deployments in the Gulf

Soviet Foreign Ministry spokesman Gennadii Gerasimov defended the deployment of US troops in Saudi Arabia at a news conference in Moscow. Referring to comments by General Vladimir Lobov, Gerasimov said there was "no connection" between the US troop buildup and US-Soviet efforts to cut forces in Europe. Gerasimov admitted that opinions were divided in the Soviet government over whether to pull Soviet advisers out of Iraq, *The Washington Post* reported on September 4.

On September 5, Gorbachev met in Moscow with a US congressional delegation headed by Senator Bob Dole to discuss the Gulf crisis. Later in the day he met with Iraqi Foreign Minister Tariq Aziz. TASS described Gorbachev's talks with Aziz as "frank." It also said Soviet officials, "for the moment at least, want to maintain permanent diplomatic contact with Iraqi leaders."

On September 6, Aziz talked to reporters in Moscow. He said the Soviet Union's military advisers in Iraq had not taken part in Iraqi military actions against Kuwait (*TASS*, September 6).

On September 7, the Soviet Union said it would be willing to provide troops for a United Nations peacekeeping force in the Persian Gulf. Foreign Ministry spokesman Gennadii Gerasimov made the announcement in Moscow, saying that the forces would have to be under a joint command that included Soviet generals (Western agencies, September 7).

In an address to the USSR Supreme Soviet on September 11, Soviet Foreign Minister Eduard Shevardnadze said that all Soviet children and most women had been evacuated from Iraq but that about 5,500 Soviet citizens remained and would be evacuated on completion of their contracts. Apparently in an attempt to justify the continuing presence of Soviet military advisers in Iraq, Shevardnadze noted the logistical difficulty of evacuating them and Moscow's desire to maintain channels of communication with Iraq. He also highlighted the fact that Moscow would lose 800 million dollars in foreign currency receipts as a result of the Gulf crisis (*TASS*, September 11).

A spokesman for the Latvian Foreign Ministry confirmed a report of September 12 that Iraqi naval personnel are being trained at the Soviet naval base at Bolderaji near Riga (*Reuters*, September 13). The deputy chairman of the Latvian Supreme Council, Andrejs Krastins, told RFE/RL on September 12 that the training of the Iraqi personnel had been reported in the Latvian media. An editor at the Latinform news agency in Riga quoted the deputy commander of the Bolderaji base, Sergei Sharov, as saying the Iraqis were learning maintenance and other "defensive" skills.

On September 14, AP reported that the Presidium of the Latvian Supreme Soviet had passed a resolution demanding that Iraqi military personnel be required to leave Latvia.

The USSR Defense Ministry also confirmed reports that Iraqi servicemen were still being trained in Latvia. Defense Minister Dmitrii Yazov said 178 Iraqi cadets were currently being trained in the USSR, including seventy-seven in the Baltic republics. He said that the latter group would return home in November at the end of their course. A Defense Ministry spokesman told TASS that Iraqi servicemen were being trained in other countries as well, including France and Italy. He also said that Soviet military advisers in Iraq were not taking part in military actions and would not be recalled until their contracts expired (*TASS*, September 15).

On September 18, Deputy Foreign Ministers Aleksandr Belonogov of the USSR and Mahmoud Vaezi of Iran held "urgent talks" in Teheran on the Gulf crisis, TASS reported. The same day, *Pravda* carried an article on the issue. The newspaper suggested that Iran stood to gain the most from an intensification of the crisis, especially in the form of a conflict between Iraq and Saudi Arabia. "Any kind of large clash between Iraq and Saudi Arabia would leave these two regional rivals of Teheran paralyzed. Whatever the outcome, they would be weakened, and Iran would emerge as the only regional superpower."

On September 22, USSR Defense Minister Dmitrii Yazov told the Turin newspaper *La Stampa* that the bombing of civilians in the Gulf would be tantamount to murder and that he saw little chance of the USSR's intervening militarily in the Gulf conflict. According to AP, Yazov said that the US military presence was now sufficient for launching an attack. He advised against this, however, saying that military action "would only demonstrate that, confronted with the strong, the weak are always guilty." While calling Saddam Hussein "a rogue" and "an aggressor," Yazov said Soviet doctrine limited the USSR to military action in defense of Soviet borders.

On September 24, Soviet Foreign Minister Eduard Shevardnadze reacted with uncharacteristic harshness to Iraqi President Saddam Hussein's threats to strike Middle East oil fields and Israel. Speaking to reporters at the United Nations, he described such threats as "inadmissible" and said "any attacks would unleash a war that would mean disaster" (*Reuters*, September 24).

On September 25, speaking at the United Nations General Assembly, Shevardnadze referred to the United Nations' will and ability to "suppress" Iraqi aggression (*TASS*, September 25). See RL 430/90.

RSFSR Takes Initiative on Economic Reform

Apparently dissatisfied with the efforts of national leaders to adopt a radical reform program on their own, Boris El'tsin made public a copy of "the 500-day program" for economic restructuring and said that the RSFSR parliament would vote on it on September 11. His strategy was to force the Union legislature to match the RSFSR's moves towards a market economy (*TASS*, September 3).

"The 500-day program" would devolve the lion's share of economic authority to the republics, leaving responsibility for defense, currency reform, disaster relief, and other "national issues" to the central government.

On September 6, El'tsin said in an interview with Novosti that 500 days would not be enough to do what needed to be done, and he expressed the hope that his economic reform program would be approved as a starting point for Russia and the Soviet Union. He said that 500 days would not be long enough to stabilize the economy or "even begin to improve the living standards of the people of Russia." El'tsin said his tour of the Russian Federation had left him with "a sense of alarm." He said Russia was in a deplorable state—"the farther from Moscow, the worse."

Up to 12 Million to Lose Their Jobs

The chairman of the USSR State Committee for Labor and Social Affairs, Vladimir Shcherbakov, was quoted as saying he expected 10-12 million people to lose their jobs in the next few months as a result of economic decline (*TASS*, September 3). He said new legislation covering retraining funds and job placement was to be presented to the Supreme Soviet. The Soviet authorities introduced a placement network several years ago, but it has been ineffective, especially in the more remote areas. Under the new legislation, the unemployment benefit would total not less than half of the worker's normal wage.

Founding Congress of Russian Communist Party Resumes

The Communist Party of the RSFSR began the second stage of its inaugural session. In opening remarks, Party First Secretary Ivan Polozkov criticized those who, he said, were trying to reintroduce capitalism in the Soviet Union. Polozkov's remarks were countered by Sergei Fedorov, a deputy from Sverdlovsk, who told the congress that Communists were leaving the new Party because of Polozkov's conservatism (*Central Television*, September 3).

On September 4, the RSFSR Communist Party Central Committee and the chairman and members of the RSFSR Party Control Committee were elected. TASS reported that a number of Moscow delegates had refused to run for election to the Central Committee in the absence of a program; they further argued against the adoption of any RSFSR Communist Party program until a CPSU program has been adopted. Colonel Nikolai Stolyarov received 70 percent of the vote to win election as chairman of the RSFSR Communist Party Control Commission, easily defeating the official candidate, Nikolai Mal'kov, first secretary of the Chita Oblast Party Committee, and two other candidates (*TASS*, September 4). Stolyarov, aged forty-three, is a lecturer in philosophy at the Gagarin Military Academy. He was nominated to run against Gorbachev for the post of CPSU general secretary in July and subsequently received a favorable notice from Novosti in a press profile as "intelligent, charming, and a talented politician."

On September 5, some delegates criticized Polozkov and called for new elections for the Party first secretary. On September 6, TASS released a statement from Polozkov saying he was not planning to resign. The congress ended later the same day amid disagreements and having failed to complete work on its program. TASS criticized the congress, saying it was nonsense for a political party not to have a program or statutes. The agency also reported that at the end of the congress Gorbachev met with some of its delegates and discussed economic problems in the Soviet Union.

At a plenum on September 7, the RSFSR Communist Party Central Committee elected its Politburo and Secretariat by secret ballot in multicandidate elections, Radio Moscow reported. Among the eighteen members of the Politburo elected were Ivan Antonovich, who will oversee relations with other parties and informal groups; Gennadii Zyuganov, who will take on the ideology portfolio; Aleksei Il'in, who will supervise cadres policy; and Nina Esilkova, who will handle women's affairs. Zyuganov is the author of several articles in the Soviet press calling for a halt to *glasnost'* in the Soviet media.

Protests in Lvov

A meeting of an estimated 100,000 people in the Western Ukrainian city of Lvov adopted a resolution against the Union treaty, TASS reported. Other meetings in that region demanded the removal of monuments to Lenin there.

No Change in Status of Russian Language in Tajikistan

A statement by the Tajik Supreme Soviet, published on September 3, said that the Tajik Law on Language, which makes Tajik the state language, does not discriminate against other languages (*TASS*, September 3). The Law on Language has been cited as one of the main reasons why some 36,000 Russian-speakers have left the republic since the beginning of 1990. Members of various work collectives have suggested that the outflow, which is damaging the Tajik economy, can only be stopped if Russian is given the same status as Tajik. While rejecting this solution, the Supreme Soviet did admit, however, that there had been many conflicts over language in daily life, and it appealed to the law-enforcement agencies to prosecute those guilty of violating the law.

Another Attempted Hijacking

Two men attempted to hijack to South Africa a plane flying from Przhevalsk to Frunze. TASS identified the hijackers as a vocational school student named Kafarov and a factory worker named Vennikov. Vennikov stabbed himself during his arrest.

On September 6, a Soviet teenager, Dmitrii Semenov, who hijacked a Soviet airliner to Sweden in June, was sentenced by the Belorussian Supreme Court to five years in a juvenile labor camp (*Reuters*, September 6).

On September 11, a Swedish court sentenced nineteen-year-old Mikhail Mokretsov to four years in jail for hijacking a domestic Aeroflot flight to Stockholm in July. The court rejected a request by the prosecution for Mokretsov to be deported following completion of his sentence. A Soviet request for Mokretsov's extradition was rejected by the Swedish Supreme Court in August, after he had tried to commit suicide in his cell (*Reuters*, September 11).

On September 25, a passenger on a Leningrad-Arkhangelsk flight threatened to blow up the plane unless it flew to the Swedish capital, Stockholm. TASS said the hijacker was arrested when the plane landed at Arkhangelsk.

Tuesday, September 4

Gorbachev Issues Decree on Military-Political Organs

Mikhail Gorbachev issued a decree ordering the restructuring of political organs in the army, KGB, and police (*Pravda*, September 5). The decree, which instructed the Defense Ministry, the Main Political Directorate of the Soviet Army and Navy, the KGB, and the Ministry of Internal Affairs to elaborate plans for the reorganization over the next three months, emphasized the principle of loyalty to the state rather than to the Communist Party. In the case of the army at least, the decree appeared to be merely a reaffirmation of a compromise decision reached at the Twenty-eighth CPSU Congress. There, it was decided that the military-political organs would be made politically neutral but that the Communist Party would be allowed to maintain its cells in the armed forces.

Shevardnadze Addresses Vladivostok Conference

Soviet Foreign Minister Eduard Shevardnadze delivered the Soviet Union's third major Asian foreign policy address since 1985 at the Vladivostok conference on Asian affairs. TASS carried the text of his remarks. Shevardnadze called for greater cooperation between Europe and Asia and suggested that the Soviet Union could act as an integrating force between the two continents. He highlighted the Soviet Union's improved relations with China, troop withdrawals from Mongolia, and recent breakthroughs in talks on Cambodia. Shevardnadze lamented the fact that military tension was still at a dangerously high level on the Korean Peninsula. He proposed a meeting of Asian foreign ministers in Vladivostok in the fall of 1993 to study problems in the region. Shevardnadze also suggested forming an organization to oversee joint European-Asian security. He also proposed that an international conference be held on the Gulf crisis.

In his speech, Shevardnadze also noted that it was in the interest of each Soviet republic to develop ties with foreign countries in the Asian-Pacific region. "The RSFSR leads in this respect," said Shevardnadze, but he also noted Uzbekistan's potential for developing ties with a number of countries in southwest Asia and the possibility of increased contact between Kazakhstan and China.

Shevardnadze Visits Japan

Soviet Foreign Minister Eduard Shevardnadze arrived in Japan on an official visit (*TASS*, September 4). On September 5, during the second round of talks between Shevardnadze and his Japanese counterpart, Taro Nakayama, the Soviet foreign minister proposed specific measures aimed at easing tensions between the USSR and Japan (*Reuters*, September 5). The ten-point plan included the following: mutual notification of large-scale maneuvers; exchanges of visits by defense ministers, military delegations, naval vessels, and aircraft; and the conclusion of a treaty similar to the US-Soviet agreement on dangerous military activities. The talks also yielded agreement on a visit by Soviet President Mikhail Gorbachev scheduled for April, 1991. The two sides agreed to prepare documents concerning Japanese technical assistance for the Soviet economy and on aid for victims of the Chernobyl' nuclear accident. Concerning the dispute over the Kurile Islands, Shevardnadze called on Japan to take a broader view of USSR-Japanese relations. The two sides agreed that five rounds of talks on the disputed islands had been useful and that working-level talks should continue (Western agencies, September 5).

On September 6, Shevardnadze ended his visit. Before leaving Tokyo he told journalists that the USSR and Japan should try to work out a compromise in their dispute over the Kurile Islands (*Reuters*, *UPI*, September 6). After Shevardnadze's departure, a Japanese Foreign Ministry spokesman said Tokyo had no plans to alter its position. He said Japan's policy remained that the four disputed islands must be returned before it could expand economic ties with Moscow (*Reuters*, September 7). On September 7, Reuters reported that, during his visit to Japan, Shevardnadze had invited Japan's Emperor Akihito to visit Moscow. See RL 433/90 and 378/90.

Developments in Armenian-Azerbaijani Dispute

The Supreme Soviets of Azerbaijan and Armenia discussed recent violence on the border between the two republics. The Azerbaijani Supreme Soviet called on Gorbachev and the USSR Supreme Soviet to take measures to disarm illegal Armenian bands, and the Armenian Supreme Soviet discussed the guaranteeing of the rights and security of Armenians living in Azerbaijan. TASS said that before the session was closed to the public two deputies reported on alleged repression by Azerbaijani authorities of Armenians in Nagorno-Karabakh. The agency quoted the authorities as saying that the situation in Nagorno-Karabakh remained difficult and unstable, with random incidents of violence.

The same day, Azerbaijani President Ayaz Mutalibov said in an interview published in *Sovetskaya Rossiya* that the USSR had abandoned his republic "to face armed extremists alone." Mutalibov said that Azerbaijanis had always linked their future with the Soviet federation but that now they had the right to start looking for partners abroad. He said Azerbaijan had cut off supplies of gas to Armenia because recent actions on the border with Armenia had exhausted Azerbaijani patience. He said it was Moscow's responsibility to normalize the situation and he also raised the possibility of holding a referendum on Nagorno-Karabakh in order to eliminate the primary cause of the conflict. (Under a law passed in 1989 the fate of Nagorno-Karabakh would be decided by the voters of the whole republic, not just those of Nagorno-Karabakh.)

The Azerbaijani parliament suspended the election campaign in several constituencies of Nagorno-Karabakh. TASS said the campaign—for the election to the republican Supreme Soviet and local soviets—would be suspended until the situation in the region normalized. The agency said the suspension was based on "the unconstructive platform and provocative acts of separatists" in the region.

Armenian Party First Secretary Vladimir Movsisyan threatened to resign from the CPSU Politburo unless the Nagorno-Karabakh issue was resolved soon. He made the threat in a statement published in the Armenian press on September 4. Movsisyan complained that a new Azerbaijani blockade of Armenia had been in place for two weeks; a gas pipeline from Azerbaijan to Armenia had been shut off; and freight trains bound for Armenia via Azerbaijan had been stopped. On September 1, gasoline was poured into the water-intake system that supplies the regional center with water. The water authority reported that 50 percent of the population was without water and that water was being delivered by tank trucks.

On September 6, the Armenian Supreme Soviet said Armenia and Azerbaijan were "on the verge of war" because of the situation in Nagorno-Karabakh. The Armenian parliament adopted a statement on the matter. As quoted by TASS, it said that the Armenian Supreme Soviet and the government were seeking negotiations to resolve the conflict but that Azerbaijan was refusing to cooperate. It said Armenians in Nagorno-Karabakh were still being "subjected to terror" by the Azerbaijani authorities and even by units of the Soviet army and MVD troops.

The leaders of the Armenian and Azerbaijani groups at the human-rights conference in Leningrad signed a joint resolution calling on both sides to end all violence and find a peaceful solution, RFE/RL's correspondent at the conference reported. The resolution was achieved after days of diplomatic efforts to get the two sides to talk to each other. The conference appealed to the UN to send urgent food aid to refugees and other victims of disorder in Armenia and Azerbaijan. It further asked the central government of the USSR and local authorities in the two republics to establish a state structure to deal with refugee affairs and to adopt a law on the federal status of refugees in the USSR. The Armenian and Azerbaijani representatives are the heads of their respective refugee organizations.

On September 10, TASS and the Azerbaijani News Agency Azerinform reported that Armenian activists had been occupying Communist Party buildings in Askeran, Gadrut, and Martuni since September 8. Armed units were also said to have attacked Azerbaijani villages, especially in the mountains along the border between Armenia and Azerbaijan. MVD troops detained nineteen activists.

On September 13, Radio Moscow reported that five Azerbaijanis had been shot and wounded and the body of an Armenian found in Nagorno-Karabakh. Meanwhile, in Askeran Raion, thirteen Party officials went on a hunger strike to protest against the dissolution of several district Party and executive committees by the Azerbaijani leadership.

Also on September 13, Armenian militants were reported to be continuing attacks against security forces. The first deputy commander of the USSR interior ministry troops, Lieutenant General Boris Smyslov, said Armenian MVD forces did not have the capacity to disarm the militants. He told TASS that, if the attacks continued, it would not be possible to meet the deadline of October 13 set by Mikhail Gorbachev for the disarmament of illegal groups.

On September 15, TASS said a television and radio center had been blown up in Stepanakert, the capital of the Nagorno-Karabakh Autonomous Oblast. TASS said that no one was hurt in the explosion, which was apparently caused by a bomb planted in the center's basement, but that it had caused tens of thousands of rubles' worth of damage.

On September 16, the Azerbaijani Foreign Ministry protested to Armenia over what it said was Armenia's annexation of an Azerbaijani village. The note said the annexation of the village of Kyarki in the Nakhechevan ASSR "cannot be regarded as anything short of aggression by one state against another" and a grave international crime. The protest note was reported by TASS and the Azerbaijani news agency.

On September 17, the Presidium of the USSR Supreme Soviet urged four Armenian members of the USSR Congress of People's Deputies to end the hunger strike they began the previous week in Moscow, TASS reported. The hunger strikers, who included eighty-two-year-old President of the Armenian Academy of Sciences Viktor Ambartsumyan, were demanding that Moscow restore local administrative powers in Nagorno-Karabakh. They said the Azerbaijani authorities were preventing elected bodies in the autonomous republic from exercising their powers. Ambartsumyan told RL's Russian service that Gorbachev had sent telegrams to the hunger strikers. He said the telegram addressed to him emphasized Gorbachev's respect for him as a leading Soviet scientist but failed to tackle the Nagorno-Karabakh issue.

On September 27, the Armenian deputies ended their fast and were hospitalized in serious condition. *Moskovskaya pravda* said other hunger strikers, including USSR people's deputy Zorii Balayan, were continuing their protest, now in its third week. The paper also quoted Balayan as saying appeals by Soviet leaders for an end to the hunger strike had not mentioned any solution to the Nagorno-Karabakh problem.

On Septembver 25, TASS said a twenty-four-hour strike was being held in Stepanakert and in other parts of the autonomous oblast. The agency said the strikers were demanding the restoration of regional organs of power dissolved in 1989.

Gosteleradio Complains of Lack of Money

The management of the USSR State Committee for Radio and Television Broadcasting said that lack of funding, poor pay for personnel, and obsolete equipment may damage the work of the state network next year, "Vremya" reported. Central Television's 1991 budget has been cut to 405 million rubles—a fact that is of particular concern to Gosteleradio in view of the forthcoming competition posed by alternative broadcasting services and the creation of an RSFSR television station.

USSR Refuses to Boost Oil Exports to Eastern Europe

The Soviet Union refused requests by Hungary, Czechoslovakia, East Germany, and Poland for increases in oil deliveries in the fourth quarter of 1990. The countries face energy shortages owing to the Gulf crisis and earlier Soviet cutbacks. Reuters quoted a Polish official as saying that bilateral negotiations would continue with the USSR and that small amounts of extra oil might be made available for hard currency.

Afghan Agent Gets Five Years for Subversion

An Afghan citizen was sentenced to five years in prison for subversive activities in Tajikistan. TASS said that the man, Amirmamad Mamadogly, had been working for Pakistani military intelligence. The news agency said Mamadogly had established contact with an anti-Soviet underground organization in Tajikistan and supplied it with literature that included calls for the creation of an Islamic state in the republic. TASS quoted the chairman of the Tajik KGB, Vladimir Petkel, as saying that subversive activities by "foreign secret services" had increased in the republic since February, when more than twenty people were killed in riots.

Work Halted on Nuclear Power Station in Bashkiria

The Supreme Soviet of Bashkiria ordered a halt to construction of a nuclear power station near the border with Tataria and Udmurtia. Radio Moscow said the decision was made during a special session of the Bashkir parliament. The radio said the halt had been ordered because of unresolved ecological and economic questions regarding construction of the power station, which had been the target of public protests in Bashkiria for two years.

Protests in the Provinces

Bus drivers in Chelyabinsk went on strike on September 4, leaving thousands of workers stranded, TASS reported. The drivers demanded higher pay, more vacation, early retirement, and better living conditions. They went back to work after reaching provisional agreement with local officials. Residents of a working-class district in Brest refused on September 3 to purchase spoiled sausage offered for sale in a local state store, and, after the police had been called, moved their protest outside to the street, where they blocked traffic. Two store employees and two city officials responsible for food supplies were fired.

Three New Parties Registered in Moscow

Soviet television reported that three new political parties had been registered by the Moscow City Soviet. They are the Moscow branches of the Democratic Party of Russia, the Russian Christian Democratic Movement, and the Democratic Platform. All three parties were formed earlier this year and are organizing branches in the RSFSR and other Union republics.

Wednesday, September 5

Decree on Protection for Servicemen

Gorbachev issued a presidential decree calling for the social and legal protection afforded to military personnel to be strengthened. According to TASS and *Pravda* (September 6), the decree is intended not only to protect servicemen assigned to maintain order in areas experiencing ethnic tensions but also to provide legal guarantees for subordinates in the event of mistreatment or negligence on the part of senior officers. The decree instructed the ministers of defense and internal affairs and the chairman of the KGB to take urgent measures to strengthen discipline and order in the armed forces. It also instructed the USSR Supreme Soviet to examine the possibility of granting servicemen the right to lodge legal complaints with military tribunals and ordered the USSR prosecutor-general to step up oversight of the military prosecutor.

Presidential Council member Valentin Rasputin told the Soviet Television program "Vremya" that Gorbachev's decree on legal protection for servicemen had been prompted by a meeting Rasputin and Evgenii Primakov had with a delegation of women two months ago. Rasputin said that the women—mothers of deceased Soviet servicemen—had asked the government for aid in stemming the large number of deaths that occur among conscripts. Rasputin suggested that the establishment of state-sponsored insurance for servicemen would be an important first step in ensuring their legal protection.

Uzbek Decree on Military Service

Uzbek President Islam Karimov issued a decree banning the conscription of Uzbeks into military units deployed outside Uzbekistan, Radio Moscow reported. The ban is to take effect this fall. The decree also called for Uzbeks to be drafted on the basis of treaties between Moscow and Uzbekistan and instructed the Uzbek government to conclude such treaties before the spring draft in 1991. As an indication of increasing concern over the number of servicemen who die during national service, the decree included a provision forbidding the drafting of young men whose brothers have died while serving in the armed forces.

Solovki Monastery to Be Returned to Church

TASS reported that the regional authorities in Arkhangelsk had decided to return the Solovki Monastery to the Russian Orthodox Church. Solovki was in the news in April, when it was learned that Aleksandr Solzhenitsyn would donate royalties to it. The Soviet press has repeatedly lamented the fact that, although restoration of the monastery, which is spread over a group of islands, was started about twenty-five years ago, little progress has been made. The Russian Orthodox Church appealed to the government in May, 1990, for the return of the ancient monastery complex to the Church.

Komsomolets Investigation Completed

A government commission was reported to have completed its investigation into the accidental sinking of a Soviet atomic submarine off the coast of Norway in April, 1989, TASS reported. The report said the accident had been caused by an electrical fire in the rear compartment of the submarine. It also said that radiation levels in the area of the accident did not exceed natural levels and added that the commission's work had prompted improvements in safety standards.

Thursday, September 6

Anti-Communist Demonstration Reported in Donetsk

A small anti-Communist demonstration was reported to have been held in the eastern Ukrainian city of Donetsk. TASS said about thirty members of "Rukh" gathered at a statue of Lenin in the city's central square and laid a wreath wrapped in barbed wire at the foot of the monument. The wreath was inscribed "to V. I. Lenin on the 72nd anniversary of Red Terror." They placed a banner on the statue that read "100 million victims." TASS criticized the action and said that some passersby had expressed surprise and indignation about the gathering. Meanwhile, the Soviet press continued to publish articles critical of Lenin. Among the many examples were pieces by Lyudmila Saraskina and Grigorii Pomerants in *Vek XX i mir*, No. 7, 1990.

Bonn and Moscow Agree on Cost of Soviet Troop Withdrawal

West Germany and the Soviet Union finally agreed on the terms of a financial agreement to pay for the withdrawal of Soviet troops from East Germany. A spokesman for the West German Finance Ministry said West Germany had agreed to build apartments for the troops in the Soviet Union and to pay for their retraining. According to West German television, Bonn will give Moscow 12 billion marks—about 7.6 billion dollars (*AP*, September 11). Moscow plans to withdraw some 370,000 troops and an estimated 150,000 dependents from East Germany over the next four years (*Reuters*, *DPA*, September 6).

The Soviet Union and West Germany also signed a treaty in Moscow that is designed to be the cornerstone of "good neighborly" relations between Moscow and a united Germany. The document, initialed by Eduard

Shevardnadze and Hans-Dietrich Genscher, included a nonaggression pledge, recognition of present-day European borders, and a commitment to increasing economic ties (*AFP*, *DPA*, September 13).

Moscow Official Says Situation Similar to That in 1917

Vladimir Karnaukhov, head of Moscow's trade office, said the Soviet economy was in almost as bad a state as it was after the 1917 revolution. Karnaukov said people had lost confidence in the ruble and, fearing inflation, were buying up everything they could. He said it was vital to restore normality but added that this would be very difficult, given the soaring demand for commodities such as bread, meat, sugar, and tobacco (*TASS*, September 6).

Ukrainian Catholics Deny Accusations by Russian Orthodox Church

Ukrainian Catholic leaders denied accusations that they were forcibly seizing thousands of Russian Orthodox churches. They told a Moscow news conference that the Ukrainian Catholic Church had "never resorted to violence." An Orthodox bishop from Lvov recently said Ukrainian Catholic leaders had detained him and had damaged his cathedral. Ukrainian Catholics are trying to regain property seized when Stalin ordered their Church to merge with the Orthodox Church in 1946. On September 6, Orthodox leaders met in Moscow with a Vatican representative to discuss the dispute (*Reuters*, September 6).

Friday, September 7

Popov Demands Ryzhkov Government's Resignation

Moscow Mayor Gavriil Popov demanded the resignation of the government of Nikolai Ryzhkov. Popov complained to the RSFSR Supreme Soviet about the fact that, on September 6, the USSR State Committee for Prices had forbidden the Moscow City Soviet to sell tobacco at commercial prices. Popov said the introduction of commercial prices was the best way of alleviating the tobacco shortage in Moscow. He said the decision of the price committee was an attempt to undermine the sovereign rights of the Moscow authorities. Popov added that pressure for Ryzhkov's resignation was mounting (*TASS*, September 7).

Gorbunovs Suspends Communist Party Membership

President of the Latvian Supreme Council Anatolijs Gorbunovs said he was suspending his activities in Latvia's independent Communist Party. The decision was reported by Radio Riga. No reason was given for the move.

Soviet-Estonian Talks Suspended

Political talks about the future of Estonia were suspended after Soviet negotiators objected to dealing with Estonia as an independent country. The talks broke off during the third round in Moscow on September 6. Estonia's official ETA news agency said the argument started when the chief Soviet negotiator, Nikolai Gritsenko, said he could conduct only "discussions" with the Estonians because "talks" were conducted "only between states, but Estonia is both de jure and de facto a Union republic" (*AP*, September 7).

Saturday, September 8

Call for Change in Status of Crimea

The Crimean Oblast Soviet voted for the abrogation of a USSR Supreme Soviet decree of 1945 and the corresponding RSFSR law that transformed the Crimean Autonomous Republic into an oblast on the grounds that they were unconstitutional, TASS reported. Members of the soviet said that the decrees "accused entire peoples of treachery" and lent legal justification to the deportation of Crimeans.

Academician Bogomolov Says He Feels Guilty about the Past

In a letter to *Ogonek* (No. 35), Academician Oleg Bogomolov said he felt guilty about what went on in the Soviet Union in the pre-*perestroika* period. Bogomolov heads a Moscow think tank that has been a source of liberal ideas and that sheltered many of today's leading reformist intellectuals in the Brezhnev era. He said that, under Brezhnev, he and his colleagues told themselves they could do more good inside the system, feeding liberal ideas to their establishment bosses, than they could outside it. But now, Bogomolov wrote, he cannot forgive himself for his failure to speak out. See RL 398/90

Sunday, September 9

Gorbachev and Bush Hold Summit

USSR President Mikhail Gorbachev and US President George Bush held a summit meeting in Helsinki. The Gulf crisis was at the top of their agenda. After seven hours of talks, Bush and Gorbachev agreed to seek a political solution to the crisis (*Reuters*, September 9). At a press conference in Helsinki, Gorbachev described Bush's pledge not to leave US forces in the Gulf zone after the crisis as "a very important statement." Bush described the presence of Soviet experts in Iraq—now numbering 150, according to Gorbachev—as "not a major irritant." Gorbachev said it should be clear to Saddam Hussein "that, if Iraq were to provoke military action, the result would be a tragedy first and foremost for the Iraqi people."

At the press conference, both leaders also said they had discussed the prospect of US aid to the Soviet Union. Reuters quoted Bush as saying, "I am very much interested in assisting to be sure that *perestroika* is successful." Gorbachev rebuffed suggestions that Moscow would play second fiddle to Washington, saying, "It would be very oversimplified and very superficial to believe that the Soviet Union could be bought for dollars" (*AP*, September 9).

Shevardnadze and Baker Meet

US Secretary of State James Baker met in Moscow with USSR Foreign Minister Eduard Shevardnadze for follow-up talks to the Bush-Gorbachev meeting, TASS reported. According to a Pentagon official, the two foreign ministers discussed the possibility of using a Soviet ship to transport US tanks to the Gulf.

On September 13, Shevardnadze and Baker discussed how to resolve differences on ceilings for NATO and Warsaw Pact troops in Europe that were delaying progress at the talks on conventional arms reduction in Vienna (*Reuters*, *TASS*, September 13).

KGB Colonel Attacks Andropov, Reveals Corruption

Sobesednik (No. 36) carried an interview with an unnamed KGB colonel who accused Yurii Andropov of pursuing "catastrophic" foreign policies during the Khrushchev and Brezhnev eras. The KGB officer said that the former head of the security services shared responsibility for the Soviet invasions of Hungary in 1956, Czechoslovakia in 1968, and Afghanistan in 1979. He said that only when historians gained access to secret archives would it be clear how many of the country's losses had been caused by Andropov and his associates. The officer also rebuffed the KGB leadership's claim that the organization was not involved in corruption under Brezhnev. He gave many examples of KGB officials' taking bribes and otherwise abusing their positions.

Parents of Servicemen Gather

The first All-Union Congress of Servicemen's Parents, organized by the informal military trade union "Shield" and the committee "Mothers against Violence," met in

Moscow over the weekend, TASS and Radio Moscow reported. Congress participants claimed that, over the past four years, 15,000-20,000 soldiers and officers had died of "noncombat-related" causes. They blamed brutality among the troops as one major cause of death and criticized military and political leaders for not being more responsive to the problem.

On September 9, *Krasnaya zvezda* carried an article criticizing the All-Union Congress of Servicemen's Parents. The newspaper accused the participants of being hysterically antimilitary and singled out for criticism a speech entitled: "The army—a machine for the destruction of our nation's future." See RL 388/90.

Destruction of Lenin Monuments Continues

Radio Moscow reported that a statue of Lenin in Ivanovo Oblast had been defaced. Commenting on this and other instances of statues of Lenin being vandalized in the Soviet Union, the radio said: "People may have different attitudes towards Lenin's heritage, but the outrage [inflicted] on monuments demonstrates a lack of civilization and the degradation of [our] society."

On September 11, a statue of Lenin in the town of Drohobych in the Lvov Oblast of Western Ukraine was demolished, Radio Kiev reported.

On September 13, Soviet television showed two rallies in Lvov. The report said that people at one of the demonstrations had demanded the removal of a statue of Lenin from the city center but that those at the other wanted it to stay. On September 14, a special session of the Lvov City Soviet decided that the monument should be taken down.

Soyuzpechat' Will Not Sell Independent Newspapers

On September 9, Soyuzpechat', the agency that holds the monopoly on retail sales of periodicals, was instructed (by whom is unknown) to refrain from selling independent newspapers such as *Democratic Russia* (the newspaper of the opposition "Democratic Russia" bloc in the RSFSR Congress of People's Deputies), *Stolitsa* (a publication of the Moscow City Soviet), *Kommersant*(published by the Union of Cooperatives), and the independent newspapers *Megapolis-express* and *Moskovskie vedomosti*. According to Andrei Mal'gin, the editor of *Stolitsa*, who reported on the decision in *Argumenty i fakty* (No. 40), post offices are also refusing to accept readers' subscriptions to these newspapers.

Soviet Fighter Plane Crashes In Italy

An SU-27 fighter plane plunged to the ground during an air show in northern Italy, killing the pilot and a steward and injuring eight spectators, UPI and AP reported. The plane crashed while performing a loop after it had passed over a crowd of 40,000 people. The pilot, Rimas Stankiavicius, was described as one of the most experienced Soviet test pilots. He had recently been appointed chief test pilot of the Soviet Union's space shuttle program, the reports said.

Group of Latvian Residents Urges Opposition to Citizenship Law

Pravda said a delegation of Latvian residents had gone to Moscow to urge the RSFSR parliament to oppose a Latvian-Russian treaty. The newspaper said the delegation wanted the Russian parliament to reject the treaty unless the Latvian parliament adopted what the group considers to be a fair law on citizenship. *Pravda* said that there were three drafts of the citizenship law in Latvia but that none were satisfactory to non-Latvian residents of the republic, who make up about 50 percent of the population.

Monday, September 10

USSR Supreme Soviet Convenes

On the opening day of the fall session, the first action of the USSR Supreme Soviet was to reject the agenda prepared by the Presidium. Chairman of the Leningrad City Soviet Anatolii Sobchak suggested that ten other items be considered, including a vote of no confidence in the USSR government, "a review of presidential decrees with reference to their lawfulness and success," and a parliamentary investigation of unpublished KGB orders and directives and their compliance with Soviet law. Sobchak also requested that control over the issue of rubles and the disposal of gold reserves be transferred from the government to the Supreme Soviet.

On September 11, USSR Supreme Soviet committees and commissions met to discuss various economic reform proposals. Prime Minister Nikolai Ryzhkov said he would not present his program in full until the group led by Abel Aganbegyan had completed its merger of the plans put forward by the government and the group led by Presidential Council member Stanislav Shatalin. (On September 7, Mikhail Gorbachev appointed Aganbegyan head of a group charged with negotiating a compromise document.) Meanwhile, Aganbegyan told Interfax that the two plans were incompatible.

Gorbachev announced the same day that he favored the Shatalin plan because it "integrates the ideas of the republics." He added, however, that he still believed that some parts of the government proposal could be incorporated in the final document.

Addressing the Supreme Soviet on September 11, Ryzhkov said: "You either replace the government or allow it to function and support it in every way possible." At a press conference on September 12, Ryzhkov claimed that the government had the country's economic situation under control and warned that, if the Supreme Soviet adopted a plan that did not match his, the government would not be able to implement it. Ryzhkov complained that his "opponents" were trying to discredit him in the eyes of the people by portraying him as determined to raise prices, while they themselves wanted to subject all prices to market forces (*Central Television*, September 12).

On September 12, a final version of the economic reform proposal was submitted to the USSR and republican parliaments. Gorbachev said it was based on Shatalin's plan and included suggestions made by representatives of the Union republics (*TASS*, September 12).

On September 14, the USSR Supreme Soviet committees heard reports from economic advisers on the reform draft. Academician Aganbegyan defended the plan, saying that government support for continuing centralism was not realistic (*Reuters*, *TASS*, September 14). Nevertheless, he stressed that the draft called for the prices of food and other staples to remain stable for a year. For his part, Shatalin said he was only trying to create a normal economy. Soviet Deputy Prime Minister Leonid Abalkin, however, who is one of the authors of the government plan, called for support for the government's cautious reform efforts. He warned of "uncontrollable inflation" if the government's views did not prevail.

On September 15, the Presidium of the USSR Supreme Soviet issued instructions on measures to stabilize society, put a stop to violence, and ensure citizens' safety. It set up several commissions to deal with these issues. The Presidium also set up a group to analyze currency and money-supply policy. The group was charged with devising ways to prevent the further devaluation of the ruble. Another commission was set up to elaborate proposals on how better to implement economic reforms in the Soviet Union (*TASS*, September 15).

On September 17, Mikhail Gorbachev addressed the USSR Supreme Soviet. He said demands for the resignation of the government were "unacceptable," because a change in government would only "intensify confrontation within society" (*TASS*, September 17). The Soviet president recommended that a national referendum be held on the question of private ownership of land, saying that people could not be forced "into new forms of economic life in defiance of social realities, the objective course of historical processes, and the peoples' interests, sentiments, psychology, and attitudes." Gorbachev said he favored the Shatalin reform plan but noted that it was not "perfect and faultless."

In his address to the USSR Supreme Soviet, Academician Abel Aganbegyan said the economic situation in the USSR was "catastrophic" and "much worse than it appears on the surface." He called the shortages, inflation, and social unrest currently affecting the USSR "a joke compared with what could happen" if radical economic reforms were not carried out immediately (*TASS*, September 17).

Aganbegyan also called for the creation of a special body, independent of the USSR Council of Ministers, to oversee the transition to a market economy, Central Television reported on September 18. Aganbegyan said the body should be jointly chaired by Gorbachev and El'tsin, since "public opinion polls carried out by Tat'yana Zaslavskaya's institute show that El'tsin enjoys the confidence of 80 percent of the population."

Stanislav Shatalin took issue with Gorbachev's call for a referendum and said that it was unfair to shift the burden of responsibility onto the people. Deputy Prime Minister Leonid Abalkin reiterated Ryzhkov's criticisms of Shatalin's proposals (*TASS*, September 17).

Sobchak Complains about Chaos in USSR

At the USSR Supreme Soviet session, Leningrad Mayor Anatolii Sobchak complained bitterly that, since adopting declarations of sovereignty, some republics had reneged on their obligations to deliver food to Leningrad. He said no economic reform program would be realizable if this continued, and he called for tough measures, including the expulsion from the Soviet Union of republics that unilaterally violated agreements.

"Reactionary Forces" Alleged to Be Blockading Moscow and Leningrad

Members of the Interregional Group of Deputies issued an appeal warning that tension in Moscow and Leningrad had reached "a dangerous level." TASS quoted the appeal as saying that the cities were the victims of a secret economic blockade imposed by "reactionary forces in the apparat." The appeal called on democratic forces not to abandon the two cities but to render all possible aid.

Israeli Officials Visit Moscow

TASS reported that Ariel Sharon, the Israeli housing minister and chairman of a cabinet committee on immigration, had arrived in Moscow on September 6 in response to an invitation from the Modul Construction Cooperative. The cooperative hopes to build apartments in Israel in exchange for the importation of Israeli fruits and vegetables to Moscow. According to TASS, Sharon addressed worshippers at Moscow's Central Synagogue on September 8, telling them: "There is a place for all of you in Israel."

On September 12, an Israeli Foreign Ministry delegation arrived in Moscow to discuss a planned UN meeting between Eduard Shevardnadze and his Israeli counterpart, David Levi (*Reuters*, September 13).

On September 14, more high-ranking Israeli officials came to Moscow for official talks. Finance Minister Yitzhak Modai and Science Minister Yuval Ne'eman came to discuss with Soviet officials Israeli agricultural sales to Moscow and a proposal to build a commercial airliner using Soviet, Israeli, and US technology (*AP*, *Reuters*, September 14). On the day of their arrival, the two Israeli ministers were received by Mikhail Gorbachev. This was the first meeting between a Soviet leader and an Israeli minister since Moscow broke off diplomatic relations with Israel in 1967 (*Central Television*, September 14).

On September 15, Modai said his "historic" meeting in Moscow with Gorbachev would boost Israel's standing in the international community. He told Radio Israel that he and Ne'eman had not expected their talks with Gorbachev to be so "thorough, long, and friendly" (*Reuters*, *UPI*, September 15). The same day, Gorbachev told the visiting Italian foreign minister, Gianni de Michelis, that he would be willing to establish full diplomatic relations with Israel if the latter agreed to participate in an international peace conference on the Middle East (*AP*, *Reuters*, September 15).

On September 16, Israeli Prime Minister Yitzhak Shamir rejected the idea of linking restoration of full Soviet-Israeli diplomatic ties to Israeli acceptance of the international conference (*AFP*, September 16).

Oleg Tumanov Versus Oleg Kalugin

A former editor for the Russian Service of Radio Liberty, Oleg Tumanov, told a correspondent from *Sobesednik* (No. 36) that a group of KGB experts led by former KGB General Oleg Kalugin had long ago advised the Soviet leadership to stop jamming RFE/RL broadcasts. Tumanov, who claims to have cooperated with the KGB before his return to the USSR in 1988, said that he personally had been against the cessation of jamming. According to *Sobesednik*, Tumanov was sent by the KGB to the Kuban region in an effort to discredit Kalugin during the latter's recent election campaign.

Russian Orthodox Priest Murdered

The Soviet media reported on September 10 that Father Aleksandr Men', a Russian Orthodox priest, had been killed the previous day by a blow to the head while going to his parish. No further details were released. Father Aleksandr, who was fifty-five, was a religious activist of long standing and a noted theologian and was regarded by the Brezhnev leadership as a dissident. Recently, a number of interviews with and articles by Father Aleksandr have been published in journals such as *Ogonek*, *Nauka i zhizn'*, and *Sobesednik*. On the eve of his death, he was chosen to become rector of the "Sunday Orthodox University."

On September 11, Gorbachev ordered a thorough investigation into the murder of Father Aleksandr (*AP*, September 11). On the following day, at the suggestion of RSFSR People's Deputy Father Gleb Yakunin, the RSFSR parliament set up its own commission to look into the murder (*Central Television*, September 11).

On September 24, TASS reported that several people had been detained in connection with the murder of Father Aleksandr.

Muslim Prayer Leader Sentenced

Imam Sokidzhon Bedimogov, a Muslim prayer leader, was sentenced to four years in prison by the Tajik Supreme Court on charges of instigating the riots in Dushanbe in February, TASS reported. TASS said Bedimogov had incited young people to commit antigovernment acts and had called for the creation of an Islamic state in Tajikistan. Bedimogov, apparently a popular figure in Tajikistan, argued at his trial that he was "a tool in the hands of people yearning for power." Seventy-seven people have now been arrested in connection with the riots.

Ukrainian Oblast Bans Political Activities by Nonlocal Groups

The Nikolaev Oblast Soviet in Ukraine banned political activities by groups from other parts of the republic. The soviet Presidium alleged that many groups were attempting to "destabilize the internal political situation and to disrupt law and order in the oblast," Radio Kiev said. The Presidium said the measures became necessary following the attempts of a group returning last month from celebrations marking the founding of the Ukrainian Cossack State to hold a demonstration.

Ukrainian Catholic Week in Lvov

The Ukrainian Catholic Week of Religious and Cultural Events took place in Lvov. According to the Rome-based Ukrainian Catholic Press Bureau, a rally on September 8 brought together about 40,000 young people in the biggest gathering of its kind since 1933 (*RFE/RL Special*, September 10).

Hungary and USSR Negotiate Costs of Ending Soviet Military Presence

The Soviet Union and Hungary started negotiations in Budapest on the costs of ending the forty-five-year Soviet military presence in Hungary. A statement issued after a preliminary meeting said the negotiators had discussed previous Soviet military withdrawals, as well as legal, financial, and environmental issues (*Radio Budapest*, September 10).

Tuesday, September 11

Shatalin Program Adopted by the RSFSR Supreme Soviet

The RSFSR Supreme Soviet approved in principle the economic reform plan drawn up under the leadership of Stanislav Shatalin. (The plan stipulated the introduction of a mixed economy in the USSR, similar to economic systems existing in Western Europe, the United States, and Japan. The plan envisaged the privatization of most Soviet enterprises and factories and the disbanding of unprofitable collective and state farms. It left only the post, railroads, and the defense industry in the hands of the central government.) The RSFSR Supreme Soviet instructed the RSFSR Council of Ministers to draw up specific measures to implement the plan. TASS quoted Boris El'tsin as saying that Ryzhkov's economic plan was incompatible with Shatalin's.

On September 13, however, the Russian parliament rejected a draft resolution on economic reform, sending it back to soviet committees for more work. TASS did not give a full account of the reasons for the move, but it did say that some deputies thought that the plan was "a sellout" and an attempt to restore capitalism in Russia. At the same session, El'tsin reiterated full support for radical economic reform. He accused the Ryzhkov government of being the main obstacle blocking the implementation of the plan and again called on the government to resign (*Central Television*, September 13).

Kazakh President Warns against Nationalism

Kazakh President Nursultan Nazarbaev warned informal groups in the republic that the authorities would take action against people who attempted to fan ethnic tensions in Kazakhstan. His warning specifically mentioned calls for the redrawing of Kazakhstan's borders and the expulsion of non-Kazakhs, according to TASS.

Nazarbaev also said that interethnic tension could hamper the transition to a market economy.

New Ambassadorial Appointments

Lev Mironov replaced Valentin Dmitriev, who has retired, as Soviet ambassador to Ethiopia. Mironov, who is fifty-seven, has served in Soviet embassies in Mongolia and Somalia. His most recent post was deputy chief of the African Countries Administration at the USSR Ministry of Foreign Affairs, where he had been since December, 1988 (*TASS*, September 11).

Yurii Myakotnykh was appointed the new Soviet ambassador to Cambodia. Myakotnykh, who is fifty-three, has served in Soviet embassies in the Republic of Congo, Italy, Malaysia, and Vietnam. Since April, 1988, Myakotnykh has been deputy head of the Asian Socialist Countries Administration at the USSR Ministry of Foreign Affairs. The current Soviet ambassador to Cambodia, Rashit Khamidulin, was "released from his duties in connection with a transfer to other work" (*TASS*, September 11).

Vladilen Nikitin replaced Oleg Kvasov as Soviet ambassador to Argentina. Born in 1940, Nikitin graduated from the International Relations Institute of Moscow State University in 1968. He served in Peru and held various posts in the USSR Ministry of Foreign Affairs in Moscow. His most recent post was first deputy head of the Latin American Administration at the Foreign Ministry (*TASS*, September 13).

Reporters Tour Lubyanka Headquarters

Reuters reported that 100 Soviet and foreign reporters had been permitted to tour the Lubyanka KGB headquarters in Moscow. They were allowed to visit part of a museum where they were shown spy equipment said to have been captured from US agents. Aleksandr Karbainov, head of the new KGB center for public contacts, told the journalists that the KGB must come under increasing public scrutiny and that it must strive to protect human rights as well as the state.

Wednesday, September 12

Rumors in Moscow of Military Coup

Two liberal Moscow journals suggested that top military officers might be considering a coup to restore order in the Soviet Union. While one of the journals—*Moscow News* (No. 36)—urged democrats to resist any such move, the other—*Literaturnaya gazeta*—said Mikhail Gorbachev should use younger generals to push through reform. In *Moscow News*, the leader of the unofficial military trade union "Shield" said he had information that the military leadership "already has a clear plan to take control of the situation in the country."

Movements by Airborne Troops in the Moscow area on September 8 and 9 sparked fears of a military coup and forced the cancellation of military exercises and rehearsals for a military parade, *Komsomol'skaya pravda* reported. According to accounts by Reuters and *The Washington Post* on September 9, Boris El'tsin told the RSFSR Supreme Soviet he had doubts about the real mission of the troops. The commander of the Airborne Troops, meanwhile, said that two regiments had been moved from Ryazan, south of Moscow, in order to prepare for the November 7 parade, while another—inexplicably dressed in combat gear—had assembled in Ryazan to help with the potato harvest.

On September 19, in a statement broadcast on Soviet television, USSR Defense Minister Dmitrii Yazov denied recent press reports that the Soviet military leadership was planning a coup. Yazov confirmed that troop movements had taken place in the Moscow area earlier this month but repeated assurances such movements involved only preparations for the parade and the potato harvest.

On September 24, a deputy told the USSR Supreme Soviet that he had information—supplied by the unofficial military union "Shield"—about suspicious troop movements in Moscow, Reuters reported. Sergei Belozertsev asked why two airborne divisions sent to Moscow several weeks before were armed with tear gas, bulletproof clothing, and weapons. He alleged that two of the divisions had been placed under KGB control, that leave for military personnel had been canceled, and that military readiness had been stepped up. KGB Chairman Vladimir Kryuchkov, however, again repeated earlier assurances that the troops were in Moscow only to prepare for the parade.

On September 25, coup rumors continued in Moscow when a Soviet colonel warned an RSFSR parliamentary committee that several army divisions and a paratroop regiment had been deployed around the capital in readiness for "a special operation." AFP quoted Colonel Sergei Kudinov—until ten days previously the deputy commander of the Ryazan Military Academy—as saying that troops had begun arriving in the Moscow region on September 9 or 10 and that "a group of about twenty officers had been set up to direct the operation around the clock."

Sovetskaya Rossiya reported on September 27 that two Supreme Soviet committees had been ordered to investigate the situation—the Committee for Questions of Defense and State Security and the Committee for Questions of *Glasnost'*.

On September 29, Yazov told *Sovetskaya Rossiya* that rumors of a military coup had been deliberately circulated by left-wing forces in order to enhance their own drive for power. Such rumors, he added, were also aimed at taking people's minds off empty shelves and at providing an excuse for expected hardships during the winter. The defense minister again reiterated the often repeated earlier assurances regarding the troop movements. He alleged that, even though the recent movements were not defense related, airborne troops were fully armed because such units must always be ready for action.

Controversy over Presidential Decree on Academy of Sciences

A TASS commentary made it clear that rank-and-file employees of the USSR Academy of Sciences were concerned about a recent presidential decree announcing that control over state property and funds at present available to the academy would be transferred to the academy. The employees were afraid that this would give a small group of the academy's leaders even greater control over the distribution of funds and equipment within that body than it already had. In an attempt to calm the situation, the leadership of the academy promised the employees of academic institutions increased participation in the affairs of the academy, as well as salary increases of 60–70 percent.

On September 19, Vice President of the USSR Academy of Sciences Oleg Nefedov was quoted by TASS as saying the academy's presidium had no intention of monopolizing the material base of Soviet research. Nefedov said the presidium had decided to distribute most of the academy's property to its institutes and laboratories. There, he said, it would be controlled by individual academic councils, not by the academy's leadership.

The RSFSR Supreme Soviet voted on September 21 to suspend the implementation of Point 2 of the presidential decree on the USSR Academy of Sciences, Radio Moscow reported. Point 2 transfers ownership and control of property and funds used by the academy from the state to the academy. The RSFSR deputies, however, argue that the USSR president does not have the authority to transfer ownership of assets located on the territory of the RSFSR. The legislature sent a request to Gorbachev asking him to change Point 2.

On September 26, *Pravda* published a letter from six leading Soviet academicians condemning the Russian parliament's decision as absurd and juridically illiterate. The letter claimed that the majority of members of the academy welcomed Gorbachev's decree.

General Speaks Out on Soldiers' Rights

Major General Leonid Ivashov told TASS that decisions made by the Soviet national leadership and various republican organs had infringed servicemen's rights, reduced them to second-class citizens, and created conditions for social tension. Identified as head of the Defense Ministry Affairs Administration, Ivashov criticized in particular the withdrawal of Soviet troops from Eastern Europe, which he said had been hastily implemented and had resulted in hardship for thousands of servicemen and their families. He voiced support for Mikhail Gorbachev's recent decree on servicemen's rights.

Lvov to Disband Draft Boards

TASS said the Presidium of the Lvov Oblast Soviet had decided to disband military draft boards in that part of Ukraine. The decision was in line with a resolution adopted by the Ukrainian Supreme Soviet in July, 1989, that called for Ukrainian soldiers to serve only in Ukraine. TASS reported that the Presidium had also decided to halt the recruitment of servicemen in Ukraine until regulations were adopted guaranteeing the implementation of the Ukrainian Supreme Soviet resolution.

Independent Uzbek Federation of Trade Unions Formed

A Federation of Independent Trade Unions, with a membership of 7.5 million, concluded its founding congress in Tashkent, TASS reported. The federation is the largest public organization in Uzbekistan and includes both official and unofficial unions. The federation permits strikes and seeks to end central control of the Soviet trade-union movement. Chairman Buri Allamuradov said that revenues gathered from Uzbek trade unions would no longer be forwarded to the central union authorities.

Uzbekistan Suffers "Brain Drain"

TASS said "Birlik," the Uzbek popular front, was urging Russian-speaking residents of Uzbekistan to remain in the republic. 177,000 Russians, many of whom are highly qualified specialists, had left Uzbekistan in 1989; out-migration has continued in 1990. Most of those who leave resettle in the RSFSR.

Thursday, September 13

Resignations in Brest

The Party first secretary and the deputy chairman of the Brest City Soviet in Belorussia resigned after residents protested about the lack of consumer goods. Anatolii Lashkov resigned as Party first secretary and Deputy Mayor Vladimir Mikhailovsky gave up his post during a meeting of the city soviet attended by angry shoppers. The chairman of Borisov City Soviet in central Belorussia also promised to resign if he was unable to satisfy residents' demands for food by September 20 (*TASS*, September 13).

El'tsin Says Leadership Made Mistakes in Nationalities Policy

Boris El'tsin said the Soviet leadership's opposition to moves towards independence or sovereignty by Soviet republics was a mistake. TASS said El'tsin told the Russian parliament that it was the Soviet leadership's opposition to the independence drive three years ago that had led to "large-scale ethnic confrontations and conflicts." He was quoted as saying that Mikhail Gorbachev should have granted independence to republics "at the very beginning" and that if he had done so "there would not have been nationalistic sentiments and centrifugal tendencies."

Explosion in Kazakhstan Provokes Panic

Izvestia said an explosion and fire at a facility that produces fuel for nuclear power plants had caused panic among local residents. The explosion took place on September 12 at the Ulbinsk metallurgical plant in the city of Ust-Kamenogorsk in eastern Kazakhstan. The newspaper said that, after the accident, city residents fled into the streets and that some left the city altogether. TASS said that gases had escaped into the air as a result of the explosion but that radiation levels were normal.

On September 14, *Izvestia* published another article on the explosion. It said residents of Ust-Kamenogorsk had long known that until recently the plant was "a top-secret brainchild" of the USSR Ministry for Atomic Power and Industry. The newspaper said the plant had been a permament test site for beryllium, a toxic metal used in nuclear reactors. The same day, *Pravda* reported that the explosion had left three workers dead and four others injured.

On September 28, Kazakh President Nursultan Nazarbaev asked Soviet Prime Minister Nikolai Ryzhkov to declare Ust-Kamenogorsk an ecological disaster area. Nazarbaev said in a telegram to Ryzhkov: "The Kazakh public and the town's population demand urgent measures and compensation for their damaged health." The local soviet also voted to ban the production of beryllium at two plants in Ust-Kamenogorsk.

Leningrad Shipping Firm Breaks Away from Ministry

Employees of one of the Soviet Union's largest marine shipping companies, the Baltic Shipping Line of Leningrad, have removed their company from the control of the USSR Merchant Marine Ministry. TASS said the employees had leased the entire company, which operates cargo ships all over the world and ferries between Leningrad, Stockholm, and Helsinki. TASS quoted the shipping line's director, Viktor Kravchenko, as saying that in the past the ministry had used profits from the shipping line to subsidize loss-making enterprises. Kravchenko also said that the ministerial system of management was too cumbersome and that it reduced the line's competitiveness on international markets.

Russians Form Intermovement in Kazakhstan

A report from Alma-Ata said that Russians in Kazakhstan had formed an unofficial "Intermovement" to represent their interests. Kial Sabdalin, a journalist in Alma-Ata, told RFE/RL that the organization had been formed earlier in September as a response to the activities of groups favoring Kazakh sovereignty. (Similar Russian groups exist in many other Union republics.) Russians make up 37 percent of the population of Kazakhstan.

Industrial Production Falls

Official statistics published in *Izvestia* showed a decline in industrial output of 0.7 percent in the period January-August, 1990, as compared with the same period in 1989. In August, production dropped 1.7 percent in comparison with August, 1989. The losses were attributed to strikes and interethnic and sociopolitical conflicts. The only republics where industrial production did not fall were Belorussia, Moldavia, Tajikistan, and Estonia.

Friday, September 14

Gorbachev Decree Declared Unconstitutional

The USSR Supreme Soviet Constitutional Oversight Committee said that a presidential decree issued earlier this year to deprive the Moscow City Soviet of the authority to regulate rallies in the Soviet capital was unconstitutional. The committee said that the decree, which transferred the right to regulate demonstrations to the USSR Council of

Ministers, infringed the powers of both the Moscow City Soviet and the Russian Federation. The committee said the decree should be suspended, pending removal of the discrepancy between it and the USSR Constitution (*TASS*, September 14). See RL 431/90.

CPSU Faces Deficit

Nikolai Kapanets, a CPSU Central Committee official, told *Pravda* that the Party was facing a deficit of about 1,500 million rubles because of declining membership and a reduction in dues. The Party is also receiving less revenue from its publishing enterprise, which, until recently, printed a majority of Soviet books and periodicals. He said that Party committees should "actively enter into business" to compensate for losses. He suggested setting up joint ventures and financing projects that would show a speedy and healthy return on investments. He said the Party might also be forced to resort to its reserve fund of about 4,900 million rubles (*Reuters*, September 14).

Fourteen Soviet-Designed Nuclear Reactors to Close Down

A high-ranking official of the International Atomic Energy Agency (IAEA) said a safety study undertaken by the organization might lead to the closure of fourteen Soviet-designed nuclear reactors in the USSR, East Germany, Czechoslovakia, and Bulgaria. Morris Rosen, assistant director in charge of nuclear safety at the IAEA in Vienna, said the study would seek to determine whether the reactors could be rebuilt to make them safe (*RFE/RL Special*, September 14).

Ukrainian Opposition to Union Treaty

Radio Kiev quoted a statement made by radical deputies from the Ukrainian Supreme Soviet criticizing Moscow's plans to conclude a new Union treaty with Soviet republics. The statement said that the treaty under preparation seemed to be aimed at increasing the power of bureaucrats and the central authorities and at preserving "the rotten colonial system." Such a treaty would mean that Moscow would requisition more bread and meat from Ukraine and result in the renewed "bondage" of Ukraine and other Union republics, the statement said.

Lithuanian Prime Minister in Czechoslovakia

Following talks with Lithuanian Prime Minister Kazimiera Prunskiene in Prague, Czechoslovak Prime Minister Marian Calfa said his country was unlikely to establish formal relations with Lithuania in the near future. He also failed to accept a Lithuanian proposal to create a special office for Czechoslovak-Lithuanian relations. He did suggest, however, that Czechoslovakia's two constituent republics could promote their own ties with Lithuania (*Reuters*, September 14). For her part, Prunskiene said she would favor the immediate establishment of direct relations with the Czechoslovak federal government, as well as with the Czech and Slovak republics (*Reuters*, September 14).

Prime Minister of Azerbaijan Visits Turkey

Azerbaijani Prime Minister Nasan Hasanova arrived in Turkey for official talks on economic cooperation, Reuters reported. Turkey and Azerbaijan agreed to open a civilian border crossing to further trade through the Nakhichevan Autonomous Oblast in Azerbaijan.

El'tsin Favors Tatar Independence

According to First Secretary of the Tatar Communist Party Mintimer Shaimiev, Boris El'tsin said he would not oppose the secession of the Tatar Autonomous Republic from the Russian Federation. Speaking on local television and radio, Shaimiev said that, when he told El'tsin during a meeting in Moscow that Tataria wanted to leave Russia to become a sovereign Union republic, El'tsin congratulated the Tatar people on their choice and said he would not oppose it (RL Tatar-Bashkir service, September 14).

Uzbek Supreme Soviet Promises Public Report on 1989 Clashes

The Supreme Soviet of Uzbekistan promised to issue a public report on the ethnic clashes in the Fergana Valley in 1989 that claimed more than 100 lives. The promise was made in response to an appeal earlier this month by the Uzbek popular front, "Birlik." A "Birlik" spokesman also said Uzbek members of the USSR Congress of Peoples Deputies had promised to ask the Congress to appoint a special committee to investigate the unrest (RL Uzbek service, September 14).

Saturday, September 15

Ryzhkov Comments on Economic Reforms

USSR Prime Minister Nikolai Ryzhkov gave an interview on Soviet television in which he discussed economic reforms and defended his own policies. Ryzhkov said that the reform plan drawn up by the group headed by Academician Stanislav Shatalin amounted to "shock therapy" and would put 270,000 coal miners out of work and lead to the closure of a quarter of the USSR's kolkhozes. Commenting on calls for his resignation, Ryzhkov said that, despite what was being said about him, he would pursue his policies. Ryzhkov said he recommended that Mikhail Gorbachev sign an emergency decree extending the powers of the current government through 1991 and preserving its present structure.

Executive Chairman of Leningrad City Soviet to Resign

Aleksandr Shchelkanov, the former stevedore who was elected chairman of the Leningrad City Soviet Executive Committee in June, announced his intention to resign, TASS reported. Shchelkanov cited a lack of support from Leningrad Soviet deputies and the inefficiency of the soviet as the reasons for his resignation.

New Ambassador to China

Nikolai Solov'ev, until now the Soviet ambassador to Japan, was appointed ambassador to China, TASS reported. Solov'ev has served in Japan (1958–61 and 1966–71), was deputy head of the Second Far Eastern Department at the USSR Foreign Ministry (1974–76), and headed the department from 1976 until his appointment as ambassador to Japan in May, 1986. His predecessor in Beijing, Oleg Troyanovsky, has retired.

Pro-Communist Lithuanian Party Adopts Program and Statutes

The pro-Moscow Lithuanian Communist Party began the final stage of its congress in Vilnius. TASS said the delegates adopted a party program and statutes, with amendments. The draft party program was presented by a senior member of the Central Committee, Juozas Jermalavicius. He said pro-Moscow Lithuanian Communists support Socialist statehood, the USSR's territorial integrity, and "the genuine sovereignty" of Lithuania within the Soviet Union. He said his party saw the formation of "a free union of sovereign Socialist states" and the signing of a new Union treaty as the means to attain these goals. The old Lithuanian Party split into proindependence and pro-Moscow parties late in 1989.

Latvian Independent Communist Party Renamed

Latvia's independent Communist Party adopted a new name. TASS said delegates at the party's second congress, which opened in Riga, voted overwhelmingly to rename the party the Democratic Party of Labor of Latvia. The congress also reelected Ivars Kezbers as party chairman. Kezbers is a USSR people's deputy.

Protesters Demand USSR Troop Withdrawal from Poland

Polish protesters staged further blockades at Soviet military installations to demand the withdrawal of Soviet troops from Poland. Radio Warsaw said the blockades were being organized by members of the Confederation for an Independent Poland, which is campaigning to have Soviet forces leave the country.

Sunday, September 16

Antigovernment Demonstration in Moscow

Moscow police were quoted by TASS as saying that 70,000 people had participated in a demonstration in the Soviet capital. At the rally, calls were heard for the resignation of the USSR government—especially of its leader, Nikolai Ryzhkov. The demonstrators also voiced support for the Shatalin economic reform program. Although the Moscow City Soviet had attempted to prevent calls for the resignation of President Mikhail Gorbachev, some banners calling for precisely that were seen.

USSR–Saudi Arabia Ties Restored

Saudi Foreign Minister Prince Saud Al-Faysal and his Soviet counterpart, Eduard Shevardnadze, met in Moscow to sign a treaty reactivating Soviet-Saudi diplomatic ties. Relations were allowed to lapse in 1938 but were never officially broken off. Sergei Kirpichenko, a Soviet Foreign Ministry official, told TASS the decision to restore ties reinforced Soviet relations with the Arab world. The Soviet Union's condemnation of the Iraqi invasion of Kuwait has helped to improve the Soviet image in Saudi Arabia and facilitated the establishment of diplomatic ties. On October 3, the USSR Foreign Ministry announced that Gennadii Tarasov would serve as ambassador to Saudi Arabia (*TASS*, October 3).

Kazakhstan Publishes Draft Sovereignty Declaration

Kazakhstan published a draft declaration of sovereignty. Radio Moscow said the draft stated that the republic had the right to suspend laws of higher Union bodies that violated the Kazakh Constitution. The draft said further that all wealth and resources on Kazakh territory were owned by the republic, and it forbade the production, storage, and testing of nuclear weapons. (The latter suggestion is significant because Kazakhstan is the main Soviet center for nuclear weapons testing.) The draft also said that Kazakhstan would form its own internal troops and public security organs and that it had the right to conduct its own international relations.

Reagans Visit USSR

Former US President Ronald Reagan and his wife arrived in Moscow as the personal guests of Mikhail Gorbachev. The Reagans, who were on a private tour of Europe, arrived in Moscow after visiting Leningrad (*Reuters*, September 16). On September 17, the Reagans visited the Kremlin, and Ronald Reagan addressed the Soviet parliament. On September 18, he visited Moscow State University. On September 19, the couple left the USSR (*TASS*, September 19).

Georgian KGB Building Ransacked

Demonstrators were reported to have stormed the KGB headquarters in Tbilisi on September 16 after a proindependence, antigovernment rally at a city stadium, according to *Krasnaya zvezda* on September 18. Interfax reported that about 100 people gained entry to the first and second stories of the building, where they smashed windows and threw furniture into the street. The KGB gave the protesters until morning to vacate the premises; they left after about two hours. The demonstrators apparently thought that an activist was being held in the building.

Chief of KGB Electronic Intelligence Presents his Service

The chief of the KGB's Eighth Main Administration of Electronic Intelligence and Counterintelligence, Lieutenant General Nikolai Andreev, said his service was shifting its focus from military intelligence to economic intelligence. Andreev told *Pravda* that in future KGB cipher officers would concentrate on protecting commercial secrets. Andreev compared his service to the US National Security Agency. He also said that no Soviet republic was in a position to maintain similar monitoring and decoding services of its own.

Explosion at Building That Houses Ukrainian City Procuracy and KGB

There was an explosion at the building housing the Prosecutor's Office in the Ukrainian city of Yenakievo in Donetsk Oblast. The explosion damaged several offices and blew out some windows in the building, which also houses the city's KGB offices. *Izvestia* (September 21) quoted city residents as saying the explosion was aimed at the Prosecutor's Office because it was investigating an arms theft.

Monday, September 17

Independent Information Agency in Kazakhstan

What appears to be the first officially recognized independent information agency in Soviet Central Asia was set up in Kazakhstan. Radio Moscow said the new agency, DANA-press, would provide objective information on interregional, interethnic, and international topics to the mass media in Central Asia and elsewhere in the USSR.

Moiseev Says Military Not Independent in Foreign Policy

The chief of the General Staff of the Soviet Armed Forces, Mikhail Moiseev, told TASS that "the Soviet Defense Ministry makes no independent political decisions on international matters." He said such questions were decided by the top organs of state power. According to Moiseev, military leaders draw up proposals and work closely with the Foreign Ministry, the KGB, and other ministries and departments. "Heated debates and clashes of opinions often occur at this level," he said. Moiseev added that the Defense Ministry today must tackle two seemingly incompatible tasks—ensuring the country's defense and implementing disarmament.

Novosti Commentator Discusses Problems of the Armed Forces

According to Novosti military commentator Valerii Pogrebenkov, Mikhail Gorbachev interrupted his summer holiday this year to address Soviet troops in Odessa because of concern about military problems. Two presidential decrees—on reform of the military-political organs and on legal protection for servicemen—resulted from that meeting, he wrote. Pogrebenkov also discussed deteriorating conditions in military life and the many problems involved in depoliticizing the armed forces. He said both presidential decrees were aimed at protecting servicemen and raising the prestige of their profession.

Biryukova Retires

TASS reported that Aleksandra Biryukova's request to retire had been granted by Gorbachev. Biryukova, a deputy chairman of the USSR Council of Ministers, relinquished her candidate membership in the Politburo at the Party Congress in July. She had been responsible for the consumer goods sector.

Rallies in Western Ukraine in Defense of Lenin

Radio Moscow and TASS reported that rallies had been held in two Western Ukrainian cities, Lutsk and Chernovtsy, in defense of Lenin. The demonstrators were also said to have demanded that Ukraine remain part of the USSR. The media made it clear that those participating in the demonstrations were mostly war veterans and Communist Party officials.

On September 21, TASS reported that a large rally had been held in the Ukrainian city of Donetsk to protest about the removals of Lenin monuments in Western

Ukraine and about attempts to take similar action in Donetsk.

Tuesday, September 18

Solzhenitsyn's Plan for Revival of Russia Published in Soviet Press

Komsomol'skaya pravda (September 18) and *Literaturnaya gazeta* (September 19) published a new work by Aleksandr Solzhenitsyn entitled *Kak nam obustroit' Rossiyu* (How We Should Reconstruct Russia). In this long essay, first published by the YMCA-Press in Paris, Solzhenitsyn said any republic desiring independence should receive it. He argued, however, that the Slavic population of the USSR (i.e., the Russians, Ukrainians, and Belorussians) should remain together. He also suggested that this union of Slavs return to the limited democratic traditions of prerevolutionary Russia—especially to the so-called *zemstva*, or local self-government bodies. This article marked the end of Solzhenitsyn's silence on the political situation in the Soviet Union, which he had kept since the beginning of *perestroika*.

On September 25, in response to a question from a USSR Supreme Soviet member from Kazakhstan, Mikhail Gorbachev criticized Solzhenitsyn's pamphlet, saying it was disrespectful to some national groups and had "a destructive character." In his remarks, which were broadcast by Soviet television, Gorbachev added, however, that he shared Solzhenitsyn's concern about the future of Russia.

The same day, a journalist in Alma-Ata informed RFE/RL that a crowd of some 6,000 people had staged peaceful demonstrations in the Kazakh capital on September 21–23 to protest against Solzhenitsyn's proposal that a new Russia include parts of Kazakhstan. The journalist said the protesters burned copies of *Komsomol'skaya pravda* and *Literaturnaya gazeta* in which Solzhenitsyn's proposal was published (RL Kazakh service, September 25).

On September 26, Novosti and Soviet television carried further comments on the pamphlet. Novosti correspondent Aleksandr Ignatov stressed that Solzhenitsyn's proposal to cut Russia off from twelve Union republics was unrealistic, given the number of problems that would result from the disintegration of the Union. USSR people's deputy and philosopher Yurii Karyakin said on "Vremya" on September 26 that he agreed with Solzhenitsyn's idea about the need for private land ownership in Russia and with his call for the Communist Party to repent the damage it has inflicted on the USSR. Karyakin also called for a careful reading of the pamphlet and asked Soviet people to refrain from misinterpreting it. He pointed out, for example, that the pamphlet contained no sign of Solzhenitsyn's adherence to monarchism. See RL 411, 412, 413, 414, 415, and 416/90.

Akhromeev Loath to Use Military Supplies to Relieve Shortages

Gorbachev's top military adviser, Marshal Sergei Akhromeev, told the USSR Supreme Soviet that he was opposed to using emergency military food and material reserves as a means of easing problems in the domestic economy. According to Radio Moscow, Akhromeev said this proposal was based on the erroneous assumption that the USSR no longer faced a military threat. While he admitted that international tensions had eased, Akhromeev cautioned that the United States was still operating from "a position of strength." He also pointed to the Soviet Union's tragic shortage of reserves in World War II.

Demonstration Held Near Iraqi Embassy in Moscow

The Zionist youth movement "Beitar" organized a demonstration near the Iraqi embassy in Moscow, according to an RFE/RL correspondent. The protesters carried banners calling for an end to the Soviet government's training of Iraqi military officers. Embassy staffers were reported to have torn banners out of the hands of protesters. Soviet police and KGB agents were at the scene but did not intervene. The "Beitar" movement was formed two months ago in Moscow.

Musical Eulogy to Tsars Proposed as New RSFSR Hymn

Music from a nineteenth-century opera eulogizing the Russian tsars will be submitted to the RSFSR Supreme Soviet for approval as the new republican hymn, TASS reported. The opera, *Zhizn' za tsarya* (A Life for the Tsar), was composed by Mikhail Glinka. After the October Revolution the title was changed to *Ivan Susanin*.

***Literaturnaya gazeta* Freed from Writers' Union Control**

The "working collective" of *Literaturnaya gazeta* was registered as the founder (*uchreditel'*) of the major literary weekly, Radio Moscow reported. The move was aimed at ending control of the USSR Writers' Union over the newspaper, according to its chief editor, Fedor Burlatsky. *Literaturnaya gazeta* had been an organ of the union, which, Burlatsky complained, had attempted to dictate editorial policy. Burlatsky promised that the newspaper would now become "a free tribune of writers." As a result of the new press law, many periodicals are trying to free themselves from the control of various organizations, including the CPSU, to which they have officially been subordinated.

United Front of Workers Attacks Democratic Forces

Interviewed in the new periodical *Politika* (No. 20), a spokesman for the United Front of Workers of Russia, Igor Malyarov, criticized market economies and "bourgeois freedoms." Confronted with the question of why major workers' movements, like the Confederation of Labor and miner's organizations, support the platforms of democratic parties—particularly that of the Democratic Party of Russia, headed by a worker, Nikolai Travkin—Malyarov suggested that all the democratically oriented workers' movements in the USSR had been bribed by members of cooperatives and by "the Soviet bourgeoisie."

More Fighter Bombers Transferred to Arctic Base

Sources in Norway said that the Soviet Union had transferred more fighter bombers to the Kola Peninsula, Reuters reported. Norway's Northern Defense Command said that a squadron of between twelve and twenty-four SU-17 combined reconnaissance and bomber planes had been redeployed. "We assume that they have been moved from Central Europe," a spokesman said. An unknown number of SU-25s have also been moved to the Kola Peninsula. Norwegian spokesmen said the Soviet Union was modernizing the Arctic base. In May, forty fighter jets were redeployed to the Kola Peninsula from Hungary.

Changes in Civil Defense Reported

The Civil Defense Forces chief of staff, Colonel General Viktor Kozhbakhteev, told *Krasnaya zvezda* that wide-ranging changes were being implemented in the civil defense sector. Kozhbakhteev said that the Civil Defense Forces were working closely with the USSR Council of Ministers State Commission on Emergency Situations. He said that well-equipped mobile rescue units had been formed and that the training system had been overhauled. Kozhbakhteev said there were plans to professionalize the service according to which recruits should be at least twenty-five years of age and would earn about 500 rubles a month. There are also plans to remove the Civil Defense Forces from their subordination to the Ministry of Defense.

War Veterans and Historian Protest about Holiday Decision

The All-Union Council of War Veterans called for a traditional celebration—complete with parades and demonstrations—of the November 7 anniversary of the

October Revolution. They rejected the proposal made by the mayors of Moscow and Leningrad to limit this year's celebration and demanded instead that November 7 continue to be considered the preeminent holiday in the Soviet Union (*TASS*, September 18). Criticism of the mayors' proposal also came from the historian Roy Medvedev, who has recently become one of the strongest defenders of Soviet orthodoxy.

Estonia to End Subsidies for Meat and Dairy Products

Estonia decided to end subsidies for most meat and dairy products on October 15 as part of a general economic reform. The official ETA news agency said the change meant prices for meat and dairy products would more than double in Estonia. ETA said part of the money saved from the subsidies would be given to nonworking pensioners and people with school-age children to compensate them for the price increases. The plan was approved by the Estonian Supreme Soviet on September 17 (RFE Estonian Service, September 18).

USSR Begins Importing Gasoline

Western oil industry officials in London said the Soviet Union had started buying gasoline on the open market to import into the Soviet Union for the first time in many years. Reports quoted the oil experts and traders as saying that it was difficult to tell precisely how much oil had been imported. The Soviet Union has been a long-time net exporter of gasoline. Reports said that through June the USSR had been exporting an estimated average of 100,000 tons of gasoline a month. Reuters quoted Western oil industry officials as saying the gasoline imports may be a result of problems in the Soviet refining industry or of cutbacks in crude oil supplies to Soviet refineries.

Latvia and Russia Sign Basic Economic Agreement

Latvia and the Russian Federation signed a basic economic agreement for 1991 and were said to be working on a further, more detailed accord, TASS reported. The agency said Latvian Prime Minister Ivars Godmanis explained the agreement at a press conference in Riga. The accord called for Latvia and the RSFSR to maintain at least this year's level of trade next year while seeking to balance trade accounts.

Pro-*Perestroika* Deputies Push for Change in Kirgizia

Frustrated by the continuing immobility of Kirgizia's conservative leadership, a group of some 120 deputies to the republican Supreme Soviet were reported to have formed a faction to push for a more rapid implementation of *perestroika.* The faction, which includes more than one-third of the members of Kirgizia's Supreme Soviet, calls itself the Deputies' Group for Democratic Renewal and Citizen Unity. The formation of the group was reported in *Izvestia.*

Wednesday, September 19

RSFSR Legislature Calls for No-Confidence Vote

The RSFSR Supreme Soviet voted 154–4, with 18 abstentions, to call for the resignation of the USSR Council of Ministers. After a lengthy debate, the deputies rejected a resolution that had been prepared on this question and sent it back to a committee for further work. On September 20, the resolution was adopted by a vote of 164 for and 1 against, with 16 abstentions, TASS reported. The resolution was then forwarded to the USSR Supreme Soviet.

Centrist Bloc Proposes Coalition Government

The Centrist Bloc of Political Parties and Movements recommended that Nikolai Ryzhkov be replaced by Anatolii Sobchak, chairman of the Leningrad City Soviet, TASS reported. The group also proposed that the USSR Council of Ministers be replaced by "a coalition government of national confidence," which would consist of only six or seven ministries. The KGB would survive, but changes in its structure were proposed; in addition, all ministries would be depoliticized. The Centrist Bloc, created in June, unites about a dozen fringe political parties and groups.

On September 20, Novosti reported that the Centrist Bloc wanted to organize a round-table discussion between new political parties and Mikhail Gorbachev.

Russian Parliament Criticizes *Sovetskaya Rossiya*

At its session, the RSFSR Supreme Soviet approved in principle a resolution setting forth the Russian legislature's disagreement with the editorial policies of the republic's major newspaper, *Sovetskaya Rossiya.* (The newspaper is a joint organ of the RSFSR parliament and Council of Ministers and the CPSU Central Committee.) TASS reported that the Supreme Soviet had instructed its Committee on the Mass Media to replace the newspaper's chief editor, Valentin Chikin, within the week. *Sovetskaya Rossiya,* which published Nina Andreeva's infamous "anti-*perestroika* manifesto," has pursued a conservative editorial line, which stands in sharp contrast to many of the pronouncements of the new RSFSR parliament.

USSR Refuses to Participate in Investigation of 1968 Invasion

A senior Czechoslovak legal official said the Soviet Union was refusing to participate in Prague's investigation of the 1968 Soviet-led invasion of Czechoslovakia. First Deputy Prosecutor-General Lubomir Veleta told the Czechoslovak parliament that prosecutors general in all the Warsaw Pact countries had been asked to release "documents that could prove the guilt of those who invited the foreign troops." He said the Soviet side had refused to cooperate (Czechoslovak Radio and Television, September 19). This revelation cast doubt on earlier reports in the Soviet press that said Soviet historians and officials were cooperating fully with their Czechoslovak counterparts in investigating the invasion (see, for instance, *Izvestia*, August 20).

Federation of Unions' Claims to Independence Dismissed

The Federation of Independent Trade Unions of the RSFSR ended its founding congress in Moscow. The new organization, formed on the basis of the official trade unions already existing in the RSFSR, was mocked by the late-night Soviet television news service, "TSN." "TSN" said only the foreign press had been taken in by the organization's claims to be independent. Radio Moscow also carried a critical commentary by a delegate from Vorkuta (a region characterized by the militancy of its coal-mining community), who said the official trade unions were on the defensive because of the growth of popular support for new, truly independent workers' movements.

Turkey and Azerbaijan Sign Economic Accord

Azerbaijani and Turkish representatives signed an economic agreement in Ankara. The agreement called for the establishment of direct road, rail, air, and telephone links between Turkey and Azerbaijan. Consular offices will also be opened in Baku and in the Turkish Black Sea port of Trabzon.

Naval Academy to Change Name

The Grechko Naval Academy—named after former Minister of Defense Marshal Andrei Grechko—will be renamed the Kuznetsov Naval Academy, TASS reported. Grechko, a ground forces commander, had little to do with the Soviet navy. Nikolai Kuznetsov headed the navy from 1939 until 1946 and was the supreme commander of Naval Forces during World War II.

"Sajudis" Elects New Chairman

The Lithuanian restructuring movement, "Sajudis," elected a new chairman. He is Juozas Tumelis, a librarian and cultural historian. Tumelis replaced Vytautas Landsbergis, who resigned in the spring when he became president of the Lithuanian Supreme Council (RFE Lithuanian service, September 19).

Thursday, September 20

Komi Government Complains of Food Shortages

Members of the government of the Komi Autonomous Republic in the northern part of the Russian Federation flew to Moscow to complain about shortages of food and consumer goods. TASS said that not only shops but also warehouses in the republic were becoming empty. It quoted local government officials as saying the growing tensions might give rise to demonstrations or even riots. TASS said the Komi representatives went to Moscow after they had failed to receive an answer to a telegram they had sent to Mikhail Gorbachev and other Soviet leaders.

RSFSR Minister Discusses Priorities of Economic Program

RSFSR Deputy Prime Minister Grigorii Yavlinsky, one of the authors of the 500-day economic plan, said he categorically opposed all measures aimed at "the dollarization of the Soviet economy." In an interview with *Sovetskaya Rossiya*, the economist said it would be wrong to give the dollar the same circulation rights as the ruble. He said this would be economically and politically dangerous. Yavlinksy said that instead priority should be given to boosting the ruble's purchasing power and forging ties among enterprises.

Future of Cuban-Soviet Relations

A member of the Presidential Council, Evgenii Primakov, said the Soviet Union's future aid and trade policies towards Cuba would not be guided simply by a desire to keep Cuban President Fidel Castro in power. Speaking in Moscow to AP, Primakov said the Soviet Union had stopped "exporting revolution in any form." But Primakov said a cut in Soviet aid would not alone bring about Castro's fall. He said he did not believe Castro's government was that unstable.

Fadeev's Last Letter Published

Izvestia published for the first time the text of a letter addressed to the Party Central Committee by writer Aleksandr Fadeev shortly before he committed suicide in 1956. In his letter, Fadeev said he had decided to take his life because of the mass repressions conducted among Soviet writers under Stalin. As head of the USSR Writers' Union, Fadeev had to give approval for the arrests of his colleagues. After Stalin's death, writers who had survived the labor camps started to return to Moscow, and some of them took Fadeev to task for his participation in the repressions against writers.

Friday, September 21

RSFSR MVD to Close Its Political Section

RSFSR Minister of Internal Affairs Viktor Barannikov said the ministry was closing down its political section and dedicating itself solely to law enforcement. *Pravda* quoted Barannikov as saying there would be no more subordination of the republic's internal affairs organs to any political party. Barannikov, who was appointed earlier this month, said the ministry would reduce the number of its departments from twenty-five to seven and encourage more initiative among its anticrime investigators.

RSFSR Forbids Sending Russians to Conflict Areas

The RSFSR Supreme Soviet said that it was unacceptable for RSFSR citizens to be sent to other Soviet republics to deal with ethnic conflicts. The statement was included in a special parliamentary resolution, which also called for the creation of special interrepublican units, made up of volunteers, to keep order in regions hit by interethnic strife and other emergency situations (*TASS*, *Radio Moscow*, September 21).

Estonian Parliament Protests about West German–Soviet Treaty

The Estonian Supreme Soviet issued a protest about the West German–Soviet treaty that was initialed in Moscow on September 13. The Estonian protest statement, approved on September 20, said the article of the treaty that recognizes all present borders in Europe amounted to the recognition of the annexation of the Baltic states by the Soviet Union. A West German Foreign Ministry spokesman said last week that the treaty did not alter West Germany's policy of not recognizing the annexation. According to Estonia's ETA news agency, the statement also called for independent Estonian participation in the Conference on Security and Cooperation in Europe (RFE Estonian service, September 21).

Kazakhs Protest after Explosion at Alma-Ata School

A report from Alma-Ata said 4,000 to 5,000 people had demonstrated there on September 20 to protest about an explosion that damaged a local school on September 19. Alma-Ata journalist Kial Sabdalin told RFE/RL on September 21 that the school had been the scene of tensions between Kazakh and ethnic Russian schoolchildren. TASS said the blast had been caused by a home-made bomb.

El'tsin Involved in Another Car Accident

Boris El'tsin was badly bruised in yet another car accident, First Deputy Chairman of the RSFSR Supreme Soviet Ruslan Khasbulatov announced to the parliament. He said a preliminary medical check had shown no signs of a fracture (*TASS*, September 21).

Georgia Invalidates South Ossetian Sovereignty Statement

Georgia invalidated a sovereignty declaration by the South Ossetian Autonomous Oblast. The Presidium of the Georgian Supreme Soviet ruled that the decision of the South Ossetian Autonomous Oblast to declare itself sovereign was unlawful and invalid. On September 20, the South Ossetian parliament proclaimed the oblast "an independent Soviet democratic republic." TASS said the parliament's session was attended only by ethnic Ossetians. The Georgian Supreme Soviet said the South Ossetian action was a "crude" violation of the Georgian constitution.

Saturday, September 22

Russian Parliament Adopts Decree on Media

The RSFSR Supreme Soviet adopted a decree on the republican media, Radio Moscow reported. The decree provided for the publication of new newspapers, such as *Delovaya Rossiya* (Business Russia), *Golos Rossii* (Voice of Russia), and *Rossiisky vestnik* (Russian Herald). The decree also expressed a lack of confidence in the newspaper *Sovetskaya Rossiya*, whose line is much more conservative than that of the Russian parliament. Radio Moscow said the parliamentary committee on the media was planning to submit a list of nominees for the post of editor in chief of the newspaper. *Moscow News* (No. 38) published a letter by a journalist from *Sovetskaya Rossiya*, who suggested that responsibility for the newspaper's conservatism lay entirely with its editor, Valentin Chikin.

Democratic Union Member Charged with Slander

Valeriya Novodvorskaya, a member of the Democratic Union who was detained after the antigovernment rally in Moscow on September 16, was charged with violating the law against slander of the USSR president, TASS reported. Novodvorskaya apparently carried a banner calling

Gorbachev "a fascist pig"; she was also said to have burned a Soviet flag.

On September 25, Gorbachev's spokesman Vitalii Ignatenko said the action against Novodvorskaya had been initiated by law-enforcement agencies, not by the president's office (*TASS*, September 25). The same day, a demonstration in support of Novodvorskaya was held in Moscow (*Central Television*, September 26). On September 26, TASS reported that Novodvorskaya had been sent for a psychiatric checkup to establish whether she was fit to stand trial.

Solzhenitsyn Fund to Be Registered in RSFSR

A fund set up in 1974 by exiled writer Aleksandr Solzhenitsyn will be officially registered in the Russian Federation, *Komsomol'skaya pravda* reported. The fund was created to help political prisoners and their families. The newspaper said agreement for the registration was reached on September 21 between RSFSR Prime Minister Ivan Silaev and Vadim Borisov, a member of the *Novyi mir* editorial board who represents Solzhenitsyn's interests in the Soviet Union. Until the advent of *perestroika*, Soviet citizens who worked for Solzhenitsyn's fund were hounded by the KGB.

Moldavia Signs Cooperation Treaty with Russia

Chairman of the Moldavian Supreme Soviet Mircea Snegur and Chairman of the RSFSR Supreme Soviet Boris El'tsin signed a treaty on "interstate relations," TASS reported. The sides recognize and undertake to respect each other's sovereignty as defined in their declarations of sovereignty. They will develop political, economic, and cultural cooperation on mutually advantageous terms and establish permanent missions in each other's capitals. In a provision especially important for Kishinev—which is facing active opposition from antireformist Russian groups—the two sides pledged to ban on their territory any activities or groups opposed to the other's state sovereignty or territorial integrity. The treaty also contained a provision allowing Moldavian residents of the RSFSR and Russian residents of Moldavia to choose the citizenship of either republic. The treaty was ratified by the Moldavian Supreme Soviet on October 1 (*TASS*, October 1).

Problems with Harvest Increase

The Presidium of the Penza City Soviet declared a state of emergency for the harvest. Radio Moscow quoted the local authorities as saying that less than 10 percent of the potato and carrot crops had been put in storage and that the situation with other vegetables was not much better.

The declaration of a state of emergency allows the authorities to require labor collectives and students to help with storing the crops. It also allows the commandeering of all freight and passenger vehicles to help with the harvest.

On September 23, in an interview on Soviet television, Prime Minister Nikolai Ryzhkov called for the mobilization of workers throughout the USSR to help with the potato and vegetable harvest.

On September 27, *Pravda* published the text of a resolution by the Soviet government calling for urgent measures to bring in the harvest and get it to market.

Latvia and Belorussia Sign Cooperation Agreement

Belorussia and Latvia signed an agreement on economic, scientific, and cultural cooperation. TASS said the agreement was signed in the Belorussian capital, Minsk, and called for the exchange of permanent diplomatic missions.

Tajiks in Uzbekistan Restore Nationality

Tajiks living in Bukhara Oblast in Uzbekistan have been given permission to correct the entry on nationality in their internal passports, TASS reported. In the 1930s many Tajiks were wrongly registered as Uzbeks. They have been trying to have this changed for at least two years. In the 1989 census the number of people claiming to be Tajik increased by no less than 56 percent over 1979—a reflection of the Tajiks' desire to reclaim their true nationality. The number of Tajiks in Tajikistan increased by only 42 percent during the same period.

Sunday, September 23

***Pravda* Says Straight Talk Needed on Transition to Market**

Pravda said it was time to give the Soviet people straightforward information about how they would be affected by the transition to a market economy. The newspaper said it was time to speak plainly and to admit that, during the first stage of the transition, some goods would become more expensive and others would be in short supply. *Pravda* said that these problems would disappear with time and that the long-awaited economic improvement would eventually bring new incentives for productive work.

Abalkin Interviewed in *Sovetskaya Rossiya*

Soviet Deputy Prime Minister Leonid Abalkin said a referendum should be used to decide whether the USSR should remain a federation. He made the proposal in an interview with *Sovetskaya Rossiya.* In his speech to the Soviet parliament on September 21, Mikhail Gorbachev said the USSR should be a federation of united, not absolutely sovereign republics.

Split with Moscow Patriarchate Continues

The parish of Svyato-Pokrovsky in Ussuriisk decided to leave the jurisdiction of the Moscow Patriarchate and to join the Russian Orthodox Church Abroad, which is based in New York (*Moscow News*, No. 38).

Monday, September 24

Gorbachev Granted Additional Powers

The USSR Supreme Soviet voted 305 to 36, with 41 abstentions, to give Mikhail Gorbachev additional powers to implement economic reforms (*TASS*, September 24; *Pravda*, September 25). For roughly 500 days, from now until March 31, 1992, Gorbachev has the power to issue decrees—"of a normative character"—"on economic problems and questions of the preservation of law and order"; he is not allowed to issue decrees that conflict with the USSR Constitution. Furthermore, the USSR Supreme Soviet has the right to reject any decrees with which it does not agree. The move was opposed by the RSFSR Supreme Soviet.

On September 25, Nikolai Petrakov, one of Gorbachev's aides, told reporters that Gorbachev would not impose martial law or introduce presidential rule, Radio Moscow reported. Petrakov said that, during the transition to a market economy, decisions would have to be made quickly and that therefore to convene the USSR Supreme Soviet each time a decision has to be made would be inefficient and would "destroy the entire fabric of the reforms."

On September 28, the Interregional Group of Deputies and the "Democratic Russia" parliamentary bloc within the RSFSR Supreme Soviet said they would ask for a review of the new law's compliance with the constitution. The deputies were quoted by Radio Moscow as saying the expansion of presidential powers could be effective only if the Soviet republics gave their consent. See RL 408/90.

USSR Supreme Soviet Adopts Compromise Reform Plan

The USSR Supreme Soviet voted to adopt a compromise program for economic reform. The program, drafted by Academician Abel Aganbegyan, incorporates elements of the more moderate Ryzhkov plan into the radical "500-day program" devised by the economist Stanislav Shatalin. It was passed by 323 to 11, with 56 abstentions, according to Western agencies. After adopting a resolution on "a united program to stabilize the economy and move towards a market economy," the deputies began to debate the program point by point. See RL 429/90.

Petroleum Minister Retires

Radio Moscow reported that Nikolai Lemaev, USSR Minister of the Chemical and Petroleum-Refining Industry, had been released from his duties by Gorbachev in connection with his retirement. Lemaev's resignation comes at a time when the Soviet energy sector is unable to provide sufficient fuel for the country. He had been minister since November, 1985.

Tatar and Kalmyk Party First Secretaries Replaced

Following the adoption of a decree by the Tatar Supreme Soviet forbidding the heads of state organs to hold any other posts, the chairman of the Tatar Supreme Soviet Mintimer Shaimiev had to give up his post as secretary of the republican Party organization, TASS reported. Revo Idiatullin, formerly a secretary of the Tatar Oblast Party Committee, was elected in his place. On September 25, Vladimir Zakharov, the first secretary of the Kalmyk Party organization, was released from this post in connection with his confirmation as head of the Department of Organizational Party and Personnel Work of the RSFSR Central Committee, Radio Moscow reported.

USSR Releases Names of Nazi Victims

AP reported that the Soviet Union had released copies of wartime documents listing 400,000 people sent to Nazi concentration camps. A spokesman for the US Red Cross said that the new material included nearly 70,000 death certificates from the Auschwitz concentration camp. He said that Soviet troops had found the records at the end of the war and that recently the Soviet government gave copies of them to the International Red Cross. Last year, *Izvestia* published a series of articles charging that for years the Soviet authorities had refused to give information about Nazi victims to the International Red Cross.

Criticism of Soviet Psychiatry Renewed

Mikhail Tsaregorodtsev, chairman of the International Independent Research Center on Psychiatry, said that little had improved in Soviet psychiatry, TASS reported.

Evidence collected by the center indicates that patients are still being treated harshly in psychiatric hospitals.

Gorbachev and Kazakh Leaders Meet US Consortium Members

TASS, in English, reported that Mikhail Gorbachev, Kazakh President and Communist Party First Secretary Nursultan Nazarbaev, and Chairman of the Kazakh Council of Ministers Uzakbai Karamanov had met with members of the American Trade Consortium, including its president, James Giffin. The discussion focused on the consortium's large-scale cooperation with Kazakhstan—joint ventures are planned in petroleum extraction, agriculture, raw materials processing, and the manufacture of agricultural machinery. The participation of Gorbachev in the discussion was a measure of the importance Moscow attaches to the Kazakh leadership's efforts to establish direct economic ties abroad and to attract foreign investment to develop the republic's resources.

Ukrainian Opposition Group Wants Party and Government Dissolved

A congress of Ukrainian parliamentary deputies called for the resignation of the Ukrainian government and the disbandment of the republican Communist Party. The deputies are part of a group called "The Association of Democratic Soviets and Democratic Blocs within Ukrainian Soviets," which was formed in July. The association's second congress has just ended in Zhitomir. Aside from the above-mentioned demands, TASS said, the deputies also called for the Communist Party's assets to be nationalized and for legal underpinning of the Ukrainian declaration of sovereignty.

Tuesday, September 25

USSR Supreme Soviet Discusses Union Treaty

The USSR Supreme Soviet discussed the concept of a new Union treaty. A report was given by the chairman of the Council of Nationalities, Rafik Nishanov, and followed by questions from deputies (*Central Television*, "Vremya," September 25). Nishanov reiterated yet again that republics wishing to secede could only do so after a referendum. He said that the basis for the talks on the new treaty was the republican declarations of sovereignty, the laws delimiting the powers of the center and the republics adopted earlier this year by the Supreme Soviet, and any new laws that were adopted in connection with the transition to a market economy. Nishanov said that it had not yet been decided whether the autonomous republics should sign the new treaty—as they have been demanding vociferously—but he said they should certainly participate in the process of preparing it.

Nishanov said three names had been suggested for the resulting federation or confederation. Gorbachev favored "Union of Sovereign States," a group of Kazakh deputies proposed "Union of Soviet Sovereign Republics," while, in 1989, the Interregional Group of Deputies had put forward the more neutral "Union of Euro-Asian Republics." The name originally suggested by Lenin for the country in 1922 was the Union of Soviet Republics of Europe and Asia (*TASS*, September 25). The USSR Supreme Soviet adopted a resolution endorsing Gorbachev's proposal to form a committee to prepare a new treaty.

Russian City Makes Solzhenitsyn Honorary Citizen

Radio Moscow said that the Russian city of Ryazan had made Aleksandr Solzhenitsyn an honorary citizen. The writer lived in Ryazan after returning from his years in labor camps and internal exile.

Defense Minister on Treaty with Iraq

USSR Defense Minister Dmitrii Yazov told Japanese journalists that the USSR had suspended the military part of its Friendship and Mutual Assistance Treaty with Iraq, Novosti reported. Yazov said that the Soviet Union would not train any more Iraqi soldiers and that deliveries of armaments and military equipment to Iraq had been discontinued. He also claimed that there were 149 Soviet military specialists in Iraq and that their withdrawal would be based on contracts signed before the Iraqi aggression. Western sources reported on September 25 that Pentagon officials believe there are between 500 and 1,000 Soviet advisers in Iraq.

Pentagon Assesses Soviet Military Power

The Pentagon's annual assessment of Soviet military capability, released on September 25, claimed that Soviet military spending fell in 1989 for the first time under Gorbachev and that the most significant reductions in Soviet arms production occurred in equipment for ground forces. The report also noted the seriousness of social and morale problems facing the army and said that some in the High Command openly opposed many of Gorbachev's reform initiatives. In the introduction, US Secretary of Defense Dick Cheney said the Soviet military threat was changing, but he cautioned that the Soviet Union "remains an enormous military superpower."

On September 26, the Pentagon's assessment was widely reviewed in the Soviet media. Reactions were mixed, with several commentators arguing that the content of this year's publication indicated that the Cold War was not over for many in the US military establishment. Foreign Ministry spokesman Gennadii Gerasimov, for example, told TASS that "images of the Cold War . . . are still alive in some US circles."

Help for Victims of Stalinism in Kazakhstan

TASS reported that Kazakh President Nursultan Nazarbaev had issued a decree authorizing additional social benefits for victims of Stalin's repressions. The decree noted that many of these people had become invalids as a result of years in prisons or labor camps but had no social protection. The decree provides for the invalids to receive medical help.

***Sobesednik* Accuses KGB of Hypocrisy**

The opening of the new KGB Public Relations Center to foreign and Soviet journalists was described by those present as "a comedy." According to *Sobesednik* (No. 38), KGB General Aleksandr Karbainov, who officiated at the opening, denied that the KGB had played a role in the persecution of dissidents and said the KGB had not been responsible for putting Vladimir Bukovsky, Petr Grigorenko, and Leonid Plyushch, among others, in psychiatric hospitals. *Sobesednik* suggested that Karbainov ought to know better: before his transfer to the public relations office, Karbainov worked in the KGB's Fifth Main Administration (ideological subversion), which was disbanded in 1989.

Wednesday, September 26

Law on Freedom of Conscience Approved in Principle

The USSR Supreme Soviet approved in principle, by a vote of 341-1, a new law on freedom of conscience and religious organization, TASS reported. Debate on individual articles continued the next day. Patriarch Aleksii participated in the debates on September 26. He noted that the Russian Orthodox Church had not asked for any special rights but only for the removal of obstacles that prevented the Church from operating freely. According to TASS, Patriarch Aleksii submitted a list of proposed amendments to the law to the Supreme Soviet for further consideration.

On September 27, the Vatican expressed "great satisfaction" with the Soviet law on freedom of conscience. A Vatican press office statement said the new law "will render justice to millions of believers in the Soviet Union" (*RFE/RL Special*, September 27). The leader of the Ukrainian Catholic Church, Cardinal Myroslav Lyubachiv'skyi, also welcomed the law. He called it the Soviet government's "first step toward true religious freedom" (*Reuters*, *AP*, September 27).

Unorthodox Communists Attempt to Salvage Party's Prestige

Members of the Marxist Platform and the moderate wing of the Democratic Platform, both of which are internal CPSU factions, said they were joining forces in a bid to revive the CPSU's declining prestige and halt "the frenzy" of anticommunism sweeping Russia (*TASS*, *Reuters*, September 26). (The radical wing of the Democratic Platform advocates the transformation of the CPSU into a social democratic party.)

Interregional Group Dissatisfied with Supreme Soviet

At an extended session, members of the Interregional Group of Deputies and the "Democratic Russia" parliamentary faction discussed their position with regard to the work of the USSR Supreme Soviet, plans to introduce a market economy, and the recent expansion of USSR President Mikhail Gorbachev's powers (*Radio Moscow*, September 26). They said they considered the USSR Supreme Soviet to have been "ineffective" and criticized that body for not adopting a more radical plan for economic reform. There was heated debate on the advantages and disadvantages of expanding Gorbachev's powers; differences of opinion between the Interregional Group and "Democratic Russia" on the question of sovereignty for the RSFSR were also reported.

Lithuania Establishes Own Secret Service

The Lithuanian government established an independent secret service to provide it with foreign and internal intelligence information. Prime Minister Kazimiera Prunskiene discussed the new secret service in an interview published in the West Berlin daily *Tageszeitung*. She said "the department for state security" was needed in Lithuania just as in any other independent state. She said her government needed to keep track of potential sources of disorder and destabilization in Lithuania.

Lithuania Adopts Law on Political Parties

The Lithuanian Supreme Council adopted a law allowing only Lithuanian citizens to become members of political parties in the republic (*Radio Vilnius*, September 26). The law also said political parties of other states may not be active or be established in Lithuania. It noted that the only party belonging to another state that is currently active in Lithuania is the CPSU. The law also forbade membership in political parties for people serving in internal affairs, state defense, state security, the courts, the prosecutor's office, the investigative organs and other legal institutions, as well as for people in the diplomatic service.

Government Adopts Resolution to Assist AIDS Sufferers

The USSR Council of Ministers approved further assistance for people with AIDS or the HIV virus. It adopted a resolution to establish financial aid for the parents of infected children under sixteen. The resolution called for the state to give financial aid to one parent of a sick child if he or she stopped work in order to care for the child. It also instructed the Union and republican governments to organize education for sick children, to provide medicines, and to reimburse expenses incurred in traveling to treatment centers (*TASS*, September 26).

Gorbachev Demands Referendum on Latvian Independence

Mikhail Gorbachev said Latvia must follow the law and subject the question of Latvian independence to a referendum. Gorbachev met in Moscow on September 26 with Latvian Prime Minister Ivars Godmanis and other Latvian officials. Gorbachev called for greater cooperation within the framework of a Union of sovereign republics. Godmanis told Gorbachev that, whatever form future relations took, there must be a restoration of full Latvian political sovereignty. He said Latvia favored interstate agreements that did not infringe its sovereignty (*TASS*, September 27).

Thursday, September 27

Gorbachev Issues Decree to Help Stabilize Economy

Mikhail Gorbachev issued his first decree since the USSR Supreme Soviet gave him broader, temporary executive powers to use during the transition to a market economy. The decree ordered businesses to respect their obligations to supply raw materials and finished products for the next fifteen months. The decree said it was unacceptable that the authorities had been interfering in the fulfillment of those obligations. The president also authorized the Soviet government to impose special work regulations in the national goods supply system, specifically on the railroads (*TASS*, September 27; *Pravda*, September 28).

Hungary and Ukraine Establish Relations

Hungary and Ukraine agreed to exchange consulates and to start talks on establishing full diplomatic relations. The agreements were reached in Kiev, on the first day of Hungarian President Arpad Goncz's visit to Ukraine. Radio Bupapest said the consulate was to be opened in the city of Uzhgorod—capital of Ukraine's Transcarpathian region. The area has a large Hungarian-speaking population.

On September 28, Ukrainian Foreign Minister Anatol Zlenko, who was attending a session of the United Nations General Assembly in New York, held discussions with several foreign ministers from other countries on the possibility of establishing consular or diplomatic relations. Among others, Zlenko met with the foreign ministers of Czechoslovakia, Poland, Romania, and Turkey (*RFE/RL Special*, September 28).

Bolshoi Asks Government to Give Up Box Seats

The Bolshoi Theater was reported to have asked the Soviet government to give up its prime seats at the theater. *Komsomol'skaya pravda* quoted Bolshoi General Director Vladimir Kokonin as saying he wanted to remove the tsar's loggia and some other seats that were permanently reserved for Soviet officials. Kokonin said this would allow him to make sixty additional seats available to the public. The daily complained that the theater had a special entrance and special stairs and elevators for those using the government seats.

Latvian Parliament Appoints Prosecutor-General

The Latvian Supreme Council appointed a republican prosecutor-general, subordinate only to the parliament. He is Janes Skrastins, the republic's former deputy prosecutor-general. On September 25, the Latvian Supreme Council adopted a law making the office accountable only to the president. Previously, the position functioned within the Union system of the USSR Prosecutor's Office (*TASS*, in English, September 27).

Estonian Parliament Starts Discussion of Border Controls

The Estonian parliament began discussion of a bill to protect the republic's domestic market, control immigration, and combat crime. TASS said the draft bill would give Estonian officials control of the movement of people and vehicles and of the export and import of goods and money across the border. TASS said border controls would be introduced in three stages. In the first stage, those crossing the border will have to present identification cards. In the second stage, they will be required to obtain a permit at the border for stays of not longer than one month. In the third stage, only people with invitations from local self-governing bodies will be given entry permits.

US and Azerbaijani Businessmen Discuss Cooperation

TASS said US and Azerbaijani businessmen were discussing economic cooperation at a symposium in Baku. TASS quoted a US banking official as saying US businesses could help develop the Azerbaijani oil, gas, chemical, and cotton industries. It quoted Azerbaijani Prime Minister Gasan Gasanov as praising the US visitors for wanting to help develop the republic's economy.

Fall in Subscriptions to Central Press

Radio Moscow reported that there had been a considerable fall in subscriptions to central newspapers compared with 1989. The number of subscribers to *Pravda* was said to have fallen by more than half, while *Izvestia* suffered a 40- to 45-percent reduction. Radio Moscow attributed the decline to the increased number of alternative publications now available. (Prior to the adoption of the press law, many of these publications existed only in *samizdat* and were difficult to obtain.) Radio Moscow said another contributing factor was the increased price of consumer goods, which has meant that some people can no longer afford newspaper subscriptions.

Friday, September 28

Seven Republics Form Direct Ties

Seven Union republics signed a protocol in Tallinn calling for direct relations among them (*TASS*, September 28). TASS said the protocol was approved by representatives of the RSFSR, the Baltic republics, Armenia, Kirgizia, and Moldavia; Tajik and Belorussian representatives also attended the meeting but did not sign the protocol. TASS said bilateral accords on economic cooperation between Lithuania and Kirgizia and between Latvia and Kirgizia were also concluded during the Tallinn conference.

USSR Agrees to Pay Hungary for Environmental Damage

The Soviet Union agreed to pay for environmental damage caused by Soviet troops stationed in Hungary. Radio Budapest said the agreement was reached during talks in Budapest on the withdrawal of Soviet forces. Hungarian Foreign Economic Relations Minister Bela Kadar signed the agreement with his Soviet counterpart Konstantin Katushev. The agreement said the amount of compensation would be determined later.

Chairman of Ukrainian Supreme Soviet Quits Party Post

The chairman of the Ukrainian Supreme Soviet, Leonid Kravchuk, quit his post as second secretary of the Ukrainian Communist Party Central Committee. TASS quoted Kravchuk as saying he had quit because he wanted to concentrate fully on his state job. A plenum of the Ukrainian Party Central Committee elected Grigorii Kharchenko to succeed Kravchuk as second secretary. Kharchenko had been first secretary of the Zaporozhe Oblast Party Committee and chairman of the oblast soviet (*TASS*, September 28).

Bonn and Moscow Initial Economic Accord

West Germany and the Soviet Union initialed an agreement on economic, industrial, scientific, and technical cooperation. A statement released by West Germany quoted Economics Minister Helmut Haussmann as saying the accord created the foundation for comprehensive and forward-looking cooperation between the Soviet Union and a united Germany and would make an important contribution to the successful implementation of economic reforms in the Soviet Union (*AFP*, September 28).

More Military Plants to Be Switched to Civilian Production

At a meeting of the Presidential Council, Mikhail Gorbachev heard a report calling for the further diversion of military resources to the civilian economy. USSR Deputy Prime Minister Igor Belousov delivered the report. Gorbachev's spokesman Vitalii Ignatenko told reporters in Moscow that the plan called for the conversion of 550 large military enterprises to civilian production by 1995. Ignatenko said the defense sector could supply consumer goods worth 270 billion rubles over the next five years (*Reuters*, September 28).

United States and Armenia Sign Assistance Treaty

The chairman of the Armenian Supreme Soviet, Levon Ter-Petrossyan, arrived in Washington at the start of a week-long private tour of the United States. He attended a ceremony at the State Department at which documents were signed granting 9.8 million dollars in humanitarian assistance to Armenia. The money will be used for medical treatment, training programs, and for the construction of housing for victims of the 1988 earthquake. It will be administered by US voluntary groups (*RFE/RL Special*, September 28).

Shevardnadze Meets Albanian Leader

Albanian leader Ramiz Alia had talks in New York with Soviet Foreign Minister Eduard Shevardnadze. TASS said this was the first meeting between leading officials of the two countries in thirty years. The Soviet Union and Albania restored diplomatic relations in July after a long rift. TASS said the two officials discussed the development of Soviet-Albanian relations. They agreed that their governments should hold foreign policy consultations and that their foreign ministers should exchange visits. The report also said Alia accepted an invitation from the Soviet leadership to visit the Soviet Union.

USSR Joins Interpol

The Soviet Union, Poland, and Czechoslovakia became members of the International Police Organization (Interpol). Raymond Kendall, the British secretary-general of Interpol, said at a news conference in Ottawa, where the Interpol annual conference is being held, that the organization now covers all of Europe except Albania (*Reuters*, *AFP*, September 28).

Another Economic Reform Plan Published

A group of economists in the Soviet defense sector added another economic reform plan to those already under study by the USSR Supreme Soviet and the Union republics. The new plan was published in *Rabochaya tribuna*. The group, which is headed by the director of an economics institute at the USSR Ministry of the Aviation Industry, was quoted as saying none of the three already existing plans—compiled by Shatalin, Ryzhkov, and Aganbegyan—would create a real market. The group said none of the plans reduced state control enough to guarantee competition.

Reformist Deputies See Antidemocratic Press Campaign

At a press conference in Moscow, members of the Interregional Group of Deputies and of the "Democratic Russia" bloc within the Russian parliament said a campaign was under way in the Soviet press to accuse democrats of plotting to destabilize the USSR and seize power. They said the campaign was being conducted by Party and government newspapers. The deputies denied calling for demonstrations and work stoppages on October 6 and 7 in connection with Soviet Constitution Day, but they said disturbances might be provoked by people seeking a pretext to introduce a state of emergency and to crush democratic forces (*Radio Moscow*, *TASS*, September 28). On September 28, *Pravda* published an article accusing radical deputies in the RSFSR Supreme Soviet and in the Leningrad and Moscow City Soviets of deliberately worsening the food supply in major Russian cities in order to overthrow the Ryzhkov government.

Saturday, September 29

Ryzhkov Warns of Economic Disorder

Prime Minister Nikolai Ryzhkov warned of spreading economic disorder and said the potato harvest must be completed to avoid a winter of hunger. In a televised interview, Ryzhkov said laws and decrees were being ignored and violated at levels not experienced for a long time. Ryzhkov said it was necessary to maintain existing economic structures until new market mechanisms were in place.

Shevardnadze Meets Jordanian Crown Prince

Soviet Foreign Minister Eduard Shevardnadze and US Secretary of State James Baker held a joint meeting in New York with Jordanian Crown Prince Hassan. Reports on the meeting, which was held on September 28, said Baker and Shevardnadze had urged Hassan to observe fully a United Nations trade embargo against Iraq and discussed ways of helping the Jordanian economy (*Reuters*, *UPI*, September 29).

Twenty-six Soviet Soldiers Ask for Asylum in Hesse

Twenty-six Soviet soldiers based in East Germany asked for asylum in the West German state of Hesse. A local Interior Ministry spokesman said the Soviet soldiers had arrived over the past few weeks (*AP*, September 29). Last week, a senior West German Defense Ministry official said that hundreds of Soviet soldiers were deserting their units in East Germany and seeking asylum in West Germany.

Estonia and Hungary Agree to Establish Consulates

Estonian Foreign Minister Lennart Meri said Estonia and Hungary had agreed to establish direct consular relations. Meri met with Hungarian Foreign Minister Geza Jeszenszky in New York, where they were attending the UN General Assembly. Meri told RFE/RL by telephone that consulates would be opened in Tallinn and Budapest.

Chukchi Autonomous Republic Declared

TASS said the soviet of the Chukchi Autonomous Okrug had declared the area an autonomous republic. TASS said deputies in Anadyr had appealed to the USSR Supreme Soviet to recognize the new republic. TASS quoted deputies as saying the main purpose of the declaration was to define more clearly the status of the native peoples of the Chukotsky Peninsula, to ensure their social protection, and to use the area's natural resources more efficiently.

Ipat'ev Site Given to Church

Komsomol'skaya pravda reported that the Sverdlovsk City Soviet had passed a resolution handing over the site of the Ipat'ev House—where Tsar Nicholas II and his family and servants were shot in 1918—to the Russian Orthodox Church. The house itself was demolished in 1978.

Ogonek(No. 38) published another installment of the book by Edvard Radzinsky about the murder of the last Russian tsar and his family. In the latest installment, Radzinsky insisted that the official Soviet version of events, according to which the Uralsk Soviet decided on its own initiative to kill the tsar's family, was a myth. In fact, Radzinsky said, the Central Party Archives contained a telegram that proved that Lenin and Sverdlov were informed in advance about the planned execution and gave their approval of it.

Sunday, September 30

Soviet-Israeli Consular Ties Reestablished

USSR Foreign Minister Eduard Shevardnadze and Israeli Foreign Minister David Levi announced at a press conference in New York that their governments would restore consular ties. Shevardnadze said they had also discussed the Middle East peace process and an accord to establish direct air links between Israel and the USSR (*Reuters*, *UPI*, September 30).

Soviet–South Korean Agreement on Diplomatic Relations

In a joint communiqué issued in New York, Soviet Foreign Minister Eduard Shevardnadze and South Korean Foreign Minister Choi Ho Joong announced that their governments would establish diplomatic relations at the ambassadorial level on January 1, 1991. Although the joint statement noted that the two governments "proceed from the premise that [the decision] will never affect their relations with third countries," it is likely to damage further the USSR's deteriorating relations with North Korea (*AFP*, September 30).

Military Official on Reform of Military-Political Organs

The head of the Main Political Directorate of the Soviet Army and Navy, Nikolai Shlyaga, told *Pravda* that the military-political organs were passing into a new stage of development where their functions would involve only service to the state. He said that the military-political organs—previously subordinate to the Communist Party—would now serve the people and the constitution of the USSR. According to TASS, Shlyaga nevertheless reiterated his belief that the Party should maintain a high profile in the armed forces.

Azerbaijan Elects New Supreme Soviet

According to TASS, early voter turnout was low in elections to the new Azerbaijani Supreme Soviet, in which some 1,200 candidates were competing for 350 seats. International observers wishing to monitor the elections were refused entry to Baku by the city's military commandant, who also banned mass rallies for weeks prior to the elections.

On October 1, a spokesman for the Azerbaijani Popular Front estimated that the organization had won about twenty-five of the 350 seats in the new republican Supreme Soviet and said that it would compete in runoff elections for a further twenty seats on October 15, according to *The Los Angeles Times*. His allegations of irregularities during the elections were rejected by the republican news agency Azerinform. Retired Politburo member and former Azerbaijani Communist Party First Secretary Geidar Aliev was elected to the new Supreme Soviet from his home village in the Nakhichevan ASSR by a large majority (*TASS*, October 1).

Georgia Votes for Unofficial National Congress

Voting began in Georgia for an unofficial "National Congress," which is envisaged by the radical wing of the Georgian opposition movement as "the sole spokesman" for the Georgian people in their campaign to regain independence (*TASS*, September 30). The congress is supported by both the radical and the liberal wing of the "Coordinating Center," which unites the majority of Georgia's alternative political parties. The Round Table and the Georgian National Front are boycotting the elections to the National Congress but will participate in the Georgian Supreme Soviet elections to be held on October 28. See RL 449/90.

On October 22, TASS announced the final results of the elections to the Georgian National Congress. Somewhat surprisingly, the National Independence Party won seventy-one of the 200 seats, six more than the coalition of democratic parties, which included the National-Democratic Party headed by Georgii Chanturia, one of the two most influential and controversial figures in the Georgian national movement. The Democratic Faction of the Georgian Communist Party, which had nominated eighty candidates, won eleven seats. Only 50.8 percent of the electorate participated in the elections.

Uzbek Decree on Military Service

The Uzbek Council of Ministers approved an Uzbek presidential decree stipulating that, starting this fall, the drafting of Uzbek youths into construction units outside the republic would end. According to a Radio Moscow account of reports from Tashkent, the decree also stipulated that potential draftees who have had a brother killed while performing military service in peacetime will not be liable for call-up.

Conference of Turkish and Caucasian Peoples Ends in Moscow

The "Founding Congress of Representatives of Democratic Organizations of the Turkic Peoples, Farsi, and the Peoples of the Caucasus" ended in Moscow. TASS said some 100 representatives of more than thirty national parties and social organizations attended. It said participants adopted resolutions on the situation in regions afflicted by interethnic conflicts. TASS said the congress criticized Aleksandr Solzhenitsyn's pamphlet on the future organization of Russia, which was published in *Komsomol'skaya pravda* on September 18. According to TASS, the delegates found Solzhenitsyn's views offensive to Central Asians.

Mormon Church Gets Recognition for First Soviet Branch

The US-based Mormon Church said its first branch in the Soviet Union had been given official recognition. A statement from the Church's headquarters in Salt Lake City said the Soviet Union's Council on Religious Affairs had registered the Leningrad branch of the Mormon Church. The Church's spokesman said Mormon missionary work in the USSR was limited and church services were being conducted in members' homes (*AP*, September 30).

The Month of October

Monday, October 1

Demonstrations and Strikes in Ukraine

On September 30, mass demonstrations were held throughout Ukraine. In Kiev, an estimated 100,000 people gathered for a rally at which leading figures in Ukraine's parliamentary opposition rejected the idea of a new Union treaty and accused the Communist Party of Ukraine of blocking the processes of democratization and national liberation. Later, during a march through the center of Kiev, the size of the crowd was reported to have doubled. Similar protests called by "Rukh" and its democratic allies were reported to have taken place in Donetsk, Ivano-Frankovsk, and other cities (*TASS*, RL Ukrainian service, September 30).

On October 1, a strike called by the republic's democratic forces took place in various cities, including Lvov, Ternopol, and Kiev. The strike was timed for the opening of the second session of the new Ukrainian parliament, in which the Communist Party, through its manipulation of electoral procedures, had managed to assure itself a majority. According to initial reports, tens of thousands of demonstrators protested outside the Ukrainian Supreme Soviet building in Kiev. According to RFE/RL sources in Lvov, employees at the city's factories, schools, and railway station were all on strike. Students from the city's higher education institutions were reported to be gathering at the university and burning portraits of Marx, Engels, and Lenin, as well as other Communist symbols.

On October 2, clashes broke out between police and demonstrators outside the Ukrainian Supreme Soviet building, leaving ten people injured, including five elderly women. The incident began when protesters tried to push their way through barricades erected by police near the parliament. This was the first violence in three straight days of protest in the Ukrainian capital. Some legislators called for an investigation (RL Ukrainian service, October 2).

On October 7, two rallies, one that defended and the other that denounced Lenin, were held in Kiev. The anti-Lenin rally was staged at the base of the city's largest statue to the Bolshevik leader. Reuters said about 10,000 people gathered there under blue-and-yellow Ukrainian flags. TASS reported that the demonstration defending Lenin had taken place at the end of a meeting of Ukrainian war veterans.

On October 13, Radio Kiev reported that more than 350 hunger strikers—mostly students—had assembled in Kiev and that at least seven of those striking were people's deputies. They were calling, inter alia, for the resignation of the Ukrainian government and for new elections. Eighty-five Ukrainian Supreme Soviet deputies were reported to have appealed to the hunger strikers to end their fast, which began on October 2.

On October 15, some 100,000 students marched through Kiev to demand the resignation of the government, the passage of a new constitution to establish the republic's independence, and the confiscation of all Party property, Reuters reported. The students were given an hour's television time on October 15 to present their demands and to publicize a call for a general strike on October 17. TASS reported that the Ukrainian Supreme Soviet had set aside its planned agenda in order to review the demands of the students.

On October 16, the protest marches in Kiev continued. The Ukrainian parliament set up a conciliatory commission to deal with the students' demands (*TASS*, *Radio Kiev*, *Reuters*, October 16).

On October 17, Western reports from Kiev said that student leaders had agreed to suspend their street protests and hunger strikes. This decision was taken in response to the issuing by the Ukrainian parliament of a resolution addressing the students' key demands. A "Rukh" spokesman said, however, that the students were skeptical about whether the parliament would honor its commitments and that they had therefore put off a decision about whether to cancel their protest until early the following week.

The parliament's resolution included several important points. The deputies agreed to hold a referendum in Ukraine in 1991 on confidence in the parliament. If the results of the vote demanded it, multiparty elections would be held (*TASS*, October 17). The resolution also said that the question of the release of Ukrainian Prime Minister Vitalii Masol from his post would be reviewed in accordance with the provisions of the Ukrainian Constitution. On October 17, Ukrainian Supreme Soviet Chairman Leonid Kravchuk promised Masol's resignation (*TASS*, *Central Television*, "Vremya," October 17).

The resolution also said recruits could perform their military service in Ukraine and would be sent to serve in the Soviet Armed Forces only on a voluntary basis. (Soviet Defense Minister Dmitrii Yazov immediately rejected this idea [*Radio Kiev*, October 17].)

The resolution said a Union treaty should not be signed before a new Ukrainian Constitution has been adopted. It said a report on nationalizing Communist Party property would be submitted to the parliament before December 1.

On October 18, First Deputy Chairman of the Ukrainian Supreme Soviet Vladimir Grinev commented on the situation in Ukraine in an interview with *Komsomol'skaya pravda*. Grinev said a new state order would emerge in the USSR as a result of moves such as those taken in the Ukraine. He said the USSR would soon become an association of free states.

Law on Freedom of Conscience Adopted

The USSR Supreme Soviet adopted by a vote of 341–2 a law on freedom of conscience and religious organizations, according to TASS (for the text of the law, see *Izvestia*, October 9). After lengthy debate, the members decided to drop from the law an article permitting the use of school buildings for religious instruction after regular hours. Radio Moscow concluded, however, that "what is not forbidden is allowed." The Supreme Soviet also voted to tax religious organizations at the same rate as businesses and to prohibit military commanders from preventing soldiers from attending religious services in their free time. See RL 480/90.

Moldavian Supreme Soviet Passes Legislation on Emergency Rule

The Moldavian Supreme Soviet adopted a law enabling its chairman and its Presidium to declare a state of emergency and other forms of emergency rule in the republic, TASS reported. Defining the prerogatives of executive power in such situations, the law added to the powers conferred on the executive by the parliament in September the right to introduce presidential rule under certain circumstances in all or part of the republic.

Moldavian Parliament Approves Economic Program

The Moldavian legislature approved in principle the republican government's draft economic program for the transition to a market economy, TASS reported. The program was broadly based on the Shatalin plan but added some elements of the USSR government plan.

Semipalatinsk Oblast Soviet Bans Nuclear Tests

TASS reported that the Semipalatinsk Oblast Soviet had banned all further nuclear explosions at the Soviet Union's main test range there. Residents in the area have been complaining for a long time about the effects of the tests on their health and on the environment, and testing has been suspended since March. Earlier, the Kazakh Supreme Soviet appealed to Moscow to close the test site, which has been the target of a mass antinuclear campaign in the republic. The Moscow authorities have promised to move nuclear weapons tests to Novaya Zemlya, but residents of the Soviet north are against the proposal.

Kazakh Informal Groups Agree Not to Stage Mass Gatherings

TASS reported that informal groups based in Alma-Ata had promised not to stage mass gatherings for a year. The promise followed a meeting between group leaders and Kazakh President Nursultan Nazarbaev.

On October 4, four unofficial Kazakh groups said they did not agree with the idea of a one-year moratorium on street rallies and demonstrations in Alma-Ata. The Jeltoqsan National Democratic Party issued a statement saying such a moratorium violated democratic processes. The same day, TASS issued a statement expressing concern about growing tension in Kazakhstan and said public rallies should be suspended because they provoked civic and ethnic unrest.

Moscow City Soviet Calls for Help with Harvest

The Presidium of the Moscow City Soviet appealed to all labor collectives and citizens of Moscow for help on October 6 and 7 with the potato and vegetable harvest, Radio Moscow reported. The city soviet said it would make transportation, gasoline, food, and tools available. The Presidium also noted that it would be "pointless" to hold meetings or demonstrations in Moscow on these days.

Lithuania to Form Economic Border Protection Force

Lithuania set up an economic border force to curb the flow of large quantities of untaxed goods out of the republic. The Lithuanian government recently adopted additional temporary measures to protect the domestic market. Radio Moscow said tourists and Lithuanian residents were smuggling goods and foodstuffs out of the country at an alarming rate. It said that, as of October 1, Lithuanian customs would be charged with the economic protection of the borders (*Radio Moscow*, September 25).

USSR Establishes Diplomatic Relations with Honduras

TASS announced that the Soviet and Honduran foreign ministers had signed a joint communiqué establishing diplomatic relations. Honduran President Rafael Callejas attended the signing ceremony, which took place in New York. Over the past few years, the Soviet Union has steadily improved its ties with several Central American governments that it had long criticized for their reactionary domestic policies and their ready acceptance of US foreign-policy initiatives in the region. The Soviet Union and Honduras signed a trade pact in 1987.

Armenian Deputies End Hunger Strike over NKAO

A group of parliamentary deputies from Armenia ended a three-week hunger strike over the Nagorno-Karabakh conflict. The hunger strikers were demanding the restoration of local elected bodies in Nagorno-Karabakh, which were dissolved earlier this year by the Azerbaijani leadership. In a statement quoted by *Izvestia*, the deputies said they were ending their action in response to appeals by the Armenian Supreme Soviet and by the head of the Armenian Apostolic Church, Catholicos Vazgen I. Several of the protesters ended their fast the previous week and were hospitalized.

On October 3, TASS reported that a delegation from the European Parliament had been expelled from Nagorno-Karabakh by the local military commandant shortly after its arrival in Stepanakert, allegedly for safety reasons, following an Azerbaijani attack on an Armenian district in retaliation for a bomb explosion that killed a nine-year-old boy. The head of the delegation expressed "outrage" at the commandant's decision.

On October 5, Armenia denied accusations that it had "annexed" the village of Kyarki in Azerbaijan's autonomous republic of Nakhichevan. TASS said on October 6 that the previous day the Armenian Foreign Ministry had called the Azerbaijani charges, made the previous week, "groundless." Armenia also said that both republics should look for ways to settle the dispute over Nagorno-Karabakh by peaceful means and to work towards the peaceful coexistence of Armenians and Azerbaijanis. TASS also said that the chairman of the Azerbaijani Supreme Soviet, Elmira Kafarova, had sent a message to USSR Supreme Soviet Chairman Anatolii Luk'yanov, accusing Armenia of trying to destabilize the situation in Nagorno-Karabakh.

The Armenian Ministry of Internal Affairs said that two people had been killed in gunfire when bandits attacked the Armenian village of Khnatsakh on October 12. The ministry said seven people had been killed since September 6 in attacks on Armenian villages. It held Azerbaijanis responsible for the attacks (*TASS*, October 13).

On October 15, TASS reported that a bomb explosion in the capital of Nagorno-Karabakh, Stepanakert, had destroyed a railcar used as the headquarters of the

Organizing Committee that took over the administration of the Nagorno-Karabakh Autonomous Oblast late in 1989 following the dissolution of Arkadii Vol'sky's Special Administration Committee and the return of the region to Azerbaijani control. No one was injured. According to USSR Minister of Internal Affairs Vadim Bakatin, this was the third attempt in two months to kill the leaders of the Organizing Committee, which is headed by Azerbaijani Communist Party Second Secretary Viktor Polyanichko.

On October 22, TASS said one man had been killed in Nagorno-Karabakh when MVD troops repulsed an attack on a convoy. TASS said residents had stoned the convoy in the village of Leninavan. It said ten passengers had had to be hospitalized and two buses and two trucks had been damaged.

On October 23, the local authorities released two Armenian deputies arrested earlier in the month in Stepanakert. *Izvestia* said the two deputies, Robert Agadzhanyan and Hamlet Grigoryan, had been released because their arrests had taken place without the sanction of the prosecutor and without formal charges. It said Chairman of the Armenian Supreme Soviet Levon Ter-Petrossyan had lodged a strong protest with RSFSR Supreme Soviet Chairman Boris El'tsin (the two Armenians were taken to a prison in the Russian city of Saratov). At the time of their arrests, the authorities accused the deputies of spreading provocative rumors and calling for mass disorder. Also on October 23, TASS reported more clashes in Nagorno-Karabakh, involving Armenians, Azerbaijanis, and troops.

On October 25, TASS reported that four Soviet MVD officials had been taken hostage in Nagorno-Karabakh. TASS said it had received an anonymous telephone call demanding the release of several Armenians detained on October 24 during a passport check before the hostages would be let go. TASS said the passport check was at a crossing point from an Azerbaijani residential area to an Armenian area in the Mardakert Raion.

Tuesday, October 2

Military Draft Woes

The USSR Defense Ministry reported that draft problems were becoming more serious. It pointed to "anticonstitutional" and "illegal" acts issued in many republics, singling out for criticism Western Ukraine, Moldavia, and Uzbekistan—all of which aim to limit the right of Moscow to draft and deploy troops from their republics. *Krasnaya zvezda* called on the USSR Supreme Soviet to overrule such laws, saying that otherwise the autumn draft would be even less successful than the spring call-up. These statements conflicted with comments made the previous week by Chief of the General Staff of the Soviet Armed Forces Mikhail Moiseev, who said ethnic strife had not significantly disrupted the military manpower system.

Light-Industry Workers Threatened with Unemployment

Interviewed in *Pravda*, Soviet parliamentarian Gennadii Kiselev said 1.5 million workers in the light-industry sector could be out of work by the end of 1991. Kiselev told *Pravda* that forty light-industry enterprises would have to close by the end of October and that the figure could rise to over 100 by the end of November. He said that this would throw 600,000 workers out of jobs and that "there could be another 900,000 added next year."

New Confrontations in Crimea Involving Tatars

New confrontations between residents of the Crimea and Crimean Tatars trying to resettle in their former homeland have occurred in the Yalta area, TASS reported. Yalta residents blocked a highway to protest against attempts by Tatars to build a tent city in a wine-growing area, and about 2,000 residents confronted the same number of Tatars in the city center. The local residents were reported to have removed a Tatar tent city from in front of the city soviet building. TASS said that more than 100,000 Tatars had returned to the Crimea but that many had refused to settle in areas where jobs and land were available and were instead choosing resort towns.

On October 7, extra police units were sent to the Crimea. The situation was reported to be still tense and all roads to Yalta closed (*Radio Moscow*, October 7). The police were trying to restrict the entry of more Crimean Tatars into the Yalta area. According to Interfax (cited by AP), there were twenty-one tent camps in the area housing more than 2,500 Crimean Tatars.

Moldavian Social Democrats Get Official Registration

TASS said the Moldavian government had granted the Moldavian Social Democratic Party's request for legal registration. According to its statutes, the party seeks to unite "the national liberation and democratic forces of the republic," irrespective of ethnicity and language, and to reflect in its ranks a broad range of social groups and interests. The party adheres to the principles of the Socialist International.

Reactions in USSR to German Unification

Speaking at the RSFSR Supreme Soviet, its first deputy chairman, Ruslan Khasbulatov, welcomed German unification and congratulated the German people. He said he was confident that a united Germany would have even stronger economic and cultural ties with Russia (*TASS*, in English, October 3). ADN reported that the Soviet and German foreign ministers had exchanged pledges of friendship and cooperation in celebration of German unification. The Ukrainian Supreme Soviet approved a statement hailing German unification as the end of "a difficult and tragic period" of German history. The statement said unification opened new prospects for lasting peace in Europe (*TASS*, in English, October 3).

The same day, the USSR Supreme Soviet canceled its fifteen-year-old treaty of friendship and mutual assistance with East Germany, which has ceased to exist (*TASS*, October 3).

Latvia Passes Law on Public Holidays

The Latvian Supreme Council passed a public holidays bill that scrapped some existing holidays, including October Revolution Day. It created instead two new holidays, commemorating "victims of Communist terror," to be held on March 25 and June 14 (*TASS*, in English, October 3).

Defense Ministry Denies Movement of Nuclear Weapons

USSR Defense Ministry spokesmen denied that the Soviet Armed Forces had transferred nuclear weapons from areas of ethnic strife to the territory of the RSFSR, TASS reported. The statement, which appeared in *Krasnaya zvezda* (October 3), labeled as inaccurate a "Vremya" report of October 1 alleging that the weapons had been moved. The statement also conflicts with comments made last week by Chief of the General Staff Mikhail Moiseev to *The Washington Post*. Such disagreement between the Defense Ministry and the General Staff on so sensitive an issue is highly unusual.

Vorkuta Miners Call for New Elections

A two-day congress of miners in Vorkuta ended with the adoption of a resolution criticizing the USSR Supreme Soviet for delaying the switch to a market economy, TASS reported. The miners called for the dissolution of the USSR Supreme Soviet and for the direct, popular election of a new parliament. They also criticized the Supreme Soviet for granting new powers to Soviet Presi dent Mikhail Gorbachev and called for the president to be directly elected and for a provision that would bar the president from simultaneously holding the post of CPSU general secretary. At the same time, the miners voiced their "complete support" for the parliament and government of the RSFSR and for its economic reform program.

Leningraders Dissatisfied with New Leaders

Reporting on the opening of the second session of the Leningrad City Soviet on October 3, Soviet television said Leningraders were losing faith in their new soviet, elected in the spring, because it had failed to alleviate the city's urgent problems. "Vremya" reported that 70 percent of the Leningraders interviewed in a recent opinion poll had said they were disappointed in their new deputies.

Ex-Minister Advocates Privatization

Nikolai Lemaev, who resigned as minister of the Soviet chemical and petroleum industry at the end of September, told *Izvestia* that the country's oil industry should be denationalized. Lemaev said that he had submitted a proposal to the Soviet government in July calling for the division of the Soviet oil industry into seven joint-stock corporations but that no action had been taken. Lemaev further said that he had resigned because he could not work under the current conditions, in which the oil industry is plagued by conflicting orders from national and local bodies, environmental protests, worthless rubles, and government indecision.

Moldavia Legalizes Private Enterprises

The Moldavian government made public a decree on the status of private enterprises, TASS reported. The decree instructed republican ministries and the local authorities to assist in the formation of private enterprises by turning over, selling, or renting production capacity to private entrepreneurs on a preferential basis. The decree also set ceilings on the number of employees in various types of private enterprise (200 in industry and construction, for example).

Primakov's Mission to the Gulf

A member of Gorbachev's Presidential Council, Evgenii Primakov, met in Jordan with King Hussein and with Yasser Arafat, the head of the Palestinian Liberation Organization. According to the Jordanian press agency, as quoted in *The New York Times* (October 4), Primakov stressed Moscow's conviction that the international community could resolve the Gulf conflict without force.

On October 4, Primakov went to Baghdad. On October 5, Primakov met with Iraqi President Saddam Hussein. The Iraqi news agency said Primakov handed the Iraqi president a letter from Mikhail Gorbachev. It was later disclosed that the letter informed Saddam Hussein that, if the United States were to engage in military action against Iraq, Moscow would do nothing to stop it (*Reuters*, October 5; *Novosti*, October 14).

USSR Foreign Minister Eduard Shevardnadze said the USSR would join any military action in the Persian Gulf authorized by the United Nations Security Council. According to *The Los Angeles Times* (September 30), Shevardnadze made his remarks during the taping of NBC's television program "Meet the Press."

On October 3, the chief of the General Staff of the Soviet Armed Forces, Mikhail Moiseev, said the United States and its allies should not use force against Iraq without prior approval by the United Nations. In an interview with *The New York Times* given jointly with his US counterpart, General Colin Powell, Moiseev said economic sanctions against Iraq were working. He said protests, uprisings, and desertions were sapping the strength of the Iraqi Armed Forces. For his part, Powell said that the United States sought a peaceful solution to the Gulf crisis but that it was not ruling out any option available to it.

On October 5, a group of Soviet deputies belonging to the parliamentary bloc "Soyuz" criticized Shevardnadze's statement on the possibility of sending a Soviet military contingent to the Gulf. In a statement carried by TASS, the group said that, while Iraq's occupation of Kuwait could only arouse indignation and condemnation, the conflict should be resolved by political means, not by military force.

On October 6, Primakov left Iraq after two days of talks with Saddam Hussein and other members of the Iraqi government, saying he was greatly satisfied. "I am not pessimistic any longer about the prospects for a peaceful solution to the crisis," Reuters quoted Primakov as saying. Saddam promised Primakov that many of the 5,000 Soviet citizens still in Iraq would soon be allowed to go home.

The same day, Moiseev said the USSR and the United States stood "shoulder to shoulder" in condemning Iraq's invasion and annexation of Kuwait. He spoke in Washington at the end of his visit to the United States. Moiseev said he hoped that the Gulf crisis could be settled by diplomatic means (*Reuters*, October 6).

On October 8, Gorbachev's military adviser Marshal Sergei Akhromeev warned that high concentrations of military forces and potential Arab resentment over the presence of US troops could lead to war in the Gulf. While conceding that the US forces were in the Gulf at the request of Saudi Arabia, Akhromeev told Novosti that their presence was destabilizing and disquieting for the Soviet military leadership. He called for a political solution to the Gulf crisis.

The same day, Soviet Deputy Prime Minister Igor Belousov said plans were in the making to bring home about 1,500 Soviet technicians from Iraq. He said many of them were insisting they be brought home before their contracts expired (*Reuters*, *AFP*, October 8).

On October 15, USSR Foreign Ministry spokesman Gennadii Gerasimov said that the Kremlin would not divulge any information about Iraq's defenses to the United States (*TASS*, October 15). But, on October 18, AP quoted KGB chief Vladimir Kryuchkov as saying that his organization was willing to share intelligence on Iraq. He said the KGB had not yet made a direct offer because, in the past, the organization's offers to cooperate with the CIA had been rejected.

On October 16, Primakov, who was in Rome continuing his mission on the Gulf crisis, met with Italian Prime Minister Giulio Andreotti for an hour. At a news conference later, Primakov expressed optimism that a peaceful solution could be found to the crisis. He said an Iraqi withdrawal from Kuwait was "possible and necessary" (*Reuters*, October 16).

On October 17, Primakov arrived in Paris to deliver a similar message on the Gulf to President François Mitterrand (*Reuters*, October 17).

On October 18, Primakov arrived in Washington to discuss the Gulf crisis with US President George Bush and Secretary of State James Baker. Talking to reporters, Primakov said military action against Iraq should be avoided if possible (*Reuters*, *AP*, October 18).

On October 19, Primakov met with Bush. After the meeting he said he and Bush had agreed that the nations of the world should not relax their insistence on an Iraqi withdrawal (*Reuters*, October 19).

On October 21, Primakov continued his discussion of the Gulf crisis with the leaders of various countries. He met in London with Foreign Secretary Douglas Hurd and later with Prime Minister Margaret Thatcher. Reuters quoted Primakov as affirming the Soviet Union's commitment to maintaining sanctions against Iraq in retaliation for its invasion of Kuwait.

On October 21, *Rabochaya tribuna* corrected a report it had carried the previous week about Soviet intelligence information on Iraq being withheld from the

Kremlin. The newspaper said the report, received from Novosti, was "a fabrication." Novosti said Soviet military intelligence knew two weeks before Iraq's invasion of Kuwait on August 2 that there was a possibility Iraq might attack. It said the Soviet Defense Ministry thought this estimate exaggerated and did not pass it on to the Kremlin. In todays report *Rabochaya tribuna* said that Novosti had been sent a letter from the chief of the General Staff of the Soviet Armed Forces, General Mikhail Moiseev, asking it to publish a Defense Ministry rebuttal.

On October 23, the conservative newspaper *Sovetskaya Rossiya* criticized Moscow's approach to the Gulf crisis and called on the Soviet Union to play a mediating role. The paper said the USSR would suffer from any military conflict in the Gulf, while Washington could benefit by building up forces and influence in the region. Noting the Soviet Union's strengths, the newspaper said, "We had and still have economic interests in Iraq (the source of a third of our hard-currency income)."

The same day, Soviet Foreign Ministry spokesman Yurii Gremitskikh said 4,300 Soviet specialists remained in Iraq. Gremitskikh said the specialists were being evacuated via two Aeroflot flights per week and were returning "as the necessary formalities are executed," TASS reported.

On October 24, Primakov traveled to Cairo at the start of a new mission aimed at settling the Gulf crisis, Reuters and AFP reported.

On October 25, Primakov met with Syrian President Hafez Assad in Damascus. AFP said he carried a message from Mikhail Gorbachev, the contents of which were not disclosed (*Reuters*, October 25). On October 26, Primakov went back to Cairo for more talks on the Gulf crisis (*AP*, *Reuters*, October 26).

Primakov returned to Baghdad on October 27 for talks with Saddam Hussein and Foreign Minister Tariq Aziz (*DPA*, October 27). On his return to Moscow, Primakov said Hussein was becoming more open to a political solution to the Gulf crisis (*Reuters* , *AP*, *AFP*, October 31).

On October 30, a Kuwaiti report said the exiled Kuwaiti government had told the Soviet Union that it appreciated efforts to reach a peaceful solution in the Gulf but had reiterated that Iraq's withdrawal from Kuwait must be unconditional (*Reuters*, *AFP*, *AP*, October 30). See RL 418/90.

Shevardnadze and Baker Call for Stronger United Nations

USSR Foreign Minister Eduard Shevardnadze and US Secretary of State James Baker issued a joint statement affirming their governments' desire to enhance the United Nations' peacekeeping functions. TASS reported that the two officials had also agreed to help strengthen the United Nations' role in supervising free elections in member countries.

Ukrainian Parliament Rejects Government 's Economic Plan

The Ukrainian Supreme Soviet rejected the Ukrainian government's economic plan, saying it did not answer the needs of the day and did not offer any prospects for the future. Deputies also rejected a government request that it be given until October 15 to rework the plan. TASS said deputies had criticized the plan for merely trying to stabilize the present situation and maintain the standard of living.

Man Sentenced for Illegal Storage of Radioactive Materials

Radio Moscow said a man had been sentenced to four years in prison in the Soviet Union's first case of illegal acquisition and storage of radioactive materials. The radio, broadcasting in English, said the man, named Abrizhnikov, had been found guilty after a trial in Mytishchi, near Moscow. It said investigators had linked Abrizhnikov to two "powerful" sources of radiation found in a cache in a forest. The radio said the investigators had been unable to determine where he had obtained the radioactive materials or what he planned to do with them.

Temporary Halt on Migration to North Ossetia

Under a decree of the Presidium of the North Ossetian ASSR Supreme Soviet "On the Temporary Restriction of Migration to the Territory of the Autonomous Republic," no one not permanently resident in the republic's territory can be hired for work, Radio Moscow reported. The reasons given were the complex sociopolitical and socioeconomic situation, difficulties with food and other supplies, and problems of employment connected with the switch to market relations. It seems possible, however, that the real reason was to stop more Ingush moving to the area around the North Ossetian capital, Vladikavkaz, which the Ingush claim as their historical homeland.

Thursday, October 4

Gorbachev Orders Limits on Profits

Mikhail Gorbachev issued a decree ordering the Soviet authorities to set limits on profits. TASS said the move was to prevent "unfounded" price increases. The news agency said that Gorbachev's decree called for excess profits to go into government budgets, both central and republican. The USSR Council of Ministers and its republican counterparts were also told to set limits on wholesale prices for a range of goods within ten days. Enterprises buying and selling among themselves were allowed to agree on wholesale prices, but only if they did not exceed fixed limits.

Official Says Shortages Getting Worse in Some Areas

Deputy Head of the USSR Ministry of Internal Affairs' Department in Charge of Combating Theft of Socialist Property and Profiteering Viktor Abrosimov said shortages of food and consumer goods were growing worse in some parts of Ukraine, Belorussia, and Azerbaijan. Abrosimov said Soviet light industry was "on the verge of disintegration" owing to a lack of material and technical resources (*TASS*, October 4).

There were also more reports of food price increases and rationing in the Soviet Union. TASS said on October 3 that bread, butter, meat, and dairy products would cost more in Estonia, beginning October 15. Prices were also expected to rise soon in Lithuania (*Radio Vilnius*, October 4). In Belorussia's Gomel Oblast, rationing of certain food products began on October 3, TASS reported.

Problems continued, too, with the Soviet harvest. Radio Moscow said on October 4 that a state of emergency had been declared the previous day in Krasnodar Krai in the RSFSR. Emergency harvesting was also under way in Belorussia's Vitebsk Oblast (*Radio Moscow*, October 4).

Violence Reported in Tbilisi

There was a report of violence in the Georgian capital, Tbilisi. The independent Iberia news agency said that two men had been killed and a third wounded on October 3 by shots fired in the headquarters of one of Georgia's two federations of opposition forces. Iberia said the two victims had been identified as members of a Georgian paramilitary organization known as the Saint George Society. The agency said it was not clear who had done the shooting or why.

Estonian Labor Camp Inmates Strike

Radio Moscow reported that inmates of Estonian labor camps were refusing to eat or work in protest against overcrowding in the camps and problems with food. The radio said that a government commission had been formed to look into the grievances. The radio said that there were four times as many inmates in one of the Estonian camps as it was intended for.

Ter-Petrossyan Continues US Tour

The chairman of the Armenian Supreme Soviet, Levon Ter-Petrossyan, met with US National Security Adviser Brent Scowcroft in Washington (*RFE/RL Special*, October 4). In an interview published the same day in *USA Today*, Ter-Petrossyan said the West should realize that the central government in the USSR was an obstacle to movement towards democracy. He said that real authority had already been transferred to the republics and that therefore the West should shift its attention to the republics. Ter-Petrossyan's visit followed the signing of a treaty in the United States granting 9.8 million dollars in humanitarian assistance to Armenia.

Abdulatipov on Sovereignty within RSFSR

At a press conference in Moscow, Chairman of the RSFSR Council of Nationalities Ramazan Abdulatipov said that the proclamations of sovereignty by some autonomous republics in the RSFSR did not mean they had become Union republics, TASS reported. Raising the status of the autonomous republics was the prerogative of the RSFSR Supreme Soviet, he said. Abdulatipov suggested that the new Union treaty should feature the autonomous formations "as equal republics in the Russian Federation."

Abdulatipov also touched on another problem—namely, demands by the oblasts of the RSFSR that they should be given equal status with the autonomous formations. He proposed that the new federal treaty being drawn up for the RSFSR should be signed by both the autonomous republics and the oblasts. Abdulatipov added that he had asked Boris El'tsin to convoke a special session of the RSFSR Supreme Soviet on interethnic relations.

New Job for Kharchev

Konstantin Kharchev, former chairman of the Council for Religious Affairs (1984-89), has finally been confirmed as ambassador to the United Arab Emirates. The eighteen-month delay in sending Kharchev abroad was, according to Infonovosti, caused by an interview Kharchev gave to *Ogonek* (No. 44, 1989), which prompted lively polemics in the Soviet press on Party and state methods of administration of religious organizations.

Independent Radio and Television Station Registered

The RSFSR Ministry of the Mass Media registered one of the USSR's first independent radio and television stations, TASS reported. The new station was founded on the basis of the all-Union public television company Nika, which was established in 1988. The founders of the company included the Soyuztelefilm Association, the USSR State

Committee for Radio and Television Broadcasting, the all-Union Komsomol Central Committee, and a Soviet-Italian company, Sovitcom. Local bureaus of Nika have been broadcasting for two years in some forty cities.

Commission on Moldavia Finishes Investigation

Krasnaya zvezda said the USSR Supreme Soviet commission appointed to examine the situation in Moldavia had formulated its conclusions. The commission, which spent most of its time with the leaders and supporters of the non-Moldavian secessionist movements, blamed the Moldavian government for "errors" in connection with the language law and asked it to "completely change its policy" towards Russian and other ethnic groups. The commission also criticized Moldavia for "[giving] its laws precedence over all-Union laws," a criticism tantamount to a direct challenge to Moldavia's declaration of sovereignty. The commission, nonetheless, endorsed the principle of the indivisibility of the republic.

Friday, October 5

RSFSR Parliament Discusses Draft Bill on Land Ownership

The RSFSR Supreme Soviet opened discussion on a draft bill allowing private ownership of land and enterprises. Sergei Krasavchenko, chairman of the parliament's Committee on Economic Reform and Ownership, said enactment of the bill would be "a truly historic event" in the federation. He said it would be the first legal act backing the transition to a market economy under a radical economic reform plan adopted by the Russian parliament. The draft bill allows for private ownership of land, enterprises, and transport facilities by Soviet citizens and foreigners. TASS said debate on the bill was split along political, economic, and psychological lines. The agency said many deputies opposed private ownership of land.

Another Hijacking Incident

A Soviet citizen hijacked a Yak-40 airliner on a flight from Novgorod to Petrozavodsk in northwest Russia. The plane landed in Helsinki (*Reuters*, *AP*, October 5). The Soviet Union said it was seeking extradition of the man, identified as Nikolai Selivanov.

Reuters and AFP reported that another Soviet hijacker, Igor Suslar, had hanged himself in a Pakistani jail. Suslar was one of eleven Soviet convicts who hijacked a Soviet airliner to Karachi in August after overpowering the guards on a domestic flight.

Left-of-Center Opposition Groups Form Bloc

TASS reported the creation of "a radical left-of-center opposition bloc," which unites a radical faction of the Moscow Popular Front, the Russian Democratic Forum, and the Association for Soviet-American Integration. TASS said the bloc wanted a free, democratic, and humane society and opposed extremism and attempts to stir up hostilities between ethnic groups. The bloc said it was willing to coexist peacefully with any political party, including the CPSU.

***Pravda* Chief Editor under Attack**

A three-day open meeting of the Party cell of the editorial staff of *Pravda* heard sharp criticism of the newspaper's editorial line and of the activities of its chief editor, Ivan Frolov. Radio Moscow said the meeting discussed the fact that the number of subscribers to the newspaper had fallen sharply. The staff blamed the situation on Frolov and demanded his resignation. Frolov rejected this criticism, however, and the Party meeting decided to ask the forthcoming CPSU Central Committee plenum to review the situation. Frolov, who replaced the extremely conservative Viktor Afanas'ev as chief editor of the newspaper in 1989, has indeed failed to change the newspaper's conservative stance.

On October 10, CPSU Deputy General Secretary Vladimir Ivashko told reporters in Moscow that the CPSU leadership would decide whether to retain Frolov as chief editor of *Pravda*, TASS reported. A *Pravda* staff member interviewed by RFE/RL also accused Frolov of being rude to his subordinates. In response to Ivashko's announcement, Frolov told TASS on October 10 that in fact his subordinates were responsible for the newspaper's conservatism.

The same day, Reuters quoted Frolov as saying he had survived "a mini-coup" by disgruntled employees of the newspaper. On October 11, *Pravda* carried a denial of reports that its Party cell had demanded Frolov's resignation.

Russian Komsomol to Change Its Name

The recently created RSFSR Komsomol announced at its second plenum that it would change the organization's name to the Federation of Youth for the Revival of Russia, *Sobesednik* (No. 39) reported. The plenum also voted to adopt as the organization's symbol the prerevolutionary Russian red, white, and blue flag. The leadership of the Russian Komsomol also complained that almost all the organization's finances, which should be in the possession of the Russian Komsomol, are still concentrated in the hands of the all-Union organization. The RSFSR

Komsomol will continue to fight to get its fair share of Komsomol money.

Saturday, October 6

Exiled Armenian Dissident Gets Citizenship Back

Reuters reported that Gorbachev had signed an order restoring Soviet citizenship to exiled Armenian activist Paruir Airikyan. Airikyan was arrested in 1988 for allegedly defaming the Soviet state after speaking publicly about the conflict in the Nagorno-Karabakh Autonomous Oblast. He was expelled from the USSR and has been living in the United States.

Separate Polish Territory within Lithuania Called For

A group of elected officials in Lithuania said there should be a Polish national territory within the republic. Radio Vilnius said the proposal was approved after five hours of discussion among elected representatives from the Vilnius area who met in Eisiskes, south of the capital. The Lithuanian Supreme Council and government expressed their disapproval of the proposal. TASS quoted a joint statement as saying: "We shall not permit narrow provincialism and ill will to inflict such serious damage" on Lithuania. TASS also quoted Lithuanian Supreme Council deputy Stanislav Peshko, who criticized his parliament's position. Peshko said the Lithuanian leadership "totally ignores" Polish interests and "we [the Poles] have always been treated as stepsons."

Latvian Popular Front Discusses New Program

A congress of the Latvian Popular Front met in Riga and began discussing a new draft program that called for the restoration of Latvian independence. TASS said the proposed program called for the complete withdrawal of the Soviet Armed Forces from Latvia, the abolition of certain agreements between the USSR and Latvia, and the cessation of activities by Soviet state institutions in Latvia.

On October 7, TASS reported that the Latvian Popular Front had elected Romualdas Razukas its new chairman. (He is a neurosurgeon born in Lithuania.) Razukas, who ran unopposed, replaced Dainis Ivans, who had led the front since its inception two years previously.

Congress of Belorussian Trade Unions; New Trade Union in Ukraine

A congress of Belorussian trade unions ended in Minsk after adopting rules barring the unions' chairman and his deputies from holding elected office in any political party. TASS said the chairman of the Belorussian trade unions,

Vladimir Goncharik, who is also a member of the buro of the Belorussian Communist Party, would have to quit one of these positions.

The same day, a new Ukrainian Trade-Union Federation held a founding congress in Kiev. TASS said that, in contrast to previous Ukrainian trade-union groupings, the new federation would promote the development of democracy in the trade-union movement and the socio-economic interests of workers.

Sunday, October 7

Moldavian Komsomol to Abjure Communist Ideology

Moldavian Komsomol First Secretary Petru Gafton has publicly called on the organization to "renounce Communist ideology," Central Television reported. The move, which echoed that already made by the Russian Komsomol, seemed designed to forestall the numerical decline in the Moldavian Komsomol and to enable it to compete more effectively with the Moldavian Popular Front and its affiliate, the Organization of Democratic Youth, for the allegiance of young Moldavians.

Moscow Protest Calls for Alternative to Military Service

Several dozen protesters rallied outside the USSR Ministry of Defense in Moscow, demanding that young men be allowed to perform community service as an alternative to the military draft. Speakers at the rally, which was sponsored by the "Memorial" society, the Committee of Soldiers' Mothers, and several youth groups, drew attention to the difficulties the Soviet army is currently experiencing in getting draftees to report for duty.

Opinion Survey on Status and Structure of RSFSR

The results of an opinion survey conducted in the RSFSR in September on how the RSFSR should be organized were published in *Moscow News* (No. 40). They showed that 58.6 percent of those questioned favored instituting the office of president and that 57.2 percent thought the president should be popularly elected. Just over half thought the center should not be able to annul or suspend the decisions of RSFSR bodies, but under half would give the RSFSR the right to annul decisions of the center. Regarding the administrative structure of the republic, 47.8 percent of the respondents thought the RSFSR should be a federation in which the national-territorial formations, krais, and oblasts were equal participants, while 55.9 percent thought that the autonomous formations should have the right to secede if a majority of the population was in favor. Close to half, however, would not give their laws priority over those of the RSFSR.

More Declarations of Sovereignty Announced

The Adigei Autonomous Oblast Soviet declared the territory an autonomous republic, Moscow Television reported. This step was part of a general trend on the part of the autonomous territories of the RSFSR to raise their status, and was a cause of concern to some RSFSR deputies.

On October 8, the Buryat Supreme Soviet adopted a declaration of sovereignty rejecting the status of autonomous republic and declaring Buryatia a Soviet Socialist republic and sovereign multinational state within the Russian republic and the Soviet Union that voluntarily delegates part of its powers to the RSFSR and the Union (*TASS*, October 8). At the same time, the republic reserved the right to suspend and object to laws of the RSFSR and the Union that violate the interests of the Buryat people. The declaration proclaimed all land, natural resources, and economic potential the property of the republic and made Buryat and Russian the state languages.

On October 9, Radio Moscow reported that the soviet of the Koryak Autonomous Okrug, which is part of Kamchatka Oblast, had declared the territory an autonomous republic. The total population of Koryakia is 40,000, of whom 70 percent are Slavs.

On October 11, after heated debates, the Bashkir Supreme Soviet accepted in principle a declaration of sovereignty for the autonomous republic. The Supreme Soviet also voted to upgrade Bashkiria's status to that of a Union republic.

On October 18, the Kalmyk Autonomous Republic declared its sovereignty but said it would remain within the RSFSR. A sovereignty declaration adopted at a special session of the republic's parliament said the Kalmyk Constitution and laws would have supremacy in the republic. It also said the republic's land, its resources, and its economic potential were the exclusive property of the Kalmyk nation. The declaration said the Kalmyk republic would stay in the RSFSR but would drop the word "autonomous" from its name. It also said the Kalmyk republic's relations with the Soviet Union, the RSFSR, and other republics would be determined by bilateral agreements (*TASS*, October 18).

The same day, the soviet of the Yamalo-Nenets Autonomous Okrug proclaimed the territory a republic, Radio Moscow reported. In 1989, the Nentsy constituted a mere 4.2 percent of the population, while Russians and Ukrainians accounted for 76.2 percent.

On October 22, the Mari Autonomous Republic in the RSFSR declared itself a Soviet Socialist republic with the new name of "Marii el," which means "Mari territory," TASS reported. Under the terms of the declaration, the republic remains part of the RSFSR. All natural resources are to be the exclusive property of the people of the republic, but TASS made no mention of Mari laws' having priority. Both Mari and Russian were declared state languages.

On October 24, the Chuvash Autonomous Republic adopted a declaration of sovereignty. TASS reported that after a sharp two-day debate the Chuvash Supreme Soviet declared Chuvashia "the Chuvash Soviet Socialist Republic—the republic of Chavash'en." The republic will remain part of the RSFSR, but all its natural resources will be the property of the republic. The state languages will be Chuvash and Russian.

On October 25, Interfax reported that the Kazakh Supreme Soviet had adopted a declaration of republican sovereignty. According to Interfax, the declaration gave the republic control over its own resources and stated that republican laws had precedence over USSR laws. The same report said the Supreme Soviet had also banned all nuclear weapons testing in the republic.

The same day, the Gorno-Altai Autonomous Oblast adopted a declaration of sovereignty and declared itself the Gorno-Altai Autonomous Soviet Socialist Republic, Radio Moscow reported. The declaration stated that the republic would remain part of the RSFSR.

On October 26, the Irkutsk Oblast in Eastern Siberia declared its sovereignty within the Russian Federation. A declaration said that, until a new Union treaty took effect, the region would have the exclusive right to manage its land and natural resources (*TASS*, October 26).

Romanian Rally in North Bukovina

For the first time since the annexation of North Bukovina by the USSR from Romania in 1945, a Romanian political rally was held in the oblast capital, Chernovtsy. The rally was organized by the Eminescu Society and other Romanian groups recently founded in the region. Local sources reported by telephone that participants in the rally were demanding a more truthful official account of Stalin's deportations of Romanians from North Bukovina, the restoration of Romanian place-names erased after the Soviet annexation, the acceptance of the Romanian tricolor alongside the Ukrainian bicolor flag in the region, the restitution of buildings confiscated from Romanian associations since the annexation, Romanian-language services in the episcopal cathedral, and the transfer of Romanian parishes to the jurisdiction of the Romanian Orthodox Church.

Suleimenov Condemns Secessionist Attitudes

Commenting on the "Founding Congress of Representatives of Democratic Organizations of the Turkic Peoples, Farsi, and Caucasian Peoples" held on September 30, Olzhas Suleimenov, the well-known Kazakh poet and USSR people's deputy, said that the participants had tried to define the role of public and informal organizations in counteracting interethnic violence in Central Asia. He condemned calls for a break with Russia, saying that "attempts to define independence as isolation from other parts of the country can only lead up a blind alley and aggravate interethnic conflicts." Suleimenov added that the peoples of the East should not copy European, and in particular Baltic, models (*TASS*, October 7).

Russian Parliament Demands Investigation

The RSFSR Supreme Soviet Committee on the Mass Media assigned a group of deputies to investigate the publication of articles in *Sovetskaya Rossiya* and *Pravda* (September 26) and *Krasnaya zvezda* and *Pravda* (October 2) in which democratic forces, particularly those in Moscow and Leningrad, were accused of deliberately exacerbating food shortages in order to cause the overthrow of the USSR Council of Ministers and take power themselves. On October 7, *Pravda* accused the parliamentary commission of violating the USSR law on the press, which proclaims the freedom of the press. *Pravda* seemed to have forgotten that the same law contains several provisions stipulating punishment for slander.

Silaev Interviewed on RSFSR Economic Plan

RSFSR Prime Minister Ivan Silaev said in an interview with *Sel'skaya zhizn'* that the first stage of the Russian Federation's economic program would focus on increasing supplies of consumer goods. Silaev said the first stage of the program would take 100 days to complete and that during that period efforts would be made to privatize shops, services, and enterprises producing consumer goods. He also said that the KGB and Defense Ministry budgets would be cut by 10 to 20 percent. Silaev said that in this first stage the prices of many goods and services could be expected to rise but that the government would control the prices of about 150 "basic necessities."

Monday, October 8

CPSU CC Holds Plenum

The CPSU Central Committee opened a two-day plenary meeting in Moscow. TASS said the meeting heard reports from General Secretary Mikhail Gorbachev, his deputy, Vladimir Ivashko, and other leading officials. Gorbachev warned Party leaders that the Party's ability to retain its leading role would depend on how it acted during the transfer to a market economy. He said "the inertia of old thinking" was "a real danger" to the Party and he called on Communists to accept that reforms were necessary. Gorbachev also said Communists should be ready to form a coalition with other political groups to deal with the crisis in Soviet society.

Gorbachev also touched on the nationalities issue in his speech. The Soviet leader said that Communists had no more important task today than to oppose separatist forces. Communist deputies at all levels must also make this their chief task because a number of soviets had adopted anticonstitutional decisions which were paralyzing the actions of the authorities and destabilizing the situation in the country, he went on. Extremists were creating an atmosphere of national hatred and terror, Gorbachev added, which should be combated with the truth and the force of the law (*TASS*, October 8; *Pravda*, October 9).

In his address to the plenum, Ivashko argued that introducing "a horizontal model" for relations between the republics, which would eliminate all-Union structures, would mean the end of the Soviet Union as a sovereign state and subject of international law—with dire consequences not only for the Union but also for each individual republic. The center must have an economic role, Ivashko said, which, in the Politburo's view, includes a single monetary system, a single customs service to defend the all-Union market, and agreement on prices for key raw materials. Ivashko described as absurd the policy of national economic self-isolation and separatism.

On October 9, the leader of the Russian Communist Party, Ivan Polozkov, complained about the failure of the Gorbachev leadership to consult Party members before deciding to move to a market economy. He also spoke bitterly about what he said was the connivance of the authorities in the defamation of Lenin's memory and in "the persecution" of Communists (see *Pravda*, October 10).

Moscow Party leader Yurii Prokof'ev, who supports the transfer to a market economy, said it could not be achieved without strong executive authority, which, he said, was currently lacking in the USSR. He urged the CPSU to take the initiative in forming a centrist bloc with other reformist forces. He recognized, however, that the mood prevailing in the Party might make the formation of such a bloc impossible.

On October 9, TASS broadcast an announcement made at the plenum by Central Committe Secretary Oleg Shenin of a radical restructuring of the central Party apparatus, which involved forming eleven new commissions: on ideology; on social policy; on socioeconomics; on agricultural policy; on nationality policy; on problems of international policy; on women and family questions; on the renewal of the activities of primary Party organizations; on science, education, and culture; on youth policy; and on military policy. These were intended to replace the six existing commissions.

In addition, twelve departments were set up: an Organizational Department (on the basis of the former Party Cadres Department), an Ideological Department, a Department for Ties with Sociopolitical Organizations, a Department for Legislative Initiatives and Questions of Law (instead of the former State and Law Department), a Department for Nationality Policy, a Socioeconomic Policy Department, a Center for Information (on the basis of the former Defense Department), an Agricultural Policy Department, an International Department, a General Department, a Press Center, and an Administration of Affairs. Shenin stressed that the commissions and departments would not interfere in government and state affairs but would elaborate recommendations for various areas of Soviet politics. There was no department envisaged for control over the KGB and army; these functions were transferred to the president and the USSR Supreme Soviet. The number of full-time employees of the central Party apparatus was reduced by 40 percent—from 1,493 to 603 people. In 1989, 536 officials were released.

Shenin further said that deputies elected to the USSR Congress of People's Deputies from the CPSU should organize themselves into a faction in order to better represent the Party line. He emphasized the need for the CPSU to form a coalition with other social groups and parties. He named Kazakhstan as a positive example, noting that the republican Party leadership had managed to stabilize the political situation by cooperating closely with the soviets and with other social organizations.

On October 10, TASS reported that, in his closing remarks to the plenum, Mikhail Gorbachev said he would propose new laws providing for tough measures against black marketeers. Gorbachev told the plenum the laws would be a powerful weapon in the hands of law-enforcement officials (see *Pravda*, October 11).

Gorbachev Drafts Decree Condemning Attacks on Lenin Monuments

In response to the destruction of numerous Lenin monuments in various Soviet cities, Gorbachev drafted a decree condemning these actions and calling on republican and local authorities to support his position. On October 13, TASS carried the text of the decree, which suspended decisions by local authorities in several republics to remove statues of Lenin and prohibited such acts in the future. Discussion of the fate of Lenin monuments has been going on in the Soviet press for some time. Liberal newspapers have condemned the existence of numerous monuments to Lenin in the Soviet Union, while the conservative press claims that the demolition of these monuments poses a serious threat to *perestroika* (see, for instance, *Krasnaya zvezda*, October 6). On October 13, TASS reported that a memorial to victims of fascism had been damaged in the Ukrainian city of Donetsk.

Central Media Correspondents Organize in Moldavia

Central Soviet media correspondents in Moldavia set up a "fully independent" association, directly subordinate to the board of the USSR Journalists' Union, TASS reported. Among the rights claimed by members was that of making "subjective assessments" of the situation in Moldavia. The move seemed designed to defend the interests of the antireform journalists assigned to report from Moldavia. Central media coverage of Moldavia often appears inspired by conservative circles in Moscow and tends to support the secessionist efforts of non-Moldavians in the republic.

Telephone Tapping May Be Declared Illegal in RSFSR

A draft version of the RSFSR Criminal Code submitted to the republican Supreme Soviet contains an article that would forbid any official monitoring of telephone conversations, Professor Valerii Savitsky told *Argumenty i Fakty* (No. 38). In June, the USSR Supreme Soviet approved an amendment—presented jointly by the KGB, the USSR Ministry of Internal Affairs, and the USSR Prosecutor's Office—that gave law-enforcement agencies the right to use audio and video means to conduct investigations. Savitsky argued, however, that the constitutional rights of individuals came before the operational needs of the police.

Party Property Nationalized in Ternopol

Ukrinform-TASS reported that the Presidium of the Ternopol City Soviet had decided to nationalize all property located within its territorial jurisdiction that belonged to regional Communist Party or Komsomol committees. It said that the property was to be transferred to the municipality and that the city prosecutor had been empowered to prosecute people who hindered implementation of the decision. The Ternopol Party authorities were quick to call the action unconstitutional and illegal. In summer, 1989, the Ternopol City Soviet, one of the most radical in Ukraine, sanctioned the dismantling of statues of Lenin and Marx.

Chapter of Islamic Renaissance Party Founded in Tajikistan

TASS reported that a constituent conference of a Tajik chapter of the Islamic Renaissance Party had been concluded in a village near Dushanbe. The conference was held despite a ruling by the Presidium of the Tajik Supreme Soviet forbidding it on the grounds that the program and rules of the party violated the republican constitution. TASS said that nearly 300 representatives from all parts of the republic attended the conference and that party members from Tatarstan and Dagestan were also invited.

On October 13, a Dushanbe court fined two organizers of the conference, TASS reported. TASS said young party activists had been demonstrating outside the court every day, spreading rumors about mass arrests of party members, and threatening the judges. "Competent" sources maintained, however, that none of the demonstrators had been arrested or charged.

Plans for Banking Reforms Discussed

Plans to reform the Soviet banking system were explained to one of the houses of the USSR Supreme Soviet. The plans called for republican banks to be sovereign but to voluntarily give the central bank the sole right to issue money and make monetary decisions (*TASS*, October 8).

On October 9, the USSR Supreme Soviet approved in principle a draft law giving control of central banking to the parliament and taking it away from the government (*TASS*, October 9).

Soviet Forces Seize Greenpeace Ship

Soviet forces boarded and seized a ship operated by the environmental group Greenpeace in the Arctic Ocean near the Soviet nuclear testing site on Novaya Zemlya. A spokesman for the KGB, which guards Soviet borders, said the ship would be taken to the Kola Bay and an inquiry conducted. He said the ship had been detained for violating Soviet territory, disobeying the authorities, and "landing people at forbidden places" (*TASS*, October 8).

Commenting on the incident on October 11, USSR Foreign Ministry spokesman Gennadii Gerasimov said the Soviet Union agreed entirely with Greenpeace's objectives and with its goal to end all nuclear testing. He added, however, that Soviet and international law must still be obeyed (*AP*, October 11).

On October 14, a member of the Greenpeace group said radiation levels on Novaya Zemlya were "frightening" (*AP*, October 14).

Tuesday, October 9

Law on Political Parties Adopted

The USSR Supreme Soviet adopted a law granting equal status to all political parties. The law provided a legal follow-up to a decision in March that ended the Communist Party's constitutional monopoly on power. According to TASS and Radio Moscow, Article 16—on political activities in the army and law-enforcement agencies—was the most contentiously debated part of the new law. Sharp clashes occurred not only between civilians and soldiers but among the military deputies themselves. One general claimed that the majority of Communists in the armed forces supported the retention of military Party organizations, while a major said a majority was opposed to them. Representatives of the Volga-Urals Military District (commanded by the ultra-conservative Al'bert Makashov) were reported to have been especially resistant. In the end, a compromise was reached that called for servicemen and law-enforcement personnel to be guided by the law and not by the decisions of any party. While a step forward, the new law leaves intact the Communist Party's extensive organizational structure in the armed forces. For the text of the new law, see *Izvestia*, October 10. See also, RL 467/90.

Supreme Soviet Ratifies Nuclear Treaties

The USSR Supreme Soviet followed the US Senate in unanimously adopting two treaties on nuclear weapons testing, TASS and AP reported. The Supreme Soviet also appealed to parliaments around the world to ban such testing altogether and called for "global nuclear disarmament." Although no details were provided, debate on the treaties—the Threshold Test Ban Treaty of 1974 and the Peaceful Nuclear Explosions Treaty of 1976—was reportedly sharp.

RSFSR Supreme Soviet Hears Economic Report

RSFSR Deputy Prime Minister Gennadii Fil'shin painted a rather grim picture of his republic's economic situation, predicting a drop in the republic's national income in 1990 of about 5–7 percent, which would make the provision of social services very difficult, TASS reported. He also rejected the all-Union plan for converting military plants to civilian production and Gorbachev's recent decree on wholesale prices. That decree, he said, would cost the USSR more than 500 billion rubles, some 300 billion of which would come from the RSFSR.

Following Fil'shin's report, the RSFSR parliament voted to begin the republic's transition to a market economy on November 1, regardless of what action the USSR Supreme Soviet decided to take. Radio Moscow (October 9) also reported that the deputies had proposed convoking "an extraordinary Congress of RSFSR People's Deputies to raise the issue of trust in the center, to appeal to voters to recall USSR people's deputies representing Russia, and to recommend that enterprise and kolkhoz managers subordinate themselves to Russian ministries and departments." The report did not make clear whether a vote was taken on the proposal.

Moiseev Pledges Continued Friendship with Cuba

Chief of the General Staff of the Soviet Armed Forces Mikhail Moiseev told reporters at Havana's International Airport that the Soviet Union would continue its longstanding cooperation with Cuba. According to Reuters, Moiseev said Moscow would honor contractual agreements—involving economic, political, and military cooperation—established during Gorbachev's visit to Cuba in April, 1989. Since the early 1960s, all weapons and equipment used by the Cuban armed forces have been Soviet-made.

TASS Director Says Agency Must Become Mouthpiece of People

The general director of TASS, Leonid Kravchenko, said his agency must stop acting as a mouthpiece of the government and become a mouthpiece of the people. DPA quoted Kravchenko's remarks from a speech prepared for a media congress in Munich. Kravchenko said that, now that the press law had abolished censorship in the Soviet Union, the main problem for Soviet journalists was to overcome psychological barriers and to do away with self-imposed censorship.

Belorussian Supreme Soviet Opens Session

Owing to the critical economic situation, the Belorussian legislature went into session one month ahead of schedule. The political caucus led by the Belorussian Popular Front submitted a package of issues for debate that included laws on citizenship, the banking system, and military policy.

On October 10, TASS reported that, at the Belorussian Supreme Soviet session, the republican prime minister, Vyacheslav Kebich, had criticized Gorbachev's recent decree on priority measures to switch to a market economy. The prime minister asserted that the decree could seriously harm his republic's industrial base and he said he might not implement those parts of it that threatened the republic's engineering industry. Kebich also criticized certain aspects of the proposed new Union treaty.

On October 12, the Belorussian Supreme Soviet approved the republican Council of Ministers' plan for the transition to a market economy, Radio Moscow reported. The plan was due to go into effect on November 1.

On October 15, The Belorussian Council of Ministers withdrew from parliamentary debate its entire package of legislation on economic reform, TASS reported. Shortly beforehand, a number of opposition deputies had left the Supreme Soviet session after none of their proposals concerning economic reform were put to a vote. Kebich said the bills would have to be substantially reworked in the light of comments by the deputies and legislative committees.

Kazakhstan Plans Slow Transition to Market Economy

A deputy chairman of the Kazakh Council of Ministers, Karatai Turysov, said that Kazakhstan's transition to a market economy would be slower than in other republics, TASS reported. A draft economic program due to be debated by the republican Supreme Soviet at its next meeting calls for stabilizing the political situation in the republic first. It provides for the first market mechanisms to be introduced in 1991 and a full market system in 1992.

Turkmenistan Devises Plan for Transition to Market

Radio Moscow reported that a plan for introducing a market economy had been worked out in Turkmenistan. The report did not say who had prepared the plan, which stresses that the republic will follow an independent policy in setting prices. Prices for essential goods and services will be frozen until the end of 1991. Wage indexation will be introduced on January 1, 1991, and major power, fuel, chemical, machinery, and cotton enterprises will be transformed into joint-stock companies in which the republic will hold a controlling number of shares.

RSFSR Signs Agreements with Turkmenia and Kirgizia

TASS reported that the RSFSR had signed trade agreements with Kirgizia and Turkmenistan. According to these agreements, signed by the chairmen of the councils of ministers of the three republics, in 1991 trade will reach at least this year's levels, and the republics will assist each other in the transition to a market economy. Both Kirgizia and Turkmenistan have recently reached similar agreements with other Union republics in an effort to ensure supplies for their industries and consumers.

Moldavians Resist Military Draft

TASS reported that the fall military draft was "encountering serious difficulties" in Moldavia. The headquarters of the Southwestern Military District issued a statement blaming "destructive elements" in Moldavia for "sowing the seeds of pacifism" and "blackening" the name of the USSR Armed Forces. The statement appealed to Moldavian draftees, their parents, the parliament, and local authorities to cooperate with the draft. It said that Moldavia's recent decisions suspending its residents' obligation to serve in the USSR Armed Forces and initiating Moldavian national military units could not be implemented before the passage of a Union treaty and a defense law. See RL 448/90.

Military Leaders in Germany Deny Press Stories

Sovetskaya Rossiya said Soviet military leaders in Germany had denied Western press reports of problems faced by Soviet troops still stationed in Germany. One unit commander denied that 400 officers' wives had asked Chancellor Kohl to allow them to remain in Germany because they were to be sent to a high-radiation area in the Soviet Union (though his statement that the unit would be redeployed 150 kilometers from Chernobyl' was unlikely to reassure anyone). Another officer denied that Soviet soldiers were selling weapons to the Germans. He claimed that his unit could account for every weapon in its inventory.

Landsbergis on Lithuanian World Role

President of the Lithuanian Supreme Council Vytautas Landsbergis said progress was being made towards full recognition of Lithuania as an independent state. In a speech broadcast by Radio Vilnius, Landsbergis said Scandinavian countries fully supported Lithuania's statehood and were moving towards establishing diplomatic relations. TASS carried excerpts from Landsbergis's speech.

On October 11, Landsbergis, who traveled that day to Paris, said he hoped Lithuania could gain full sovereignty as a nation within "one year" (*RFE/RL Special*, October 11).

The same day, Landsbergis met with French President François Mitterrand. Speaking to reporters after the meeting, he said France was willing to return immediately Lithuanian gold it had been keeping safe since the outbreak of World War II (*Reuters*, October 11).

"Pamyat'" Activist Nominated for Moscow City Council

The leader of one of the branches of the anti-Semitic "Pamyat'" society, Konstantin Smirnov-Ostashvili, who was on trial for shouting anti-Semitic slogans at a meeting of the Moscow literary organization "April," was reported to have been proposed as a candidate for a seat on the Moscow City Soviet. *Moskovskaya pravda* said a constituency in Moscow's Kuibyshev Raion had nominated Ostashvili for the seat. TASS said the Moscow election commission was expected to make a decision on his candidacy before October 15. (See also *Izvestia*, October 6.)

On October 12, Ostashvili was sentenced to a two-year term in a labor camp. This decision marked the first time in Soviet history that a sentence had been handed down under the law banning violations of the equality of all nationalities.

In an interview with Soviet television, Andrei Makarov, a prominent Moscow lawyer who assisted the prosecution in the Ostashvili trial, named Ivan Polozkov, first secretary of the RSFSR Communist Party, as "the real ideologue" of "Pamyat'." Makarov cited the close ties between Polozkov and Ostashvili.

Eight Soldiers Dead in Shooting Spree

Three Soviet soldiers seized weapons and ammunition from a military depot in southern Ukraine and opened fire, killing eight other soldiers, news agencies reported on October 10. The USSR Defense Ministry said that two of the three soldiers were later captured, while the third remained at large. Spokesmen gave no motive for the shooting. According to Interfax, the victims included a lieutenant colonel and seven privates. The attackers were all privates.

Wednesday, October 10

Gorbachev Issues Decree on Military Parades

Mikhail Gorbachev issued a decree ordering military parades in Moscow and the capitals of the Union republics to mark the November 7 holiday, Radio Moscow reported (see *Pravda*, October 11). The decree also called for parades to be held in towns and cities where the staffs of army and navy districts were located. The parade in Moscow is to be reviewed by Defense Minister Dmitrii

Yazov. The presidential decree was welcomed by military leaders, who had urged that the anniversary of the October revolution continue to be observed. The reformist mayors of Moscow and Leningrad had asked Gorbachev to limit this year's celebration.

Interregional Group Criticizes Gorbachev

Speaking on behalf of the Interregional Group of Deputies, economist Academician Oleg Bogomolov criticized Gorbachev for issuing presidential decrees without waiting for the USSR Supreme Soviet's decision on economic reform. According to TASS, Bogomolov also warned Gorbachev against attempting to overrule the RSFSR authorities. He said that, even with the aid of "military authority and fear of repression," Gorbachev could not save the economic situation. On October 9, Radio Moscow broadcast a statement by RSFSR Deputy Prime Minister Gennadii Fil'shin criticizing Gorbachev for issuing presidential decrees that supported the realization of Prime Minister Nikolai Ryzhkov's economic reform plan rather than that of Academician Stanislav Shatalin.

USSR Signs Accord with Wall Street

The New York Stock Exchange (NYSE) signed a cooperation accord with the Soviet Union. The accord called for regular consultations, sharing of financial information and experts, and cooperation in training in an effort to help the USSR establish an effective stock market, according to Western news agencies. Currently there are about 400 joint-stock companies in the Soviet Union, but the vast majority of shares are held by the state. Reuters quoted NYSE chairman John Chalsty as saying that "an exchange can be established by year-end, but it won't have much to do until there is private ownership out there."

Ukrainian Resolution on Draft

The Ukrainian Supreme Soviet passed a resolution stipulating the conditions under which Ukrainian conscripts can serve in the Soviet army. The resolution banned the use of Ukrainian conscripts to solve ethnic conflicts outside Ukraine without the republic's permission and required that Ukrainians currently serving in such units return home by December. It said that most Ukrainian conscripts would be sent to units in Ukraine and called for quotas for the number of conscripts drafted into the Soviet army (*TASS*, October 10).

RSFSR Supreme Soviet Calls Lower Bodies to Order

The RSFSR Supreme Soviet adopted a law proclaiming the laws of the republic binding for all organs and all citizens on the territory of the RSFSR, Radio Moscow reported. The law established a system of fines ranging from 500 to 10,000 rubles to be imposed on officials who deliberately fail to implement the laws of the RSFSR, the decrees of the Presidium of its Supreme Soviet, or orders of the Council of Ministers and its Presidium.

The new law also prohibited local soviets from interfering in the operational work of the local executive committees and required raion soviets to obey orders issued by their superior oblast and city soviets. The law was passed on the initiative of the mayors of Moscow and Leningrad, where a number of raion soviets have issued declarations of independence.

Party History Institute in Uzbekistan Closed

Trud reported that the Central Committee of the Uzbek Communist Party had closed the republican Institute of Party History and the interrepublican branch of the Institute of Religious Studies and Atheism of the CPSU Central Committee Academy of Social Sciences. The two institutes will be replaced by an Institute of Sociopolitical Problems under the sponsorship of the republican Central Committee. There was also discussion of closing the Higher Party School in Tashkent and creating an institute for political science to train sociologists, specialists in management and marketing, and diplomats, as well as political scientists.

First Cases in Osh Affair Handed Over to Courts

The late-night television news program TSN reported that the first cases arising from the violence in Osh Oblast in June and July had been handed over to the courts. The report noted that the number of deaths in the Osh events was now set at 250. Although 135 people have been arrested, the investigators are not convinced that they included the true organizers of the violence and, according to the report, the investigators are unsure whether they will ever find the ringleaders. They also have evidence that both Kirgiz and Uzbeks in Osh Oblast are stockpiling weapons.

Sverdlovsk Oblast Warns of Food Shortages

Deputies in the Sverdlovsk Oblast Soviet set a one-week deadline for an improvement in the oblast's food supplies and adopted a statement that said the oblast reserved the right to take "extreme measures to defend the interests of the population." It said those measures included a halt in deliveries to other parts of the USSR of industrial products and raw materials produced in Sverdlovsk Oblast, effective November 1. According to Radio Moscow, the statement was sent to Gorbachev as well as to the Union and republican governments.

On October 18, the food supply crisis in Sverdlovsk was reported to have worsened. *Rabochaya tribuna* said people could not get their monthly allotment of sugar and sausage even with ration coupons. The daily said dairy products were not being delivered to shops. It said workers at two dairy factories were on strike and more strikes had been announced. The newspaper said working conditions at the factories did not meet even "elementary requirements."

Thursday, October 11

USSR to Demand Hard Currency for Training Foreign Servicemen

The Soviet Union decided to demand hard-currency payments for training foreign military personnel starting in 1991. TASS said the average cost of training a foreign serviceman was the equivalent of 1,500 US dollars. It said fees charged for training foreign military personnel had been kept low until now for political reasons. TASS said the new rules would affect more than 1,000 servicemen from twenty-nine countries now studying at twelve military academies in Leningrad. The largest contingents are from Bulgaria, Afghanistan, and Angola.

Russian Parliament Approves New Government Members

The RSFSR Supreme Soviet elected members to two new committees that will be charged with overseeing the development of northern Russia and supervising the cleanup of contamination in the republic caused by the Chernobyl' accident. The deputies approved the nomination of Murmansk Oblast Party Secretary Evgenii Komarov to head a new State Committee for the Economic and Social Development of the North. The deputies also approved Semen Voloshchuk to head a State Committee on the Effects of Chernobyl'. Voloshchuk has chaired the so-called Chernobyl' Union in Moscow.

Also approved was a career diplomat, Andrei Kozyrev, as foreign minister of the republic. TASS said the deputies had approved these and two other nominees but rejected Prime Minister Ivan Silaev's nomination of Sergei Ivchenko as minister for social security. Ivchenko is a deputy minister for social security and an RSFSR people's deputy.

Estonia Changes State Holidays

The Estonian Supreme Soviet decreed that the anniversary of the October Revolution would no longer be a state holiday in the republic. The decree, issued by the parliament's Presidium and carried by TASS, also abolished as a holiday Soviet Victory Day on May 9. The decree said Estonia would again officially celebrate the republic's independence day on February 24. Another new holiday is June 23, to be marked as Victory Day. It was on June 23, 1919, that the Estonians defeated German forces that had tried to conquer Estonia and Latvia in the war of independence. Yet another new state holiday is November 16, to be known as Day of Revival. That is the date in 1988 when Estonia adopted a declaration of sovereignty (RFE Estonian service, October 11).

CPSU Weekly Severely Criticizes Russian Minister

After a lull of several weeks, criticism of RSFSR Minister of the Press and Mass Media Mikhail Poltoranin resumed with the publication of an article in the latest issue of the new CPSU Central Committee weekly, *Glasnost'*. The weekly criticized a speech by Poltoranin broadcast on Soviet television last month, in which he said that Party journalists who did not change their conservative line were "playing a dangerous game and not thinking of their families' futures." *Glasnost'* stressed that Poltoranin was himself once a Party journalist and called him a renegade. The weekly also asked Boris El'tsin to take a stand on Poltoranin's statement.

Shatalin and Baker Discuss Soviet Reforms

The US State Department said a meeting between US Secretary of State James Baker and economist Stanislav Shatalin, who is a member of the Presidential Council, had focused chiefly on the state of the Soviet economy and efforts to reform it. Shatalin told Baker about his economic reform plan and complained about a lack of understanding in the Soviet Union of how a free market works. Shatalin is in the second week of a private visit to the United States for talks with senior US officials and businessmen (*RFE/RL Special*, October 11).

Lenin Monument Destroyed in Urals Village

A Lenin monument was reported to have been destroyed in the village of Kashtak near the Urals city of Chelyabinsk. TASS said a man called the Chelyabinsk television station and claimed responsibility on behalf of the "Pamyat'" society, and warned that a Lenin statue in Chelyabinsk's Revolution Square would also be destroyed.

Soviet Rocket Explosion Damages Space Center

A Soviet booster rocket used to launch satellites broke up just seconds after lift-off from the Baikonur Space Center in Kazakhstan a week ago. In a report on the accident,

TASS said that the explosion had damaged one of the launch pads but that no one had been hurt.

Friday, October 12

Gorbachev Issues Decree on Property

Mikhail Gorbachev issued a decree on "the inviolability of the right of ownership in the USSR," the primary aim of which is to safeguard Party property and reassure others that their investments, businesses, homes, and property will not be expropriated. If necessary, USSR Ministry of Internal Affairs troops will be used to guard "state and [collectively owned] property" (*TASS*, October 12; *Pravda*, October 13).

Ryzhkov Presents Measures to Strengthen Law and Order

Chairman of the USSR Council of Ministers Nikolai Ryzhkov presented a package of "urgent measures" to protect citizens' rights and security and to fight crime. Speaking on Central Television, Ryzhkov said he approved of the KGB's proposal to create new special units to fight organized crime. He also talked about a program to increase the size of the police force. The number of MVD personnel dealing with crime will be increased to 52,000, and the MVD will get 24,000 new police cars and 140,000 radios and other pieces of equipment. Ryzhkov also called for the revamping of the so-called People's Volunteer Detachments and Workers' Militia and the creation of a single central body to coordinate MVD and KGB activities.

MVD to Expand

At a press conference on October 22, USSR Minister of Internal Affairs Vadim Bakatin said his agency had submitted a draft plan for a nationwide campaign to combat organized crime to the USSR Supreme Soviet (*TASS*, *Radio Moscow*, October 22). The program called for a substantial increase in the MVD's budget.

Furor Grows over Military Exercises

An air force pilot who took part in controversial military exercises around Moscow in early September charged in *Komsomol'skaya pravda* that the Defense Ministry was hiding the real purpose of the maneuvers. According to Major Mikhail Pustobaev, those participating in the maneuvers—which later raised fears of a military coup—believed themselves to be on a genuine alert. On October 12, however, high-ranking military officers were quoted in *Sovetskaya Rossiya* as again rejecting the coup rumors and saying that the troop movements around Moscow had been planned in August and had been kept secret deliberately in order to test the readiness of the forces.

On October 16, Pustobaev published an apology in *Sovetskaya Rossiya*. Pustobaev said he was now convinced that he had been mistaken and he believed that the troop movements were "normal exercises." Pustobaev's superior, Air Force Commander General Evgenii Shaposhnikov, said an investigation would be conducted to establish whether Pustobaev had disclosed any military secrets.

Gorbachev's Message to Moldavia

Addressing the people of Moldavia on Radio Moscow, Gorbachev warned that interethnic tensions had placed "Moldavia's integrity under threat," and he called for "an immediate start to dialogue among all interested sides" and for "a mutually acceptable compromise." Urging a resolution that would "preserve the integrity of the republic," Gorbachev asserted that "a renewed Union of sovereign states can reliably guarantee this" and that "such a Union accords with the basic interests of the people of Moldavia." Kishinev, however, wants a confederal arrangement instead of "a renewed Union" and is refusing to negotiate with the two breakaway republics on its territory.

El'tsin Back at Work

After a three-week recuperation period following an automobile accident, Chairman of the RSFSR Supreme Soviet Boris El'tsin was back at work, TASS reported. After the accident, the RSFSR legislature placed an order for armored limousines for El'tsin and for Chairman of the RSFSR Council of Ministers Ivan Silaev, but the KGB did not approve the request. A Soviet firm that specializes in armored van production for banks has since volunteered to build a car for El'tsin.

Russian Orthodox Church Statement

The Holy Synod of the Russian Orthodox Church issued a statement on relations with the Ukrainian Catholic Church in connection with the situation in Western Ukraine, TASS reported. The statement said that normal Church life in Western Ukraine had been disrupted as a result of aggressive actions by Catholics of the Eastern Rite, and it described measures undertaken by the leadership of the Russian Orthodox Church to ease tensions. The Holy Synod appealed to Ukrainian Catholics to realize the graveness of the present situation and to accept that only dialogue could solve their problems.

Communists Open Own Bank

The CPSU Central Committee recently set up the first commercial bank controlled by Communists, Reuters reported. Arkadii Krutikhin, formerly general administrator of the Leningrad Oblast Party Committee and now chairman of the new bank, said the bank would open with a capital base of 3 million rubles drawn from Party sources. Bank Rossiya plans to finance joint ventures of the CPSU and restoration projects in Leningrad.

Saturday, October 13

Moldavian President Disavows Reunification with Romania

Addressing the people of the republic on radio and television, Moldavian President Mircea Snegur disavowed any idea of reunification with Romania, TASS reported. "We did not proclaim our full sovereignty in order to unite with anyone, but in order to become masters of our house," Snegur was quoted as saying.

Republics Take Stand on Military Service

On October 13, TASS reported that, after consultations with the USSR Ministry of Defense, the KGB, and other agencies, the Azerbaijani Council of Ministers had ruled that 50 percent of the draftees scheduled for call-up this fall would perform their military service within Azerbaijan, where they will build homes for Azerbaijani refugees from Armenia and for the families of servicemen.

A meeting organized on October 14 in Moscow to urge the immediate establishment of alternative service for conscripts revealed growing opposition to military service among draft-age youth. A representative of the Moscow City Soviet warned that, unless they were given the option of alternative service, large numbers of youths in the capital would evade the draft this fall. Officers questioned how conscientious objector status would be determined and argued that draft deferral regulations already freed 50 percent of the draft contingent from service nationwide and 70 percent in the Moscow and Leningrad areas. They also complained that only 292 of the 6,647 people who evaded the draft in 1989 had been convicted. The meeting was carried by Central Television.

On October 17, TASS reported that the Armenian Supreme Soviet had passed a resolution suspending the all-Union law on compulsory military service and making provision for draftees to perform their military service on Armenian territory in the future.

Kommunist Tadzhikistana (October 9) reported that the Tajik Supreme Soviet had adopted a resolution stipulating that republican conscripts called up into construction battalions must serve in the Turkestan Military District and primarily in Tajikistan.

Moldavian MVD Plans New Force

Moldavian Minister of Internal Affairs Major General Ion Costas told a press conference that the draft for Moldavia's planned 10,000-strong force of "Carabinieri" would begin in spring, 1991, TASS reported. Costas announced that Kishinev opposed the idea of subordination of the republican MVD to the all-Union organization and insisted that sovereign republics were entitled to their own internal affairs ministries and troops. Three specialized schools to be opened shortly will train senior staff officers, operations officers, and NCOs; some officers will also be sent to Romania for training. Costas complained that his ministry was underequipped and underfinanced.

New Tatar Party

The formation of the Tatar People's Democratic Party "Vatan" (Homeland) was formally announced in Moscow, TASS reported. The party's aim is "the recreation of Tatar statehood" either within the USSR or outside it, on the territory of the former Astrakhan, Kazan, and Siberian khanates. Party members said these lands were occupied by the Russian state in the sixteenth century and had been under occupation ever since. They base their case on the UN declaration of 1960 "On granting independence to colonized countries and peoples."

On October 14, a day of mourning was held in Kazan to commemorate those who died 438 years ago during the capture of Kazan by Ivan the Terrible. The initiators were the Tatar Public Center and the independent "Ittifak" party. Interviewed by Radio Moscow, Tatarstan deputy Fandas Safiullin denied that Tatarstan wanted to secede from the RSFSR, saying that it only wished to "get out of the system of subordination" and be able to control its own affairs.

Yakutia Signs Agreement with South Korean Firm

Under an agreement concluded between the major South Korean corporation "Khende" and Yakutia, "Khende" will participate in the exploitation of the El'gin coal deposits, TASS reported. It said the South Korean firm planned to build a 320-kilometer railway line linking the major coalfield to the BAM railway. About 850,000 tons of coal are scheduled to be delivered to South Korea in 1991 and 1 million tons in 1992.

KAMAZ Shares for Sale

The Soviet Union's largest truck manufacturer, KAMAZ, has started selling shares of stock in the company, TASS reported. Soviet enterprises and organizations have already signed up for shares worth more than 1.5 billion rubles; KAMAZ plans to sell more than 2 billion rubles' worth of shares by 1992.

First Service in Seven Decades in Red Square Cathedral

An Orthodox service was conducted for the first time in seven decades at the St. Basil's Cathedral in Red Square in Moscow. TASS said the service was conducted to mark the holiday on October 14 of the Virgin Mary, one of the most important Orthodox holidays.

Poland Signs Agreements with Ukraine, Belorussia, RSFSR

Poland and Ukraine signed a declaration on bilateral relations as "sovereign states." The declaration was signed in Kiev by Polish Foreign Minister Krzysztof Skubiszewski and Ukrainian Foreign Minister Anatol Zlenko. The Polish news agency PAP said Warsaw and Kiev would also establish consular relations.

In contrast, the planned signing of a Belorussian-Polish agreement in Minsk on October 15 was called off after the Belorussian side complained of discrimination against Poland's Belorussian minority and refused to recognize that the frontier between the two countries, established by a Polish-Soviet treaty in 1945, was immutable (*Reuters* citing *Warsaw Television*, October 16). A representative of Belorussia's parliamentary opposition claimed that Poland's Bialystok province was ethnically Belorussian. The Polish side, for its part, cited problems in Belorussia, including difficulties in practising religion. Poland had been prepared to sign a trade agreement, Radio Warsaw reported, and to agree to the opening of a Belorussian consulate in Bialystok.

On October 16, the foreign ministers of the RSFSR and Poland signed a declaration of friendship and cooperation that called for an exchange of diplomatic and consular missions, TASS and Radio Warsaw reported. RSFSR Prime Minister Ivan Silaev said the declaration was the first to be signed by the RSFSR with a foreign country and ended the years in which "Russia had no face of its own in international relations." The treaty recognizes the current border between the

RSFSR and Poland and states that neither has territorial claims against the other.

Sunday, October 14

Party Cards for Sale

Black-market prices for CPSU membership cards start at thirty dollars, with cards of former *apparatchiki* being the most desirable, according to Soviet television's late-night news.

USSR and Iran Agree to Set up Rail Link

Iran and the Soviet Union agreed to establish a passenger rail link between Teheran and Moscow in 1991. The Iranian media said an agreement had been signed by Iranian Transport Minister Mohammad Saidi-Kia and Soviet Minister of Railways Nikolai Konarev (*Reuters*, October 14).

New Trade Union in Karaganda

A new trade union was formed in Karaganda, a coal-mining region in Kazakhstan. Radio Moscow said the union's founding conference was called by the local workers' committee. That committee evolved from the strike committee formed during the miners' strikes in 1989. The report said the Karaganda authorities intended to cooperate with the new union in social, economic, and political matters.

Another Cossack Organization Formed

A new Cossack organization held its founding congress in the city of Krasnodar. The participants came from Kuban, a region in the southern RSFSR. Radio Moscow said that congress participants proposed, among other things, changes in the drafting of Cossacks into the Soviet Armed Forces. It gave no details. Similar meetings, the first in decades, were held earlier this year by Cossack groups from other regions of the Soviet Union.

Ethnic Attitudes towards Secession, Democracy

The results of a public opinion survey published in *Moscow News* (No. 41) confirmed that Russians in the non-Russian republics cannot be treated as a homogeneous group. The survey also provided data on the degree of support among the Soviet Union's various nationalities for secession and for various political systems and documented their views on whether or not *perestroika* had improved their lives. Ninety-one percent of Balts and 92 percent of Georgians, but only 24 percent of Central

Asians, approved of secession. The Russians in the Union republics were more or less equally divided in favor of and against it, except in Belorussia, where a majority were in favor.

Monday, October 15

Gorbachev Grants Autonomy to Universities

Gorbachev issued a decree granting administrative and financial autonomy to the Soviet Union's universities. The decree, released by TASS, stipulated that institutions of higher education should run their own affairs and make their own rules in conformity with USSR and republican laws (see *Pravda*, October 16). The decree also transferred ownership of all the universities' present property and state funds to them. Gorbachev issued a similar decree in August granting autonomy to the USSR Academy of Sciences, but it has proved difficult to implement.

USSR Prosecutor-General to Resign

"Vremya" reported that USSR Prosecutor-General Aleksandr Sukharev had asked the USSR Supreme Soviet to release him from his post on the grounds of ill health. In April, the USSR Supreme Soviet recommended "[strengthening] the leadership of the office of the USSR prosecutor- general" as a result of its handling of the case of investigators Tel'man Gdlyan and Nikolai Ivanov. While he was in office, Sukharev's department justified the arbitrary behavior of conservative Party and state officials and demonstrated a complete disregard for the law. Demands for Sukharev's resignation have been heard frequently in connection with calls for the resignation of Prime Minister Nikolai Ryzhkov and his government.

Gorbachev Awarded Nobel Peace Prize

Mikhail Gorbachev was awarded the 1990 Nobel Peace Prize (*TASS*, October 15). Gorbachev was applauded briefly by members of the USSR Supreme Soviet when the news was announced. Former Politburo member Egor Ligachev said the award "means that we are finally met with confidence in the world," AP reported. President of the Lithuanian Supreme Council Vytautas Landsbergis said he had sent a message of congratulations to Gorbachev. Landsbergis told the Lithuanian information agency ELTA that Gorbachev's merit in preventing a destructive war was indisputable. He added, however, that Soviet policy towards Lithuania had been ill-disposed and even hostile (*TASS*, October 15).

Western leaders congratulated Gorbachev on the award, which they said he certainly deserved. The reaction among Soviet citizens was not so positive, however. In a commentary on October 16, Novosti political observer Aleksandr Ignatov said that the Nobel Peace Prize would not increase Gorbachev's prestige at home, which has been seriously undermined by the USSR's severe economic problems.

Shevardnadze Defends Foreign Policy

Soviet Foreign Minister Eduard Shevardnadze reported to the USSR Supreme Soviet on the policies that only hours before had earned Gorbachev the Nobel Peace Prize (*TASS*, October 15). According to Soviet and Western news agencies, Shevardnadze focused on Soviet policy towards Eastern Europe, Germany, the Persian Gulf, and on disarmament. Arguing that the policies of the Cold War had failed to meet Soviet defense needs, Shevardnadze rejected a suggestion that "new political thinking" had resulted from the Soviet Union's economic weakness. He said that the Warsaw Pact was being restructured in a realistic fashion, and he defended Moscow's acquiescence on German reunification. "After the withdrawal of Soviet troops from Germany," he said, "there will be no confrontation on the continent, the number of Bundeswehr troops will be cut considerably, as will the number of US troops on the continent." Shevardnadze also defended recent US-Soviet agreements on nuclear and conventional arms-control issues.

Shevardnadze's speech drew fire from hardline deputies. Colonel Nikolai Petrushenko, a cochairman of the conservative "Soyuz" group of deputies, said "new thinking" had led to unilateral losses for the Soviet Union. He also criticized the Foreign Ministry for failing to keep the legislature informed of foreign policy decisions. Colonel Viktor Alksnis, chairman of "Soyuz," said that "for the first time in its history the Soviet Union has no more potential enemies, but neither has it any allies."

The debate over Soviet policy vis-à-vis Iraq was particularly sharp. Petrushenko and others criticized the Kremlin for abandoning the Iraqi alliance without consulting the legislature. Petrushenko also charged the Foreign Ministry with "a casual approach to the possible use of military force" in the Gulf. He said that any such action by Moscow, even under the aegis of the United Nations, would damage Moscow's relations with Iraq, undermine Soviet ties with other Arab states, and strengthen the military position of the United States in the Gulf. Shevardnadze said any use of Soviet troops outside the country required parliamentary approval (*TASS*, October 15).

USSR Submits Military Budget Figures

In a memorandum sent to United Nations Secretary-General Javier Perez de Cuellar, Moscow told the United Nations that its 1990 military budget was 71 billion rubles. The document also contained details of the numerical strength and main types of armaments of the Soviet Armed Forces. Deputy Foreign Minister Vladimir Petrovsky told a UN press conference that the memorandum provided "a detailed picture of Soviet military capability" (*RFE/RL Special*, October 15).

Newspapers Suffer Loss in Subscriptions

According to statistics published by *Pravda*, the number of subscribers to that newspaper has fallen from 6.8 million in January, 1990, to 504,000. Subscriptions to *Komsomol'skaya pravda* have fallen from 21 million to 4 million over the same period. *Argumenty i fakty*, which enjoyed the highest number of subscribers of any Soviet publication, has lost half of its 31 million subscribers.

Interfax reported on October 15 that *Argumenty i fakty* had dropped all restrictions on subscriptions. (Previously it was impossible to subscribe to this periodical in many provincial Soviet cities.) In addition, using the right offered by the new law on the press, *Argumenty i fakty* has escaped from the supervision of the all-Union "Znanie" society to which it was subordinate. Interfax said that the USSR State Committee for the Press had issued a registration certificate to the journal's collective, making it the sole producer of the publication. In obtaining its independent status, *Argumenty i fakty* has followed the example of other leading Soviet periodicals, including *Ogonek* and *Literaturnaya gazeta*. On October 13, *Sovetskaya kul'tura* reported that it had broken its ties with the CPSU Central Committee.

Moldavian and Ukrainian Movements Confer

Moldavian Popular Front delegates, headed by First Deputy Chairman of the Moldavian Supreme Soviet Iurie Rosca, conferred in Kiev over the weekend with leaders of the Ukrainian popular movement "Rukh" Ivan Drach and Mykhailo Horyn, Moldavian participants told RFE/RL on October 15. The two groups agreed to initiate steps in the republican legislatures to provide native-language education for Moldavians in Ukraine and Ukrainians in Moldavia. Concerning disputed territories, they agreed to continue consultations with a view to preventing conservative forces in Moscow from setting the two republics against one another. The participants also agreed to promote the creation of a mechanism for consultation among popular fronts and movements in various Soviet republics.

USSR Ambassador to Chile Appointed

Seventeen years after the severance of diplomatic relations between the Soviet Union and Chile, Moscow appointed career diplomat Yurii Pavlov ambassador to Chile, TASS reported. Pavlov had been chief of the Ministry of Foreign Affairs' Administration for Latin America since 1989. From 1987 to 1989, he headed the First Latin America Department and from 1982 to 1987 served as Soviet ambassador to Costa Rica. From 1980 to 1982, Pavlov worked as deputy chief of the Second European Department, responsible for Australia, Canada, Ireland, Malta, New Zealand, and Great Britain.

Iranian Minister Visits Azerbaijan

Iran sent its finance minister, Mohsen Nurbakhsh, and its roads and transport minister, Mohammad Saidi-Kia, to the Azerbaijani capital, Baku, for discussions on trade, economic links, transportation, and other issues (*Reuters*, October 15).

On October 19, TASS reported that Azerbaijan and Iran had signed an agreement on the development of border trade between Azerbaijan and the Iranian provinces of western Azerbaijan and Gilan. The possibilities for automobile, railway, and air traffic and for tourist exchanges were discussed.

Estonian Minister on Moscow-Tallinn Negotiations

The Estonian government minister responsible for negotiations with Moscow, Endel Lippmaa, said that the talks were completely deadlocked and that there was "not even a glimmer of a solution." Lippmaa said the deadlock had arisen because Estonia would accept nothing less than independence while Moscow wanted to keep Estonia within the USSR in one form or another. Lippmaa was interviewed in this week's issue of the German magazine *Der Spiegel*.

Tuesday, October 16

Gorbachev Submits Compromise Plan to Supreme Soviet

Disappointing leading Soviet reformers, Mikhail Gorbachev submitted a compromise plan for economic reform that was a watered-down version of the Shatalin "500-day" program. TASS summaries of the document noted that it proposed a less ambitious privatization program and the retention of more central economic levers than the Shatalin plan. It also failed to set a timetable (although the program was divided into four "stages").

The first stage focused on legislative measures and economic "stabilization," above all, getting the Soviet financial house in order. Reductions in state budgetary spending and increased incentives to save were likely measures. Stage two was devoted mainly to the freeing of prices. The logic in delaying this stage was that the restrictive monetary and fiscal measures of the first stage would help to minimize inflationary pressures of the "demand-push" variety. Stage three would attempt to "stabilize market relations," especially in the consumer goods sphere; no details on what that would entail were available. Stage four was reserved for demonopolization and the development of a competitive market. Implementation of the four stages was supposed to take about two years.

On October 13, Gorbachev met with leaders of eleven Union republics to discuss his compromise economic reform program. TASS and Soviet television ("Vremya") said the republican leaders on the whole supported the direction of the program and made some suggestions. TASS said speakers stressed that the republics should have broad independence in deciding how to implement the reforms. Leaders from Georgia and the Baltic republics did not attend.

On October 19, the USSR Supreme Soviet approved at its first reading Gorbachev's blueprint for economic reform (for details of the plan, see *Izvestia*, October 27). In his speech to the Supreme Soviet committees on October 18, Academician Abel Aganbegyan said that Gorbachev's plan would allow republican legislatures to forge their own reform plans and move to the market at their own speed (*TASS*, October 19). See RL 488/90.

El'tsin Rejects Gorbachev's Plan

On October 16, RSFSR Supreme Soviet Chairman Boris El'tsin rejected Gorbachev's compromise program. In a speech to the RSFSR Supreme Soviet, reported by TASS, El'tsin said the plan represented an attempt to "maintain the command-administered system."

He warned that, if the central authorities did not stop discrediting the RSFSR Supreme Soviet, people would protest in the streets. He said that regions and cities where democratic forces had a majority were victims of outright sabotage. He called for the resignation of Prime Minister Nikolai Ryzhkov and the abolition of central government structures. Some key ministerial posts should be kept, El'tsin proposed, but they should be filled in part with Gorbachev nominees and in part with republican-approved candidates. As an example, he suggested that Gorbachev choose the KGB chairman but that the republics select the defence minister.

RSFSR Adopts Law on a Referendum

The RSFSR Supreme Soviet adopted a law on a referendum, TASS reported. Under the new law, a referendum can be held on the most important questions of state and public life and its results have supreme juridical force. A referendum can be held at the request of the republican Congress of People's Deputies, of the Supreme Soviet, or of not less than one million citizens or one-third of the total number of Congress or Supreme Soviet deputies. For its results to be valid, at least 50 percent of voters must take part. The motion is regarded as carried if over half of those voting vote in favor.

USSR Wants Worldwide Referendum on Nuclear Testing

The USSR proposed that elected parliaments around the world hold referenda on nuclear testing. The proposal was presented to the UN General Assembly's Political and Security Committee by Soviet Deputy Foreign Minister Vladimir Petrovsky (*Reuters*, October 17).

Moldavian CP Condemns Secessionist Movements

Addressing a Moldavian Communist Party Central Committee plenum, First Secretary Petru Lucinschi condemned "all forms of separatism" and called for the preservation of Moldavia's territorial integrity and sovereignty within a renewed Union. In an appeal to Communists and citizens in the south and east of the republic, the Central Committee condemned the drives to form Dniester and Gagauz Soviet republics and to secede from Moldavia (*TASS*, October 16).

USSR to Receive 2 Billion Dollars in Aid from Italy

The Italian government approved an economic aid package worth 2 billion dollars for the Soviet Union, AP reported. A communiqué issued by Prime Minister Giulio Andreotti's cabinet said that the initiative was aimed at helping to maintain economic stability during "the current delicate phase of economic reform."

Kalugin to Join KGB Watchdog Committee

Former KGB general Oleg Kalugin said he had been invited to join the USSR Supreme Soviet committee that oversees the Soviet army and the KGB, TASS reported. Kalugin told TASS that, if he became a permanent member, the parliamentary Committee for Defense and State Security would become more objective and thus more competent.

Bonn and Moscow Sign Disaster Aid Pact

Germany and the Soviet Union signed an agreement on mutual aid in cases of disaster. A German government official said a strong foundation of good cooperation had been laid after the earthquake in Armenia in 1988. He said the accord created a contractual basis for such aid. The official said the accord also provided for cooperation to prevent disasters. He cited exchanges of information and practical experience, joint training and research, and joint exercises (*RFE/RL Special*, October 16).

Murmansk Party Organization Blames Gorbachev for Crisis

A letter sharply criticizing Gorbachev was approved at a recent Murmansk Oblast Party conference, Novosti reported. The Soviet Union's present situation, the letter stated, is the result of "major political and economic errors" committed by the leadership. The Murmansk Communists appealed for the imposition of temporary emergency measures to end lawlessness and anarchy.

Alternative Draft Sovereignty Declaration in Kirgizia

The "Kyrgyzstan" movement proposed its own draft sovereignty declaration, TASS reported. In contrast to the parliamentary draft proclaiming Kirgizia a Socialist multinational state, the alternative document described it as "a free, democratic, legal, and parliamentary state." The alternative draft advocated only republican citizenship, instead of dual republican and USSR citizenship, and suggested that the republic set up its own MVD troops, security forces, and, if need be, army.

Wednesday, October 17

Party Membership and Financial Losses Detailed

Politburo member Oleg Shenin told a press conference in Moscow that 800,000 people had left the Party so far this year, while only 200,000 had joined, TASS reported. Party membership now stands at 17,725,914. Shenin also revealed that this year Party revenues would fall by about 60 percent rather than by the 40 percent previously forecast. As a result, the Party will have a deficit of over 1 billion rubles, which will be made up out of reserve funds. Every Party organization in the country—with the exception of those in Moscow and Leningrad—will require subsidization. Revenue losses were attributed to arrears in dues, lower dues, and dramatically lower subscription rates to Party periodicals.

CPSU CC Secretariat on Political Organs

At its weekly meeting, the Secretariat of the CPSU Central Committee criticized the policies of the parliaments of Estonia, Lithuania, and Moldavia and of the Moscow City

Soviet that would ban CPSU organs in the army, KGB, and MVD. The Secretariat called such attempts to exert "moral pressure" on Communists an infringement of human rights. USSR Minister of Internal Affairs Vadim Bakatin, however, suggested at the Secretariat's meeting that the political organs in his ministry should be abandoned because they had become obsolete.

Record Grain Harvest Reported

According to a senior official at the USSR State Committee for Statistics, the Soviet harvest "will be not less than 240 million tons," about 3 million tons more than the bumper crop of 1978 (*Reuters*, October 17). State purchases should total 73–75 million tons. In 1989, the state purchased 59 million tons.

40 Million Living in Poverty

Izvestia reported that more than 40 million of the Soviet Union's 288.8 million citizens were destitute. The official poverty line is set at an income level of 78 rubles per month. *Izvestia* noted that if the poverty line was adjusted to 100 rubles—a figure many Soviet experts believe is more realistic—the number of poor would rise to 70.9 million.

Yavlinsky's Resignation Refused

The RSFSR Supreme Soviet refused to accept the resignation of republican Deputy Prime Minister Grigorii Yavlinsky, who, together with Stanislav Shatalin, coauthored the "500-day" program for economic reform. Yavlinsky offered his resignation in protest against the compromise economic reform program presented to the USSR Supreme Soviet by President Mikhail Gorbachev. Yavlinsky said the compromise plan was unrealistic and would lead to rapid inflation. RSFSR Prime Minister Ivan Silaev told the republican parliament that Yavlinsky's departure could be damaging, and the deputies rejected it.

RSFSR to Use CPSU Printing Facilities

Viktor Yugin, the chairman of the RSFSR Supreme Soviet Information Commission, told the RSFSR Supreme Soviet that the CPSU had agreed to put some of its publishing facilities at the disposal of the Russian parliament and government. Yugin was quoted by TASS as saying the agreement had been reached after prolonged negotiations with the CPSU Central Committee. The fact that the CPSU still owns most of the USSR's printing facilities is seriously hampering implementation of the Soviet press law. The current agreement between the RSFSR parliament and the CPSU seems to be an important victory in the campaign to decrease the CPSU's role in the media.

RSFSR Redefines Its Foreign Policy

Andrei Kozyrev, the newly appointed RSFSR foreign minister, told Radio Moscow that the republic must lay "an entirely new foundation" for its relationship with Western Europe and pursue the goal of "a single and unified European system" without "senseless ideological claims." RSFSR politicians will, he said, have to prove to the United States and Canada that they do not wish to drive a wedge between those countries and Western Europe and that the RSFSR supports the US presence in both Europe and Asia. Kozyrev referred to the Eastern European countries as "the Soviet Union's former allies." His first act as minister was to sign a treaty establishing diplomatic relations between the RSFSR and Poland.

Uzbekistan Publishes Market Plan

Uzbekistan's program for the transition to a market economy was published for republican-wide discussion, TASS reported. The plan was worked out by a government group. TASS said that Uzbekistan intended to privatize small and medium-sized enterprises but that the state would retain control of basic economic resources. There will be no privatization of land, but the development of cooperative and leasing arrangements is foreseen. According to TASS, the program's authors think that private ownership of land is alien to Uzbek traditions. The program contains measures for social protection, including unemployment benefits.

Ukrainian-Belorussian Agreements Signed

The chairmen of the Belorussian and Ukrainian Supreme Soviets signed a document on promoting political, economic, scientific, and cultural ties between their two "sovereign states," TASS reported. The two sides also signed a government-to-government agreement on trade and on economic and technological cooperation. Leonid Kravchuk, chairman of the Ukrainian Supreme Soviet, said the agreements would take precedence over any Union agreements and that Ukrainian and Belorussian enterprises would reach agreements independent of the central authorities.

New Chairman of Mordovian Supreme Soviet Elected

Radio Moscow said the Supreme Soviet of Mordovia had replaced its chairman, Anatolii Berezin, with his deputy Nikolai Biryukov, Radio Moscow reported. The question of a vote of no confidence in Berezin, a Brezhnev-era figure who has headed the Mordovian Party organization since 1971, had been raised at the previous session of the Supreme Soviet. On the eve and the first day of the latest session—at which Berezin submitted his resignation—thousands gathered in the central square of Saransk, the Mordovian capital, demanding that he resign immediately.

Leningrad Dam Project Halted

The Leningrad City Soviet decided to halt work on one of the largest construction projects in the world—a dam in the Gulf of Finland designed to control flooding in Leningrad—TASS reported. The soviet voted to rechannel the construction funds into other local infrastructure projects. In support of its decision, the soviet cited a USSR Academy of Sciences report concluding that pollution in Leningrad's Neva River and the Gulf of Finland had increased threefold since the project began in the late 1970s.

"Democratic Russia" in Kaluga

A local branch of the "Democratic Russia" political bloc was set up in the Russian city of Kaluga, Radio Moscow said. The bloc unites members of the Democratic Platform within the CPSU, the Democratic and Social Democratic Parties of Russia, and the city's electoral club "Izbiratel'" (Voter). The bloc reportedly refused to accept as participants CPSU members who did not share the position of the Democratic Platform.

Cheney Visits Moscow

US Defense Secretary Dick Cheney was received by Gorbachev and Foreign Minister Eduard Shevardnadze, TASS reported. He also addressed the USSR Supreme Soviet. Gorbachev told Cheney about steps he intended to take in order to stabilize the political and economic situation in the country. Shevardnadze stressed US-Soviet cooperation in solving regional conflicts and in combating drug trafficking and illegal arms trading. Cheney pointed out that Washington was still concerned about Soviet "capabilities" because the USSR continues to produce more weapons than the United States.

On October 18, Cheney continued his visit to the Soviet Union with tours of Soviet military installations (*DPA*, October 18).

On October 19, Cheney wrapped up his Soviet tour, saying he had "a very positive" impression of Soviet reforms. Cheney said that, if progress continued, the United States might no longer consider the USSR an adversary. Soviet Defense Minister Dmitrii Yazov said he and Cheney had had the frankest talks ever about strategic nuclear weapons. He said a pending strategic nuclear arms treaty might be followed by a 50-percent reduction in Soviet missile production (*TASS*, *AP*, October 19).

Future of USSR Writers' Union in Question

The leadership of the USSR Writers' Union held a press conference in Moscow. First Secretary Vladimir Karpov said the organization may not survive financially, since a number of its leading publications have made use of the new Soviet law on the press to achieve independence from the union. Karpov said that the union's Board would hold a plenary session to discuss the decision of *Literaturnaya gazeta* to become independent of the Writers' Union. The previous week, the Union took legal action to protest against a similar move by the monthly journal *Znamya*.

Rodionov Blames KGB, MVD and Political Leadership for Tbilisi Deaths

In its actions in Sumgait, Tbilisi, Baku, Nagorno-Karabakh, and Vilnius, the army followed the direct orders of the top political leadership, but "with clenched teeth," Colonel General Igor Rodionov wrote in *Molodaya gvardiya* (No. 9). General Rodionov, who commanded the troops that suppressed a peaceful demonstration in Tbilisi in April, 1989, also said it would not have been necessary to use the army in Tbilisi had the KGB and MVD done their jobs properly. Instead, he charged, they "hid behind the broad back of the army."

Details of Brezhnev Assassination Attempt

Literaturnaya gazeta published the first central press account of Soviet Army Lieutenant Viktor Ilyin's attempt to assassinate Leonid Brezhnev in 1969. Wearing a policeman's uniform, Ilyin posted himself inside the Kremlin and awaited the arrival of Brezhnev's motorcade. Ilyin fired sixteen shots into the Zil limousine that he thought carried Brezhnev, but Brezhnev was in a different car and arrived through a different entrance. The driver of the limousine was killed. Ilyin, then twenty-two, was arrested and subsequently diagnosed as suffering from "sluggish schizophrenia." He spent nineteen years in solitary confinement. In 1988, he was transferred to a hospital in Leningrad.

Sweden Supports Baltic Request

A second Nordic country said it supported the Baltic republics' request for observer status at the Conference on Security and Cooperation in Europe (CSCE) meeting in November. Swedish Prime Minister Ingvar Carlsson joined Norway in supporting the request. Carlsson made the comments at a joint news conference with Lithuanian Prime Minister Kazimiera Prunskiene in Stockholm. Prunskiene said Lithuania would prefer to attend the CSCE meeting as a full member (*AP*, October 17).

Thursday, October 18

Cabinet Approves Soviet Troop Accords

The German cabinet formally approved two agreements with the Soviet Union on the deployment and withdrawal of Soviet troops from former East Germany. One of the accords covered financial arrangements involving German payment of more than 12 billion marks. The other set rules governing the activities of the Soviet troops (*RFE/RL Special*, October 18).

Meanwhile, Soviet lawyer Oleg Lyamin appealed to the German Foreign Minister Hans-Dietrich Genscher to help put a stop to violations of the human rights of Soviet soldiers in Germany. Lyamin said in an open letter to Genscher that Soviet soldiers were being mistreated to make them hand over marks. The letter said that crime was increasing among Soviet soldiers and that their plight was posing a threat to Germans. Lyamin asked Germany to provide additional legal protection and humanitarian aid to Soviet soldiers (*RFE/RL Special*, October 18). Lyamin recently defended a Soviet soldier who defected from his unit in Germany because army racketeers were trying to force him to give them marks. The soldier received a suspended two-year sentence last week.

Popov Wants Gorbachev to Head Coalition Government

Gavriil Popov, chairman of the Moscow City Soviet, suggested that Mikhail Gorbachev head a nationwide coalition government composed of left- and right-wing forces. Radio Moscow quoted excerpts from Popov's interview with *Moscow News* (No. 42), in which he said Gorbachev should take personal responsibility for foreign and domestic affairs, defense, and security, and should protect small property owners and set up a market system. He stressed that such a coalition would consolidate executive and judicial power.

Film about Wallenberg in Preparation

Ukrainian filmmakers joined with a Swedish television crew to produce a film about Swedish diplomat Raoul Wallenberg. The film's director, Aleksandr Rodnyansky, was quoted by TASS as saying the project stemmed from dissatisfaction with the official Soviet claim that Wallenberg died in a Moscow prison in 1947. The director said the film crew had visited prisons and labor camps where Wallenberg was reportedly seen alive in the 1950s and 1960s.

Siberian Labor Movement in Crisis

According to Yurii Butchenko, a leader of the Kuzbass Union of Workers, the workers' movement there is undergoing "a severe crisis," stemming from factional infighting, personal political ambition, and too much involvement with the Soviet government and the CPSU. Butchenko spoke to reporters at the Helsinki Watch organization in Washington. Butchenko is trying to establish an independent labor movement in the Kuzbass; he has been in the United States for two months at the invitation of the AFL-CIO (*RFE/RL Special*, October 18).

RSFSR to Publish Foreign Policy Journal

The RSFSR Supreme Soviet will publish a foreign policy journal, TASS reported. To be published in four languages, the journal will concentrate on questions of RSFSR foreign policy. Financed by the Russian parliament, the USSR Academy of Sciences, and a Russian-US joint-venture, the first issue of *Evropa plyus Amerika* was scheduled to appear in December. According to chief editor Yurii Korolev, the first issue will include an interview with Presidential Council members Veniamin Yarin and Stanislav Shatalin.

Russian Poet Odoevtseva Dies

TASS said Russian poet Irina Odoevtseva had died at the age of eighty-nine. Odoevtseva's literary career began in 1922 with the publication of her first collection of poems. Soon afterwards she emigrated to France where she actively participated in émigré life. Three years ago Odoevtseva returned to Leningrad and spent her last years there.

Friday, October 19

Government Makes Deal with Oil Workers

The Soviet oil industry will be allowed to spend up to 1 billion dollars in hard-currency earnings on equipment and consumer goods for its workers, the *Financial Times* reported. The offer was reported to have been made earlier this month but not publicized. Some 40,000 field engineers, angry over having to pay fines for failing to observe security and environmental regulations, were reported to be considering walking off the job.

Armenia to Extend Food Rationing

Radio Moscow reported that Armenia was to introduce ration coupons for the sale of cereals, cheese, and tobacco on November 1. Sugar, butter, and, on occasion, meat and coffee have been rationed for the past few years. The *Frankfurter Allgemeine Zeitung* reported six weeks earlier that, as a result of the sporadic rail blockade imposed by Azerbaijan, the only foods regularly available in Erevan were tomatoes, cucumbers, cabbage, and chives.

GNP Down in USSR

Government statistics released for the first nine months of 1990 showed that the Soviet Gross National Product had declined 1.5 percent over the same period last year. The figures showed a drop of nearly 1 percent in the volume of industrial products manufactured during that period. They also showed an increase of 1.4 percent in food production and of more than 13 million rubles in the value of the consumer goods produced during the period. But the government said that consumer prices were skyrocketing, labor productivity was down, and that there were an estimated 2 million unemployed people in the country (*TASS*, October 19).

Saturday, October 20

Long-Range Nuclear Missiles Housed in Slavic Republics

USSR Defense Minister Dmitrii Yazov revealed that Soviet long-range missiles armed with nuclear warheads were based only in the RSFSR, Ukraine, and Belorussia, according to *The Washington Post*. Yazov did not comment on the location of short-range nuclear weapons.

Weapons Confiscation Continues

Between July 26 and October 18, the USSR Ministry of Internal Affairs confiscated 20,200 firearms, three tons of explosives, 700,000 rounds of ammunition, 100 radios, and 711 stolen vehicles, according to TASS. Twenty-four paramilitary groups were disbanded, and 364 criminal cases concerning the seizure of weapons and attacks on MVD and army troops were filed. One hundred thirty-two thousand different weapons depots were inventoried, and more than 500,000 weapons were confiscated from training centers, DOSAAF units, and enterprises. Some 34,000 depots were shut down.

KGB Discussed in Media

KGB First Deputy Chairman Filip Bobkov, not his boss, Vladimir Kryuchkov, is the real master of the KGB, retired KGB officer Valentin Korolev told the Soviet television show "Vzglyad" on October 19. Korolev claimed that Bobkov—who became a KGB deputy chairman after Yurii Andropov moved to the CPSU Central Committee Secretariat in May, 1982—was "the architect" of the "Pamyat'" movement, which, he said, was in fact a branch of the KGB. Korolev noted that Bobkov's son, Sergei, was on the editorial board of the national-Bolshevik journal *Molodaya gvardiya*. An article by Korolev entitled "Secrets of the Secret Services" was published in *Ogonek* (No. 43).

Responding to Korolev's accusations, two officers from the KGB Public Relations Center told "Vzglyad" that Korolev's criticism of Kryuchkov was unfair. Colonel Igor Prelin said that Kryuchkov's contribution to greater *glasnost'* in the KGB must be apparent. Referring to Kryuchkov's frequent contacts with Western journalists and politicians, Prelin said Westerners were better informed and more positive about the KGB than Soviet critics of the agency.

On October 24, *Literaturnaya gazeta* carried two articles, by an NKVD and a KGB agent, in which they confessed to having worked for the secret police.

Second Latvian Official Resigns after Publication of Gordievsky Book

Reports from Riga said a second senior Latvian Foreign Ministry official had resigned after being identified as a KGB agent in a book by KGB defector Oleg Gordievsky. On October 19, the Latvian Popular Front and Radio Riga named the official as Foreign Ministry press attaché Dainis Zelmenis. Another ministry official, Deputy Foreign Minister Nikolajs Neilands, resigned earlier. Both were named as KGB agents in Gordievsky's book *The KGB—The Inside Story*, which was published in Britain this week (RFE Latvian service, October 20).

Moldavian Dispute Intensifies

The Moldavian government and Supreme Soviet daily *Moldova Suverana* printed an appeal from the Moldavian Popular Front and a number of other public organizations, including the Moldavian Writers' Union, for the formation of "volunteer units" to defend Moldavia's territorial integrity and sovereignty. As summarized by TASS, the appeal proposed that the units be formed at workplaces and places of residence. Blaming secessionist movements in the east and south of the republic for "bringing Moldavia to the brink of civil war," the appeal urged "all democratic forces, irrespective of political tendency and ethnicity," to help Moldavia "develop as a free, integral, and sovereign state." The alternative is its "disintegration into small principalities and its disappearance from the world map," the appeal said.

The USSR in October, 1990

In an interview with *Izvestia* on October 22, Moldavian President Mircea Snegur said that Gorbachev's recent address to the people of Moldavia had "buried the hopes of the separatists" who sought to create new Soviet republics in Moldavia. Gorbachev endorsed Moldavia's territorial integrity and called for the resolution of interethnic problems by parliamentary means. In his interview, Snegur held out the prospect of a new administrative law in Moldavia under which "counties" would be created reflecting the separate cultural identity of the Russians and Gagauz in Moldavia.

In a message to the Gagauz ethnic group, Snegur said that secession drives by Gagauz in the south and by Russian leaders in the east of the republic aimed to "dismember Moldavia" and had brought the republic "to the brink of civil war," TASS reported. Snegur urged the Gagauz to renounce plans to elect a Gagauz Supreme Soviet on October 28 and called on them to continue political dialogue with a special commission set up by the Moldavian parliament. He warned at the same time that he would use his powers "to prevent a tragedy and preserve the territorial integrity of the republic."

On October 23, Igor Smirnov, self-styled president of the "Dniester Soviet Republic," told Radio Moscow that the would-be republic had "more than 40,000 military men" and that any attempt by Kishinev to reimpose its authority in eastern Moldavia "could well result in civil war." Interviewed on the same program, Snegur threatened economic sanctions against the breakaway area, while Moldavian Minister of Internal Affairs Ion Costas confirmed that Moldavian civilians had begun forming paramilitary "volunteer units."

On October 24, Reuters and Interfax reported that the Gagauz leaders were determined to proceed with elections as scheduled. The agencies quoted a member of the self-styled "Gagauz Republic Provisional Committee" as a source. As quoted by Reuters, Interfax reported that the committee wanted Gorbachev to place the Gagauz under the direct rule of the USSR president.

On October 25, TASS reported that elections had begun "spontaneously" in a number of Gagauz villages. The Moldavian parliament opened an emergency session to discuss the situation, described by TASS as "very tense." Snegur told the parliament that he had talked on the telephone with Gorbachev and that they had agreed that only peaceful means should be used to preserve Moldavia's territorial integrity. In the meantime, a large force of Moldavian police and civilian volunteers was sent to the borders of the self-proclaimed Gagauz Republic. Later the same day, Snegur went to the main Gagauz town of

Komrat to try to persuade the Gagauz not to proceed with "unlawful elections."

On October 26, the Moldavian Supreme Soviet declared a state of emergency in areas inhabited by the Gagauz. The Moldavian parliament also called on Moldavian volunteers to stay away from Gagauz areas. In its turn, the Gagauz Provisional Committee set up a commission to start negotiations with Moldavia (*TASS*, *Reuters*, October 26).

At an extraordinary session on October 26, the Moldavian Supreme Soviet voted to suspend Moldavia's participation in negotiations on a new Union treaty, the Soviet media reported on October 27. The resolution said Moldavia would not return to the negotiations until the threat to its territorial integrity was removed and the republic's sovereignty was appropriately guaranteed. Deputies who spoke in favor of the resolution, including moderates and Communist Party members, accused Moscow of encouraging the secession movements among the Gagauz and Russian inhabitants of the republic.

On October 27, TASS reported that the Soviet government had decided to send MVD troops to the Gagauz region. TASS said the decision had been taken in response to requests by Snegur and representatives of the Gagauz population.

The same day, negotiations between a delegation of the Moldavian Supreme Soviet and Gagauz deputies began in the town of Chimishlia on the edge of the Gagauz-inhabited area (*TASS*, October 27). On October 28, TASS reported that the Gagauz community had agreed to temporarily suspend elections to its self-proclaimed parliament.

On October 30, the Moldavian Supreme Soviet expelled ten of the thirteen deputies representing the Gagauz region. TASS said the ten included four members of the would-be Gagauz republic's provisional governing body. They were accused of shunning their duties, provoking citizens to break the law, and organizing general elections in the Gagauz area.

Later that day, talks between Moldavian negotiators and representatives of the self-proclaimed Gagauz Republic broke off without agreement. The Gagauz representatives were reported to be continuing to insist on the creation of a separate Gagauz republic. No new talks were scheduled. Spokesmen for the Moldavian presidential press office said that, as a result of the failure of the talks, the Moldavian government had decided to declare a state of emergency in the Gagauz area. The area was reported to be calm (RFE Romanian Research, October 30). On October 31, militant Moldavian volunteers returning from the Gagauz region were reported to have attacked border crossings and taken over local Party buildings in Moldavia. TASS said two border crossing points with Romania had been attacked during the night by more than 3,000 militants demanding the withdrawal of MVD troops from southern Moldavia. Moldavian officials were flown to the border and persuaded the militants to withdraw after several hours of talks. AFP quoted a border official as saying the situation had then returned to normal. A spokesman for the independent organization Democratic Youth denied that Moldavians had damaged Communist Party buildings when they took them over. *The Los Angeles Times*, however, quoted Iurie Rosca of the Moldavian Popular Front as saying "people are destroying Lenin monuments and hate everything associated with the USSR, the Soviet army, and the Communist Party." Rosca also said Moldavia should consider secession from the USSR if Moscow did not help it protect its territorial integrity (*Radio Moscow*, November 1).

The same day, the Supreme Soviet of the self-proclaimed Gagauz republic was reported to have held its first session in the town of Komrat and elected a chairman—Stepan Topal, a fifty-two-year-old civil engineer. He was also one of the deputies expelled from the Moldavian parliament on October 30 (*TASS*, October 30).

Developments in Kirgizia

The Communist Party of Kirgizia put forward proposals on introducing a market economy and cutting the republic's budget deficit at its Central Committee plenum in the republican capital, Frunze. The plenum discussed the proposed privatization of some of the republic's enterprises and the creation of joint-stock companies. The plenum also proposed to halt government subsidies to loss-making enterprises and to cancel some construction projects and other programs that yielded no immediate benefit (*TASS*, October 20).

On October 22, the Kirgiz Supreme Soviet met to discuss a number of political and economic issues, among them a declaration of republican sovereignty and the institution of an executive presidency, TASS reported. The "Democratic Renewal" group of deputies, which published its own agenda for the session last month, is demanding more radical measures than those proposed by the government. The "Kyrgyzstan" movement has also advanced a program for the creation of a sovereign national state.

On October 24, the Kirgiz Supreme Soviet became the latest republican parliament to approve a plan for the transition to a market economy (*Radio Moscow*, October 24).

On October 25, *Izvestia* reported that on October 24 the Kirgiz Supreme Soviet had created the post of president of the republic. There was no mention of nominees for the new post. TASS said members of "Kyrgyzstan" were staging a hunger strike in front of the Supreme Soviet building to press demands for the resignation of Supreme Soviet Chairman and Communist Party First Secretary Absamat Masaliev and his deputy, Renat Kul'matov, the former Party first secretary of Osh Oblast, who was blamed for ignoring the interethnic tensions that led to the riots in summer, 1989. "Kyrgyzstan" also called for the Supreme Soviet to adopt a law on public organizations.

Belated Recognition of Soviet German Wartime Contribution

A monument to deported Soviet Germans who died at the beginning of the 1940s from hunger, cold, and sickness while building the Chelyabinsk Metallurgical Works was unveiled in Chelyabinsk, TASS reported. According to preliminary estimates, about 20,000 Soviet Germans in the so-called Labor Army, who lived and worked behind barbed wire, died there. The ceremony came at the end of a week of German culture organized by the local German Cultural Center. About 40,000 Germans live in Chelyabinsk Oblast today.

Head of Ukrainian Orthodox Church Arrives in Kiev

The patriarch of the Ukrainian Autocephalous Orthodox Church arrived in Kiev. Metropolitan Mstyslav Skrypnyk, a resident of the United States, was chosen as patriarch in June of this year. TASS said that during his visit the patriarch would conduct church services, attend a Synod of the Church, and then visit several towns in Western Ukraine. The appointment of Skrypynyk as patriarch emphasized the independence of the Ukrainian Autocephalous Church, which was suppressed in the 1930s and not rehabilitated until 1989. There is another, separate Ukrainian Orthodox Church that is a part of the Moscow Patriarchate.

On October 22, TASS and Radio Kiev reported that the Autocephalous Orthodox Church in Ukraine and the Moscow Patriarchate faced a dispute over property. The Ukrainian Autocephalous Church wants to reclaim churches that it lost after being suppressed in the 1930s.

European Community Talks with USSR

A Soviet delegation, headed by Deputy Chairman of the USSR Council of Ministers Stepan Sitaryan, and a group of European Community officials, led by EC Commission President Jacques Delors, met in Brussels for talks on EC aid to the Soviet Union (*Reuters*, October 20). On October 22, a meeting of foreign ministers of the European Community decided that this was not the time to offer the Soviet Union a big short-term aid package. British Foreign Secretary Douglas Hurd said the Soviet economy was too fluid (*Reuters*, October 22).

Sunday, October 21

"Democratic Russia" Holds Congress

A two-day congress of the "Democratic Russia" movement held over the weekend was attended by 1,700 deputies and delegates from seventy-eight oblasts, krais, and autonomous regions who represented newly founded non-Communist political parties and movements in the Russian republic. Other participants included representatives from democratic movements in Poland, Hungary, Bulgaria, Czechoslovakia, and Germany, Radio Mosow reported. One of the organizers of the congress, RSFSR people's deputy Lev Ponomarev, said in an opening address that the movement considered itself an alternative to the CPSU. The congress called for the resignation of the USSR government and the confiscation of CPSU property. A commission to find ways to create a market economy in the RSFSR was set up. "Democratic Russia" also created a commission to organize civil disobedience; specifics were not disclosed, but the movement rejects violence (*TASS*, Western agencies, October 20 and 21).

Activities of the Russian Communist Party

The archconservative wing of the Russian Communist Party, the so-called "Initiative Congress," met in Leningrad to discuss its "Program for Action." (The Russian Communist Party, headed by Ivan Polozkov, has attempted to dissociate itself from this faction.) TASS said the "Program for Action" called for the revival of Russia and said that the Communist program was the only right one. TASS correspondents were refused accreditation to the congress, despite having submitted the necessary paperwork.

On October 19, *Sovetskaya Rossiya* carried the draft of "the Main Directions of Activity" of the main wing of the RSFSR Communist Party. This document was intended to fill the void created in September when the Party's Constituent Congress failed to adopt a program. The RSFSR Communist Party's original draft program was rejected when reformers pointed out that its antimarket slant contradicted the official programmatic declaration adopted by the CPSU at its Twenty-eighth Congress. The RSFSR Communist Party's latest draft grudgingly took note of these objections; in the words of Nikolai Travkin, it contained some "*rynochnye prosvetleniya*" ("gleams of the market").

The same issue of *Sovetskaya Rossiya* printed an offer by the Central Committee of the RSFSR Communist Party to cooperate with the liberal "Democratic Russia" forum.

Remains of Former Estonian President Reburied

The remains of former Estonian President Konstantin Pats were reburied in the Estonian capital, Tallinn. Pats was president of independent Estonia until 1940, when Soviet forces occupied the republic. He was deported to Russia and died in a psychiatric clinic near Kalinin (now renamed Tver) in 1956. The search for and identification of the former president's remains was initiated by Estonian activists in 1989 (*TASS*, October 21).

***Moscow News* Publishes Excerpts from Allilueva's New Book**

Moscow News (No. 42) carried excerpts from a new book by Stalin's daughter, Svetlana Allilueva, entitled *Kniga dlya vnuchek* (A Book for Grandchildren). The excerpts detailed Stalin's death and his funeral. *Komsomol'skaya pravda* (October 13) carried the text of a short telephone interview its correspondent conducted with Allilueva, who now lives in London. Allilueva explained why she left the USSR again after returning to live there for two years (1986–88).

Deputy Director of TASS Condemns Its Policies

TASS should stop serving the interests of only the conservative wing of the CPSU, the agency's deputy director general, A. Krasikov, told *Moscow News* (No. 42). In his letter to the newspaper, Krasikov said that many staff members of TASS did not support the conservative line of its director general, Leonid Kravchenko, who attacked *glasnost'* in a speech at the latest CPSU Central Committee plenum. Krasikov also stressed that he and other TASS commentators were ashamed of a commentary by their colleague Vladimir Petrunya that accused democrats in Moscow and Leningrad of deliberately aggravating economic problems in the USSR. The publication of Petrunya's commentary in several conservative newspapers, including *Pravda*, provoked strong criticism by the Interregional Group of Deputies.

Destruction of Graves of Stalin Victims Proclaimed Criminal Offense

The RSFSR State Prosecutor's Office declared the destruction of graves in the city of Kolpashevo (near Tomsk) in Siberia a criminal offense, according to *Komsomol'skaya pravda*. In 1979, after a flood exposed the corpses of many hundreds of victims executed during the Stalin era, the local authorities decided to grind up the bodies using ship propellers and then to dispose of them in the Ob River. This action was authorized by Egor Ligachev, then the first secretary of the Tomsk Oblast Party Committee. Although the story was first made public by *Pravda* on May 11, 1989, *Komsomol'skaya pravda* noted that the Prosecutor's Office had only now—after Ligachev's resignation from the Party leadership—decided to act.

Monday, October 22

Supreme Soviet Adopts Tough Measures against Black Market

In accordance with a law adopted by the USSR Supreme Soviet, "the resale for a profit of goods bought at state prices" will be punishable by a term of up to three years in prison and the confiscation of the goods, with longer sentences and higher fines imposed for large-scale offenses, TASS reported. Commenting on the new law at a Moscow press conference, KGB Chairman Vladimir Kryuchkov said that organized crime and black-market activity had increased beyond all predictions. He also said that joint ventures with Western firms had become a front for large-scale economic crime. Kryuchkov noted that during the transition to a market economy more order would be needed. USSR Minister of Internal Affairs Vadim Bakatin said that black-market operators understood market relations but that their "criminal tendencies must be held in check."

Supreme Soviet Adopts Resolution on Foreign Policy

The USSR Supreme Soviet adopted a resolution supporting the Soviet Union's current foreign policy course and the principles of "the new thinking." The Supreme Soviet Committees on International Affairs and Defense and National Security resolved to hold closed meetings with the Defense and Foreign Affairs Ministries to discuss Soviet national security problems. The Committees for Afghan Veterans, International Affairs, and Defense and National Security resolved to discuss problems in Soviet-Afghan relations, TASS reported.

New Regulations on State Secrets Revealed

Following the end of preliminary censorship in connection with the adoption of the new press law, new arrangements have been made to prevent the appearance of state secrets in the media, *Pravitel'stvennyi vestnik* (No. 40) reported. The former censorship body, Glavlit, was transformed in August into the Main Administration for the Preservation of State Secrets in the Mass Media (GUOT SSSR). Glavlit used to compile annual secret lists of topics that could not be discussed in the Soviet press, many of which were politically sensitive issues. The lists compiled by GUOT are supposed to include only real state secrets, mostly in the military sphere, and, in contrast to the Glavlit lists, those of GUOT will be published in the open press.

The report in *Pravitel'stvennyi vestnik*, however, contradicted an article published in *Izvestia* on October 9. *Izvestia* reported that GUOT had started its activities by issuing a secret list of forbidden topics. The list, which was not for publication in the press, reportedly included not only military secrets, but also such subjects as cattle viruses.

Election Official Sentenced

A member of a local electoral commission in Tver was sentenced to two years in a labor camp for falsifying election results, Radio Moscow reported. The official, identified only as Golovin, was found to have cast ballots under the names of people who did not actually vote. The sentence was suspended for one year because Golovin's action had not changed the outcome of the elections.

Moscow Brezhnev-Era Dissidents to Be Rehabilitated

KGB Chairman Vladimir Kryuchkov said that most of those convicted for anti-Soviet agitation and propaganda in the 1960s and 1970s should be rehabilitated. Kryuchkov told a Moscow press conference that the cases of 7,250 people were currently under review (*Radio Moscow*, October 22).

Miners' Congress Held in Donetsk

A miners' congress opened in the Ukrainian city of Donetsk. Radio Moscow said about 900 miners from coal mines across the USSR attended. One of the main topics on the agenda was the creation of an independent miners' union. *Pravda* said another topic was how the coal mining industry, which has always operated at a loss, could be brought into a market economy. Mikhail Gorbachev sent an appeal to the congress asking miners to support his economic reform plan (*TASS*, in English, October 22).

On October 23, TASS reported that the miners' congress had called for the resignation of the government of Nikolai Ryzhkov and proposed holding presidential elections by direct vote.

On October 24, TASS reported that little progress had been made after two days of debates. TASS said no consensus had been reached on the central issue of the congress—namely, whether to reconstitute the existing miners' union as an independent trade union. TASS said the delegation from the Kuzbass favored only a loosening of union structures, while miners from Ukraine wanted a more radical reorganization. On October 25, however, an independent coal miners' union was declared by a group of trade unionists who broke with the majority at the congress. AP said the new union represented miners from Ukraine, Kazakhstan, and Siberia.

The same day, the congress was addressed by Minister of the Coal Industry Mikhail Shchadov, who told the miners that they should have a wage increase and a degree of control over their own mines. He also said, however, that they should be patient while the government drafted a new plan to improve their lives (*AP*, October 25).

On October 26, the miners' congress followed the move of its breakaway faction and voted to form a new confederation of independent miners' unions (*TASS*, October 26).

Moscow Ponders Mixed System of Rationing and Free Trade

The Presidium of the Moscow City Soviet proposed that rationing cards for basic foodstuffs be introduced in the Soviet capital but that, at the same time, private traders be allowed to sell goods at a profit. Radio Moscow did not specify which goods would be affected. According to this plan, price rises for goods on the free market would be kept in check by a system of progressive taxation. The radio said that, if the city soviet approved the proposals, Moscow would ask the RSFSR Supreme Soviet to introduce this system throughout the republic.

Independent Journalists' Union Formed in Ukraine

Ukrainian journalists set up an independent union to guarantee freedom of speech and conscience and to protect journalists' professional and social rights. Radio Moscow said the union had been formed at the seventh congress of the official Ukrainian Journalists' Union.

Landsbergis Visits Budapest

President of the Lithuanian Supreme Council Vytautas Landsbergis arrived in the Hungarian capital, Budapest. He told the Hungarian news agency MTI that he would hold talks on expanding Hungarian-Lithuanian economic, political, and cultural collaboration.

On October 23, Landsbergis met with Hungarian President Arpad Goncz and discussed bilateral relations with him. The same day, Landsbergis took part in ceremonies commemorating the anniversary of the start of the 1956 revolution in Hungary. Landsbergis said Lithuania should take as an example Hungary's struggle against communism in 1956 (*Radio Budapest*, October 23).

On October 25, Landsbergis told RFE/RL that he was discussing with Hungarian leaders the possibility of restoring diplomatic ties between their countries.

Tuesday, October 23

Gorbachev Meets with Leaders of Autonomous Republics

Gorbachev met with the leaders of the autonomous republics at their request, TASS reported. The discussion centered on the role of the autonomous territories in the drawing up of the new Union treaty and their place in a renewed Union. TASS said participants were in favor of accelerating work on the treaty. The TASS report said nothing about what was probably the main demand of the autonomous republics—namely, that they should be direct parties to the Union treaty, a demand that is unlikely to be met.

Aitmatov to Quit Presidential Council

Chingiz Aitmatov, the internationally renowned Kirgiz novelist and public activist, told AP that he was resigning from the USSR Presidential Council to become Soviet ambassador to Luxembourg and to resume writing. Commenting on the future of the USSR, Aitmatov described the country as "a boiling pot [in which] history is making its porridge" and as "a sick organism, but a living one." Aitmatov—the only representative of the Muslim republics in the Presidential Council—criticized politicians who call for the dismantling of the Soviet Union, saying that this would benefit no one.

Trade-Union Congress Held

The official Soviet trade unions met in Moscow to discuss disbanding the highly unpopular All-Union Central Council of Trade Unions (AUCCTU) and replacing it with a more loosely organized general confederation. TASS described the proceedings as "unexpectedly stormy." Georgia and the Baltic republics sent no delegations. In his opening address, the acting chairman of the trade-union council, Vladimir Shcherbakov, recognized that the new confederation would have no monopoly over trade-union activity in the country but would have to cooperate with new, independent movements.

Shcherbakov called for emergency measures to protect the low-paid during the transition to a market economy. He said that between 70 and 80 million Soviet citizens currently lived on subsistence wages. (The official minimum monthly wage is 70 rubles per person, but the unions say this figure is too low, since it fails to take account of the fact that, because of widespread shortages in state stores, even the poorest members of the population have to buy goods at kolkhoz markets where prices are higher.)

On October 24, acknowledging that the official trade unions were out of touch with the country's workers and unable to cope with the present economic crisis, delegates to the congress decided to disband the All-Union Central Council of Trade Unions and replace it with an organization provisionally entitled the All-Union Confederation of Trade Unions of the USSR (*TASS*, October 24).

On October 24, the congress was addressed by USSR Prime Minister Nikolai Ryzhkov. Ryzhkov said his government opposed "layoffs on a mass scale" during the transition to a market economy and described the right to work as the main issue of social policy at the present time.

The trade-union congress also complained to the USSR Supreme Soviet that a law on trade-union rights had not yet been adopted. The bill was tabled for consideration at the present parliamentary session but is not high on the agenda (*TASS*, October 24).

On October 27, the General Confederation of Trade Unions ended its week-long congress and elected Vladimir Shcherbakov as its chairman. Shcherbakov replaced Gennadii Yanaev, who was appointed a CPSU Central Committee Secretary during the summer (*TASS*, October 27). He earlier held the post of chairman of the Moscow City Trade-Union Council for four years and came under attack for his "bad-tempered style of leadership," but he was also noted for his criticism of the way the AUCCTU was run.

Masol Finally Steps Down

The Ukrainian Supreme Soviet voted 254 to eighty-three to accept the resignation of republican Prime Minister Vitalii Masol, Interfax reported. The agency said Masol had denounced the vote as "moral terrorism." He has been succeeded temporarily by Vitol'd Fokin, chairman of the USSR State Committee on the Economy. The resignation of Masol was one of the demands made during mass demonstrations in Ukraine.

Sverdlovsk Granted Right to Conclude Foreign Deals

The Moscow authorities have given the city of Sverdlovsk permission to conclude transactions with foreign countries, Radio Moscow reported. The decision came after what Radio Moscow described as a long hard fight by the Sverdlovsk Oblast Soviet. The city will be allowed to keep 5 percent of its foreign earnings, which will amount to some 1 billion rubles.

Lidiya Chukovskaya Awarded Sakharov Prize

Soviet writer Lidiya Chukovskaya has been awarded the recently created Andrei Sakharov prize, *Moskovskaya pravda* reported. The prize was established by the liberal writers' association "April" and is awarded to writers for civic courage in both their lives and their literary work. During the Stalin era, Chukovskaya wrote stories detailing her impressions of the mass arrests of 1937 and 1949 (she narrowly escaped arrest herself). Chukovskaya was expelled from the USSR Writers' Union in 1974 for defending persecuted Soviet writers, including Aleksandr Solzhenitsyn. She has returned to official public life in the USSR under Gorbachev.

Kalugin Hearings Adjourned

The Moscow City Court adjourned its hearing of former KGB general Oleg Kalugin's case against KGB Chairman Vladimir Kryuchkov because the USSR Council of Ministers and the Chief Military Prosecutor had not yet responded to the court's request for a number of documents and information, TASS reported. Kalugin told TASS that he thought the court was linking his case against Kryuchkov and Chairman of the USSR Council of Ministers Nikolai Ryzhkov (which concerns the loss of his rank and pension) with the criminal case under investigation by the Military Prosecutor's Office (which concerns Kalugin's possible divulgence of military secrets) in order to use the criminal court's decision as legal support for the annulment of his pension.

Wednesday, October 24

Center Versus Republics

The USSR Supreme Soviet passed a law establishing the precedence of all-Union laws throughout the Soviet Union until the conclusion of a new Union treaty, the Soviet media reported. (For the text of the law, see *Izvestia*, October 26.) A few hours later, the RSFSR Supreme Soviet adoped a law stating that laws and other acts of the all-Union authorities—including presidential decrees—would take effect in the RSFSR only "after their ratification by the RSFSR Supreme Soviet" (*TASS*, October 24). A similar law requires that orders of the USSR Council of Ministers be approved by the RSFSR Council of Ministers. The Ukrainian Supreme Soviet also proclaimed the precedence of republican laws over national laws and stipulated that only national laws ratified by the republican parliament would be in force. On October 26, Belorussia followed suit by asserting the supremacy of republican laws over those of the USSR (*TASS*, October 26).

On October 25, the RSFSR Supreme Soviet called for the creation of a panel to define the powers held by the central and republican governments while a new Union treaty was being devised. The parliament also proposed the creation of an interrepublican economic committee (*TASS*, October 25).

Greater Powers for Gorbachev Rejected

Article 4 of the draft law proclaiming the precedence of national laws in all Soviet republics proposed granting President Mikhail Gorbachev the right to dismiss the directors and employees of enterprises, associations, and organizations if they failed to comply with national laws and orders. A specially formed conciliation commission amended this article to grant Gorbachev the right only to dismiss the heads of state enterprises, associations, and organizations that are directly subordinate to all-Union bodies, "Vremya" reported. According to *The Times*, the draft also gave Gorbachev the right to limit the powers of local soviets and their executive councils should they fail to observe national laws and decisions.

Soviet Veterans Club Established

Soviet war veterans have formed a Club of Heroes of the Soviet Union, TASS reported. The founding congress of the club, held in Moscow, was attended by 400 Heroes of the Soviet Union. The club, which was set up by the Main Political Directorate of the Soviet Army and Navy, proclaimed the struggle against antimilitary propaganda as its major goal. Defense Minister Dmitrii Yazov named *Komsomol'skaya pravda* as an example of a newspaper that reports negatively on the armed forces.

Projects to Increase *Pravda*'s Sales Discussed

Pravda, troubled by steep falls in readership, hopes to launch into the world market, chief editor Ivan Frolov told a news conference. TASS quoted Frolov as saying that on October 23 the Party leadership had discussed proposals to turn the newspaper into a sort of "combine," generating its own profits through advertising and having greater independence. Frolov said the CPSU Central Committee Secretariat had also proposed the creation of an international edition of *Pravda* to be produced in collaboration with newspapers in the United States, Japan, Britain, and France. (Foreign language digests of *Pravda* have already been issued in several European countries and in the United States.)

CPSU Wants Its Own Television Company

At the same press conference, Frolov revealed that the CPSU Central Committee Secretariat had also discussed the possibility of setting up a Party television company. "There is a project to rent a television studio and make our own films, which would then be shown on television," Frolov said (*Reuters*, *TASS*, October 24). Conservative Communists have complained that Moscow and Leningrad television, once loyal mouthpieces of the CPSU, are now being used by radicals to undermine the Soviet system. Democratically oriented political parties and people's deputies, on the other hand, have complained that the director of Gosteleradio, Mikhail Nenashev, still too often bases broadcasting policy on the point of view of conservative Communists.

"Union of Persecuted" Formed in Moscow

The inhabitants of Red Square's "tent city" formed a new organization to defend their interests and those of all Moscow's petitioners. It is to be called "the Union of the Persecuted" (*Soyuz gonimykh SSSR*). Every year, the central authorities receive about 5 million letters or personal visits from Soviet citizens who believe they have been unjustly treated. Known as "truth-seekers," these people form a vast Soviet underclass of unknown proportions.

Underground Nuclear Test Held in Arctic

The Soviet Union conducted its first underground nuclear test in more than a year, TASS reported. The test was conducted on the island of Novaya Zemlya; the force of the explosion was rated at between 20 and 150 kilotons.

The test was condemned by the chairman of the State Committee for the Protection of the Environment, Nikolai Vorontsov, in an address to the RSFSR Supreme Soviet. Vorontsov said that the Soviet military complex, which conducted the test, had failed to inform either Vorontsov's committee or the local authorities at Novaya Zemlya of its plans in advance (*Central Television*, October 25).

On October 25, Norwegian Prime Minister Jan Syse also condemned the test and said an investigation had been ordered into its effects. In response to the test,

Finland renewed a call for a global ban on underground testing (*Reuters*, *AP*, October 25).

On October 26, *Komsomol'skaya pravda* said deputies from Arkhangel'sk Oblast planned to make an official protest to the USSR Supreme Soviet Presidium over the testing. The Soviet branch of the organization Physicians for the Prevention of Nuclear War also protested (*TASS*, October 26).

On October 29, eleven members of the USSR Supreme Soviet read a joint statement to the Supreme Soviet in which they claimed that the test on Novaya Zemlya had had two goals: first, to discredit Gorbachev, who had just been awarded the Nobel Peace Prize; and second, to provoke a conflict between Moscow and the RSFSR, which has said it does not want nuclear tests conducted on its territory. Vorontsov said Gorbachev did not know about the test in advance and he described it as a blow by the military-industrial complex against Gorbachev.

On October 31, the USSR Supreme Soviet criticized the government for not informing parliament sooner about the test. It said the test had made it difficult to develop cooperation with north European countries aimed at improving the ecological situation in the region. A resolution issued by the Supreme Soviet asked the government to provide advance notice of any future tests to the state's highest competent bodies.

Belorussian Parliament Supports Draft Bill on Citizenship

The Belorussian Supreme Soviet decided to support a draft bill on citizenship prepared by the republican popular front. TASS said this was the first time that deputies supporting the front had won a majority vote in the parliament. After winning support in principle, the bill was sent back to a committee for further work. TASS said the two drafts—one from the popular front and the other from the Belorussian government—differed mainly over the question of whether citizens of other republics residing in Belorussia should have equal rights and be allowed to hold dual citizenship. The popular front opposed granting that right. TASS said the front's draft stressed that people would have to prove at least seven years of residence in Belorussia, a permanent source of income, and knowledge of the Belorussian language and republican laws. But Belorussian Supreme Soviet deputy Sergei Navumchyk told RFE/RL that in fact the front's draft did not require knowledge of the Belorussian language in order to obtain citizenship. He said the draft did call for "state protection" of the Belorussian language.

"Rukh" Congress Opens

On October 25, at the opening of the second congress of "Rukh," its chairman, Ivan Drach, called for the full restoration of an independent Ukrainian state. Other "Rukh" leaders pledged to unite with students and other reform groups in the republic to achieve this aim. They also said they would seek to remove the Ukrainian Communist Party from power by democratic means (*Reuters*, October 25). Also addressing the congress was the leader of the Belorussian Popular Front, Zyanon Paznyak, who called for the creation of a Baltic-Belorussian-Ukrainian organization to work for "decolonization of the republics" (*DPA*, RL Ukrainian service, October 25).

On October 27, in a surprise move, the congress reelected Ivan Drach as chairman of "Rukh," even after he had stated that he wanted to step down. The organization also created fifteen new councils, each focused on a specific issue. Human-rights activist Mykhailo Horyn was put in charge of the political affairs council. "Rukh" declared itself formally in opposition to the Communist Party and effectively banned members of the CPSU from its ranks (*TASS*, RL Ukrainian service, October 28).

Conflicting Views on Danger of Disorder, Coup in USSR

The well-known Soviet military historian Professor Vyacheslav Dashichev said he saw the danger of a coup attempt in the USSR if the supply situation deteriorated further. He said that if there were fresh outrages within the next two years there would be a threat of a revolution from below. He said in this event the armed forces might intervene to restore order. Dashichev made his remarks in an interview with the German newspaper *Neue Osnabrücker Zeitung*.

A different point of view was expressed by USSR Minister of Internal Affairs Vadim Bakatin in a separate interview published in *Die Zeit* (October 26). Bakatin said that, although the situation in the Soviet Union was very serious, with problems such as hunger and cold threatening to trigger new tension and push the situation out of control, speculation about a military coup was unfounded.

The director of the CIA, William Webster, also joined the debate on the potential for destabilization of the Soviet Union. He said he was concerned about nuclear weapons falling into the wrong hands if nationalist strife broke up the Soviet Union. Webster said there was currently very little danger of this happening, because of the tight central control over Soviet nuclear weapons.

But he said that, if the Soviet Union should disintegrate, "then we would have to see who are the people moving to take control over those particular weapons" (*Reuters*, October 25).

Soviet General Envisages Europe without Military Blocs

The chief of the General Staff of the Soviet Armed Forces, General Mikhail Moiseev, said he envisaged a Europe without military blocs. Moiseev was addressing the NATO chiefs of staff in Brussels at the end of a two-day meeting on NATO's future. He was the highest-ranking Soviet military officer ever to address NATO (*Reuters*, *AP*, October 25).

On October 26, speaking to reporters in Brussels after finishing the talks with NATO officials, Moiseev suggested direct phone links between NATO and Soviet command posts. He said such a move would reflect the dramatic thaw in East-West relations (*AP*, *AFP*, October 26).

Moscow Party School to Become Institute of Political Sciences

The Moscow Higher Party School, a power base of the Democratic Platform within the CPSU, has been renamed the Russian Institute of Political Sciences and Social Prognosis, Radio Moscow reported. The scientific council of the school sent a request to the CPSU Central Committee to approve the decision. The institute, set up on the basis of the Party school, will accept students regardless of whether they are members of the CPSU.

USSR and Argentina Sign Agreement

USSR President Mikhail Gorbachev and his Argentinian counterpart, Carlos Menem, signed a cooperation agreement in Moscow. TASS quoted Menem as saying the two countries had many similar problems. Soviet Foreign Minister Eduard Shevardnadze and Argentine Foreign Minister Domingo Cavallo also signed agreements covering cooperation in the peaceful uses of atomic energy and space and in efforts to combat drug trafficking (*TASS*, in English, October 25).

Tajiks Seek Work Abroad

A private employment agency has opened in Tajikistan to find people work abroad. According to TASS, it has already found employment for several applicants.

Congress of Russian Social Democrats

The second congress of the RSFSR Social Democratic Party opened in Sverdlovsk. TASS quoted the party's cochairman, RSFSR people's deputy Oleg Rumyantsev, as saying the congress discussed the party's draft program, which stresses as the party's main goal the establishment of social guarantees for working people at a time when the country is moving towards a market economy. Rumyantsev also said that the congress marked the transformation of the social democratic movement into a real, normally functioning party. He said that previously the movement, although called a party, was in fact an informal group.

Two New Ambassadors Appointed

Gennadii Il'ichev has been appointed ambassador to Lebanon, TASS reported. Il'ichev, born in 1938, is a graduate of the Moscow Foreign Relations Institute. His previous postings include Kuwait, Syria, the Yemen Arab Republic, and the People's Democratic Republic of Yemen. Il'ichev served most recently as the senior counsellor of the Near East and North African Countries Administration. TASS also reported the appointment of Anatolii Tishchenko as ambassador to Norway. Tishchenko, born in 1935, is also a graduate of the Moscow Foreign Relations Institute. He has served as deputy head of the Scandinavian Countries Department at the Foreign Ministry and as minister-counsellor at the Soviet embassy in Helsinki. Most recently, Tishchenko served as deputy head of the Main Administration of Personnel and Educational Institutions at the Foreign Ministry.

Friday, October 26

Gorbachev Visits Spain

Mikhail Gorbachev, accompanied by Soviet Foreign Minister Eduard Shevardnadze and Kazakh President Nursultan Nazarbaev, arrived in Madrid for talks with Spanish officials (*TASS*, October 26). He met first with Prime Minister Felipe Gonzalez to discuss trade and other forms of economic cooperation. In an interview with *El Pais*, Gorbachev said that one of the goals of *perestroika* was to integrate the Soviet Union into the European and world economies as an equal partner.

Later that day, Gorbachev addressed the Spanish parliament and asked for understanding for his reform program in the Soviet Union. He said his reforms were aimed at laying the foundation for a new Soviet state. He said such a process was necessarily painful. During the visit, several agreements were signed between the USSR and Spain, covering Spanish economic assistance to the Soviet Union and cooperation over military contacts, visa procedures, tourism, and the fight against drug trafficking.

Speaking at a Madrid news conference at the end of two days of talks with Spanish leaders, Mikhail Gorbachev stressed similarities in the Spanish and Soviet political experiences and described his visit to Spain as one of "great dimensions." The visit yielded sixteen agreements, including a 1.5-billion-dollar Spanish credit (*Reuters*, *TASS*, October 27). The credit will be spread over a three-year period and will be tied to Soviet purchases of Spanish goods and services, news agencies reported on October 28. On October 28, Gorbachev left Spain for France. On his way he visited the Spanish city of Barcelona (*TASS*, October 28).

Committee Says Residence Permits Should be Abolished

The USSR Committee for Constitutional Oversight said that the residence permits (*propiski*) required of Soviet citizens violated human rights and should be abolished. At present Soviet citizens are required to obtain a residence permit every time they change their domicile. This procedure is very complicated, especially for people wishing to reside in Moscow or in other major Soviet cities. The committee said this requirement interfered with citizens' rights to migrate, work, and receive an education (*TASS*, October 26). (The committee was established by the USSR Supreme Soviet to review the legality of disputed laws and other acts.)

Soviet Official Says Arms Trade Remains State Monopoly

First Deputy Chairman of the USSR Council of Ministers Lev Voronin said the Soviet state would retain its monopoly on the weapons trade. He told TASS that no change in the situation was possible. He said that trade in military equipment was the prerogative of the state "strictly within the framework of intergovernmental agreements and with the observance of international standards." Voronin was commenting on a recent report in *Komsomol'skaya pravda* that several defense-industry firms had been allowed to sell military equipment abroad.

Gorbachev Issues Decree on Foreign Investment

Gorbachev issued a decree allowing foreign investors to control up to 100 percent of enterprises they are involved in inside the Soviet Union. In accordance with the decree, foreign investors can also set up businesses in the USSR on their own, without Soviet partners, and can reinvest their profits in the USSR or transfer them abroad. The decree is aimed at attracting more foreign investment.

Another decree issued the same day lowered the commercial exchange rate for the ruble to 1.8 to the dollar—about one third its present value—effective

November 1. The commercial rate is the exchange rate used for foreign-trade transactions. The change was aimed at increasing the ability of Soviet enterprises to sell their products abroad by making Soviet goods cheaper on the world market and imports more expensive (*TASS*, October 26). See RL 468/90 and RL 490/90.

German Communist Party Leader Visits Moscow

Gregor Gysi, the leader of the Party for Democratic Socialism (PDS), formerly the East German Socialist Unity Party, visited Moscow on October 25 to clear up mysterious financial transfers that prompted a police raid on his party headquarters, Reuters reported on October 26. The party had transferred about 100 million marks abroad using a Soviet firm as an intermediary. The German authorities say the PDS broke the law by transferring the money without the permission of a state trustee agency that is supervising its finances.

Landsbergis Compares Annexation of Lithuania with Kuwait

President of the Lithuanian Supreme Council Vytautas Landsbergis said on Soviet television that not many Lithuanians would want to be a part of the Soviet Union. He compared the annexation of Lithuania by the Soviet Union in 1940 with Iraq's annexation of Kuwait.

Saturday, October 27

Results of Russian Orthodox Bishops Council

Kirill, archbishop of Smolensk and Kaliningrad, who is chairman of the Department of External Church Relations and a representative of the Russian Orthodox Bishops Council, announced at a press conference on October 27 that the council had passed a resolution, the first part of which granted "rights of independence" to the Ukrainian Orthodox Church. The second part welcomed the new USSR law on freedom of conscience as a document that corresponded with the basic principles of the UN Declaration on Human Rights. The resolution also stated, however, that some important principles, in particular, the recognition of the Church as a juridical entity, had been excluded from the law despite the fact that the Church had repeatedly emphasized their importance (*TASS*, October 27).

Meanwhile, Aleksii, patriarch of Moscow and all Russia, visited Ukraine. Thousands of supporters of the Ukrainian Autocephalous Orthodox Church rallied outside Saint Sophia's Cathedral in Kiev to protest against his visit (RL Ukrainian service, October 28).

Niyazov Elected President of Turkmenistan

Turkmen Communist Party First Secretary Saparmurad Niyazov was elected president of the republic in a direct popular election, TASS reported. He was the only candidate for the post. Turkmenistan is so far the only republic to have elected a president directly.

Kazakhstan Prohibits Export of Consumer Goods

Radio Moscow reported that the Kazakh Council of Ministers had prohibited the export from the republic of forty types of consumer goods in order to end growing shortages of such goods. Earlier in the year, the export of certain industrial products was prohibited for the same reason, causing a protest by factory managers who wanted to make their own decisions about where to sell their products.

Christian Democrats Hold Congress

The Christian Democratic Movement of Russia, which held its second congress over the weekend in Moscow, stated that Communist doctrine should not be the government's official ideology. The movement also rejected the state's official policy of atheism. TASS quoted the movement's leader, Viktor Aksyuchits, as saying the movement now has about 15,000 members. The main result of the congress was the movement's decision to join "Democratic Russia," the main bloc of democratic forces in the RSFSR (*TASS*, October 28).

Soviet Journal Reassesses Activities of General Vlasov

New Times (No. 43) published an article reassessing the activities of Soviet General Andrei Vlasov, who was captured by the Germans during World War II and used by them in actions against the Soviet Union. The article broke with the traditional Soviet portrayal of Vlasov as a traitor who should be categorically condemned. The article was based on a major study of Vlasov by German historian Joachim Hoffmann, for whom Vlasov is a complicated and tragic figure, a man caught between two evils—Stalinism and Nazism.

Congress of Estonia Ends Session in Tallinn

The Congress of Estonia ended a two-day session held in Tallinn. The congress is an official body elected earlier this year by citizens of prewar Estonia and their descendants. It met for the first time in March and then again in May. The congress supports full Estonian independence and regards the Soviet Union as an occupying power. The agenda of the session included the reelection of the congress' leading body, "the Committee of Estonia," and the adoption of resolutions on the political situation in the republic (RFE Estonian service, October 27).

Sunday, October 28

Gorbachev in France

After leaving Spain, Gorbachev arrived in Paris for a short visit during which he signed a series of cooperation accords with France. One of the agreements provided for French credits to the Soviet Union totalling 1 billion dollars (*AFP*, October 28). (On October 31, AFP reported that the Soviet Union intended to use part of the French credit to buy 3–4 million tons of grain.) During his visit, Gorbachev also held talks with French President François Mitterrand. The Gulf crisis was one of the topics they discussed.

On October 29, France and the Soviet Union signed a treaty of "entente" that gave each side the right to call consultations should its national security be threatened. The treaty called on both sides to "harmonize their positions" (*Reuters*, October 29).

Before leaving Paris, Gorbachev held a press conference at which he called for an Arab initiative on the Gulf crisis. He suggested Saudi Arabia initiate "an inter-Arab conference" to resolve the crisis (*Reuters*, *TASS*, October 29).

Soviet Economic Official Ends Visit to Saudi Arabia

USSR Minister of Foreign Economic Relations Konstantin Katushev ended a visit to Saudi Arabia after several days of talks aimed at expanding trade relations. Katushev's visit followed the decision taken by the USSR and Saudi Arabia in September to restore full diplomatic ties, which had been allowed to lapse in 1938 owing to various disputes. AP reported that Katushev had urged Saudi Arabia to use some of its enormous oil profits to invest in the developing Soviet economy.

Magadan Party First Secretary Resigns

Viktor Vichkanov resigned as Communist Party first secretary in the Far Eastern city of Magadan, saying he was disappointed in *perestroika*. Radio Moscow quoted him as telling a plenum of the city Party committee that he did not believe any more that the transition to a market economy would improve the life of the people.

Leading Scientist Elected President of Kirgizia

The Kirgiz Supreme Soviet elected Askar Akaev as executive president of the republic. Akaev is president of the republican Academy of Sciences. Radio Moscow said he had defeated five other candidates in a secret ballot.

On October 29, TASS reported that Akaev would be concentrating on restoring interethnic relations and popular consensus, stabilizing the economy, and strengthening the republican Supreme Soviet's authority.

The same day, RFE/RL learned that Akaev had met with protesters who had been staging a hunger strike outside the building of the republican Communist Party Central Committee. One of them, Topchubek Turgunaliev, cochairman of the "Kyrgyzstan" democratic movement, said they had been demanding the introduction of an executive presidency and were satisfied with Akaev's election. He added, however, that they also wanted a reassessment of the violence in Osh Oblast and the resignation of Absamat Masaliev from his post as chairman of the republic's Supreme Soviet. See RL 493/90.

Elections in Georgia

Elections to the republican Supreme Soviet were held in Georgia. Bewildered by the similar programs of the thirty-four competing parties, most of the electorate were reported to have voted either for the Georgian Communist Party or for the Round Table, the non-Communist opposition movement (*AP*, October 28). There was some delay in reporting the full results of the poll, owing to the complicated electoral system: 125 delegates to the Supreme Soviet were to be elected in single-candidate constituencies, with the remaining 125 seats to be divided among thirteen separate alliances and parties according to the proportion of the total vote received by each. Separatist organizations in Abkhazia and South Ossetia called for a boycott of the vote after being banned from participating.

On November 1, the Round Table was reported to have won over 54 percent of the vote, thus taking over power from the Communist Party, which won just under 30 percent. TASS said the results meant the Round Table would have at least 147 deputies in the 250-seat parliament and the Communists at least seventy-six. Seven other candidates also won seats. The leader of the Round Table, Zviad Gamsakhurdia, told Soviet television that he was only partly pleased with the results. He alleged that there had been violations of the election laws. See RL 472/90.

Monday, October 29

RSFSR and Kazakhstan Sign Cooperation Agreement

TASS reported that the RSFSR and Kazakhstan had signed an intergovernmental agreement on trade and the development of cultural relations for 1991. They aim to keep trade at at least 1990 levels.

Tuesday, October 30

Gosbank Raises Interest Rates

The Soviet Union's central bank—Gosbank—announced higher interest rates on deposits and loans for businesses and organizations, effective November 1. A Gosbank statement carried by TASS said rates would range from 6 percent on loans for one year or less to 11 percent on credits for more than five years. The interest on deposits will range from 2 to 8 percent. Reports said the move was aimed at cutting inflation.

Western Firms to Be Allowed to Exchange Rubles for Hard Currency

The New York Times quoted Gosbank officials as saying that Western businesses would be allowed to exchange their ruble profits into hard currency starting in January, 1991. Current Soviet law bans the expatriation of ruble profits by Western companies.

No Agreement at Estonian-Soviet Military Consultations

At a meeting in Moscow, Estonian and Soviet officials failed to reach agreement on two important military issues—Estonia's demands to set up its own army and to have its conscripts serve only in Estonia. The Estonian delegation said that Estonia wanted to be a neutral state and that such neutrality must have reliable protection. The Soviet side countered that the creation of a separate Estonian armed force would create numerous problems (*TASS*, October 30).

Office to Monitor Human Rights Opened in USSR

Soviet and US sponsors said they had opened the first independent office to monitor human rights in the USSR. The office, which opened on October 29 in Moscow, is called the Bureau on Exit, Human Rights, and Rule of Law. It was sanctioned by the Soviet authorities. The organizers said the office would monitor anti-Semitism in the USSR and help people leave the country for Israel and elsewhere. The US sponsor of the office is the Washington-based Union of Councils for Soviet Jews. The Soviet sponsor is the Public Committee on Exit and Entrance and Other Human Rights, which is a Moscow-based rights monitoring group (Western agencies, October 30).

Opinion Poll Shows Citizens Disenchanted with Socialism

According to the results of an opinion poll carried by *Komsomol'skaya pravda*, Soviet citizens are increasingly disenchanted with socialism, with only 14 percent of those questioned expressing support for the Communist Party. Tat'yana Zaslavskaya, head of the Soviet public opinion research center, told the newspaper that only 1.5 percent of people interviewed in September had faith in the future. She said people were also worried about chaos in the country, about the dislocation of the economy, and about the increase in crime. Polls carried out on the economic reform program proposed by Stanislav Shatalin suggested that, while 36 percent of respondents supported the plan and 12 percent opposed it, up to 52 percent said they did not know enough about it to express an opinion. The poll showed that confidence in the government of Nikolai Ryzhkov had slipped to 14 percent.

South Korea Opens Embassy in Moscow

South Korea officially opened its embassy in the Soviet Union, a month after Moscow and Seoul had established full diplomatic relations. The South Korean Foreign Ministry said Gong Ro-Myung, former head of the South Korean consular department in Moscow, had been appointed ambassador.

KGB Denies Involvement in Illegal Financial Moves

The KGB denied any involvement in illegal financial transactions of the former East German Socialist Unity Party (SED). The denial came after an admission by the SED—renamed the Party for Democratic Socialism—that two high-ranking Communist officials had secretly transferred 107 million marks to the Soviet Union without the party's knowledge or permission. Reports said the officials were trying to anticipate expropriation of party assets after German unification (*TASS*, October 30).

Senior Police Official Murdered in Erevan

A senior police official was reported to have been killed during a shootout with gunmen in the Armenian capital, Erevan. The Soviet media identified the official as MVD Lieutenant Colonel Andreyasan (*TASS*, *Radio Moscow*, October 30).

More Food Rationing Introduced in Chelyabinsk

The authorities in Chelyabinsk have decided to ration food further and distribute it only to local citizens beginning November 1. Radio Moscow said rationing would apply to such goods as meat, eggs, cooking oil, cereals and flour, tobacco products, and vodka and wine. The radio said the rationing would not be likely to alleviate supply problems in Chelyabinsk.

USSR and Czechoslovakia Conclude New Oil Deal

Czechoslovakia and the Soviet Union concluded a new deal for deliveries of Soviet oil to Czechoslovakia in 1991.

The prime ministers of the USSR and Czechoslovakia—Nikolai Ryzhkov and Marian Calfa—signed an agreement in Moscow that called for the Soviet Union to deliver 13 million tons of oil to Czechoslovakia in 1991. That is about 20 percent less than the figure outlined in the old agreement. TASS said Czechoslovakia would pay for the oil with "oil equipment," consumer goods, and hard currency.

Monument to Victims of Totalitarianism Unveiled in Moscow

Thousands of people gathered in central Moscow to dedicate a monument to "the victims of totalitarianism." The monument is located near the Lubyanka prison and the headquarters of the KGB. It consists of a large piece of rock taken from the Solovetsky Islands, where the Soviet prison camp system was founded in the 1920s. Hundreds of people took part in a march to the unveiling ceremonies. The march was led by a priest and people carrying icons. Some of those marching wore prison numbers or carried signs bearing the names of Soviet prison camps. The ceremonies were addressed by Deputy Chairman of the Moscow City Soviet Sergei Stankevich and people's deputy Yurii Afanas'ev, among others (*Central Television*, "Vremya," October 30).

Lithuanian Supreme Council Urges Youths to Avoid Draft

The Lithuanian Supreme Council said Lithuanians were not required to—and should not—serve in the army of a foreign country. A resolution passed by the Supreme Council stated that most Lithuanian youths had not responded to the Soviet spring conscription drive and would probably ignore the fall drive. It said that, while the Lithuanian government did not forbid Lithuanian youths to join the Soviet army, it encouraged them not to do so (RFE Lithuanian service, October 30).

Sobchak Sees Leningrad Economic Zone as Test Case for Nation

At a news conference in Washington, Chairman of the Leningrad City Soviet Anatolii Sobchak said the creation of a free-enterprise economic zone in Leningrad would be the fastest way for the city to move to a free market system. He said such a zone could be "a sort of test case for the rest of the country." He said the Leningrad government's aim in this experiment "is to have a moral, economic, and cultural rebirth" of Leningrad-Petersburg as the spiritual center of Russia and as the center of scientific and technological progress. Sobchak was in Washington to meet US Secretary of State James Baker and other leading US officials as well as US businessmen (*RFE/RL Special*, October 30).

Wednesday, October 31

RSFSR Begins 500-Day Program

The RSFSR parliament began a 500-day economic reform program by approving overwhelmingly a law that transfered control of most resources and property from the USSR to the RSFSR. The law was designed to give a legal basis to the RSFSR's declaration of sovereignty that the parliament adopted in June. The declaration proclaimed the republic's right to ownership of its resources (*Reuters*, *TASS*, October 31).

Lawmakers Announce Symbolic Trial of Communist Party

Two Soviet officials said they planned to hold a symbolic public trial of the Communist Party in the hope of exposing abuses and spurring changes in Party operations. Lev Balashev, a member of the Moscow City Soviet, and Stepan Sulakshin, a member of the USSR Congress of People's Deputies, were quoted as saying they wanted the trial to address criticism of the Party in "a civilized manner" (*AP*, October 31).

USSR and Romania Initial Agreement on Visa-Free Travel

Romania and the Soviet Union were reported to have reached agreement in principle on a document that would end the visa requirement that now exists for travel between the two countries. TASS said the agreement was expected to be signed before the end of November and would go into effect thirty days later.

Soviet Army Says War Graves Desecrated in Hungary

The Soviet army complained that graves of its soldiers killed during World War II were being desecrated in parts of Hungary. Officers showed journalists' photographs of broken graves and pulled-down headstones at military cemeteries. Almost 150,000 Red Army troops died during the liberation of Hungary from Nazi occupation, and their bodies are interred at 1,000 cemeteries around the country. Soviet officers, speaking at the main military garrison in Budapest, said the worst-affected graves were in areas where Soviet forces had already left or were preparing to depart (*Reuters*, October 31).

Ukraine Approves Coupon Plan

The Ukrainian Supreme Soviet has decided to go ahead with an interim step on the way to introducing a separate currency in the republic. The Ukrainian parliament today approved implementation of a plan that would pay Ukrainians 70 percent of their salaries in coupons. Reports said most food and consumer goods sold in state stores would be available only for coupons or for a mixture of coupons and rubles. Ukrainian acting Prime Minister Vitol'd Fokin said the coupons system was only a temporary measure until a separate Ukrainian currency is created (*TASS*, October 31).

The Month of November

Thursday, November 1

Situation in Moldavia

On November 1, Stepan Topal, chairman of the Supreme Soviet of the would-be Gagauz Republic, said the withdrawal of Moldavian volunteers from the Gagauz region had created a favorable atmosphere for negotiations (*TASS*, November 1). The same day, the Moldavian Supreme Soviet said it would debate the situation in the Gagauz area in closed session. The Moldavian Popular Front called on the parliament to demand the immediate withdrawal of MVD troops and KGB forces from Moldavia and to ask the United Nations to send peace-keeping troops to Moldavia. It also called on Romania to take unspecified "firmer actions" to support Moldavia (RFE Romanian Research, November 1).

On November 2, Moldavian police clashed with "an internationalist detachment" of Russian workers that had taken control of the town of Dubasari on the left bank of the Dniester (*TASS*, November 2). The police had been ordered to recapture government buildings and bridges seized by the Russian workers, who had arrived from Tiraspol and Rybnitsa the preceding day. It was the first major clash since the outbreak of interethnic strife in Moldavia. Kishinev put the casualty toll at three dead and sixteen injured. The Moldavian parliament and the USSR Prosecutor's Office both launched investigations.

Hours after the clash, the Moldavian police withdrew from Dubasari to the right bank of the Dniester, leaving the Russian detachment in control. The Dubasari district, whose population is overwhelmingly Moldavian, was Kishinev's last stronghold on the left bank. The authorities of the would-be Dniester SSR were in control of the other four districts on the left bank. Much of the left bank was thus rendered practically out of bounds for Kishinev, as were the Gagauz-inhabited districts in the south of the republic.

On November 2, USSR President Mikhail Gorbachev received a Moldavian Communist Party delegation headed by First Secretary Petru Lucinschi, who pleaded for Moldavia's territorial integrity and condemned the secession movements, the Moldavian media reported. On November 3, Gorbachev, USSR Prime Minister Nikolai Ryzhkov, Chairman of the USSR Supreme Soviet Anatolii

Luk'yanov, and members of the Presidential Council conferred in Moscow with delegations from Moldavia headed by President Mircea Snegur and the would-be leaders of the Gagauz SSR and Dniester SSR, Stepan Topal and Igor Smirnov. In statements on Central Television on November 2 and 3, Gorbachev and Ryzhkov outlined a compromise based on observance of Moldavia's territorial integrity "as part of the USSR," resistance to "all types of secessionism," the immediate dissolution of all paramilitary detachments in all parts of the republic, a mutual suspension of both the Gagauz and left-bank secession proclamations and of Kishinev's decisions to invalidate them, and the creation of a republican parliamentary commission for reconciliation consisting of deputies from all ethnic groups.

In an address to Moldavian television viewers on November 4, Snegur said he had opposed the Soviet leaders' proposal to send USSR MVD troops to the left bank of the Dniester. The previous day, the Moldavian government of Mircea Druc had also rejected the proposal, a move that was endorsed by the Moldavian Supreme Soviet. (Meanwhile, the central press repeated Topal's and Smirnov's attacks on Druc. Both leaders had demanded Druc's resignation.) Intervention nonetheless appeared imminent: the commander in chief of USSR MVD troops, Colonel General Yurii Shatalin, told "Vremya" on November 3 that troops were ready to be sent in "in the next few hours." At the same time, the Soviet media publicized urgent demands from representatives of the population on the left bank that troops be sent.

On November 4, TASS reported that the RSFSR Supreme Soviet had sent a delegation to Moldavia to analyze the situation there. The agency said Boris El'tsin had sent the delegation in response to an appeal by representatives of the Russian-speaking population of Moldavia. On November 7, TASS quoted a member of the delegation, former political prisoner Sergei Kovalev, as saying the Russian deputies would not interfere in Moldavia's internal affairs. He said they would try to understand the situation, to advise, and to see how Russians and other citizens were getting along.

On November 4, thousands of people demonstrated in the Romanian capital, Bucharest, calling for reunification with Moldavia (*Reuters*, November 4). At a late-night session, the Moldavian Supreme Soviet adopted the compromise solution agreed to by Gorbachev, Snegur, and Russian and Gagauz leaders in Moscow on November 3. Snegur and First Deputy Chairman of the Moldavian Supreme Soviet Ion Hadirca told the session that they had narrowly avoided the dispatch of USSR MVD troops to the left bank of the Dniester and that they had been warned that any further ethnic unrest would lead to the sending of troops and the imposition of a state of emergency throughout the republic. Snegur and Hadirca disclosed that Gorbachev and Ryzhkov had confronted Kishinev with additional demands, including changes in personnel policy in favor of non-Moldavians, the rescindment of some provisions in legislation on language passed in 1989, and adherence by Kishinev to the concept of "a union of states" as opposed to that of "a confederation of sovereign states," which Kishinev has sought in the negotiations on a new Union treaty. TASS and Western agencies said the Moldavian parliament had passed a resolution urging Moldavian, Russian, Ukrainian, and Gagauz volunteer units to disband within two hours. The reports said the parliament would create a commission of accord made up of representatives of the Moldavian government and the Gagauz and Dniester regions to discuss the republic's future.

On November 6, TASS carried several reports saying that the Moscow decisions of November 3, though accepted by the Moldavian Supreme Soviet, were not being implemented on the left bank of the Dniester. Local Russian leaders who had proclaimed secession from Moldavia were reported to be continuing the electoral campaign for a Supreme Soviet of "a Dniester SSR." The Russian workers' detachments created by local enterprises of all-Union subordination were not being disbanded, and roadblocks and checkpoints impeding access from the right to the left bank were not being removed. On November 5, however, TASS reported that the Moldavian volunteer detachments had been disbanded.

On November 6, TASS reported that thousands of people had gathered in Dubasari on the left bank of the Dniester to bury and honor three men killed in clashes with the Moldavian police on November 2.

On November 8, the Moldavian Popular Front appealed for calm in the republic (RFE Romanian service, November 8).

On November 10, the Moldavian Communist Party Central Committee ended a plenum in Kishinev. Interviewed by TASS, several participants—all with Russian names—said that the plenum had once again demonstrated that "the Moldavian Party can do nothing to help" and that "scarcely anyone listens to the opinion of Communists in Moldavia nowadays."

In a telephone interview with RFE/RL, a member of the Moldavian government's special committee appointed to administer the state of emergency in Gagauz-inhabited areas said the situation there was one of "dual power."

The special committee, which was operating out of the police headquarters of the three raions affected, had authority only in Moldavian and other non-Gagauz localities. In the Gagauz localities, however, power was being exercised by the self-proclaimed Gagauz government. In a news conference reported by the Soviet media on November 11, Moldavian Minister of Internal Affairs Ion Costas repeated the accusation that the USSR MVD troops deployed in the area were deliberately failing to fulfill their mandate to enforce the state of emergency.

On November 11, a delegation from the RSFSR Supreme Soviet left Kishinev after spending a week in Moldavia investigating conditions in the republic. It had met the previous day with Snegur. TASS said they had agreed that existing problems should be resolved legally and that the republic should remain whole.

On November 13, Lucinschi, who was chairman of the Moldavian conciliation commission, presented to the Moldavian Supreme Soviet a package of measures to normalize the situation in the republic. As summarized by TASS, the proposals included the creation of a Gagauz "administrative-territorial formation," the creation of a government department for national "minority" affairs, proportional representation of "minorities" in the republican government, Moldavia's return to the negotiations on a Union treaty, and official disavowal by the Moldavian leadership of any intent to join Moldavia to Romania.

On November 14, the Moldavian Supreme Soviet appealed to the USSR Supreme Soviet to help prevent the formation of the would-be Dniester SSR in eastern Moldavia. Adopted at the suggestion of writer Ion Drutse, the document said such a development could set a dangerous precedent for all Union republics (*TASS*, November 14). The same day, a delegation of the Moldavian Supreme Soviet flew to Moscow to hand over the document to the USSR Supreme Soviet and to convey a formal invitation to Gorbachev to visit Moldavia as soon as possible. The invitation, couched in flattering terms, was adopted by the same session of the Moldavian Supreme Soviet.

The same session of the Moldavian Supreme Soviet also adopted a package of measures designed to reassure non-Moldavians. The package suspended Kishinev's earlier decision to invalidate the formation of a Gagauz territorial-administrative unit within Moldavia (the wording allowed for the creation of a "national raion"-type unit), created a department of the Moldavian government on nationality relations, instructed state institutions that the republic's ethnic composition should be reflected in their hiring policy, created a commission to monitor the implementation of language laws with a view to ensuring that the rights of non-Moldavians be observed, and instructed the Supreme Soviet Presidium to draft a special law on the rights of ethnic groups. In a separate resolution, addressed to the people of the republic, the Supreme Soviet declined all responsibility for "rumors" that Moldavia was preparing to rejoin Romania (*TASS*, November 14).

On November 16, the Moldavian Supreme Soviet rejected a proposal to declare a state of emergency in Kishinev following disturbances there on November 15 (*TASS*, November 16). (Two ethnic Russian parliamentary deputies were beaten up during the violence.)

On November 18, following the Moldavian Supreme Soviet's decision on "Urgent Measures to Achieve Civil Accord," the Moldavian government established a State Department for Nationality Affairs. The department, whose head must by statute be non-Moldavian, was empowered to represent the interests of non-Moldavian ethnic groups in the government and to monitor the observance of those groups' rights. A law "On the Defense of the Rights of National Minorities" and related acts are being drafted urgently, Moldovapres reported.

On November 19, Marshal Sergei Akhromeev came to Moldavia to mediate the interethnic disputes there. TASS said Akhromeev held talks with Moldavian leaders.

On November 21, Moldavian President Mircea Snegur called for a boycott of the elections called by the self-proclaimed "Dniester Republic." In an appeal on television, Snegur said the elections jeopardized Moldavia's sovereignty and territorial integrity. The same day, the Moldavian CP first secretary, Petru Lucinschi, called for "a moratorium" on the elections to be declared (*TASS*, November 21).

Elections to the legislature of the self-proclaimed Dniester SSR were conducted between November 21 and 25 on the left bank of the Dniester River under the supervision of local Russian officials, who were backing the move for separation from Moldavia. According to TASS and Moldovapres dispatches of November 23 and 24, the elections were conducted under a state of emergency, declared unilaterally in the main towns, that restricted access to the area, mobilized the Russian "workers' detachments," and forbade authorities of "another republic"—meaning Moldavia—to enter. Moldavian sources in the area told RFE/RL by telephone that the local Moldavian population followed Kishinev's call to boycott the elections en masse and that some ethnically Ukrainian villages also refused to take part.

On November 27, the Moldavian Supreme Soviet declared the elections null and void. Information presented to the Moldavian Supreme Soviet purported to show that the elections had been rigged, TASS reported. Moldovapres reported that elections in most constituencies had not been contested, that most candidates had been nominated by the local organization of the Communist Party, that there were no independent observers of the balloting, and that the local Moldavian population had followed Kishinev's call to boycott the elections.

On November 30, TASS announced that the visit to Kishinev Mikhail Gorbachev had planned for that day was being canceled. Reuters and AFP, citing Gorbachev's presidential office, initially blamed bad weather, but Snegur gave the republican Supreme Soviet more substantial reasons for the cancellation. On the basis of his account of a telephone conversation with Gorbachev, Snegur said the Soviet president had decided to postpone his visit when it transpired that the deputies from the left bank of the Dniester River had refused an invitation to attend the Moldavian Supreme Soviet session at which Gorbachev was to speak. Gorbachev reportedly said he would visit the republic when the situation became more clear there (*Reuters*, November 30).

Monthly Record Set for Soviet Jewish Emigration

An American Jewish group said Jews emigrated from the Soviet Union in record numbers in October. Statistics compiled by the New York–based National Conference on Soviet Jewry showed that 20,500 Jews had left the USSR in October, with the great majority of them settling in Israel (*RFE/RL Special*, November 1).

Czechoslovakia and Lithuania to Set Up Diplomatic Missions

Czechoslovakia and Lithuania agreed to set up diplomatic missions in each other's capitals. The official Czechoslovak news agency said the agreement had been reached in talks between Czechoslovak Deputy Foreign Minister Robert Harencar and Lithuanian Deputy Foreign Minister Ramustas Grizas (*Reuters*, November 1).

Six Killed in Blast at Chemical Plant

An explosion at a chemical plant in the Urals killed fifteen people and injured twenty-two others. TASS said the explosion tore through an experimental workshop at the end of a shift. The plant, located near the town of Asbest, produces explosives for the mining industry. On November 5, Boris El'tsin visited the plant and talked to members of the commission investigating the accident.

Soviet Doctor Says 500,000 Affected by Semipalatinsk Tests

A Soviet doctor said atmospheric nuclear tests at Semipalatinsk in Kazakhstan between 1949 and 1963 had affected half a million people. Professor Maira Zhangelova told an antinuclear congress of Swedish doctors that one-third of the children born since the tests began were deformed. She also said there had been a major increase in the incidence of cancer, leukemia, and immune deficiency–related diseases. Zhangelova said details of the medical effects of the tests had been secret until 1989. She explained that she was studying the effects of radiation on the basis of documents to be published in the next few months (*AFP*, November 1).

On November 13, the head of the USSR's Radiology Research Institute, Boris Gusev, told journalists in Hiroshima that half a million people had been affected by radiation from the Semipalatinsk nuclear weapons testing site and that 100,000 of them had died of radiation-induced cancers (*AFP*, November 13). The people affected live within a 550-kilometer radius of the testing site, according to Gusev.

Students Stage Hunger Strike outside Kremlin

About forty Moscow students staged what they called a warning hunger strike outside the Kremlin. They demanded the resignation of the Soviet government and the seizure of Communist Party property. Earlier in the day, Gorbachev and Prime Minister Nikolai Ryzhkov met student leaders for talks that TASS described as "sometimes rather sharp." In an interview with *Moskovsky komsomolets*, Ryzhkov said he would stay on as prime minister despite strong criticism of his government over economic policy (*TASS*, *Reuters*, November 1).

Fifth Reactor Phased Out in Chelyabinsk Chemical Plant

Reports said the fifth reactor at the "Mayak" chemical plant in Chelyabinsk was to be shut down today. Radio Moscow said the reactor had been used to produce plutonium for military purposes. The "Mayak" plant produced the first Soviet atom bomb and was for a long time a top-secret site. The radio said the ceremony shutting down the reactor would be open to journalists.

General Dismisses Reports of Desertions

A Soviet army general dismissed as ridiculous Western news reports about hundreds of desertions and sales of large quantities of weapons by soldiers serving in Eastern Europe. Major General Kozlov, a member of the military council of the forces based in Eastern Europe, told TASS the army was aware of only fifteen cases of soldiers' deserting to the West. German officials have said hundreds of Soviet soldiers are seeking asylum in Germany.

Gorbachev Meets with Soldiers' Parents

Mikhail Gorbachev met for over three hours with the parents of Soviet soldiers who have died while serving in the Soviet army in peacetime. According to RFE/RL sources in Moscow, the meeting was filmed by a television crew from "Vremya" but was not broadcast, because it was felt that no one would allow their sons to serve in the Soviet army after seeing the horrifying pictures parents displayed of mistreated conscripts. Gorbachev was said to have agreed to all the demands put by the parents, including calls for a declaration of mistrust in both the USSR Prosecutor-General and the USSR Military Prosecutor. The parents also said they did not trust Presidential Council member Veniamin Yarin, who was appointed chairman of a commission set up by the USSR Supreme Soviet to investigate peacetime deaths in the army. The parents said they wanted Yarin to be replaced by Aleksandr Yakovlev, who is also a member of the Presidential Council.

Friday, November 2

Presidential Decree on Hard-Currency Earnings

USSR President Mikhail Gorbachev issued a decree stipulating that 40 percent of all hard-currency export revenues would be used to repay the country's foreign debt in 1991 (*TASS*, November 2; *Pravada*, November 3). The decree allowed enterprises and organizations that exported goods for hard currency to keep a negotiated share of their hard-currency revenues but ruled that they must sell the rest to the state for rubles at the new commercial rate. It said 90 percent of the hard-currency revenues would go into a special national hard-currency fund and 10 percent would be deposited in the hard-currency funds of republican and local governments. A committee including representatives from each Union republic would decide how the national fund was used (*Reuters*, October 30).

RSFSR Signs Foreign-Trade Agreement

The RSFSR and Malta signed a five-year trade accord and concluded a contract to deliver 60,000 tons of coal to Malta in return for deliveries of consumer goods to the RSFSR's coal-mining regions (*Reuters*, November 4). The deal involved coal produced in Kemerovo in excess of its annual quota. RSFSR Minister of Foreign Economic Relations Viktor Yaroshenko also reported that the republican government would abide by all trade agreements reached by the center.

Hungary Tells USSR of Strains in Ties

The chairman of the Foreign Affairs Committee of the Hungarian Parliament, Gyula Horn, told the Soviet Union that its failure to honor commitments was straining bilateral relations. His comments came in a letter to the chairman of the Foreign Affairs Committee of the USSR Supreme Soviet, Aleksandr Dzasokhov. Horn's letter was released on November 2 by the Hungarian government. Horn stressed Hungary's efforts to achieve harmonious relations with the USSR but lamented "the huge damage" caused to the "already crisis-ridden" Hungarian economy by the Soviet "habit of tearing up contracts" and its failure to deliver oil, electricity, and raw materials as agreed (*Radio Budapest*, November 2).

On October 30, the Soviet Union had told Hungary it would no longer accept rubles as payment for oil deliveries as of December 1. Officials at Hungary's National Oil and Gas Trust said Soviet oil would be available only for hard currency. They said the Soviet Union had also changed the conditions for November and was offering Hungary only 143,000 tons of oil for rubles—if Hungary wanted the remaining 200,000 tons it must pay for it in barter with Western goods (*Radio Budapest*, October 30).

***Trud* Gives Statistics on Literacy**

According to *Trud*, there are 4.3 million illiterate people in the USSR. The percentage of those who cannot read or write is highest in Moldavia. The lowest percentages are in Estonia and Latvia.

Saturday, November 3

The Soviet Union and the Gulf Crisis

Speaking on Soviet television's "Mezhdunarodnaya panorama" show on November 3, Presidential Council member Evgenii Primakov noted that Iraq and its neighbors both had legitimate concerns. On the one hand, he said, Iraq must withdraw from Kuwait unrewarded for its aggression; but, on the other hand, he added, it is also "a must" that Saddam Hussein be given an opportunity to save face.

On November 5, Georgii Arbatov, Director of the United States and Canada Institute, denied that there were "conflicts or rifts" between the Soviet and US positions on the Gulf crisis. At the same time, during an interview with

NBC television, Arbatov stressed that the Soviet Union would agree to the use of force only in the event of a UN resolution's calling for such force. Arbatov pointed out that any UN resolution on the Gulf would require Soviet acquiescence.

On November 8, US Secretary of State James Baker arrived in Moscow together with senior US officials from the arms negotiations in Vienna. Baker held talks with Soviet Foreign Minister Eduard Shevardnadze in which the situation in the Gulf was the main issue. TASS quoted Shevardnadze as saying that using force in the Gulf was undesirable and that priority should be given to enforcing UN economic sanctions against Iraq.

On November 15, two Soviet envoys—Deputy Foreign Ministers Vladimir Petrovsky and Aleksandr Belonogov—began a tour of Arab states aimed at finding an end to the Gulf crisis. While Petrovsky held talks with Tunisian President Zine El Abidine Ben Ali and PLO leader Yasser Arafat before flying on to Libya, Belonogov visited Egypt and Syria. Petrovsky concluded his visit to Tunisia saying that the Arab states should plan to take an active role in securing a peaceful resolution to the Gulf crisis.

Speaking at a news conference in Paris on November 21 while attending the CSCE summit, Gorbachev said the UN Security Council should meet without delay to decide what to do about the Gulf crisis (*Reuters*, November 21). Interviewed the same day by Soviet and French television, Gorbachev said Iraqi President Saddam Hussein should not be allowed "to bring the whole of the world community to its knees." A parallel meeting between the US and Soviet foreign ministers, James Baker and Eduard Shevardnadze, produced a statement of Soviet support for new action by the United Nations Security Council against Iraq. Neither Baker nor Shevardnadze said specifically that a new resolution should permit the use of force (Western agencies, November 20).

Speaking before the USSR Supreme Soviet on November 26, Mikhail Gorbachev said: "Aggression is impermissible. It should be punished." The statement marked a shift from Gorbachev's previous formulation that Iraq should "not be rewarded" for its aggression. Gorbachev and Eduard Shevardnadze later met with Iraqi Foreign Minister Tariq Aziz in the Kremlin. According to TASS, Gorbachev told Aziz Iraq must show its willingness to resolve the situation by leaving Kuwait and releasing the hostages. Gorbachev warned that otherwise "a tough resolution" would be adopted by the UN. Afterwards, Soviet Foreign Ministry spokesman Vitalii Churkin described Iraq's preventing the departure of Soviet citizens as "totally abnormal and unacceptable."

Yurii Blokhin, a member of the "Soyuz" group of parliamentary deputies, said the same day that the USSR Supreme Soviet would not back the dispatch of Soviet troops to the Gulf, Reuters reported on November 27. Blokhin went on to say that the USSR Supreme Soviet would insist on a parliamentary debate before the USSR voted on a UN Security Council resolution authorizing the use of force against Iraq.

On November 29, the Soviet Union joined the United States in sponsoring the UN Security Council resolution to authorize the use of force to get Iraq out of Kuwait. The resolution gave Iraq until January 15 to withdraw, after which date members of the UN would be authorized to use "all necessary means" (Western agencies, November 29). See RL 487/90.

Law on Political Parties in Action

The first official announcement, at least at the all-Union level, of the election of a member of a political party other than the CPSU was published in *Izvestia*. Georgii Petruk-Popik, a secretary of the Ternopol writers' organization and a member of the Ukrainian Democratic Party, was reported to have been registered as a USSR people's deputy by the Central Electoral Commission. Previously, official information on a deputy's political affiliation was limited to "a member of the CPSU" or "a non-Party member."

Central Coordinating Council of "Intermovements" Created

A conference of "Intermovements" held on November 2 issued a statement on forming a Central Coordinating Council of "Intermovements" of the USSR, *Sovetskaya Rossiya* reported on November 3 and 6. The conference, which was attended by representatives from the Baltic republics, Moldavia, Western Ukraine, and the Central Asian republics, as well as by USSR deputies belonging to the "Soyuz" parliamentary group, expressed concern about the lack of legal protection for ethnic minorities in the republics and criticized the president and the USSR Supreme Soviet on this account. The participants strongly denied, however, that leaders of "Intermovements" had called at a press conference for the removal of Gorbachev and El'tsin.

Shevardnadze Meets USIA Chief

Soviet Foreign Minister Eduard Shevardnadze met in Moscow with the chairman of the US Information Agency, Bruce Gelb. Gelb was leading a US delegation at the fourth US-Soviet meeting on information and cultural cooperation. TASS said Shevardnadze and Gelb had discussed deepening and developing cooperation in information and cultural contacts between the United States and the USSR.

USSR and North Korea Sign New Trade Payment Treaty

The Soviet Union and North Korea signed an agreement that based future trade on payment in hard currency. TASS said the agreement, which was to take effect in January, 1991, had been signed after negotiations in Moscow. The USSR said it intended to replace all its former international trade agreements with agreements calling for hard-currency payments.

Ukrainian Parliament Approves Plan for Independence

The Ukrainian Supreme Soviet approved a plan for Ukraine's "complete economic and political independence," TASS reported. Acting Chairman of the republican Council of Ministers Vitol'd Fokin (the parliament has been unable to agree upon a replacement for Vitalii Masol, who resigned in the wake of mass student protests in October) said the plan would lead to the privatization of property, the denationalization of thousands of enterprises, market-based consumer prices, and a Ukrainian currency. Ukraine would also seek separate membership in the IMF and other international agencies. Fokin indicated further that "profound constitutional changes" lay ahead.

More Revelations by Oleg Kalugin

The number of MVD troops today is close to 500,000, according to former KGB General Oleg Kalugin, writing in *Vechernyaya Moskva* on November 3. There are more policemen in Moscow and Leningrad than in all of Italy, a country with "a complicated criminal environment," Kalugin noted. The exact number of KGB personnel remains a state secret, Kalugin said, but it greatly exceeds the prewar staff of the NKVD. The publication of Kalugin's article coincided with the appearance of his book, *The View from the Lubyanka.*

In an article published in *Leningradskaya pravda* on October 21, Kalugin said that what was called the Left, or the democratic movement, in the USSR was to a significant degree under the control and, in some ways, under the "guidance" of the KGB organs. Kalugin maintained that many prominent leaders of "the democratic camp" were, for many years, KGB informers; for ethical reasons he refused to reveal their names. Should they continue to attempt to disrupt the democratic process, however, Kalugin said he would consider it his "civic duty" to reveal their names.

Sunday, November 4

New Youth Organization in RSFSR

A new political youth organization, the Association of Democratic Youth of Russia, was reported to have been set up in the RSFSR. According to Radio Moscow, four youth groups adhering to the platform of the "Democratic Russia" movement participated in the creation of the new association. The formation of the new group came at a time when the republican Komsomol was also attempting to transform itself into a democratic youth association.

Warsaw Pact Agreement Reached

Warsaw Pact officials meeting in Budapest over the weekend signed an agreement concerning the division of conventional forces to be retained in Europe by member countries. The agreement, which defined the number of tanks, artillery, armored vehicles, combat aircraft, and combat helicopters to be allocated to each country, allowed the Soviet Union to keep the most in each category. At a news conference on November 4, the Hungarian and Romanian foreign ministers said that the Warsaw Pact had no future either as a military or as a political alliance (*RFE/RL Special*, November 3).

Leading Economists Say Transition Period Will Be Painful

A group of Soviet economists said the USSR Supreme Soviet's failure to adopt a radical economic reform plan meant that economic recovery would be much more painful. The economists included Stanislav Shatalin and Nikolai Petrakov, senior economic advisers to Mikhail Gorbachev. In a letter published in *Komsomol'skaya pravda*, the economists said government plans for price rises accompanied by monetary compensation would lead to hyperinflation. They said the worsening economic situation meant that a steep decline in living standards was inevitable.

On November 5, Deputy Prime Minister of the RSFSR Gennadii Fil'shin also criticized Gorbachev over the economy. He said Gorbachev's economic decrees were bad for the Russian republic. In an interview with *Der Spiegel*, Fil'shin said that what the country needed was a real law on investment, not inconsequential orders from above that excluded important facts such as motivation and protection for foreign investors. Fil'shin said that the Russian republic would pass its own law on investment but that such a law would continue to be blocked at the all-Union level for ideological reasons.

Tensions in Kazakhstan Described

An article in *Moscow News* (No. 44) said that the primary cause of tension in Kazakhstan was the question of whether the Kazakhs should have greater rights than other nationalities in the republic. The author, Ol'ga Bychkova, argued that the recently adopted declaration of republican sovereignty had tried to paper over the divisions between ethnic groups and that the level of tension remained high. She said a balance was maintained only by the rough parity between Kazakhs and Russians in the republic's population and by the limited effect of extremist ideas. Bychkova called for a willingness on the part of both nationalities to find agreement and avoid a possible outbreak of violence.

On November 6, a council of civic accord was reported to have been set up in Alma-Ata. The council included representatives of various political parties and civic and youth groups, as well as of the national cultural centers (*TASS*, November 6).

Lithuanian Official Terms Economic Talks with Moscow "a Fiasco"

Lithuanian Minister for Material Resources Romualdas Kosyrovicius said recent discussions with Moscow on the economic plan for 1991 had been "a complete fiasco." Kosyrovicius told journalists in Vilnius that Moscow's attitude in last week's talks at expert level had been such that he saw little chance of agreement. Radio Vilnius quoted Kosyrovicius as saying that Soviet economic bodies had refused to sign a purchase and sales agreement with Lithuania. He compared these developments to the economic blockade imposed by Moscow against Lithuania earlier in 1990.

Convent Reopened in Central Russia

TASS reported that the Akatov-Alekseev convent near Voronezh had been returned to the Russian Orthodox Church. The convent, built in the seventeenth century, is under restoration and will become a center for Church charitable activities: the nuns help the sick, lonely, and poor.

On November 4, Patriarch Aleksii blessed the cornerstone for a cathedral to be built on the site of the Cathedral of our Lady of Kazan, which was destroyed in the 1930s under Stalin, TASS reported. Thousands of people attended the ceremony.

Famine Victims Commemorated in Ukraine

A day commemorating the victims of the 1932–33 famine was observed in many places in Ukraine. The first Sunday in November was declared an official holiday this year by the authorities in Lvov Oblast. Radio Kiev did not say whether commemorative rallies and church services were held republic-wide. Radio Kiev said it was now officially acknowledged that the famine had been caused deliberately by Stalin's policies.

Battle over Ivan Polozkov's Flat in Moscow

CPSU officials were reported to be continuing to put pressure on the Moscow City Soviet to provide special housing for Russian Communist Party First Secretary Ivan Polozkov. According to *Moscow News* (No. 44), the latest letter to Moscow Mayor Gavriil Popov was signed by Nikolai Kruchina, the administrator of affairs of the CPSU Central Committee. Kruchina urged the city soviet to give Polozkov a permit to live in the apartment originally chosen for him, albeit at that time in his capacity as a member of the CPSU Politburo, not as the first secretary of the RSFSR Communist Party. The apartment in question, the weekly reported, consists of eighty square meters of living space, far more than his family of four is entitled to. Radio Moscow reported on November 6, however, that the Moscow City Soviet had again refused to issue a residence permit to Polozkov. The radio said it was the first time such action had ever been taken against a Politburo member, and it called it "a sensation."

***Pravda* Attacks Yakovlev, Defends Stalin**

Pravda published an interview in which two senior officials claimed that neither Stalin nor the People's Commissariat of Internal Affairs had played any part in the assassination in 1934 of Leningrad Party chief Sergei Kirov. One of those interviewed, a KGB colonel, went so far as to allege that Aleksandr Yakovlev (chairman of the Politburo commission investigating Stalin's crimes) had used the same methods as those who covered up crimes under Khrushchev and Brezhnev. Yakovlev told a meeting of reformist Communists during the CPSU Congress in July that he disagreed with the KGB's assertion of Stalin's innocence, and the Party Congress recommended that his speech be published in *Pravda* (*Central Television*, July 13). For some reason, however, the newspaper of the CPSU Central Committee ignored the order.

Soviet Section of Fourth International to Be Set Up

A seminar was held in Moscow on November 3 and 4 by the "Committee for the Creation of the Soviet Section of the Fourth International," Novosti reported on November 5. The committee includes the Leningrad Trotskyist organization, the Union of Left Socialists from Kiev, and the Revolutionary Marxist Group from Novosibirsk. The seminar was also attended by representatives of the

British Communist Party. Novosti said that the participants in the seminar (nine people) had agreed to set up a coalition in the Soviet Union of ultraleft forces that still adhere to revolutionary Marxism.

Monday, November 5

Crime Rising in USSR

At a press briefing in Moscow, the USSR Ministry of Internal Affairs announced that, in the first nine months of 1990, crime had risen by 12.3 percent over the same period in 1989, TASS reported. Premeditated murder, assault, and rape increased by 26.4 percent. A total of 775 police and MVD troops were killed on active duty between January and September, 1990; 6,799 were injured. The MVD was reported to have asked for a substantial budget increase—from 11 billion rubles in 1990 to 20 billion in 1991, 53 percent of which should come from central state funds and the rest from republican budgets.

On November 11, however, USSR Minister of Internal Affairs Vadim Bakatin pointed out that crime was growing less quickly in 1990 than in 1989. Appearing on the television show "Pravovoi kanal," Bakatin observed that statistics could be manipulated: "One can [state] that the increase in crime this year is one-third as great as last year, but one can also assert that the total number of crimes is ten times as high this year as last year." His deputy had asserted two days earlier that fears were being aroused unnecessarily among the population, and Bakatin admitted that the mass media's coverage of crime was "not always justified."

Iranian Mining Minister in Moscow

Iranian Mines and Metals Minister Mohammad Hosein Mahlujchi met with Soviet Prime Minister Nikolai Ryzhkov to discuss the implementation of economic and political accords agreed to in June, 1989. Ryzhkov and Mahlujchi also discussed border relations, possible solutions to the Gulf crisis, and Soviet-Iranian joint ventures in the metals and mining industries, TASS said.

USSR and South Korea Set Up Direct Telephone Links

The Soviet Union and South Korea opened four direct telephone circuits linking their two countries. Previously, calls were relayed—with little success—via Britain, Italy, or Greece. The South Korean Communications Ministry said calls between the two countries had increased from four in all of 1987 to more than 5,000 per month in 1990, AP reported.

Tuesday, November 6

Goskompechat' on Registration of Periodicals

In an interview with *Argumenty i fakty* (No. 41), the deputy chairman of the USSR State Committee for the Press (Goskompechat'), Aleksandr Gorkovlyuk, explained how his agency had dealt with the registration of the periodicals of political parties during the period between August 1 (when the new law on the press went into effect) and October 9 (when the new law on public associations was adopted). Gorkovlyuk said that, during this period, his agency should, strictly speaking, have refused to register the periodicals of any political party. Gorkovlyuk said his agency had decided, however, to approach the situation realistically: since the CPSU was mentioned in the Soviet constitution, all its periodicals were registered by Goskompechat' as constitutional. The periodicals of other political parties were registered as periodicals founded by private individuals.

The executive committee of the Leningrad City Soviet took a different stand, however. According to *Komsomol'skaya pravda* (November 1), the committee refused to register the Leningrad regional Komsomol newspaper, *Smena*, as well as some of its other periodicals. The reason given for the refusal was that at the time of the application the law on public associations was not in force. Therefore, the executive committee could not register the newspaper, because it was an organ of a political organization that had no legal basis for existence. Although *Smena* was finally registered by the RSFSR Ministry of Mass Media, the Leningrad Komsomol intends to clarify its conflict with the Leningrad executive committee in court.

Turkmen Religious Figure Criticizes Nationalist Agitators

Radio Moscow broadcast an interview with Ishankuli Medzhidov, head of the executive organ of Muslim societies in Turkmenistan, on believers' attitudes towards interethnic violence in the USSR. Medzhidov said that recently several agitators had come to his mosque and, after asking why the Turkmen were lagging behind other nationalities, suggested that they drive the Russians and others out of the republic. Medzhidov said that the council of elders and religious council had told the troublemakers to get out of Turkmenistan. This appeared to be the first indication of this type of agitation in the republic.

Shepherd Recovered Hydrogen Bomb

Sobesednik (No. 44) reported on the results of an inquiry launched by the USSR Ministry of Defense in response to a report issued by the Kazakh antinuclear movement,"Nevada-Semipalatinsk," entitled "On the Loss of a Hydrogen Bomb in 1957 near the Semipalatinsk Nuclear Test Site." An unidentified USSR people's deputy quoted a telephone message from the USSR Ministry of Defense to the local military commandant: "In 1957, in the village of Beketai in the Maisky Raion of Pavlodar Oblast, shepherd B. Kishpaev found a hydrogen bomb that had not exploded."

Uzbek Communists Want Independence from CPSU

The Communist Party of Uzbekistan was reported to be considering new statutes that would give it organizational and political independence from the CPSU. The draft statutes, published in Tashkent on November 6, said the Uzbek Communist Party should be free to work out its own programs and financial and personnel issues. They said the Party's policy should aim to ensure Uzbekistan's political and economic sovereignty (*TASS*, November 6).

Wednesday, November 7

Celebrations of October Revolution Anniversary

Mikhail Gorbachev addressed a specially invited crowd on Red Square on the seventy-third anniversary of the October Revolution. (Gorbachev, Nikolai Ryzhkov, Boris El'tsin, Anatolii Luk'yanov, and other officials took their positions on the viewing stand on top of Lenin's Masoleum. Noticeable for his absence was the Russian Communist Party first secretary, Ivan Polozkov.) In his speech, Gorbachev called on the country not to panic in the face of radical changes. He also acknowledged the failures of the system set up in the USSR as a result of the October Revolution. He insisted, however, that it was "not the fault of those who took part [in the revolution] that the goals they dreamed of were not fulfilled."

A military parade took place on Red Square. Soviet television said the parade was being held not on the instructions of the Defense Ministry but on the orders of the president. The report said its purpose was not to demonstrate the USSR's military might but to continue a tradition dating back to the time of Tsar Peter the Great. The parade was followed by an official demonstration during which a man fired two shots into the air 200 meters away from the mausoleum. Reuters quoted KGB officials later in the day as saying that the man, who was immediately detained, was "probably mad." On November 8, a KGB spokesman, Aleksei Kandaurov, identified the man as Aleksandr Shmonov, an unemployed metal worker from Leningrad. Psychiatric tests were ordered for Shmonov, who is thirty-eight (*TASS*, November 8).

There was also an alternative demonstration in Moscow organized by the leaders of new political movements.

In Kiev, the anniversary was observed with a civilian parade in the middle of the city and a counterdemonstration. The Kiev City Soviet had voted to ban a traditional military parade in the center of the city (RL Ukrainian service, November 7). A small-scale military celebration was authorized on Victory Square.

According to RFE/RL sources in Minsk, veterans and schoolchildren were bused in to the Belorussian capital to take part in the official ceremony, which was confined to speeches and was over quickly. A larger counter-demonstration was attended by an estimated 30,000 people. Participants carried placards saying "Down with the Communist Party of Belorussia," "Down with the KGB," and "Farewell to Communism."

TASS reported that celebrations were held in all the Central Asian republics. The traditional parade in Frunze was joined by a group representing the democratic opposition movement, "Kyrgyzstan," carrying banners calling for an independent democratic state based on the rule of law, freedom of the press, and the separation of Communist Party and state power.

The TASS report indicated that informal groups were allowed to participate in the parade in Alma-Ata but did not name the groups. Parades in other capitals were apparently traditional.

The Armenian Supreme Soviet ruled in October not to hold a military parade but nonetheless declared a public holiday. In Baku, the military commandant also canceled the military parade, citing the state of emergency still in force in the city. The military commandant of Nagorno-Karabakh acted likewise. In Georgia, a parade was held at the military garrison in Tbilisi, but there was no other celebration. Many people reported for work. Georgian television refused to relay coverage of the military parade in Moscow.

In Leningrad, riot police kicked and beat demonstrators who were protesting against the official ceremonies, RFE/RL sources in Leningrad reported. City soviet member Aleksandr Rodin told those present at the counterdemonstration that the October Revolution had established "Communist terror" and that the anniversary should be marked as "a day of mourning." Shortly thereafter, riot police moved in. Rodin and two other members of the city soviet were among those beaten.

No parade of any kind took place in Kishinev and no ceremonies were organized by the Moldavian authorities anywhere in the republic. The Moldavian Supreme Soviet refused to ratify Gorbachev's decree of October on holding military parades in Union republican capitals. Civilian demonstrations and various ceremonies to honor November 7 were staged only by Russian communities in eastern Moldavia and by Gagauz leaders in Komrat. Elsewhere, local Russian groups held low-key ceremonies in front of Soviet monuments or inside Party conference halls. Some Moldavian anti-Communist demonstrations began in Kishinev and elsewhere, but they were stopped by marshals of the Moldavian Popular Front in an effort to avoid an escalation of tensions (*TASS*, RFE Romanian Research, November 7).

In Tallinn, a military parade was held against the wishes of the Estonian parliament. TASS said there were no serious incidents during the parade. In Vilnius, a military parade was thrown off course by two men who lay down in the street in front of approaching vehicles (*DPA*, November 7).

Soviet ICBM Unveiled

The Soviet Armed Forces publicly displayed their new SS-25 mobile intercontinental ballistic missile for the first time during the November 7 parade in Moscow, Reuters reported. The appearance of twelve SS-25's marked a reversal of Soviet policy of recent years, during which ICBMs were not included in the military parade. According to the Pentagon's *Soviet Military Power* for 1990, the missile has a range of 6,500 miles and carries a single nuclear warhead. It was first deployed in early 1985, and, as of September, 270 were in service.

Ukraine Wants Participation in Conference on Security and Cooperation

The TASS correspondent at the UN reported that Ukraine had asked to be made an equal participant in the Conference on Security and Cooperation in Europe. The request came in the form of a letter from Ukrainian Foreign Affairs Minister Anatol Zlenko to his French counterpart, Roland Dumas. Ukraine's envoy to the UN, Gennadii Udovenko, said he had emphasized to UN officials that, although his country had discussed its request with the USSR Ministry of Foreign Affairs, the latter had no right to dictate its wishes to a sovereign Ukraine.

Solzhenitsyn's Dictionary Published in USSR

The main publishing house of the USSR Academy of Sciences, "Nauka," has published Aleksandr Solzhenitsyn's

Dictionary for the Enrichment of the Russian Language. The dictionary contains many dialectal as well as old Russian words and phrases that are no longer used but that Solzhenitsyn thinks should be returned to the Russian language (*TASS*, November 7).

New Attack on *Pravda*'s Chief Editor

The chief editor of *Pravda*, Ivan Frolov, was attacked again, this time by the editorial staff of the journal *Rodina*. In issue No. 5, the journal's "editorial collective" said that, after being named chief editor of *Pravda* in October, 1989, Frolov had immediately started a campaign to close *Rodina*, which at the time was a subsidiary publication of *Pravda*. Frolov accused the journal of being anti-Soviet, anti-Leninist, promonarchist, and "Zionist." *Rodina* was saved by the RSFSR Ministry of Mass Media, headed by Mikhail Poltoranin, who helped the journal free itself from the supervision of *Pravda* and registered *Rodina* as an organ of the RSFSR Supreme Soviet and Council of Ministers.

Official Defends Nuclear Test

USSR Deputy Minister for Atomic Energy Professor Viktor Mikhailov defended Moscow's recent decision to carry out an underground nuclear weapons test on the arctic island of Novaya Zemlya, TASS reported. While stating that the USSR remained opposed in principle to nuclear testing, Mikhailov told *Trud* that continued testing by the United States, France, and China obligated the USSR to continue its own program. Mikhailov has made similar statements in the past.

Thursday, November 8

Second Uzbek Women's Group Set Up

A second women's organization, called the Eastern Women's Association, was established in Uzbekistan. The new group was reported to be associated with the "Erk" democratic movement (RL Uzbek service, November 8). The first women's group in Uzbekistan, the "Tomaris" association, was founded at the begining of the year in association with "Birlik," the Uzbek popular front.

Armenian Communists Protest Depolitization

The Armenian Communist Party criticized the republican Supreme Soviet's decision to depoliticize various state and economic bodies. Radio Moscow quoted a statement by the Presidium of the Twenty-ninth Armenian Party Congress as saying the Supreme Soviet decision did not comply with the Armenian Constitution. The Presidium alleged that the decision was an attempt to destabilize the situation in the republic. (The Armenian parliament voted on November 6 to abandon Party organizations in state bodies, enterprises, institutions, schools, and military subunits.)

Monarchists Demonstrate in Moscow

A demonstration in which forty "monarchists" participated took place in Moscow, TASS reported. It was held to commemorate members of the White Army who died during the Civil War. Although the demonstration was not authorized by the Moscow City Soviet, the police did not interfere.

Friday, November 9

Gorbachev in Germany

Soviet President Mikhail Gorbachev started a two-day visit to Germany. He held talks with German Chancellor Helmut Kohl and signed a treaty with him covering German-Soviet relations in general. Two other treaties, on economic and social cooperation, were signed by German and Soviet officials. Kohl and Gorbachev hailed the treaties as further evidence that the Cold War era had come to an end (*DPA*, November 9).

The same day, Gorbachev said in Bonn that he was deeply worried about Soviet army troops in former East Germany, and he urged Germans to show understanding for the 380,000 Soviet troops in their country, AP and Reuters reported the next day. Kohl said he would soon visit Soviet barracks in an effort to ease tensions there. *Der Spiegel*, meanwhile, said that more than 200 Soviet soldiers had deserted in the past week alone and that assault rifles and other weapons were being sold on the black market by Soviet soldiers.

On November 10, Gorbachev met with German Foreign Minister Hans-Dietrich Genscher and other German officials outside Bonn before taking a tour of Chancellor Helmut Kohl's home state of Rheinland-Pfalz. Gorbachev and Genscher were reported to have agreed that it was important to create a Europe in which borders would no longer play a role. Genscher also thanked Gorbachev for his contribution to German unity. Gorbachev also met with the chairman of the Free Democratic Party, Otto Lambsdorff, with Kohl's Social Democratic challenger in the all-German December election, Oskar Lafontaine, and with German Finance Minister Theodor Waigel (*Reuters*, *DPA*, November 10). The same day,

Gorbachev left Germany for home. In a radio interview, Genscher urged Western countries to aid Moscow financially.

Finland Will Not Question Borders

Finnish Foreign Minister Pertti Paasio said on November 9 that it was "not in our interest to call [Finland's borders] into question." He added: "Finland's borders have been defined after two wars and in three peace treaties." The broaching of the issue by the Finnish parliament reflects a concern among many Finns that nearly 10,000 square miles of territory in southeastern Karelia will never be returned to Finland. The minister also said Finland had no intention of opening talks to modify the wording of the draft Soviet-Finnish Friendship Treaty. The treaty mentions Germany as a possible source of aggression (*Reuters*, November 9).

Another Historical Revelation

The weekly *Nedelya* (No. 44) continued its historical series by publishing archival materials on the arrest, investigation, trial, and execution of one of Stalin's MGB (Ministry of State Security) chiefs, Viktor Abakumov, who was arrested in 1951 and executed in 1954 after Stalin's death. *Nedelya* provided many interesting details about the functioning of Stalin's secret police. In particular, it revealed the central role played by Stalin in all the major fabricated cases. This undermines Khrushchev's claim that after 1934 the NKVD-MGB put itself above the Party and functioned almost independently of any external control.

Saturday, November 10

Leaders of Baltic Republics in Moscow for Trade Talks

Leaders of the Baltic republics arrived in Moscow for talks with the Soviet government on future trade relations. Estonia was represented by Prime Minister Edgar Savisaar, Lithuania by Prime Minister Kazimiera Prunskiene, and Latvia by Deputy Prime Minister Arnis Kalnins. The Soviet side was represented by Prime Minister Nikolai Ryzhkov and his first deputy, Yurii Maslyukov (*TASS*, November 10). TASS quoted Prunskiene as saying that the three Baltic leaders had coordinated their stands on trade with the USSR and prepared for presentation to Soviet officials a draft plan for trade between the Baltic republics and the Soviet Union in 1991.

On November 12, Lithuanian and Latvian officials said they would not agree to Soviet conditions outlined at the talks. They complained that during the talks Ryzhkov had issued an ultimatum to the Baltic republics, ordering them to abandon their tax systems and their policies regarding prices, currency, and foreign relations (*TASS*, in English, RFE Lithuanian service, November 12). Ryzhkov threatened that, if the Baltic republics did not comply with his demand, all subsidies to them would be cut.

On November 16, Prunskiene said "the bridges have been burned" between Vilnius and Moscow. She told the Lithuanian Supreme Council that there was no point in further negotiations with the Soviet government on Lithuanian independence. She also reiterated her fears of a new economic blockade following the inconclusive economic talks with Moscow (*DPA*, November 16).

Censorship by Print Shop

Trud reported that the local print shop had refused to print the November 7 issue of the Siberian youth newspaper, *Krasnoyarsky komsomolets*, because workers at the shop disliked certain jokes that were supposed to appear in the issue. The newspaper's editors refused to cut the offending passages, and the print shop therefore refused to print the newspaper.

RSFSR Minister of Foreign Affairs in Washington

The RSFSR's new foreign minister, Andrei Kozyrev, arrived in Washington on a visit aimed at establishing independent ties with the United States, RFE/RL's Washington correspondent reported on November 10. Kozyrev met Deputy Secretary of State Lawrence Eagleburger and addressed a press conference. Kozyrev told his audience that the RSFSR was engaged in intense negotiations to shape a new relationship with the central government and with all the republics of the Union. Treaties with the three Baltic republics and with Ukraine could be signed in a month or so, he said. Kozyrev added that, as the richest and largest republic, the RSFSR expected to be consulted on key aspects of foreign policy and was developing independent positions on, among other things, foreign military aid and the long-standing territorial dispute with Japan.

Sunday, November 11

Gorbachev Meets with El'tsin

Mikhail Gorbachev and Boris El'tsin met for over two hours in the Kremlin. They began the meeting alone but were joined later by Nikolai Ryzhkov and Ivan Silaev, prime ministers of the USSR and RSFSR, and by El'tsin's deputy, Ruslan Khasbulatov.

On November 12, TASS and Western agencies reported that, as a result of their meeting, Gorbachev and El'tsin had agreed to negotiate over key issues of economic management and the division of the country's resources before the signing of a new Union treaty. El'tsin said that, before the meeting, the RSFSR was being urged "to sign a new Union treaty first and settle all other issues later." Reporting on the meeting to a plenary session of the RSFSR Constitutional Commission on November 12, El'tsin scotched speculation that the RSFSR was dissolving the Union, declaring unequivocally that the RSFSR was in favor of a strong union with the USSR and a Union treaty. As TASS observer Andrei Orlov commented, El'tsin had realized that the RSFSR could not conduct its radical reform without Gorbachev's support. At the same time, Gorbachev cannot proceed without the RSFSR.

In his address to the RSFSR Supreme Soviet on November 13, El'tsin gave more information on his meeting with Gorbachev. El'tsin said that Gorbachev had agreed "in principle" to El'tsin's proposal that "a government of unity" should be formed and that the RSFSR should name key ministers. El'tsin said the RSFSR would insist on nominating the prime minister, the defense minister, and the finance minister (*TASS*, November 13).

El'tsin added that there had been many "misunderstandings" following his August meeting with Gorbachev and that, in order to avoid such misunderstandings in future, he and Gorbachev had agreed to sign a protocol to serve as the basis for carrying out the decisions taken at the meeting of November 11.

Also discussed at the Gorbachev-El'tsin session were the problems faced by Russian-speakers in the non-Russian republics and by Russian recruits who perform military service outside their home republic.

Shmonov Charged with Attempted Terrorism

Aleksandr Shmonov, the man who fired two shots into the air on Red Square on November 7, has been charged with attempted terrorism, according to *The Los Angeles Times*. On November 10, *Sovetskaya Rossiya* published a profile of Shmonov, in which it reported that he was a member of a voters' association in Leningrad that organized rallies "marked by scandal" during last spring's elections and that he had sold literature of the Democratic Union door-to-door. Valerii Terekhov, a leader of the Democratic Union's Leningrad branch, said Shmonov was not a Democratic Union member but belonged to the Free Democratic Party. Marina Sal'e, a member of the Leningrad

City Soviet and leader of the FDP, refused to confirm or deny Shmonov's membership.

On November 15, KGB chief investigator Petr Sokolov stated that Shmonov had wanted to assassinate Mikhail Gorbachev. Sokolov said that a note had been found in Shmonov's pocket during a body search that clearly expressed his intention to kill the president. Sokolov said Shmonov had been preparing the attack for more than two years and had written the note in case he was killed during the attempt (*TASS*, November 15).

Exiled Armenian Dissident Returns

Citing an Armenpress dispatch, Reuters reported that veteran Armenian dissident Paruir Airikyan intended to return to Armenia to take up his seat in the Armenian parliament. Airikyan was arrested in March, 1988, for his participation in the campaign for the transfer of Nagorno-Karabakh from Azerbaijan to Armenia and exiled to Ethiopia in July of that year. He later went to the United States. His Soviet citizenship was restored in October. On November 12, Interfax said Airikyan had returned to Armenia.

Relations with Foreign Parties Discussed by Secretariat

The CPSU Central Committee Secretariat has decided to transfer the planning and organization of cooperation with foreign parties to republican and local Party organizations, TASS reported. The agency reported that West European Socialist and Social Democratic parties were interested in expanding contacts with the CPSU. The leaders of "renewed East European parties" were also said to be interested in restoring traditional contacts with the CPSU, which broke off in 1989. Meanwhile, on November 14, TASS reported that the leaders of five former ruling Communist parties (from Poland, Czechoslovakia, Hungary, Bulgaria, and the former GDR) had met in Moscow with CPSU members. The situation in Eastern Europe was the main topic of discussion.

Union-Republican Foreign-Currency Committee Meets

The USSR's new Union-Republican Foreign-Currency Committee held its first meeting in Moscow. The committee was formed by a decree issued by Gorbachev earlier this month. At the session, chaired by Nikolai Ryzhkov, the committee passed measures regarding its future work on resolving the country's foreign-currency and other financial problems. The committee also discussed importing raw materials, medicine, food, and consumer goods. TASS said there was no representative from Lithuania at the session.

Use of Force Reportedly Planned in 1981 Submarine Incident

A Soviet officer said in an interview published on November 11 that the Soviet Union had been prepared to use force to free a submarine stranded in Swedish waters nine years ago, AP reported. Vasilii Besedin, who was aboard the submarine, told *Dagens Nyheter* that Soviet warships had been waiting off the Swedish coast poised to save the submarine in the event of the Swedish authorities' trying to seize it. A Swedish navy captain disagreed, however, saying "the Soviet fleet that was there would not have had enough strength for the job." Besedin said he had lost his commission following the incident but was now once again a political officer in a coastal unit.

Popov Says Moscow Needs Own Market Plan

Chairman of the Moscow City Soviet Gavriil Popov said the city should not wait for Soviet and Russian leaders to negotiate economic reforms but should immediately take its own urgent measures. In a report on the state of the city, Popov told the city soviet that Moscow had become a unique symbol of the crisis of *perestroika*, with the administrative-command system no longer working and the market mechanism not yet created. Radio Moscow said Popov's proposals included measures to create a free market, to privatize housing and trade, to introduce a new system of taxation, and to improve preschool education.

Top NATO Generals in USSR

Two of NATO's top generals arrived in Moscow on an official visit. General John Galvin, the supreme allied commander in Europe, and Vigleik Eide, chairman of the NATO Military Committee, were met at a Moscow airport by Chief of the General Staff of the Soviet Armed Forces General Mikhail Moiseev (*DPA*, November 11).

On November 12, the NATO officials held talks with Soviet Defense Minister Dmitrii Yazov and later had separate meetings with Moiseev and Foreign Minister Eduard Shevardnadze. TASS reported that the two generals also visited the Taman motorized rifle division near Moscow. After the talks, Yazov said that meetings between leaders of the two military alliances should be held on a monthly basis. Talks with Shevardnadze reportedly focused on building a new peaceful order in Europe and on the forthcoming Paris summit.

On November 13, Galvin and Eide met with Gorbachev. The NATO officials were quoted by Reuters and AFP as saying Soviet officials agreed that conventional arms-reduction talks should continue after the signing of a treaty on conventional military forces.

On November 14, the NATO officials started a tour of the Soviet Union. Galvin visited Kiev and the Black Sea naval base at Sevastopol. Eide visited Leningrad (*TASS*, November 14).

Election Rerun; New Parliament Meets in Georgia

In the second round of elections to the new Georgian Supreme Soviet on November 11, the Round Table/Free Georgia coalition increased its majority, gaining 155 of the total of 250 seats. The Georgian Communist Party, in second place, won an additional three seats, giving it sixty-four in all. The Georgian Popular Front won a total of twelve seats, the "Democratic Georgia" bloc, four, and the "Liberation and Economic Rebirth" bloc and the Rustaveli Society, one seat each. Nine independent candidates were elected. Four seats remained unfilled (*TASS*, November 12).

At its first session on November 14, the new Georgian Supreme Soviet elected as its chairman veteran dissident Zviad Gamsakhurdia, the leader of the Round Table/Free Georgia coalition. The parliament also voted (following the example of Armenia) to drop the words "Soviet" and "Socialist" from the republic's name—it will henceforth be known as the Republic of Georgia. The parliament also restored the state hymn, flag, and seal of the short-lived independent Georgian republic (1918–21). Gamsakhurdia envisaged a five-year transition period to full Georgian independence. He told Interfax that he advocated "an economy totally independent of the central authorities, a maximum of privatization, and business contacts with all other states on a mutually beneficial basis." The same day, the Georgian government submitted its resignation but was requested by the parliament to continue discharging its duties until the formation of a new Council of Ministers.

On November 15, the Georgian Supreme Soviet appointed a member of the Round Table/Free Georgia Coalition, Tengiz Singua, as chairman of the Georgian Council of Ministers. TASS said Singua, a fifty-six-year-old professor, was chairman of the Rustaveli Society, an opposition group (*TASS*, November 15).

On November 16, the Georgian parliament elected Akakii Asatiani as first deputy chairman and Nemo Burchuladze as deputy chairman of the republican legislature. The Georgian Supreme Soviet also endorsed a resolution on protecting human rights and on "enhancing" law and order. TASS also reported that the parliament had passed a law that barred Georgian draftees from doing military service outside Georgia.

Monday, November 12

Gorbachev's Books to Be Shredded

Sobesednik (No. 45) reported that books and publications written by Gorbachev, Shevardnadze, and Ryzhkov were destined to be shredded because no one wanted to buy them. The order to shred the books was issued by a special commission of "Moskniga," the body in charge of book sales in Moscow. *Sobesednik* quoted an official at one Moscow bookstore as saying that the order had come as a shock, since the shredding of books by leaders who were still in power had previously been classified as a state crime.

Presidential Decree Needed to Relocate Chernenko Bust

A decree issued today ordered the bust of former CPSU General Secretary Konstantin Chernenko at present located in the city of Krasnoyarsk to be moved to the nearby village of Anash, where Chernenko was born, TASS reported. According to current legislation, busts of top Soviet leaders are to be erected after their deaths in the places of their birth. Citing this legislation, Krasnoyarsk officials had demanded the removal of Chernenko's bust from the city.

Referendum to Be Held on Status of Crimea

An extraordinary session of the Crimean Oblast Soviet voted in favor of adopting a declaration on the restoration of the statehood of the Crimea and of holding a referendum on its future status, Ukrinform-TASS reported. According to Radio Moscow, speakers agreed that, since the deportation of the Crimean Tatars had been illegal, the decrees abolishing the Crimean ASSR in 1945 and transferring the territory to Ukraine in 1954 were invalid. They were divided, however, over whether the Crimea should be an autonomous republic in Ukraine, should be returned to the RSFSR, or should be a Union republic. Not only current residents of the Crimea but all Crimean Tatars elsewhere will be able to vote in the referendum. The importance of the issue was underlined by the presence at the session of the chairman of the Ukrainian Supreme Soviet, Leonid Kravchuk, and USSR and Ukrainian deputies.

Ecological Situation Causes Tensions in Ust-Kamenogorsk

Central Television reported that public anger over lack of ministerial concern about environmental conditions in Ust-Kamenogorsk in Eastern Kazakhstan had led to tensions and the creation of strike committees. An explosion in September at a plant producing beryllium focused outside attention on toxic pollution from Ust-Kamenogorsk's metallurgical works, but the incident was only one manifestation of a problem that is extensive and long-standing. The television report showed Kazakh President Nursultan Nazarbaev visiting the city and expressing his understanding of citizens' concerns.

Meeting on Conversion Held

A meeting held in Moscow between the Russian Federation leadership and more than 280 top defense industry officials on the issue of conversion ended in a stalemate, TASS reported. RSFSR Prime Minister Ivan Silaev, stating that the defense industries accounted for approximately 55 percent of all industrial production in the RSFSR, promised government cooperation. He later told reporters, however, that leaders of the military industry had made no constructive proposals at the meeting and that they needed to "restructure their psychology." Defense industry officials, meanwhile, complained that they were losing qualified personnel to the cooperatives and called for greater investment in the conversion process.

Troop Movements Opposed

Protests at airports in Ukraine and Karelia by families of Soviet servicemen have disrupted attempts to transfer troops from those areas, Interfax reported. AFP said approximately 100 family members of air force pilots serving near Zaporozhe had blocked the local civilian airport runway for several hours as a protest against the redeployment of the regiment to Central Asia. At an air base near Petrozavodsk in Karelia, meanwhile, about 100 women and children staged a similar demonstration. Redeployments resulting from troop reductions and withdrawals from Eastern Europe have raised tensions in the military community.

Soviet–North Korean Consultations

The Soviet Union and North Korea held political consultations on November 10 and 12 to discuss "Soviet-Korean" relations and the situation in the Asia-Pacific region, TASS reported on November 12. TASS's reference to "Soviet-Korean" relations was ambiguous and departed from the usual practice of referring to North and South Korea as the Democratic People's Republic of Korea and the Republic of Korea, respectively. The use of such vague language comes at a time when Pyongyang is particularly sensitive to signals indicating whether or not Moscow is continuing to support the existence of North Korea as a sovereign state.

Berlin-Moscow Agreement

City officials of Moscow and Berlin met in the Soviet capital and said they were committed to friendship and cooperation between their two cities. In a joint statement, West Berlin Mayor Walter Momper, East Berlin Mayor Tino Schwierzina, and First Deputy Chairman of the Moscow City Soviet Sergei Stankevich said an agreement between the cities would open the way for political, cultural, economic, and technical cooperation. The aim of Momper's and Schwierzina's two-day visit was to extend an existing partnership between East Berlin and Moscow to all of Berlin (*ADN*, November 12).

College Graduate Sent to Jail for Damaging Monument

A court in Chernovtsy in Western Ukraine sentenced a graduate of a local industrial college to thirty months in prison for damaging a Lenin monument. Radio Kiev said the parents of the man, identified as Valerii Malik, had paid for the damage. In a separate development, a Lenin monument recently removed from one of Ternopol's squares was reerected on a main street in the Western Ukrainian city's military zone.

Ukrainian Policemen Demonstrate at Parliament Building

Several thousand policemen picketed the Ukrainian Supreme Soviet building in Kiev, demanding immediate adoption of legislation to protect policemen's professional and social rights. Radio Moscow, reporting from Kiev, said Ukrainian parliamentary commissions had been told to draft a law on the police and to present it to the Supreme Soviet the following week.

Landsbergis Goes to Britain

President of the Lithuanian Supreme Council Vytautas Landsbergis traveled to London for talks on Lithuania's desire for international recognition (*Reuters*, November 12). On November 13, Landsbergis held talks with British Prime Minister Margaret Thatcher. After the talks, Thatcher was quoted as saying Britain would "do nothing to let down the Baltic republics." But she also made clear that Britain did not want to make the position of Mikhail Gorbachev more difficult. She said Britain had never accepted as legal the Soviet annexation of the Baltic states, but she stressed that currently the situation could only be resolved through negotiations. Speaking at a news conference after the talks, Landsbergis complained that Moscow had hardened in its attitude towards Baltic independence, with recent threats and ultimatums. He referred to Ryzhkov's ultimatum at the trade talks between Soviet and Baltic officials on November 10–12 (*RFE/RL Special*, November 13).

Stock Exchange Set Up in Moscow

The Soviet Union has created its first stock exchange since October, 1917, TASS reported. The agency said the Moscow stock exchange had been founded by 187 Soviet enterprises and banks. It did not say when trading would begin.

Tuesday, November 13

Gorbachev Meets with Military Deputies

Mikhail Gorbachev met with an assembly of more than 1,000 soldiers elected to various levels of public office, TASS and Western news agencies reported. In an attempt to reassure the disgruntled officers, Gorbachev dismissed rumors of a planned military coup and called for the retention of both a single, unified army and conscription. He also expressed sympathy for the hardships currently being faced by the officer corps and criticized liberal and nationalist attacks on it. Gorbachev balanced his statements, however, by continuing to defend his "new thinking" in foreign policy. He argued that reduced international tensions and the Soviet Union's domestic economic problems continued to make military reform imperative. He tied the military reform process closely to the evolving relations between the center and the periphery and to accelerating economic reform.

Gorbachev's speech to the officers followed a long and often acrimonious discussion among the military deputies themselves concerning reform in society and within the armed forces. Concerns were voiced regarding a broad spectrum of issues, including resistance to military service in the non-Russian republics. Defense Minister Dmitrii Yazov complained that morale was low and dissension high in the armed forces as a result of antiarmy attacks by emerging political forces and the press. He also lamented the erosion of living standards in the armed forces stemming from the massive troop withdrawals from Eastern Europe.

Tyumen Oblast Soviet Rejects Yamalo-Nenets Republic

A session of the Tyumen Oblast Soviet decided to ask the RSFSR Supreme Soviet to refuse to recognize the self-proclaimed Yamalo-Nenets Republic, Radio Moscow reported. The Yamalo-Nenets Autonomous Okrug, which declared its sovereignty on October 18, accounts for just over half the territory of Tyumen Oblast. The Khanty-Mansi Autonomous Okrug, which accounts for another third of the oblast's territory, has declined to adopt a declaration of sovereignty for the time being.

Kazakhstan Supreme Soviet Considers Law on Land Seizure

Radio Moscow reported that the Kazakh Supreme Soviet had added to its agenda consideration of a law increasing the penalties for seizure of existing living quarters or land on which to build homes. A severe housing shortage in the republic, officially described as one of the causes of the riots in Alma-Ata in 1986, was supposed to be cured by a crash program of housing construction, which has, however, had limited effect. In the past year, there have been numerous reports of seizures of vacant apartments and unused land, particularly in Alma-Ata.

Ligachev Does Not Want to Leave Political Arena

Former Politburo member Egor Ligachev told *Argumenty i fakty* (No. 43) that he did not intend to leave the Soviet political scene altogether. In his capacity as a member of the USSR Congress of People's Deputies, Ligachev said he would be more active and would probably join the "Soyuz" group of conservative deputies that opposes some of Gorbachev's policies. *Literaturnaya gazeta* (No. 45) published an appeal written by two prominent activists of the "Memorial" society that urged Ligachev's recall as a USSR people's deputy in the light of recent revelations concerning his alleged role in the desecration of a mass grave unearthed near Tomsk in 1979.

Arbatov's Memoirs Published

Znamya (Nos. 9 and 10) published the memoirs of Academician Georgii Arbatov, the head of the USA and Canada Institute, whose opposition to the political and economic stance taken by the Soviet military-industrial complex has recently received wide publicity. Arbatov recalled his work with Brezhnev, Andropov, and Chernenko and said he had been particularly close to Yurii Andropov, whom he recalled in warm terms. Andropov was not, according to Arbatov, a liberal. Andropov erred, in Arbatov's opinion, when he promoted such conservatives as Georgii Romanov, Geidar Aliev, and Egor Ligachev.

Demand for More Information on State of USSR

A letter published in *Moscow News* (No. 46) demanded that the Soviet authorities give a frank assessment of the situation in the USSR. The letter called for a full disclosure of the state of the economy and the detailing of the army and KGB budgets. It demanded the nationalization of Communist Party property and a ban on political activities by the CPSU within the army and security organs. Among the signers of the letter were USSR people's deputies Galina Starovoitova and Vladimir Tikhonov. Academicians Oleg Bogomolov and Tat'yana Zaslavskaya also signed the letter.

Reduction of Soviet Deliveries of Oil to Cuba

Manuel Aguilera, executive secretary of the Cuban National Energy Committee, told reporters in Rio de Janeiro that the Soviet Union had cut its oil supplies to Cuba by 20 percent this year. Aguilera said Cuba was coping with the cutback by imposing rationing and did not envisage seeking other oil suppliers. Meanwhile, the Soviet press continued to debate the question of Soviet aid to Cuba. See, for instance, an article by Aleksandr Oskin in *Rabochaya tribuna*, November 10.

Moscow Signs Three European Conventions

The USSR signed three conventions of the Council of Europe. It was the first time Moscow had pledged to adhere to such agreements since it was given guest status at the council. Soviet Ambassador to France Yurii Dubinin signed the conventions in Strasbourg. One convention protects animals being transported across national borders, another protects archaeological sites, and the third preserves historical monuments (*TASS*, November 13).

***Pravda* Launches Attack on Pornography**

Pravda launched an attack on pornography, saying it was engulfing culture and degrading the USSR. The CPSU daily criticized newspapers aimed at the youth market for making heroines out of women it described as "butterflies of the night." The paper deplored the use of enticing photos to increase newspaper subscriptions. Meanwhile, *Pravda* itself has been strongly hit by a decrease in subscriptions. Elsewhere in the same issue, the newspaper appealed to readers to renew their subscriptions to it.

Wednesday, November 14

USSR Supreme Soviet Convenes

Members of the USSR Supreme Soviet, returning after a twelve-day recess, voted overwhelmingly to change their agenda and to demand that President Mikhail Gorbachev deliver a report on the nationwide crisis, the proposed Union treaty, and his recent meeting with RSFSR Supreme Soviet Chairman Boris El'tsin, TASS reported.

On November 16, in response to demands by deputies, Mikhail Gorbachev presented a major report to the USSR Supreme Soviet on the economic and political situation in the USSR and on the prospects for a new Union treaty.

Gorbachev said he believed that the crisis in the USSR could be overcome not through confrontation but through the consolidation of all forces backing restructuring, and he rejected accusations that the central government had no plan for overcoming the crisis. He criticized what he called "vile rumors" that the Soviet population would be hungry and cold this winter, saying that there was enough food in the country to meet reasonable requirements. In his speech, Gorbachev said there would soon be a government reshuffle and that the armed forces would be reformed. He told the parliament that "respected people" must be brought in to set up a government with a broad social base—a view he said was shared by Prime Minister Nikolai Ryzhkov. Gorbachev also expressed great hope that the new Union treaty would improve relations between the republics and the center (*Radio Moscow-2*, November 16).

Representatives of Latvia, Estonia, and Georgia, however, told the USSR Supreme Soviet that they would not sign the planned Union treaty. (Lithuanian representatives did not attend the session.) First Deputy Chairman of the Georgian Supreme Soviet Akakii Asatiani said he had been mandated to tell the Soviet parliament of Georgia's decision not to sign the Union treaty. Chairman of the Armenian Supreme Soviet Levon Ter-Petrossyan said Armenia would not ratify any proposed treaty until it recovered its sovereignty. Representatives of Moldavia also expressed doubts about the treaty.

The session was also addressed by El'tsin, who called for the resignation of the Ryzhkov government and proposed setting up "an extraordinary anticrisis committee." He said that the committee should be a coalition body and that Gorbachev should be given two weeks to consult with the republics about the idea (*TASS*, November 16).

Council of Ministers Frees Prices of Luxuries

The USSR Council of Ministers issued a resolution freeing the prices of many luxury goods, according to TASS (see *Pravda*, November 15). The resolution, which covered goods such as jewelry, furs, crystal, high-quality furniture, and audio and video equipment, took effect on November 15. It was designed to spur production by giving producers increased incentives.

Several hours after the publication of the text of the resolution, in apparent contradiction of the new spirit of cooperation recently announced, the RSFSR Supreme Soviet declared that the measure was not binding on the republic's territory. After a series of stormy debates, the chairman of the Committee on Legislation, Sergei Shakhrai, proposed the adoption of an RSFSR decree that "practically blocks the fulfillment of the normative act of the Union government," TASS reported. The RSFSR Supreme Soviet immediately informed the legislatures of autonomous and Union republics of its decision and asked them, in the interest of economic stability, to adopt similar measures.

On November 15, the Moscow City Soviet suspended on the city's territory the resolution freeing prices (*TASS*, November 15). On November 16, the Kazakhstan Supreme Soviet rejected the resolution (*TASS*, November 16). Azerbaijan suspended the resolution on November 21. On November 28, the Moldavian Supreme Soviet ratified the resolution.

Economic Slide Continues

Izvestia published preliminary economic figures for October that indicated that the Soviet economic slide was continuing unabated. Over the course of the year, Soviet industry failed to deliver production worth some 12.8 billion rubles, a little over 1 percent of expected annual gross industrial output. Gas production continued to exceed the plan, but coal and oil production continued to fall, in part because of the closure of spent wells. Consumer goods production through October was up 6.5 percent over the same period in 1989, but money incomes rose twice as fast as planned. The result was increased black-market activities at the expense of empty store shelves. Output of a whole range of foods, including meat, canned goods, and oats, fell by between 3 and 4 percent.

Soviet Media Officials Reshuffled

Mikhail Nenashev was transferred from his post as chairman of the USSR State Committee for Television and Radio (Gosteleradio) to chairman of the USSR State Committee for the Press (Goskompechat'), Soviet media reported. (The post of Goskompechat' chairman had been vacant since July, 1990, when Nikolai Efimov was transferred to head *Izvestia*.) Nenashev's transfer marked his return to the position he held from February, 1986, until May, 1989, when the committee was known as the USSR State Committee for Publishing (Goskomizdat). While head of Goskomizdat, Nenashev was considered a supporter of *glasnost'*, but after his transfer to Gosteleradio he followed a much more conservative line.

The post of Gosteleradio chairman, left vacant by Nenashev's transfer, was filled by Leonid Kravchenko, also a conservative, who until then headed the news agency TASS and earlier held the post of deputy chairman of Gosteleradio. Earlier in 1990, *Moscow News* reported that staff members of TASS were dissatisfied with what they regarded as Kravchenko's unbalanced support of the CPSU's conservative wing.

Figures on Unemployment Given

For the first time, an official figure on the number of unemployed was released. The State Committee for Statistics said there were 2 million unemployed in the USSR in the first nine months of 1990, according to the ILO's definition of unemployment, *Ekonomika i zhizn'* (No. 43) reported. The ILO defines an unemployed person as someone who is without work, actively seeking work, and available to start work immediately.

Demonstrations in Alma-Ata

A journalist in Alma-Ata informed RFE/RL that members of Kazakh informal groups were picketing the republican Supreme Soviet building and demanding publication of the final report of the commission that investigated the 1986 disturbances in Alma-Ata. When the republican Supreme Soviet formally approved the commission's report in September, publication of the findings was promised.

Nentsy Declare Sovereignty; Dagestanis Discussing It

At an extraordinary session, the Nenets Okrug Soviet declared the Nenets Autonomous Okrug the Nenets Autonomous Soviet Republic, Radio Moscow reported. The chairman of the soviet said the reason for the change was that the soviet was not sure whether the interests of autonomous okrugs would be safeguarded under the future RSFSR federal treaty. Radio Moscow also reported that the second congress of people's deputies of the Dagestan ASSR would discuss a declaration of sovereignty that would possibly turn Dagestan into a Union republic.

Kalugin Continues Legal Battle

The RSFSR Supreme Court rejected the USSR prosecutor-general's protest against former KGB General Oleg Kalugin's suit against Prime Minister Nikolai Ryzhkov. The Prosecutor's Office had claimed that the actions of the head of the Soviet government could be overruled only by the USSR Supreme Soviet and not by the courts, *Izvestia* reported.

Independent Trade Union of Priests and Monks

Soyuz (No. 39) carried a report on a recent discussion with one of the leaders of the Independent Trade Union of Priests and Monks, Father Ilya. He said the aim of his organization was to help believers, especially priests and monks, to surmount their financial problems. Father Ilya is a follower of the True Orthodox Church, which—like the True Orthodox Christian Church—once belonged to the so-called Catacomb Church. Both the civil authorities and the Moscow Patriarchate still consider these groups illegal.

Luk'yanov in Japan

Japan told the USSR that it could not expect any economic aid until the dispute over the Kurile Islands was settled. Chairman of the USSR Supreme Soviet Anatolii Luk'yanov was seeking aid in talks with Japanese Prime Minister Toshiki Kaifu and Foreign Minister Taro Nakayama (*Reuters*, *AP*, November 14). (Luk'yanov visited Tokyo to attend the enthronement of Emperor Akihito on November 12 and to discuss Gorbachev's planned visit to Japan in April, 1991.)

Akhromeev's Article in *Sovetskaya Rossiya*

Gorbachev's military adviser, Marshal Sergei Akhromeev, said the armed forces might be used to maintain the country's integrity and Socialist system if they were threatened by anticonstitutional forces. He said, however, that force would only be used following a decision by the Soviet parliament or the president. In an article in *Sovetskaya Rossiya*, he said the armed forces would recognize the victory in elections of non-Communist parties only if this victory came about by constitutional means.

Eight Dead in Soviet Industrial Accident

A report from Moscow said eight people were dead and six were missing following an explosion at a factory in Biisk in Altai Krai in the RSFSR. Interfax said the explosion had occurred at a weapons factory. It said a building had been destroyed and ten people injured.

***Komsomol'skaya pravda* Says Vietnam Bans Soviet Periodicals**

Komsomol'skaya pravda said that Vietnam had "virtually banned" some Soviet magazines for ideological reasons. Such periodicals as *Moskovskie novosti* and the digest of the Soviet press for foreign readers, *Sputnik*, as well as some other titles, were listed in a Vietnamese catalogue for subscribers. *Komsomol'skaya pravda* said, however, that "the Vietnamese who wanted to read them invariably meet with refusal."

Thursday, November 15

Gorbachev Issues Decree on Soldiers' Deaths in Peacetime

Mikhail Gorbachev ordered the creation of a special commission to investigate the peacetime deaths or injuries of Soviet soldiers. TASS said the commission would include USSR and republican-level people's deputies, representatives of the USSR Prosecutor's Office and Justice Ministry, and the Committee of Soldiers' Mothers. The agency said Gorbachev's decree authorizing the commission had been issued at the request of the mothers' committee (see *Pravda*, November 16).

Rationing in Leningrad

Because of severe food shortages, the Leningrad City Soviet voted overwhelmingly to begin rationing many food products on December 1. AP said the items to be rationed included meat, eggs, butter, flour, and cooking oil. Sugar and vodka were already rationed. TASS reported the same day that officials in several Soviet regions had appealed to Gorbachev to help solve food shortages in their areas. The appeals came from Chelyabinsk, the Karelian Autonomous Republic, Novgorod, and Pskov as well as Leningrad.

Arrest of Ukrainian Deputy Sparks Protests

Some Ukrainian members of parliament and workers in the West Ukrainian city of Lvov voiced their support for a deputy who was stripped of his parliamentary immunity on November 14. The deputy, Stepan Khmara, who is from Chervonograd, was accused of taking part in an assault on a policeman in central Kiev on November 7. A group of Ukrainian parliamentary deputies from the opposition faction "Narodna Rada" told a press conference in Kiev that the vote on Khmara violated legal and procedural norms. They said a group of deputies had declared a one-day hunger strike to demand that a parliamentary commission examine the case. It was reported that workers in Lvov were considering strikes in support of Khmara (*Radio Kiev*, November 15).

On the evening of November 17, plainclothes policemen entered the Ukrainian Supreme Soviet building and arrested Khmara. RL's Ukrainian service learned on November 18 that a meeting protesting against Khmara's arrest had been held in Kiev. The Ukrainian Republican Party also condemned the arrest.

On November 26, Khmara announced from his prison cell in Kiev that he was staging a hunger strike to protest against what he called "the falsified criminal case" against him (RL Ukrainian service, November 26).

Another Hijacking

A Soviet man hijacked an Aeroflot jet to Helsinki. He had originally demanded that the plane fly to Stockholm, but when it landed in Helsinki he surrendered and asked for political asylum. The plane was on a flight from Leningrad to Moscow. Aeroflot identified the man as thirty-one-year-old Aleksandr Vilesov of Perm Oblast (*TASS*, November 15). On November 16, the USSR requested the extradition of Vilesov, TASS reported.

On November 16, another Soviet citizen undertook an unsuccessful attempt to hijack a passenger jet en route between Moscow and Tallinn. He wanted the plane to fly to Sweden, but the pilot managed to land safely in Tallinn (*Reuters*, November 16).

Czechoslovak Minister in Moscow for Economic Talks

Czechoslovak Finance Minister Vaclav Klaus arrived in Moscow for a day of talks about Czechoslovak-Soviet economic relations. He met with Soviet Finance Minister Valentin Pavlov. One of the major economic problems between the USSR and Czechoslovakia is the supply of Soviet oil to Czechoslovakia (*CTK*, November 15).

On November 19, the Czechoslovak and Soviet finance ministers initialed a payments agreement between the two countries to take effect on January 1, 1991. The agreement stipulated that trade payments would be conducted in convertible currencies (*TASS*, November 16).

KGB Meets Victims of Stalin's Repressions

In an attempt to improve its image and dissociate itself from Stalin's NKVD, the KGB organized a meeting of its officials with representatives of "the Association of the Victims of [Stalin's] Terror." At the meeting, the members of the association demanded information on mass graves of executed victims, the opening of the NKVD archives, and the publication of lists of the names of those repressed. TASS said that the deputy head of the KGB Center for Public Relations, Aleksei Kandaurov, had revealed during the meeting that the KGB was participating in the preparation of a law on material support for Stalin's victims and their relatives.

Friday, November 16

Changes in Turkmen Leadership

The Supreme Soviet of Turkmenia elected a new parliamentary speaker and reappointed the incumbent prime minister, Khan Akhmedov. The new speaker is Sokhat Muradov, the former first deputy speaker. He replaced Saparmurad Niyazov, who was chosen as executive president of Turkmenia in a popular election in October (*Central Television*, "Vremya," November 16).

Latvia and RSFSR Agree on Farming Cooperation and Food Trade

Latvia and the Russian Federation signed an agreement on bilateral trade in farm produce and raw materials. The agreement, signed in Riga by representatives of the two republics' agriculture ministries, also provided for cooperation in agricultural science and technology. Radio Moscow said that the agreement opened possibilities for direct contracts between Latvia and the enterprises and organizations of the Russian Republic. The broadcast did not say how long the agreement would be in force.

Lithuanian Parliamentary Committee Appeals to Germany

The Foreign Affairs Committee of the Lithuanian parliament expressed concern about a clause in the recently concluded German-Soviet Friendship Treaty. The committee appealed to the German government not to interpret the clause as recognizing the Soviet Union's annexation of Lithuania. It also urged Germany not to encourage the Soviet Union to make such an interpretation. The appeal, issued on November 15, focused on the clause in the treaty that commits Germany and the Soviet Union to respecting Europe's present borders. The committee sent a similar appeal to the USSR Supreme Soviet (RFE Lithuanian service, November 16).

USSR's Instability Obstacle to Trade, Clark Tells El'tsin

Visiting the USSR, Canadian Foreign Minister Joe Clark said Canadian businessmen considered Soviet instability a possible obstacle to the development of trade relations with the USSR. TASS said Clark made the comments during a meeting with Boris El'tsin at which El'tsin expressed willingness on the part of the RSFSR to conclude a bilateral treaty with Canada. Later the same day, Clark met with his Soviet counterpart, Eduard Shevardnadze.

Landsbergis Welcomes Decision to Invite Baltic Republics as Guests

President of the Lithuanian Supreme Council Vytautas Landsbergis welcomed the decision to invite the Baltic republics as special guests to the Paris summit Conference on Security and Cooperation in Europe (CSCE). The CSCE summit opened on November 19. The Baltic republics had sought observer status, but that would have required the consent of all thirty-four states taking part. Landsbergis said in an interview with RFE/RL that the decision to invite the Balts as special guests was a positive step away from "the policy of stagnation" that he said the West had adopted towards the Baltic republics.

Saturday, November 17

Gorbachev Outlines Changes in Power Structure

For the third time in 1990, Mikhail Gorbachev asked the Soviet parliament to grant him fresh powers. In a brief speech to the USSR Supreme Soviet, Gorbachev proposed: (1) transforming the Council of the Federation from a consultative into a policy-making body able to coordinate the activities of the center and the republics; (2) dissolving the Presidential Council and creating a Security Council directly subordinated to the president; (3) appointing presidential representatives to monitor the implementation of the center's decisions in the regions; (4) creating the post of vice president. The USSR Supreme Soviet approved the proposals "on the whole."

Gorbachev proposed that the Council of the Federation (the consultative body set up in March) should be given new powers to approve all decisions affecting the interests of the republics. Gorbachev said the Council should hold regular meetings and its deliberations should be published. A new Interrepublican Committee would handle the day-to-day work of the Council of the Federation, Gorbachev said.

Gorbachev proposed dissolving the Presidential Council (also set up in March) and replacing it with a new body, directly subordinated to the president, to be called the Security Council. Gorbachev told the Supreme Soviet he wanted to have all activities concerned with maintaining the law under his direct control.

Gorbachev also proposed the creation of a presidential supervisory body that would monitor the implementation of all-Union laws and presidential decrees in the regions. Gorbachev would station personal representatives "with full powers" in each of the republics (*TASS*, November 17).

Speaking in Kiev on November 19, Boris El'tsin rejected Gorbachev's proposals for state and government reorganization, saying they would only make a bad situation worse. "The president's proposals are aimed at strengthening the center," Interfax quoted El'tsin as saying. "He thinks he can get along without consulting the sovereign republics, but that is already impossible. Russia, for one, will not accept it." El'tsin said the RSFSR was prepared to propose a vote of no confidence in Gorbachev's continued presidency and in the government of Prime Minister Nikolai Ryzhkov. Interfax said El'tsin did not reject Gorbachev's proposals outright but that he was clearly not prepared to accept them in their present form. On November 21, El'sin called for a national referendum on Gorbachev's proposals (*AP*, November 21).

On November 23, the USSR Supreme Soviet gave Gorbachev two weeks to present details of his plan to increase his presidential powers (*TASS*, November 23).

Democratic Platform Forms Republican Party of Russia

At a two-day founding congress in Moscow over the weekend, "the Democratic Platform outside the CPSU" set up a new political party, to be called the Republican Party of Russia. This was the part of the Democratic Platform that announced its departure from the Party at the Twenty-eighth CPSU Congress in July. Radio Moscow reported on November 17 that 235 delegates from forty-eight autonomous republics and oblasts of the RSFSR had attended the gathering. The new party advocates a mixed economy and political and ideological pluralism.

Democratic Movements within CPSU Hold Their Own Meeting

A number of groups calling themselves "democratic movements within the CPSU" held their own conference in Moscow. The groups included "the Democratic Platform within the CPSU," "the Marxist Platform within the CPSU," "Democratic Unity" and other organizations that oppose what they see as the introduction of capitalism in the USSR. The conference, which discussed Soviet economic reform, called for the CPSU to hold its Twenty-ninth Congress in 1991 in order to adopt a Party Program, which the CPSU presently lacks. The meeting was attended by the CPSU Central Committee secretary in charge of relations with new political movements, Valentin Kuptsov (*TASS*, *Radio Moscow*, November 17).

Azerbaijani CP Proposes Changing Republic's Name

TASS reported that the Azerbaijan Communist Party, whose victory in September's Supreme Soviet elections was called into question by the republic's informal groups, had decided to recommend to the Azerbaijani Supreme Soviet that the republic be renamed the Republic of Azerbaijan. Armenia and Georgia implemented similar changes following the victory of non-Communist coalitions in their respective Supreme Soviet elections.

Karachai Deputies Proclaim Sovereign Karachai Republic

A congress of Karachai deputies at all levels in Karachaevsk in the Karachai-Cherkess Autonomous Oblast adopted a declaration proclaiming the Karachai territory the Karachai Soviet Socialist Republic within the RSFSR, TASS reported. The Karachai had been campaigning to recover their own autonomous formation, which they lost when they were deported en masse in 1943. Soviet ethnographers recently expressed the view that this demand was justified and warned that, although things appeared quiet in the Karachai-Cherkess Autonomous Oblast, the storm clouds were beginning to gather.

Opposition Leader Named to Presidential Council in Kirgizia

Kazat Akmatov, one of the cochairman of the democratic movement "Kyrgyzstan," told RFE/RL he had been named a member of Kirgizia's Presidential Council by the newly elected president, Askar Akaev. Akmatov concluded that Akaev wanted to step up the pace of democratization and *perestroika* in Kirgizia. Other council members included KGB Chairman Dzhumabek Asankulov, Chairman of the Council of Ministers Apas Dzhumagulov, and Deputy Minister of Internal Affairs Feliks Kulov, who is in charge of troops enforcing the state of emergency in Osh Oblast.

Turkmen Parliament Holds Session on Ecology

TASS and Radio Moscow carried reports of an extraordinary session of the Turkmen Supreme Soviet devoted to the effects of the Aral Sea catastrophe on the parts of the republic nearest the sea. The session was held in Tashauz Oblast, one of the regions worst affected, and subsequently declared the Tashauz, Mary, and Chardzhou Oblasts ecological disaster areas. The declaration included a demand that environmentally harmful enterprises be shut down and an appeal to the Supreme Soviets of Uzbekistan and Tajikistan to stop discharging untreated waste water containing high concentrations of pesticides and herbicides into the Amu Darya River.

Shatalin Hospitalized

AFP reported from Moscow that economist Stanislav Shatalin, the author of the radical "500-day" economic reform program, had been hospitalized with heart and lung problems.

Sunday, November 18

Gorbachev Visits Italy

Mikhail Gorbachev left Moscow for a four-day trip to Italy and France. TASS said he was accompanied by Foreign Minister Eduard Shevardnadze and Defense Minister Dmitrii Yazov.

The same day, Gorbachev met in the Vatican with Pope John Paul II. The Soviet president described his talk with the Pope as "very satisfying," adding that they had discussed "the most important problems in Europe and the world." Gorbachev's spokesman, Vitalii Ignatenko, quoted Gorbachev as saying the next meeting between Gorbachev and the Pope would "perhaps, or probably, be in the USSR," AP reported.

Reuters reported that the Italian government had put together a 6-billion-dollar credit package for the Soviet Union to be paid out over the next five years. Prime Minister Giulio Andreotti on November 18 approved a credit line worth 900 million dollars as "the first in a series of financial measures in support of *perestroika*." The Italian Foreign Ministry said Italy would provide 1.9 billion dollars in direct loans, about half of which would be used to clear debts to Italian firms. The other 4.3 billion would cover export credit guarantees.

Also on November 18, Gorbachev and Andreotti signed a Treaty of Friendship and Cooperation. The treaty included a nonaggression clause similar to that included in the Soviet-German friendship treaty signed recently. The treaty also included provisions to set up a hotline between Moscow and Rome and commited each side to cooperate in fighting organized crime, terrorism, and drug smuggling, Reuters reported.

Clashes outside Army Base in Lithuania

Senior Lithuanian officials appealed for calm after five people were injured in a clash between protesters and Soviet soldiers outside an army base in Vilnius. Witnesses said that, during the clash the previous night, Soviet soldiers had beaten demonstrators with ammunition belts and fired shots into the air after attempts to disperse the crowd failed. A similar protest by Lithuanians took place peacefully on November 18 outside an army base in Kaunas (*Radio Vilnius*, *Reuters*, *Komsomol'skaya pravda*, November 18).

General Staff Chief on Reform

Chief of the General Staff of the Soviet Armed Forces Mikhail Moiseev said in *Krasnaya zvezda* that the draft of a ten-year, three-stage plan for military reform had been sent to the USSR Supreme Soviet, Western news agencies reported. The first stage involves East-West arms accords and includes the withdrawal of Soviet forces from Eastern Europe and Mongolia. The second calls for the strategic regrouping of forces in the USSR and envisages a reorganization of the command structure and of the military districts. The third envisions a 50-percent cut in strategic offensive weapons by the year 2000 and a reduction in manpower to about 3 million men. Moiseev also said that the military draft would continue but that alternative service on religious grounds would be allowed.

Lithuania Supports Moldavia

The Lithuanian Supreme Council issued a statement signed by its president, Vytautas Landsbergis, protesting about "the criminal policy of dismembering Moldavia," the news agency Moldovapres, cited by Radio Bucharest, reported. Condemning "the creation of artificial state entities on Moldavia's territory" and the use of military pressure against Kishinev, the statement blamed the situation on "reactionary" and "imperialist" forces of the USSR seeking to force Moldavia to sign a Union treaty "favorable only to the center." The statement said similar methods were being used against other republics.

Starovoitova Initiates Court Case against Petrunya

USSR people's deputy Galina Starovoitova accused TASS correspondent Vladimir Petrunya of libel. Petrunya's commentaries, which have appeared in *Pravda*, *Sovetskaya Rossiya*, and *Krasnaya zvezda*, suggested that certain reformist deputies to local Soviets in the RSFSR had deliberately tried to exacerbate the food shortage in an attempt to discredit the central government and win power. Interviewed in *Argumenty i fakty* (No. 43), Starovoitova said she had decided to go to court after Petrunya's allegations appeared in the main CPSU daily.

Murder of Orthodox Priest

TASS reported that a Russian Orthodox priest from a village in Western Ukraine had been found shot dead. A police official said only that the murder did not appear to be a case of robbery.

El'tsin in Ukraine

Chairman of the RSFSR Supreme Soviet Boris El'tsin arrived in Kiev for talks with Ukrainian officials. TASS said the purpose of the visit was the signing of a treaty on the fundamental principles of relations between the two republics and the discussion of a Union treaty.

On November 19, the Ukraine and the RSFSR signed a ten-year bilateral agreement covering a broad range of political, economic, cultural, and other issues. The document was signed by El'tsin and the chairman of the Ukrainian Supreme Soviet, Leonid Kravchuk. At a subsequent press conference, the Russian and Ukrainian leaders stressed that the agreement was between two sovereign and equal states. On November 20, *Izvestia* noted that the document pointedly omitted any references to a Union treaty or the USSR Constitution. In addition to the formal agreement, the two sides issued a joint statement demanding that the sovereignty of the two republics be consistently respected by the USSR Supreme Soviet.

On November 22, the Ukrainian Supreme Soviet ratified the agreement with the RSFSR. The Russian parliament ratified the treaty on November 23, TASS reported. TASS reported on November 22 that Ukraine had signed a five-year cooperation treaty with Uzbekistan.

Opinion Poll Indicates Fear of Right-Wing Coup

An opinion poll published by *Moscow News* (No. 46) showed that 33 percent of those polled feared that a right-wing coup was possible in the USSR; this compared with 17 percent who thought the threat to the country's future came from left-wing forces. The poll also showed that the reunification of Germany was a matter of concern for many—31 percent of those polled had negative feelings about reunification and 32 percent thought that it was a blow to the Soviet Union's achievements in World War II. A third regarded reunification positively. The poll showed that a majority (62 percent) feared most the possibility of famine during the winter. Regarding how the country is to get out of the present crisis, those polled showed very great uncertainty and a lack of concrete ideas. The proposition that secured the highest level of approval (25 percent) was to allow the republics to decide their own future. Least support (3 percent) was given to the Ryzhkov-Abalkin economic reform program.

Turkmen Activist Committed to Psychiatric Hospital

Moscow News (No. 46) reported that an activist of the Democratic Platform, Kurbanberdy Karabalakov, had been incarcerated in a psychiatric hospital in Ashkhabad, apparently because he tried to set up a branch of the Democratic Platform in Turkmenistan. The coordinating council of the Democratic Platform in Moscow said it had a medical report declaring Karabalakov completely sane.

Monday, November 19

Gorbachev Attends CSCE

On November 19, Gorbachev arrived in Paris to attend the Conference on Security and Cooperation in Europe. Speaking at the opening of the conference, Gorbachev stressed the importance of building new institutions encouraging European integration and, as a corollary, including the Soviet Union. His remarks were carried by TASS. Gorbachev also praised US-Soviet cooperation, especially with regard to arms control and the Gulf crisis. In contrast to his statements during earlier visits to Spain and France, Gorbachev spoke warmly of the United States and Canada as parts of Europe. He described Europe as "passing beyond the geographical limits of the Atlantic to the Urals . . . stretching from the shores of the Pacific Ocean to the USA and Canada."

While in Paris, Gorbachev held meetings with British Prime Minister Margaret Thatcher, with whom he discussed the Gulf crisis. He also discussed bilateral relations and Soviet economic problems with Polish and Hungarian leaders (*PAP*, *Central Television*, "Vremya," November 20).

Moiseev on CFE Agreement

Chief of the General Staff of the Soviet Armed Forces Mikhail Moiseev hailed the accord on Conventional Forces in Europe signed on November 19 as reaching further than any other in history and said that sharp reductions in tanks and men throughout Europe "ensure the Soviet Union's dependable defense capacity," TASS and Reuters reported. Moiseev's comments contrasted with criticism he and other members of the High Command had leveled at Gorbachev's peace initiatives in the past. Political commentators Aleksandr Bovin and Yurii Kovalenko called in *Izvestia* for NATO to be disbanded along with the Warsaw Pact.

Ukraine and Baltic Republics Protest about Their Status in Helsinki Process

Ukrainian Foreign Minister Anatol Zlenko withdrew from the Soviet delegation to the Paris CSCE summit in protest against Moscow's refusal to allow Ukraine separate representation at the conference. According to the deputy head of the Foreign Affairs Commission of the Presidium of the Ukrainian Supreme Soviet, Bohdan Horyn, Soviet Foreign Minister Eduard Shevardnadze refused to recognize Ukraine's claim, as a sovereign republic, to separate representation in Paris. Horyn said the Ukrainian delegation intended to distribute an appeal to the participants in the CSCE summit, signed by the chairman of the Ukrainian Supreme Soviet, Leonid Kravchuk, stressing Ukraine's desire to participate in the Helsinki process as a sovereign and independent actor (RL Ukrainian service, November 19).

Meanwhile, the three Baltic foreign ministers said their status as "distinguished guests" at the CSCE had been revoked. The French government denied that the three had ever been given such a status. A French minister was quoted by Reuters as saying the government had decided not to proceed with the granting of such status at the request of the Soviet Union. Later, Soviet official Vitalii Zhurkin told another news conference that, until they became independent, the three Baltic republics had no right to representation at the CSCE summit.The Baltic republics were supported by Polish Prime Minister Tadeusz Mazowiecki, who told the CSCE leaders in his address that Lithuania, which borders Poland, and the other Baltic republics should not be absent from the Helsinki process (RFE Polish service, November 20).

Sobchak Appeals for Aid

Chairman of the Leningrad City Soviet Anatolii Sobchak appealed to the West for emergency aid to avoid famine and prevent public opinion from turning against democratic reforms, the AP reported. In an interview with the news agency, Sobchak said he no longer thought the USSR could get by without foreign aid. He warned that, by the time steps were taken to increase stockpiles and improve distribution, major Soviet cities could already be in danger of famine.

The same day, German Chancellor Helmut Kohl said he supported the idea of individual citizens' sending food packages to the Soviet Union. The idea of sending aid directly to Soviet homes is designed to circumvent the problems of the Soviet Union's delivery system. Kohl said the German government would continue its emergency food aid program to the USSR, despite its limited success, wire services reported.

CPSU Still Attempts to Control Media

A senior editor of the Bryansk Oblast Committee on Television and Radio complained that in his region the Party bosses were still trying to control the press, even though such interference was forbidden by the press law (*Zhurnalist*, No. 11). The editor complained that, although his committee was subordinated to the oblast soviet, it was not the soviet but the Party Committee that dictated the political line to the local radio and television by banning outspoken programs.

Peasants' Union to Be Formed in Kirgizia

A peasants' union is in the process of creation in Kirgizia, but an official on the organizing committee has complained that attempts are already being made to take over the new organization, TASS reported. The official said that everyone involved in agriculture, including leaseholders and members of agricultural cooperatives, scientific establishments, and educational institutions, was welcome to join the new union, which he hoped would be able to withstand pressures to incorporate it into "the administrative-bureaucratic system."

Program to Preserve German Culture in Kazakhstan

Novosti reported that the Kazakh Council of Ministers had adopted a program to preserve and develop German language and culture within the republic. It includes plans to expand the teaching of German in schools and kindergartens and to invite professors from Germany. In 1987, the republican Supreme Soviet ordered measures to encourage the teaching of German in the hope that this would reduce German emigration from the republic. Various officials have expressed concern, however, that many Germans still want to leave.

International Conference on Drugs in Moscow

Law-enforcement officials from thirty countries gathered in Moscow for a conference designed to increase East-West cooperation in fighting the illegal drugs trade. The conference was sponsored by the United Nations. USSR Minister of Internal Affairs Vadim Bakatin told the opening session of the conference that the process of building a common European home would help law-enforcement agencies work together to fight the drug trade (*TASS*, November 19).

On November 21, the Soviet delegation at the congress presented a report stating that more than 1,000 attempts to smuggle drugs across Soviet borders had been detected since 1985 and that the problem was growing (*TASS*, November 21).

Tuesday, November 20

RSFSR CP Appeals to Population

An appeal by the Politburo of the RSFSR Communist Party was published in *Pravda*, *Sovetskaya Rossiya*, and *Sel'skaya zhizn'*. It called on the working class, the peasantry, and the working intelligentsia to struggle against "the forces striving for the disintegration of the Union, internal strife, and feud."

Almost 2,000 Soviet Citizens Seek Asylum in Germany

The German Interior Ministry said that 1,791 Soviet citizens had already sought asylum in Germany this year. The ministry said that among the asylum-seekers were fifty-nine Soviet servicemen who had defected from their units in what was formerly East Germany. Unofficial reports said the number of deserters seeking asylum was much higher (*DPA*, November 20).

More Problems with the Draft

Deputy Chief of the General Staff Colonel General Grigorii Krivosheev said that the draft was proceeding smoothly in parts of Russia and Soviet Central Asia but that the situation was "much worse" in Transcaucasia and the Baltic republics. Krivosheev said that in Georgia little more than 2 percent of conscripts for the fall draft had registered. He said the figure for Armenia was just over 5 percent. As quoted by TASS, he gave no figures for the response to the draft in the Baltic republics.

RSFSR Adopts Pension Law

A new law adopted by the RSFSR Supreme Soviet provided for minimum pensions in the Russian Federation to be higher than in the rest of the USSR. According to the law, pensions in the republics will be based on a minimum requirement for living established annually by the republican parliament. TASS said the minimum pension had been set at 100 rubles per month for 1991. Across the Union, the minimum pension is 70 rubles per month.

Ligachev Questioned about Desecration of Siberian Mass Grave

The Moscow City Prosecutor's Office questioned former Politburo member Egor Ligachev about the desecration of a mass grave of victims of repression under Stalin (*Izvestia*, November 23). The incident happened in 1979 in Tomsk Oblast in Western Siberia, where Ligachev was at the time the Communist Party first secretary. The Ob river flooded and uncovered the bodies of people believed to have been executed by the NKVD in the 1930s. Reports said the authorities had ordered the bodies to be ground up using ship propellers and then disposed of in the river. Ligachev's testimony lasted two hours.

Wednesday, November 21

RSFSR Signs Agreement with Kazakhstan

The Russian Federation and Kazakhstan signed a bilateral cooperation agreement. The treaty was signed in Moscow by the chairmen of the republics' Supreme Soviets, Boris El'tsin and Nursultan Nazarbaev. TASS said that under the treaty the Russian Federation and Kazakhstan agreed to recognize each other's sovereignty and guarantee equal rights to citizens, regardless of their ethnic origin.

RSFSR Supreme Soviet Appoints Two More Government Members

The RSFSR Supreme Soviet appointed two more members of the republic's government. They were Mikhail Malei, who was named chairman of the State Committee for the Administration of State Property, and Leonid Prokop'ev, who became chairman of the State Committee for Nationality Affairs. TASS quoted Malei as saying he thought it possible to transfer national defense enterprises located on Russian soil to the ownership of the Russian Federation.

Gorbachev Says Majority in Favor of Preserving Union

In an interview with French and Soviet television reported by TASS, Gorbachev once again expressed his conviction that the majority of the population of the USSR wished to preserve the Union. He said that more people had celebrated the recent anniversary of the October Revolution in Riga than in Moscow and that he had been told that, after the Lithuanian authorities had refused to react to provocations against the armed forces in Lithuania, people had demonstrated in support of the Soviet army. Gorbachev once again implied that the reason the Lithuanians were unwilling to hold a referendum on secession was because the mass of the population was for the Union.

Gorbachev's statements provoked sharp criticism in the Baltic republics. On November 21, the presidents of the three republics met in Jurmala and issued a joint appeal to the USSR Supreme Soviet. The appeal called for a halt to "the escalation of the policy of threats . . . and intimidation" directed against the Baltic republics. The three Baltic leaders told a news conference that they "must try to seek possible ways to react to efforts by Gorbachev to preserve a unitary state at all costs" (*Radio Riga*, November 21). The same day, a leader of the Latvian Popular Front, Romualdas Razukas, said on Radio Riga that Latvians should prepare for "civil disobedience" if the USSR tried to impose direct presidential rule on the Baltic states.

"Soyuz" Deputy Attacks Gorbachev

In an interview with *Sovetskaya Rossiya*, the leader of the "Soyuz" faction of deputies in the USSR Supreme Soviet, Viktor Alksnis, criticized Mikhail Gorbachev. He said that, if Gorbachev stuck to his promise to prevent the breakup of the Soviet Union, he would have the group's support. But he also said that, if "everything is again limited to verbal maneuvers, we shall demand his resignation." Alksnis said, "A veritable civil war is getting under way in the country."

Two Die in NKAO Violence

There was more fighting in Nagorno-Karabakh, TASS reported. The agency said two Azerbaijanis were killed on November 20 by unidentified assailants in the village of Zabukh in the Lachin district. It said Soviet troops sent to the scene were ambushed, and reinforcements were called in.

USSR Writers' Union Discusses Reorganization

Leaders of the USSR Writers' Union held a two-day meeting in Moscow. They debated a "Declaration of Renewal," which redefined the union as a voluntary association of equal republican unions. Some Soviet writers have questioned whether there is a need at all for the conservative Writers' Union, while several leading Soviet periodicals have used the new law on the press to break their relations with the union, which had previously supervised them. Among the periodicals is the main Soviet writers' newspaper, *Literaturnaya gazeta*. The fate of this newspaper was one of the topics discussed by the union.

On November 22, amid sharp debate, Vladimir Karpov, the first secretary of the board of the Writers' Union, offered his resignation (*Radio Moscow-1*, November 22).

MVD Troops to Remain under Central Control

The commander of USSR Ministry of Internal Affairs troops, Yurii Shatalin, said the force should remain under central control. Shatalin said that to allow the troops to be under the command of local authorities would mean allowing them to "degenerate into ethnic units." He said this could lead to "unpredictable consequences" if units were used to prevent interethnic strife. Writing in *Krasnaya zvezda*, Shatalin said the MVD was working on a legislative proposal that would ensure the force remained under central control.

State of Emergency Lifted in Frunze

By order of the president of Kirgizia, Askar Akaev, the state of emergency was lifted in the Kirgiz capital, Frunze (*TASS*, November 21). The state of emergency had been in force since early June, when rioting broke out in Frunze following ethnic clashes in Osh Oblast.

RSFSR Minister on Reorganization of Republican Press

The RSFSR minister of the mass media, Mikhail Poltoranin, told Novosti that plans were under way to create a Russian information agency. This agency would unite the independent news agencies Postfaktum and Interfax, which were set up earlier in 1990. Poltoranin also announced the creation of a center, to be attached to the new agency, for the study of public opinion and the analysis of the political situation in the RSFSR. He added that the RSFSR Supreme Soviet planned to launch several new periodicals.

Thursday, November 22

Comments on Soviet Economic Situation

Gorbachev's economic adviser Nikolai Petrakov told *Izvestia* he believed that the democratic process in the

Soviet Union was seriously threatened by the economic crisis. He added that there was no more pressing task than "to recreate a market economy" in the USSR. Petrakov said the most important means of creating a market in the USSR was "restoring the purchasing power of the ruble."

The same day, the chairman of the RSFSR Council of Ministers, Ivan Silaev, said that the RSFSR could carry out much of the "500-day" economic plan but not all of it. Silaev told the RSFSR Supreme Soviet that the RSFSR could not carry out the plan in full, because to do so depended on integration with the program of the USSR (*TASS*, November 22). Silaev also asked the Russian parliament for additional powers to make changes in his government in the interests of efficiency. He said he wanted more control over his government's ministers. He also called for more effective enforcement of RSFSR law throughout the republic.

Yavlinsky Resigns

Deputy Chairman of the RSFSR Council of Ministers Grigorii Yavlinsky resigned his post. The RSFSR Supreme Soviet accepted the resignation. TASS said the chairman of the RSFSR Council of Ministers, Ivan Silaev, expressed regret at the resignation. Yavlinsky is coauthor of the "500-day" economic reform plan adopted by the Russian parliament. Yavlinsky expressed his desire to resign earlier this fall. TASS quoted the first deputy chairman of the RSFSR Supreme Soviet, Ruslan Khasbulatov, as saying that he had offered Yavlinsky the chairmanship of the economic advisory council to the chairman of the RSFSR Supreme Soviet, Boris El'tsin.

Vadim Medvedev in Seoul

After meeting with officials in the South Korean capital, Seoul, Soviet Presidential Council member Vadim Medvedev said it was time to dispose of the vestiges of the Cold War in Asia and the Pacific region. Medvedev said it was important for the United States and the USSR to recognize each other as partners, not military adversaries, in the Asia-Pacific region. He said the United States and the USSR had made positive progress in their economic and political cooperation in the region, but Medvedev said there had been virtually no change in the military field. Medvedev said Moscow supported a North Korean proposal for the withdrawal of US forces from South Korea and backed the North Korean demands that the divided peninsula be made into a nuclear-free zone. He proposed that leaders in Asia meet for multicultural military consultations to speed up the arms-control talks and force cutbacks (*Reuters*, *AP*, November 22). The agencies also reported that Medvedev was seeking loans in Seoul to finance Soviet economic reform.

On November 23, the Soviet and South Kroean delegations conducting talks in Seoul initialed a series of agreements on trade and cooperation. The most important agreement eliminated double taxation, allowing each country to extend most-favored-nation trading status to the other (*AP*, *Reuters*, November 23).

The same day, the president of Kazakhstan, Nursultan Nazarbaev, arrived in South Korea on an eight-day visit to promote investment in his republic (*AP*, November 23).

USSR Defense Ministry Plans Budget Cut

TASS said the USSR Ministry of Defense planned to reduce its budget for 1991 by about 4.5. billion rubles—a cut of more than 6 percent. TASS quoted the head of the Defense Ministry's financial administration, Colonel General Vladimir Bab'ev, as saying that the USSR Supreme Soviet Committee for Defense and State Security backed the proposed cuts but that a final decision had to be made by the Soviet government. Bab'ev said the cuts reflected the process of disarmament.

Tatar Activist Heads New Committee to Help Crimean Tatars

The Crimean Oblast Soviet set up a committee to deal with the problems of Tatars returning to the Crimea. The eleven-member committee is headed by Yurii Osmanov, an engineer who was twice sent to a labor camp for taking part in the Crimean Tatar national movement. TASS said he also spent two years in a psychiatric clinic. TASS said the committee included other Tatar activists. TASS did not say when the committee was formed, but, according to Osmanov, its members helped settle some recent disputes involving Tatars in the towns of Yalta and Evpatoria.

Shelved Nuclear Reactor Project Revived in Chelyabinsk

TASS said construction of a nuclear power plant in the region of Chelybinsk in the Southern Urals was to resume. The Chelyabinsk Oblast Soviet reversed its earlier decision to suspend the reactor project, which had been taken in response to public pressure. TASS said the deputies were now pinning their hopes on a particular design of reactor said to be less dangerous.

Soviet Court Sentences Man for Spying

In Moscow a man identified as Anatolii Khobta was convicted of selling military secrets to a Western country and sentenced to ten years' imprisonment. TASS said Khobta, born in 1954, pleaded guilty and said he had attempted to pass classified military information, which he had obained during service in the armed forces, to representatives of the secret service of a Western country. The country was not identified.

Latvia Calls for Supervised Removal of Soviet Troops

The Latvian Supreme Council called for the removal of Soviet troops from Latvia under international supervision. The Supreme Council asked the United Nations or the Conference on Security and Cooperation in Europe to oversee the operation. The call came in a note to the USSR Supreme Soviet and Mikhail Gorbachev (RFE Latvian service, November 22). Meanwhile, the Latvian and Estonian foreign ministers arrived in Strasbourg seeking support for the independence of the Baltic republics. Their plan was to ask political factions of the European Parliament for a resolution in favor of Baltic self-determination. They met with representatives of the Christian Democrat and Social Democrat factions (*Radio Riga*, November 21).

RSFSR Supreme Soviet Approves Farmstead Bill

The RSFSR Supreme Soviet approved a law giving citizens of the RSFSR aged eighteen or older the right to set up a farmstead and to receive a plot of land for that purpose. The law stated that a farmstead would be recognized as the equal in the republic's economic system of a state, collective, or other body (*TASS*, November 22).

Shevardnadze Goes to China

Soviet Foreign Minister Eduard Shevardnadze left Moscow for a visit to China. Radio Moscow said he would discuss with Chinese leaders Sino-Soviet relations and the situation in the Gulf region.

On November 23, Shevardnadze met with his Chinese counterpart, Qian Qichen, in the city of Urumchi in the west of China for private talks throughout the day concerning the Gulf crisis. The Xinhua news agency quoted Qian as saying China and the USSR were firmly opposed to Iraq's invasion and annexation of Kuwait and as calling on Iraq to comply with the United Nations resolution to withdraw from Kuwait as soon as possible.

Friday, November 23

Draft Union Treaty Published

The draft of the new Union treaty was sent to the USSR and republican Supreme Soviets on November 23 and published in the press the next day. The treaty provided for a federation—rather than a confederation—with federal law having priority in matters of exclusive federal competence—for example, the imposition of federal taxes and a common currency.

The draft Union treaty provided for an executive president, a vice president, a policy-making Council of the Federation, and a cabinet (replacing the Council of Ministers). All the members of the cabinet would be nominated by the president—at present he nominates only the chairman of the Council of Ministers, who in turn chooses his ministers.

Under the terms of the draft Union treaty, legislative power in the Union would be exercised by the USSR Supreme Soviet, implying that the USSR Congress of People's Deputies would be abolished. A constitutional court would replace the present Committee for Constitutional Oversight.

Gorbachev on New Union Treaty

In answer to questions about the new Union treaty at a press conference on November 23, Mikhail Gorbachev adopted an extremely tough line, warning that bloodshed could result if attempts were made to split up the Soviet Union. He also warned of the international consequences if the Soviet Union disintegrated. Gorbachev reiterated that any republic that chose not to sign the Union treaty would have to abide by the law on secession, which requires that a referendum be conducted. He further made clear that he intended to do all in his power as president to hold the country together (*TASS*, November 23).

Five Killed in Siberian Mine Accident

Five miners were killed by an explosion at a coal mine in the Kuzbass region of Western Siberia on the night of November 22, TASS and Radio Moscow reported. The media said the explosion was caused by combustion of coal dust and methane during shaft-sinking at the Anzherskaya mine. They said the accident was probably due to a violation of safety regulations governing the use of explosives. A state commission was investigating the accident.

Soviet Guard Killed in Attack on Erevan Munitions Store

TASS said one Soviet border guard was killed and another wounded in an attack on an arms depot in Erevan, the capital of Armenia. The deputy head of the Transcaucasian Border District Forces, Major General L. Vysotsky, said the troops had been attacked by a group of five or six assailants who fled when reinforcements arrived. TASS reported that this was the second such attack within a year; there were no casualties reported in the earlier incident.

RSFSR Journalists' Union Created

Representatives of sixty regional journalists' organizations signed an agreement setting up an RSFSR Journalists' Union. TASS said that the Union would be independent of government bodies and political parties and that its main task would be to defend journalists against the continuing attempts of the authorities to impose restrictions on them. TASS noted, however, that the journalists' organizations of Moscow and Leningrad had not signed the agreement. TASS gave no reason for this, but earlier reports said journalists from the two cities were unhappy that the planning stage of the new union had been so dominated by editors of conservative periodicals.

Saturday, November 24

Soviet Troops in Germany

Soviet lawyer Oleg Lyamin told *Junge Welt* that at least 800 Soviet soldiers had died in East Germany in 1988 and that he was dealing with 2,000 cases of unexplained deaths in the armed forces overall. He said soldiers had been beaten and raped, some had been killed, and others had committed suicide. Lyamin also claimed that hundreds more had deserted and many had turned to crime. The commander of the Western Group of Forces, Army General Boris Snetkov, has denied Lyamin's claims, the *Chicago Tribune* reported on November 25. He said that only eighty-four soldiers had died in East Germany in 1988, many in traffic accidents or training mishaps.

On November 26, a leader of the German Social Democratic Party said the Soviet Union was confining conscripts in eastern Germany to their bases, AP reported. Manfred Opel said that the order was aimed at keeping Soviet soldiers from seeking asylum or selling their weapons. German Defense and Foreign Ministry officials noted, however, that Soviet enlisted men had long been restricted to their bases, saying that "this is nothing new." Opel's comments nevertheless indicate the rising tensions surrounding the continued presence of Soviet soldiers in Germany.

On November 29, the Soviet Union and the German armed forces set up a telephone hotline to coordinate the gradual withdrawal of Soviet troops from eastern Germany. Bonn's liaison office said the link was between the senior German military commander in eastern Germany, Lieutenant General Jörg Schönbohm, and Snetkov (*DPA*, November 29).

Meanwhile, police in the state of Thuringia in eastern Germany reported an incident involving a Soviet army deserter who took refuge in a police station in Saalfeld on November 28. The police said that Soviet troops briefly surrounded the building but later left. The police refused to disclose where the soldier had gone after he left the station, as they feared that doing so could endanger his life (*DPA*, November 29).

Cuba Counters Allegations in Khrushchev's Memoirs

Cuba's Communist Party newspaper, *Granma*, rebutted charges that Fidel Castro had favored a preemptive nuclear strike during the Cuban missile crisis. These allegations were contained in Nikita Khrushchev's newly released memoirs, excerpts from which were serialized in *Time* during September. *Granma*, as well as *Le Monde*, published the text of five messages exchanged between Khrushchev and Castro at the height of the crisis in 1962. *Granma*'s accompanying commentary described *Time*'s publication of the Khrushchev memoirs as "an attempt to stoke up anti-Cuban hysteria in the United States and the world."

Exodus from CPSU Continues

Vechernyaya Moskva said that as many as forty-two employees of the Youth Institute (formerly the Higher Komsomol School and alma mater of many Party officials) resigned from the CPSU between the Twenty-eighth Party Congress in July and September 11. The exodus from the Party of such popular figures as Boris El'tsin, Gavriil Popov, and Anatolii Sobchak, the newspaper said, had begun the process of the total collapse of the CPSU.

Deported Peoples Found Confederation

A confederation of peoples of the RSFSR who were victims of repression under Stalin was founded in Moscow, TASS reported. Representatives of the Balkars, Ingush, Kalmyks, Karachai, Crimean Tatars, Soviet Germans, and Chechens said they wanted to achieve the restoration of their land and the legal status of the territories of their peoples. The chairman of the presidium of the new confederation, Ismail Aliev, said the confederation would employ exclusively parliamentary methods to achieve its aims. The headquarters of the new confederation is Karachaevsk in the Karachai-Cherkess Autonomous Oblast.

Stalin's Bunker Opened to Public

Authorities in the city of Kuibyshev in the RSFSR opened Stalin's wartime bunker to the public. TASS said the bunker had been built during World War II as headquarters for the military supreme command and for Stalin personally. The agency said that Stalin had not made use of the bunker and that, until recently, it had been set aside as an administrative center for the region to be used in case of war. Local authorities had decided to turn it into a museum of civil defense.

Sunday, November 25

Yazov Calls for Unity in the Army

In an unscheduled ten-minute television appearance, Soviet Defense Minister Dmitrii Yazov harshly criticized nationalist forces in the Soviet republics and demanded that the army's unity be maintained. Yazov also dismissed as "absurd" a recent RSFSR resolution aimed at controlling the number and disposition of troops in the Russian Federation. Yazov saved some of his strongest criticism for the Baltic republics, warning that the Soviet army "will not permit anyone to taunt it." He was referring to recent clashes in Lithuania between civilians and military personnel and to reports from Latvia that local authorities were cutting off supplies to military bases.

Calls for Indigenous Officers to Be Replaced

Komsomol'skaya pravda reported that a USSR Defense Ministry order dated November 15 required that officers of local origin who command munitions depots be replaced by December 1, 1990. The newspaper said the order was aimed at local authorities in the Baltic republics, Transcaucasia, Moldavia, and parts of Ukraine who were alleged to be raiding weapons dumps in order to equip local military formations. The defense minister ordered that all such officers be assigned to equivalent duties elsewhere, and that those suspected of illicitly dispensing arms be dismissed from the army.

Akhromeev on Troop Withdrawal Problems

Marshal Sergei Akhromeev told the Finnish paper *Keskisuomalainen* that the half-million Soviet soldiers returning from Europe would worsen the USSR's social problems and require changes in defense policy, AP reported. Akhromeev tried to calm fears that troop build-ups on the Finnish border would be the result, saying: "We will not position the troops we are withdrawing from central Europe in the vicinity of Finland." Spokesmen for the Nordic countries argued, however, that the Soviet Union would have to station forces on the Finnish border and that "the front line of Soviet defense is already being pushed farther east and north . . . closer to us."

Deputies Set Up Pro-Union Council in Riga

Parliamentary deputies from several Soviet republics met in the Latvian capital, Riga, on November 24 and formed a council in support of the proposed new Union treaty, TASS reported on November 25. TASS said the group, called the Interparliamentary Council, included deputies from the Baltic, USSR, and Belorussian parliaments and also some members of the Moscow and Leningrad City Soviets. These deputies advocate the preservation of the Soviet Union. According to TASS, the group views itself as an alternative to the Baltic Council, which is seeking independence for the Baltic republics.

Tajik Democratic Party Leaders on Hunger Strike

Komsomol'skaya pravda reported that the Presidium of the Tajik Supreme Soviet had promulgated a decree prohibiting hunger strikes just half an hour before such a strike by leaders of the Democratic Party of Tajikistan was scheduled to begin. Members of the Democratic Party who appeared at the Supreme Soviet building were detained by policemen enforcing the decree. According to the report, the dispute originated with a request by the Democratic Party to hold a congress at the beginning of December. The Supreme Soviet Presidium ruled that the congress could be held only after December 15, when the current session of the republican Supreme Soviet is scheduled to end.

On November 28, in a move apparently intended to reduce tensions in Dushanbe, the Presidium of the Tajik Supreme Soviet reversed its earlier decision and gave the Democratic Party of Tajikistan permission to hold a congress on December 1, according to Radio Dushanbe. The report said party leaders had promised to end a hunger strike in protest against the original decision. The late news on Central Television reported, however, that the strike continued on November 28, with the number of participants having grown to 200. According to the report, the strikers were also demanding the direct election of the republic's president and an end to the harassment of informal groups.

Chechen and Ingush Proclaim Sovereignty

A congress of the Chechen people unanimously adopted a declaration of state sovereignty of the Chechen republic, TASS reported. The congress—which was attended by about a thousand elected delegates, guests from other parts of the Soviet Union, and representatives of the

Chechen diaspora—asked the Supreme Soviet of the Checheno-Ingush ASSR to ratify the decision.

On November 26, people's deputies of the Checheno-Ingush ASSR adopted a declaration of sovereignty proclaiming the Checheno-Ingush Republic and stated that the republic did not form part of either the Russian Federation or the USSR, TASS reported on November 27. This goes further than any other autonomous republic. The declaration does state, however, that the republic can enter into treaty relations with other states and join a union of states. November 27 was declared the day of national rebirth of the Chechen and Ingush peoples.

Deputies from Four Republics Back Community of Interests

Members of the Supreme Soviets of four Union republics met in Minsk and agreed to promote the establishment of a loosely knit confederation stretching from the Gulf of Finland to the Black Sea. The deputies signed a declaration proposing a community of interests for Latvia, Lithuania, Belorussia, and Ukraine. One of its purposes would be to provide mutual aid if the center should impose an economic blockade (RL Belorussian service, November 26).

Kozyrev Says RSFSR Does Not Seek Superpower Role

The foreign minister of the Russian Republic, Andrei Kozyrev, urged the West not to concentrate on Gorbachev alone in formulating foreign policy but to take account of the growing influence of the republics. Writing in *The New York Times*, he said foreign policy in the USSR was no longer under the sole direction of the USSR Foreign Ministry. Kozyrev argued that the desire of Ukraine, Belorussia, and the Baltic republics to establish nuclear-free zones on their territories implied that the RSFSR would remain in sole possession of nuclear weapons. The RSFSR, Kozyrev concluded, does not seek superpower status; rather, it favors cuts in Soviet military potential.

Monday, November 26

USSR Supreme Soviet Discusses 1991 Budget and Plan

The USSR Supreme Soviet met to discuss the 1991 budget and plan for the country's economic and social development. Supreme Soviet Chairman Anatolii Luk'yanov said the 1991 budget and plan were of special significance as instruments for implementing emergency measures to stabilize the economy and consumer market. First Deputy Prime Minister Yurii Maslyukov introduced the plan. He said the USSR's economic situation had considerably worsened because of political and economic developments, as well as steps by the republics to assert the supremacy of their laws over all-Union laws. Maslyukov said there was a crisis in the governing of the USSR and that economic instability was increasing (*TASS*, November 26).

On November 28, Novosti reported that the Soviet government intended to impose a 3-percent sales tax in 1991 to increase government revenue. The new tax will be levied on both producers and consumers.

Khasbulatov on Draft Union Treaty

A senior RSFSR official added harsh criticism to the mixed reviews of President Gorbachev's draft Union treaty. First Deputy Chairman of the RSFSR Supreme Soviet Ruslan Khasbulatov told the *Financial Times* the plan was unacceptable even to the RSFSR, which does not want to leave the Union. "This Union treaty is a big coffin for all of us to lie in," Khasbulatov said.

Complaints Judged Groundless

The Soviet television news program "Vremya" reported the findings of a special commission set up by the Presidium of the USSR Supreme Soviet to examine the cases of the approximately 200 desperate people who have, since July, sought to draw attention to their complaints by camping in a shanty town outside the Hotel Rossiya on Red Square. A commission spokeswoman said the commission had found the majority of the complaints to be without foundation, while one member of the commission said he and his colleagues were not afraid to recommend the use of force to "liquidate" the protest.

Cattle Diseases Still Classified as State Secrets

Five people contracted brucellosis (undulant fever) from contact with infected cattle in Tula Oblast in the RSFSR. TASS said those infected were stockbreeders at a state farm and that foreign livestock had been identified as the source of the infection. TASS went on to point out, however, that the disease would not have spread to humans had the regional health service not initially concealed the fact that the imported livestock were diseased. Diseases in cattle are still treated as state secrets in the USSR, according to a recent list compiled by the Main Administration for the Preservation of State Secrets in the Mass Media.

Moscow Leader Says City Needs Foreign Aid

The deputy chairman of the Moscow City Soviet, Sergei Stankevich, said the city would need "urgent" foreign assistance with certain types of food over the winter. Addressing a news conference in Moscow, Stankevich said the city had stocks of powdered milk sufficient to last for only three days. Nine regions bordering Moscow said they intended to halt or severely reduce their milk deliveries to the capital. Stankevich suggested that this was an organized campaign aimed at worsening the food situation in the Soviet capital. He said that the city authorities had already turned to foreign firms and that food was beginning to reach the city, but he called for further aid from foreign charities and other public organizations (*AFP*, November 26).

Meanwhile, addressing a special session of the RSFSR Congress of People's Deputies, Boris El'tsin said that feeding the nation was more important than political confrontation. He said that "the threat of famine" made confrontation between the RSFSR and the center a luxury that politicians could not afford (*Central Television*, November 27).

On November 29, the first aircraft delivering food from Germany landed in Moscow (*DPA*, November 29). On November 30, the chairman of the Moscow City Soviet, Gavriil Popov, blamed the Soviet Union's acute shortages on the distribution system and on hoarding. Speaking at a conference of the Moscow City Party organization, he criticized collective and state farmers, whom he accused of refusing to sell commodities to the state (*Postfaktum*, *Radio Moscow-1*, November 30).

Agreements on Cooperation between Republics

The governments of Ukraine and Kazakhstan signed an agreement on developing economic and cultural cooperation during 1991–95. TASS said the agreement was signed in the Ukrainian capital, Kiev. The agency said the two governments pledged to make every effort to develop strong economies in their republics and to satisfy demand for food and consumer goods. Kazakhstan and Ukraine recently signed similar agreements with the Russian Federation. TASS also said Georgia and Estonia had started talks in Tbilisi on political, economic, social, and cultural cooperation, which led to the signing of a treaty on November 27 in the Georgian capital.

On November 29, agreement on economic and cultural cooperation from 1991 to 1995 between Estonia, Latvia, and Ukraine was reached in Kiev, according to an Ukrinform dispatch. The agreements established mechanisms for coordinating cooperation between the signatories. The same day, Radio Riga reported agreement between the Latvian and Georgian governments to exchange "permanent representatives."

Moldavia Considers Measures to Combat Shortages

Moldavian Trade Minister Valeriu Bobutac told Moldovapres that "accelerated privatization" and the introduction of republican ration coupons were the only way to alleviate the shortages of consumer goods on the Moldavian market. Bobutac said that, notwithstanding the draft Union treaty, which provides for a common financial policy and all-Union currency, Moldavia would have to protect its consumer market by issuing "its own coupons, essentially a national currency," whose value would be higher than the ruble by virtue of being tied to goods on the republican market.

Tuesday, November 27

Yazov and Gorbachev Approve Use of Force in Strife-Torn Republics

USSR Defense Minister Dmitrii Yazov told Soviet television audiences that the armed forces had been ordered to use force if necessary to protect military installations and personnel in areas torn by ethnic strife. Acting on orders from President Gorbachev, Yazov condemned "illegal actions" in a number of republics, which he said were undermining national security. He also said nuclear weapons would remain under the control of the central authorities. Earlier in the day, Gorbachev issued a presidential decree protecting the rights of servicemen in the non-Russian republics (*TASS*, November 27).

On November 28, Lithuanian officials criticized Yazov's statement. The president of the Lithuanian Supreme Council, Vytautas Landsbergis, said Yazov was "playing with fire" (RFE/Lithuanian service, November 28). Yazov's statement was criticized by officials of other Baltic republics. A deputy to the Belorussian Supreme Soviet, Sergei Navumchyk, told RFE/RL he thought Yazov's edict meant that "the military is beginning to set the tone" in Moscow (RL Belorussian service, November 28). See RL 495/90.

Moiseev Says Military Discharges May Be Delayed

Chief of the General Staff of the Soviet Armed Forces Mikhail Moiseev said recruits due for discharge may have to serve longer because of problems with the draft this fall. Moiseev was addressing the Ukrainian Supreme Soviet. The Ukrainian parliament adopted a resolution in October that required most Ukrainian conscripts to serve in their own republic. Moiseev said this had caused the Soviet Armed Forces difficulties because young Ukrainians make up a fifth of all those drafted. He also said 3,000 Soviet servicemen had deserted this year, 184 of them Ukrainians. Moiseev said the USSR Defense Ministry was taking into consideration the decisions of the Ukrainian parliament when planning special measures to meet the interests of Ukrainian citizens (*TASS*, November 27).

Gorbachev Says Lithuanian Law on Parties Illegal

Mikhail Gorbachev issued a decree declaring a recent law on political parties adopted by the Lithuanian Supreme Council illegal. He said the law violated the USSR Constitution and he urged people not to obey it. In September, the Lithuanian parliament adopted a law saying only Lithuanian citizens could join political parties in the republic. The law also forbade the establishment of parties of other states in Lithuania or the conduct by them of political activity. Radio Vilnius said that when the law was passed only one party from another state was active in Lithuania—the CPSU. Gorbachev's decree said this part of the law overtly discriminated against Soviet Communists in Lithuania (*TASS*, November 27; *Pravda*, November 28).

On November 28, the president of the Lithuanian Supreme Council, Vytautas Landsbergis, denied that the law on political parties was discriminatory. He also said Gorbachev's decree had no legal force, because it was directed at the "Lithuanian SSR" and there was no such entity (RFE Lithuanian service, November 28).

Ol'ga Shatunovskaya Dies

Ol'ga Shatunovskaya, an Old Bolshevik and a longtime prisoner in the labor camps under Stalin, died in Moscow on November 23, *Pravda* reported on November 27. Rehabilitated by Khrushchev, Shatunovskaya resumed an active role in Party affairs and became a member of the Party Control Committee and of the commission set up in 1960 by the Presidium of the CPSU Central Committee to investigate Kirov's murder. In a letter to *Argumenty i fakty* (No. 22) earlier this year, Shatunovskaya said the Kirov commission had assembled convincing evidence of Stalin's responsibility for the murder. The commission's conclusions were not made public, however, and Shatunovskaya claimed that key documents on Stalin's involvement had been destroyed after Khrushchev's ouster.

Court Case against Gorbachev Critic

A representative of the USSR Prosecutor's Office visited the office of *Argumenty i fakty* to seize the original of a letter, published in issue No. 42 of the periodical, that accused Mikhail Gorbachev of being "an agent of world imperialism" and of undermining Soviet power. *Argumenty i fakty* (No. 45) reported that a court case had been initiated against the author of the letter, R. Shumkevich, who is charged with violating the law on the defense of the honor and dignity of the Soviet president. *Argumenty i fakty* said that, although the editorial board did not share Shumkevich's views, it opposed the decision to initiate proceedings. The newspaper added that Shumkevich's letter was typical of many it had received recently.

Hijackers Sentenced in Leningrad Court

Four men received sentences of up to eight years in prison for the attempted hijacking of a Soviet airliner on July 10. A Leningrad court sentenced Georgii Apkhazava of Georgia to eight years' hard labor for the attempted hijacking to Sweden of a Tupolev-154. The court also sentenced three teenage men in connection with a separate attempted hijacking on July 12. Vladislav Lebedev was sentenced to two years in a labor camp, Aleksei Kudryavtsev to two and a half years, and Aleksandr Korablev to two years (*AFP*, November 27).

Samaranch Confirms Decision to Bar Baltic Teams from Olympics

At a press conference in Varna, Bulgaria, on November 27, International Olympic Committee President Juan Antonio Samaranch confirmed the IOC's decision to bar teams representing the Baltic republics from competing in the Olympic Games until Estonia, Latvia, and Lithuania were independent of the Soviet Union. Samaranch added that he would welcome Baltic Olympic committees, but, he said, "before that, they must solve their political problems" (*Reuters*, *DPA*, November 28).

Soviet Delegation in South Africa

Andrei Chernuchin, director general of the state industry and technology enterprise Ekonprom, headed a nine-man Soviet delegation to explore trade and academic contacts with South Africa (*Reuters*, November 28). Chernuchin addressed South African leaders of commerce, industry, and science in Pretoria. Chernuchin asked for assistance in the resettlement of people displaced by the Chernobyl' nuclear accident. In August, 1989, Pretoria pledged help with cleanup efforts. While the two countries have no diplomatic relations, the Soviet side has recently indicated an interest in establishing ties.

Creation of Soviet Zionist Federation

The inaugural congress of the USSR Zionist Federation opened in Moscow, TASS reported. A spokesman for the congress, Eli Lifshitz, said that representatives of Jewish communities in fifty cities were participating. On November 28, the congress adopted its program, TASS reported. The main initiator of the congress was the Zionist organization "Irgun Tsioni." Among the aims of the federation are assisting the migration of Soviet Jews to Israel, "fighting anti-Semitism at the political level," participating in elections, and trying to persuade the USSR government to be less hostile towards Israel in its Middle Eastern policy. Members of "Pamyat'" and a group of Arab students in Moscow, numbering about a hundred in all, held a protest demonstration on November 28 outside the building where the congress met. TASS reported that the demonstrators chanted anti-Zionist slogans and burned the Israeli flag.

Wednesday, November 28

Politburo Asks Gorbachev for Action on Lithuania

The CPSU Politburo asked President Gorbachev to take all necessary measures to guarantee Soviet citizens' rights in Lithuania. The Politburo criticized what it called "antidemocratic acts" and "human-rights violations" in Lithuania. The statement said non-Lithuanians and Soviet soldiers had been attacked and provoked in the republic. It especially criticized the Lithuanian law on political parties (*TASS*, November 28; *Pravda*, November 29).

Gorbachev Meets Cultural Figures

Mikhail Gorbachev met in Moscow with cultural figures from all of the Union republics. In a speech to them, he took responsibility for the failure of his reform policies but said he would carry on. Gorbachev said he would not give in either to people who wanted to turn the clock back or to those who wanted to lead the country into "adventures." A declaration was adopted at the meeting, urging citizens of the Soviet Union to unite in order to get the country out of the present crisis (*Central Television*, "Vremya"; *TASS*, November 28).

Latvians Unenthusiastic about Union Treaty

Radio Riga said a recent public opinion poll showed that only 8 percent of the Latvians and 54 percent of the non-Latvians living in Latvia endorsed the new Union treaty. The same poll also indicated that 91 percent of Latvians and 41 percent of non-Latvians believed that in 1940 the Soviet Union occupied and subsequently annexed the Baltic states.

Speculation on Troop Movements

Komsomol'skaya pravda carried a lengthy article on a recent USSR Supreme Soviet report on mysterious troop movements around Moscow in early September. The article questioned the thoroughness of the report, which was compiled by the Supreme Soviet Committee for Defense and State Security and the Committee for Questions of *Glasnost'*, arguing that it had failed to answer a number of crucial questions, among them why the Soviet Air Force had failed to record any flights by heavy aircraft from Belorussia to Moscow and Ryazan at that time, why airborne troops did not fire a single shot in the alleged training exercise, and why the maneuvers were suddenly terminated.

Dollar Falls against Ruble

In the last two rounds of currency auctions in Moscow, the ruble traded at 20.88 to the US dollar. This compared with an exchange rate of 22.6 rubles to the dollar on October 9. New data published in *Ekonomika i zhizn'* (No. 48) indicated that the volume of currency exchanged at auction had grown to 24.3 million hard-currency rubles on November 15 from only 11.7 million on October 25.

New Chief of TASS Appointed

Lev Spiridonov, a candidate of philosophical sciences, was appointed head of the main Soviet news agency, TASS. Spiridonov replaced Leonid Kravchenko, who earlier in November became the chairman of the USSR State Committee for Television and Radio Broadcasting. Spiridonov was previously first deputy chief editor of *Pravda*.

El'tsin Issues Appeal to Peoples of Northern Caucasus

Chairman of the RSFSR Supreme Soviet Boris El'tsin appealed to the peoples of the Northern Caucasus in the name of the RSFSR Supreme Soviet to "maintain calm and show wisdom and restraint," TASS reported. The appeal noted with regret the exacerbation of interethnic tensions in the Northern Caucasus and attempts to split up the existing state and territorial formations. El'tsin assured the people of the area that the RSFSR parliament would guarantee them equality of rights, which would be reflected in the new RSFSR federal treaty and constitution.

Chernobyl' Death Toll

Volodymyr Yavorivs'kyi, a deputy to the USSR and Ukrainian parliaments, told reporters at the United Nations that the Soviet authorities had suppressed information about the extent of the death toll from the Chernobyl' catastrophe in 1986 and had falsified death certificates. He said that he personally knew of 540 deaths resulting directly from the accident. The official toll is thirty-one.

Yavorivs'kyi blamed the low official figure on an unpublicized government decree aimed at keeping all data on Chernobyl' secret. Yavorivs'kyi is chairman of the Ukrainian Supreme Soviet Commission on Questions of the Chernobyl' Catastrophe (*Reuters*, RL Ukrainian service, November 28).

Thursday, November 29

Gorbachev Says CPSU Stands Guilty before Working Class

Speaking at a conference of the Moscow City Party Committee, Mikhail Gorbachev said he was aware of the worsening of the country's food situation and its ethnic problems. "We stand guilty before the working class, I think, all of us and me personally," Gorbachev added. He also said that agreements had been reached with Estonia, Ukraine, and Kazakhstan for deliveries of dairy products to the Soviet capital, TASS reported.

On November 29, the conference reelected Yurii Prokof'ev first secretary of the Moscow City Party Committee (*TASS*, November 30).

On November 30, Radio Moscow-1 and the Postfactum news agency reported that the conference was addressed by the chairman of the Moscow City Soviet, Gavriil Popov, who complained about problems with the supply of food to the Soviet capital and called on Gorbachev to issue a special decree on the situation in Moscow.

Difficulties in Military-Plant Conversion

Difficulties were reported in the conversion of Soviet military plants to civilian production. *Komsomol'skaya pravda* said that, of 400 defense enterprises scheduled for conversion, only five or six had been fully switched to manufacturing consumer goods. The article said the products from those factories "are a far cry from world standards." The newspaper also complained that conversions were undermining "the only sound sector of the economy."

Georgian Patriarch Attacked in Abkhazia

TASS reported that the motorcade of Georgian Patriarch Ilia II had been attacked on November 27, while traveling in the Abkhaz ASSR, by a crowd of 2,000 Abkhaz. The patriarch escaped uninjured, but one car was forcibly overturned and a passenger beaten. Some twenty people were killed in clashes between Georgians and Abkhaz in July, 1989, and the Abkhaz Popular Front, which is campaigning for the separation of Abkhazia from Georgia and its upgrading to the status of a

Union republic, was banned from participating in the Georgian elections in October. Ilia II recently issued a proclamation condemning as "an enemy of the Georgian people" any individual who murdered an ethnic Georgian, regardless of circumstances.

Gorbachev Protests against Replacement of Georgian KGB Leader

"Vremya," the television news program, reported that Gorbachev had declared illegal and unconstitutional a decision by the newly elected Georgian parliament to replace the republic's KGB leader. The new Georgian government named the previous week did not include the post of KGB chairman, but Supreme Soviet Chairman Zviad Gamsakhurdia's personal bodyguard was named minister of internal affairs.

Armenian Party Congress Votes on Party Status, Elects First Secretary

At the second stage of the Armenian Communist Party Congress, delegates adopted a resolution declaring the Party to be independent within the framework of the CPSU, TASS reported. (Prior to the first stage of the congress in September, it had been proposed to hold a referendum among Party members to determine whether the republican Party should break its ties with the CPSU.) The congress also elected a new Party first secretary to replace Vladimir Movsisyan, who stood down for health reasons (*TASS*, November 30). His successor was Stepan Pogosyan, a fifty-eight-year-old historian, who had also served as the Party first secretary in the Armenian capital, Erevan.

Uzbek-Chinese Economic Agreement Signed

An agreement was signed on establishing joint Uzbek-Chinese enterprises in Uzbekistan and in the Uigur autonomous region of northwestern China. Radio Tashkent said the enterprises would be involved in agriculture and consumer goods production.

Latvian Parliament Bars Soviet Soldiers from Voting

The Latvian Supreme Soviet voted 111 to 39 in favor of changing the Latvian Constitution to bar Soviet soldiers from voting with effect from December 1. Some deputies expressed fear that the Latvian decision could be seen in Moscow as a provocation, but Supreme Council Deputy Chairman Dainis Ivans said the decision should have been made long ago. In Lithuania, only natives of Lithuania serving in the army may vote. In Estonia, Soviet soldiers may vote only to fill four Supreme Soviet seats reserved for the armed forces (RFE Latvian service, November 29).

"Intermovement" Representative Meets with Marshal Akhromeev

Igor Lopatin, a representative of the organizational buro of the recently formed USSR "Intermovement," met with Marshal Sergei Akhromeev, Novosti reported. On November 30 Lopatin informed Akhromeev of the aims of the USSR "Intermovement" and the plans of the Latvian branch to stage a series of mass protests against the infringement of the rights of servicemen in the republic. He also asked Akhromeev to inform Gorbachev of the readiness of his organization to cooperate with the central authorities in order to stabilize the country and preserve the unity of the Soviet Union.

Friday, November 30

Gorbachev Orders Workers to Control Supplies of Food and Consumer Goods

Mikhail Gorbachev ordered the creation of special workers' committees to monitor the distribution of food and consumer goods. A decree by Gorbachev stated that the committees would strictly supervise the distribution system, from producer to consumer. The decree's declared purpose was to limit hoarding, spoilage, theft, and speculation. The committees were instructed to work closely with the KGB and the USSR Ministry of Internal Affairs (*TASS*, November 30; *Pravda*, December 1). The KGB was also reported to have set up an agency to direct the distribution of food aid sent to the USSR. TASS said that this had been approved by the USSR Supreme Soviet and that the KGB would concentrate on ensuring the food aid moved efficiently through the Soviet Union's distribution system.

Soviet Official Says USSR May Have Miscalculated Arms Figures

A Soviet arms negotiator, Oleg Grinevsky, said the USSR might have miscalculated the number of arms it must scrap under the new CFE treaty reducing conventional forces in Europe. Grinevsky told a news conference that "mistakes cannot be excluded" and, if found, "they will be corrected." Grinevsky heads the Soviet delegation at the NATO–Warsaw Pact talks in Vienna on reducing the number of troops in Europe. He was questioned about Western concerns that the USSR had deliberately moved a lot of military equipment east of the Urals, where it is outside the zone covered by the conventional arms treaty. Grinevsky responded that "nothing dangerous [or] surprising is going on." He said 8,000 modern tanks and many other weapons were moved east as part of a unilateral withdrawal of forces announced by Mikhail Gorbachev in 1988 (*Reuters*, *AP*, November 30).

Lvov Oblast Soviet Head Granted Emergency Powers

The oblast soviet of Lvov in western Ukraine decided to grant special powers to its chairman, former political prisoner Vyacheslav Chornovil. Radio Kiev said the powers may be used in an emergency and when there was not time to convene the Presidium of the soviet. The soviet also imposed a ban on political activity in the workplace and demanded the release from detention of Stepan Khmara, a deputy to the Ukrainian Supreme Soviet accused of attacking a policeman in Kiev.

Makhkamov Elected President of Tajikistan

Kakhar Makhkamov, the first secretary of the Tajik Communist Party, was elected president of Tajikistan. His election by the Tajik Supreme Soviet was announced by Radio Dushanbe. In addition to his Party post, Makhkamov was chairman of the Tajik Supreme Soviet. The Tajik parliament decided to institute an executive presidency on November 29.

Sino-Soviet Talks on Armed Forces Reductions Resume

The Soviet Union and China resumed talks in Beijing on mutual reduction in armed forces along their common border. TASS said the Soviet delegation was headed by Genrikh Kireev, head of the USSR Foreign Ministry's department concerned with Socialist countries in Asia, and by Liu Guangzhi, head of the Chinese Foreign Ministry's Soviet and East European Department (*TASS*, November 30).

The Month of December

Saturday, December 1

Congress of "Soyuz"

On December 1, "Vremya" led with a report on the weekend congress of the conservative "Soyuz" group of deputies. The group is dedicated to the preservation of the integrity of the Soviet Union. The meeting was presided over by Chairman of the USSR Supreme Soviet Council of Nationalities Rafik Nishanov, and the group was lionized by the moderator of "Vremya"—a program that always reflects the official point of view.

During the two-day gathering of "Soyuz," members demanded the resignation of Minister of Internal Affairs Vadim Bakatin; they also called for the selection of a conservative for the post of vice president. Some delegates at the gathering said that, if Gorbachev did not meet their demands, "Soyuz" intended to put foward a motion of no-confidence in the president during the forthcoming session of the USSR Supreme Soviet, AFP reported. The gathering was addressed by Anatolii Luk'yanov, chairman of the USSR Supreme Soviet, who warned the group against veering to the right. The meeting formally set up the all-Union "Soyuz" Association of Deputies at all levels, TASS reported on December 2.

Gorbachev Issues Decree on Armed Forces

Mikhail Gorbachev issued a presidential decree declaring null and void any republican laws that threaten Soviet defense capability and stipulating that republics had no right to form their own armed forces, TASS reported (see also *Pravda*, December 2). The decree ruled specifically against republican laws allowing local young men to perform military service in their home republics. A number of republics have passed such legislation, and military leaders have complained bitterly that the military manpower system is being undermined. Gorbachev has moved increasingly to embrace the generals' views.

Joint Session of Baltic Parliaments

An unprecedented joint session of the parliaments of the Baltic republics was held in Vilnius. Parliamentary delegations from Estonia, Latvia, and Lithuania approved documents calling for a withdrawal of Soviet troops from their republics, the recognition of Baltic independence by governments in the West, and the start of negotiations with the USSR on Baltic independence (*AP*, *Radio Vilnius*, December 1).

In their appeal to the residents of the Baltic republics and Soviet soldiers, the legislators called for the prompt withdrawal of Soviet troops as part of a process of establishing the de facto independence of Estonia, Latvia, and Lithuania. They stressed that the Baltic people did not consider Soviet soldiers their enemies, since the soldiers were victims of an imperialist policy toward the Baltics.

Yazov Again Threatens to Use Force

In an interview in *Komsomol'skaya pravda*, Defense Minister Dmitrii Yazov reiterated that Soviet troops would seize supply facilities if local authorities cut off services to military garrisons. Yazov, pointing especially to the Baltic republics, said that local authorities were "threatening" the army. He warned: "We will take the electric power stations, the thermal electric power stations, and the water supply under our protection if the need arises." This was Yazov's third statement threatening force in one week, and it came as Gorbachev moved to intimidate supporters of independence in the Baltic and elsewhere.

Switzerland to Send Soldiers as Relief Workers

During meetings in Moscow on November 30 and December 1, Switzerland and the Soviet Union signed agreements providing for Swiss assistance to the USSR. According to Swiss Foreign Minister Rene Felber, one agreement provided for a special Swiss army emergency intervention corps to be sent to the Soviet Union (*Swiss Radio*, December 2).

Two Hijacking Attempts Foiled

Soviet army intelligence foiled a plot by soldiers in Siberia to hijack an airplane to the United States and join the mafia. The story, appearing in *Rabochaya tribuna* (December 1), alleged that the soldiers had intended to take their commander and his wife hostage but were apprehended while their planning for the operation was still in its early stages. On December 2, it was reported that an unidentified Soviet man had tried to hijack a Murmansk-Leningrad flight to Sweden. AFP said the man had given himself up and the plane had landed in Leningrad as planned.

There was another hijack attempt on December 12. A man on an Aeroflot flight from Baku to Tbilisi demanded that the pilot fly to Turkey, TASS reported. The crew persuaded the man, identified as Raul Mursalov, that the plane needed to land in Tbilisi to refuel and settle other matters connected with the flight to Turkey. TASS said police arrested the man upon the plane's arrival in the Georgian capital and a criminal investigation was initiated against him.

Democratic Party of Tajikistan Holds Congress

The Democratic Party of Tajikistan opened a controversial congress that was the subject of conflict between the organization and the republican authorities. The authorities had initially ordered the congress to be delayed until after the current session of the Supreme Soviet, but then moved forward the date of the legislative session so that the presidential election would take place before the Democrats could meet. TASS reported that the party program adopted by the Democrats on December 1 called for a law on citizenship based on the Universal Declaration of Human Rights and for the depoliticization of the judiciary, KGB, and MVD.

Situation in Moldavia

At a mass rally in Kishinev on December 1, the Moldavian Popular Front made public the text of a statement that was to have been read in the front's name in the Moldavian Supreme Soviet on November 30 during Gorbachev's planned visit. In the statement the front appealed to Gorbachev to end his policy of pressure and threats against the Baltic and other republics aspiring to more independence. Noting Gorbachev's contribution to ending East-West tensions, the front urged him not to use "Cold War methods" inside the USSR to govern relations between the center and the republics. It protested against attempts to make Moldavia's territorial integrity conditional on its agreement to sign the proposed Union treaty, saying that Moldavia could not sign as long as "occupation troops" remained on its territory (*RFE/RL Special*, December 1).

On November 30, a congress of deputies of the self-proclaimed Dniester Republic named a delegation to go to Moscow to meet with Gorbachev, Radio Moscow reported on December 1.

On December 3, USSR Foreign Ministry spokesman Vitalii Churkin criticized Romanian Prime Minister Petre Roman for his comments on Moldavia. Churkin told a briefing in Moscow that Roman's remarks on Soviet Moldavia in an interview with *Die Welt* (November 28) constituted "unacceptable interference in the domestic affairs of the USSR," TASS reported. He quoted Roman as saying that it was Romania's task to "fight for Moldavia's independence." In Bucharest a government spokesman responded that Roman had used the term "sovereignty," not independence, Radio Bucharest reported on December 4. In fact,

Die Welt had quoted Roman as saying that "a struggle for independence" was under way in Soviet Moldavia and that reunification with Romania was "entirely possible" later on in "the natural course of history."

On December 5, the Moldavian Supreme Soviet adopted at its first reading a draft law on the police, TASS reported. As summarized by TASS, the law subordinated the police directly to the republican leadership without any mention of dual republican and all-Union jurisdiction. It stipulated that the activities of political parties would not be allowed in police units. The law also raised policemen's salaries to at least double the average salary in the republic.

On December 6, TASS reported that the Moldavian Supreme Soviet had lifted the state of emergency imposed on parts of the republic populated by the Gagauz minority. The state of emergency was imposed in late October when the Gagauz began electing a parliament for their self-declared republic.

Moldavian Prime Minister Mircea Druc, on his way home after a business trip to Italy, stopped over in Bucharest on December 7 for a day of talks with Romanian Prime Minister Petre Roman. The two prime ministers told the Romanian media after their session that they had discussed creating "an institutionalized framework" for economic cooperation, which they described as a matter of "high priority" for their governments. It was Druc's first-ever trip to Romania and the highest-level Romanian-Moldavian meeting thus far.

On December 8, the Moldavian Supreme Soviet adopted at its first reading a draft law whose avowed aim was to "stop immigration that has pushed Moldavia's population density to 140 people per square kilometer, the highest in the USSR." As summarized by TASS, the preamble also stated that immigrants' claims to jobs and housing "may not infringe on the interests of the republic's citizens." The law empowered the Moldavian government to set immigration quotas on the basis of specific requests to be submitted by local administrative bodies.

On December 11, the would-be Dniester SSR and Gagauz Republic decided to join together in a federation, TASS reported. A joint declaration by their self-styled Supreme Soviets announced this decision and proclaimed the two republics' adherence to the new Union treaty as members of the "renewed" USSR. The declaration invited Moldavia to join the two republics in a tripartite federation.

Belorussian Party Chief Replaced

In a surprise development, Party First Secretary Efrem Sokolov did not stand for reelection at the Thirty-first

Congress of the Belorussian Communist Party. He apparently did not want to take part in a secret ballot election. The new republican Party first secretary is Anatolii Malofeev, former first secretary of Minsk Oblast. He only narrowly defeated Vladimir Brovikov, the former Soviet ambassador to Poland, who has been an outspoken critic of Gorbachev's policies. Malofeev sharply criticized the situation in Belorussia, called for the speedy conclusion of the Union treaty, and indicated that there would be a personnel shakeup.

Armenian Parliament Grants Special Powers to Prime Minister

The Armenian Supreme Soviet granted special powers to the republic's government and to Prime Minister Vazgen Manukyan. TASS quoted *Izvestia* as saying the measure had been made necessary by "the extremely tense situation" that had arisen in the republic's economy, particularly in the consumer market. Manukyan's additional powers will be valid for one year. They include the right to appoint and fire members of the republic's government.

Karachai-Cherkess Sovereignty Declaration

The Karachai-Cherkess Autonomous Oblast Soviet declared the territory a sovereign state, the Karachai-Cherkess SSR, within the RSFSR, TASS reported. While the declaration was in line with similar moves made by many other autonomous territories, it also seemed to be intended to act as a counterweight to the recent decision of a congress of Karachai deputies to proclaim a separate Karachai republic. After dwelling on the supposed community of culture, traditions, and customs of the disparate peoples inhabiting the oblast, the declaration stated that its raised status would make it possible to deal with pressing social and economic problems "on the basis of preserving national-territorial integrity."

Sunday, December 2

Gorbachev Replaces Minister of Internal Affairs

Mikhail Gorbachev replaced the relatively liberal minister of internal affairs, Vadim Bakatin, with Boriss Pugo, who headed the KGB in Latvia in the early 1980s (*TASS*, December 2). (Until this new appointment, Pugo was chairman of the CPSU Party Control Commission.) Colonel General Boris Gromov, the last commander of Soviet Forces in Afghanistan, was named first deputy minister. The move appeared to presage a switch to tougher policies in the law and order sphere and a virtual takeover of the ministry of internal affairs by the secret police and the army.

On December 3, Latvian deputy Colonel Viktor Alksnis, who is a leader of "Soyuz," welcomed the appointment of Pugo. Alksnis told TASS that Bakatin was "not only passive but rendered concrete support to separatist forces in the republics." A USSR Supreme Soviet deputy from Estonia joined Alksnis in praising Gorbachev's shakeup of the Ministry of Internal Affairs. Evgenii Kogan, leader of the "Intermovement" and also a member of "Soyuz," emphasized that "Soyuz" had persuaded Gorbachev to replace Bakatin with Pugo. Kogan told Reuters on December 3 that "the turn of other people who do not suit 'Soyuz' will come very soon."

On December 6, Pugo appealed to the Soviet people to help the police fight crime. Pugo also called on the USSR Supreme Soviet to approve quickly a law to give law-enforcement bodies a stronger legal basis for their work (*Central Television*, "Vremya," December 6).

On December 10, the USSR Supreme Soviet failed to approve Bakatin's resignation and the appointment of Pugo and his deputy, Boris Gromov, TASS reported. Supreme Soviet Chairman Anatolii Luk'yanov blamed the Interregional Group of Deputies for the failure. He accused the liberal deputies of conspiring against Gorbachev and his policies (*Central Television*, December 12).

A report carried by the "Vremya" television news program claimed that the Supreme Soviet had failed to approve Bakatin's replacement because of the lack of a quorum. Reports reaching Radio Liberty from Moscow, on the other hand, maintained that Gorbachev's attempt to replace Bakatin had been stalled by the refusal of two parliamentary committees to recommend it to the Supreme Soviet; according to these sources, the committees demanded that Gorbachev explain the reasons for his decision.

Democratic Party of Russia Holds Congress

The Democratic Party of Russia held its first congress over the weekend. (The Party was founded in May, 1990.) Almost 700 delegates attended the congress, TASS said. Some called for the "constitutional overthrow" of the Communist Party and the reconstruction of an independent Russian democratic state. The congress elected Nikolai Travkin as the party's chairman. Travkin told the congress that the party was openly anti-Communist, but he dissociated himself from calls from some members of the party for the prosecution of the Communist Party.

Sharp Debate on Yakut Sakha Constitution

The draft of the new constitution of the Yakut Sakha SSR was adopted at its first reading after what Radio Moscow described as an unprecedentedly heated debate. At one stage a group of deputies left the Supreme Soviet session in order to deprive it of a quorum. Radio Moscow did not reveal what caused the dissension. The draft introduced republican citizenship, made Yakut and Russian the state languages, and declared the Yakut Sakha SSR part of Russia and a subject of the USSR. Natural resources were declared to be the exclusive property of the republic, which is to be a nuclear-free zone.

Gorno-Altai Communists on Adoption of Union Treaty

The participants in the Gorno-Altai Oblast Party conference that ended on December 2 called on RSFSR deputies not to examine the draft RSFSR Constitution before a new Union treaty was concluded, Radio Moscow reported. No reason was given for this appeal. The RSFSR leadership is against the autonomous republics' being cosignatories of the Union treaty, and the official draft of the new Russian Constitution subordinates the autonomous territories firmly to the central authorities of the Russian republic. For this reason, many autonomous oblasts feel that their interests will be better safeguarded by the Union treaty.

New Ukrainian Political Party

The Party of the Democratic Rebirth of Ukraine concluded its founding congress on December 2, according to TASS. The new party traces its origins to members and adherents of the Democratic Platform in Ukraine and numbers about 3,500 supporters. The party will work through legal means towards abolishing Soviet statehood and towards the signing of a collective interrepublican treaty declaring the Soviet Constitution invalid.

Azerbaijan to Drop "Soviet Socialist" from Its Name

Azerbaijani President Ayaz Mutalibov issued a decree ordering that the words "Soviet" and "Socialist" be dropped from the name of the Azerbaijani republic. The president also said in his decree that a new flag composed of three horizontal stripes of blue, red (carrying a white crescent moon and eight-point star) and green would be introduced. TASS quoted the decree as saying the changes were linked to the growth of national self-awareness and the development of Azerbaijani statehood.

New Violence on Armenian-Azerbaijani Border

Four Azerbaijani policemen and three Armenian militants were killed in a clash in Azerbaijan's Khanlar Raion, TASS reported. Two other policemen were reported missing.

Soviet media coverage of the situation remained misleading, in that TASS reported only incidents in which Armenians appeared to be the aggressors. Radio Erevan claimed on November 30 that Azerbaijanis had launched a new wave of killings, arson, and hostage-taking in Nagorno-Karabakh.

Foreign Aid to USSR

On December 2, medicine shipped to the Soviet Union by a private US relief group arrived in Moscow. It was delivered to a clinic for infants (*AP*, December 2).

On December 3, Mikhail Gorbachev issued a directive setting up a special committee headed by First Deputy Prime Minister Lev Voronin to receive and distribute international humanitarian aid arriving in the USSR, "Vremya" reported. Gorbachev also discussed the Soviet food situation and the international aid to the USSR at length in an address to the USSR Supreme Soviet on December 4 (*TASS*, December 4).

On December 4, a convoy of eight German trucks arrived in Moscow with food aid, Western agencies reported. An Israeli plane arrived in Moscow the same day with ten tons of fruit and vegetables. Another planeload containing fifteen tons of powdered milk was shipped on December 5.

On December 5, Radio Moscow reported that food to the value of 170,000 rubles had been found by Leningrad deputies and workers' controllers in the warehouses of major Leningrad food stores whose counters were empty. Implying that the shortage of food in the city was mainly the result of organized sabotage, the radio said directors of stores who kept but did not sell food would be punished.

The same day, Visvaldis Brinkmanis, deputy chairman of the Committee of Latvia, urged Germany to send food aid to Estonia, Latvia, and Lithuania, and not just to Russia, since the store shelves were just as empty in the Baltic as in the RSFSR (RFE Latvian service, December 5).

On December 18, Japan announced a 108-million-dollar loan package of emergency food and medical aid to the Soviet Union, AP reported. Prime Minister Toshiki Kaifu stressed, however, that the policy of withholding ordinary assistance to the USSR would remain unchanged as long as the territorial dispute between Japan and the USSR remained unresolved.

On December 26, Soviet Foreign Ministry spokesman Vitalii Churkin said the USSR had received more than 16,000 tons of emergency food and other aid. Churkin said that the donations were mostly from Germany but that twenty-four other countries had also sent help. AFP reported that on December 26 alone forty tons of medicine and baby food from a French humanitarian group had arrived in Moscow.

On December 24, Western agencies reported that the Soviet Union had asked for another loan from Germany. The reports quoted officials of the major German association of industrialists. They said that the Soviet Union had asked for 2 billion German marks to support the Soviet economy and that the German government had been asked to guarantee repayment of the loan.

Monday, December 3

RSFSR to Permit Private Land Ownership

In a historic decision, a special session of the RSFSR Congress of People's Deputies voted to allow farmers to own land for the first time in sixty years. The vote was 602 for, 369 against, with 40 abstentions. As a result of strong conservative opposition, however, the bill was approved only after the adoption of an amendment stipulating that land could be privately owned only if it was used for growing farm produce. The amendment also said privately owned land could be sold only if it had been owned for at least ten years and only to the state (*TASS*, *Central Television*, December 3).

USSR Supreme Soviet Endorses Draft Union Treaty

After a short but sharp discussion, the USSR Supreme Soviet endorsed the draft of the new Union treaty, TASS reported. The chairman of the Supreme Soviet's Commission on Nationalities Policy, Georgii Tarazevich, claimed during the debate that a recent public opinion study in all the republics had shown that 73 percent of the population favored preserving the Soviet Union's present frontiers and only 16 percent opposed this.

Rafik Nishanov, who presented the draft, was critical of those political figures (i.e., Boris El'tsin) who proposed to construct a new Union on the basis of bilateral treaties between individual republics. Nishanov said this would be a step backwards. He added that the 1922 treaty would remain in force for those republics that did not sign the new treaty and reiterated that they would have to observe the procedures stipulated by the law on secession.

Estonia Names Envoy to Latvia

The Estonian government named Henn Tuherm to serve as Estonia's envoy to Latvia (*ETA*, December 4). Until his appointment, Tuherm headed the Department of Woodwork at the Latvian Academy of Agriculture. The government named Mart Tarmak, former press secretary of the popular front, as envoy to Lithuania in spring, 1990.

Estonia Approves Use of Hard Currency

The Estonian government approved a decree legalizing the use of hard currency, ETA reported. Starting December 4, residents of Estonia may conduct commercial transactions in hard currency. Director General of the State Department for Foreign Economic Relations Mehis Pilv reassured consumers not in possession of foreign currency, saying that Estonian businesses would not be able to sell their wares for hard currency until they had fulfilled their state plans.

USSR States Official Position on Cuba

Valerii Nikolaenko, head of the Soviet Foreign Ministry's Latin American Department, and Georgii Mamedov, head of its USA and Canada Department, told a news conference in Moscow that the Soviet Union wanted the United States to drop its demands for democratic change in Cuba as preconditions for normalizing ties. The two officials described themselves as special envoys of Soviet President Mikhail Gorbachev. Nikolaenko stressed that the Soviet Union "with all its problems, is ready to continue economic cooperation with Cuba," and went on to say: "Our position is firm in continuing our friendship with the revolutionary government of Cuba. . . . We respect and support the course taken by that government." Nikolaenko also said that a possible reduction in future Soviet military aid to Cuba would depend on what progress was made in normalizing ties between Washington and Havana, Reuters reported.

Violence in Uzbekistan

On December 3, TASS reported that five MVD troops and three civilians had been killed in Namangan on the night of December 2, after young people clashed with MVD soldiers returning from leave on a public bus. The report said that a crowd of some 3,000 people surrounded the bus and beat four of the soldiers to death. A group of unarmed troops tried to intervene, but had stones and metal rods flung at them. Armed reinforcements were called, backed by 700 police, and weapons were used to break up the disorder, which lasted several hours. The TASS report said that the Presidium of the Uzbek Supreme Soviet had sent a commission to the city to investigate the incident and that the families of MVD troops were under protection.

A crowd of 500 people gathered in front of the police headquarters in Namangan on December 4 and forced the police to release persons detained in connection with the riot on December 2, according to *Trud*. On December 5, *Izvestia* said that the city was being regularly patrolled and that special civilian groups were being formed to help keep order. Contradicting an earlier statement by the Uzbek minister of internal affairs that the situation in Namangan was under control, the *Trud* report said that gunfire could be heard and that groups of youths were assembling in the city center. The republican authorities were reported to have forbidden the local media to report on the events in Namangan, and residents of Uzbekistan were said to have learned about them only from the central press and television.

Kiev Residents Polled on Sovereignty and Independence

A recent opinion poll in Kiev conducted by the Institute of Sociology of the Ukrainian SSR revealed that a little more than 38 percent of those questioned in the Ukrainian capital favored an independent Ukrainian state outside the USSR, Radio Kiev reported. Close to 40 percent supported an independent state within a Soviet confederation, and another 18.5 percent were for a sovereign Ukraine in a federated USSR. A poll held in Kiev in September had shown 25 percent in favor of Ukraine's secession from the USSR.

Low Draft Turn-Out in Ukraine

Radio Moscow reported that not one recruit had been dispatched from Lvov Oblast in Ukraine to serve in the Soviet Armed Forces and that there had also been problems in Ukraine's Ivano-Frankovsk and Rovno Oblasts. According to the report, the draft has, in practical terms, been suspended in Western parts of the republic. It also indicated that there had been difficulties in Moldavia, Georgia, Azerbaijan, and Armenia. Soviet officials and military leaders have blamed many of the problems on legislation passed in the republics.

Victory for Soldiers' Wives

A group of air defense servicemen's wives in the Ukrainian city of Zaporozhe ended their protest after winning concessions from the armed forces, Radio Moscow reported. The women had been demonstrating against the transfer of their husbands to a region in Kazakhstan that they claimed was polluted and lacked facilities for families. Earlier, the wives blocked a runway at the local airport and later declared a hunger strike. A senior air defense officer said that some of the husbands would be sent to Kazakhstan but that living conditions would be improved. Others would be sent to the reserve forces.

Soviet Spokesman Appeals for "Humanism" in Honecker Case

Soviet Foreign Ministry spokesman Vitalii Churkin said the USSR hoped Germany would be guided by "the principles of humanism" in dealing with former East German Communist Party Secretary General Erich Honecker. The Berlin Justice Office has issued an arrest warrant for Honecker, charging him with manslaughter for ordering East German border guards to shoot to kill people fleeing to the West. Honecker is staying at a Soviet military facility (*AP, AFP*, December 3).

Popov Says Moscow Soviet Is Not Working Properly

Since many deputies to the Moscow City Soviet hold opposing political views, the Soviet cannot function properly, its chairman, Gavriil Popov, said. According to APN (December 5), Popov made the statement after the soviet had failed once again to approve the membership of its Presidium. Popov suggested that, if the situation did not improve in the near future, the USSR Supreme Soviet should sanction new elections for the Moscow soviet or take some other measures to restructure it.

Meanwhile, complaints about the functioning of other local soviets continued to be published in the Soviet press. *Izvestia* (November 29) published an article saying that the oblast soviet in Karaganda (Kazakhstan) could not perform its duties because its bureaucratic apparatus was too large.

Tuesday, December 4

Supreme Soviet Approves Gorbachev's Request for More Power

The USSR Supreme Soviet approved in principle President Mikhail Gorbachev's proposed changes to the structure of the Soviet government. These would concentrate executive powers in the hands of the president, transform the Council of Ministers into a cabinet of ministers subordinated directly to the president, and create the post of vice president. The Council of the Federation, which includes the president and the heads of state of the Union republics, would be changed from an advisory body into a decision-making organ coordinating policy between Moscow and the republics. Such changes require constitutional amendments, and the Supreme Soviet voted to recommend that the Congress of People's Deputies should make the necessary changes when it convened on December 17.

Sobchak Proposes Expelling Unruly Republics from Union

The chairman of the Leningrad City Soviet, Anatolii Sobchak, suggested that, if the USSR could not impose order in unruly republics, it ought to expel them from the

Union. Sobchak made the proposal in an interview with Novosti in which he also said the Soviet Union needed disciplinary measures because "crime is rampant, and state and other functionaries are outrageously irresponsible." Sobchak said that Gorbachev should demonstrate political will and "resolve" to rectify the situation.

Russian Democracy "Hopeless," Journal Says

"Democrats elected to local Soviets and to the RSFSR Supreme Soviet are failing to defend the interests of the Russian Republic," according to one of the most liberal and outspoken Soviet journals, *Sobesednik* (No.48). The journal charged that the leadership of the RSFSR was protecting neither Russians living in other Union republics, nor Russian interests in economic agreements with other republics, nor the territorial integrity of the republic against separatist forces. *Sobesednik* called on "honest democrats" to unite with "honest patriots" in a joint effort to rescue Russia from chaos. The publication of such an article in a liberal journal provided an indication of the depth of the crisis afflicting democratic forces in the RSFSR.

Yet Another Poll Shows Drop in Gorbachev's Popularity

Preliminary findings from an opinion poll conducted in the RSFSR by *Sobesednik* (No. 48) indicated a further decrease in Gorbachev's popularity. Boris El'tsin was overwhelmingly named as the most popular leader, with Leningrad's Anatolii Sobchak in second place. (Sobchak collected only a quarter of the number of votes El'tsin won, however.) RSFSR Prime Minister Ivan Silaev also came out well in the poll, occupying fourth place (following Moscow's Gavriil Popov.) Asked which of the year's events they regarded as most significant, the majority of those polled cited El'tsin's election as chairman of the RSFSR Supreme Soviet. In second place was the country's embarkation on the road to a market economy. Third was the demolition of statues of Lenin.

Only Volunteers to Be Sent to Transcaucasus

Defense Minister Dmitrii Yazov ordered that military units in the Transcaucasus henceforth be manned only with servicemen from other parts of the country on a voluntary basis. Deputy Chief of the General Staff of the Soviet Armed Forces Grigorii Krivosheev told TASS that the decision had been prompted by the dangerous conditions for servicemen currently existing in the region. Krivosheev blamed that situation on so-called antiarmy groups in the Transcaucasus and said that a recent statement by Yazov instructing servicemen to protect themselves against civilian attacks had been welcomed by the troops.

Yazov on Publication of *Mein Kampf*

Defense Minister Dmitrii Yazov told TASS that it was wrong for *Voenno-istorichesky zhurnal* to publish excerpts from Adolf Hitler's book, *Mein Kampf.* The November issue of the military journal published the excerpts, claiming that it was responding to requests by readers. Yazov called the book "an ominous compendium of anticommunism, racism, and militarism." He implied that he would take steps to stop the publication of any further excerpts.

RSFSR Council of Nationalities Appeals to Republican Parliaments

The Council of Nationalities of the RSFSR Supreme Soviet adopted an appeal to the Supreme Soviets of the other republics on the situation of Russians and other indigenous peoples of the RSFSR (*rossiyane*) in the non-Russian republics, Radio Moscow reported. The appeal called on the republican parliamentarians to use all their influence to prevent the discrimination and violence against Russians in their republics that has deprived people of their jobs and made them want to abandon their long-established homes.

New Strikes, Protests in Georgia

Five weeks after the electoral victory of the non-Communist Round Table/Free Georgia coalition, unofficial Georgian news agencies reported that the newly appointed chairman of the State Committee for Television and Radio, thirty-seven-year-old Teimuraz Kvantaliani, a member of the Georgian Helsinki Union, had been fired after television personnel went on strike to protest about his refusal to allow groups professing views other than those of the ruling coalition access to the media. Sixty members of Mkhedrioni, the paramilitary organization of the unofficial National Congress, began a hunger strike on December 4, likewise to demand free access to the mass media.

Ukraine and Azerbaijan Sign Agreement

Ukraine and Azerbaijan signed a bilateral agreement covering economic, scientific-technical, and cultural cooperation, Radio Kiev and Radio Moscow reported.

Japan Sends Drilling Equipment to USSR

Japan's Marubeni Corporation said it had exported oil-drilling and recovery equipment worth over 11.5 million dollars to the Soviet Union. Marubeni officials said the export followed the issue of a letter of credit for the USSR

Ministry of the Oil and Gas Industry by the Soviet Bank for External Economic Relations, AFP reported.

Wednesday, December 5

El'tsin Warns Army against Intervention in Politics

Boris El'tsin said a military coup would lead the Soviet Union to catastrophe. The chairman of the RSFSR Supreme Soviet was speaking at the Dzerzhinsky Military Academy in Moscow. He said that soldiers had an important role to play in society but that armed force could not solve economic problems. El'tsin said military intervention in the USSR's current political crisis would deprive the country of its last chance to find a positive outcome and that a coup could lead to civil war (*TASS*, December 5).

Army Supports Gorbachev

The head of the Volga-Urals Military District's Political Directorate denied Viktor Alksnis's claim that Gorbachev had "lost" the army, Radio Moscow reported. Boris Tarasov also said that recent actions by Gorbachev and the High Command fully addressed demands made by disgruntled officers at a meeting last month between the president and uniformed deputies. He added that most officers supported Gorbachev's reform program but were unhappy about attacks on the army and the state. Tarasov's comments are interesting because the Volga-Urals Military District is commanded by the notorious Colonel General Al'bert Makashov, and is reputed to be a hotbed of conservatism.

Gromov on Discipline and Army's Loyalty

Boris Gromov, the former commander of the Kiev Military District and recent appointee as deputy minister of internal affairs, was featured in interviews in *Rabochaya tribuna* and *Sovetskaya Rossiya*. In the first, Gromov said that the USSR needed order and discipline in order to improve living standards but that this should be based on understanding and respect for the law and the state rather than on force. In the second, he reaffirmed his and the army's loyalty to the state. He also said that the passage of sovereignty declarations by various Soviet republics had stalled reform.

Army Provides Own Food Supplies

The chief of the Defense Ministry's Rear Services told *Pravda* that there was no need to use any state stocks of food or equipment to support the army. According to Army General Vladimir Arkhipov, the total output from the army's eighty-three agricultural enterprises makes the armed forces self-sufficient in food. He said existing difficulties in providing troops with food were due partly to steep price rises and partly to mismanagement.

"Deutsche Welle" Broadcasts Program for Ethnic Germans

It was reported from Volgograd that, on November 29, local television began transmitting an information program from the television service of Germany's Deutsche Welle for the Volga Germans. The half-hour program in the German language "Around Europe" was scheduled to go out twice a month.

Tajik Supreme Soviet Approves Draft Union Treaty

TASS and Radio Moscow reported that, after a sharp debate, the Tajik Supreme Soviet had approved the draft Union treaty with amendments. These included the creation of a single-chamber USSR Supreme Soviet, in which all states making up the Union would have an equal number of representatives, regardless of the size of their populations or territories. The Tajik deputies also wanted republics to have the right to suspend the operation of all-Union laws on their territories if the laws were deemed to run counter to the republics' interests.

Tajik Supreme Soviet Elects Vice President

The Supreme Soviet of Tajikistan approved the creation of the post of republican vice president and elected Izatullo Khaeev, chairman of the Council of Ministers, to fill it, according to TASS and Radio Moscow. Khaeev was one of the leaders whose resignation was demanded by demonstrators during the disturbances in Dushanbe in February. The reports of his election did not say whether he retained his previous job or whether newly elected President Kakhar Makhkamov intended to abolish the Council of Ministers and replace it with a ministerial cabinet subordinate to himself.

Ukrainian Parliament Discusses Economy

Radio Kiev (December 4 and 5) reported that the Ukrainian Supreme Soviet had adopted new laws on prices, taxation, and the budget but failed to adopt a new law on land ownership. The new pricing policy will preserve fixed retail and wholesale state prices for most agricultural products but will be independent of the Union pricing policy. In view of the large budget deficit, the deputies annulled all tax breaks and required the government in future to account for its expenditure. The new land code, based on the statement in the Ukrainian declaration of sovereignty that all land belongs to the Ukrainian people, would have forbidden the private sale of land; it failed to win approval by the Ukrainian Supreme Soviet, however, and, after two days' debate, was postponed for further discussion.

Political Group Calls for State of Emergency

A newly formed Soviet political group called on Mikhail Gorbachev to impose a nationwide state of emergency to restore order in the Soviet Union, TASS reported. The group asked Gorbachev to suspend the operation of political parties and send central government officials to replace elected officials in some republics, including Georgia, Lithuania, Moldavia, and the RSFSR. The group, calling itself the National Salvation Committee, said at a press conference in Moscow that it hoped to end the influence in the USSR of radical groups on the right and left. One spokesman, lawyer Vladimir Zhirinovsky of the Liberal Democratic Party, told AP that the new group had about 18 percent of the votes in the Congress of People's Deputies. Many members of the new group came from the Centrist Bloc of Political Parties and Movements, formed in summer, 1990, which some observers have depicted as a Communist Party front. Others come from the conservative "Soyuz" organization.

On December 7, Ivan Laptev, chairman of the Council of the Union, one of the two chambers of the USSR Supreme Soviet, met with members of the "Soyuz" group and of the Centrist Bloc to discuss their call for the introduction of a state of emergency in the country. Laptev did not seem to take the group seriously, however. "The loudness of the declaration hardly corresponds with the extent of the bloc's influence," Reuters quoted him as saying.

Novodvorskaya Fined for Insulting Gorbachev

A court in the city of Sverdlovsk fined a leader of the anti-Communist Democratic Union, Valeriya Novodvorskaya, 400 rubles for insulting the Soviet president and for trying to hold an unsanctioned meeting in the city, Radio Moscow reported on December 5. A similar case has also been brought against Novodvorskaya in Moscow. The latter case was initiated by the Moscow Public Prosecutor's Office after Novodvorskaya was detained for holding an antigovernment demonstration in the Soviet capital in September, at which she reportedly carried a banner calling Gorbachev a fascist criminal and burned a Soviet flag.

Thursday, December 6

State Managers Criticize *Perestroika*

Managers of Soviet state enterprises sharply criticized Gorbachev's reforms, saying they were causing the economy to disintegrate. The criticism came at a Moscow meeting of 3,500 managers and senior Soviet officials, including the Soviet president. One manager said *perestroika* had been launched without any concept and had now failed. The managers loudly applauded this remark. When, in response, Gorbachev asked if the Soviet Union should return to its old ways, his comment was drowned out by "a hum of indignant voices," TASS said.

Ryzhkov Says State Industries Will Be Around a Long Time

Speaking at the same meeting of managers of state-run enterprises, the chairman of the USSR Council of Ministers, Nikolai Ryzhkov, said state-owned industries would be a feature of Soviet life for a long time. He said that, in view of the tasks facing the country, it was necessary to allow industries with other forms of ownership to operate with equal rights. But, the prime minister said, the state would continue to control key branches of the economy in the short and long term (*TASS*, December 6).

Gorbachev Orders Antipornography Commission

In his latest decree, Mikhail Gorbachev ordered the establishment of an antipornography commission to take urgent measures to protect public morals. Chaired by USSR Minister of Culture Nikolai Gubenko, the commission is to study the experience of other countries in fighting pornography, TASS reported (*Pravda*, December 7). Earlier in 1990, *Pravda* published a call by conservative cultural figures demanding that the Soviet leadership take measures against pornography in the mass media. Gorbachev's commission was set up in response to this call.

Chelyabinsk City Soviet Proposes Referendum on Plant

The Chelyabinsk City Soviet decided to hold a referendum on whether to continue construction of a local nuclear power plant, TASS reported. Construction of the plant in the Southern Urals had been stopped after local protests. The Chelyabinsk Oblast Soviet, however, recently called for construction to be resumed.

Turkmenian Official Finds Fault with Union Treaty

Writing for Novosti press agency, Turkmen First Deputy Prime Minister Ata Char'ev said that, from Turkmenia's point of view, the draft Union treaty was flawed. Char'ev said the draft should give republics control over their own natural resources and their foreign economic ties. He said

Turkmenia was generally in favor of the new Union treaty but wanted changes made to give Turkmenia and other republics more economic rights.

Monuments and Graves of Latvian Legion Damaged

Latvian Supreme Soviet deputy Eduards Berklavs said a monument to the Latvian legion had been blown up in Latvia on December 3 and graves of legion members desecrated. (The legion was made up of Latvians who fought for an independent Latvia on the German side in World War I.) Berklavs told RFE/RL on December 6 that the incident would be discussed by the Supreme Soviet and that he expected the legislature to instruct the state prosecutor to investigate.

Commander Says MVD Troops Often Blocked from Duties

First Deputy Commander Lieutenant General Boris Smyslov told *Izvestia* that, because mass disturbances were in many cases supported by the local authorities, MVD troops were often prevented from performing their functions. Smyslov said this had happened in Armenia and Azerbaijan. He said it was often the case that neither the instigators of mass disturbances, nor the organizers, nor those directly involved were prosecuted. He said that laws aimed at averting mass disturbances in extreme situations did not work and that therefore the MVD bodies should not be blamed for their ineffectiveness.

US Group Names Gerasimov "Communicator of the Year"

A US group called the National Association of Government Communicators named outgoing Soviet Foreign Ministry spokesman Gennadii Gerasimov as "communicator of the year." Gerasimov was popular with United States journalists for his wit and fluent English (*AFP*, December 6).

Ukrainian Deputies Stage Boycott over Khmara Case

TASS reported that opposition deputies had boycotted a session of the Ukrainian Supreme Soviet to protest about the detention of a deputy, Stepan Khmara, arrested on charges of assaulting a policeman. TASS said only 274 of the 448 deputies attended the session. TASS said the "Narodna Rada" opposition faction would stay away from parliamentary sessions until Khmara's case was cleared up.

On December 13, Khmara ended the hunger strike he was staging in a Kiev prison. He told visitors that he was ending the fast at the request of the metropolitan of the Ukrainian Catholic Church, Volodymyr Sternyuk of Lvov (RL Ukrainian service, December 13).

Friday, December 7

Conference on Military Doctrine

The USSR Ministry of Defense hosted an all-Union conference devoted to Soviet military doctrine. According to TASS, discussion centered on the military aspects of a new comprehensive security system based on giving priority to political rather than military means and on observance of the principle of reasonable sufficiency for defense. Chief of the General Staff of the Soviet Armed Forces Mikhail Moiseev and other speakers emphasized the need to minimize resources expended on defense but also called for maintenance of a single, unified Soviet army. For the first time, representatives of various republican governments took part in the meeting.

RSFSR to Introduce Convertible Ruble in Two Years

Deputy Chairman of the RSFSR Council of Ministers Gennadii Fil'shin said the Russian Federation planned to make the ruble convertible in two years. TASS quoted Fil'shin as telling a seminar in Moscow that the change would be introduced gradually on foreign exchange markets with the aim of preventing a sharp drop in the value of the ruble. No further details of Filshin's plan were made public, but TASS said conference participants expressed doubts about whether the RSFSR could sustain a convertible ruble on its own.

Silaev's Plan for Economic Stabilization Adopted by RSFSR Congress

The RSFSR Congress of People's Deputies adopted a resolution approving the plan for economic stabilization and the transfer to a market economy that Prime Minister Ivan Silaev first presented to the Congress on December 5 (*TASS*, December 7).

After a sharp debate, the Congress also adopted an amendment to its draft decree on the activity of the government in stabilizing the economy, saying that the country's diamond and gold reserves were the common property of the Union republics and that therefore the central authorities and the Union republics should agree jointly on how to dispose of them (*TASS*, December 7). A large group of deputies had wanted them to be shared out only between the RSFSR and the USSR.

Lithuanian-Ukrainian Agreement Signed

Radio Vilnius reported that Lithuanian Prime Minister Kazimiera Prunskiene and Ukrainian Prime Minister Vitol'd Fokin had signed an agreement in Kiev on economic and cultural cooperation during the period 1990–95. Ukraine accounts for 15 percent of Lithuania's trade, sending coal, metals, machines, tractors, vegetable oil, and grain, and receiving machine tools, precision instruments, building materials, light industry products, and food.

General Wants "Vzglyad" Banned

On December 7, viewers of the iconoclastic television chat show "Vzglyad" were shown a leaflet in which, moderators said, Colonel General Igor Rodionov—notorious for his decision to use poison gas and clubs against peaceful demonstrators in Tbilisi in April, 1989—spelled out his ideas for military reform. Alongside what "Vzglyad" described as sensible measures such as outlawing bullying in the army, Rodionov demanded a stop to what he called an "antiarmy" campaign in the mass media and called specifically for "Vzglyad" to be taken off the air. Moderator Aleksandr Lyubimov said "Vzglyad" would happily go into voluntary liquidation if it thought the army's problems would be so easily solved.

Ukrainian Supreme Soviet Adopts Land Ownership Law

Radio Kiev and TASS reported that the Ukrainian Supreme Soviet had finally adopted the law on land ownership proposed by the government. The new law allows the transfer of land to individuals for "perpetual" hereditary ownership for the purposes of maintaining subsidiary farms and orchards and of building private housing. It does not, however, permit the sale of land.

Armenian Earthquake Rebuilding Program "in Ruins"

Marking the second anniversary of the Armenian earthquake in which a minimum of 25,000 people are known to have died, "Vremya" reported on December 7 that the two-year government program to rebuild the devastated area had "collapsed completely." It noted, however, that the situation had been aggravated by the fact that no one had anticipated either the arrival of 300,000 Armenian refugees from Azerbaijan, who swelled the number of homeless, or the periodic blockade of all rail traffic into Armenia by Azerbaijan. Hundreds of thousands of people are spending their third winter in tents and rail cars.

Georgian CP Elects New Secretary

The Georgian Communist Party convened a special congress on December 7–8 to assess its future, following its resounding defeat in the October elections to the Supreme Soviet. On December 7, Givi Gumbaridze, who was elected Georgian Party first secretary after the reprisals against peaceful demonstrators in Tbilisi in April, 1989, stepped down, saying that the Party needed a new leader to build "a strong opposition" (*TASS*,

December 7). The congress elected as his successor Avtandil Margiani.

Mamedov Appointed Head of USA-Canada Department

TASS reported that Georgii Mamedov had been appointed head of the Soviet Foreign Ministry's United States and Canada Department. He was previously a deputy chief of this department and has held various positions at the Soviet embassy in Washington.

Saturday, December 8

RSFSR People's Deputies Urge Discussion of Union Treaty

About 150 deputies asked to speak during the discussion of the draft Union treaty in the RSFSR Congress of People's Deputies, TASS reported. Opinions of the draft varied widely. Deputy Yurii Slobodkin from Moscow Oblast described the draft as fully acceptable, and North Ossetian deputy Askharbek Galazov said any delay in signing it would only "push the country into the abyss." In contrast, Galina Starovoitova of the "Democratic Russia" movement was sharply critical, maintaining that the draft was "a cosmetic renewal" of the 1922 treaty and failed to turn the empire into a free association of equal states. Dmitrii Volkogonov, while agreeing on the need for a Union treaty, said the draft still left far too many powers with the center. Ruslan Khasbulatov, first deputy chairman of the RSFSR Supreme Soviet, said that the draft had many shortcomings but that the Russian Federation was committed to the idea of a new treaty.

On December 11, the RSFSR Congress of People's Deputies adopted a resolution confirming that the Russian Republic would be "a full member of a renewed USSR on the basis of a new Union treaty," TASS and Radio Moscow reported.

In a speech to the RSFSR Congress carried by Radio Moscow on December 11, Boris El'tsin reiterated that the RSFSR was in favor of the Union, but he criticized the center for showing undue haste.

Moscow Does Not Face Famine, Deputy Mayor Says

The deputy chairman of the Moscow City Soviet, Sergei Stankevich, told a press conference that Moscow was not facing famine. Stankevich said that, although the major Soviet cities desperately needed the food aid now flowing in from the West, he believed that present food stocks were sufficient to secure Moscow against "famine, civil war, and food riots." "The situation in the capital is not comparable with that in Ethiopia," he commented (*TASS*, December 8).

Similar statements were made by other Soviet officials. On December 13, Soviet First Deputy Prime Minister Lev Voronin said that there was no real famine in the Soviet Union and that he did not expect there to be one (*TASS*, December 13). The chairman of the Leningrad City Soviet, Anatolii Sobchak, also said that, although the food situation in his city was "catastrophic," there was no threat of famine (*TASS*, December 13).

KGB Reports on Food Theft and Distribution Problems

The KGB said theft by organized criminals and distribution problems were to blame for acute shortages of food and other goods in the USSR. The KGB said it had uncovered several incidents of organized groups' diverting food. The report also said imported cargoes, including food, were stuck in ports and railyards because of inefficient transport (*TASS*, December 8).

The same day, Aleksandr Perelygin, a member of a special commission overseeing the distribution of aid, said no Western aid shipments had disappeared and no one had been caught trying to steal or divert any of the relief supplies that had arrived so far in the USSR, Reuters reported.

On December 13, the head of the KGB's public relations center, Aleksandr Karbainov, told reporters in Moscow that the KGB was preparing to fight economic sabotage and was waiting for a law to be passed covering it. He stressed that the existing criminal codes did not cover economic sabotage (*TASS*, December 13).

Congress of Lithuanian CP

On December 8 and 9, the independent Lithuanian Communist Party held a congress that voted to change the party's name to the Lithuanian Democratic Labor Party. Radio Vilnius reported on December 9 that Algirdas Brazauskas had been reelected first secretary. The congress approved a new program describing the party as "a parliamentary political organization of the Social Democratic type" whose main aim is "the building in the Republic of Lithuania of a democratic civil society that embodies humanist values." The party has about 56,000 members.

Anti-independence Demonstration in Vilnius

About 80,000 people rallied in Vilnius in protest against Lithuanian independence and called on President Gorbachev to impose presidential rule in the republic, DPA reported on December 9. The rally approved a resolution calling on the Lithuanian parliament and government to make way for "a provisional government created on the basis of a coalition of all the democratic forces in Lithuania."

Georgian CP Congress Continues

Continuing its congress on December 8, the Georgian Communist Party adopted a new set of rules defining it as "an independent political organization operating on the basis of its own program and Party rules within the constitution of Georgia." The congress also adopted a resolution affirming that the Party would work for the restoration of full Georgian sovereignty. Adoption of a new Party program was postponed for one month after delegates failed to agree on a new name for the Party (*TASS*, December 8).

The Georgian Communist Party's decision to proclaim independence from the CPSU was rejected, however, by delegates to the congress from Abkhazia and South Ossetia (*TASS*, December 8). Both areas are campaigning for secession from Georgia.

After splitting from the CPSU, the Georgian CP removed from its headquarters all portraits of Gorbachev, Lenin, Marx, and Engels, Reuters reported on December 11.

Mordovia Adopts Watered-Down Sovereignty Declaration

Faced with strong opposition to a declaration of sovereignty, presumably from the majority Russian element in the territory's population, the Mordovian Supreme Soviet dropped the word "sovereignty" from the title and adopted a declaration "On the state-legal status of the Mordovian SSR," TASS reported. The final text omitted any mention of Mordovian laws' taking precedence over those of the USSR and the RSFSR. The declaration declared Mordovian-Erzya, Mordovian-Moksha, and Russian the state languages.

Sunday, December 9

Demonstration in Moscow against Totalitarianism

Thousands of people gathered in the center of Moscow to commemorate the victims of Stalin's repressions. TASS said among those attending the rally were leaders of sociopolitical organizations, as well as people's deputies of the USSR, RSFSR, Moscow City Soviet, and district Soviets. After the rally there was a candle-lit procession to Dzerzhinsky Square, the site of the KGB headquarters.

Demonstration in Kiev

Radio Kiev reported that about 15,000 people had taken part in a sanctioned meeting in Kiev to mark the forty-second anniversary of the UN Declaration of Human Rights. The meeting was organized by "Rukh" and the Ukrainian Republican Party. Demonstrators called for the release of Ukrainian people's deputy Stepan Khmara, a boycott of the Union treaty, refusal by Ukrainian citizens to perform military service outside the republic, and the organization of strike committees at factories.

Ukrainian Parliament Ignores Union Treaty

Radio Kiev reported that discussion of the draft Union treaty had not been included on the agenda of the Ukrainian Supreme Soviet. Volodymyr Hryn'ov, deputy chairman of the Ukrainian Supreme Soviet, said in an interview that both the conservative majority and the opposition were "unanimous" in their belief that the draft treaty was incompatible with the Ukrainian declaration of state sovereignty.

Landsbergis in Washington

President of the Lithuanian Supreme Council Vytautas Landsbergis arrived in Washington from Toronto, where he had spent three days talking to Canadian officials and businessmen and meeting with the Lithuanian Canadian community. On December 10, Landsbergis had lunch with senior State Department officials, followed by a meeting with President George Bush (*Reuters*, *AP*, December 9 and 10). Landsbergis told reporters that the meeting had given him a great deal of confidence in the United States. Landsbergis said he had urged Bush to make clear statements supporting Lithuanian independence. He said Bush had promised to consider various ways of helping Lithuania, but he did not elaborate (*Reuters*, December 10).

On December 11, Landsbergis told a news conference in Washington that the Soviet Union was threatening to impose an economic blockade on Lithuania. Landsbergis said Moscow was demanding that Lithuania remain in the central USSR planning, finance, and taxation system and that it give its hard-currency earnings to the Soviet Union (*RFE/RL Special*, December 12). He said that, if Lithuania refused to comply with these demands, the Soviet Union would stop its deliveries of food, fuel, raw materials, metal and wood products, electronic goods, and construction materials on January 1, 1991.

Soviet Private Businessmen Set Up Political Party

Soviet private businessmen met in Moscow to found their own political party, to be called the Free Labor Party. Radio Moscow did not say how many delegates attended the meeting and gave no details of the new party's platform. It quoted a delegate, Valerii Makeev of Naberezhnye Chelny, as saying that the new party was intended to be a counterweight to workers' political movements, such as the miners' strike committees.

Gorbachev Sides with Polozkov against Moscow Soviet

Moscow leader Gavriil Popov revealed that Gorbachev had personally lobbied the Moscow City Soviet in an effort to persuade it to grant the leader of the RSFSR Communist Party, Ivan Polozkov, a Moscow residence permit (*The New York Times*, December 9). Popov said Gorbachev was very angry with him for announcing that the city soviet was no longer prepared to provide subsidized housing for Party officials from outside the capital while Muscovites had to wait decades for housing.

Monday, December 10

CPSU CC Plenum

The CPSU Central Committee began a plenum in Moscow to debate the strategy for the USSR Congress of People's Deputies' session due to convene on December 17.

In his report to the plenum on the draft Union treaty, Gorbachev set forth once again his arguments in favor of concluding a new Union treaty and described militant nationalism and interethnic strife as the main dangers facing the Soviet Union. He maintained that the draft treaty provided a good basis for the Union and had been supported in the main. Gorbachev rejected arguments that the Union treaty should not be signed until the republics had adopted new constitutions and said that bilateral interrepublican agreements were only of benefit if they were not aimed against the Union treaty and the all-Union market. The dropping of the word "Socialist" from the country's name did not, Gorbachev argued, change the country's fundamental orientation towards socialism (see *Pravda*, December 11).

On December 11, TASS reported that the plenum had shown that the Central Committee was unanimous in the view that Communists should do everything to preserve the Union, TASS reported.

The plenum relieved the former Party first secretaries of Belorussia and Armenia, Efrem Sokolov and Vladimir Movsisyan, of their duties in the Politburo. Their replacements, Anatolii Malofeev and Stepan Pogosyan, were made new members of the Politburo (*TASS*, December 11; *Pravda*, December 12). (Republican first secretaries are ex officio members of the Politburo.) The TASS report of the changes in the Politburo made no mention, however, of the new Georgian Party first secretary, Avtandil Margiani, who theoretically also qualifies for Politburo membership. This may have been because the Georgian Communist Party voted on December 8 to split from the CPSU.

On December 11, the plenum adopted a resolution stating that the conclusion of a new Union treaty was vital to the solution of economic, social, interethnic, political, and legal problems and to ensuring the consolidation of the USSR's international position. Implicitly rejecting the dropping of the word "Socialist" from the country's name, it called for a precise definition of the Socialist character of the renewal of the Union. Membership in the Union should be decided by a free expression of the will of the people, including by referendum, it said. The resolution also called for meetings on the Union treaty to be held in all primary Party organizations and for the Party to bring home to every individual the importance of preserving the Union. The resolution called for the creation of a special television channel, "Sodruzhestvo," to deal with interethnic relations and entrusted the CPSU Secretariat with the creation of a special scientific center and periodical on the theory and practice of state relations.For the text of the resolution, see *Pravda*, December 13.

Protest in Moscow against Awarding of Peace Prize to Gorbachev

There was a protest outside the Norwegian embassy in Moscow by about forty people who were opposed to Mikhail Gorbachev's receiving this year's Nobel Peace Prize. Some of the demonstrators blamed the Soviet president for ethnic and political violence in the Soviet Union. Reuters reported that protesters waved the flags of Estonia, Georgia, Azerbaijan, Armenia, and Ukraine.

In Oslo, First Deputy Foreign Minister Anatolii Kovalev accepted the Nobel prize on Gorbachev's behalf. Gorbachev did not travel to Oslo to accept the prize personally, because of tensions in the USSR. In a message to participants in the awarding ceremony, Gorbachev said he did not regard the peace prize as an award to him personally but as a recognition of *perestroika* and innovative political thinking (*AP*, *DPA*, December 10).

On December 14, Gorbachev announced that he would donate the money he had received along with the prize—about 715,000 dollars—to childrens' hospitals, TASS reported.

Radio Rossii Goes on the Air

A new radio station called Radio Rossii went on the air. The station, a division of the All-Russian Radio and Television Company, is provisionally using Gosteleradio frequencies but is administratively independent of the state body and receives its financing from the RSFSR. The bulk of the Radio Rossii team is composed of young journalists from Radio Yunost, a youth channel sponsored by the Komsomol.

To celebrate its own birthday and International Human-Rights Day, Radio Rossii started with a reading from *Govorit Moskva* by the late Yulii Daniel. In 1966, Daniel was sentenced to five years in a labor camp for writing this story and publishing it abroad.

Call to Stop Conscripts' Being Used to Control Ethnic Unrest

A draft document proposing to prohibit the use of army conscripts in the resolution of ethnic conflicts was circulated by RSFSR deputies at an extraordinary session of the RSFSR Congress of People's Deputies, Novosti reported. The draft said that the use of military force to resolve ethnic conflicts would only lead to further escalation of hostilities and the deaths of servicemen. The document called upon the USSR Supreme Soviet to work with the republics towards the creation of special interrepublican units to be used in such situations.

Deaths of Servicemen

The chief military prosecutor, Lieutenant General Aleksandr Katusev, announced that one-third of all noncombat deaths among Soviet servicemen were the result of criminal acts, while two-thirds resulted from accidents, Novosti reported. It said that most of the accidental deaths were caused by the misuse of weapons or other equipment and that one in every four deaths was suicide. Katusev's comments were consistent with other official statements with regard to deaths in the Soviet Armed Forces. Critics have charged that some 15,000 soldiers have died over the past five years.

Trade-Union Law Adopted

The USSR Supreme Soviet adopted a law detailing the rights of trade unions, TASS reported. The new law declared the unions independent of state organs, and gave them full financial autonomy. The new law appeared not to grant the unions the powers they had demanded to prevent the closure of loss-making enterprises. Instead, it merely required the owners of enterprises to notify the unions at least three months in advance of a closure or suspension of production.

Finland Begins Meat Shipments to Soviet Karelia

Finnish farmers began shipping 300 tons of meat to Soviet Karelia, a region of the Soviet Union that used to belong to Finland. The shipment was part of an agreement signed in October for Finland to ship 1,600 tons of beef and 3,500 tons of potatoes to the USSR, Reuters reported.

EC Proposes 2.4 Billion Dollars in Aid

The European Community proposed a 2.4 billion dollar grant in food and economic assistance to the USSR for

1991 and 1992. The package envisaged 1 billion dollars in food aid for 1991, 560 million dollars for technical assistance in 1991, and 840 million dollars for technical assistance in 1992 (*AP*, December 10).

Masaliev Resigns from Supreme Soviet Post

Radio Moscow reported that Kirgiz Communist Party First Secretary Absamat Masaliev had resigned from his post as chairman of the Kirgiz Supreme Soviet. In November, the conservative Masaliev failed to be elected president of the republic and saw the job go instead to a liberal scientist, Askar Akaev. During the Supreme Soviet session that elected Akaev, representatives of the informal political group "Kyrgyzstan" staged a hunger strike, demanding among other things Masaliev's resignation. Masaliev told the Supreme Soviet on December 10 that he intended to concentrate on his Party job (*TASS*, December 10).

On December 11, the Communist Party apparat won an apparent victory in the Kirgiz Supreme Soviet when Ideology Secretary Medetkan Sherimkulov was elected to replace Masaliev as chairman of the Supreme Soviet. Sherimkulov is a conservative but may be somewhat more flexible than Masaliev. He has been an active supporter of Kirgiz national interests.

Uzbekistan Abolishes Gosplan

Izvestia reported that the State Planning Committee in Uzbekistan had been abolished. In its place a Committee on Economics has been created by presidential order to prepare prognoses and define the parameters of the republic's short- and long-term economic development.

Gorbachev and RSFSR Congress Send Greetings to Walesa

Mikhail Gorbachev wished Lech Walesa success as Poland's new president. In a message to Walesa, quoted by TASS, Gorbachev said history had shown the need for Poland and the USSR to cooperate, and he said he hoped the two countries would have good relations.

Tuesday, December 11

KGB Will Prevent Disintegration of USSR, Kryuchkov Says

Appearing on Soviet television, KGB Chairman Vladimir Kryuchkov alleged that extremist groups, some supported from abroad, were being formed across the country and were seeking to push the country towards chaos. Kryuchkov stressed that he was speaking on behalf of

Mikhail Gorbachev. Kryuchkov said the KGB was committed to preserving the integrity of the Soviet state. This was the first time for many months that the KGB chairman had mentioned "foreign secret services," which, he alleged, were conducting "a secret war" against the USSR.

Solzhenitsyn Rejects RSFSR State Prize

"Vremya" quoted Aleksandr Solzhenitsyn as saying that "under no circumstances" would he accept the RSFSR state prize offered to him for *The Gulag Archipelago*. Solzhenitsyn was awarded this prize by a commission appointed by the new RSFSR leadership. The list of 1990's RSFSR state prize winners was published on December 11 in *Sovetskaya Rossiya*. Solzhenitsyn cited three reasons for rejecting the prize: first, the fact that copies of *The Gulag Archipelago* are in short supply in the RSFSR and ordinary people can obtain them only by paying huge sums on the black market; second, that former Gulag prisoners are living in poverty in the USSR and have received no compensation for their sufferings; and third, that the state has no role to play in literary matters and that he therefore rejects any state prize for literary works on principle.

RSFSR Writers' Union Congress Opens

A congress of the RSFSR Writers' Union opened in Moscow's Soviet Army Theater, the Soviet media reported. Virtually no liberal or best-selling authors were elected delegates. (The RSFSR Communist Party leader, Ivan Polozkov, attended the session as a guest of honor, but even this conservative gathering refused to elect him to the congress presidium.)

Shatalin on Integrity of MVD Forces

Colonel General Yurii Shatalin, the commander of Soviet MVD Forces, said in *Krasnaya zvezda* that MVD forces could be organizationally divided into Union and Union-republican units but should remain, as in the past, a single Union organization. Shatalin also called for the MVD forces to be manned on a mixed principle, including both extraterritorial conscript soldiers and volunteers serving on a contract basis. He said that MVD troops serving in the republics could be ordered into action by the republican authorities but he warned against efforts by republican governments to form their own armed detachments.

Georgian Parliament Abolishes South Ossetian Autonomy

The Georgian parliament voted to abolish the South Ossetian Autonomous Oblast as a separate administrative unit within the Republic of Georgia on the grounds that the Ossetians' ongoing campaign for the unification of the oblast with the North Ossetian Autonomous Oblast in the RSFSR could jeopardize Georgia's own campaign for independence (*TASS*, December 11). The South Ossetian Oblast Soviet passed a sovereignty decree in September and appealed to the USSR Supreme Soviet then for the new South Ossetian Soviet Democratic Republic to be recognized as an independent member of the Soviet federation. This appeal was rejected by both Moscow and Tbilisi as a violation of both the USSR and the Georgian Constitutions. Georgian Supreme Soviet Chairman Zviad Gamsakhurdia affirmed in November that he would preserve both Ossetian and Abkhaz autonomy within Georgia.

On December 12, the Georgian parliament declared a state of emergency in the South Ossetian capital, Tskhinvali, and in the neighboring Dzhava Raion following "a terrorist act" in Tskhinvali in which three people were killed. MVD and KGB troops were instructed to patrol the area and enforce a curfew; demonstrations and strikes were banned (*TASS*, December 12).

The same day, former South Ossetian Oblast Party Committee First Secretary Anatolii Chekhoev appealed to Mikhail Gorbachev and the USSR Supreme Soviet to "defend the rights of the South Ossetian people." USSR Supreme Soviet Chairman Anatolii Luk'yanov subsequently told reporters in Moscow that the decision by the Georgian parliament to abolish South Ossetian autonomy violated the USSR Constitution.

On December 13, the chairman of the South Ossetian Supreme Soviet, Torez Kulombegov, was quoted by TASS as calling for a peaceful dialogue between the South Ossetian authorities and Georgian officials about the new tensions in the region. The same day, a spokesman for the USSR Ministry of Internal Affairs said the ministry had sent investigators to the South Ossetian region, TASS reported.

On December 14, the Presidium of the Supreme Soviet of North Ossetia protested against Georgia's revocation of the autonomy of South Ossetia. The protest called the Georgian action "an unprecedented act of trampling on the rights of a small ethnic group" (*TASS*, December 14). The same day, the Presidium of the USSR Supreme Soviet also criticized Georgia's decision to rescind the autonomous status of South Ossetia, TASS reported.

On December 16, the South Ossetian Oblast Soviet appealed to Mikhail Gorbachev to impose a state of emergency in the region and to send USSR MVD troops to stabilize the situation (*TASS*, December 16). The oblast was already under a state of emergency imposed by the Georgian authorities on December 12.

On December 18, a senior officer of the USSR MVD troops, General Genrikh Malyushkin, told TASS that the situation in South Ossetia remained tense and that, on December 17, a group had tried to attack soldiers at a military settlement. Interfax reported on December 18 that some 2,500 supporters of the unofficial Georgian National Congress had for two days held unsanctioned meetings in Tbilisi to express support for the Georgian Supreme Soviet's decision to abolish South Ossetian autonomy.

On December 19, the Presidium of the Georgian Supreme Soviet accused the USSR MVD troops of siding with separatists in South Ossetia. TASS said the Presidium had sent a statement on the matter to the USSR Congress of People's Deputies.

On December 24, Georgian, Soviet, and South Ossetian officials met to discuss the crisis in South Ossetia. A state of emergency remained in force in some South Ossetian districts. TASS said those taking part in the talks, held in the Georgian capital, Tbilisi, included the chairman of the Georgian Supreme Soviet, Zviad Gamsakhurdia, the commander of the Soviet MVD troops, and South Ossetian representatives.

On December 26, *Krasnaya zvezda* reported that people were fleeing from South Ossetia to North Ossetia (in the RSFSR). The report also spoke of armed civilians blocking roads to South Ossetia. The report said the roadblocks had prevented food and other essentials from reaching South Ossetia.

On December 27, Gamsakhurdia rejected criticism by North Ossetia of the Georgian Supreme Soviet's decision to revoke the autonomy of South Ossetia. The Georgian newspaper *Zarya Vostoka* carried a letter from Gamsakhurdia saying the North Ossetian protest was "crude interference" in Georgia's affairs.

TASS reported on December 28 that some 2,000 people had stormed police headquarters in the South Ossetian capital, Tskhinvali, on December 27 and taken a group of Georgian policemen hostage. The hostages were released only after police set free a local man arrested for illegal possession of a firearm. Gorbachev's personal envoy in Georgia, Leonid Gorshkov, described the situation in Tskhinvali and the neighboring Dzhava Raion as tense.

"Agzybirlik" Leader Sentenced

RFE/RL learned that Turkmen poet Shiraly Nurmyradov, one of the leaders of the popular front "Agzybirlik," had been sentenced to seven years in prison on a charge of having defrauded a woman of money. "Agzybirlik" contended that Nurmyradov had been framed because he had ridiculed Turkmen President Saparmurad Niyazov. Another leader of "Agzybirlik" said that the group would ask the republican Supreme Soviet for permission to hold a rally in support of Nurmyradov, and it threatened to stage a hunger strike if this were denied (RL Turkmen service, December 11).

Estonia Rejects Western Food Aid

Estonian Prime Minister Edgar Savisaar told Soviet officials in Moscow that Estonia would not accept shipments of Western food aid, ETA reported. Savisaar sent a telegram to Deputy Chairman of the USSR Council of Ministers Lev Voronin saying the Estonian government "does not feel it necessary to appeal for any of the emergency food aid being sent to the Soviet Union." The telegram, sent in response to Voronin's earlier request that Estonia form an ad hoc commission to distribute incoming aid, said Estonia would accept medicine and Christmas packages intended for children and the elderly, as well as packages from sister cities abroad.

Two Police Chiefs in Leningrad

The city of Leningrad was reported to have two police chiefs—one appointed by the Leningrad City Soviet and the other by the USSR MVD. Radio Moscow quoted Major General Gennadii Voshchinin as saying he was still the city's police chief, despite the appointment by the city soviet of another person to the post. Voshchinin said the city soviet had no right to replace him.

Sakharov's Exile Home in Gorky Turned into Museum

The building where the late Andrei Sakharov spent almost seven years in internal exile is to be made into a museum. This was decided by the city authorities of Nizhnii Novgorod (formerly Gorky), TASS reported.

Wednesday, December 12

United States Announces 1-Million-Dollar Food Credit

Following talks with USSR Foreign Minister Eduard Shevardnadze, US President George Bush announced that the United States would provide the USSR with up to 1 billion dollars in credits to purchase food, AP reported. Commenting on the package, Bush said, "I want *perestroika* to succeed."

CPSU Official Says Assets Barely 5 Billion

Deputy CPSU General Secretary Vladimir Ivashko said the CPSU had assets of no more than 5 billion rubles. Ivashko told reporters in Moscow that recent unofficial estimates putting the Party's wealth at up to 200 billion rubles were "a myth." He said the Party's assets were worth exactly 4.4 billion rubles plus 600 million rubles in foreign exchange. He also said there was nothing to forbid the Party earning money. He added that the just-concluded CPSU plenum had decided to appoint a special committee responsible for economic and financial affairs.

RSFSR Deputies Discuss Changes in Constitution

The RSFSR Congress of People's Deputies excluded all references to "socialism" from the preface and first ten articles of the RSFSR Constitution. Soviet television reported that the deputies planned to make as many as fifty-seven changes to the old constitution and thereupon to call a referendum to adopt a new, non-Communist constitution.

New Prosecutor and Justice Minister Appointed

The USSR Supreme Soviet approved the appointment of a new minister of justice—thirty-nine-year-old Sergei Lushchikov, formerly deputy chairman of the USSR Supreme Soviet's Legislation Committee—and of a new prosecutor-general—fifty-nine-year-old Nikolai Turbin, who was formerly RSFSR public prosecutor. The USSR Supreme Soviet also approved the appointment of former USSR Justice Minister Veniamin Yakovlev as USSR Chief State Arbitrator (*TASS*, December 12). All these appointments were suggested by Gorbachev.

New Commander for Western Group of Forces

TASS reported that fifty-five-year-old Colonel General Matvei Burlakov had been named the new commander in chief of Soviet forces in Germany. Burlakov had, since 1988, been commander of the Southern Group of Forces, based in Hungary. His new appointment was reportedly a reward for his successful handling of the Soviet troop withdrawal from Hungary and for maintaining a high level of combat readiness while in command there. Burlakov replaced Army General Boris Snetkov, who, it was later revealed, was dismissed following the discovery on November 29 that two of his senior officers had deserted, taking antitank missiles and antiaircraft weapons with them.

Shevardnadze on Military Action in Gulf

TASS quoted a letter from Shevardnadze to Soviet parliamentarians as saying the USSR "has not and never had any plan" to take part in military conflict in the Gulf. Shevardnadze was responding to accusations from conservative members of the Supreme Soviet that he was leading the

USSR into participation in a Gulf war. Shevardnadze reiterated, however, that "if the life and security of Soviet citizens appear endangered" and if "rapid and decisive action is necessary to save them," Soviet troops would be sent to the Gulf without the approval of the USSR Supreme Soviet.

Shevardnadze Meets Savimbi

Shevardnadze met for the first time with UNITA leader Jonas Savimbi at the Soviet embassy in Washington. The meeting was part of a coordinated US-Soviet effort to help end Angola's civil war. After the meeting, Shevardnadze said that, if the Marxist government and the anti-Communist forces were able to reach a cease-fire agreement, "then it would be easier for us to address the possibility of a cutoff of arms," Western agencies reported.

Plenum of "Democratic Russia"

Representatives of various branches of the "Democratic Russia" bloc held a press conference to report on the results of the first plenum of the movement, which took place on December 8 and 9 in Moscow. Radio Moscow said the plenum discussed the draft RSFSR Constitution, the Union treaty, and nationality problems. The plenum also set up a coordinating council of the movement, which includes USSR people's deputies Il'ya Zaslavsky, Yurii Chernichenko, Yurii Afanas'ev, and Gavriil Popov. It was stressed that "Democratic Russia" did not favor a complete ban on the CPSU's political activities but did want the Communist Party to give up the privileges that it enjoyed over other political groups.

Popular Television Journalist Wounded

Radio Moscow reported that Aleksandr Nevzorov had been shot and wounded by an unknown assailant in a Leningrad suburb. Nevzorov, compere of the television show "600 Seconds," is Leningrad's most popular investigative journalist and a self-described "anti-Communist." Reuters quoted Nevzorov's Soviet colleagues as saying his hard-hitting commentaries had brought him a number of death threats.

The attack on Nevzorov even provoked a reaction from Gorbachev. The presidential spokesman said Gorbachev was "deeply outraged" by the incident and he urged the chairman of the Leningrad City Soviet, Anatolii Sobchak, to take "the most active measures" to find Nevzorov's assailant (*TASS*, December 13).

Kirgiz SSR Changes Its Name

TASS reported that the Kirgiz Supreme Soviet had voted to drop the words "Soviet" and "Socialist" from the republic's name. The move came during discussion and voting on the articles of the republican declaration of sovereignty. The articles adopted defined the republic as "an independent sovereign state" in which all-Union laws would apply only after they had been approved by the republican Supreme Soviet. The TASS report said that discussion was continuing, and it speculated that the draft Union treaty, the next item on the agenda, would face an even sharper debate.

Bill on Private Ownership of Land Adopted by Belorussian Parliament

After several days of stormy debate, the Belorussian Supreme Soviet voted to allow individuals to own land and pass it on to their heirs. They will not, however, be permitted to sell it. TASS said on December 12 that the deputies were divided into two irreconcilable camps over the issue. The liberal opposition submitted an alternative law that provided for the private sale of land, but it was voted down by the conservative majority. A similar bill of land ownership was approved on December 3 by the Congress of People's Deputies of the RSFSR.

International Scientific Group on Leningrad Dam

An international environmental study group hired by the Soviet government was quoted as saying the flood-control dam being built across the Gulf of Finland had caused minimal impact on waters in the Leningrad area. TASS quoted the study group's chairman, Dutchman Hein Angel, as telling reporters that damage to bodies of water in the Leningrad area came mainly from the city's sewage and not from the dam project. The international experts were hired to study the dam's impact on the Neva River estuary and the Gulf of Finland. TASS quoted representatives of the Leningrad City Soviet commission on the dam as saying they respected but did not share the opinion of the international commission.

Independence for USSR State Bank Approved

The USSR Supreme Soviet adopted a law making the USSR State Bank an independent institution, reporting only to the Soviet parliament. It had previously been controlled by the Soviet government. The law also brought the USSR State Bank and the republican central banks into a unified system based on a single currency. The Central Council of the USSR State Bank is to be made up of the chairmen of the republican central banks. The USSR State Bank and the republican central banks will issue money, control commercial banks, service the debts of the USSR and the Union republics, and deal with securities and foreign currency.

Bomb Damages Latvian CP Building

AP and TASS reported that a bomb had exploded near the entrance of the Sociopolitical Center of the Latvian Communist Party Central Committee in Riga. Several windows were broken but nobody was injured. TASS said the explosion had been politically motivated, claiming that "destructive forces are still planning to do away with the Latvian Communist Party."

On December 13, a member of the Latvian Supreme Soviet, Janis Freimanis, said the bomb had in fact caused very little damage. He said it looked as if the bombing had deliberately been planned to make a political statement without causing major damage (RFE Latvian service, December 13).

On December 14, TASS reported that a bomb had exploded at the entrance to the KGB headquarters in Riga. TASS quoted Latvian KGB officials as saying the bomb was homemade and not very powerful. No one was killed or injured.

On the night of December 17, small "explosive devices" went off near the offices of the Latvian Communist Party, the Military Prosecutor's Office, and a monument to Lenin, *The Washington Post* reported on December 18. Windows were broken, but no one was hurt. While the Latvian mission in Moscow accused "forces hostile to the Latvian people" of carrying out the attacks in order to create an impression of disorder and pave the way for presidential rule, a Latvian army officer told Soviet television that the blasts were the work of nationalists hoping to provoke the army into "interfering in Latvia's internal affairs."

On December 19, Latvian Minister of Internal Affairs Aloizs Vaznis offered a new Soviet-built car as a reward for information about who planted the explosive devices (RFE Latvian service, December 19).

There was an explosion on the night of December 21 at the higher military-political school in Riga, TASS reported. The agency said there were no injuries. On December 27, four more bombs exploded in Riga. The explosions took place in a kindergarten and at a railroad workers' hospital. Nobody was hurt, but there was damage to doors and windows (RFE Latvian service, December 27).

Chairman of Armenian Supreme Soviet Says Time Has Run Out for Union Treaty

Chairman of the Armenian Supreme Soviet Levon Ter-Petrossyan said time had run out to write a new Union treaty for the Soviet Union. Ter-Petrossyan said it was too late for "such a compromise" because the situation had deteriorated to the point where only brute force could prevent the dissolution of the USSR. He criticized Mikhail Gorbachev, saying the Soviet president had made many political mistakes. Ter-Petrossyan made his comments in an interview with the Oslo daily *Arbederbladet*. Meanwhile, a report from Erevan said Armenia's deputies had decided not to attend the session of the USSR Congress of People's Deputies, opening December 17. The boycott was a protest against the failure of the central government to settle the Nagorno-Karabakh conflict (*RFE/RL Special*, December 14).

Thursday, December 13

Gorbachev Urges Foreign Businesses to Invest in USSR

In an interview to be published in the December 17 issue of the US business magazine *Fortune*, Mikhail Gorbachev said there was much room for US businesses to cooperate with Soviet industry. He also said that US investors were welcome to invest in the Soviet defense industry and that the Soviet Union was seeking long-term loans with favorable terms. He said the Soviet Union especially needed help in modernizing its factories in the areas of light industry, food processing, electric power, engineering, and defense (*AP*, December 13).

Kohl and Silaev Hold Economic Talks

German Chancellor Helmut Kohl and Chairman of the RSFSR Council of Ministers Ivan Silaev held talks in Bonn on economic cooperation between Germany and the Russian republic. A statement said their talks also covered aid shipments to the Soviet Union, DPA reported. The same day, Silaev also met with Foreign Minister Hans-Dietrich Genscher and President Richard von Weizsäcker.

USSR and Germany Sign Accord on Troop Housing

German and Soviet officials signed a protocol on the construction of homes in the USSR for Soviet troops withdrawing from former East Germany. The protocol regulated the obligations of the two countries and the joint organizational and financial procedures for the program. The construction plan was part of an earlier agreement between Bonn and Moscow covering the withdrawal of all 360,000 Soviet forces from East Germany by the end of 1994 (*RFE/RL Special*, December 13).

***Krasnaya zvezda* Says Gorbachev Opposes Cut in Research**

Krasnaya zvezda said the Soviet government wanted to cut military spending in 1991. It said one of the cuts the government wanted to make was to take 23 percent from spending on military research and development. It added, however, that Mikhail Gorbachev wanted research funding maintained at the 1989 level.

South Korean President in Moscow

South Korean President Roh Tae Woo arrived in Moscow at the start of an official visit to the Soviet Union, TASS reported. The same day he met in the Kremlin with Mikhail Gorbachev. TASS said the two officials held a brief conversation. On December 14, Roh held formal talks with Gorbachev. A joint declaration on bilateral relations was signed by the two leaders. It called for a "just and fair" settlement of the division of Korea by peaceful and democratic means (*TASS*, December 14).

Shevardnadze in Turkey

USSR Foreign Minister Eduard Shevardnadze arrived in Turkey for a two-day visit to discuss the Gulf crisis and Soviet-Turkish relations. It was the first visit to Turkey by a Soviet foreign minister in twenty-five years (*Reuters*, December 13).

On December 14, Shevardnadze held talks in Ankara with Turkish President Turgut Ozal. Speaking to reporters after the talks, Shevardnadze said the proposed US-Iraqi talks were very important and should be held as soon as possible. Shevardnadze said everything must be done to find a peaceful solution to the Gulf crisis (*Reuters*, December 14).

Earlier the same day, the Soviet foreign minister met with Turkish Prime Minister Yildirim Akbulut and Finance Minister Adnan Kahveci, Reuters reported.

Ukrainian Communists Begin Second Stage of Party Congress

The Ukrainian Communist Party opened the second stage of its congress in Kiev. TASS said the main speech was delivered by Party First Secretary Stanislav Hurenko, who was elected during the first stage of the congress in June. Ukrainian sovereignty, the transition to a market economy, the draft Union treaty, and a new Party program were on the agenda of the congress. On December 12, TASS quoted Ukrainian Party Second Secretary Grigorii Kharchenko as saying the Ukrainian Party had lost 223,000 members. He did not specify, however, over what period this had taken place (*Radio Kiev*, December 12).

Georgia Suspends Local Soviets' Powers

The Georgian Supreme Soviet suspended the powers of local Soviets until new local elections were held in March, 1991. It transferred local authority from the soviets to provisional commissions formed by parliamentary deputies elected in November's multiparty elections. TASS said the move was designed to "dismantle Soviet power structures" in the republic.

Friday, December 14

Gorbachev Decree on Economic Disorganization

Mikhail Gorbachev issued a decree designed to overcome "industrial disorganization." The decree said the disorganization was caused by enterprises that failed to fulfill contracts to deliver goods to the state. It said all public companies must sign contracts by the end of December undertaking to guarantee deliveries in 1991 based on present agreements. Gorbachev's decree also ordered Soviet republics and enterprises to stop most of their direct trading with each other and with foreign partners (*TASS*, December 14; *Pravda*, December 15).

Soviet General on Payment Dispute

The outgoing commander of Soviet forces in Hungary, General Matvei Burlakov, said Budapest should pay 600–700 million rubles in compensation for property left behind by withdrawing Soviet troops. Burlakov said that this was in fact only half the property's value but that the rest could be set off against Hungarian demands for compensation for environmental damage caused by Soviet forces. Hungary disputed the Soviet figures, however, saying the property was worth far less than the Soviet Union claimed (*AFP*, December 14).

Anniversary of Andrei Sakharov's Death

Soviet citizens payed homage to Academician Andrei Sakharov, who died on December 14, 1989. Dozens of mourners laid flowers and wreaths on Sakharov's grave at a cemetery in southeast Moscow. Newspapers also praised him and some reprinted his speeches.

Gorbunovs on Direct Presidential Rule in Latvia

TASS quoted Chairman of the Latvian Supreme Council Anatolijs Gorbunovs as saying Gorbachev planned to declare direct presidential rule in the Baltic republics. Gorbunovs did not say what his statement was based on, but he told reporters in Riga that direct presidential rule in the Baltics could be justified only if local leaders proved incapable of coping with economic and political problems.

Tataria Agrees to Sign Draft Union Treaty

It was announced that Tataria had decided to sign the new Union treaty but wanted some changes made to the draft.

The decision was made at a meeting of the Tatar Supreme Soviet in Kazan on December 13 (RL Tatar-Bashkir service, December 14). A deputy, Tatar Public Center Chairman Marat Molukov, said the deputies had agreed that Tataria would sign the treaty as "a sovereign republic."

Church and Government Officials Discuss Property

Russian Orthodox Church leaders met with various government officials in Moscow to discuss the status of Church property expropriated after the Bolshevik Revolution. The officials were from the USSR and RSFSR governments, as well as from the Moscow City Soviet. TASS said the talks were heated, with some officials expressing doubts about whether the Church could care for the valuable art and architectural sites in question. The meeting took place after the patriarch of Moscow and Russia, Aleksii, had sent a letter to the Russian government demanding the return of the property, including sixty-one monasteries, 375 buildings, and many artistic works.

Karakalpak Autonomous Republic Declares Sovereignty

The Karakalpak Autonomous Republic declared itself sovereign within the republic of Uzbekistan. The decision was made by the Supreme Soviet of the Karakalpak ASSR. The sovereignty declaration said that the republic would now determine its state structure, territorial and administrative divisions, and legal system. TASS said the republic would also in future be known as Karakalpakstan.

Gromov Sues Ukrainian Komsomol Paper

Proceedings opened in Kiev in a lawsuit filed by Army General Boris Gromov against the Ukrainian Komsomol triweekly *Komsomol'skoe znamya*. Gromov accused the Komsomol paper of insulting him by printing an interview quoting another military officer as saying Gromov was one of the people in the USSR capable of initiating a military coup (*Radio Moscow*, World Service, December 14). Gromov was the last commander of Soviet troops in Afghanistan. He was commander of the Ukrainian Military District until his recent appointment as USSR first deputy minister of internal affairs.

Georgian MVD Demands Disarmament of Paramilitary Groups

The Ministry of Internal Affairs in Georgia ordered all unauthorized paramilitary groups to turn in their weapons or face prosecution. *Zarya Vostoka* said there were roughly 17,000 armed members of illegal groups in Georgia.

RSFSR Supreme Soviet Instructed to Draft Law on Presidency

The RSFSR Congress of People's Deputies instructed the republican Supreme Soviet to draft a law on the election of the RSFSR president, TASS said. The RSFSR president, the Congress ordained, should be elected by universal suffrage on a multicandidate basis. The introduction of a republican presidency ran into resistance from the conservative deputies.

More on Antidemocratic Campaign in the Press

Radio Rossii broadcast a program in which Vladimir Lysenko, Galina Starovoitova, and Lev Ponomarev commented on a series of articles in which TASS correspondent Vladimir Petrunya accused democrats of conspiring against Gorbachev and the Soviet government. Petrunya supported his accusation with quotations from a document called "Action Program-90." The democratic leaders speaking on the radio said the authors of the program belonged to no democratic group. They alleged, however, that KGB Chairman Vladimir Kryuchkov had used the document at a meeting of the Presidential Council to persuade Gorbachev not to cooperate with leaders of the country's democratic forces.

Saturday, December 15

"Soyuz" Softens towards Gorbachev

The "Soyuz" group of deputies met to discuss its position at the USSR Congress of People's Deputies. The group was far less critical of Gorbachev than it was in November and seemed to be satisfied with the president's latest statements in support of the preservation of the Soviet Union. According to TASS, the group agreed that members of "Soyuz" would support the draft Union treaty and rejected a call by one of its leading members, Viktor Alksnis, for the ouster of both Gorbachev and El'tsin.

"Shield" Holds Congress

The military union "Shield," which seeks better living conditions and legal protection for servicemen, held its second congress over the weekend. TASS reported that the union provided "enhanced security" at the congress because many of the union's members are former military officers and a number have left the Communist Party. The congress opened with a mass conducted by priest and RSFSR people's deputy Gleb Yakunin for those who had died while performing military service. Boris El'tsin also addressed the congress. Cochairman of the union Vitalii Urazhtsev told the congress that membership had reached 200,000.

Baklanov on the Armed Forces

CPSU Central Committee Secretary Oleg Baklanov said in *Sovetskaya Rossiya* that efforts to eliminate the Communist Party's influence in the army could lead to dangerous levels of confrontation. He strongly condemned efforts in the republics to form national armies, arguing that they would be economically inefficient, could lead to a new arms race, and would lower Soviet defense capability. Baklanov warned that the creation of national armies could lead to nuclear destabilization, a specter that has been raised often by those who oppose republican sovereignty.

RSFSR Congress Decides to Set Up New Security Committee

The RSFSR Congress of People's Deputies decided to set up a new republican security committee. TASS said the congress had adopted a resolution to form the committee and hand over to it all KGB organizations on RSFSR territory. Boris El'tsin told deputies that earlier consultations with KGB Chairman Vladimir Kryuchkov had shown that he would not oppose the decision "in principle."

New Organization of Communist Youth Created

The inaugural congress of a new group, called the Communist Initiative, proclaimed as its aim the revival of a union of Communist youth. TASS quoted one of the organizers of the congress as saying the Komsomol and the Communist Party had been discredited by "a bureaucratic elite" that had used the ideas of socialism and collectivism for its own purposes and had brought the Soviet Union's Communist organizations to a state of crisis.

PLO Rejects Soviet Invitation

PLO Chairman Yasser Arafat rejected an invitation to meet with Eduard Shevardnadze during his recent visit to Turkey. Shevardnadze was reported to have invited Arafat to a meeting in Ankara. Speaking on December 15 during a visit to Jordan, Arafat allegedly referred to Gorbachev as "Gorbush" and stressed the PLO's disagreement with the US and Soviet positions on the Middle East, AP reported.

Tajik Branch of Islamic Party Outlawed

Radio Moscow reported that the Supreme Soviet of Tajikistan had outlawed the Tajik branch of the all-Union Islamic Renaissance Party on the grounds that its activities violated the republic's constitution. The Supreme Soviet instructed the Ministry of Internal Affairs, the KGB, and the republican prosecutor's office to prevent any further activity by the party. The Supreme Soviet tried in October to prevent the creation of the republican branch of the organization, and its leaders have been heavily fined for defying the ban. The party reportedly frightens non-Tajik inhabitants of the republic.

Latvian Popular Front Under Fire from Prosecutor

TASS issued a statement that seemed designed to discredit the Latvian Popular Front. The statement said the grass-roots movement could plunge Latvia into economic chaos, "possible social conflict, and even a bloodbath." The Latvian public prosecutor has threatened to press charges against the popular front for allegedly advocating an anti-Soviet campaign of civil disobedience. The Latvian parliament, where the popular front holds a majority, recently declared that civil disobedience could occur if demands for the removal of Soviet troops and for other measures were not met.

Latvian Communist Party First Secretary Alfreds Rubiks joined the public prosecutor in criticizing the popular front. Rubiks told TASS the same day that those who opposed Gorbachev's new Union treaty were "guided by narrow political and nationalist ambitions."

Independent and Pro-Moscow Estonian CPs Hold Meetings

Both branches of the Estonian Communist Party met over the weekend, an RFE/RL correspondent in Tallinn reported. The pro-Moscow party, which held its Twenty-first Congress, named Lembit Annus to replace Aleksandr Gusev as first secretary and reiterated its support for the new Union treaty. The independent Estonian Communist Party held a conference, reelecting Enn-Arno Sillari as its leader.

Sunday, December 16

KGB Intelligence Chief Says He Knew of Kuwait Invasion

"The invasion of Kuwait was not a surprise for us," the head of KGB intelligence, Leonid Shebarshin, told Soviet television. Shebarshin did not explain why, if this was the case, USSR Foreign Minister Eduard Shevardnadze and other Soviet officials had told US officials on the eve of the Gulf crisis that they did not believe Iraq would invade Kuwait. Suggestions have appeared in the Soviet media that both the GRU and the KGB had advance warning of Baghdad's intentions but that the Soviet political leadership failed to react.

USSR Apologizes for KAL-007 Shooting

Local press reports in the South Korean capital, Seoul, said the Soviet Union had for the first time apologized for the shooting down in 1983 of Korean Airlines flight 007. The apology was reported to have been offered in a meeting between Shevardnadze and South Korean Foreign Minster Choi Ho Joong in Moscow on December 15. Choi quoted Shevardnadze as saying: "I regret that the incident cost innocent lives, although the tragedy has an aspect involving our rights to self-defense," AFP reported.

Opposition to Union Treaty in Moldavia

Several thousand people held a rally in Kishinev to express their opposition to the proposed Union treaty. Moldavian Prime Minister Mircea Druc was quoted as telling the crowd that the new Union treaty was "not worth discussing" (*AFP*, *TASS*, December 16). The same day, the Moldavian Supreme Soviet Presidium authorized a Grand National Assembly to begin on December 16 in Kishinev. The assembly had been requested by the Moldavian Popular Front and other public organizations and was supported by the government (RFE Romanian service, December 16). The assembly approved a number of resolutions. One said Moldavia would sign the Union treaty, while the other called for the return to Moldavia of Southern Bessarabia and Northern Bukovina, which is now part of Ukraine.

Three Killed in Ambush in Nagorno-Karabakh

More people were killed in clashes in Nagorno-Karabakh. TASS said three people were killed when a truck carrying ten people from the Azerbaijani village of Dzhamillu was ambushed. Two of the victims were members of the armed forces and one was a citizen of Dzhamillu.

On December 19, a bomb was reported to have exploded outside the Communist Party headquarters in the capital of Nagorno-Karabakh, Stepanakert. There were no reports of any injuries, but TASS said damage to the Party building was considerable.

On December 23, TASS reported that there had been another bomb attack in Nagorno-Karabakh. The agency said an attempt had been made on December 22 to blow up a bus carrying a group of MVD troops. One serviceman was injured.

First Foreign Encyclopedia to Be Published in USSR

A Soviet publisher and the US-based Encyclopedia Britannica, Inc. plan to publish the first foreign encyclopedia in the USSR since 1917. Britannica said it and the USSR's state-owned Progress Publishers had agreed to begin translating a twelve-volume edition of the encyclopedia. The project is expected to take five years (*AP*, December 16).

Monday, December 17

USSR Congress of People's Deputies Opens Session; Shevardnadze Resigns

The fourth session of the USSR Congress of People's Deputies was opened in the Kremlin by Chairman Anatolii Luk'yanov. Soviet television provided live coverage of the event. At the first day of the Congress, 1,979 deputies registered out of a total membership of 2,240. Lithuania was boycotting the session on the grounds that it considered the USSR a foreign state. Latvian and Estonian deputies planned to stay at the Congress session only long enough to hear Mikhail Gorbachev's address. Armenian deputies said they would not take part in the actual work of the session (*Radio Moscow*, December 17). On the Congress, see *Pravda*, December 18-28

The first speaker, a Chechen woman named Sazhi Umalatova who is a deputy elected to represent the CPSU and a member of the USSR Supreme Soviet, called for a vote of no confidence in President Gorbachev. Umalatova appeared to speak on her own initiative; she was not supported by "Soyuz." Her proposal that a vote of no confidence be included on the Congress agenda was defeated by a vote of 1,288 to 426, with 183 abstentions.

In his address to the Congress, Mikhail Gorbachev admitted that the situation in the USSR was extremely difficult, but he made a point of stressing positive aspects of *perestroika* as well, saying that people were no longer persecuted for their views. Gorbachev harshly criticized separatist tendencies in the republics, saying that they were mainly to blame for the country's being in a state of chaos. He endorsed the idea of strong presidential power and called for the strengthening of executive organs in the country.

The Soviet president called for a nationwide referendum on the future of the USSR, and he said every citizen should be allowed to vote in favor of, or against, the new Union treaty establishing a federation of sovereign republics. "The results of the referendum in each republic," Gorbachev said, "will be a final verdict." Gorbachev also officially proposed holding a referendum in each Union republic on whether or not to permit private ownership of the land.

Speaking to reporters during a break in the congress, Egor Ligachev said he fully supported the basic ideas in Gorbachev's report, especially those dealing with greater presidential power and bringing order to the country (*TASS*, December 17). Commenting in his turn on Gorbachev's speech, Boris El'tsin asserted that a referendum on the future of the USSR would be "a waste of time" (*AP*, December 17).

A radical speech was made at the congress by Kazakh President Nursultan Nazarbaev, who attacked Ryzhkov's economic policies and Gorbachev's decrees as, respectively, "hidden sabotage" and "purest bluff." Nazarbaev, whose outspoken remarks were carried by Radio Mayak and summarized by TASS, also said the breakup of the empire was a natural and objective process, since "it was not the republics that gathered round the center," but the center that forcibly attached the republics to itself.

On December 18, the Congress rejected two proposed additions to its agenda. One was a call by a young deputy named Sokolov for the adoption of a law on free trade; the other was an attempt by Estonian deputy Viktor Palm to persuade the deputies to formally recognize the declarations on sovereignty adopted by the parliaments of the Union republics. At the request of the deputies, the morning session ended with a report by USSR Prime Minister Nikolai Ryzhkov. Ryzhkov told deputies that, "in the form in which it was originally conceived, *perestroika* has failed to be realized," TASS reported. Ryzhkov appealed to the deputies "to resist attempts to change the nature of the social system."

Speaking to reporters during a break in the proceedings, Gorbachev defended his need for more power to hold the Soviet Union together, saying that he could have become a dictator but had not done so. He said that national authority was being destroyed, which was why he had raised the issue of greater presidential power (*Reuters*, *AP*, December 18).

Speaking at the Congress session the same day, President of the Estonian Supreme Council Arnold Ruutel told the deputies that Estonia's incorporation into the Soviet Union in 1940 had not been based on the free will of the Estonian people. He stated that Estonia had never voluntarily joined the USSR and said that what had happened to Estonia that year represented "one of the many major crimes of the Stalinist regime." Ruutel reiterated Estonia's refusal to sign the new Union treaty but called for good-neighborly relations between the USSR and Estonia.

During the Congress proceedings Radio Mayak broadcast speeches in full, but those aired by the second channel of Soviet television were heavily censored. Soviet television cut all criticism of Gorbachev in a speech made on December 18 by Nikolai Travkin, leader of the Democratic Party of Russia. Travkin said the only part of Gorbachev's speech that had any relevance to the needs of ordinary people was his call for a fight against pornography. Referring to the cinemas reserved under

Brezhnev for the elite, Travkin said only the *nomenklatura* should be allowed to watch pornographic movies, because nothing could make them more corrupt than they were already.

On December 19, the Congress resumed its session by continuing to discuss Gorbachev's report. Meanwhile, the three Baltic republics issued an appeal to deputies urging the USSR to recognize their independence and begin negotiations with them as soon as possible (*TASS*, *Radio Moscow*, December 19). In contrast, fifty-three Soviet officials and USSR Congress deputies, including the Leningrad Party chief, Boris Gidaspov, Chief of the General Staff Mikhail Moiseev, Patriarch of all-Russia Aleksii, USSR Minister of Culture Nikolai Gubenko, and writer Yurii Bondarev, called on Gorbachev to declare a state of emergency and rule by decree in tense areas.

In response to this appeal, Gorbachev told the Congress that he was considering introducing "a state of emergency or presidential rule" in major conflict zones. Gorbachev did not say which areas he had in mind.

The same day, El'tsin said the new powers requested by Gorbachev could bring back dictatorship. He told the Congress that the powers sought by Gorbachev were more comprehensive than those legally granted to either Stalin or Brezhnev. He called the present Soviet leadership "a government of national distrust" that was trying to stay in power at any price (*TASS*, December 19).

Addressing the Congress on December 19, the chairman of the Council of Nationalities, Rafik Nishanov, said it would take time for a new Union treaty to be signed and he denied that the Baltic republics were being coerced into signing the document. The chairman of the Ukrainian Supreme Soviet, Leonid Kravchuk, told the Congress that the treaty in its present form was not in the best interests of Ukraine. He said his republic should put it to a referendum.

Thirty-nine deputies from Moldavia left the Congress session, saying they would not return until Gorbachev issued a decree banning the unilaterally declared Gagauz and Dniester Republics in Moldavia. On December 20, APN reported that Mikhail Gorbachev intended to meet with the deputies from Moldavia.

On December 20, USSR Foreign Minister Eduard Shevardnadze announced his resignation to the Congress and warned that "dictatorship is coming" to the USSR, TASS reported. "If you create a dictatorship, no one can say who will become the dictator," Shevardnadze said. He told deputies he could no longer stand silent while elected legislative bodies surrendered their power to the

Soviet president. According to TASS, Shevardnadze said he had been motivated to resign by "persecution" from political opponents, whom he characterized as "reactionary." Suggesting that Gorbachev should have come to his defense, Shevardnadze lamented that "not a single person...stood up" against his critics when they accused him of "unilateral concessions, incompetence, and illiteracy." Shevardnadze described his speech as "one of the shortest and saddest" of his life.

Members of the conservative faction in the congress, "Soyuz," responded with joy to the announcement of Shevardnadze's resignation. A leader of the faction, Colonel Viktor Alksnis, told reporters it was "a step in the right direction." Another leader of the group, Colonel Nikolai Petrushenko, said he did not take the resignation seriously but interpreted it as a tactical maneuver (*TASS*, December 20).

In contrast, members of the Interregional Group of Deputies were upset by the resignation. Academician Yurii Ryzhov said Shevardnadze's statement was an implicit warning of an approaching right-wing coup. Political figures and people's deputies in the Baltic republics also expressed concern over Shevardnadze's resignation. The President of the Lithuanian Supreme Council Vytautas Landsbergis said the resignation was "a very serious signal" to supporters of democracy.

Mikhail Gorbachev condemned Shevardnadze's decision to resign. He told the Congress it was unforgivable on Shevardnadze's part to do such a thing without even consulting with the president. He called on Shevardnadze to reconsider his decision. He added that, before Shevardandze spoke, he had been planning to recommend him for the new post of vice president.

Talking to reporters, presidential spokesman Vitalii Ignatenko said the resignation must be endorsed. He said this was up to the president and the USSR Supreme Soviet (*TASS*, December 20).

The news of Shevardnadze's resignation was received with concern and regret abroad. Leaders around the world said they were saddened by the loss of Shevardnadze in world diplomacy. US Secretary of State James Baker and his German counterpart, Hans-Dietrich Genscher, said they would miss Shevardnadze as a friend as well as a colleague. Western leaders, as well as NATO headquarters and the European Community, expressed deep concern that the situation in the Soviet Union was deteriorating further (Western agencies, December 20).

On December 21, the Congress debated Mikhail Gorbachev's plan for expanded presidential powers.

Views differed sharply over the wisdom of such a move. A member of the Presidential Council, Aleksandr Yakovlev, spoke in support of the plan, saying it would be an efficient way to carry out the will of the parliament. Ukrainian deputy Volodymyr Chernyak rejected the proposal. He said the plan was a symptom of "the quiet, creeping, right-wing reactionary coup d'état" being staged in the USSR (*TASS*, *DPA*, December 21).

On December 24, the Congress approved Gorbachev's plan to hold referendums on the Union treaty and on land ownership, TASS said. Deputies also voted overwhelmingly to support the Union treaty in principle. They then began formal debate on the draft of the treaty. (The draft has been sharply criticized by many republics because it does not give them as much autonomy as they want.) The Congress voted to preserve the Soviet Union as a federation of sovereign and equal republics. Deputies also voted to retain the name of the country—the Union of Soviet Socialist Republics. (Several suggestions had been voiced at the Congress for renaming the Soviet Union.)

The same day, the Congress rejected a proposed moratorium on all strikes for 1991. The chairman of the USSR Supreme Soviet, Anatolii Luk'yanov, presented the moratorium proposal to the deputies on December 24. Several deputies were quoted by Radio Moscow as saying a moratorium would violate labor laws recently enacted by the USSR Supreme Soviet.

On December 25, the Congress approved a constitutional amendment giving more power to the Soviet president. AFP said deputies approved the amendment with slightly more than the required two-thirds majority. Earlier the same day, Boris El'tsin said he would vote against expanding the presidential powers. He said there was already too much power in the president's hands. The new executive powers of the president include the creation of a new, smaller cabinet of ministers to be directly subordinated to Gorbachev and a powerful vice president, also subordinate to Gorbachev.

Speaking to the Congress on December 25, Mikhail Gorbachev repeated that he had no intention of giving up his post as CPSU general secretary. TASS said he was responding to a call by the chairman of the RSFSR Social Democratic Party, Aleksandr Obolensky, to "decide where he belongs."

On December 26, Gorbachev nominated Politburo member Gennadii Yanaev for the newly created post of vice president, TASS reported. Addressing the Congress, Yanaev promised that, if elected, he would work to stabilize the economy and to promote economic reform.

The same day, the Congress voted 1,555 to 110 with eighty-three abstentions to give Gorbachev expanded presidential powers and to reorganize the government. The Congress also nominated a number of candidates for seats in the USSR Supreme Soviet (*TASS*, December 26). The seats were to be opened up by the annual "renewal" of the USSR Supreme Soviet that is stipulated by the Soviet Constitution. On December 27, the Congress elected 193 members of the Soviet parliament. Four seats still remained vacant after the elections. TASS said this was because one candidate from Ukraine and another from Armenia did not win the majority of votes required for election. The agency also said the Estonian and Lithuanian delegations were supposed to nominate one candidate each but failed to do so.

On December 27, the last day of the session, the Congress initially failed to elect Yanaev as vice president. Gorbachev proposed a second ballot and called for further debate on Yanaev's qualifications. This time Yanaev was elected; he won by 117 votes.

The same day, the Congress approved the holding of referendums to change Soviet laws or write new ones. TASS said the law as approved did not permit a referendum on changing the borders of the USSR or its republics. The law allows referendums to be held at the request of Soviet citizens, the USSR Congress of People's Deputies, the USSR Supreme Soviet or its chambers, the Soviet president, or higher legislative bodies of the Union republics. For the text of the law, see *Pravda*, December 29.

In his final address, Gorbachev told the Russian parliament to stop challenging the Soviet Constitution and USSR laws, TASS reported.

Students Reject Empire

About 200 students from the RSFSR, Ukraine, Armenia, Kazakhstan, and Estonia accosted USSR people's deputies near the Hotel Rossiya behind Red Square, protesting against the Union treaty. One banner carried by the students demanded to know whether the RSFSR was an independent state or "a puppet of the [all-Union] center." Waving the tricolor banner of prerevolutionary Russia, one student told Soviet television that the text of the treaty, as published in the Soviet press, furthered "the preservation of the empire" and that "this way is unacceptable to us."

Petition against Union Treaty Tops One Million in Latvia

Radio Riga reported that 1,002,829 people in Latvia had signed a petition opposing Latvia's inclusion in the new USSR Union treaty. This was a significant number, since the population of Latvia is about 2,600,000. The Popular Front of Latvia began gathering signatures at the beginning of the month.

Calls for State of Emergency in Estonia

Demonstrators at a rally in support of the Union treaty demanded that a state of emergency be imposed in Estonia, according to Radio Tallinn. The Tallinn rally, organized by the United Council of Work Collectives, protested against the Estonian government's opposition to the treaty and featured speeches calling for unity among the Soviet Union's "Intermovements."

Media on Troops in Latvia

In an interview with TASS, a high-ranking political officer alleged that Soviet soldiers in Latvia were being mistreated by Latvian citizens. "Vremya" also claimed that Soviet soldiers were being victimized in Latvia and it interviewed a Lithuanian conscript who claimed he had been attacked by Latvians.

Soviet television also claimed the same day that Lithuania's deputy head of territorial defense had made inquiries into purchasing Soviet military equipment from the former East German army. The broadcast referred to a report in the German *Berliner Zeitung*, which alleged that the weapons would be used to equip the future armed forces of Lithuania.

Workers in Southern Urals Protest about Industrial Problems

Some 15,000 workers in clothing and shoe factories in the Southern Urals attended meetings to protest about problems in the RSFSR's light industries. TASS said forty enterprises in the Russian republic that were supposed to produce shoes, textiles, and clothing had shut down because of a lack of raw materials. The news agency said the meetings were substitutes for an industry-wide strike originally called for today. The strike was postponed after workers met with Prime Minister Nikolai Ryzhkov, but, TASS commented, "workers do not yet have complete faith in the decisions of the country's leadership."

Elections to USSR Academy of Sciences

TASS reported that, following recent elections, the USSR Academy of Sciences had an additional forty-five full and 136 corresponding members. Seven places for academicians and eighteen for corresponding members remained unfilled, however. Most of these vacancies were in the departments of philosophy and law. This unprecedented situation can be explained by the fact that in the USSR the social sciences have come to be regarded as mere servants of the regime.

Kontinent to Be Published in USSR

TASS reported that the Paris-based Russian émigré journal *Kontinent* would be published in the USSR starting in 1991. The Soviet edition will be published in Moscow with the same frequency as in Paris (once quarterly) and will have an initial circulation of 100,000. Soviet representatives of *Kontinent* stressed at a press conference in Moscow that until recently it was forbidden to take the magazine into the Soviet Union.

USSR to Compensate Iraq for Early Return of Personnel

Soviet Foreign Ministry spokesman Vitalii Churkin said that 751 Soviet citizens had returned to the Soviet Union from Iraq between December 7 and 17 and that a total of 2,565 Soviet citizens remained there. Iraq and the Soviet Union were reported to be locked in negotiations over how much Iraq should be paid, and when, for the USSR's breach of contract. On December 17, Vladimir Mordvinov, a deputy minister of foreign economic relations, met with Hussein Kamel, acting oil minister in Iraq. AP said negotiations were being delayed because Iraq had not received an official Soviet pledge of payment and the two sides had not agreed on an amount. In the meantime, Baghdad slowed down the processing of exit visas.

On December 18, Churkin called on Soviet experts to return home in the interests of their own security, while special envoy Evgenii Primakov told TASS that there were about 1,000 Soviet experts in Iraq who wished to remain and complete their contracts. On December 19, Churkin said the USSR would try to bring home all its citizens from Iraq by January 15, the UN deadline for Iraqi withdrawal from Kuwait (*TASS*, December 19).

On December 26, the Soviet Union sent two envoys, Deputy Prime Minister Igor Belousov and head of the USSR Foreign Ministry's Middle East Department Vasilii Kolotusha to Baghdad to complete plans for evacuating 1,700 Soviet experts and advisers still working under contract in Iraq. Soviet Foreign Ministry spokesman Vitalii Churkin said the USSR's goal was to bring home those who wanted to leave by January 10 (*TASS*, December 26).

On December 27, Belousov held talks with Iraqi President Saddam Hussein on the Gulf crisis (*AFP*, December 27).

Ukrainian Democratic Party Strives for Independence

The Democratic Party of Ukraine held its founding congress in Kiev on December 16. Dmytro Pavlychko, a "Rukh" leader and the chairman of the Foreign Affairs Commission of the Ukrainian Supreme Soviet, told Radio Moscow on December 17 that the new party's main goals were a measured transition to national independence and the dismantling of Communist Party supremacy. The party will be headed by the long-time political prisoner Yurii Badz'o.

USSR and Czechoslovakia Sign Trade Agreement

The Soviet Union and Czechoslovakia signed a bilateral trade agreement for 1991. The accord was signed in Moscow by Soviet Foreign Minister Konstantin Katushev and Czechoslovak Deputy Prime Minister Vaclav Vales. The agreement covered the change to trade in convertible currency starting on January 1 and also dealt with sales of Soviet oil (*CTK*, December 17).

On December 18, TASS reported that the USSR would supply Czechoslovakia with 7.5 million tons of oil in 1991. In exchange, Czechoslovakia will provide equipment for the Soviet oil industry.

Calls for Prunskiene's Resignation

TASS reported that a conference in Siauliai had called for the resignation of Lithuanian Prime Minister Kazimiera Prunskiene. Representatives of the Independence Party, Christian Democratic Party, Democratic Party, Green Party, and a number of Lithuanian unions said the government had been "slow in implementing radical reforms" and they accused the prime minister and her cabinet of maintaining ties with "corrupted elements of the *nomenklatura*."

Events of 1986 Commemorated in Alma-Ata

Some 20,000 people gathered in Alma-Ata to commemorate the protests of 1986, now officially recognized in the republic as "the first democratic action of young people against the totalitarian system" (*TASS*, December 17). The Alma-Ata City Soviet designated December 17, the anniversary of the protests, as a "Day of Democratic Renewal"; the city's mayor told the meeting that a commemorative plaque was being erected. The imam of Alma-Ata's main mosque read from the Koran. Similar meetings were held in Gurev, Dzhambul, Kzyl-Orda, and Chimkent.

Tuesday, December 18

New USSR MVD Chief Wants More Power

The Soviet Union's new minister of internal affairs, Boriss Pugo, said the draft Union treaty gave his ministry too little power. The draft said the USSR MVD should coordinate the work of law-enforcement bodies. In an interview with TASS, Pugo said this was insufficient.

NATO Foreign Ministers Express Support for Baltic Independence

NATO foreign ministers expressed their support for Baltic independence in a communiqué issued on December 18, agencies reported. The statement, issued after a two-day meeting in Brussels, said: "We support the expectations and legitimate aspirations of the Baltic peoples. We call on the Soviet authorities to continue to seek, through just and open dialogue with the democratically elected leaders of the three Baltic republics, a negotiated solution."

Food Prices to Rise in Latvia

TASS reported that the Latvian Council of Ministers proposed to increase the prices of many food items—including bread, meat, and milk—by as much as 300 percent on January 3, 1991. The price of a kilo of butter will rise from 3.4 rubles to 10 rubles, of cheese to 8 rubles, of grade-one beef to 7.2 rubles, and of boiled sausage to more than 12 rubles. The price hikes will be offset by increased payments to nonworking pensioners (46 rubles per month) and students, plus higher child allowances. It is also proposed that wages should increase by an average of 66 rubles per month.

Draft Problems in Armenia

Deputy Chief of the General Staff of the Soviet Armed Forces Grigorii Krivosheev said that the military draft was being "practically ignored" in Armenia and that to date only 25 percent of eligible draftees had been conscripted, TASS reported. The colonel general met with the deputy chairman of the Armenian Supreme Soviet Commission on Defense, Vagan Shirkhonyan. Krivosheev rejected a suggestion that Armenian conscripts should be allowed to serve in Armenia, arguing that the armed forces were organized on "an extraterritorial principle" according to which conscripts are sent where they are needed. Only 7.5 percent of eligible draftees in Armenia were conscripted this past spring.

Pravitel'stvennyi vestnik (No. 48) carried an interview in which Krivosheev detailed draft shortfalls throughout the USSR. He criticized draft-dodging in the Baltic republics but also mentioned picketing at a draft office in Moscow on October 25.

Trade-Union Official Jailed in Minsk

An official of an independent Soviet trade-union group has been jailed in Minsk on charges of disturbing the peace by engaging in public protests. A Minsk journalist,

Yaz Valoshka, told RFE/RL that Mikhail Sobol' had been taken into custody five days ago and was now serving a fifteen-day jail sentence. Sobol' is one of three cochairman of the independent Confederation of Labor and chairman of the independent Belorussian Workers' Union.

Russia and Belorussia Sign Cooperation Treaty

The RSFSR and Belorussia signed an agreement on bilateral cooperation. The treaty was signed in Moscow by the chairmen of the Supreme Soviets of the two republics, Boris El'tsin and Nikolai Dementei. In the treaty, the RSFSR and Belorussia agreed not to take economic measures that could harm each other. TASS quoted El'tsin as saying this was the sort of "horizontal" treaty between republics that could be a basis for the new all-Union treaty.

Uzbekistan Adopts Its Own Economic Program

Uzbekistan decided it would overrule any increase in the price of bread, flour, and bakery products that might take place in the USSR. TASS said this decision had been made by the Uzbek Council of Ministers as part of a program to stabilize the consumer market in the republic next year.

Wednesday, December 19

Soviet General Threatens Latvians

Lieutenant General Petr Chaus, commander of the Baltic Military District, warned Latvians against pushing the army "to extreme measures." The warning was given on December 18 by Chaus to the Latvian prime minister, Ivars Godmanis. The general said the army would make every effort to make sure that soldiers and their dependents were not left without heat, water, electricity, or bread (*TASS*, December 19). In November, the Latvian Supreme Soviet instructed municipalities to stop providing supplies and social services to the Soviet Armed Forces in Latvia.

On December 19, Godmanis said it was possible that the Soviet Union would intervene in the Baltic republics. The prime minister said Mikhail Gorbachev could soon use the armed forces to depose the Baltic parliaments and governments. Godmanis said he expected no US or West European support if the USSR intervened in the Baltic republics (*DPA*, December 19).

US State Department spokesman Richard Boucher again urged the Soviet government to resolve its dispute with the Baltic republics through peaceful means. Boucher said that "threats, intimidation, and coercion should not be used" (*RFE/RL Special*, December 19).

The same day, Colonel General Al'bert Makashov, a leading military conservative, told Interfax that the Soviet Union had "vital" strategic and economic interests in the Baltic republics and could not simply allow them to go their own way.

Estonian Parliament Calls for Civil Disobedience

On December 18, the Estonian Supreme Council called for civil disobedience in the event of a Soviet military crackdown, *Rahva Haal* reported on December 19. The resolution, passed by fifty-one votes to fifteen with seven abstentions, stated that, if "the USSR . . . [tries] to impede the Republic of Estonia's laws and state authority with the use of force, the first priority is the preservation of the Estonian people. This excludes using force as a means of resistance." The resolution called for "civil disobedience and [legal] acts passed by the Republic of Estonia's Supreme Council to guide actions." The resolution was passed before Soviet President Mikhail Gorbachev issued his threat to impose a state of emergency or direct presidential rule.

Kirgizia Hedges on Approval of Union Treaty

The Kirgiz Supreme Soviet approved in principle the draft Union treaty but wanted some changes made in it. Frunze journalist Kadyraly Konkobaev told RFE/RL that the republican Supreme Soviet had completed work on a declaration of Kirgiz sovereignty on December 15 and declared that day an official holiday to commemorate the declaration (RL Kirgiz service, December 19).

Belorussian CP Chief Claims Belorussians Support Union

The first secretary of the Belorussian Communist Party, Anatolii Malofeev, said he believed the majority of Belorussians supported a Union of Soviet republics. Malofeev told *Pravda* that Belorussians wanted a Union on a new basis. He said it was important for republics to join the new federation voluntarily and at the same time to preserve their sovereignty. He also said he saw no problem if some republics failed to join a new Union in the first stage of its reorganization. He said they would still have time to decide on their future.

New Moscow Group to Help Manage Soviet Privatization

Soviet and Western businessmen formed a group to help advise Soviet enterprises on how best to prepare for privatization. The group, the Moscow International Center of Enterprise and Privatization, aims to link Soviet firms with Western experts and organize foreign investment. Aleksandr Vladislavlev, a member of the Moscow City

Soviet's Executive Committee, said Soviet enterprises needed examples. He said the main obstacle to joint Western-Soviet investment was the lack of experience and competence in the USSR (*Reuters*, December 19).

Lithuanian-Moldavian Cooperation Agreement Signed

In Vilnius, Lithuanian Prime Minister Kazimiera Prunskiene and Moldavian Prime Minister Mircea Druc signed a bilateral agreement covering trade and economic, technical, and cultural cooperation for 1991, Radio Vilnius reported.

Shevardnadze Pledges Support for Decolonization

Eduard Shevardnadze said the USSR intended to support the United Nations' efforts to establish "an integral system of global partnership." The UN released Shevardnadze's message marking the thirtieth anniversary of "the UN declaration on the granting of independence to colonial countries and peoples." Shevardnadze said the proposed global partnership should be based on "a balance of interests, political realism, and responsible behavior of states." He also advocated "protection of democracy and human rights and adherence to a worldwide system of law and order based on the charter of the United Nations" (*RFE/RL Special*, September 19).

Yazov on Housing for Soviet Armed Forces

Soviet Defense Minister Dmitrii Yazov said the Defense Ministry had built 66,000 apartments for military personnel in 1990. Moscow television quoted Yazov as saying the ministry would get another 11,000 apartments from local governments, bringing the total new housing units available to military personnel in 1990 to 77,000. Yazov also noted that Germany had agreed to finance the construction of 36,000 additional flats in the next four years for soldiers withdrawing from former East German territory.

Thursday, December 20

Afanas'ev Says USSR Moving towards Dictatorship

Echoing what was said by Eduard Shevardnadze when he announced his resignation as Soviet foreign minister, reformist Professor Yurii Afanas'ev said the Soviet Union was moving towards a dictatorship. Afanas'ev made the comments in an article for the new Soviet weekly *Nezavisimaya gazeta*, which appeared on December 21. In his article, Afanas'ev said Gorbachev had been under heavy pressure from a coalition of "conservative and reactionary forces" to slow down his reforms. Afanas'ev cited the CPSU apparatus, the KGB, and military commanders as major elements of the coalition. Afanas'ev said that Gorbachev himself was "sufficiently conservative-minded" to be affected by the pressure of the coalition.

Two Parties in RSFSR Announce Intention to Unite

Two parties in the Russian Federation claiming to hold Social Democratic positions announced their intention to merge, Novosti reported. These were the Social Democratic Party, led by Oleg Rumyantsev, and the Republican Party, headed by Vyacheslav Shostakovsky. The latter party was set up earlier in 1990 on the basis of the radical faction of the Democratic Platform in the CPSU.

Latvia Extends Parliamentary Session, Recalls Congress Deputies

The Latvian Supreme Council decided to stay in session during the forthcoming holidays and recalled its members from the USSR Congress of People's Deputies. A deputy of the Latvian Supreme Council, Eduards Berklavs, told RFE/RL that the parliament had decided to stay in session because of the volatile situation in the Baltic republics. He said the only break in the session would be on December 25 and 26. The Latvian Supreme Council also issued an order barring Latvian Supreme Council deputies from participating in any way as Latvian representatives on USSR bodies (RFE Latvian service, December 20).

Friday, December 21

Gorbachev's Message to Gulf Cooperation Council

In a move calculated to signal that the USSR's foreign policy remained unchanged despite Shevardnadze's resignation, Gorbachev sent a message to the Gulf Cooperation Council reaffirming Moscow's support for the UN Security Council resolution demanding Iraq's withdrawal from Kuwait. "I would like to confirm the determination of the Soviet Union to stand by international law and achieve restoration of the sovereignty and territorial integrity of Kuwait," Gorbachev said in a message carried by TASS.

Interregional Group Calls for Unity of Democratic Forces

The Interregional Group of Deputies called for a revitalized coalition of democratic deputies to counter what the group's members described as resurgent hard-line Communists. The group appealed specifically to deputies from the Russian Federation, asking them to work against forces favoring a return to authoritarian rule in the USSR. The statement also called on Mikhail Gorbachev and

Boris El'tsin to settle their differences and throw their weight behind democratic reforms (*Reuters*, December 21).

Two New Western Studies of Soviet Economic Situation

Two new Western studies of the Soviet Union's economic situation opposed large-scale, direct aid for the country until an economic reform program was firmly in place. One study, led by the International Monetary Fund, said the USSR's old planning system "has broken down but has not been dismantled." It said aid would be of little value because significant reforms were still needed. But the report did say humanitarian and technical assistance could be justified. The second study, by the European Community, also supported small-scale projects and food aid for the USSR. The EC report said "firm and concerted action" was needed to reform the Soviet economic system (*AP*, *Reuters*, December 21).

Soviet economic experts praised the IMF report. Academician Stanislav Shatalin said the report was "unbiased, fundamentally solid, not malicious." But he and Gorbachev's economic adviser Nikolai Petrakov said they were not sure the Soviet government would follow the report's recommendations (*Reuters*, December 22).

RSFSR Supreme Soviet Adopts Law on Rural Areas

The RSFSR Supreme Soviet adopted a law outlining social development in rural areas. The law called for accelerated housing construction, for priority to be given to the construction of public health facilities and roads, and for easier credit for agricultural workers. The law also set annual financial support for the agricultural sector at a level of no less than 15 percent of the federation's national income (*TASS*, December 21).

Soviet Army in Baltic Appeals for Presidential Rule

Representatives of the Soviet army in the three Baltic republics appealed to the USSR Congress of People's Deputies to introduce presidential rule there. Radio Riga and TASS said about 500 army representatives met in the Latvian capital, Riga. The appeal said if presidential rule were not effective a state of emergency should be introduced nationwide. It said if the USSR Congress of People's Deputies did not take action to ensure political stability the army would be compelled to adopt "all measures, including extraordinary ones, in order to protect the soldiers' rights and human dignity."

Meanwhile, TASS reported that Soviet troops were patrolling the streets of the Lithuanian city of Klaipeda in spite of protests by Lithuanian officials. The armed soldiers were authorized by their garrison commander to check citizens' documents and arrest anyone who resisted, TASS reported.

Several Thousand Bureaucrats to Lose Jobs in Kazakhstan

Kazakh President Nursultan Nazarbaev ordered a restructuring of the government that would eliminate the jobs of several thousand state employees. TASS quoted the deputy chairman of the Kazakh Supreme Economic Council, Daulet Sembaev, as saying those dismissed would get new jobs in industry. He said there was no danger of unemployment, because there was "an acute shortage" of skilled workers, engineers, and managers. Nazarbaev's restructuring called for the elimination of nine ministries and eight state committees and the creation of two new ministries and eight new state committees. TASS said the details of the restructuring were published in the Kazakh press on December 21.

Saturday, December 22

Kryuchkov Addresses USSR Congress of People's Deputies

In a toughly worded speech to the USSR Congress of People's Deputies, carried by TASS and broadcast by Soviet television, the chairman of the USSR KGB, Vladimir Kryuchkov, accused foreign intelligence services of aggravating ethnic tensions in the Soviet Union by supporting nationalist organizations. Kryuchkov singled out the CIA, saying it had set up a special service to collect information on new political movements in the USSR. The KGB chief also attacked Western firms for taking advantage of the Soviet economic crisis, accusing them of selling Moscow substandard goods and radioactive food.

Kryuchkov emphasized, however, that "the internal subversion" facing the USSR was stronger than "the external one." He said that, if ethnic violence continued to develop in the Soviet Union, the country would be unable to avoid "very grave upheavals." He stressed that the USSR must be prepared to accept the possibility of bloodshed if order was to be restored in republics where there was ethnic unrest. Kryuchkov said: "Society has a right to be defended. . . . It would be best to solve political problems with political measures, but if one witnesses the use of force, with certain political groups using terror and weapons, then what is one to do?"

On December 24, the US State Department said Kryuchkov had made "unfounded and inaccurate" statements about foreign involvement in Soviet affairs. State Department spokesman Richard Boucher said the United States was concerned that a senior Soviet official should use such outdated and inflammatory rhetoric (*AP*, December 24). On December 25, Kryuchkov said his remarks about foreign involvement in Soviet affairs had been "misunderstood." He stressed that they did not signal a return to a Cold War mentality. Speaking to reporters in Moscow, the KGB chairman said he had not meant to accuse the majority of foreign enterprises, and he welcomed international aid to the USSR (*AP*, *AFP*, December 25).

Gorbachev Threatens Steps to Restore Order in Moldavia

Mikhail Gorbachev threatened to use his presidential powers unless Moldavian leaders and minority groups acted within ten days to end ethnic conflict. The warning came in a decree carried by TASS. TASS said Gorbachev had ordered the dissolution of the republics proclaimed by the Gagauz minority and the nonindigenous residents of the Dniester region. He also called for changes in Moldavia's language law so that the interests of ethnic groups could be respected.

On December 23, the Soviet media said there had been clashes between opposing groups at a rally in the Moldavian capital, Kishinev. TASS said speakers at the Communist Party-sponsored rally supported Gorbachev's decree on Moldavia. The agency said another group of people held a counter rally, chanting "Invaders go home." TASS said people from both sides started a brawl, and police intervened (*Central Television*, "Vremya," December 23).

TASS reported on December 30 that the Moldavian Supreme Soviet had accepted Gorbachev's decree aimed at ending the republic's ethnic conflicts. The parliament noted that many of the president's demands had already been implemented, including "the dissolution of volunteer detachments and the annulment of unconstitutional decisions concerning the setting up of the so-called Gagauz and Dniester Republics."

The chairman of the Supreme Soviet of the would-be Gagauz Republic, Stepan Topal, claimed on December 28 that Moldavia's Gagauz minority was ready to meet Gorbachev's terms. But, in a statement carried by TASS, Topal said he was not sure the Moldavian authorities were ready to observe all parts of the decree.

El'tsin on Shevardnadze's Resignation

The chairman of the RSFSR Supreme Soviet, Boris El'tsin, said he believed Eduard Shevardnadze had made a mistake in resigning. El'tsin told reporters that Shevardnadze's resignation would not shock Soviet leaders into introducing further reforms. The same day, Ukrainian Foreign Minister Anatol Zlenko said Shevardnadze's resignation had caused apprehension throughout the world. But he added that he believed that the reforms of the past five years had set a new direction for Soviet foreign policy that would not be changed by one man's resignation (*TASS*, *Radio Kiev*, December 22).

Prunskiene Urges West to Take Tougher Stance

Lithuanian Prime Minister Kazimiera Prunskiene urged Western governments to take a tougher stance against Mikhail Gorbachev. In an interview with Reuters, she said Western powers should threaten to withhold support and aid for the Soviet Union. She said it was absurd to back Gorbachev regardless of his domestic policies. Prunskiene described Shevardnadze's resignation as a dramatic warning to the world that reactionaries in the old Communist Party elite and some parts of the armed forces were gaining control in the USSR. Prunskiene was speaking during a visit to Tokyo (*AP*, December 24).

On December 22, the president of the Lithuanian Supreme Council, Vytautas Landsbergis, said the Baltic republics should prepare to resist the imposition of presidential rule. Speaking at a meeting of "Sajudis" in Vilnius, Landsbergis said the Lithuanian restructuring movement should prepare its own program of resistance in the event of the Kremlin's "introducing an overtly occupationist form of rule in Lithuania" (*Reuters*, December 22).

Sunday, December 23

Pro-Democratic Rally in Moscow

About 2,500 people gathered at a rally in Moscow to criticize Mikhail Gorbachev and protest against what they saw as the danger of a dictatorship in the USSR. The rally was organized by the Interregional Group of Deputies and other reformist organizations. Some placards carried slogans supporting Shevardnadze and warning Gorbachev about the danger of losing his closest allies in the government. Several speakers criticized the speech by KGB Chairman Vladimir Kryuchkov at the USSR Congress of People's Deputies (*AP*, December 23).

Armenian CP Leader Expelled from Nagorno-Karabakh

Radio Baku said the Armenian Communist Party first secretary, Stepan Pogosyan, had been expelled from Nagorno-Karabakh. Giving details of the incident, Radio Baku said Pogosyan had arrived in Stepanakert on December 22 without having cleared his visit with the Azerbaijani authorities. The military commandant of Nagorno-Karabakh therefore demanded that he leave immediately.

Soviet Jewish Emigration Reaches Record High

The Israeli media said the rate of Soviet Jews immigrating to Israel had reached a record high of 100 arrivals an hour. A spokesman for the Israeli agency that handles immigration said that more than 7,000 Soviet Jews had landed in Tel Aviv since flights were increased earlier in the week. Israeli officials said the rise in immigration was due to fears of political and economic instability in the Soviet Union (*Reuters*, *AP*, December 23).

Train Explosion Kills Eleven

Eleven people were killed and forty-eight injured when a rail tanker filled with liquid gas exploded, causing two passenger trains to crash near Belgorod in Central Russia. TASS said the gas tanker was parked on a siding at Elnikovo-pod-Belgorodom station and that it blew up as the Kislovodsk-Leningrad express passed by. The blast threw the electric locomotive of the express into the path of a passenger train traveling between Moscow and Novorossisk. Carriages of both trains caught fire, and sixteen carriages burned out.

Belorussia Introduces Anti-Inflation Measures

A report said the first legal act in the USSR to protect the population from inflation had been adopted in Belorussia. TASS said that the Belorussian authorities would begin calculating consumer price indexes and making adjustments to incomes. It said incomes would be indexed after each rise of 5 percent in the consumer price index and that income adjustments would begin in January, 1991.

RSFSR Sets Up Food Commission

The RSFSR Supreme Soviet set up an emergency food commission. An extraordinary session of the RSFSR Congress of Peoples' Deputies had earlier in December ordered the commission to be set up to stabilize food supplies and investigate why shortages were occurring. TASS said that Boris El'tsin was to head the commission and that RSFSR Prime Minister Ivan Silaev was among its members.

Monday, December 24

Congress Gets Results of Poll on Union

According to a poll conducted for the USSR Congress of Peoples' Deputies, slightly more than half (53 percent) of the people surveyed around the country thought a breakup of the USSR was impossible. About one-third (27 percent), however, thought such a breakup was inevitable. The results of the poll were circulated at the Congress. TASS said the poll had been taken in the past few days by the Soviet parliamentary poll service. It questioned people in twenty-three cities and villages in all regions and republics.

Another survey, this one conducted among the Congress deputies themselves, indicated that about one-quarter of them belonged to the conservative "Soyuz" faction. The Soviet media said that Congress deputies had officially registered with eighteen factions and that the "Soyuz" faction had 561 members. The survey showed that the Communists formed the largest faction in the Congress, with 730 members. That is about one-third of the Congress' total membership of 2,250 deputies. Other large groups registered included farmers (431), workers (400), and the liberal Interregional Group of Deputies (229). Other factions represented ecologists (220), women (216), centrists (153), young deputies (125), and Afghan war veterans (52). Deputies were allowed to register with more than one faction (*Central Television*, "Vremya," December 24).

Antimilitary Demonstration in Moscow

More than 300 mothers whose sons had been killed serving in the Soviet Armed Forces demonstrated in front of the Defense Ministry in Moscow. According to TASS, they were demonstrating against "the disastrous situation in the army." It said the women failed to meet any of the ministry's leading officials.

Soviet Deputy Defense Minister Appointed

A presidential decree appointed Colonel General Vladislav Achalov a deputy defense minister. TASS said Achalov was filling a newly created post. Achalov became commander of the Soviet airborne troops last year. He was previously chief of staff of the Leningrad Military District. TASS said General Pavel Grachev had been appointed the new commander of the airborne troops. Grachev is an Afghan war veteran.

"Soyuz" Issues Resolution on Gulf

The conservative "Soyuz" faction within the USSR Congress of People's Deputies demanded a strong role for the Soviet parliament in determining Soviet policy on the Persian Gulf. In a resolution, "Soyuz" asked the Congress to require the Soviet Foreign Ministry to give the USSR Supreme Soviet daily reports on the Gulf crisis. The group also called for a special Supreme Soviet session on January 14, the day before the United Nations deadline for Iraq to leave Kuwait or face possible attack. "Soyuz" said the Soviet parliament should have to approve any deployment of Soviet troops to the Gulf (*Reuters*, *TASS*, December 24).

Raisa Gorbacheva Visits Chernobyl' Victims

Raisa Gorbacheva visited victims of the Chernobyl' nuclear accident at a Moscow hospital. She told Soviet television: "Chernobyl' is our common pain" and the grief of many people. Gorbacheva also formally accepted a private gift from a Japanese foundation of 38 million dollars' worth of medical equipment for use in treating Chernobyl' victims (*AP*, December 24).

Soviet Bank Warns Foreigners against Accepting Rubles

The USSR State Bank warned foreign companies working in the USSR not to accept payments in rubles from Soviet firms and institutions. In a statement issued on December 24, the bank said a growing number of payments were being made through financial documents denominated in rubles. It said that these totaled thousands of millions of rubles and emphasized that neither the State Bank nor the USSR Finance Ministry had offered to guarantee these payments. The bank's statement reminded foreign companies that Soviet law bans the export of Soviet currency. The bank also denounced the practice in some business contracts of setting an exchange rate for the ruble that is lower than the official commercial level (*TASS*, December 24).

RSFSR Passes Law on Property

The RSFSR Supreme Soviet adopted a law on property (*TASS*, December 25). The law gave foreign companies and Soviet citizens the right to own factories and other enterprises as well as buildings and other property in the republic. TASS said the law nullified the activities of state bodies and other economic partners that contravene the sovereignty and economic interests of the RSFSR. TASS said most features of the law would take effect on January 1, 1991, and would regulate all matters of property in Russia. The bill included a section on private land ownership that was to take effect on January 15, 1991.

Tuesday, December 25

El'tsin Says Dual Citizenship to Be Introduced in RSFSR

Boris El'tsin said a policy of dual citizenship would be introduced in the RSFSR for Russians living abroad. El'tsin told a news conference that Russians who had taken citizenship in other countries would be able to enjoy "all rights and responsibilities" in the republic. He called for the restoration of "broken-off relations between the homeland and its children abroad," TASS reported.

Krasnaya zvezda on Shevardnadze's Resignation

Writing in *Krasnaya zvezda*, USSR people's deputy Major General Mikhail Surkov denied that the USSR Defense Ministry had put pressure on Eduard Shevardnadze to resign as Soviet foreign minister. Surkov complained that democratic deputies had leveled accusations to this effect against the Soviet Armed Forces at the USSR Congress of People's Deputies.

USSR and Israel Formally Exchange Consuls

The Soviet Union and Israel formally exchanged consuls general at ceremonies in Jerusalem and Moscow, TASS and AP reported. The moves raised the countries' official representation to the highest level since the USSR cut off diplomatic relations with Israel during the Middle East war in 1967. Full diplomatic ties have been blocked by Soviet-Israeli disagreement over a Middle East peace conference that would include Palestinians.

Patriarch Asks That Christmas and Good Friday Be Holidays

Patriarch of Moscow and All Russia Aleksii asked the RSFSR Supreme Soviet to declare Christmas and Good Friday public holidays. (The Russian Orthodox Church celebrates Christmas on January 7.) In asking for the holidays, the patriarch cited the republican law on freedom of conscience. That law says the republic can declare holidays at the request of major religious organizations (*TASS*, December 25). On December 27, the RSFSR Supreme Soviet fulfilled the patriarch's request and declared the Orthodox Christmas an official holiday, TASS reported.

On December 26, the Moldavian Supreme Soviet issued a list of republican holidays that included Christmas (January 7–8). The list excluded November 7, the anniversary of the October Revolution (*TASS*, December 25). The same day, the Ukrainian Supreme Soviet declared January 7 a public holiday (*TASS*, December 26).

Unit to Fight Economic Crime Set Up in Leningrad

The city of Leningrad set up a special unit to fight economic crime. The unit leader, Police General Evgenii Ratkovsky, said the new body was necessary to combat increased corruption and black market activities. TASS quoted experts as saying that some 60 percent of goods meant for general distribution ended up on the black market, earning marketeers annual profits of about 150,000 million rubles.

Woman Goes on Trial for Slandering Gorbachev

A student of a higher educational institution in the RSFSR city of Tver (formerly Kalinin), identified by TASS as Tamara Tselikova, went on trial for insulting Mikhail Gorbachev. TASS said Tselikova had been detained in September putting up leaflets that said Gorbachev had "stained his hands with blood in Baku and Tbilisi." The leaflets also said Gorbachev was "a fascist criminal, just like Lenin, Stalin, and Khrushchev."

North Korea Condemns Roh Visit to Moscow

North Korea criticized the recent visit to Moscow by South Korean President Roh Tae Woo. The Pyongyang Workers' Party newspaper *Rodong Sinum* said the tour was "antipeace and anti–North Korean." The newspaper also said the aim of Roh's "treacherous" trip was to absorb North Korea with the support of Moscow and Washington (*Reuters*, *AP*, December 25).

Kiev Military District Has New Commander

Lieutenant General Viktor Chechevatov was appointed commander of the Kiev Military District.

Wednesday, December 26

Ryzhkov Hospitalized with Heart Attack

Soviet Prime Minister Nikolai Ryzhkov was hospitalized after suffering a heart attack. Yurii Tyun'kov, a USSR Council of Ministers spokesman, told AP that Ryzhkov was out of danger. The heart attack was announced by Mikhail Gorbachev to the USSR Congress of People's Deputies (*TASS*, December 26).

On December 27, Gorbachev told the Congress that Ryzhkov's condition was serious but not worsening. Interviewed the same day by TASS, Ryzhkov's wife Lyudmila attributed her husband's heart attack to exhaustion and sharp criticism of his economic policies.

Armenia Accuses Azerbaijan of Cutting Natural Gas

A report from Erevan said Azerbaijan had reduced by half the flow of natural gas through the main pipeline to Armenia. Radio Erevan quoted Naytransgaz, the Armenian transportation association, as saying only about 13 million cubic meters of gas were flowing daily to Armenia from Azerbaijan. The radio did not say when the disruption had begun.

North Ossetia Declares Itself a Soviet Socialist Republic

North Ossetia, which has been an autonomous republic within the RSFSR, declared itself a Soviet Socialist republic within the RSFSR and the USSR. The decision was made by the North Ossetian Supreme Soviet, which also adopted a declaration of state sovereignty for North Ossetia that said all resources in the republic belonged to the people living there and that the state languages of the republic were Ossetian and Russian (*TASS*, December 26).

Thursday, December 27

German Police on Crimes of Soviet Troops in East Germany

Die Welt quoted Hans Ludwig Zachert, president of the Investigation Office of the German Federal Police, as saying Soviet troops in East Germany were committing up to thirty criminal offenses a day and were posing a growing security problem to the recently united Germany. The police official said these offenses, mainly theft and traffic violations, irritated Germans and aroused animosity towards the Soviet forces. He also said morale was worsening among Soviet troops in East Germany and that fifteen to thirty of them were deserting every week.

On December 29, USSR Foreign Ministry spokesman Vitalii Churkin disputed the claim of the German police that Soviet soldiers had been committing up to thirty crimes a day in the former GDR. Churkin said the German figure was some ten times higher than the Soviet estimate, but he added that Soviet and German officials could be using different data. He suggested that the German figures could include soldiers on temporary leave from their garrisons (*Reuters*, *DPA*, December 29).

RSFSR Finance Minister Resigns

The newspaper of the RSFSR Supreme Soviet, *Rossiiskaya gazeta*, reported that the republican finance minister, Boris Fedorov, had resigned because of the lack of progress in economic reform. The paper quoted Fedorov as saying the republic had not advanced in its transition to a market economy. He said proposed reforms got lost for months "in the depths of the apparatus."

The Presidium of the RSFSR Supreme Soviet accepted Fedorov's resignation on December 29. RSFSR Deputy Prime Minister Yurii Skokov told TASS that Federov was a "sound" economist but said there had been "differences" over the pace of economic reform in the republic.

Anniversary of Invasion of Afghanistan Marked

In a special commentary devoted to the eleventh anniversary of the Soviet invasion of Afghanistan, TASS said the nine-year war there had brought "untold sorrow" to the people of both the Soviet Union and Afghanistan. It said Soviet soldiers had "paid with their blood for the mistake made by the country's political leaders." The RSFSR Supreme Soviet stood up to mark the memory of soldiers who died in the war (*Moscow Television*, December 27).

Friday, December 28

Fraud Alleged in Yanaev Election

Members of the Interregional Group of Deputies said that Gennadii Yanaev's election as USSR vice president may have involved fraud. A spokesman for the group, Arkadii Murashov, told reporters that the election had not been properly monitored and that there had been discrepancies in the counting of the ballots. Murashov said the Interregional Group would ask the Committee for Constitutional Oversight to investigate the matter. In a statement issued the same day, the Interregional Group warned that the USSR was in danger of being ruled by a dictatorship under which violence would be the primary means of resolving internal political issues.

Popular Soviet Television Show Banned

The presenters of the popular television show "Vzglyad," Aleksandr Lyubimov and Aleksandr Politkovsky, told RFE/RL that their commentary on the resignation of USSR Foreign Minister Eduard Shevardnadze had been withdrawn by Chairman of the State Committee for Radio and Television Broadcasting Leonid Kravchenko. Kravchenko subsequently banned the entire December 28 edition of the show, during which the two men had planned to reveal that Shevardnadze's resignation had not come as a surprise to President Mikhail Gorbachev and other Soviet politicians.

Interviewed by Central Television on December 30, Kravchenko denied that he had banned the December 28 edition of "Vzglyad." He admitted, however, that he had advised the "Vzglyad" team that interviewing Shevardnadze would be inappropriate. Kravchenko explained: "The president had asked people not to get drawn into . . . such a debate. There was a great deal that still needed to be weighed up and assessed." His words implied that the Kremlin had not yet adopted an official line on the foreign minister's resignation.

On January 4, however, "Vzglyad" was banned again because its producers planned to discuss the resignation of Shevardnadze. Announcer Igor Kirillov told the viewers of "Orbita" on the evening of January 4: "There will be no 'Vzglyad' today, for the same political reasons as last week. Any suggestions that the program is not ready for broadcasting are groundless."

Kebich Says Belorussia Facing Bankruptcy

Belorussian Prime Minister Vyacheslav Kebich said his republic was near bankruptcy. *Rabochaya tribuna* quoted Kebich as saying that Belorussia's 1991 budget deficit could run into billions of rubles owing to the rising costs of livestock feed and of raw materials needed by many Belorussian enterprises. Price increases were forcing Belorussia to become a net importer rather than an exporter, he said, adding that the republic should be allowed to export goods on its own account instead of through central trade agencies. Kebich said the central government seemed to agree with this idea but was nevertheless "putting up obstacles."

Economic Adviser Favors Dual Currency System

An economic adviser to Gorbachev, Nikolai Petrakov, said he favored the creation of a convertible Soviet ruble that would exist alongside the present nonconvertible currency. Noting that extreme measures were required to revive the Soviet economy, Petrakov told *Trud* that the convertible ruble could be used to purchase both foreign currencies and goods on the world market. Petrakov was elected a full member of the USSR Academy of Sciences in December, 1990.

Saturday, December 29

Gorbachev Orders 5-Percent Sales Tax

A nationwide 5-percent sales tax on consumer goods and services, with the exception of food, was imposed on the country as of January 1, 1991. TASS said the money raised would be used for social security benefits and some public-sector salaries and would also help offset the state budget deficit. Some 70 percent of the revenues from the new tax will go to the republics, the rest to central government.

In his decree announcing the tax, Gorbachev also said a stabilization fund had been created to help enterprises hurt by the new economic reforms. Finance Minister Valentin Pavlov told Central Television on December 29 that the fund would help alleviate the effects of unemployment and hardship due to price increases. Money for the fund will come from taxes on profits from state enterprises that exceed guidelines set by the USSR Supreme Soviet and on proceeds from the privatization of state properties (see *Pravda*, December 30).

Glasnost' Is a Guarantee against Dictatorship, Aide Says

A presidential aide, Georgii Shakhnazarov, said public debate and *glasnost'* would prevent Gorbachev from abusing his new powers. Interviewed by *Rabochaya tribuna*, Shakhnazarov noted: "The president's every move and word are discussed by the people and the press in an ever more open manner, so we have the main remedy against dictatorship."

Soldiers Allowed Weapons for Self-Defense

The Soviet Defense Ministry said servicemen would be allowed to carry personal firearms for self-defense. TASS quoted the ministry press center as saying that incidents of violence against servicemen and their families had been increasing. The ministry said that all regular officers, naval and army warrant officers, and servicemen on extended or temporary duty in regions where such violence was highest could carry personal firearms.

Belorussia and Ukraine Sign Ten-Year Accord

The chairmen of the Belorussian and Ukrainian Supreme Soviets signed a ten-year accord recognizing each other's republics as sovereign and pledging equal treatment for Belorussians or Ukrainians on each other's territory. Radio Moscow said the accord, signed in the Belorussian capital, Minsk, guaranteed the rights and liberties of citizens of the neighboring republics, including the right to cultural, linguistic, and ethnic independence.

Erevan Mayor Cites Worsening Conditions in City

The chairman of the Erevan City Soviet, Ambartsum Galstyan, told Radio Moscow that food shops in the Armenian capital were virtually empty and that public transport had stopped operating. Galstyan said Erevan had been receiving only about 40–45 percent of its food provisions. Nearly 1,500 of the city's buildings were in such poor condition that their inhabitants would have to be evacuated immediately, he added.

Gasoline Shortage in Eastern USSR

TASS reported that the supply of gasoline and other fuels was running extremely low in the outlying eastern regions of the USSR. The agency said almost 90 percent of the cars in Vladivostok were idle because filling stations had no gasoline.

Ukrainian Orthodox Believers on Hunger Strike

About forty clergymen and laymen of the Ukrainian Autonomous Orthodox Church were reported to have been on hunger strike in the Ukrainian city of Ivano-Frankovsk for more than twenty days, TASS reported. The hunger strikers were protesting about the loss of their churches to Ukrainian Uniate Catholics.

Sunday, December 30

Moscow's "Tent City" Razed

The police moved in with bulldozers to clear away the "tent city" in Red Square. The tents, occupied by citizens from all over the USSR who had come to Moscow to seek redress for their grievances, appeared in July during the Twenty-eighth CPSU Congress. According to Reuters, forty-seven people were taken into custody. Some were to be sent back to their original places of residence, while others were due to receive psychiatric attention.

No Professional Armed Forces

Soviet Defense Minister Dmitrii Yazov was quoted by *Komsomol'skaya pravda* as saying that a move to begin creating a volunteer army in the USSR had failed. Yazov said the General Staff's proposal to pay volunteer soldiers more than enlisted men had been rejected by the USSR Finance Ministry. He said the plan had been tried this month in Transcaucasia. In another interview carried the same day by TASS, Yazov said 177,000 families of Soviet officers had nowhere to live.

Soviet Teachers Close to Poverty Line

TASS reported that the Presidium of the Council of the USSR Confederation of Trade Unions had called for higher salaries for Soviet teachers in institutions of secondary education. The Presidium said teachers' salaries had reached their lowest level since the revolution. Teachers currently earn only two-thirds the average wage accorded a specialist in industry, putting their salaries close to the poverty line, according to the Presidium.

Drink Shortage Sparks Rioting in Siberian City

TASS reported that angry crowds rioted in the east Siberian city of Chita to protest about the shortage of liquor for the New Year's holiday. TASS said the disturbance occurred because thousands of people were unable to redeem ration coupons for wine and vodka.

Monday, December 31

Gorbachev Says 1991 Will Be Critical

In a New Year's message broadcast by Central Television to the Soviet population on December 31, Soviet President Mikhail Gorbachev said there was "no cause more sacred" than the preservation and renewal of the USSR. Gorbachev said 1991 would be a critical year because it would resolve "the fate of our multiethnic state."

Presidents of US and USSR Exchange Greetings

Presidents George Bush and Mikhail Gorbachev sent New Year's messages to the people of each other's country. Gorbachev predicted that the Moscow summit scheduled for early 1991 would further improve US-Soviet relations, which, he said, were still hampered by some "old obstacles." Economic, scientific, and technological cooperation, Gorbachev said, "still do not correspond to the spirit of the times." Bush's message to the USSR was carried by TASS on December 31 and was shown on the main Soviet television new program, "Vremya," on January 1. For its part, "Vremya" marked the New Year with a low-key commentary expressing the hope that the coming year would be "no worse" than the last.

Kohl Sends USSR New Year's Greetings

German Chancellor Helmut Kohl extended to the Soviet population "heartfelt greetings and good wishes" for the New Year from the united Germany. He said in a New Year's speech on Central Television that 1990 had been a milestone in the histories of both countries. Kohl also repeated his support for Moscow's "difficult political and economic reforms."

Problems with Soviet Underground Transport

The chief of the USSR Ministry of Railways Main Department of Underground Railroads, Viktor Pakhomov, said some services would stop on January 10 because there was no money to pay wages or for electricity. Pakhomov told Central Television that beginning January 1 the metro services would no longer be maintained out of the revenues of the all-Union railroads but instead by individual republics and cities. The official said five such systems had found a solution to their financing problems. He cited Minsk, Leningrad, Tbilisi, Erevan, and Tashkent. He said the Leningrad metro would raise its fare to fifteen kopeks.

"Donetsk Coal" Output Down by 400,000 Tons

The coal output of the "Donetsk Coal" enterprise in Ukraine during 1990 was reported to be some 400,000 tons below the annual target. Radio Kiev said only six of the enterprise's mines had managed to meet their targets, while fifteen others had failed to do so. The radio said it was the first time in ten years that "Donetsk Coal" had failed to meet its overall plan target.

Key

to Articles Published in *Report on the USSR* in 1990

RL Numbers	Issue Number	Date of Issue
1–12	1	January 5
13–24	2	January 12
25–35	3	January 19
36–49	4	January 26
50–60	5	February 2
61–70	6	February 9
71–81	7	February 16
82–95	8	Februrary 23
96–108	9	March 2
109–120	10	March 9
121–131	11	March 16
132–143	12	March 23
144–155	13	March 30
156–166	14	April 6
167–177	15	April 13
178–185	16	April 20
186–192	17	April 27
193–205	18	May 4
206–216	19	May 11
217–226	20	May 18
227–236	21	May 25
237–245	22	June 1
246–255	23	June 8
256-265	24	June 15
266–277	25	June 22
278-287	26	June 29
288–296	27	July 6
297–306	28	July 13
307–319	29	July 20
320–328	30	July 27
329–336	31	August 3
337–347	32	August 10

RL Numbers	Issue Number	Date of Issue
348–353	33	August 17
354–360	34	August 24
361–369	35	August 31
370–375	36	September 7
376–386	37	September 14
387–396	38	September 21
397–407	39	September 28
408–417	40	October 5
418–428	41	October 12
429–440	42	October 19
441–450	43	October 26
451–456	44	November 2
457–466	45	November 9
467–476	46	November 16
477–486	47	November 23
487–494	48	November 30
495–502	49	December 7
503–509	50	December 14
510–516	51	December 21
517–525	52	December 28

Name Index

Subject Index

About the Book and Editors

A unique, day-by-day chronology of important events and trends related to the USSR, this reference annual draws from a wide variety of sources, including Soviet and international media reports. The volume's comprehensive indexes to persons and places provide easy access to specific information being sought. Entries are brief but substantial, providing the context necessary in order to understand current developments.

Vera Tolz is a senior analyst in the research department at Radio Liberty, and **Melanie Newton** is an editor of *Report on the USSR*, a weekly publication of Radio Free Europe/ Radio Liberty, Inc.